TEXTBOOK OF
Abnormal Psychology

THE MACMILLAN COMPANY
NEW YORK · BOSTON · CHICAGO · DALLAS
ATLANTA · SAN FRANCISCO
MACMILLAN AND CO., Limited
LONDON · BOMBAY · CALCUTTA · MADRAS
MELBOURNE
THE MACMILLAN COMPANY
OF CANADA, Limited
TORONTO

TEXTBOOK OF

Abnormal Psychology

CARNEY LANDIS

PROFESSOR OF PSYCHOLOGY, COLUMBIA UNIVERSITY
PRINCIPAL RESEARCH PSYCHOLOGIST
PSYCHIATRIC INSTITUTE AND HOSPITAL

M. MARJORIE BOLLES

FORMERLY RESEARCH ASSISTANT
PSYCHIATRIC INSTITUTE AND HOSPITAL

THE MACMILLAN COMPANY · NEW YORK

1947

Reprinted March, 1947

This textbook has been written primarily for the use of the under-graduate student. The material is directed to those students who are majoring in psychology, education, sociology, biology, or the-ology. It should be of particular value to those who hope to go into clinical psychology, teaching, or social work, as well as to medical, premedical, and prelaw students.

Much of the material presented is new so far as textbook inclusion is concerned. Every attempt has been made to obtain and make use of experimental evidence and careful clinical observation. No one theoretical formulation has been completely accepted or followed. Rather, an eclectic standpoint has been taken so that the best and most rational explanations might be provided for the student. We believe that psychology, in so far as possible, should be an objective science. In light of this belief, the student is entitled to have all relevant facts and theories placed before him so that he may be stimulated to weigh the evidence and draw his own conclusions. In a field which comprises so much that is uncertain, irrational, and unclear as abnormal psychology, there is no place for dogma and propaganda. Only a healthy respect for careful observation and experimentation can provide a sound basis for adequate conclusions or stimulation to further work and exploration which may answer many of these puzzles of behavior and mental life.

As psychologists, we believe that the most important, difficult, and interesting problems in contemporary psychology are in the realm of psychopathology. Answers or relevant information bearing on the nature of schizophrenia, amentia, aphasia, amnesia, or any of the other mysteries of abnormal psychology constitute the greatest contribution which any psychologist can make to his science. If the student can be stimulated to work actively in this field, or if in later life he may have an adequate appreciation of the problems of ab-normal psychology and the possible answers to its enigmas, then this course is fully justified in any college curriculum.

We are most grateful for the assistance given us by many indi-viduals and institutions. They have in many ways aided us in the production of this book. Among our colleagues at the New York State Psychiatric Institute and Hospital we are especially indebted to Drs. Franz Kallmann and Joseph Zubin who provided much material and corrected many of the more obvious errors. Drs. Nolan D. C. Lewis and Paul Hoch have provided helpful criticism. Dr. Jacob Shatzky facilitated the bibliographical work.

To Mrs. Jane Cushman we are especially grateful for technical assistance at every step, as well as for her artistic skill in producing many of the figures and drawings. Miss Marjorie MacMullen afforded much technical assistance. Mrs. Helen Marcin and Mrs. Kathleen Gallagher gave stenographic assistance. Mr. Hans Gehrung made many of the photographic reproductions.

Professors R. S. Woodworth, Calvin P. Stone, and Henry W. Nissen have read and corrected parts of the manuscript. For reading and correcting all or parts of the following chapters we are indebted to the following persons: Chap. X, Mental Deficiency, Dr. Elaine F. Kinder; Chap. XXXI, The Law, Judge John Bolles and Mr. E. L. La Crosse; Chap. XXXIII, Psychotherapy, Dr. John Cotton; and the Glossary, Mrs. Jane Noll. The staff of the Library of the New York Academy of Medicine assisted in the procuring of material for Plates 2, 3, 12, 15, 18, and 19.

Students in our classes in abnormal psychology for years past have sat in judgment and assisted in the formulation of many of the ideas here presented. Their questions have led to many of the experiments which have been done in this laboratory and elsewhere. They have been a continuing stimulus to the production of this textbook as it now stands.

We acknowledge all this assistance and inspiration with gratitude. Needless to say, all errors of omission and commission as may occur are the sole responsibility of the authors.

C. L.
M. M. B.

New York City

CONTENTS

vii

ACKNOWLEDGMENTS

The authors and publishers express their appreciation for permission to reproduce the following:

Plates

1. The Library of the New York State Psychiatric Institute and Hospital — 16
2. The Alien Property Custodian under License No. JA-887. "Copyright vested in the Alien Property Custodian, 1945, pursuant to law" — 26
3. Estate of Doris Ulman, copyright owner — 31
4, 5. Nervous and Mental Disease Publishing Company, Washington, D.C., copyright owner — 35, 37
6, 7, 8. Jane F. Cushman — 136, 138, 139
9, 10. Nervous and Mental Disease Publishing Company, Washington, D.C., copyright owner — 152, 201
11. Jane F. Cushman — 220
12. The Library of the New York Academy of Medicine — 261
13. Jane F. Cushman — 432
14. Press Association, New York, copyright owner — 445
15. Progress Medical — 460
16. H. H. Goddard — 464
17. H. H. Goddard and George B. Thom, Vineland Training School — 466
18, 19. The Library of the New York Academy of Medicine — 497, 515

Figures

1. Modified from W. G. Lennox, *Science and Seizures;* by permission of Paul B. Hoeber, Inc., New York, copyright owner — 121
2, 3, 4. T. J. Putnam, *Convulsive Seizures;* by permission of J. B. Lippincott Company, Philadelphia, copyright owner — 123, 124
5. Modified from W. G. Lennox, *Science and Seizures;* by permission of Paul B. Hoeber, Inc., New York, copyright owner — 127
6. Journal of Studies on Alcohol, Inc., New Haven, Conn., copyright owner — 188

Tables

DIRECT QUOTATIONS

The authors and publishers acknowledge their gratitude to the following holders of copyrights or authors of original material for their courtesy in granting permission to reproduce certain passages. The Roman numeral at left indicates chapter number and the Arabic numerals at right the pages on which the quotations occur.

TEXTBOOK OF
Abnormal Psychology

Chapter I

INTRODUCTION

MOST of us are quite confident that we have a fair degree of understanding of other people. We understand (or think we can) most of their actions and thoughts; we can explain (more or less adequately) their behavior; we can predict (to our own satisfaction) their future behavior; and we feel that if we exerted ourselves sufficiently we could control other people's behavior, although most of us doubt that we could control their thinking. In short, most of us are fairly confident that we understand the thoughts and actions of most people that we meet.

Every now and then we meet, are told about, or read about actions or experiences of some person, which seem to us not understandable. His words and actions are somehow foreign to our own notions of common sense and behavior. So we say to ourselves (or to someone else) that this person is odd, peculiar, bizarre, unusual, astonishing, or "crazy." We are astonished or bewildered by his behavior because it does not "make sense" to us. We try to find some explanation for this behavior. At times we attribute its strangeness to the fact that our knowledge of the person is incomplete; at other times we distort or read something into the peculiar behavior, so forcing it into a pattern which is understandable to us; and at still other times we merely give the behavior a name and having named it we feel as though we had explained it.

Every one of us has had one or more periods when we could not understand or control our own actions or thoughts; we thought that we were "out of our minds," possessed, confused, or crazy. Usually such periods have been short, and not too frequent. We soon forgot them or rationalized them to ourselves and to others. If they seemed too peculiar, occurred too frequently, or lasted too long, we may have started discreet questioning among our friends, gone to see a doctor, or started reading books on psychology. Hence, although we understand most people (and ourselves) most of the time, it does happen that on occasion we are baffled or astonished by behavior in ourselves and others which is odd or unusual.

Scientific psychology is organized knowledge which deals with the behavior and mental life of mankind and is usually directed toward the better understanding, prediction, and control of mental experience and behavior. As subdivisions of this field of knowledge, general or normal psychology deals with the usual, while abnormal psychology deals with the behavior or mental life which is odd or unusual.

It is possible to define abnormal psychology in many other ways and in much stricter terms. Abnormal psychology can be considered as the psychology of those who are sick; the psychology of persons who are at the extremes of the normal distribution of humanity; the psychology of those who are badly adjusted within themselves or to the world they live in; the psychology of the occult; the psychology of the insane. Essentially, the definition or delimitation of any field of knowledge depends on the formulation of the problem or problems to be answered. The student of psychology may reasonably expect to find somewhere in the entirety of scientific psychology a description and discussion of the kinds of human behavior and experiences which are not clearly reasonable or understandable in terms of his own experience or in terms of common sense.

In abnormal psychology the student may expect to find enlightenment, but not always the answer, to questions such as the following:

What is a neurotic? Am I neurotic? What are my chances of becoming insane? Will overwork, emotional frustration, physical injury, or disease cause me to lose my mind? My mother (or some other relative) has been in a mental hospital; will I too develop a mental disease?

Is alcoholism a symptom of mental illness or is the mental illness a result of the alcoholism? Are epileptics crazy or does epilepsy lead to mental deterioration?

What are the causes of mental illness in soldiers? Does the stress of wartime increase the number of persons with mental disorder?

What does it "feel like" to be mentally ill? Why doesn't the insane person exert his will and force himself to get over his peculiar ideas? Is mental abnormality only an exaggeration of the sort of personality which a person has had all of his life? Isn't a great deal of crazy behavior just a form of malingering to escape some sort of unpleasant duty?

What is the status of the mind-body problem in the field of abnormal psychology? What is meant by such terms as repression, inhibition, rationalization, inferiority complex, or Oedipus complex?

What is the effect of severe brain injury on personality? Is there a typical epileptic personality? Does feeblemindedness run in families? Does an unhappy childhood lead to mental illness? How can the personality changes of old age be explained?

What disturbances in memory, perception, and attention occur in mental illness? Do normal people ever have vague feelings of fear or anxiety without known cause? Is mental deterioration an irreversible process? Do the insane ever really get well?

Are mental diseases increasing or decreasing? What are the chances of recovery from different kinds of mental illness? Is ours a neurotic civilization? Would changing our political and economic social structure increase or decrease the frequency of mental abnormality?

What is psychotherapy? How do physicians and psychologists treat mentally ill persons and how do different forms of treatment compare in effectiveness?

The student may expect to find questions such as these dealt with in abnormal psychology. To certain of these questions there are answers based on fact; to others, there are logical and consistent interpretations which fit the observed data; but to many there are only vague theories and hypotheses which do not cover the available material and which have only partial acceptance by workers in the field.

There are other questions which the student might also expect to encounter in a book on abnormal psychology but with which we will not be concerned. For example, the student will find hypnosis treated as a therapeutic measure with but little information on its essential nature. This is because we regard the hypnotic state as a special mental condition which is not definitely related to the main body of abnormal phenomena. Nothing is included which deals with the psychology of the occult, spiritualism, or telepathy. Nor will morbid, fantastic, or astounding case-history material be included, not because such material does not occur, but because such histories rarely shed light on the basic problems concerned. The details of *medical* procedure and therapy will not be taken up, since such considerations are not properly in the scope of abnormal psychology. (Psychotherapy will be considered.)

It is unfortunate that many people cling to the idea that mental disorders of any sort are horrible and disgraceful. Any educated person should try to understand, and, in so far as possible, help to correct conditions which may favor abnormal psychological states. Civilization is based on increased knowledge, on understanding, on control and correction of conditions which are unfavorable to human existence. In brief, civilization is based on the substitution of scientific thought for magical thinking. Mental abnormalities are not due to magic, nor can they be cured by magic.

A further value comes from understanding abnormal psychology. Many of the mental states and patterns of behavior shown by the deranged person are exaggerations or caricatures of normal mental life or behavior. Seeing and understanding the caricature makes it easier to understand the psychology of everyday life.

We do not advocate any particular school of thought, theory, or explanation as central or all important. Rather, our viewpoint is eclectic, meaning that we select and report portions of different systems of thought and theory wherever they seem to be valid and useful. Eclecticism sacrifices a certain amount of consistency, but it affords the student the opportunity for examination of all viewpoints so that he may draw his own conclusions in the light of his own general attitude toward life and its problems. Furthermore, the field of abnormal psychology is still made up of much descriptive material for which many speculative answers may be advanced without opportunity for the complete proof of the truth of any of the speculations. It is better to maintain an open-minded, tolerant attitude in the hope that the future will bring explanations which can then be placed in their proper setting among all of the diverse explanations which exist at present.

In general, abnormal psychology should not be viewed as a field of psychopathology, extreme deviation, or bizarre phenomena isolated from the rest of psychology and the other sciences. The goal of the psychologist should be to make these not-immediately-understood phenomena comprehensible and coherent through a knowledge of the conditions under which they arise and the various factors — neurological, physiological, or psychological — which enter into their production. There are so many gaps in our present knowledge that complete understanding of these phenomena is not yet possible, nor does it seem that we will have answers to some of the questions for many years to come. Some of the occurrences seem as alien to normal attitudes, beliefs, and experiences as the experience of color is alien to the completely color-blind person. It has been found that the visual experiences of the color-blind person are equivalent to gradations of gray. The person with color vision, knowing this fact, can now understand and appreciate how the world of color looks to the color-blind person. In the same way, the mentally normal person should reach a better understanding of the mentally abnormal when analogies and similarities between his ways of thinking and feeling and those of the mentally abnormal are formulated for him.

In the presentation of the field of abnormal psychology the following plan will be used. First, in Chaps. II and III will be given the terms and concepts with which to describe and to start to classify the varieties of human abnormality. Next, in Chaps. IV to XVII, inclusive, the different groups (diagnostic categories) of abnormal persons will be described. In Chaps. XVIII, XIX, and XX the general basic explanatory concepts which are used to explain abnormality will be presented. Chapters XXI to XXVII, inclusive, will deal with psychopathology; that is, with the different aspects of disorders of mental life without direct reference to the diagnostic category in which they occur. Finally, Chaps. XXVIII to XXXIV, inclusive, will take up certain of the contributions which have been made, are being made, and may be made in the future, by the various sciences, education, and the law, to our knowledge and understanding of the phenomena of abnormal psychology.

Chapter II

DESCRIPTION, CLASSIFICATION AND TERMINOLOGY

LIKE any other division of science abnormal psychology is based on description, classification, and explanation; on counting and measuring. When we are unable to understand, immediately, the behavior of some other person, we may start making careful and extensive observations of that person. We try to describe the conditions under which his strange and unusual behavior takes place, as well as the characteristics of the behavior itself. Next, we try to work out the patterns or elements that are common to his behavior and to that of other persons who somehow resemble him. The process of grouping together patterns of behavior which appear to be similar or equivalent is, of course, classification. From such classifications we try to go on to the development of explanations stated as principles, rules, or laws which serve to clarify our understanding of the specific behavior manifestations which puzzled us. Often the description can be made so full and complete that no additional interpretation is necessary, the course of events seeming logical and orderly when all circumstances are known. In other instances, conjecture or speculation must supply the missing elements that cannot be had by direct observation, but which are necessary to make the particular behavior understandable.

Description in Abnormal Psychology

But how can one describe what one does not understand? The answer to this question is not simple and does not depend upon any one method. Scientists attempt to be objective. They attempt to put aside preconceptions and prejudices, describing in as simple a fashion as possible that which actually occurs. In theory, a sound motion picture offers a truly objective record of an event. But even such a record is of no use unless it is clearly understood by a majority of observers. Two people reporting the same event may mention or be impressed by completely different points. In general, one's interests, beliefs, and previously formed concepts will determine what is reported and, to some

6

extent, what is actually perceived. Thus, the verbal description of an event serves an essentially different end from a photographic record. The former is more akin to a photograph taken through a filter which allowed only certain qualities to go through and make an impression. In other words, all verbal description is selective; and the scientific approach, by emphasizing counting and measuring, guards against these selective factors, preventing, in part, distorted views and distorted reports.

If the same occurrence is witnessed or experienced time after time, one's description will be more complete since various details that are important may have been missed in the first observations. After many students have observed many unusual persons their observations and descriptions may be brought together, compared, and checked one against the other. In this way, we arrive at what one might call an "average" or "typical" description of some particular deviation, together with the variations and varieties of this particular abnormality. At the same time, we frequently gain knowledge of the relationship which exists between some particular abnormality, such as a tendency to falsify memory, and certain other deviations which may occur together with it in the same person, for example, emotional instability.

In order to make such descriptions accurate, we sometimes need to invent new words or attach new meanings to old words. Specialists in the field of abnormal psychology are criticized because of the freeness with which they coin such new words or redefine old words. This criticism is unjustified. If we could accurately and easily describe or understand the condition to start with, it would not be part of abnormal psychology. Here, as in most other developing fields of science, a new and specialized vocabulary must be built up so that we may accurately describe the events with which we are dealing.

In the description of unusual and strange experience and behavior the student will meet words such as "hallucination," "aphasia," or "phobia." We will explain each of these terms when it first occurs. In the same way, specialized meanings will be given to words which are used otherwise than in everyday speech, such as "anxiety," "intelligence," and "compensation." (A glossary of terms will be found beginning on page 547.)

Sources of Information

So far we have spoken only of direct observation of the behavior of the abnormal individual, but actually there are many other available sources of information about him. One of the most obvious ways of getting information concerning an abnormal person is to ask him to tell us all about himself. This may take considerable time and be quite revealing. When we are dealing with an abnormal individual we must be exceedingly cautious in our acceptance of his self-description. We must inquire repeatedly and at length in order to find out what the words, phrases, and ideas he uses in self-description really mean to him. We frequently find that his words and ideas have a different meaning and a different reference from that which we commonly accept. Only repeated questioning can clarify our understanding of such self-description. These descriptive accounts are valuable in that they furnish us with an understanding of what it is like to undergo some psychopathological experience. We must remember, however, that these are abnormal individuals and their concepts and explanations may be colored by their abnormality so that we cannot accept as factual everything they say about themselves. The abnormal person will tell his story over and over again, using much the same language and ideas. His account is consistent from one time to the next; his report is "reliable," in the statistical sense. On the other hand, judged by all ordinary standards, what he is saying and the explanations which he gives are incorrect. It is, in part, this incorrectness which causes us to classify him as abnormal.

The next step in obtaining information concerning such abnormal persons is to interview extensively all of the friends, acquaintances, relatives, and others who have known these individuals more or less intimately. Such material must be very carefully evaluated. It has been demonstrated experimentally that the more informants one has concerning any individual, the more inconsistent becomes the information. This inconsistency grows from the fact that only rarely are the informants trained observers. In addition, it may be that they have never had opportunity really to study the person in question. Some mothers are unable to give correctly the age of their own children. Husbands will be unable to report anything concerning the names or family history of their wife's parents and relatives. Children will be unable to say anything about the places where their parents have lived, the work that they have done, or the education which they may have received. Such a lack of information is mainly due to sheer ignorance of the facts.

Another source of error in information gained from interviews works out as follows: If anyone of us should be asked to report all that he knows concerning some friend or acquaintance who has become mentally ill, we would tend to recount instances in which the person in question has behaved in an odd or peculiar fashion at some previous time; that is, we will tend to overemphasize instances which indicate peculiarity and neglect to report the evidence which indicates that the individual was for the most part normal and rational. Again, it may be that this particular individual has been a source of annoyance or concern to us. If this is true, one may expect that the report will, to say the least, emphasize peculiarities of behavior at the expense of the usual normal activity. In our evaluation we must remember that even the most peculiar and abnormal individual is apparently normal in much of his everyday existence.

The art of obtaining accurate and meaningful information from either the patient or from those who know the patient is one which is at present acquired only by experience and supervised training. In the basic training of the psychiatrist, the social worker, or the psychologist who is going to specialize in this field, much time and attention has to be given to proper and adequate training in the art of obtaining a life history which is truly representative. A great deal of the confusion which exists in the field of abnormal psychology is due to reports which have been taken by individuals who were inadequately trained or who were more or less blinded by prejudice or preconception concerning the nature of the deviation which they were trying to describe.

Psychologists have attempted, with varying degrees of success, to make use of tests, rating scales, or other experimental procedures which have been standardized with normal persons, in order to determine the kind or amount of deviation exhibited by the abnormal individual. The use of intelligence tests with the feeble-minded is an outstanding example of such an application. We will consider from time to time the results which such objective procedures add to our knowledge of psychopathology. At present most information and consequent knowledge are based on the life history, with the more objective test material used to support and supplement.

Classification in Abnormal Psychology

Any classification of material describing deviations in behavior or in mental life is done for some particular purpose or some particular end. There is no evidence which would indicate that the basic factors operating in the deviations have changed in any way during the period of recorded history. The way in which the deviations have been classified or explained has depended upon the philosophical views or concepts of life which the leading thinkers of any particular time have adopted.

At present there are operating in the field of abnormal psychology three major types of classification: (*a*) classifications dealing with normal versus abnormal; (*b*) classification of groups among those who are abnormal; and (*c*) descriptive categories of reactions which are not oriented to either normality or abnormality. The classifications which have to do with normality versus abnormality have grown out of the ancient beliefs of the moralists or religious groups and constitute the legal viewpoint toward mental abnormality. The moralists have tended to associate normality with goodness and abnormality with evil, or the losing of the mind with the activity of the Devil. In the law, a sharp line of distinction has been drawn between sanity and insanity so that the notion of responsibility or lack of responsibility might hold as a fixed point of reference in legal thinking. In sociology and in anthropology, emphasis has been placed upon classifications which have been related to the social and cultural standards and to the changing of those standards as civilization has changed. The statisticians have identified normal with the middle portion of the distribution of general descriptions of human behavior and abnormal with the extremes of such grouped data. Psychologists have tended to identify normal with well-adjusted and abnormal with maladjusted behavior.

The second of the major systems of classification is based primarily upon the clinical studies of physicians who are trying to differentiate types of reaction within the general group of abnormal individuals who have been institutionalized, usually through some court of law, and who are, so far as the law is concerned, considered insane. The principal systems used at present are those of Kraepelin, of Meyer, and of Freud. The third of the major systems of classification, namely, that dealing with categories of reaction, falls, for the most part, into the general field of personality study. Here psychologists have been interested in describing and classifying those dimensions of human reactions upon which all individuals can be compared. For our present purposes we will take up this sort of classification only when it contributes to our knowledge of the behavior of the abnormal person.

This textbook presents abnormal psychology from an eclectic standpoint. Hence, it is worth while to consider somewhat more closely the everyday concepts which enter into this formulation and see which are valid and which should be rejected. It will become more and more apparent as we go along that many of our notions with respect to normality and abnormality are based upon preconceptions and prejudices which have little or no basis in fact. Most of us in our everyday dealings with social and mental deviants accept the notion that their deviation is a result of some fault, shortcoming, sin, or unwillingness on their own part or on the part of their relatives and close friends. It is common to explain insanity, feeble-mindedness, and other gross deviations in behavior or in mental life in terms of praise and blame. It is common to act as if some form of major deviation had been adopted willingly by the abnormal person, and if he would only exert his will power he might overcome his difficulty. This attitude, which is characteristic of the everyday viewpoint, is a carry-over from the classification system which was followed for many centuries by the moralists and religious leaders. In spite of the almost universal acceptance of this common-sense belief, it has been most unproductive for either the prevention, cure, or understanding of abnormality. The application of this viewpoint in legal procedure does serve to protect society from the abnormal person (the lunatic) and to protect the lunatic from himself or from being taken advantage of because of his disability.

Most of the more marked forms of abnormal behavior are dealt with by the courts, where they are classified according to certain legal concepts. In the eyes of the law a person whose behavior is grossly disordered or grossly defective is judged and classified on the basis of such subjective tests or standards as having the ability to distinguish between right and wrong or being "possessed of an insane and irresistible impulse." Such persons who are, or may be, dangerous either to themselves or to others are adjudged mentally incompetent or irresponsible, so that a guardian is appointed who will assume responsibility for the care and protection of this particular person. Since both care and protection are apt to be prolonged and to involve segregation from society, the actual guardianship is assigned, in most instances, to the superintendent, warden, or director of some institution which takes over the care and treatment of the individual. The classification in the eyes of the law is of two major varieties: those whose intellect is and has been from an early age of such character that they are unable to care for themselves or to compete in any fashion with their fellows; and those whose alienation of mind is such that they can no longer distinguish right from wrong and hence are not responsible for their own acts, possibly endangering their own life and safety.

Another grouping of abnormal persons derives from social standards and customs. From this standpoint, any person, whom for one reason or another his fellows wish to segregate, is called abnormal. This applies equally to the defective, the delinquent, or the diseased. The rational basis for the segregation may constantly change. The basis is neither medical, psychological, legal, moral, ethical, religious, nor biological, although these factors enter into the system of segregation in varying degrees at different times. If a central idea does exist in this social concept, it is that a group of persons decide (or are told) that the behavior of one or more individuals in their group is not "reasonable," and that these individuals cannot be appealed to by the same forms of logic or reason which will activate the majority of that group. This reasonableness exists only at a particular place, a particular time, and with a particular group. It changes as the ideas and times and groups change. In this sense there is no fixed meaning for the word "abnormal."

Another system of classification is more or less statistical in nature. Much of psychological experimentation is coupled with psychological measurement. When we measure psychological traits, behaviors, or attitudes we generally obtain a normal distribution in which most individuals show about the same amount of the characteristic in question, with a few showing a gross excess and a few a gross deficit. We can, on the basis of our measurements, give the average, the standard deviation, and other statistical values which enable us to state the degree of normality or deviation in statistical terms. This particular concept has worked very well in classifying most varieties of feeble-mindedness. It has not been found to be of much use with other varieties of abnormality.

Still another method of psychological classification grows out of human and animal experimentation. Here attempts have been made to establish abnormal behavior patterns experimentally. Knowledge of such patterns might lead to the better understanding of the operation of similar abnormal behavior as it is met in everyday life.

The system of classification used most extensively in abnormal psychology is that developed by psychiatry, based on a combination of medical and psychological observations. This system of classification of abnormalities and deviations of behavior, which has been accepted by organized medicine and which is partially recognized in the courts of law, has the most widespread acceptance of any in present use. No one believes that this system has any degree of finality about it, but it does serve as the best available way of holding together the various descriptive categories so that they can be studied and (to a degree) understood. Most of this classification is based upon the formulations of Kraepelin, the German psychiatrist, and is called the "Kraepelinian classification." In dealing with the main groups of deviants, this particular system will be followed.

General Terminology

We have already mentioned that new terms would be defined as they occurred and that the definitions for many of these terms will be found in the glossary at the end of this book. There are, however, certain medical, statistical, and sociological terms and concepts which should be made clear before proceeding further.

Health and disease are contrasting terms. *Health* means soundness of body and mind so that bodily or mental functions are duly discharged. *Disease* means a condition of the body or mind, or some part of the body or mind, in which its functions are disturbed or deranged. *Adjustment* (or adaptation) is a means of maintaining health. *Maladjustment* is a characteristic of disease, since it is a breaking down of the integrity of the organism and so may lead to death. *Pathology* is the science or study of disease; *psychopathology*, the science or study of mental disease. *Etiology* is that part of science which investigates the causes of disease. *Diagnosis* is the determination of the nature of a diseased condition. *Prognosis* is a forecast of the probable course of disease in some individual. A *symptom* is a bodily or mental phenomenon, circumstance, or change of condition arising from and accompanying a disease and constituting an indication or evidence of it. A *syndrome* is the concurrence or combination of several symptoms in a disease.

The words "disorder," "deviation," "defect," and "disease" are used more or less interchangeably. *Defect* is more frequently applied to conditions of feeble-mindedness; *disorder* or *deviation* to less severe forms of abnormality, but the student will have to rely on the context of the statement for any shades of difference in meaning which may be implied.

With respect to the outcome of disease, the terms *cured, alleviated, remission, improved, ameliorated,* or *unimproved* are used. There is no standard which has been agreed upon which will cover the variety of meanings which can be attached to the word "cured." Hence, this term must be used with a great deal of caution. *Remission,* meaning that the particular symptoms which were markedly apparent at some earlier time have subsided or disappeared, is more exact and descriptive. The terms *ameliorated, alleviated, improved,* or *unimproved* are properly used to compare the present condition with some previously described status. A person may be very deviant at present and at the same time much improved, in contrast to his disorder at some previous time.

The difference between *predisposing* and *precipitating* causes is one which the student should have clearly in mind. A predisposing cause refers to some factor or factors in the general background of the individual: his heredity, his history of health and sickness, his physical constitution, his social or economic status. A precipitating cause refers to the particular incident or combination of incidents which led either to his seeking or being brought to the attention of authorities. For example, the case of an unhealthy, poorly educated, poorly nourished, shy, timid boy of poor heredity (predisposing factors) whose mother has died, leaving him alone in the world (precipitating incident), who is brought to the hospital because of his strange and apathetic behavior, provides an illustration of the operation of these two factors.

Organic and *functional* are terms which are used quite often in abnormal psychology. Where the word "organic" is used it is a token that evidence has been established indicating that in this oddly behaving person there is a change in the structure of the nervous system, or some one or more of the other organic systems of the body. We have real and substantial evidence that an actual physical change has taken place to which we may attribute the psychological deviations. All those deviant conditions in which we have not so far been able to establish organic change or deviation are termed *functional disorders*. This does not mean that no organic changes exist; it does mean that scientific methods which are at present available have been unable to isolate and identify changes which may have occurred. It is, of course, equally possible that there is no organic change, but that there has been a change in the functional relationship between bodily organs or a conflict among the habit systems which has led to the odd and peculiar behavior which brought this person to our attention.

In the background material bearing on the major behavior deviations considered in abnormal psychology, concepts which occur frequently, should be clarified. Most of our information concerning the number of abnormal individuals comes from official reports based on hospital, institution, prison, special school, and other specialized population samples. One figure given in such reports is that of *resident population*. This means the number of persons residing as patients at the particular institution on some particular date. Since the length of residence varies tremendously among the different kinds of abnormal persons, it is unfair to measure their relative frequency on the basis of residence alone. Furthermore, some types of abnormality are recurrent, bringing the individual to the institution on several occasions. To meet these two difficulties a great deal of reporting is done in terms of the number of *first-admissions*, which is merely the count of the number of individuals who come to an institution for the first time in a given year. Any subsequent appearances are termed *readmissions*. First-admissions plus readmissions are *total admissions*. Resident populations and first-admission figures are of themselves difficult to compare until they are expressed as rates per thousand of the general population. Hence, such figures are usually reported as first-admissions per 10,000 or per 100,000 of the general population, of the same age and sex.

In reporting the outcome of treatment, it is customary to give the number of patients who have improved or ameliorated per 100 patients of the same classification under treatment during some given period of time. For example, 40 per cent of chronic alcoholics were reported to have recovered during the course of a year. The discharge rate of any institution is figured in the same way as the outcome rate, except that the question of improvement or remission is omitted. For example, we may find that 80 per cent of patients who had delirium tremens were discharged during a year, which would mean that out of every 100 such patients 80 left the institution either unimproved or improved.

We will take up, wherever possible, evidence concerning certain genetic and constitutional relationships which bear on our understanding of psychopathology. By *heredity* is meant the sum total of those characteristics (either physical or mental) which are passed from parent to child by means of the biological carriers — the chromosomes and genes. By *constitution* we will refer to the relatively constant biological make-up of the individual, which governs the adjustment which that individual makes to disease or health. It is not a specific concept but refers to those positive factors leading toward normal, healthy adjustment. It is the result of two components, heredity and environment.

Psychoanalytic Terminology

A special development in the field of abnormal psychology has evolved from the therapeutic discoveries and theoretical explanations of Sigmund Freud. The finer details of this portion of the field of psychopathology will be taken up subsequently; but since much of the terminology which Freud and his followers developed is now in regular use throughout the field of abnormal psychology, it is well to have certain of these terms and concepts defined before proceeding further into the field.

Originally Freud* divided consciousness (or the mind) into the

* The simplest statement of Freud's system will be found in S. Freud, *The Problem of Lay-Analysis*. New York, Brentano, 1927. The theories and terminology of psychoanalysis are well formulated in W. Healy, A. F. Bronner, and A. M. Bowers, *The Structure and Meaning of Psychoanalysis*. New York, Knopf, 1931.

fore-conscious, the subconscious, and the unconscious, meaning by these terms about the same thing that they mean in everyday usage. Later he revised this usage and spoke of the three parts which make up the anatomy of the mind; namely, the *Ego* ("I will"), *Superego* ("One must not"), and *Id* ("It wants"). The Ego corresponds to what we usually speak of as conscious experience and awareness as we know them in our own everyday life. The Superego corresponds to the usual ways in which we use the word "conscience." The Id is that part of

PLATE I

SIGMUND FREUD (1856–1939)

the mind which we would ordinarily speak of as "the unconscious" but to which the psychoanalysts have attached certain specialized meanings. They hold that in the Id are found all of the dynamic forces of human existence which are ordinarily called "motives," "urges," "wishes," "drives," "yearnings," or "instinct." It also possesses a generalized dynamic force which is termed *libido* and may be defined as that force by which the sexual instinct is represented in the mind, or the energy of those instincts which have to do with all that may be comprised under the word "love." It should be noted that the essential dynamic force of the Id is sexual (in the broadest sense of that term) in nature. The ways in which the libido shows itself in the conscious life of the individual have been loosely referred to as instincts, meaning the general tendencies toward expression which are common in all human beings and grow out of the psychosexuality of the individual.

Since many of the instincts or wishes which grow out of the Id are either mutually contradictory or are inhibited in their expression by moral and ethical considerations, there is set up in the unconscious life of the person a *conflict*. These conflicts give rise to many of the symptoms and abnormalities of mind and behavior shown by the person suffering from some mental disorder. They also show themselves in various ways in the everyday life of the normal person. Conflicts can be most easily observed and analyzed through the study and interpretation of dreams, since it has been found that in dreams many common elements, ideas, concepts, and figures of speech refer to rather simple wishes or instincts which have come into conflict.

The ways in which these conflicts which exist either in the Id itself or grow out of repression by either the Ego or the Superego are resolved, are spoken of as *mental mechanisms*. This term may be defined as unconscious or conscious stylized processes whereby the inner conflict situation is eliminated or reduced in its severity. These conflicts may be resolved in many ways. Outlets for such situations may be provided in terms of socially acceptable equivalents for the repressed wish. Barriers or defenses may be raised against the exhibition of any of these conflicts, so that neither the individual himself nor others recognize that a conflict is present. The more common ways in which these mental mechanisms operate, together with the names applied to the process, are as follows:

One of the most common of the mechanisms is *repression,* which is the exclusion of painful and unpleasant material from expression in either the behavior or the mental life of the person. It is a process of active forgetting which is carried out, usually, without any volition on the part of the individual. If, for example, one has told a lie and been caught in the act, the memory of the event may be put out of mind and we say that, so far as we can remember, the event never happened. Another general way of dealing with conflict is by a process of *catharsis,* which in this connection means expression through talking (or some other form of behavior) of the unpleasant emotional experience, so that the very act of talking about it somehow seems to drain off the acute unpleasantness. For example, everyone is familiar with the feeling of relief which comes from "talking out" some problem with a close friend.

Two very common means of solving conflicts are spoken of as *sublimation* and *rationalization*. By sublimation is meant the unconscious exchanging of overt expressions of sexual desires and wishes for other types of behavior which are socially, morally, or ethically approved. An example of sublimation is the composition of sonnets by the young man who is in love. Rationalization is a process which arises from the need which we all have for accounting or justifying to ourselves certain feelings, ideas, acts, or emotions which are not rational. As reasonable human beings we all feel that we ought to be able to account for ourselves in terms which indicate that we have behaved and thought according to the best of our ability. Since much of our behavior is not of this sort, we explain an irrational action by an unconscious manipulation and revision of the events so that we essentially fool ourselves.

Another method of solving mental conflicts is that of *symbolization*, which is an unconscious process built up on the basis of association and similarity so that one object or idea comes to represent or stand for (symbolize) some other object or idea through some aspect which the two have in common. In this process there is also the taking over of the emotional value attached to the original object or idea by its symbol. For example, an exaggerated fear which one might have of fire might be a symbolization of one's own fear of sexual expression: "Playing with fire is dangerous." When the symbolization is expressed in some form of physical or physiological representation, it is spoken of as *conversion*. If a person seems to have an actual blindness in one eye without any physiological reason for the blindness, we may find that by the process of conversion the unpleasant sights are kept away: "If thy right eye offend thee, pluck it out, and cast it from thee."

Another way in which conflicts are met is by a process which is spoken of as *regression*. This refers to the symbolical act of returning to some earlier period in one's life and acting and thinking as if one were a child or an infant. We often remark that the person who has been disappointed in love acts like a baby. If the psychological and emotional development of an individual seems to remain at a behavioral level which was appropriate at an earlier period in the life of that individual, it is spoken of as *fixation*. For example, this term is used to describe the adult who shows a childlike emotional dependence upon his mother or father.

The term *transference* refers to the reproduction of forgotten and repressed experiences of early childhood. This transference shows itself in the form of emotional storms directed toward the object of one's affections. Usually in these storms the person is angry and reproachful toward the person who is the center of his love attachment. The jealous behavior of the lover is a good example of transference behavior, in that it usually is expressed as a small child would express his resentment at anyone who interfered with his mother's attentions to him.

By *projection* is meant the process of attributing to another the rejected or unpleasant ideas, emotions, or motives which really belong to oneself. When we blame someone else for our own shortcomings and mistakes, we are making use of the projection mechanism. The reverse of projection is *identification*. Here we have an unconscious molding of our own Ego after the fashion and pattern of someone that we have taken as an ideal or as a model. Such identification is most clearly seen in the behavior of the small boy who copies the habits and mannerisms of his father. Adults use this same mechanism to strengthen themselves against their own inner reproaches by behaving in the same fashion as they believe someone who is strong and well adjusted would do or does do.

Unconscious fantasies are those which have been formed or elaborated in the unconscious and appear as daydreaming fragments in everyday consciousness. Such fantasies modify and determine the course of much of our daydreaming. For example, the desire to be ill is derived from the unconscious fantasy that if one is sick, one will get love and attention which is not obtained so long as one is well and healthy.

Psychologists, Psychiatrists, and Psychoanalysts

A good deal of confusion exists in the minds of many concerning the similarities and differences which exist between psychiatrists, psychoanalysts, and psychologists. The term *psychiatrist* as it is used at present is restricted to those individuals holding the degree of Doctor of Medicine and who specialize in the diagnosis, care, and treatment of patients suffering from nervous and mental diseases. Psychoanalysts are usually medically trained individuals who make use of the special therapeutic technique of psychoanalysis in their care and treatment of the mentally disturbed individual. There are a few psychoanalysts who do not have medical training. They are called "lay-analysts." Professional psychologists usually hold the degree of Doctor of Philosophy (or, at least, Master of Arts) and are concerned with all of the problems of human behavior and mental life. Abnormal psychologists are those professional psychologists who specialize in the scientific study of the cause, cure, and explanation of mental disabilities. Their interest is different from that of the psychiatrist in that the psychiatrist is a physician attempting to heal the mentally sick, while the abnormal psychologist is the research specialist who is attempting to provide understanding and new methods which the psychiatrist can put to use. Clinical psychologists are professional psychologists who either specialize in the application of standardized psychological tests to persons in order to measure certain special abilities, as intelligence or reading comprehension, so that guidance based on objective tests may be given, or who apply special psychological therapeutic procedures, as hypnosis or reeducation, to help in the adjustment of persons who find marked difficulty in meeting the problems of everyday life.

Chapter III

ORIENTING CONCEPTS

THE MORE unusual members of any community are said to be either "crazy," "peculiar," or "idiotic." Generally speaking, the word "crazy" is reserved for those individuals whose behavior is very disorderly, incoherent, or violent, and who seem to have lost contact with the common rules of conduct to which most of us respond. The peculiar individuals are those whose behavior is odd and somewhat unpredictable, but not too far removed from the same rules and regulations by which most of us govern our everyday life. The idiotic person is the one who is stupid — the feeble-minded person who seems unable to acquire knowledge by means of ordinary instruction and who fails to benefit from his own experience, whether that experience be painful or pleasant.

Varieties of Abnormal People

The everyday ways in which abnormal people are characterized are descriptive but not systematic. They do not lend themselves to a better understanding of the nature, cause, or remedy of the abnormality. It is possible to separate several major groups, each of which has certain common features and characteristics.

1. The most marked deviation from normal human behavior is shown by those individuals who are insane. These persons are suffering from a real derangement of their mental life, which is so severe that they do not respond to any of the usual methods of reason and logic which are sufficient to guide ordinary human beings. For the most part, these persons have very little or no insight into their own condition. These major mental deviations are spoken of as *psychoses*. (The term *psychosis* is reserved for the major mental diseases or derangements — the loss of mind.) Usually such persons come before the courts and are legally committed to mental hospitals. In the milder stages, in partial recovery after an acute outbreak, or when the economic situation of the family is such that adequate home care can be given, the condi-

21

tion may be camouflaged by some such name as *nervousness, run-down condition, nervous prostration, emotional instability,* or *nervous breakdown.*

2. There are many people who suffer from milder mental disorders. Such persons recognize the abnormality of their own symptoms and their need for help. They have considerable insight into their own condition. They are able to carry on their daily life after a fashion, although with nowhere near the efficiency which might be expected of them were not their mental life occupied by morbid fears, anxieties, compulsions, and obsessions. Such individuals are said to be suffering from an essential *neurosis.* (The term *neurosis* refers to the milder mental disorders which are usually found to be without physical or environmental basis, and which are recognized by the patient as abnormal, but over which he has no voluntary control.)

3. Closely allied to the neuroses are the psychological disturbances which produce, or are produced by, many kinds of physical illness or invalidism, and which are termed *psychosomatic* (mind-body) medical problems. These persons are not necessarily considered to be peculiar or insane. Their symptoms are commonly thought to be allied in some way to their physical disability.

4. There are a number of persons who, without having shown or having been conscious of any definite disorder of behavior or experience, feel that their general responses to the demands of everyday life are unsatisfactory. They are forced to seek guidance in order to achieve a better adjustment to the ordinary problems of existence. Such individuals complain of feelings of inferiority, feelings of discrimination, jealousy, unwarranted suspicion, overenthusiasm, exaggerated emotional reactions, mild depressions, chronic irritability, violent likes and dislikes, and so on. Some of these persons are said to have a *character neurosis,* and others have been called "members of the lunatic fringe."

5. There is another group of people who are, as a rule, not mentally or physically ill, but whose behavior is socially disturbing and socially inadequate. Either the person himself or the authorities may realize the unsatisfactory nature of his behavior and attempt to arrive at some basis of better life adjustment. This group includes delinquents, criminals, some alcoholics, and the sexually abnormal. Usually such persons are termed *psychopathic personalities.* They differ from the neurotics and psychotics in that they are not troubled by their own feelings; rather, their behavior is disturbing to others.

6. There are those who, from a very early age, lack the ability to acquire knowledge or to profit from experience and training. They are

unable to care for themselves adequately. These persons we term *mentally deficient* or feeble-minded.

These six groups include the majority of human beings who are called "abnormal" and whose behavior and experience constitute the subject matter of abnormal psychology. There is much variability in the composition of each of the groups. Considering the diversity of behaviors, it will be apparent why abnormal persons present so many puzzling problems. By way of illustration, suppose that any one of us knew five hundred persons. Among that five hundred there would probably be fifteen or twenty who are considered abnormal. Of these fifteen or twenty, three or four would be feeble-minded, three or four would be criminal or delinquent, three or four would be insane, and one might have epilepsy. The remainder would be neurotic.[7]* Since any one of these groups is but a small percentage of our entire acquaintance, we have no basis either for comprehending their problems or for devising adequate ways for dealing with them, unless we have special training or information made available to us. Abnormal psychology provides both information and speculation which adds to our understanding of these problems.

The Medical Concept of Psychopathology

The art and science of medicine is concerned with the treatment of disease and with the maintenance of health. It is possible — indeed, it is assumed by many thoughtful people — that most of the problems of abnormal psychology are essentially varieties of disease and hence medical problems. This viewpoint and attitude represent a marked change in human thinking which has taken place during the past century and a half. Before that time only rarely did anyone consider the possibility that abnormal behavior was a disease. Most varieties of abnormality were thought of in terms of poor self-control or willfulness, religious manifestations, possession by the Devil, loss of mind, and so forth. Due to certain discoveries, it has been established beyond all doubt that some varieties of psychopathology are disease conditions that may be adequately treated by medical methods. Therefore, the present viewpoint is that most, if not all, forms of psychopathology are essentially forms of disease. However, the ways in which the diseases may manifest themselves are thought to depend, in part, on differences in personality types.

* The numbers inserted in the text in this fashion refer to the number of the references which are listed at the end of each chapter.

Personality Types and Traits

No two human beings are exactly alike in personality structure and no single individual is completely consistent in the way he reacts at different times to the same situation. This axiomatic statement, of the uniqueness of the individual does not mean that descriptive categories of reaction are impossible. There are similarities among different individuals and consistencies in the behavior of any one individual. Attempts to describe and classify human behavior, either normal or abnormal, are based on these similarities and consistencies. The classes are named so that they may be analyzed and discussed more easily. Classification may be made on the basis of specific forms of behavior that "look" alike, that seem to arise from the same motive, or that seem to produce the same effect. Such procedures result in the grouping together of bits of behavior that seem highly diverse, but which are interpreted as having some sort of dynamic unity. The interpretations and consequent organizations depend both on the phases of behavior which are under consideration, and also upon the viewpoint of the observer.

In a sense, no individual is actually a "type." Instead of saying that some person is "typical" (as we do in everyday speech), it would be better to say that the type represents him.[5] In other words, a type gives an integrated view of the different styles of behavior. Types may be set up in two different ways. They may be developed empirically through observation of many individuals over a long period of time, or they may be developed intuitively. In the latter approach, it is understood that a certain amount of observation has taken place before the types are formulated, but the descriptive unity is formed by a sort of rapid mental synthesis which defies later analysis.

The types with which we are concerned are those which have been found of value in describing the reactions of abnormal people. Some have been derived from the study of the differences between normal and abnormal; while others although not differential, have been of value in describing general reactions of individuals with specific varieties of mental disorder.

Some otherwise normal people have personality traits which are similar to, though not necessarily identical with, the symptoms observed in one or another of the major mental diseases. Those who resemble the dementia praecox or schizophrenic patients (see Chap. IV) are spoken of as *schizoid* or autistic personalities. They are shy, close mouthed, given to daydreaming and wishful thinking, self-centered, incapable of overt emotional display, and not particularly interested in social or group activity.

The *cycloid* or cyclothymic personality resembles, in part, the symptoms shown in the manic-depressive psychosis (Chap. V). The cycloid person is boisterous, emotionally unstable, has marked swings in mood between elation and depression, is interested in social events, and likes to be the "life of the party."

The *epileptoid* person tends to be self-centered, pedantic, monotonous in speech and thought, shallow in emotion, often fanatic in his identification with some cause, and sometimes given to violent outbursts of anger and hostility. Whether or not the epileptoid has anything to do with epilepsy is a matter of debate (Chap. IX).

In addition to these three types, which are more or less related to varieties of mental diseases, there are several other personality descriptions or types which are commonly used in abnormal psychology. Among these are introversion-extroversion and dominance-submission.

Introversion-extroversion are terms that were introduced by Jung[4] which have come into popular usage. The extroverted individual is distinguished by his striving toward objects and persons around him, his identification with and his dependence on these objects and persons. The introvert shows a minimum of consideration for the objective world; his fundamental interest is directed toward himself. As Allport[1] phrased it, "The extrovert usually considers the introvert a sick soul; the introvert is often of the opinion that the extrovert is a Philistine and a bore."

Somewhat similar divisions were made by other investigators before and after the time of Jung's formulations. Stern[8] had distinguished between the subjective and objective types, and James[2] referred to the difference between tender-minded and tough-minded individuals. The tender-minded individual was described as rational, intellectual, idealistic, religious, free-willed, and dogmatic; whereas the tough-minded individual was sensationalistic, materialistic, fatalistic, and skeptical.

Types related to dominance-submission also have been of interest to the abnormal psychologist. The dominant person is the one who controls or tries to control the actions of others, who is aggressive in social relationships, and who tends to be a leader. In contrast, the submissive person tends to be unassertive, passive, and controlled by the actions of others. In describing specific varieties of abnormal persons, this submissive tendency or lack of self-assertiveness is frequently used. It is not enough, however, to know whether the person *acts* in a dominant or submissive fashion. Actually, it is more important to know whether he *feels* dominant or submissive. Dominance feeling, which amounts to high self-confidence, does not necessarily correspond to an actual dominant status with other individuals, and a dominant status

PLATE 2

CARL G. JUNG (1875–   )

does not mean that the person will have a strong feeling of dominance. He may consider himself as very ineffectual, timid, and controlled by others even when this is not the case.

Another variety of typology is that which relates the psychology or the personality of any person to his physical constitution or body-build. It is commonplace, not only for the psychologist or physician, but for any observant person to say, "That fellow looks like a day-dreamer," or "That woman looks frustrated." When anyone is asked to give the basis for such a statement, he usually resorts to generalities, taking it for granted that anyone else who looks at the individual would say the same thing. There has been for many centuries a persistent belief that there does exist some sort of a relationship between physique and mental characteristics. Systems such as phrenology or physiognomy for the analysis of temperament, personality, or character have risen, have been followed, and, having been found wanting, have disappeared. When each system was subjected to careful scrutiny, it was found lacking in value for new generations and new times.

Although the experimental evidence for the existence of clear-cut differences in physique, which will permit them to be grouped as types, is far from satisfactory, it is, nevertheless, quite common to describe any person, using one or another of the systems which have been put forth from time to time. In psychopathology, a great deal of use is made of Kretschmer's[6] classifications. He divided mental patients into three physical types: the *pyknic* (compact, round, fleshy), *asthenic* (slender, long bones, little muscular strength), and *athletic* (strong, solid, muscular). He later added a fourth group, the *dysplastic*, to describe those persons whose physical dimensions showed a conspicuous disharmony due to some dysfunction in the secretion of the endocrine glands. He held that there was a clear biological affinity between the pyknic body type and the cycloid or cyclothymic temperament and manic-depressive insanity. He believed also that there was a close connection between the asthenic group and the retiring personality characteristic of both the schizoid temperament and dementia praecox. The athletic and dysplastic groups tend to be associated with the schizoid personalities much more frequently than with the cycloid.

All of these types or traits are used either for description or explanation in abnormal psychology. They form part of the concepts which the student must understand in order to obtain a clearer knowledge of the field.

Explanatory Concepts Used in Abnormal Psychology

Modern scientific psychology regards human behavior and mentality in terms of heredity, physical constitution, physical and mental growth and development, and the influence of physical, mental, and social environment. Students of other sciences, arts, or disciplines may find it more advantageous to make some other basic assumptions. The psychologist, as a scientist, has organized his knowledge on the basic assumption that man is a biological organism and that his behavior must be explained in terms of this assumption.

Many of the explanatory concepts used in psychopathology are of the "either-or" variety; that is, the explanation is put in terms which imply that all of the factors belong to either one system of explanation or to some contrasted system. For example, we have the contrast between explanation in terms of heredity and explanation in terms of environment. We have explanations in terms of medical concepts and in terms of legal concepts. Since much of everyday explanation of abnormal behavior is related to heredity or environment, these two concepts may be briefly stated. They will be examined at length in Chaps. XVIII and XIX.

HEREDITY-ENVIRONMENT

It is generally accepted that many of our outstanding physical characteristics are genetically determined — the color of our eyes, our stature, our skin color. Many deviations and disorders, both mental and physical, are known to run in families. Finally, among the varieties of abnormal behavior there are those which are clearly genetically determined; others where heredity seems to play no role; and still others where the role of genetics is complicated by the effect of many other influences — physical, social and personal.

The use of environmental concepts in the explanation of psychopathology is widespread and, to a large extent, composed of a hodge-podge of cause-effect statements and observations, with but little guiding logic assumed. Such explanations as: "He went crazy because his business failed," "She has been despondent ever since her baby died," "He belonged to the Baptist Church but his neighbors argued religion with him till he went crazy," "He has never been right since he was hit on the head in that accident," "The judge sent him up for six months and he has been queer ever since," "Her mother and father were divorced, so that made her a queer person," are frequently heard. Usually the basic assumption is that there is an unusual social event, a profound emotional shock, an injury or an illness, or some deviation in family life which caused the abnormality. Basically it is assumed that if enough stress is placed on any person, he will "lose his mind." Since this is assumed to be a possible explanation in practically every instance of abnormal human behavior, it is necessary to examine the concept again and again as each variety of abnormality is discussed. In addition to a direct appeal to either heredity or environment, there is a group of explanatory concepts which partake from both sources, but are largely independent schemes of explanation.

INFANTILE TRAITS AND CHILDHOOD TRAINING

Since the effect of training and experience, which are had in infancy, is more or less clearly related to the fundamental attitudes, motives, and styles of reaction seen in later life, many observations and speculations are available bearing on the dynamic effect of this early experience. This particular concept has been greatly stressed by the psychoanalysts and is thought to be of real importance in the formation of the personality structure which any adult may show in later life. It is possible in certain patients to trace back the psychopathological symptoms shown in adult life to similar tendencies which their parents noted in the first year of life, as, for example, gross emotional instability related to a later cycloid personality.

Even more attention is placed on the effect of early training, early habit formation, and emotional expression as they influence later personality development. The question of thumb-sucking, the acquisition of toilet habits, the process of weaning, early home discipline, the amount of physical cuddling which the young child receives — these and other common events in everyone's life have come under scientific investigation and are thought to be of importance in personality formation.

It has been mentioned that injury or shocks in adult life are commonly thought to cause mental disorder. This concept is the next that should be clarified.

PHYSICAL AND PSYCHOLOGICAL TRAUMA

Trauma means an injury or a wound. There is good evidence that it is possible to produce deviant and disordered behavior and gross psychopathology by intense and long-continued emotional experience. Some men who were under enemy bombardment for a long period of time, certain persons who were buried in the wreckage of a house following aerial bombing, some wives with incorrigibly adulterous husbands, a few children who have harsh, ununderstanding parents — many of these have been shown to have the tendency to develop anxieties, nightmares, obsessions, and uncontrolled outbursts of emotional behavior which can be directly related to the situations in which

PLATE 3

ADOLF MEYER (1866–)

they have found themselves. Most persons, however, recover from acute symptoms which have been set up in this way when they are removed from the particular situation and are no longer forced to make adjustments under the intense strain of the situation. It is also known that the susceptibility to stress is, in many instances, related in some fashion to an innate predisposition. Some persons succumb, others do not, to apparently equivalent trauma or stress.

ADJUSTMENT

By *adjustment* is meant the arranging, composing, and harmonizing of differences, conflicts, and decisions which must be made in everyday life; the regulation or systematization of the elements of our behavior in relation to the larger components of existence. In many of the minor character and personality disturbances we commonly refer to the trouble as a defect in the adjustment which such a person is making to the problems of his existence. Meyer has stated certain of the usages of the concept of adjustment as follows:

The greatest difficulty in life, the greatest source of disharmony, apart from the influences of heredity, infectious disease, and poor feeding, and poor chance for growth, is the discrepancy between impulse, yearning and ambition on the one hand and the actual opportunities and the actual efficiency of performance on the other. We know of people who try continually to put square pegs into round holes. They are unwilling or unable to learn to know and to accept their own nature and the world as it is, and to shape their aims according to their assets.

In a large percentage of cases in which persons come to grief in their mental and moral health, the trouble is of just that kind. Failing with what is frequently impossible and undesirable anyhow, these persons develop emotional attitudes and habits and tendencies to fumble or to brood or to puzzle or to be apprehensive until what students of the functional diseases of the heart call "a break of compensation" occurs, a break of nature's system of maintaining the balance, with a more or less sudden slump and implication of collateral functions. In our field this is oftenest in the form of a declaration of a simple "minor psychosis" in which the patient maintains his or her general understanding of the situation and of human relations, but develops exhaustibility along with inability to rest, insomnia, various derangements and collisions of function, that should work smoothly, not only of sleep, but also of digestion, of the heart action, of the breathing, of the thyroid function. . . . Or the patient develops obsessions, fear of death or of going insane, doubts . . . gets into a way of paying attention to various queer feelings and conditions of special parts and organs which really are normal. . . . These conflicts and emotional states then are apt to rise to the surface as peculiar dreamy states, fancies, outbreaks of emotions. . . . The real relation, however, of these manifestations to the actual difficulties remains concealed from the layman and often actually hidden from the patient. . . . The condition is like an evasion, not a real disease of the organs but a disorder of balance by evasion or substitution, a disorder of management, adaptation and adjustment.*

An Eclectic Viewpoint

There are many different viewpoints which can be taken toward the facts of mental disorder. The simplest working viewpoint to be

* H. S. Jennings, J. B. Watson, A. Meyer, and W. I. Thomas. *Suggestions of Modern Science Concerning Education*. New York, Macmillan, 1917, 201–204.

assumed by the student who is beginning his study in this field can be stated somewhat as follows: Some human beings are born with physical or psychological weaknesses or defects which will *permit* them to acquire a mental disease or a physical disease if the proper circumstance, infection, or trauma occurs. If none of these events happen, then the person will go through life without developing the particular disability. For example, a native of some island in the South Pacific might inherit a physiological lack of resistance to tuberculosis. So long as he never came in contact with any person who had tuberculosis, he could never develop the disease. If he did come in contact with a tuberculous person, he might develop the disease, depending on his general health and other factors which operate for or against the infection. For many varieties of mental disease, it seems that the individual must have the genetic potentiality before any circumstance can provoke a derangement. For other varieties of mental illness, there is no evidence of any innate predisposition. In general, one may assume, unless good evidence is presented to the contrary, that most psychoses develop on the basis of some genetically determined susceptibility. The existence of a genetically determined predisposition, which may lead to the development of a neurosis if proper circumstances occur, is not so clearly established.

The advantage of this particular viewpoint is that it permits one to recognize the influence of heredity and constitution without minimizing the effect of social, developmental, or cultural factors. It also makes it possible to eliminate many persons from consideration as potential psychopathological patients. If a person has sufficient constitutional resistance and lacks specific susceptibility, he cannot develop the disorder in question. Those individuals who are predisposed may develop the disorder. The life conditions can then be studied very carefully to see which will favor health and which may provoke some form of psychopathology. The particular merit of this viewpoint is that it encourages the student to think about the problems of abnormal psychology with a minimum of bias and bewilderment.

REFERENCES

1. Allport, G. W., *Personality: A Psychological Interpretation*. New York, Holt, 1937.
2. James, W., *Principles of Psychology*, Vol. I. New York, Holt, 1890.
3. Jennings, H. S., J. B. Watson, A. Meyer, and W. I. Thomas, *Suggestions of Modern Science Concerning Education*. New York, Macmillan, 1917.
4. Jung, C. G., *Psychological Types*. New York, Harcourt, 1923.

5. Klüver, H., "Do Personality Types Exist?" *Amer. Jour. Psychiat.*, 1931, *10*, 781–788.
6. Kretschmer, E., *Physique and Character*. New York, Harcourt, 1925.
7. Landis, C., and J. D. Page, *Modern Society and Mental Disease*. New York, Rinehart, 1938.
8. Stern, W., *General Psychology*. New York, Macmillan, 1938.

Chapter IV

DEMENTIA PRAECOX

O F ALL of the varieties of mental abnormality, the most bizarre, crazy, or insane is that which is called "dementia praecox" or "schizophrenia" — the two terms refer to the same mental condition and are used interchangeably. The true nature, the cause, and the treatment of this group of symptoms are largely unknown. There are those who hold that it is an organic disease; those who say it is but a way of reacting, the inevitable development of unhealthy habits of thought; those who say it is but a name for a group of symptoms which may be due to a variety of causes; and those who say it is a group of diseases with certain symptoms in common. In any event, there are certain common symptoms, and common psychological and personality changes in which elements of similarity may be seen. Dealing with this symptom-complex and its subvarieties as though it were a single disease (which assumption may or may not be true) provides a way of presenting the facts in a simple fashion.

This disease is the most disabling of all varieties of mental illness; it lasts longer, has fewer recoveries, and is the most difficult for the patient, his relatives, and his friends to understand. It does not seem to be directly related to occurrences in the patient's life. In most cases it has a slow, insidious onset. It is most prevalent in the age group 22–32 years. It complicates the picture of many of the so-called senseless crimes. It is really one of the greatest medical and psychological problems of our day.

Case Histories

There are four varieties of this disease which can best be illustrated by a history of the characteristic behavior of each. The most common variety is termed *hebephrenia* or hebephrenic dementia praecox. The following history is illustrative:

CASE 1: At the age of twenty-one, he was admitted to a mental hospital because he had attempted suicide, refused to eat for fear that the food was poisoned, imagined that his sister was dead (and blamed himself for it), and feared that people were going to kill him. These acute symptoms had existed for ten days prior to admission, but for three years he had been suspicious of people around him, particularly his schoolmates, and felt that they were "ganged up against him."

He had been a good student until the last two years of high school. His teachers always liked him but he made no close friendships with his schoolmates. Sometimes, when his mother or father berated him for not looking for

PLATE 4

FACIAL EXPRESSION IN HEBEPHRENIC DEMENTIA PRAECOX[17]

a job, he became very irritable and sullen and refused to speak to them for several days. He was inconsiderate of their feelings and his mother complained that he seemed to have no affection for his father or herself. On one occasion his sister, in the course of an argument, said to him, "You're cockeyed." He became extremely excited and annoyed, declaring there was nothing wrong with his eyes. He stood in front of a mirror for a long time staring at himself. He complained that the neighbors kept their shades up so they could watch him, and finally made a scene with one of them about it. His family pointed out to him that the neighbors had always left their shades up at night but he could not be shaken from the belief that they were spying on him. Outbursts of anger at trivial happenings in the home became more frequent. One morning he slashed one wrist and threatened to shoot himself. The family doctor advised that he be taken to a mental hospital for observation.

At the time of admission he was cheerful and happy and smiled without any particular reason. He said that everything would be all right, that he would sleep, that everyone would sleep, and that everyone needed a lot of fresh air. In an exalted mood he would walk up and down the ward. In a few days his mood changed and he became somewhat depressed, suspicious, and hopeless. He said that he felt guilty and thought that he should die, but there was very little apparent emotion associated with this statement: "Everybody is sick because of me. I am to blame for everything." He was frequently preoccupied with the thought that he was part male and part female both mentally and physically. He hugged and kissed himself and murmured words of endearment to himself, stating that the male part of him was making love to the female part.

Later he became more and more talkative and carried on a rapid stream of conversation whenever he could get an audience. He offered solutions for all world problems and was anxious to act as mediator between the nations. He delighted in complicated forms of expression and wrote on such topics as "The Internity of Our Dimensionality," "Physical and Thought Strength — Technocracy's Mistake," and "Relativity, Life Cycles, the Comprehensive Cycle."

He had a rapid-fire manner of conversation and would produce in a quick matter-of-fact voice such statements as, "Tell me, darling nurse, why do I have such a passion for basins? Please put me in one.", or, "Go away, I am in conference with God." He moved the furniture from the walls to insulate it from the cosmic forces in the walls. While playing checkers he explained that he was amplifying existence by giving a personality to each of the pieces and moving them as puppets in the drama of life.

This patient was under observation for six years, during which time there were many shifts and changes in the particular symptoms shown. In the earlier phase he thought that certain individuals and the United States government were after him; and believed he was affected by cosmic forces. Throughout this time there was a gradual loss in mental control and a deterioration in personal and social habits. He became more preoccupied and irritable when interfered with. His verbal productions became more rapid, incoherent, and filled with made-up words (neologisms). He ate pieces of dirt that he found on his shoe and was untidy in his personal habits.

Among the symptoms mentioned one should note the infantile behavior, the regression and seeming deterioration, the shallow emotional responses, the senseless and illogical thought processes, the possible evidence of homosexuality, the delusions, and the hallucinations. These are all symptomatic of hebephrenia.

Another variety of dementia praecox is *catatonia*. The following history is illustrative of the course of this psychosis:

CASE 2: A laborer, aged twenty-seven, had led a normal, uneventful life. He had no special abilities or talents and left school at the age of sixteen. He was always very friendly among men but shy with women. He was cheerful, considerate, and affectionate toward his parents. He participated in sports, such as baseball and basketball. His work habits were steady and he had never been discharged from a job. Three weeks prior to admission to the mental hospital he became insomnious, seclusive, unusually untidy, and very irritable toward his brother and sister.

The first psychopathic behavior occurred when he was at a bar. A man he had known all his life came over to him and offered to buy him a drink. He turned to the man and replied vehemently, "Every time any one of you

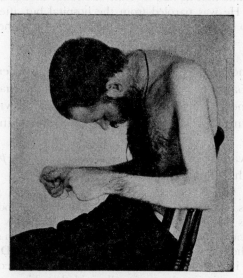

PLATE 5
RIGID CATATONIC STUPOR[17]

buys me a beer you go out and talk about it. You always talk behind my back, but you won't come out in the open and fight like a man." He became very excited and assaultive. His friends finally succeeded in getting him home where he stood at the window shouting and spitting at people in the street because he thought they were trying to get him.

When he was brought to the hospital he gave either monosyllabic responses or none at all. His face bore a blank, staring expression, his gait was slow, and he was incontinent. In the next few days he became oblivious to his environment and completely mute. He was observed standing against the wall with his arms raised above his head, and on one occasion stood with one arm bent over his head with his index finger extended as if pointing. Since he refused to eat, tube feeding was necessary. At times he became extremely resistive and assaultive to the nurses on the ward. He showed these severe symptoms for nearly five weeks and then became somewhat more cooperative. He no longer had to be tube fed and would eat from a spoon or at times feed himself. His extreme apathy changed to fearfulness and he appeared to be afraid of everything and everyone about him. After a year of hospitalization he rarely answered questions and was still disoriented. There came to be days during which he would enter into activities with the other patients and help with the ward routines. His limited conversation showed that he sometimes had auditory hallucinations. Occasionally there was impulsive, assaultive behavior.

He gradually made a better social adjustment and his personal habits improved. He was alert and cooperative and, in general, friendly. He wanted to go home and felt that he was well enough to start looking for a job. He said at the time that he had no fears or strange thoughts and that he felt "natural-like." He was paroled from the hospital but after ten months at home he had to be readmitted due to the recurrence of the previous symptoms.

It will be noted that the major psychological differences between the catatonic patient and the hebephrenic are the inaccessibility, the muscular stiffness, and the general negativism shown in catatonia. The motor symptoms are of especial importance in the catatonic syndrome.

The third variety of this disorder is *simple dementia praecox*, which is illustrated by the following case:

CASE 3: Miss S, aged twenty-seven, has had three periods of residence in mental hospitals since the age of nineteen. She was a slow but not unusual student in common school and in the first two years of high school. Until she was seventeen she was a normal child, with many friends. During the second and third years in high school she became apathetic and complained of loss of energy, vague pains, and occasionally said that things seemed unreal to her. Her parents said that there seemed to be a slow but pronounced change in character and that she seemed to lose all interest in things which she had formerly enjoyed. There was no evidence of delusions or hallucinations.

Because of her apathy and slovenliness, she was finally brought to a mental hospital, where she became even more disinterested and apathetic. She appeared to be mentally deteriorated, so that after six months her behavior and conversation were similar to that of a feeble-minded person. Her family took her home from the hospital on two different occasions, hoping that home surroundings would stimulate her and make her more normal in behavior. At home she continued in the same deteriorated fashion. Her lack of attention to her person and her untidiness interfered with the family life to such an extent that she had to be returned to the hospital on each occasion. At age twenty-seven she behaved like a stupid girl of six or seven, giving no evidence of any of the intellectual ability which had enabled her to reach high school.

These simple dementia praecox cases are marked by their apparent and long-lasting deterioration and scarcity of acute psychotic symptoms. Their indifference, their lack of judgment and foresight make them seem feeble-minded rather than psychotic. In general, they are rather inadequate persons who seem to "run down" and rarely, if ever, regain interest in normal life.

The fourth subvariety is *paranoid dementia praecox*. The following case is illustrative of the more outstanding symptoms:

CASE 4: Mr. P., aged twenty-six, was seen and this history was obtained in a mental hygiene out-patient clinic while he was working as a shipbuilder. He had been under observation in a psychopathic ward of a general hospital on several occasions. He was an only child; a high-school graduate with an average record. His mother said that he had always been suspicious and irritable and had never had very many friends or confidants.

He was firmly convinced that he had a special gift from God which enabled him to hear the voices of angels who informed him how the world should be governed and how he should comport himself with his fellow men. He wrote letters to famous people telling them what they should do to save the world. Some of these letters contained threats which had led to his arrest and observation in a psychopathic hospital. He felt that his arrest was due to the fact that he was being persecuted and that it was only an example of fact that the Devil was compelling others to make trouble for him. He systematically varied the restaurants at which he ate so that there would not be so much danger of getting poison in his food. He changed jobs and went under assumed names to avoid evil influences. He came to the mental hygiene clinic seeking advice on how to increase his will power so that he might combat the evil influence of certain labor leaders who, he claimed, were trying to kill him by changing the hours of his work. He had no insight into his fantastic and peculiar beliefs, feeling that he was divinely correct and all of the rest of the world was wrong.

He subsequently got into a fight with a workman at his place of employment and was committed to a mental hospital where he has since resided. He has not markedly deteriorated and does maintain a certain amount of interest in his surroundings, but he is irritable and makes a good deal of trouble in the hospital because of his belief in his divine mission.

The major difficulty of the paranoid dementia praecox patient revolves around his delusions in thought, belief, and action. These delusions are usually fantastic, not well organized, and are only partially incorporated into the thoughts and life of the patient. They seem to grow out of the hallucinations which the patient has, and are one way in which these patients are able to explain their bizarre experiences to themselves.

From the study of many cases the following symptoms have been shown to be more or less common to all forms of dementia praecox: hallucinations, especially of hearing, sight, and touch; incoherent associations; poor judgment; deterioration of feeling and emotion with an apparent apathy; impulsive, irritable behavior; negativism or uncooperativeness; delusions; disorder in the process of thought; and an apparent mental deterioration. Not all of these symptoms occur in every case, but it is quite usual for any case to have many of these symptoms at one time or another.

Personal Experience

The case histories and the list of symptoms describe the way in which the dementia praecox patient appears to anyone who comes into contact with him. The personal experience which the patient himself has is not very well understood for a variety of reasons. Most of the descriptions of their inner life are difficult for us to understand or appreciate. Often such a patient will say that there are no words to describe the way he feels. There have been a few schizophrenic patients who possessed a good descriptive vocabulary and the ability to analyze and report their experiences. It may be that such reports are not truly representative, but they furnish the best available psychological data.

The most outstanding difference, from normal experience, that such patients describe is the subjective effect of hallucination,* which is, to them, identical with normal sensation and perception. The only way the patient can differentiate hallucination from normal perception is through clues in the surrounding situation, such as obvious incompatibility with reality; appearance and disappearance of the perception without normal cause, and the like. Hallucinations occur without antecedents and without any connection with the conscious content of the moment. For example, the first hallucinatory voice that one well-educated patient[11, 12] heard claimed to be God, and since he was a skeptic rather than a religious man, the voice did not fit in with his mental trends. Later, as these experiences continued, they would appear and disappear without reference to what was going on around him, or what he happened to be thinking about. On numerous occasions he tried to produce hallucinations voluntarily and was always unsuccessful. Neither could he voluntarily change the nature of an

---

* Hallucination is a false experience of sensation or perception. There is no known adequate stimulus, but the experience seems real.

hallucination as it was progressing. From his inability to induce or control the appearance of hallucinations, he concluded that they were not the product of the activity of his conscious self and that attempts to explain them in this way were wrong. The hallucinations appeared to him as fully organized and complex experience; not as a vague, amorphous quantity which gradually took structure. At times, he noticed that the hallucination was of such a substantial quality that it blocked out the real external stimulation. This patient referred to the experience as an anesthesia, for factors of actual external stimulation which competed with the hallucinatory pattern were blocked out by it. For example, an hallucinated figure of a woman was completely opaque in that she seemed to block out part of the doorway in which she was standing, and her voice blocked out the actual words spoken at the same time by a real person.

Another typically schizophrenic symptom that this patient described was the auditory hallucination of hearing his thoughts clearly spoken out loud. At times they appeared to be his own thoughts which he heard, and again the voice claimed to be that of God or some other person. He had the feeling of being objectively separated from this voice. This patient experienced thoughts-out-loud as much as 90 per cent of his waking time. According to his report, the voice sometimes expressed his own thoughts, and sometimes thoughts which were foreign to him. In either case, the voice seemed to come from a point in external space, slightly above his ear. During these thoughts-out-loud he was able to recognize a certain amount of tonus in his vocal muscles and a sensation which he called "proprioceptive pressure." The pressure was said to be sometimes static and at other times vibratory. It occurred usually in the back of the upper part of the head. The vibratory phase resembled a wave passing between two poles, one at the back of the head and the other near the mouth. When he felt his pulse at the same time he seemed to notice a correlation between the pulse rate and the rhythm of the pressure.

The subjective account of hallucinatory experiences indicates that they are not initiated or controllable by the conscious self, that they appear spontaneously and do not grow out of phantasy or other conscious trends, and that they are identical in kind with normal conscious sensation and perception.

Another outstanding symptom in the schizophrenic is *loss of affect*, emotional flattening, or emotional deterioration. Judging from the subjective account given by such patients, this loss of affectivity is more apparent than real. One patient[13] believed that there was some loss in feeling tone, but that the more important change was in the direction of the feelings. Instead of attachment to persons and events in the immediate environment, the schizophrenic patient is more concerned with ideas, and about these he may have intense emotional reactions. Ideas have much more value and importance to him than do external events. In his own case he was able to notice the gradual, progressive shift in the direction of interest toward ideas and away from people and things. He believed that the dominant psychological change brought about by his psychosis was the overemphasis on ideological aspects of his mental organization at the expense of interest in the environment and its effect on him. With this overemphasis went an increased affectivity concerning ideas and a decrease concerning the other aspects of experience.

Still another aspect of schizophrenic affectivity that is frequently mentioned is its apparent inappropriateness.[7] The patient cries or laughs without known cause, or shows emotion which is inappropriate to the situation. Specifically, the patient sits and laughs and giggles to himself; when told that his wife has just died he makes no greater show of concern than if he had been told that it was raining. It has been suggested that these responses which are apparently inappropriate would be understandable and coherent if we only knew and appreciated what was going on in the patient's mind. This belief is supported by occasional instances in which the patients report later what they had been thinking and feeling, but even when these reports are made, they are somewhat incongruous. It has been suggested, also, that they are appropriate responses to the hallucinations which may be going on.

The account of the schizophrenic patient previously mentioned[13] gives interesting information about such reactions. He experienced strong affective states, such as exaltation, pleasure, or sadness which occurred spontaneously. He could not attribute them to any particular environmental occurrence, or even to his mental trends immediately previous to the emotion. He said that the time relationship between the hallucination and the affect was as follows: during an indifferent affective state, a pleasant affective state would spontaneously occur without any known stimulus, either actual or hallucinatory, to initiate it. Immediately following, a thought-out-loud would occur to which the pleasant affect was appropriate. The amount of time lapsing between the affect and the hallucination was never more than a matter of seconds. The important point here is that the affective state was never delayed until after the hallucination. This patient interpreted his experiences as evidence that both the hallucination and the affect were organized and brought about by some factor outside the conscious self. Whatever the interpretation, the evidence does indicate that the relation of the affect or emotion to the hallucination is not on the same basis as the relation of the affect to external stimuli under normal conditions. That the affect is appropriate to the ideation seems to be true, but the normal connection of cause and effect in emotional response does not seem to obtain here.

Another subjective phenomenon very frequently reported by schizophrenics is the feeling of unreality or depersonalization.[14] They say that they see or feel themselves reacting as if they were inwardly divided and one part could watch the other part. Ordinary events in the world seem to be happening at a great distance away from them and seem to have an unreal quality.

In regard to false interpretations and delusions, there are few subjective data available. Even with marked improvement many of these patients still fail to gain insight into their previous false beliefs. When questioned, they often maintain that there may have been some truth in their previous delusions. Some recovered patients have said that they do not believe that any arguments, no matter how logical, could have shaken them from the beliefs they previously held.

Facts and Figures[10]

In the entire United States in 1942 there were between 250,000 and 260,000 patients suffering from dementia praecox, resident in hospitals. There were 22,155 new schizophrenic patients admitted to hospitals for the first time during 1941. They constitute over 45 per cent of the total resident mental hospital population and over 20 per cent of the first-admissions. Of every 100,000 of the general population of the United States aged between 25 and 69 years, 243 were schizophrenic and resident in a state mental hospital (1933). Of every 1000 children born alive, 16 will spend some part of their lives in a state mental hospital suffering from this disease. The average age at first-admission for men is 30 years; for women, 34 years.

Dementia praecox has been found to occur in all races of mankind and in every country. Analysis of the rates of first-admission to mental hospitals in America indicates that during the past forty years there has been a slight increase. This increase is associated with increased hospital facilities, and with the increasing average age of the general population. The increase is not associated with war or economic depression. Among those admitted to state mental hospitals, there are 15 per cent more men than women, but there are little or no differences between urban and rural populations, or among racial and religious groups.

Out of every 100 schizophrenic patients under treatment during any given year, from 6 to 25 leave the hospital in an improved condition. This wide variation in rate of recovery is a function of the kind of patients treated, nature of treatment, and definition of the term *improved condition*. In one follow-up study of 100 cases it was found that 46 were still in the hospital after 10 years and 38 at the end of 15 years. The average number of years spent in the hospital (New York State hospitals, 1941) by those who died in the hospital was 18 years.

While many dementia praecox patients are of an asthenic constitution, this is far from uniformly true. Special studies of the personality and temperament which were said to have characterized the schizophrenic patient before hospitalization indicated that 53 per cent were shy or seclusive (schizoid), while 27 per cent were normal; in other words, there is a tendency for the psychotic state to appear as an exaggeration of the prepsychotic, but this tendency is far from universal.

The results of investigations of heredity[5] in this disease must be oriented to the fact that it occurs in about 0.85 per cent of the general population. When the family history of patients suffering from this disease is investigated, 10 per cent of the parents of such patients are found to have been schizophrenic, about 14 per cent of the brothers and sisters, 16 per cent of the children, 4.3 per cent of grandchildren, and about 4 per cent of other relatives. In studies of twins it has been shown that when one of a pair of identical twins is schizophrenic, in 80 to 90 per cent of the cases their co-twins will also be schizophrenic; in fraternal twins, about 14 per cent of the co-twins will have schizophrenic co-twins. Investigations of geneticists[6] have established the fact that whenever co-twins or other blood-relatives of schizophrenic patients are found to be psychotic, a schizophrenic type of psychosis will almost always be found, indicating a specific type of heredity.

History of the Concept of Dementia Praecox

In 1860 Morel, a French psychiatrist, used the term *démence précoce* to describe the mental condition of a boy aged fourteen who was showing marked mental deterioration and loss of memory. He emphasized the very early onset of mental deterioration. Kraepelin[9] in 1896 took over this term, *dementia praecox*, as a name for a group of symptoms which he thought were basically characteristic of a single disease. Originally, he held that the essential symptoms were the onset of mental abnormality in adolescence or early adulthood, a progression toward a state of dementia, and certain personality traits, such as shyness, irritability, and capriciousness noticeable in early childhood and becoming exaggerated with the onset of the disease. He observed that 26 per cent of dementia praecox patients improved, while 8 per cent of hebephrenics and 13 per cent of catatonics recovered. The majority of dementia praecox cases showed a progressive dementia which was not altered by any of the available therapeutic procedures. The essential characteristic of this disease, according to Kraepelin, depended upon a weakening and loss of the usual intimate connections in the mental life between emotional, volitional, and intellectual reactions. Kraepelin revised and modified the details of this concept during the thirty years following his original formulation. He always held that this condition was really a single disease of a biological nature with a large element of hereditary determination, which in all probability was due to some disturbance in metabolism or in the physiological chemistry of the body. His formulation was so well put together that no one has subsequently been able to do more than shift the emphasis with respect to the importance of certain details.

Bleuler[1] modified the concept more than anyone else. He objected to the name *dementia praecox* in that the illness does not necessarily begin in puberty and does not always terminate in dementia. He coined the name *schizophrenia*, meaning "the splitting of the mental life" which he regarded as the main characteristic of the disorder. He also held that schizophrenia was not a single disease, but rather a group of symptoms of varying origin. He did agree that the essential characteristics of the schizophrenic patient are, as Kraepelin had said, specific disorders in thought and emotion, together with a disordered relation to the external world. The thought disorder, he believed, consisted in a loss of coherence in the normal associations between ideas. The stream of thought was only partially guided by one or another central idea, such as the normal person would use in his thinking. Because of this, words of similar sound, alliteration, generalizations, nonsense words, and the like enter into their thought process making it illogical, odd, and incomprehensible. The affective disorders he believed to be particularly marked by a flattening of emotion. The sudden senseless outbursts of excitement, anger, or irritation resulted from the lack of cohesion or harmony in both intellectual and emotional integration. Of these patients' difficulty in their relation with the external world, he said, "One feels emotionally more in touch with an idiot who does not utter a word than with a schizophrenic who can still converse intellectually, but who is inwardly unapproachable." He held that schizophrenic thought was not dependent upon psychic influences, but solely upon the seriousness of the basic organic pathological process which was probably toxic in nature.

Like Bleuler, Adolf Meyer[16] took issue with Kraepelin on certain points concerning the dementia praecox concept. He held that in those patients where deterioration was not the outstanding disturbance, the diagnosis should be "allied to dementia praecox," implying that there was probably not one single disease process. Kraepelin had been impressed with the generally unfavorable course of this disease, pointing out that very few recovered. Meyer emphasized, not this failure of recovery, but rather the assets and possibilities which a patient might have which would lead to his recovery. So far as he was concerned, the symptoms themselves were only incidental and the central point of interest was the patient's elasticity which governed the chances of his recovery or his progressive dementia. Instead of dementia praecox, Meyer preferred to call this condition "parergasia," meaning a false integration of performance and behavior. He also held that on the basis of all of the physiological, anatomical, and biochemical investigations, there was no real evidence indicating that this disease was biologically determined. Rather, he pointed out that comprehensive clinical and psychological studies showed that the essential deterioration and disorder could be traced back to very early deviations from normal personality development. These initially small disorders gradually developed into the more and more complete psychopathology which constitutes the final actual psychosis. He held that the study of the prepsychotic life of such patients revealed an astonishing frequency of peculiarities in the personality make-up long before any psychopathology manifested itself. Of the deteriorated patients, those few who did subsequently recover showed from the very beginning of their disorder essential differences from those who failed to recover. Observations of this sort led Meyer to conclude that, instead of blaming heredity, toxins, metabolism, or biology, it was sounder to consider the responsible factors in terms of untimely evocation of instincts and longings and ensuing habit-conflicts.

Various writers[3] who have been influenced by the psychoanalytic formulations of psychopathology have developed still a different notion concerning the essential nature of dementia praecox. In general, they hold that in schizophrenia there is an extensive mental regression, so that the patient adopts modes of thinking and modes of behavior typical of the very earliest years of any person's life. They point both to the fact that some catatonic patients adopt the same posture which the foetus has before birth, and also to the lip and mouth movements of sucking which are quite similar to those shown by the nursing infant. The dreamlike quality of the thought and mental associations is said to come from the predominant importance of basic instincts which have no relationship to logic as we know it in adult life. The splitting between emotion and intellect in the mental life is interpreted as a return to an early level where emotion and intellect have not yet been differentiated. The condition itself, they believe, develops mainly out of the conflicts of adolescence. These patients are unable to adjust to the demands of personal and social responsibilities of adult life and so turn back to an infantile level of behavior and thought in order that they may avoid difficulties in adjustment. Many of the schizophrenics have, they say, particularly strong, unconscious homosexual wishes and desires which they cannot overcome or outgrow, and so retreat to an infantile state as a form of adjustment which they can tolerate.

Chemistry, Physiology, and Anatomy

Due both to the fact that this syndrome is fairly well defined in many patients, and to the fact that Kraepelin and Bleuler both had believed in the organic basis for the condition, there has been since 1896 a tremendous amount of work done in the fields of physiology, anatomy, and chemistry of the schizophrenic patient.[15] The work on physiological chemistry has been extended to all types of metabolic relationships that might be disordered in these persons. Attempts have been made to relate various metabolic variations to the psychological state of the patient. The subvarieties of catatonia and hebephrenia have been studied and compared to see whether there were any metabolic differences. A great variety of studies of protein and carbohydrate metabolism, liver function, oxygen and CO_2 metabolism have failed to establish any essential relationship between these functions and schizophrenia.

The hypothesis that the cause of the condition might be some toxic substance[8] produced by the body has received a great deal of attention. Studies of the blood and, indeed, of all of the fluids and most of the tissues of the body have been made, in the hope that such a toxin could be identified. So far, no distinctly positive results have been found. Other investigators, thinking that some disorder in the functions of the glands of internal secretion might be the basis of the symptoms, have made elaborate surveys of thyroid function, pituitary function, gonad function, and functions of other ductless glands. Again, the results have been disappointing.

Anatomists and neurologists have made searching and far-reaching investigations of the structural organization and the functional efficiency of both the central and autonomic nervous systems in schizophrenic patients. There is evidence of a deficiency in certain of the processes controlled by the nervous system; but just how this is related to the disease still lacks specific identification. One group of physiologists and psychologists have pointed out that the term *withdrawal* could be applied to both the psychological and physiological changes. Withdrawal is expressed psychologically in a lack of interest, apathy, and indifference; physiologically, it is expressed in a general hyporeactivity, a diminution of organic bodily responsiveness to various stimuli. This physiological withdrawal has been found to mark most schizophrenic patients, but the real meaning of the lack of physiological responsiveness is still unknown.

It seems incredible that a group of human beings as numerous as the schizophrenics could exhibit such well-marked changes without evidence of some specific peculiarities with respect to the biological processes which must be somehow involved. Whether these physiological alterations cause the disorder or are merely associated with it is a debatable point; but there can be no debate on the fact that there should be, somewhere, a differentiating organic pattern of response which accompanies the very marked and well-differentiated psychopathology. So far, research scientists have been unable to specify what this deficit, toxin, or disorder really is.

Psychology

All sorts of psychological studies have been made of the mental functions, as well as of the development and the disorders of the total personality of the schizophrenic patient. Just as is the case with organic, physical methods of investigation, there is no psychological test or group of tests on which one can make a clear and indisputable diagnosis of dementia praecox. The disorder shows itself in such a complicated way that test procedures are no more than confirmatory of the general impression which such a person makes when interviewed. Even a detailed case history which is descriptive of the individual can only point out certain symptoms and general relationships which are common to all patients of this variety. These patterns of symptoms are based on alterations of thinking, feeling, and responding to the external world. The schizophrenic tends to withdraw from reality into what seems like a dream world of his own creation. Whether such a patient really creates a dream world (intentionally and purposefully), or whether he finds himself in one is debatable. The degree of withdrawal from reality varies from a preference for solitary pastimes and activities to a condition where the individual sits on a bench day after day, mute, unresponsive, and resistive to all people and events about him. Such patients seem unable to cope with ordinary reality in an adequate way; and their needs, dreams, and wishes seem satisfied by their fantasy world. They seem unable to distinguish between real and unreal, logical and illogical, fact and dream.

The thought processes of the schizophrenic patient are strange and illogical. Associations in thought lose coherence. Two or more ideas may be condensed into one. Perseverative tendencies occur, as shown by the appearance and reappearance of some single idea which will govern for a period of time the stream of thought. Frequently the associations in thought seem to have only superficial linkage, so that successive ideas are essentially unrelated and the patient himself is unable to indicate what the essential relationship (if any) might have been. Directive ideas are repeatedly lost, so that irrelevancies and incoherencies predominate. Thoughts or ideas which are somehow opposed to the wishes or momentary emotions of the patient are excluded from the stream of consciousness, so that the patient seems no longer concerned or even aware of his inconsistencies. Two terms have been used to describe certain phases of these thought disturbances. Higher mental thought processes which deviate from the ordinary laws which govern logical thinking, and logical experiencing are termed *dereist*. Subjective thinking in which objective occurrences in the world about the individual are given personal subjective meaning and emphasis, is spoken of as *autism*.

Disorders in thought can be most adequately studied by recording the conversation of such patients.[18] It has been found that the schizophrenic uses superficially conventional language to express vague, emotional states rather than common ideas. He condenses many complex ideas and many different associations into a single word or a short phrase. He uses metaphors or words which he himself makes up and which have purely personal meanings, without making any effort to define or otherwise make them meaningful to the listener. The more deteriorated patients tend to condense whole sentences into one word or a phrase, the personal meaning of which is unprecise and changeable.

The emotional life of the dementia praecox patient is quite different from that of the normal individual or of any of the other groups of mental cases. These patients show what is called "inappropriate affect," meaning that their expression of emotion is inappropriate to the circumstances or situations in which it occurs. The inappropriate laughter and silliness which are outstanding symptoms in the hebephrenic patient were studied[7] in order to obtain information about the mechanism of the hilarity. It was found that laughing was activated more easily after the onset of the illness than in normal life, and that it seemed to relieve a feeling of inner tension. The descriptions implied that the psychosis had resulted in a disintegration of personality, which was followed by an overwhelming sense of frustration to which the patient reacted, not with despair, but rather with helpless mirth. This mirth probably is a form of cynical laughter in the early stages of the disease and later becomes stereotyped, having no longer any essential relationship to the patients' thoughts, but being merely a reaction without particular content.

Although changes in the intellectual and emotional life are frequently said to be the "primary manifestations" of this disorder, they are not the most striking feature so far as the patient, himself, is concerned. The hallucinations and delusions are, from the standpoint of the patient, the most impressive experience of psychological deviation which accompanies his psychosis. Schizophrenic hallucinations are most commonly of the auditory type. Hallucinations of vision, olfaction, kinesthesis, taste, and the like do occur, but most usually in combination with auditory hallucinations. The patient, particularly in the earlier stages of his disease, is usually unwilling to admit that he hears voices or experiences any kind of hallucinations, and when questioned on the subject tends to be evasive. The compelling, pervasive nature of the hallucinations leads him to form delusions (false beliefs) with which he accounts for his odd experience. These delusions are unshaken by contradictory, objective evidence. They frequently involve misinterpretations of actions, events, and motives of others. Most of the delusions are persecutory in nature, although some of an erotic, grandiose, or religious nature do occur.

The delusions are associated with a disturbance of insight. Insight has been defined as a peculiar characteristic of consciousness, which attaches to a belief that is based on adequate evidence; in other words, it is self-understanding. In this particular sense, insight refers to the awareness of psychological changes and to the ability of making a self-judgment as to whether these phenomena (hallucinations, feelings) are natural or morbid. In the mind of the psychotic patient such phenomena are sometimes believed to be the result of demoniacal possession, religious influence, or supernatural effects. The patient contemplates his experience with a disordered mind in which defective intellect and emotion are further complicated by hallucination. In certain patients statements which superficially indicate insight are of particular interest. Far from being insightful, they are the result of severe disturbances in emotion or hallucination, so that the patient will remark, "I must be crazy," or "I ought to be in an asylum," only to conceal from others the experience which he is having and concerning which he has no real insight.[4] Because of the splitting between psychological functions and the deficit of efficiency in many mental functions, the delusions are of a fantastic, changeable nature but are completely refractory to reason and logic. No amount of argument or demonstration will convince the patient of the falsity of his beliefs.

Another outstanding characteristic of the schizophrenic is the display of odd, distorted behavior. The forms of this behavior are too various to be summarized in any specific way. Such a patient may walk around tapping furniture with a mysterious air; he may collect meaningless scraps of paper and finger them continually; he may tie a bit of cloth to his ear or a bandage around his head. To the casual observer these performances are peculiar, purposeless, and insane. The patient himself may give either an illogical, incoherent explanation of them, or no explanation at all. His habits of personal cleanliness frequently deteriorate. Such deterioration has been called "regressive behavior" in that it is similar in form to reactions which occur in the early years of life. The psychoanalyst believes that this regression is a real psychological return to an emotional and intellectual infantilism. A similar deterioration in behavior is seen in the dementia of practically all forms of psychosis. Hence, a simpler explanation is that the mentality of a demented patient becomes so disordered and deficient that he can no longer follow the habitual responses which marked his lifetime of training in personal hygiene and cleanliness.

From the standpoint of the psychologist the outstanding characteristics of the schizophrenic patient are the weakening and splitting of the mental life (particularly in its intellectual, voluntary, and emotional aspects), the apparent arrest in personality development, the hallucinations, and the delusions.

Attention should be drawn to the possible relationship between the so-called schizoid personality and the schizophrenic psychosis. There are otherwise normal, healthy people who are of schizoid personality. They are more or less shy, uncommunicative, given to fantasy, show few external interests, and are not interested in participating in social pleasures.[2] They frequently employ dereistic and autistic thinking.

This type of personality is qualitatively similar to the exaggerated reactions seen in the schizophrenic patient. To some extent the student of human nature can gain knowledge concerning the personality reactions of the schizoid through the study of the more marked deviations shown by the schizophrenic patient. There is a note of caution which must be sounded; namely, that the similarity is often more apparent than real. So far, no standardized psychological test or procedure has indicated any fundamental similarity or necessary connection between the schizoid personality and schizophrenia.

Summary

It is strange that a condition which disables so many thousands of persons every year, which is responsible for the holding in mental hospitals of countless other thousands, is still so incompletely understood. Whether it is one disease, a group of diseases, a system of bad habits, or only a group of psychological symptoms is debatable. The weight of the evidence from all fields of research indicates that the simplest way of thinking about this problem is to view it as a "nuclear" condition — a disease — which is complicated by a number of other disorders which have been called "allied to dementia praecox." The nuclear condition is genetically determined in that some persons are born with the potentiality of developing dementia praecox while the rest of humanity does not have this potentiality. The former do not inevitably develop the disease. They do develop it when proper provoking circumstances are also present. Among such circumstances which may bring out dementia praecox in those so disposed are malnutrition, pregnancy and childbirth, exhausting physical disease, prolonged physical fatigue, and prolonged emotional stress. However, these circumstances are effective only when the potentiality is present; that is, their action alone is not sufficient to cause dementia praecox. There are also certain other mental disorders having somewhat similar symptoms which in all probability have basic causes other than nuclear dementia praecox. These are the conditions called "allied to dementia praecox."

REFERENCES

1. Bleuler, E., *A Textbook of Psychiatry* (trans., A. A. Brill). New York, Macmillan, 1924.
2. Bowman, K. M., and A. F. Raymond, "A Statistical Study of the Personality in Schizophrenic Patients," *Proc. Asso. Res. Nerv. Ment. Dis.*, 1931, *10*, 48–74.

3. Brown, J. F., *The Psychodynamics of Abnormal Behavior*. New York, Mc-Graw-Hill, 1940.

4. Campbell, M. M., "The Judgment of Insight," *Amer. Jour. Psychiat.*, 1940, *96*, 945–950.

5. Kallmann, F. J., *The Genetics of Schizophrenia*. New York, Augustin, 1938.

6. ———, "The Operation of Genetic Factors in the Pathogenesis of Mental Disorders," *N. Y. S. Jour. Med.*, 1941, *41*, 1352–1357.

7. Kant, O., " 'Inappropriate Laughter' and 'Silliness' in Schizophrenia," *Jour. Abn. Soc. Psychol.*, 1942, *37*, 398–402.

8. Kopeloff, N., *Bacteriology in Neuropsychiatry*. Springfield, Ill., C. C. Thomas, 1941.

9. Kraepelin, E., *Dementia Praecox and Paraphrenia* (trans., R. M. Barclay). Edinburgh, Livingstone, 1919.

10. Landis, C., and J. D. Page, *Modern Society and Mental Disease*. New York, Rinehart, 1938.

11. Lang, J., "The Other Side of Hallucination," I, *American Jour. Psychiat.*, 1938, *94*, 1089–1097.

12. ———, "The Other Side of Hallucination," II, *Amer. Jour. Psychiat.*, 1939, *96*, 423–430.

13. ———, "The Other Side of the Affective Aspects of Schizophrenia," *Psychiatry*, 1939, *2*, 195–202.

14. ———, "The Other Side of the Ideological Aspects of Schizophrenia," *Psychiatry*, 1940, *3*, 389–393.

15. McFarland, R. A., and H. Goldstein, "The Biochemistry of Dementia Praecox," *Amer. Jour. Psychiat.*, 1938, *95*, 509–552.

16. Meyer, A., "Fundamental Conceptions of Dementia Praecox," *Brit. Med. Jour.*, 1906, *2*, 757–760.

17. White, W. A., *Outline of Psychiatry* (12th ed.). New York, Nervous and Mental Disease Monographs, 1929.

18. Woods, W. L., "Language Study in Schizophrenia," *Jour. Nerv. Ment. Dis.*, 1938, *87*, 290–316.

Chapter V

MANIC–DEPRESSIVE PSYCHOSIS

NEXT TO dementia praecox in importance among the major forms of psychopathology is the manic-depressive psychosis. This illness is marked by either (or both) an acute press of activity and excitement (mania), or by an unreasonable melancholia (depression). Like dementia praecox, the true nature, the cause, and the treatment of this disease are controversial. Also, as in dementia praecox, there are those who hold that manic-depressive psychosis is one disease; those who say that it is two or more diseases; those who say that it is only a group of psychological symptoms without a common basis; and those who say that it is the inevitable outcome of unhealthy habits of thought and behavior. Just as we have considered dementia praecox as one disease — in spite of the possible doubt of the assumption — so shall we deal with manic-depressive states as a disease with a fairly well-defined psychopathology.

The manic-depressive psychosis occurs in about half as many persons as dementia praecox, but in spite of the severity of its course and symptoms it has a high rate of remission or recovery. Generally speaking, it seems more "sensible." In most instances we think we can understand why the patient behaves as he does and we can, without too much effort, imagine ourselves behaving similarly. Although the mania and the depression seem vastly different, psychological analysis shows them to be fundamentally similar.

Case History

CASE 5: Miss M was admitted to a mental hospital early in February. She was excited and confused but said she was eager to be in the hospital and to receive treatment because she could not stand other people suffering because of her. She, and her family, said that her acutely emotional state was due to a frustrated love affair. Within two days she became quiet, depressed, slow-moving, soft-spoken, and tearful. She complained of a feeling of worthlessness, at the same time giving an impression of being quite egotistical and resentful. Mental examination showed that she was well oriented as to time, place, and person; her memory was good; her thinking capacity diminished because of her hopeless attitude; her insight faulty; and her judgment poor. All findings on physical examination were negative.

Her condition improved so that early in March she was allowed to go home to her family. The improvement proved transient and she was returned to the hospital in May in an acutely melancholic condition. This depression gradually lessened so that in September she seemed cheerful, although timid and thoughtful. Until mid-October she vacillated between periods of confused depression and bursts of excited, boisterous activity. One day she announced that she had a sudden feeling that she was well again and that all her trouble was over. She became overactive, talkative, and elated. She compared her elation to her depression by saying: "This condition is going on increasingly more and more, both mentally and physically. Thoughts are going through my head. It is now excruciatingly wonderful; before it was excruciatingly awful. I am so happy I want to cry. Before, no emotion was genuine, sincere, or pleasant. At times I thought I was happy but I felt I never was sure. Now it is wonderful and just as intense in the other extreme. It is something uncomfortable. I remember how I used to feel and I don't ever want to feel that way again."

She had to be transferred to a disturbed ward where her overactivity and excitement increased day by day. She was given sedatives and continuous baths but remained very noisy and obtained little sleep. She was frequently placed in a continuous bath for the purpose of relaxation but continued her rapid fire of conversation throughout the day. She showed flight of ideas, rhyming, singing, and screaming. On one occasion she said, "How did you get to know Dr. Carr? I know, in a Ford. I will show you a ticket. [A ticket for what?] For Mary, Queen of Scot! [Who played in Mary of Scotland?] Mary Browning, the Barretts of Wimpole Street! What pole? The thinker, the trolley horse. [Whose horse?] The horse on a treasure hunt." [Upon observing the doctor writing] "Did I ever explain to you that a sheet of paper is an inclined plane? A sheet of paper with lines on it is an ink-lined plane. An inclined plane is a slope up and a slow pup is a lazy dog." On the ward she would strip off her clothing, yell, dance, spit on others, curse and scream obscenities. This conduct continued for three weeks before she grew somewhat quieter; but she remained talkative and excitable until early December when she calmed down to such an extent that she could again be sent to the convalescent ward. During January and February she continued to be somewhat overactive, excitable, talkative, and irritable. Early in March her behavior was once more normal, so that she was finally discharged from the hospital. Her entire first cycle of depression and mania lasted a little over a year. During six years following this original illness she has been in a mental hospital on two occasions, once for eight months and once for thirteen months, each time with symptoms similar to her first attack.

Not all patients of this sort show both the depression and the mania. Kraepelin[12] found that the first attack is a depression in 60 to 70 per cent of patients. Two thirds of the depressions are followed by a remission; one third by mania and then usually by remission. When mania is first, two thirds are followed by remission and one third by depression and then usually by remission. More recently Pollock[23] reported that in more than half of over 8000 patients there was no recurrence of attack of sufficient severity to cause readmission to a mental hospital. Patients who were aged between 20 and 40 at first-admission had fewer recurrences than those whose first-admission occurred before 20 or after 40.

There are certain psychological changes which are marked in both the mania and the depression, and other symptoms which are peculiar to only one of the conditions. In both states there is a basic mental inhibition, a partial paralysis of volition, attention, perception, and association. Except in delirious states, consciousness is clear and hallucinations rare or inconsequential. Memory remains unimpaired for the life before the illness, while, because of the emotional disturbance and unclear perception, memory for events during the illness is fragmentary. Judgment is defective, with frequent delusions which fit the predominant emotion — expansive in mania, hypochondriacal and self-accusatory in depression. There is no real dementia during or following either state.

The following mental functions are markedly disturbed in apparently opposite but fundamentally similar ways in depression and mania:

Both Phases	Manic Phase	Depressive Phase
a. Attention weakened	Distractibility	Inattention and conflict of attention
b. Affectivity: inhibition of altruistic feelings	Pleasantness, elation, euphoria	Unpleasantness, anxiety, gloom
c. Associations retarded	Flight of ideas (no "Goal Idea")	"Thinking difficulty" and fixed ideas
d. Action: inhibition of voluntary action	Psychomotor excitement or "Pressure of Activity" with absence of fatigue	Psychomotor retardation, and exaggerated feelings of effort and fatigue*

Personal Experience

Since most persons who suffer from this disease recover, and since only rarely is there any mental enfeeblement or deviation during subsequent normality, many excellent accounts† have been published.

---

* Bridges, J. W., *Outline of Abnormal Psychology* (2d ed.). Columbus, R. G. Adam,s 1921, 144.

† Beers, C., *The Mind That Found Itself*. New York, Longmans, 1908.

Krauch, E., *A Mind Restored*. New York, Putnam, 1937.

Hillyer, J., *Reluctantly Told*. New York, Macmillan, 1927.

Kindwald, J. A. and E. F. Kinder, "Postscript on a Benign Psychosis," *Psychiatry*, 1940, *3*, 527–534.

Although these accounts differ among themselves, it is possible to pick out from them many elements in common and so to understand better the psychological experiences and psychotic manifestations which occur during the illness.

Initially, there is a marked diminution or loss of self-control, which loss the person recognizes, at least for a short period of time. The depression or the excitement is recognized as being exaggerated and ill founded but uncontrollable. This results in a variety of dissociation which persists in varying degree throughout the illness. Kipling's lines, "Stood beside an' watched myself be'avin' like a bloomin' fool," characterize such an experience very well, since they indicate that the person has some knowledge of the fact that he is acting strangely. There are lapses in the memory of the patient for periods of time during the illness. On recovery there may be blanks for days, weeks, or months which are totally missing. Usually these lapses correspond to the more severe phases of the excitement or depression as observed and recorded at the hospital.

Both the excited and depressed phases are marked in the mind of the patient by an exaggerated irritability and sensitivity. They remember being greatly hurt and unreasonably irritated by events or chance remarks which were in reality innocuous. One patient described this state which occurred when she was in a manic phase as follows:

"Although I was quite willing to acknowledge that the hospital was doing the best that it could, nevertheless suspicion was there too, and I was eager to support it. The best that could be done! Just that had been known to fail so often! Surely there might have been some other way! All the while, down underneath there was resentment, seething, turbulent, threatening, something unaccountable that thumbed its nose at mental processes and formulae. Just then I wanted more than anything else, someone who would question the judgment of the hospital, someone who would dispute it to the bitter end. There came back to me a well-remembered saying of Dr. Meyer's: 'The psychosis is an experiment of nature.' The phrase which I had always enjoyed, now roused a violent protest. 'Why should I be one of nature's guinea pigs?' Feebly, the logical counter query rose: 'Why, pray, should I not?' I had no satisfactory answer for either question . . . As the nurse and I walked back to my room, everything seemed hushed and still. 'You will have to keep quiet now,' she said, 'You must go to sleep.' Oh, I *must* go to sleep, must I! was my unspoken reply . . . Bars! Human stupidity and callousness. What lay beneath the well-regulated surface of this hospital? What worship of routine and habit would I find here? Since all society was honeycombed with these, surely this place would not be free of them! I had little hope that the hospital would help me. I had begun to feel that, possibly, the physician might; but that would be through something of himself, not because of any observations by nurses. I wouldn't have given a fig, just then, for all the notes of all the nurses on the place." *

The disorganization of thought which marked the acute manic confusion was described by this same patient as follows:

"There appeared increasing use of bizarre symbolism, progressive fragmentation, and loss of sense of continuity. . . . [The] memory of making a cake illustrates the fragmentation and the gradual intrusion of symbolic ideas. . . . I tried to follow what the instructor was saying. I kept hearing her voice, caught phrases, separate bits of what she said, and found myself wondering why all this seemed difficult. As the work progressed, a change came. The ingredients of the cake began to have a special meaning. The process became a ritual. At certain stages the stirring must be counterclockwise; at another time it was necessary to stand up and beat the batter toward the east; the egg whites must be folded in from left to right; for each thing that had to be done there were complicated reasons. I recognized that these were new, unfamiliar, and unexpected, but did not question them. They carried a finality that was effective. Each compelling impulse was accompanied by an equally compelling explanation." †

The acute mental distress and suffering which are the outstanding experience during the phase of depression were described by another patient in this way:

"Suffer? And what is the verdict of people who have undergone the most excruciating physical pain, and then been mentally ill? These people say: 'Rather all the physical illnesses — every one of them — over again, than mental breakdown.' Or, more simply, 'That's the real hell.' Torture. There is never any getting away from it. Your body seems shaken by it. It gives you no rest. It is like a mental flagellation — always, day and night. The minute you wake up it is there. All day long it is there. Whatever you try to do it stands in your way. And sometimes it is like a big, threatening obstacle. But you have to put up with it. You think: 'Isn't there something the doctor can cut away?' It is like a monster, it is like a growth. It presses down on you. It mocks you. It exhausts you. It makes your thoughts go spinning around like a squirrel in a cage, and it wears you out just as going around in a circle physically would wear you out. 'If I could only press a lever to stop this whirring,' you say to yourself. Yet you *cannot stop.* You cannot 'snap out of it.' If only you might. For just a minute, for just a second. No wonder so many depressives long for death.

"Perhaps the best way to explain it is to say that it is like an unpleasant noise; but a much more unpleasant and awful noise than any one who is sane could ever imagine. Think of a noise like that, the worst, most grating, most nerve-racking noise you ever heard; then imagine that it never stops,

---

* Kindwald, J. A. and E. F. Kinder, "Postscript on a Benign Psychosis," *Psychiatry*, 1940, *3*, 529.

† Kindwald, J. A. and E. F. Kinder, *ibid.*, 530.

never, never for an instant. Imagine that you recognize this; that you know the noise will never stop. That it will go on in this way forever, tearing at your nerves, pulling at your muscles, goading at your mind, deriding you, reproaching you, sneering at you! Then maybe you will not blame us for thinking of suicide. Then maybe you will no longer say, 'They do not suffer.' Yes, we suffer."*

Another common experience is "mental weakness," particularly during recovery. It is as if the mania or depression had so exhausted the mental processes that the patient can only think, respond, or decide with the greatest difficulty. This weakness is described by others as confusion, indecision, or unwarranted sensitivity. Return to normal mental vigor seems to be mainly governed by time. The recovery is *slow* but relatively constant and complete.

Facts and Figures[14]

Among the first-admission patients to the mental hospitals of the entire United States in 1941, there were 10,551 manic-depressive patients who constituted 10 per cent of the new admissions. There were between 35,000 and 40,000 manic-depressive patients resident in the mental hospitals of the entire United States during the same year, constituting about 12 per cent of the entire resident population of mental hospitals. Of every 1000 children born alive in the United States, according to present expectancy, 5 will at some time during their lives be hospitalized for this disease. The average age of patients admitted to the hospitals with this diagnosis has been steadily increasing from 30 years in 1913 to 37 in 1941.[15] The disease is 20 per cent more prevalent among women than among men.

During the past thirty years the annual rate of first-admissions to mental hospitals in the United States of persons suffering from manic-depressive psychosis has decreased from 12 to 8 per 100,000 of the general population of the country aged over fifteen.[21] This decrease is probably due to the more frequent use of other psychiatric diagnoses, since there is no comparative decrease (actually there is a slight increase) in the number of hospitalized mental patients in the same age range which includes manic-depressive psychosis. The decreasing rate is not associated with any economic or social change, wars, or depressions. There is no real difference between the frequency of the appearance of this disease among persons who live in the city and persons who live in a rural environment. In New York State hospitalization for this

* Krauch, E., *A Mind Restored*. New York, Putnam, 1937, 95–96.

disease is about 50 per cent more common among Negroes than among the white population, and somewhat more common among those of Irish birth or Irish parentage than among those of other national origin.

Of every 100 manic-depressive patients under treatment during any year, about two thirds will be discharged as greatly improved or recovered. The disease usually ends in complete remission, in the sense that the individual gradually loses his psychotic symptoms and is said by his friends and relatives to be of the same personality and intellectual status as he was before the onset of his disease. A follow-up study of cases who had been admitted to mental hospitals fifteen years previously indicated that during the first year 41 per cent of such cases were discharged and not later readmitted to a hospital, while 18 per cent were later readmitted. At the end of the fifteenth year 13 per cent of the original group were still in the hospital, 17 per cent had died, and 67 per cent had been discharged and never readmitted.

The statistical reports indicate that the onset of the psychosis often follows physical illness, loss of employment, or financial loss. A pyknic type of physical constitution and a cycloid type of prepsychotic personality make-up are found in many of these patients. The cycloid form of temperament is said to be characterized by emotional instability, irritability, and a tendency to egocentricity and minor mood swings, which, in a diluted form, duplicate the manic and depressive episodes of the disease itself. According to a report of Bowman and Raymond,[3] about one third of manic-depressive patients showed a cycloid type of prepsychotic personality, while another third revealed unusual personality traits other than cycloid. The remainder were classified as normal, since no unusual personality traits had been noticeable before the onset of the disease.

Manic-depressive psychosis occurs in 0.44 per cent of the general population irrespective of their genetic background. Various investigations have reported that from 15 to 39 per cent of the parents of these patients suffered from the same disease; 7 per cent of their brothers or sisters; and 3 per cent of the grandparents. In one study of identical twins it was found that in 16 of 23 pairs both members were affected by the disease, while in the remaining 7 pairs only one member was affected. Generally speaking, geneticists hold that the genetic determination of the disease is specific; that if any person has inherited this specific determiner, he may develop manic-depressive psychosis (not dementia praecox or some other psychosis), though he will not inevitably do so if the proper precipitating circumstances do not occur.[9]

Various investigators have given evidence that the environmental precipitating circumstances are not so significant for the development of manic-depressive psychosis as they are for dementia praecox.

History of the Manic-Depressive Concept

The description of mania and of melancholia as forms of abnormal behavior survives among the fragments of the most ancient medical literature extant.[7] The phenomena marking these types of disordered behavior were described in the Bible and in the early Greek tragedies, as well as in ancient medical descriptions. The long, involved history of description and theory dealing with mania and melancholia need not concern us at present. The interested student can find as good a summary of this material as is available in Burton's *Anatomy of Melancholy*, first published in 1621.*

Falret and Baillarger between 1850 and 1854 brought together a number of observations which led them to believe that, in addition to mania and melancholia as separate disorders, there was a circular or double form in which the two appeared alternately. In spite of this formulation, most writers and systematists continued to speak of many different forms of mania and melancholia with but little reference to the fact that the two might possibly be associated. In 1899 in the sixth edition of his *Textbook of Psychiatry*, Kraepelin first formulated the concept of the manic-depressive psychosis. He said, "In the course of years I have been more and more convinced that all of these pictures are but forms of a single disease process. Certain fundamental features recur in these morbid states notwithstanding manifold external differences."† Essentially, he held that this was a disease which included all of the periodic and circular forms of psychosis, as well as simple mania and simple depression, together with their mixtures and combinations.[12] He believed that this condition was marked by certain fundamental recurring features which give a uniform stamp to all of the varieties of clinical manifestations and afford a fixed point for the prediction of the outcome of the illness. He further held that these forms of abnormal behavior pass over from one to the other without recognizable boundaries, so that they may, and often do, replace each other in one and the same case. He pointed out the general favorable prognosis for any single attack, the tendency for repetition of attacks, and the

* See F. Dell and P. Jordan-Smith, editors of R. Burton, *The Anatomy of Melancholy.* New York, Rinehart, 1927.

† Kraepelin, E., quoted from S. E. Jelliffe, "Some Historical Phases of Manic-Depressive Synthesis," *Proc. Asso. Res. Nerv. Ment. Dis.*, 1930, *11*, 6.

significance of heredity and of the physical constitution in the determination of the disorder. Lange, who followed Kraepelin, pointed out in 1928 the following facts which he believed to be of particular importance.

(1) We have to do with a very definite hereditary illness, the features of which are very complicated. At times in families with members with circular psychoses simple direct inheritance of marked temperaments is evident. The tendency to the development of cyclic psychical as well as somatic disorders is striking. Circular metabolic developments, 'arthritic' in character, are frequent in these families. (2) Mania and melancholia, as observations on one-cell twins show, are not separable on an hereditary basis. (3) The time of onset of circular disorders is hereditarily fixed, even though at times, outside constellation factors may modify the cycles. (4) Critical times are paramount in the circular phasic disorders, thus, puberty, pregnancy, birth, menopause and also severe infections. *

Meyer[18] took issue with the concept of manic-depressive psychosis as it was formulated by Kraepelin. He held that this condition was not a disease, as such, but rather a behavioral deviation shown in the total integration of the organism in which definite situations, reactions, and types of personality must be evaluated. He called this condition "thymergasia." He insisted that all factors entering into the disorder, such as infections, metabolic disturbances, toxic processes, physical constitution, and the life history of the person, must be considered in determining our understanding of the condition as it exists in any particular person. The depressive reaction types, he held, were essentially a withdrawal by the patient from an overwhelming environmental or personal situation which he could not handle. The withdrawal took the form of depression because of the particular constitutional make-up of that person. Excitement or mania he thought of as a violent rebellion of the patient in response to definite life difficulties and this outbreak was determined by the previous personality of the particular person. Analysis of the thought content of the patient during the more acute stages of the disorder indicated that the basis of the excitement or the depression was formed by the previous habits of the individual and by his reactions to a certain life situation in which he found himself.

The psychoanalytic explanations of this type of disorder have mainly been directed toward the understanding of depression or melancholia, although a few studies have been made of the manic phase. In general, the analysts have held that the depression represents

* Lange, J., quoted from S. E. Jelliffe, *ibid.*, 12.

an assimilation (introjection) by the person of the hostility which he formerly felt toward some lost love object. This hostility was previously neutralized by affection which was mixed with the hostility, but following the loss the individual turns the entire hostility back on himself. Hence, he hates himself both for his previous hate and love and for his inability to make up for the loved object which he has lost. In normal grief there is a conflict between love and hatred which is at least partially recognized; but in melancholia this recognition is lost. This particular concept was further developed by Abraham,[1] who stated that the psychopathology of the depression may be characterized (according to Oberndorf and Meyer[20]) as follows: "A state of depression is precipitated when the patient is obliged to make a definite decision as regards the attitude and application of his libido, as for example, when about to fall in love. . . . [The conflict is formalized as follows:] I cannot love because of my hate; the result is I am hated and so I am depressed and hate back."

The analytic formulation of the manic phase is not so specific, but, in general, the behavior is related to the law of retribution and retaliation. In childhood we found that punishment serves to wipe out the consequences of our sins, and so all religions and societies have institutions and rituals for easing both the individual and social conscience. In the manic phase there is a release of instinctive drives toward retribution in which normal inhibition by conscience (Superego) disappears. The manic allows himself every possible form of psychological retaliation — abusive language, excessive love-making, screaming, obscenities. He is driven by a vague sense of impending doom since his conscience is not completely lost. In mania the patient retaliates directly; while in depression, being overwhelmed by his conscience, the only retaliative satisfaction he gets comes from the discomfort which his suffering causes others.

It is evident that there is no essential unity between the various schools of thought with respect to the basic psychological nature of manic-depressive psychosis. Kraepelin emphasized constitutional predisposition; Meyer emphasized life situations and habit patterns; while the psychoanalysts emphasized the interplay between love and hate, retaliation and retribution.

Anatomy, Neurology, and Physiology

The extremes of agitated excitement and dejected depression shown by these patients are among the most profound deviations of both feeling and behavior which are exhibited by any type of psychotic or neurotic patient. Since they are so extreme it seems only logical that they should be accompanied by marked changes in the biological functions of the individual, which could be determined by the methods of anatomy, physiology, or biochemistry. It may be that the disorder is psychological in origin, or it may be that it is physiological; but in either event, one would expect that such marked psychological changes would be accompanied by gross and easily detectable physiological alterations.

There is a tendency for these cases to have a slightly increased blood sugar; for some of the acutely depressed to be defective in sugar tolerance; for the manics to have a slightly increased blood calcium; and for the fat content of the blood to be rather high in both the manic and the depressive patient.[17] However, every one of these tendencies is well within the limits of normal variation so that the findings are not particularly significant or definitive. Some investigators have not been able to find relationships between the sugar content of the blood and the mental state, whether depressed or manic; while others have reported high blood-sugar values, particularly in the depressed state. It may be that the increases which have been found are due to the immediate emotional reaction to the withdrawal of the blood sample, rather than to the psychotic disturbance itself. High blood sugar in the normal person does not produce an emotional reaction. There is usually an increase with marked physiological activity, so that one might expect that there would be an increase in the agitated state, but this has not been found.

The very intense and prolonged activity of the manic patient in contrast to the marked retardation in activity of the depressed patient would lead one to believe that there should be a marked variability in the rate of basal metabolism, that is, the rate at which sugar is consumed by the body. In such patients as were cooperative enough to secure satisfactory measurements, extremes in metabolic rate were not found, the rates for the most part falling within the limits of normal variability.

The agitation which some of these patients show suggests that there might be some gross disturbance in the glands of internal secretion, particularly the thyroid gland. However, no one of the studies which have been directed at the detection of thyroid dysfunction in this psychotic condition has produced results which were outside of normal variability. Since the psychosis occurs more frequently in women than in men, and since it is frequently associated in onset with the menstrual cycle, the possibility that it might be associated with disturbances in the gonadal secretions of the ovaries has been studied. Again, no significant results have been obtained.

Some years ago various investigators made studies of the brains of manic-depressive patients who had died during their psychoses. No findings of special significance were established by the neuropathological examinations.

Lewis[16] made an anatomical study of eight cases in which the symptoms during life had indicated that the disorder was a clear-cut manic-depressive psychosis. He stated that very few anomalies could be found from physical examination or during autopsy. There was some evidence of an enlargement of the heart and vascular system, some evidence of previous hemorrhage into the thyroid gland, and, in general, a possible increase in the size of the various glands of internal secretion. He believed that in these particular individuals the circulatory and endocrine systems had reacted in a compensatory way in excess of that usually found in those dying at about the same age as these particular patients.

The rate of secretion of saliva by the parotid gland has been shown to vary markedly in depressed patients as compared to normal persons.[25] The depressed patient frequently complains of a dry mouth and of difficulty in swallowing. His complaint is borne out by the finding that there is an excessively small amount of saliva secreted over long periods of time. The rate of secretion for the manic patients is approximately the same as that found in normal individuals. Although this finding is based on a small number of cases, it does have promise as an indicating device for the differentiation of the truly depressed individual from patients in whom the depression is complicated by other symptoms so that one cannot be sure of the true nature of the disorder. Why this particular physiological deficit should occur in depression and not in mania is not understood.

From an extensive review of the literature bearing on the biochemistry of this disorder, one investigation concluded that the variability exhibited in emotional control might, in turn, be related to a defective homeostasis.[17] By this was meant that the physiological control of the interrelationship between the various organic systems of the body was defective and that the physiological defect was somehow associated with the psychological defect.

It is generally thought, at present, that the lack of positive findings of physiological disturbance in this condition is due either to (*a*) the fact that very few patients have been studied over a long enough period of time to relate the tests satisfactorily to the psychological alterations;

or to (*b*) the present lack of any suitable indicator or measure for the physiological changes which do take place. This second point is plausible if one considers the analogy of the manic-depressive psychosis to that of morphine addiction. There is in both states a very marked disorder of behavior and of psychological experience. No one has yet been able to demonstrate just what the physiological effects of morphine are, either in the way it produces the addiction or in the way in which it produces mental disturbances. Usually, this lack of positive information is said to be related to our ignorance of proper tests.

Psychology

Many psychopathologists have held that there is a fundamental relationship between the cycloid personality and the manic-depressive psychosis. Such a cycloid person has periods of time in his life during which he feels elated, full of energy, possessed of many ideas, hopeful, and overactive. When in this condition, he actually is exceedingly productive and accomplishes much. Many such accomplishments would be impossible for the ordinary person because the average man lacks the necessary energy and spirited motivation. At other times, the cycloid individual will have periods of mild depression or "the blues." It just does not seem worth while to expend the energy to accomplish anything. Life appears somewhat futile and there is no particular point in working hard. In some persons these mood swings are always in one direction, either elation or depression; while in others there is an alternation. Psychologically, these changes may be regarded as a kind of defense against the problems of everyday life. When things worry us we often become restless, pace up and down, are unable to sit still, or try to keep busy so that we do not have to think. At other times we simply sit with our head hung down and our hands folded, refusing to take part in anything that is going on around us, so defending ourselves by the simple means of shutting out the world.

There is an obvious psychological similarity between the gross behavior disturbances shown by the manic-depressive patient and the minor emotional changes shown by the cycloid personality. Since the similarity is so plain, it seems only reasonable to believe that the psychotic condition might be but an exaggeration of the behavior and mental experience of the individual with the cycloid personality.

In spite of the difficulties encountered in getting information about prepsychotic personalities, it has been possible to secure relatively adequate characterizations of groups of patients in which the diagnosis was not a matter of doubt. Surprisingly enough, these investigations, which were carried on with both dementia praecox and manic-depressive patients, failed to show that the prepsychotic personality was uniformly associated with the type of disease which the individual developed.[3] Generally speaking, it may be concluded from the work of different investigators that about half of dementia praecox patients had a prepsychotic schizoid personality, and that but one third of manic-depressive patients were cycloid personalities. Stated in a different way, the information which is obtainable from friends and relatives indicates that the distinctive psychotic symptoms occur as often as not in personalities or temperaments which were called "normal" before the onset of the disease. It seems possible that, if any person has the basic potentiality to develop either of these major psychoses, he may show the symptoms in mild degree for a number of years before the onset of the acute disturbance; but in an equal number of instances no evidence of behavior similar to that shown in the disease itself will be found until the disorder appears in a rather abrupt fashion.

Several investigators have held that in dementia praecox the pattern of response which was obtained on certain of the standard intelligence tests could be used as a *schizophrenic index*.[10] This index, although not too well defined or established in all cases, does have some psychological value in that it reflects the splitting of the personality, the peculiarity of associations, and the contradictory nature of the ideas in the thought process. Attempts which have been made to derive a similar *cycloid index* have not been successful. There is no evidence that the manic-depressive patient in either phase of the disorder performs in any unique way on an intelligence examination.[24] It is true that the depressed patient frequently gives a performance which is much below his actual intellectual capacity. He either will not, or cannot, cooperate to an extent which will provide an index of his true intellectual level. The same sort of inferior intellectual performance is occasionally obtained from manic patients who are too preoccupied and flighty to pay attention to the details of the examination.

It will be recalled that Jung[8] characterized the outlook on life of different persons into two groupings, introversion and extroversion. The introvert, he said, is primarily interested in himself; while the extrovert is interested in the world about him and the way he can take part in it. Jung suggested that marked introversion was associated with the schizoid personality and schizophrenia, while extroversion was associated with the cycloid personality and the manic-depressive psychosis.

A great many psychological studies have been carried on with respect to the possibility that human beings could be characterized as predominantly introverted or extroverted. In general, it has been found that most persons are ambiverts; that is, neither predominantly introverted nor extroverted. Applications of the more or less standardized psychological tests of introversion-extroversion to groups of psychiatric patients have shown that some, but not all, schizophrenics obtain high introversion scores; while some, but not all, manic-depressives obtain high extroversion scores.[19] This is not too remarkable, since most of these tests have been drawn up to be descriptive of the outstanding psychological symptoms of the schizophrenic and the manic-depressive patient and one should, therefore, find some agreement between the test results and the personalities which they were supposed to describe.

A major drawback of the questionnaire type of investigation, applied to psychiatric cases, comes from the fact that the patient does not see himself or think of himself in the same terms that the normal observer does. Several years ago Page, Landis, and Katz[22] drew up a series of 54 statements to which the schizophrenic patient might be expected to give specific answers. These statements were put together in a questionnaire form and given to a fairly large group of dementia praecox, manic-depressive, and normal individuals. Each of the 54 questions was supposed to be characteristic of the schizophrenic patient (he should be expected to answer Yes) and to distinguish him from either the manic-depressive or the normal person. The average patient in the schizophrenic group gave the answer Yes to 17.6 of the 54 items; the average manic-depressive gave the answer Yes to 14.0 of the items; while the average normal person answered Yes to 18 of the 54 questions. From this, it may be concluded that the patients do not think of themselves as possessing the psychological traits which we normal persons attribute to them. Also, there is no particular distinction between the self-descriptions afforded by schizophrenic and manic-depressive patients in this type of investigation.

Many other varieties of psychological tests and experiments have been tried with manic-depressive patients who were cooperative enough to provide valid responses. No one of the standard test procedures, nor any combination of these procedures, has been found to be of particular significance. These patients vary so much among themselves that the test results do little more than confirm the presence or absence of outstanding psychological deviations which are obvious to any careful observer who has had some experience with this type of disorder. Just as there is an absence of positive association between the physiological and biological experimental findings and this disease, so is there a lack of association between any of the standardized psychological test procedures and the manic-depressive psychosis.

With the possible exception of a more-than-chance number of persons said to be of cycloid personality before they develop this disorder, we are forced to the conclusion that this particular variety of psychopathology appears most frequently in individuals who have been "normal," both physically and mentally, before the onset of their illness. By normal we mean that most of these patients had no distinguishing or outstanding psychological or physiological deviations which called particular attention to them. The predisposition to manic-depressive psychosis is not detectable or predictable on the basis of any test or measurement now available.

In view of these general findings, we may return to the original notion of Kraepelin, that this disorder may be toxic in nature and that the reactions shown during the psychosis may be a result of this unknown and unspecified toxin. It should be remembered that no biochemical evidence exists indicating the presence of any true toxic agent. It may be possible that some toxin causes the radical psychological alterations which we can accurately describe even though we do not really understand them. However, the explanations of the psychological changes are as hypothetical as are the toxins.

Summary

Manic-depressive psychosis, which is relatively common among the mental disorders, is one in which the manifest symptoms are more clearcut and seemingly understandable than are those of almost any other of the mental disorders. We can, without difficulty, imagine ourselves behaving like, or feeling like, the manic-depressive patient. In spite of the commonness of the disorder, and in spite of our ability to identify ourselves psychologically with such patients, the true nature of this disorder is far from being understood. It is really a major puzzle why, in a state of disorder of behavior and experience so profound as this, physiological or psychological research investigations have made so little positive progress. There are, to be sure, numerous theories and explanations which have been put forward to account for either the physiology or the psychology. It must be emphasized that all of them are, strictly speaking, hypotheses or guesses which may lead to future scientific verification.

REFERENCES

1. Abraham, K., *Selected Papers*. London, Hogarth, 1927.
2. Beers, C., *The Mind that Found Itself*. New York, Longmans, 1908.
3. Bowman, K. M., and A. F. Raymond, "A Statistical Study of the Personality in Schizophrenic Patients," *Proc. Asso. Res. Nerv. Ment. Dis.*, 1931, *10*, 48–74.
4. Bridges, J. W., *Outline of Abnormal Psychology* (2d ed.). Columbus, R. G. Adams, 1921.
5. Burton, R., *The Anatomy of Melancholy* (ed., F. Dell and P. Jordan-Smith). New York, Rinehart, 1927.
6. Hillyer, J., *Reluctantly Told*. New York, Macmillan, 1927.
7. Jelliffe, S. E., "Some Historical Phases of the Manic-Depressive Synthesis," *Proc. Asso. Res. Nerv. Ment. Dis.*, 1931, *11*, 3–47.
8. Jung, C. J., *Psychological Types*. New York, Harcourt, 1923.
9. Kallmann, F. J., "Heredity and Eugenics," *Amer. Jour. Psychiat.*, 1944, *100*, 551–553.
10. Kendig, I., and W. V. Richmond, *Psychological Studies in Dementia Praecox*. Ann Arbor, Edwards Bros., 1940.
11. Kindwald, J. A., and E. F. Kinder, "Postscript on a Benign Psychosis," *Psychiatry*, 1940, *3*, 527–534.
12. Kraepelin, E., *Manic-Depressive Insanity and Paranoia* (trans., R. M. Barclay). Edinburgh, Livingstone, 1921.
13. Krauch, E., *A Mind Restored*. New York, Putnam, 1937.
14. Landis, C., and J. D. Page, *Modern Society and Mental Disease*. New York, Rinehart, 1938.
15. ———, and J. E. Farwell, "A Trend Analysis of Age at First-Admission, Age at Death and Years of Residence for State Mental Hospitals, 1913–1941," *Jour. Abn. Soc. Psychol.*, 1944, *39*, 3–23.
16. Lewis, N. D. C., "The Pathology of Manic-Depressive Reactions," *Proc. Asso. Res. Nerv. Ment. Dis.*, 1930, *11*, 340–373.
17. McFarland, R. A., and H. Goldstein, "The Biochemistry of Manic-Depressive Psychosis," *Amer. Jour. Psychiat.*, 1939, *96*, 21–58.
18. Muncie, W., *Psychobiology and Psychiatry*. St. Louis, Mosby, 1939.
19. Neymann, C. A., and G. K. Yacorzynski, "Studies of Introversion-Extroversion and Conflict of Motives in the Psychoses," *Jour. Genl. Psychol.*, 1942, *27*, 241–255.
20. Oberndorf, C. P., and M. A. Meyer, "Psychoanalytic Sidelights on the Manic-Depressive Psychosis," *Proc. Asso. Res. Nerv. Ment. Dis.*, 1930, *11*, 450–467.
21. Page, J. D., and C. Landis, "Trends in Mental Disease, 1910–1940," *Jour. Abn. Soc. Psychol.*, 1943, *38*, 518–524.
22. ———, ———, and S. E. Katz, "Schizophrenic Traits in the Func-

tional Psychoses and in Normal Individuals," *Amer. Jour. Psychiat.*, 1934, *13*, 1213–1225.

23. Pollock, H. M., "Recurrence of Attacks in Manic-Depressive Psychoses," *Proc. Asso. Res. Nerv. Ment. Dis.*, 1931, *11*, 668–675.
24. Rabin, A. I., "Differentiating Psychometric Patterns in Schizophrenia and Manic-Depressive Psychosis," *Jour. Abn. Soc. Psychol.*, 1942, *37*, 270–272.
25. Strongin, E. I., and L. E. Hinsie, "Parotid Gland Secretions in Manic-Depressive Patients," *Amer. Jour. Psychiat.*, 1938, *94*, 1459–1466.

Chapter VI

THE NEUROSES

THE ABNORMALITIES which are grouped under the general concept of neurosis are so diverse that it is best to speak of the neuroses in the plural. The word "neurosis" originally meant a disorder of the nerves. The growth of knowledge showed that this concept was not wholly true, so the term *psychoneurosis* was coined — illness of mind and nerves. This was no improvement. Today, it is usual to speak of *the neuroses* or to speak of *neurasthenia, hysteria, anxiety neurosis, compulsion neurosis,* or *reactive neurosis,* when one wishes to be more specific.

In general, the neuroses are characterized by markedly inefficient and imperfect adjustment to the environment and by feelings of uneasiness and disturbance about oneself. Specifically, the neuroses are a group of psychological abnormalities in which occur anxiety, phobias, compulsions, obsessions, and conversion symptoms (physical ailments substituted for mental troubles). The pattern of symptoms varies among individual cases. The different varieties of neuroses are distinguished by the particular symptoms which predominate. In practically every case, many types of symptoms are present. The outstanding symptoms,[2] in order of frequency, are tenseness, depression, anxiety, sexual preoccupation, hypochondriasis, obsessions and compulsions, fear of insanity, and weakness.

The neurotic has a tendency to worry over little things and to be unable to make up his mind. He feels inadequate and socially uncomfortable; he is tense and unable to sleep at night; he has illogical fears and is pursued by troublesome thoughts. Everyone can probably truthfully say of at least one of these characteristics, "Why, that's true of me," and ask, "Am I neurotic?" The occurrence of experiences of this sort is certainly too common to justify anyone's calling them "pathological" as such, but they are nonadaptive reactions. Under strong emotional upset or stress, anyone may be temporarily disorganized psychologically, but *in the neurotic these reactions are persistent and chronic* and constitute a style of reaction in a wide range of different situations. In the neurotic, they interfere so extensively with his efficiency that they must be viewed as a mental disorder.

Are we justified in speaking of neurotic tendencies in a basically normal person? On the basis of the frequency of episodic neurotic reactions, the answer is Yes. Many people who show these episodic neurotic mechanisms are not incapacitated socially or vocationally, but their lives are filled with periods of annoyance, real suffering, unhappiness, and wasted energy. Is it justifiable to place these "normal" neurotics at some point on a scale ranging from normality to severe neurosis? The findings of the psychoanalysts support such placement. Also, a public health survey[8] made in one part of Baltimore showed that the persons in the general population who were said to be "nervous" had a sex, age, and race distribution similar to that of those who had been diagnosed neurotic in that area.

What is the relation between neurosis and psychosis? Some have held that there is no difference in kind, but only in degree; that the neurosis is a mild form of the condition called "psychosis." Certainly, the symptoms of neurosis are less deviant from the normal than are those of psychosis, and in this sense, it is but a matter of degree. But does this mean that they are based on the same processes? The best answer is No, because neuroses do not develop into psychoses, except in rare instances.[14] Different follow-up studies have shown that, of patients originally thought to be neurotic, less than 10 per cent have later developed a psychosis, and most of these cases which later became psychotic were seen and diagnosed as neurotic before the psychosis had fully developed, or were insufficiently studied in the first place. It is very probable that neurotic features sometimes occur in psychotic patients, usually in the early stages of onset, but the conditions themselves are really different in kind.

The psychotic is a *danger* to himself and others, while the neurotic is a *nuisance* to himself and others. The classic differences between neuroses and psychoses are that the *neurotic is in better contact with reality and shows more insight into his condition.* The psychoses usually involve a change in the whole personality of the subject, whereas in the neuroses only part of the personality is affected.

Varieties of Neurosis

NEURASTHENIA

Originally the term *neurasthenia* was used to designate all cases where the mental conflicts were transferred to, and showed themselves as, organic dysfunctions or ailments. Today, the use of the term is restricted to those cases showing chronic mental and physical fatigue, together with many physical complaints which are of a hypochondriacal nature. Inability to concentrate, insomnia, and loss of appetite may form part of the psychological picture. The patients frequently attribute their symptoms to overwork, but it has been conclusively shown that rest brings no solution to their problems. Although autointoxication was once believed to be a cause, biochemical studies have failed to support this contention. The most generally accepted interpretation today is that the condition results from profound and prolonged emotional maladjustment. The physical complaints which are a prominent part of many of the cases are believed to be secondary accompaniments rather than causes. Persistent emotional states are fatiguing. Preoccupation with some mental conflict or insoluble problem is known to shift over to preoccupation with one's physical condition. Hence, the fatigue and the shift of attention are thought to bring into prominence the physical complaints.

The following history is that of typical condition of neurasthenia:

CASE 6: A forty-eight-year-old man has had a series of physical complaints for the past seventeen years. At first he began to feel "run-down" and had numerous gastric symptoms. Repeated visits to doctors brought him their assurance that there was nothing wrong with him except "nerves," but he did not accept their statements. His symptoms continued in relatively mild form until seven months before the present admission to the hospital, when they finally became accentuated to such a degree that he had to enter the hospital. There he complained of indigestion, a feeling of distention in the abdomen, and pains around his heart. He said that he felt weak and that he was obsessed by the thought that he was going to die. While in the hospital he continued to complain of aches and pains and believed that he must have some "dreadful disease, possibly brain tumor." He kept after the physician to give him repeated physical examinations, especially of his chest. Such an examination would give him some reassurance that there was no organic defect, but after a few days he would resume his complaints. He claimed to have had poor health all his life. Actually, there was no history of any definite illness or pathology. The mental examination showed no evidence of memory disturbance, thinking difficulty, hallucination, or delusion. His mood was one of rather complacent hopelessness, but with no evidence of a true depression. He realized that he thought too much about his physical condition, but, even after extensive treatment in regard to his hypochondriacal symptoms, he said: "I am always tired. I can't sleep at night, but I am sleepy all day. Sometimes I think it's my head, sometimes I think it's my stomach. I know there is something wrong with me, even if the doctor can't find it. I don't know if it's in the head or in the body." During the nine months of his hospitalization, he lost some of his physical complaints, but continued apprehensive about his "ill health."

ANXIETY STATES

The distinction between anxiety hysteria and anxiety neurosis, as originally made by Freud, has been replaced by the broader concept of anxiety states. The psychological picture in these conditions is one of episodes of anxiety, together with definite physical complaints. These symptoms are of diverse form and degree, but mostly they are the common physical signs of fear: palpitation of the heart, breathlessness, dry mouth, various gastrointestinal sensations, and tremors.

In some cases the source of fear may be some simple, relatively harmless object in the environment. These morbid fears or *phobias* are usually a fear of the recurrence of an anxiety attack. The person has an attitude of exaggerated fearfulness toward the situation, or some element in the situation in which a previous anxiety attack occurred. In some cases the situations which produce anxiety seem to do so because they revive anxieties which occurred during infancy or early childhood; in other cases, the emotion seems to have been displaced onto a neutral object or situation for which the person need feel no sense of responsibility. In other words, the patient's troubled mind (his internal conflict) is the prime mover of the feeling of anxiety, but this may suffer a displacement to some object in his environment, such as dogs, open spaces, or infection by germs. The symptom picture of anxiety is probably the most common of all the forms of neurosis. The feelings of apprehensiveness, phobia, or panic which are experienced by these persons are so severe that the sufferers will go to any length to avoid the situation which originally aroused them, or which will now set them off. The following history is illustrative of the anxiety state:

CASE 7: A thirty-three-year-old man suffered an acute attack of anxiety one year prior to admission to the hospital and has had repeated attacks of the same type since then. At the time of the first attack, he complained of severe pains in his heart, great difficulty in breathing, and fear of death. His wife said he was pale and trembling during an attack. These attacks occurred frequently during the night. He would awaken, gasping for breath, belching, and panic-stricken. He said that there did not seem to be any specific factor that brought them on but that they were more severe when he was alone. During his hospitalization it was noted, however, that his symptoms seemed more exaggerated when he had an audience. He talked at great length of his suffering to anyone who would listen. He was of very superior intelligence with excellent educational and cultural background. Throughout his school days he had been a trouble maker. This same pattern continued in the hospital. He was extremely critical of the hospital and uncooperative with its routines. He complained that his family had always rejected him, which complaint was not supported by any actual evidence. He was unable to adjust himself in his marriage with an intelligent, emotionally stable woman. He had always been hypercritical of others, although resistant and resentful of any criticism of himself. He was described by his family as thoughtless, selfish, and "touchy." He made many demands upon his family and wife but refused to accept any responsibility as far as they were concerned.

COMPULSION NEUROSIS

Persons suffering from this type of neurosis feel impelled to carry out certain actions over and over, although they usually realize that there is no logical reason for such repetition. If questioned as to why they must do these things, they may say that they feel uncomfortable and uneasy unless they do them. Forms of compulsion or obsession which are fairly common are handwashing, object touching, or object counting. Such repetitious tendencies may occur in mental as well as motor activities. Certain thoughts, over which they have no control, may keep running through their minds. The obsessive compulsion is sometimes so strong that the individual may require hours to carry out such simple tasks as dressing or eating. These conditions are extremely difficult to treat. The following history is illustrative of the condition:

CASE 8: During the fifteen years of her marriage, a thirty-six-year-old woman showed marked inefficiency in running her home and in keeping social appointments. She continually scrubbed, cleaned, and washed, so that she did not finish her housework until the early hours of the morning. She did not get around to fixing her own breakfast until six o'clock in the evening. While dressing, she had to wash her face ten or fifteen times. She felt impelled to choose some definite number and then fulfill the next daily task this number of times. There were set formulae that she had to carry out in regard to putting on her clothes, in writing a letter, or in ordering groceries. When this routine was disturbed, she had to start over again from the beginning. She did not allow anyone to use the furniture in her living room, which she continually polished, because she was afraid it might get scratched.

She believed that these tendencies started when she was eight years old. A friend told her to touch a doorway through which they were walking, saying it would bring her good luck. Since that time she felt that she must touch certain objects in order to bring luck. She was never able to keep appointments because her rituals in preparation for them took so much time. Frequently, dinner in her household was not prepared until ten or eleven o'clock at night. She said, "Whenever I did not like to do something or go somewhere, I was purposely late." In general, she had little insight into her condition and felt that people were unfair to object as they did to her being late. She did not feel that she was mentally ill and saw no reason why she should have started. or should continue, psychiatric treatment.

REACTIVE NEUROSIS

In some neurotics the outstanding symptom is depression. This depression differs from the psychotic depression, seen in the manic-depressive psychosis or in involutional melancholia, in that here the depression seems to be fittingly related to some event or existing condition. These neurotics are actually overreacting to a real situation. There is something real in their lives about which to be depressed. We can, to an extent, understand their feelings, although there seems no reason for the prolonged grief. Most people "snap out of it"; "forget it"; "quit crying over spilt milk." These neurotics cannot quit.

They are serious suicide risks. Not many neurotics are truly suicidal, but those who do commit suicide or attempt suicide are usually of the depressive variety.

If the situation to which the patients attribute the depression changes for the better, they usually recover, although they require more time for the recovery than does the average person. Other individuals of this type recover rapidly following electric convulsive therapy. This condition is typified by the following case description:

CASE 9: A thirty-seven-year-old businessman became extremely depressed, tearful, and unable to carry on his work. He had always been well liked, vocationally competent, and well adjusted in his marriage. There had previously been no evidence of mental instability. At the time when his business began to fail and his savings were lost, he became despondent. He lost his appetite, developed insomnia, and wept frequently. He felt very guilty over the fact that he could no longer support his wife adequately. He finally became so depressed that he was completely unable to go to work. He became sexually impotent and developed feelings of hopelessness. After his admission to a hospital, he came to realize that his difficulty was entirely within himself and believed there were no external influences except his financial losses which determined his condition. His plans for the future were obscured by feelings of hopelessness. He complained of a "feeling of fog" in his head. He also had some gastrointestinal complaints which were relieved by a controlled diet. Later, he complained of pains in his arms and shoulders, which were of neurotic origin. The patient showed improvement after four months in the hospital. After discharge, he obtained a new position and carried out his new duties in a successful fashion.

Personal Experience

There is a great deal of information available as to what a neurosis feels like from the inside. Many neurotics enjoy recounting their symptoms in detail. The tendency to be introspective is a characteristic part of the picture. Because so many of their feelings and attitudes are, in part, common to us all, we can understand their reports; whereas it is often impossible to understand the reports of psychotic patients.

The autobiography of Leonard* provides an excellent and intelligent report of many neurotic symptoms. He was a college professor who suffered from a severe neurosis over a long period of years. In his autobiography he took issue with the concept that overreaction is an outstanding characteristic of the neurotic person. He held that such strong emotional reactions are specific to those situations which bring out the neurosis. To such situations, which are essentially different from any of those faced by the normal, the reaction of the neurotic is appropriate and not truly an overreaction, according to Leonard. Again, taking exception to the view that egotism is a prime neurotic symptom, he pointed out that in some cases it may also be the result of compelling physical symptoms, such as pain and the problem of relief from this pain.

In writing of his physical symptoms, Leonard described the two years of agony he suffered from his eyes. He tried glasses and new glasses; oculists and new oculists, all of whom gave the report that there was nothing wrong with his eyes; but the feeling of half-ache, half-shooting pain continued. He said that he experienced many different kinds of suffering. For two weeks he had a pain localized in his jaw, for which the dentist could find no organic cause. While napping one afternoon, it became fiercely acute. At another time, he experienced excruciating pain in the region of the rectum, lasting for five to twenty minutes. He later came to attribute these pains to reinstatement of specific pains experienced in early childhood. At another time, sounds tortured him so, that all bells in his home had to be plugged and everyone had to tiptoe across the floor. In this hypersensitive state, he said all sounds had to him the nerve-racking quality of chalk squeaking on a blackboard.

He developed a strange fear of water, and when only a short distance from shore in a boat or in swimming, he experienced feelings of dread and terror. He later interpreted these as a feeling of distance from safety, believing that the land was equivalent to safety to him. He recognized the phobic nature of these feelings, but no attempt at mastery or cure was effective. Later, these fears spread so that the feeling of insecurity recurred in extreme form when he was any distance (even a block or two) from his own home. This became the

---

* Leonard, W. E., *The Locomotive God.* New York, Appleton-Century, 1927; Taylor, W. S. and E. Culler, "The Problem of the Locomotive God," *Jour. Abn. Soc. Psychol.*, 1929, *24*, 342–399.

most disabling phase of his neurosis. He described feelings of a sinking loneliness, an uneasy, weird isolation, as though he were all alone in the universe, of sudden and nameless horror at being separated from home and its security. At times, he became panicky over his panic. The recognition of these feelings as mentally abnormal, precipitated a secondary panic. In other words, he became increasingly upset at the thought that this abnormality was a desperately critical symptom. These feelings are commonly reported in people having anxiety attacks; they are afraid of becoming afraid.

From prolonged introspection, Leonard found that these phobic experiences started in a state of terror without content. Generated by past experiences, this state ranged in severity from vague anxiety to intense feelings of impending death. Sometimes, the form which these feelings took was determined by the original experience. At other times the form seemed to be determined by the intellect trying to seek adequate explanation for the feelings. Thus, the mind rationalized the terrors into secondary forms or pseudo explanations. The real causes were unknown to the neurotic sufferer; therefore he made up the causes, frequently in the form of a physical illness or disease. For example, a rapid pulse accompanied by gasping breathing (physical manifestations of fear) was falsely interpreted as evidence of a serious cardiac disease.

The relation between neurotic symptoms and early traumatic history, which Leonard worked out over a period of many years, is both long and complicated, but it is an interesting psychological document. He objected to many of the classic formulations regarding the neuroses. (For example, the "sickness benefit" of many neurotic symptoms.) He maintained that fifteen years of thinking about and experiencing neurotic symptoms had given him a firmer basis for theory than have the secondhand reports upon which the psychopathologist depends.

Facts and Figures

No one can do more than guess how many neurotics there are in the general population. Some physicians and surgeons in the general practice of medicine have estimated that two thirds to three fourths of the patients who come to them with complaints of some organic illness are primarily neurotics whose organic symptoms are merely an expression of their neurosis. Other medical men say that they rarely see a neurotic patient. Estimates of the incidence of neurotic persons have been based on surveys made of college populations and on industrial disability of persons for whom medical care was automatically provided. These estimates vary between 5 and 27 per cent of the groups studied. A conservative estimate would be that about 3 per cent of the adult general population (more than two million persons in the United States) are more or less disabled by neurosis at any one time.

This disability is not so severe that it requires hospitalization, save in a relatively small number of cases; 4470 individuals, diagnosed as neurotic, were first-admitted to all the mental hospitals in the United States in 1942. Hospitalization for neurosis is rare before the age of 14, or after the age of 64. The most frequent age at hospitalization for women is between 25 and 35, and for men, between 35 and 45. The hospitalization rate is 4.1 per 100,000 of the general population between the ages of 25 and 69. Among first-admissions of neurotics to our mental hospitals, we find that nearly 50 per cent more come from urban communities than from rural communities. Of hospitalized neurotic patients, 84 per cent are in dependent or marginal economic circumstances; while the educational achievement is high school or better in 30 per cent of the cases. The educational level is higher than in most other types of mental disorder and corresponds closely to that of the general population. There are no reliable data concerning the incidence of neuroses in different national and racial groups.

Studies of the onset of neurosis show that the following circumstances may precede hospitalization: financial troubles, deaths in the family, sex conflicts, and marital difficulties. Investigations of the general nature of the personality of these individuals before hospitalization indicate that the majority of cases showed personality deviations for the greater part of their lives. Exaggerations of these symptoms to the point at which they were disabling led most of the patients to hospitalization. The personalities of these patients frequently show the following characteristics: overwhelming need for affection and approval, hypersensitivity, feelings of inadequacy, and overconscientiousness.

It is a common observation that similar stress situations produce neurotic symptoms in some persons, and no such symptoms in others. The fact that some individuals do succumb to neurosis is attributed to poor childhood care and training, faulty habit organization, prolonged malnutrition, physical disability due to injury or illness, or to a genetically determined lack of resistance, that is, poor heredity. Since nothing can be done about heredity, the bulk of attention has been directed toward the other factors which may cause the neurosis.

The amount of "psychopathic tainting" (blood relatives who have had some form of nervous or mental disorder) varies considerably among the various types of neurosis. Different investigators have reported that between 10 and 60 per cent of all relatives have this tainting, with 4 to 7 per cent having the same sort of symptoms as the patient whose family history is under investigation.[11,13]

The general consensus seems to be that there is a constitutional predisposition (a genetically determined lack of resistance) to neurotic behavior, so that the amount of stress necessary to bring out such reactions varies among individuals. Thus, it is reasonable to assume that, if there are relatively few stresses in the environment, a person may not show obvious neurotic tendencies, even though a constitutional inadequacy is present. For example, observers have noted that some patients were able to carry on without too much trouble with one or two constant sources of tension, but broke when a third or fourth was added. Such a person might get along in an unhappy marriage, plus living with his wife's relatives, so long as his job was secure and interesting; but shifting to another job which he disliked would precipitate a breakdown. There seems to be wide individual difference in the tolerance for stress and tension before actual neurosis occurs, just as there are individual differences in recuperative power. Some patients recover almost as soon as the immediate stress is removed, others recover more or less slowly, and a few never recover.

Slater[15] has made a most careful study of all background factors and concluded that the neurotic constitution is preponderantly determined by a very large number of genes, each of which has small effect. The effect of genes which are qualitatively similar is additive and becomes manifest by producing a reduced resistance to some form of environmental stress, and so facilitates the appearance of neurosis. The effect of genes qualitatively dissimilar is to produce the different types of neurotic symptoms. In brief, the neurotic person has more than average susceptibility to environmental stress.

History of the Concept of Neurosis

The concept of neurosis is a relatively new one in the history of medical psychology. Charcot was the first to study neurotic cases as a group. He recognized psychological influences in the determination of symptoms, but he did not realize that they were primary causes of the illness. He made use of suggestion and hypnosis in treating the symptoms of these cases. S. Weir Mitchell, an early American psychiatrist and a famous figure in this field, believed that neurotic patients were suffering from an actual physical exhaustion of the nervous system. As a method of treatment he used complete and utter rest carried to an almost unbelievable degree, in which the patient was not allowed even to turn over in bed, but was turned by an attendant. This treatment had a great vogue, but now is viewed as worse than useless.

Janet[6] introduced systematization into the study of neurotic disorders, dividing the patients into those who were suffering from hysteria and those suffering from psychasthenia. Under the latter, he included morbid fears, undue fatiguability, obsessions, and compulsions. He held that neurosis was an evidence of weakness of the central nervous system because the level or amount of psychic tension was lowered or disturbed. This lowering or disturbance brought with it feelings of fatigue (without physical basis), feelings of weakness, self-dissatisfaction, and a lack of will power. Although his description is essentially a psychological one, he believed that nervous tension could be lowered by physical factors, such as disease, fatigue, emotion, or the changes at puberty.

Another outstanding figure in the historical development of this concept was Freud.[17] His early work with Breuer on cases of hysteria marked the beginning of his psychoanalytic psychology. Although some of his original concepts were derived from Charcot, he went on to develop a broad and systematic formulation of the problem of neurosis. His explanation of the neuroses,[4] although popularly quoted as a psychogenic interpretation, actually emphasized that they were serious, constitutionally determined disorders, evidenced over long periods of life. The psychogenic components received more attention from his followers because they lent themselves to investigation and active treatment. Freud separated what he termed the *true neuroses* from the *psychoneuroses;* the former were believed to arise from the present sexual life of the patient, and the latter from abnormal instinctive endowment, plus factors in the early sexual history. From his analysis of neurotic patients of the hysterical variety, Freud originally assumed that the symptomatology derived from early sexual trauma. Later, he revised this opinion and pointed out that these reported incidents were memories of childhood fantasies. The symptoms of neurasthenia were usually interpreted by him as the result of excessive masturbation, with extreme mental conflict resulting from the practice, which constituted inadequate sex gratification for an adult.

To account for the symptom-forming power of psychosexual factors of infancy and childhood, Freud introduced the concept of repression. Painful or socially taboo memories are pushed out of consciousness, he said, but survive and remain active agents in the unconscious. If successfully "forgotten" there are no bad after effects, but if inadequately repressed the psychic energy of these ideas may be converted into physical symptoms. These are symbols or substitutes for the repressed memory, and on deeper analysis are found to represent an unconscious wish. Compulsive acts may arise as an attempt to ward off anxiety. The obsessive thought arises as a protection, in the same way, by displacing a painful memory and keeping it out of consciousness. The symptoms are the result of the operation of displacement, substitution, and symbolism. Their function is to prevent the unpleasant from appearing in consciousness.

Horney[5] has recently presented a new development of psychoanalytic psychology. She holds that neurotic trends develop, early in life, from combined temperamental and environmental influences. These trends are attempts to handle feelings of fear, helplessness, loneliness, and insecurity. In this sense, they are psychological protective devices. She stresses the importance of specific cultural conditions in determining the nature and form of neurotic reactions. The person who becomes neurotic has experienced the difficulties peculiar to his particular culture in an accentuated form, and, mainly because of certain unfortunate childhood experiences, his solution of these difficulties is inadequate. In this newer interpretation, as well as in many of the older psychoanalytic interpretations of the neuroses, the importance of conflict is stressed. This conflict is between the forces of the Ego and those of the unconscious (Id). In other terms, it has been formulated as a struggle between different instinctive drives, between personal drives and the pattern of culture, or between ideals and practical necessities. The concept of conflict is probably the most basic idea that Freud and his followers have offered in explanation of neurosis. One should bear in mind that it is still open to question whether the conflict precipitates the neurosis (in the neurotically inclined), produces the neurosis, or is itself the product of neurosis.

The psychobiological viewpoint of Meyer[12] explains the common characteristics of neurosis as (a) constitutional traits, providing a preparedness for the later development of the neurotic reaction, (b) experiential factors acting on the personal make-up, and (c) substituted activity resulting when there is an ineffectual performance in the situation. There are a large number of young people who remain children of the moment, distractible, swayed by desires and casual opportunities, showing flashes of enthusiasm and emotional display, but without cohesion or sound plan and consistency. Such persons may be said to possess a "neurotic constitution," and in them changes for the worse may be anticipated.

Riggs[14] formulated the problem of neurosis as maladjustment of intrinsically normal individuals to what, in the vast majority of cases, proves to be an environment also within the normal range. He believed that a tendency to overmobilization of energy, irrespective of need, is the commonest form of inefficiency in these cases. He held that these conditions are curable and avoidable, and that self-understanding is the best assurance against neurosis. He pointed out that the symptoms of potential neurosis are sensitiveness to the disagreeable and painful, overbalance of one or more instincts, faulty application of intelligence and ideals to instinctive forces, and unevenness in the relative development of the physical, mental, and moral sides during growth. These constitute defects in integration or adaptation of the whole individual.

G. V. Hamilton[3] made a study of two hundred cases which came to him seeking psychiatric aid. He had previously done work in comparative psychology studying habit formation and reactions to frustration or baffling situations in various kinds of animals. The most common neurotic behavior, he described as a persistent, nonadjustive, affective reaction to some form of baffling situation. It is common practice to attribute a feeling of inner tension, overfatigue, and "nervous" aches and pains to frustration. Hamilton found that he could experimentally produce equivalent symptoms in humans and animals when he subjected them to prolonged and baffling disadvantage. Some individuals in these situations showed persistent repetition of nonadjustive responses; others showed an alternation of adjustive effort with nonadjustive efforts; others showed persistent trial-and-error responses with no evidence of benefit of learning when they did occasionally hit on the correct adjustive response; others showed indirect reactions to instinctive or emotional urges; and, finally, some showed the direct evidence of a conditioned emotional response to some previous experience which was somewhat similar in nature.

Hamilton's presentation is more a description than an explanation. Since it does tie in with much of the experimental psychology of learning, it has possibilities for future development, thus far not realized.

Physiology and Pathology

The palpitations of the heart, the dilated pupils, the digestive disturbances, the shallow, rapid breathing, the vertigo, and disorders in sweating are, any or all of them, frequent occurrences during a neurotic episode. All of these physiological changes are functions of the autonomic nervous system. Investigations of these changes made by physiologists and biochemists have produced confused and confusing results.[10] On one day a patient may show marked evidence of disordered function; the next day, no disorder whatever. There is good evidence of increased variability of function in the neurotic, as compared to the normal. There is a high correlation in the neurotic group between the variability on tests of physiological function and (*a*) poor cardiovascular reactions, (*b*) impairment in psychological test performance, and (*c*) frequency of neurotic complaints. In spite of the high correlation, there is no good basis for individual prediction of the relationship between any of these functions. The variability probably implies some sort of fatigue, together with over- or undercorrection or loss of adaptability of physiological function, which ultimately results in irritability, and dysfunction of certain organic mechanisms.

Evidence from a somewhat different viewpoint has been given by Comroe.[1] He made a follow-up study of 100 patients who had been examined in an excellent outpatient clinic of a large hospital and diagnosed as neurotic. After an average period of eight months, the follow-up showed that 40 were improved, the condition was unchanged in 34, and worse in 2. In the remaining 24 cases, there was definite incontrovertible evidence of organic disease which had been present when the original diagnosis of neurosis was made. From this, one may conclude that a fair number of neurotics do have an organic disease, the symptoms of which are atypical or so obscure that a diagnosis of neurosis appears appropriate. In such cases the diagnosis simply means that the true basis of the complaints has been missed by the physician.

In spite of much evidence to the contrary, both] from physiology and pathology, it is commonly held that neurosis is psychogenic and that the physiological changes are associated phenomena, just as indigestion is associated with intense fear. This viewpoint is largely due to the fact that psychotherapy has been relatively effective in bringing about improvements in these neurotic conditions, while organic therapies have been relatively ineffective.

Psychology

A great many investigations have been made of the psychological alterations in neurosis. Usually, the findings have emphasized one or another particular function. The results obtained, using the methods of developmental psychology as they shed light on the entire personality of the neurotic, are of particular interest at the present point.

Landis et al.,[7] made a study of the growth and development of personality in 153 normal women and 142 female psychiatric patients, of whom 50 were hospitalized neurotics. Since much of our present-day thinking concerning the nature of neurosis has emphasized the role of psychosexuality in the development of the neurotic personality, special attention was devoted to the early sex development in every individual, although adequate information was obtained on other factors which influence the developing personality.

In spite of the fact that these neurotic women showed a wide range of reaction patterns during childhood and adult life, there were certain characteristics which were common to many of them. The history of the psychological growth and development of the psychotic and normal women was found to be essentially similar, while that of the neurotic women was different from either the normal or the psychotic. The neurotics did not report particular experiences that differentiated them from either the psychotics or the normals in the sense that something had *happened* to them, but they did report differences in their style of life, which differences were apparent from early childhood onward. *The neurotic style of life was characteristically emotionally non-adaptive.* While there were no differences from the normal in the type of early sex information which these women reported that they had obtained, their complaints and criticisms of their families in this respect were severe. Many of them blamed their disgust concerning sexual matters upon the unpleasantness of their early sex information, or upon their ignorance of the subject. In describing their relationships with other members of the family, they frequently cited instances of family conflict. There was no evidence that the actual past situations were different from those lived through by the normal women, yet it was clear that the neurotics reacted more strongly to these situations. They reported excessive anxiety concerning masturbation. While the number of neurotic women who reported childhood sex aggressions was no greater than that in the normal group, the emotional significance which they placed on the experience was much greater than that placed by the normals. The neurotic women did not deviate from the normals with respect to physical constitution, physical development, or medical history.

The environment in which the neurotic women had developed showed no essential differences from that in which the normal women had grown up. However, the way in which the neurotic women described these environmental influences was reported in very different terms from those used by the normal person. The parental relationship and home situation were said to have been sources of conflict, instability, and friction. There was evidence of factors in the early home background that might be expected to produce unhealthy emotional development. The adult heterosexual interests and attachments of the neurotic women were somewhat different from those of the normal women. They were apt to continue a childish sort of emotional relationship to their parents and to individuals outside of their family, and were rather late in reaching any independent adult status. More neurotics than normals told of general incompatibility in marriage.

The neurotic style of life showed a clear, consistent trend from early childhood to adult life. Such women tended to view themselves as unfortunate individuals and to blame their parents for most of their difficulties. The neurotic style was manifested in their reaction to early sex information, contact with other children, attitude toward sex, attitude toward discipline and affection shown by the parents, inability to free themselves from family ties, general inability to get along and handle their own problems in life, and inability to adjust in marriage.

Certain of these neurotic personality characteristics were particularly related to the immediate symptoms of the disorder — the preoccupation with personal problems to the exclusion of any outside interests; the feelings of self-reproach, inadequacy, and guilt; the inability to get along in the usual environment; and the prevailing anxious mood. These are all characteristics of the present neurosis. Before these symptoms became acute, the story of their life history revealed that similar or equivalent tendencies had always been common to them.

The neurotic style of life developed in a person, probably of psychologically inadequate constitution, who had been exposed to factors conducive to insecurity and instability in early childhood. It seemed likely that one unfortunate combination of events and reactions in infancy or early childhood led to another, and that the series of such unhappy experiences gave rise to the immediate symptoms of neurosis in adult life.

Summary

Although it is common to speak of neurosis as though it existed as a psychological entity, it is more probable that there are several different forms of neuroses which merely have certain psychological symptoms in common. The lack of the ability to make emotional adjustments and adaptations to everyday life constitutes a central symptom. Associated with this are the fears, compulsions, anxieties, obsessions, and feelings of guilt. Certain physical symptoms, generally of a vague and indefinite nature, are also associated; for example, insomnia, indigestion, shortness of breath, and cardiac distress. These physical symptoms probably depend upon an unstable autonomic nervous system.

There are no specific, precipitating factors for neurosis. Neurotic symptoms are most apt to come out when new and more difficult adjustments are called for. Having neurotic parents and an unhappy childhood home, or serious and frequent illness in childhood may act as a predisposing factor. The neurotic tends to break down more readily in difficult situations than does the normal person. However, there is a great deal of individual variation among neurotics, some being able to stand quite a lot of stress before becoming disabled.

Neurosis, in its various forms, represents a style of life which is consistent from a very early age. The style is not due to the effects of any one incident, but rather, is a gradually developed mode of emotional maladjustment. This style may be the result of a basic constitutional inadequacy exposed to factors conducive to insecurity and instability in childhood.

REFERENCES

1. Comroe, B. I., "Follow-up Study of 100 Patients Diagnosed as 'Neurosis'," *Jour. Nerv. Ment. Dis.*, 1936, *83*, 679–684.
2. Hamilton, D. M., and J. H. Wall, "Hospital Treatment of Patients with Psychoneurotic Disorders," *Amer. Jour. Psychiat.*, 1942, *98*, 551–557.
3. Hamilton, G. V., *An Introduction to Objective Psychopathology*. St. Louis, Mosby, 1925.
4. Hendrick, I., *Facts and Theories of Psychoanalysis* (2d ed.). New York, Knopf, 1939.
5. Horney, K., *New Ways in Psychoanalysis*. New York, Norton, 1939.
6. Janet, P., *The Major Symptoms of Hysteria* (rev.). New York, Macmillan, 1920.
7. Landis, C., *et al.*, *Sex in Development*. New York, Hoeber, 1940.
8. Lemkau, I., C. Tietze, and M. Cooper, "Complaint of Nervousness and the Psychoneuroses," *Amer. Jour. Orthopsychiat.*, 1942, *12*, 214–223.
9. Leonard, W. E., *The Locomotive God*. New York, Appleton-Century, 1927.
10. McFarland, R. A., and H. Goldstein, "Biochemistry of the Psychoneuroses — a Review," *Amer. Jour. Psychiat.*, 1937, *93*, 1073–1095.
11. McInnes, R. G., "Observations on Heredity in Neurosis," *Proc. Roy. Soc. Med.*, 1937, *30*, 895–904.

12. Muncie, W., *Psychobiology and Psychiatry*. St. Louis, Mosby, 1939.

13. Paskind, H. A., "Heredity of Patients with Psychasthenia," *Arch. Neurol. Psychiat.*, 1933, *29*, 1305–1317.

14. Ross, T. A., *An Inquiry into Prognosis in the Neuroses*. London, Cambridge University Press, 1936.

15. Slater, E., and P. Slater, "A Heuristic Theory of Neurosis," *Jour. Neurol· Neurosurg. Psychiat.*, 1944, 7, 49–55.

16. Taylor, W. S., and E. Culler, "The Problem of the Locomotive God," *Jour. Abn. Soc. Psychol.*, 1929, *24*, 342–399.

17. Zilboorg, G., and G. W. Henry, *A History of Medical Psychology*. New York, Norton, 1941.

Chapter VII

HYSTERIA AND DISSOCIATED PERSONALITY

HYSTERIA and dissociated personality are forms of neurosis. Both the history of these concepts and their psychological implications are important to abnormal psychology. Hysteria differs from other forms of neurosis in that there are losses of bodily functions or disturbed and uncontrolled functions for which no physiological or organic causes can be demonstrated. The symptoms of the hysteric patient seem, at first glance, to indicate clearly either that there is something organically wrong with him, or that he is consciously falsifying his complaints. The essential point is that neither of these suppositions is true. No organic basis sufficient to explain the symptoms can be found, and upon close examination they frequently turn out to be only "reasonable facsimiles" of organically determined symptoms. On the other hand, they are not consciously falsified by the patient. He is not a malingerer, since he is unconscious of the basis or meaning of his symptoms. It may be found that the symptoms do serve a purpose for him; for example, they may get him out of some uncomfortable or disagreeable situation, but he himself is not conscious of any such motivation.

From the psychological point of view, hysteria is especially interesting because of the highly dramatic nature of the symptoms, and because the scientific study of abnormal psychology started with the investigation of these cases. These investigations have furnished the basic concepts which are used in the field of psychopathology. Such insight as we have concerning the mental mechanisms and the operation of unconscious motives and drives came first from the study of the hysterical patient. His symptoms are more dramatic, more easily understood, and less involved than those of the other forms of neurosis or psychosis. In addition, it has been found that many of the mechanisms manifested by the hysterical patient give us added insight into the mental life of the normal person and so add to our ability to understand normal behavior.

Case Histories

No single case history can give any notion of the wide range of symptoms that can occur in hysterical patients. The following history illustrates the style of the abnormal behavior, rather than the variety and extent of grosser physical symptoms.

CASE 10: "A young girl twenty years old, called Irène, whom despair, caused by her mother's death, had made ill. We must remember that this woman's death has been very moving and dramatic. The poor woman, who had reached the last stage of consumption, lived alone with her daughter in a poor garret. Death came slowly, with suffocation, blood-vomiting, and all its frightful procession of symptoms. The girl struggled hopelessly against the impossible. She watched her mother during sixty nights, working at her sewing-machine to earn a few pennies necessary to sustain their lives. After the mother's death she tried to revive the corpse, to call the breath back again; then, as she put the limbs upright, the body fell to the floor, and it took infinite exertion to lift it again into the bed. You may picture to yourself all that frightful scene. Some time after the funeral, curious and impressive symptoms began.

"The crises last for hours, and they show a splendid dramatic performance, for no actress could rehearse those lugubrious scenes with such perfection. The young girl had the singular habit of acting again all the events that took place at her mother's death, without forgetting the least detail. Sometimes she only spoke, relating all that happened with great volubility, putting questions and answers in turn, or asking questions only, and seeming to listen for the answer; sometimes she only saw the sight, looking with frightened face and staring on the various scenes, and acting according to what she saw. At other times, she combined all hallucinations, words, and acts, and seemed to play a very singular drama. When, in her drama, death has taken place, she carried on the same idea, and made everything ready for her own suicide. She discussed it aloud, seemed to speak with her mother, to receive advice from her; she fancied she would try to be run over by a locomotive. That detail was also a recollection of a real event of her life. She fancied she was on the way, and stretched herself out on the floor of the room, waiting for death, with mingled dread and impatience. She posed, and wore on her face expressions really worthy of admiration, which remained fixed during several minutes. The train arrived before her staring eyes, she uttered a terrible shriek, and fell back motionless, as if she were dead. She soon got up and began acting over again one of the preceding scenes." *

One of the characteristics of such hysterical somnambulisms is that they repeat themselves indefinitely. Not only are the different attacks alike, repeating the same movements, expressions, and words, but in the course of the same attack, when it has lasted a certain time, the

* Modified from P. Janet, *The Major Symptoms of Hysteria* (2d ed.). New York, Macmillan, 1920, 29–31.

same scene may be repeated again, in exactly the same way, five or ten times. Finally, the agitation seems to wear out, the dream grows less clear, and, gradually or suddenly, according to the case, the patient comes back to normal consciousness, taking up the ordinary business of life without being too much disturbed by what has happened.

In other forms of hysteria, which make up a larger proportion of the cases, physical symptoms (conversion phenomena) are the outstanding part of the picture, as is shown in the following case:

CASE 11: Miss H, aged twenty-three, was said to have been a very fearful child, easily frightened by cats and dogs, and liable to scream at the slightest provocation. She said that her father had been cruel and abusive, both to herself and to her mother, and that her parents had been divorced when she was sixteen. The patient underwent an appendectomy at age twenty. She later complained of intense pain all over her body and developed a peculiar shuffling gait, at times limping on the right side and at times on the left side. For weeks at a time she remained in a wheel chair. Careful examination showed that there was no organic, neurological, or muscular disorder. The pattern of her gait did not correspond to any known type of motor disability. Since there were no true organic findings, she was referred to a psychiatric hospital. At this time it was found that she had a changeable cutaneous anesthesia over her upper chest. With extensive psychotherapy the disturbance in gait improved and, when she became interested in some particular physical activity, it disappeared completely. Although this patient had had a definite organic illness, it was clear from the history that her neurotic tendencies antedated it. During hospitalization, she complained of intense earache and throbbing pain in the eyes. These different types of bodily complaints were of short duration. Some of the symptoms were quickly removed with suggestion, and others disappeared after extensive psychotherapeutic interviews designed to show her the significance of the symptoms. In describing her motor symptoms, she said: "I've been told it is from my nerves, but it feels worse with the changing of the weather, and it is much worse at night. Both legs feel like logs. My arms feel that way too. I used to get it in my fingers. It was a drawing, pulling feeling. Sometimes, my feet get numb, from the ankles down."

Over a period of time, this patient manifested a wide range of symptoms, such as temporary blindness in one eye, fainting, and deafness. She left the hospital in a much improved condition, but she had so little self-understanding that there was every reason to believe that new symptoms would appear.

The Symptoms of Hysteria

The symptoms of hysteria are so varied in nature that practically any organ or function of the body may be involved. These disturbances have been, and still are, the most common source of surgical blunders — unnecessary appendectomies, nerve sections, and the like. It is impossible to pick any one symptom which is characteristic, but certain forms of disorder occur more frequently than others. One large category into which many of the symptoms fall is loss of function. Under this heading come anesthesias, blindness, deafness, and motor paralysis.

The presence of insensitive areas of the skin in hysterical states has been noted for many years. Charcot[3] stated that they constituted the preeminent *stigma* of hysteria. It is a matter of historical interest that in the Middle Ages when a woman was suspected of being a witch because she had trances or spells, she was tested in the following way. A sharp needle point was applied over all the body surface and the discovery of an insensitive area, or "Devil's Claw," as it was called, was taken to be a certain sign of witchcraft.

' The skin anesthesias found in hysterical patients have certain distinctive marks. In the first place, the area involved follows the lines of what the patient conceives the disorder to be. That is, a "verbally" distinct part of the body, such as a leg or hand (the stocking and glove anesthesias), will be affected; and not a pattern determined by the nerve distribution, the area that would be involved if there were something actually organically wrong with the nerve supply. Second, these anesthetic skin areas appear suddenly and disappear just as suddenly. They can be induced, removed, or shifted through the suggestions of a skilled therapist.

In determining whether blindness or deafness is hysterical, the physician must first exclude any possible organic basis for the condition. After he has seen that there is nothing organically wrong with the eyes or the ears, he must next investigate the conditions under which the loss of function occurred. Frequently, these prove to be situations which were difficult, embarrassing, or traumatic to the patient. The classic illustration is that of a man who was about to address a large audience and felt very nervous about it. He suddenly became blind just before the time for him to speak. The connection may not always be so direct as this, but usually the study of the personal history will bring out relationships of this type.

In hysterical paralysis, the neurological examination will show an absence of the reflex alteration which typically accompanies a true organic paralysis; and frequently, the limb is carried differently than it is in a true paralysis. The reflexes remain normal and no atrophy of the muscles occurs, even after years of hysterical paralysis. In organic paralysis, the atrophy or wasting away of the muscles is generally pronounced. Again, the diagnosis of hysteria may be made upon the fact that a peculiar part, or pattern of parts, of the body is involved.

Just as in the skin anesthesias, the dysfunction will not follow the true anatomical distribution of muscle function, or it may involve only some specific function. Certain functions of the muscles may be lost, while the same muscles can function perfectly well in a different activity. An example is writer's cramp, where writing becomes impossible although the hand can still be employed in all other sorts of fine motor coordinations.

In the case of an hysterical seizure, the patient may fall and go through a series of contortions and convulsions, but the performance is carried out in such a way that he does not injure himself in falling (he falls easily, or on a soft spot). Also, such seizures occur only when there is an audience present. These extreme attacks are now only rarely seen, although Charcot had hundreds of patients of this sort.

Other hysterical symptoms take the form of amnesia (loss of memory) and various trance states. In these, the normal consciousness is disturbed and the person responds in an automatic way. The patient may be possessed by one idea or a set of ideas to the exclusion of all else. Some portion of his normal memories and habits is not available to him. He may not remember his name, his family, or his former life, but may realize something is lost and actually attempt to find out what it is. When he recovers from this condition, he has no memory for it or the things that happened in it. When this tendency to behave in an automatic way is combined with an unconscious desire to run away, he may wander many miles away from his home with no memory of his name or where he came from. These amnestic periods are usually of short duration and the memory of the events transpiring during the state can usually be recovered under hypnosis. One case was described in which a middle-aged embezzler recalled events that had occurred during a fugue state more than twenty years earlier, although he had not been able to remember them during the entire twenty years.

Dissociation and Multiple Personality

An unusual disorder of behavior which occurs in a few hysterical persons is so interesting that it deserves, and has received, special study. Dissociation is but an exaggeration of the amnesic states just mentioned. When the periods of automatic behavior are prolonged and systematized, independent of the usual personality, they are called "double" or "multiple personality." In this condition, there exist two or more personalities, each of which is so well developed and integrated as to have a relatively coordinated, rich, unified, and stable life of its own. Actually, such cases are rare. Various accounts of cases of this type have been published since 1817.[10] Dual personality was made familiar to the general public through Stevenson's fictional account of Dr. Jekyll and Mr. Hyde, but many of the true histories are quite as startling.

Probably the best known and certainly the most extensively investigated was the case of Miss Beauchamp,* studied by Morton Prince, over a period of years. Miss Beauchamp was a quiet, reserved, New England girl of good intellectual ability. Following a somewhat traumatic event, a transient state appeared in which she showed a different type of personality. The personality of Miss Beauchamp disappeared and was replaced by that of *Sally*, a mischievous little girl who delighted in tricks and practical jokes (which Sally played even upon Miss Beauchamp). While under the care of Dr. Prince, she developed several other distinct and different personalities. Each personality had its own train of thoughts, views, tastes, habits, experiences, and memories.

Personal Experience of Dissociation

One of the cases that Morton Prince worked with has reported in her own words the feelings and attitudes that went along with the change in her personality. Miss B. C. A.† was treated by Prince for two years.

In her description of the development of the dissociated state (which was, of course, influenced by what she had read and what she was told by Dr. Prince), she stated that the first cleavage in her personality was a result of emotional shock. This emotion was one of fright and led to rebellion against the conditions of her life, forming a small, vague complex which recurred from time to time, but was immediately repressed. A second shock twelve years later (the knowledge that her husband had an incurable disease) revived the emotions of fright and rebellion. Consequent anxiety and sorrow at her husband's death were followed by four years of strain. There was a conflict between her ideals of duty and responsibility, on the one hand, and a longing for happiness, which made her rebellious against a situation which forced her to give up the pleasures of life. The development of these rebellious thoughts into a separate emotional complex resulted in a split of her consciousness into two personalities, A and B.

* Pronounced Beech-am.
† B. C. A., "My Life as a Dissociated Personality," in M. Prince, *Clinical and Experimental Studies in Personality*. Cambridge, Mass., Sci.-Art, 1929, 211–254.

These were both dissociated states and were finally organized into a normally integrated state, C. Personality A was characterized by numerous physical complaints, fatigue, moral doubts, and scruples. State B was free from the depressive mood and physical complaints of A, and its predominant mood was one of exaltation. State B was both an alternating and co-conscious personality; that is, at times it was in complete control, and at other times, existed along with state A as a co-conscious state which had full knowledge and memories of state A. Personality A had an imperfect memory for personality B. There was a marked difference between the two states in regard to moods, tastes, points of view, habits of thought, and controlling ideas.

In describing her subsequent experiences, this woman said that, following her husband's death, she had feelings of being alone, hopeless, and desolate beyond description. Then, after several weeks, came another emotional shock, so that for a few minutes these desperate ideas flashed through her mind, and then all was changed. The distressing ideas disappeared suddenly, and she looked back upon the emotional situation as a lark. There was no loss of memory for the ideas, but her way of viewing them changed completely. This state, which she referred to as personality B, appeared to others as a perfectly normal person but, while in it, she herself felt like a different person. As B, she was lighthearted and happy; felt really alive and vigorous. She experienced no discomfort of fatigue from strenuous physical activity, which previously she had avoided. She felt much younger, and the change in her expression was remarked on by others. She lost the formality and reserve that had previously characterized her. She remained in this state for some weeks, enjoying walking, boating, and other activities in a way that was utterly foreign to her previous semi-invalidism.

A new emotional shock produced a shift from condition B back to personality A, in which she again had headaches, insomnia, loss of appetite, and almost complete physical prostration. She now felt a horror for the way she had been acting as B and was really shocked. In mood, point of view, and ideals she was personality A, but she did some of the things she would have done as B, although she disapproved of them thoroughly. She said this was due to B existing in her coconscious at the same time that A was dominant in consciousness.

Another shift to B followed. She believed that these shifts back and forth between A and B were due to successive emotional shocks. It was only in retrospect that she recognized these changes as being complete, for, until she came to Dr. Prince for treatment, she had never heard of "change of personality." These changes had felt to her like awakening from a dream, rather than a real change in personality.

As A, she remembered the way she had acted when B, and she would think, "*Why* did I do as I did? *How* could I have done it? Why did it seem right? What would my friends think if they knew? I was mad! I *was not myself*." She then began to alternate frequently from one state to the other, and state A had a complete amnesia for her whole life as B. B remained as a co-conscious with A, sharing all its memories.

The periods of amnesia that she had as A made her life very difficult. "How can I describe or give any clear idea of what it is to wake suddenly, as it were, and not to know the day of the week, the time of the day, or why one is in any given position? I would come to myself as A, perhaps on the street, with no idea of where I had been or where I was going; fortunate if I found myself alone, for if I was carrying on a conversation, I knew nothing of what it had been; fortunate indeed, in that case, if I did not contradict something I had said; for, as B, my attitude toward all things was quite the opposite of that taken by A. Often it happened that I came to myself at some social gathering — a dinner, perhaps — to find I had been taking wine (a thing, as A, I felt bound not to do) and what was to me most shocking and horrifying, smoking a cigarette; never in my life had I done such a thing and my humiliation was deep and keen."[8]

As B, her attitude toward A was that of an irresponsible, gay girl toward a more serious-minded sister, having no patience with all her scruples and morbid ideas, and, in fact, feeling a little sorry for her. B did not look upon A as any part of herself and felt herself to be a distinct personality. A, on the other hand, recognized no division of personality. As B, she was very extravagant and bought things which, as A, she felt she could not afford. B, fond of gaiety, made social appointments which A, less social, did not want to be part of. Even her tastes in reading and dresses varied between the two states. Black was distasteful to B and, so far as possible, she wore white. (At the time of the first appearance of dissociation, she was in mourning.) She described one particularly distressing day in which, as A, she felt ill and had to lie down. As B, she felt fine and went around at the work at hand. She changed back and forth from one state to the other at least half a dozen times during that one day, shifting from a state of suffering to one of health and activity.

After prolonged study, Prince, by the use of hypnosis, brought together a normal personality, C, which possessed the combined memories of A and B and was free of the pathological symptoms which had characterized both. In her account, she said that she was unable to describe how this new change took place because everything was done during hypnosis. She only knew that she went to see Dr. Prince one day in a particularly disintegrated state, was hypnotized, and woke up with a feeling of strength and poise which had long been lacking, and with no blanks in her memory.

This account illustrates the subjective side of a personality dissociation that had proceeded to an extreme degree. While automatic activity in the normal individual remains under the control of consciousness, in cases such as this one, the secondary activities become involuntary and uncontrollable. If, by way of analogy, one conceives of consciousness as being made up of many interlacing streams of thought, then some of these may meet obstacles in the form of emotional conflicts or fixations and form whirlpools which separate from the main currents of thought. When large and powerful, they may assume the form of secondary personalities, any one of which may become dominant under certain conditions.

Background

Actually, there is no way of estimating the incidence of hysteria in the general population. Many real physical complaints may be covered by an overcast of hysterical symptoms, while hysterical features may be mixed with other symptoms in many types of mental disease. The statistical data on the neuroses as a group, given in the previous chapter, included those for hysteria. It is generally believed that hysteria is more common in the lower intellectual strata, but this thesis has never been conclusively demonstrated. It is usually stated that hysteria is more frequent among women than men, but even this is not always true.[9] As to the hereditary or constitutional factors involved, some such predisposition has been postulated, but, again, the evidence either pro or con is meager.[5]

There is more information available about the personality traits of hysterical persons than of many of the other types of patients. In addition to a strong tendency to dissociation, hysterics are usually "infantile," both physically and psychologically, particularly with respect to their emotional reactions. They tend to be egocentric and selfish in a childish way. They show a lack of self-control and general immaturity of impulse and motivation. They claim attention from others and enjoy being the center of attention. They avoid taking responsibility, and many of their reactions can be viewed as methods of escaping from unpleasant situations, although they may not be consciously aware of it. They act like "spoiled children." Most of the character traits of the hysterics appear early in life and are clearly developed by the time of adolescence. According to Jung[4] hysteria usually occurs in persons of the extroverted type. Extroverts and hysterics have many personality characteristics in common. Both enjoy being the center of attention, direct many of their activities toward attention-getting, and are strongly controlled by their feelings and emotions.

The usual concept of hysterical reactions should be separated from the concept of hysterical personality. Hysterical reactions may occur in practically anyone, if the stress of the situation is sufficiently painful or unpleasant, and if dissociation or physical complaints offer a possible mode of escape. The hysterical personality, on the other hand, is a consistently maladjusted style of life distinguished by its infantilism, egocentricity, poor integration, and a strong tendency to dissociation. This basic inadequacy may be genetically determined or it may be due to the persistence of childish habit patterns in adult life. There is no conclusive evidence for or against either hypothesis.

History of the Concept of Hysteria

The history of the concept of hysteria shows that for centuries there has been an attempt to find and formulate some sort of unity behind the diverse hysterical symptoms that appear and disappear without sufficient organic or physical basis (or even psychological basis). Widely different views have been advanced.

Going back to Hippocrates (460–377 B.C.) we find that he described vague and fluctuating symptoms of hysteria in women, which he attributed to the wandering of the uterus throughout the body. He believed that the hysterical symptoms were caused by the temporary pressure of the uterus upon the different parts of the body. In the early part of the seventeenth century, Lepois extended the concept of hysteria to include certain types of paralysis, deafness, blindness, and anesthesias. He claimed that hysteria occurred in both men and women and attributed the source of the disturbance to the brain, but this theory was not commonly accepted. In the latter part of the seventeenth century, a still broader range of symptoms was included and all the symptoms were attributed to demonic possession. It was finally recognized that hysterical manifestations could simulate almost every known disease, the distinguishing marks being the lack of any sufficient organic basis and the great changeability of the symptoms.

The first systematic description of hysteria came with the work of

Charcot and his students. Charcot, in the 1880's, showed that hysterical symptoms could be produced and removed by suggestion. The therapeutic results obtained by him were so astonishing that his treatments had a great vogue. Charcot believed that the cause of hysteria was an inherited degeneracy of the nervous system. The patient was assumed to be so susceptible because of this degeneracy that symptoms could be set up by suggestion.

Janet, at the end of the nineteenth century, was the first to formulate a psychological explanation of the disorder by showing how mental factors operate in producing the symptoms. He considered hysteria the result of faulty mental reactions. The major symptoms were attributed to a retraction of the field of consciousness, and to the tendency for the dissociation of systems of ideas and functions. He held that the particular symptoms were in some cases due to suggestion; in some other instances the functions involved were those which were most difficult for the person; in still other instances, the functions involved had been in full activity at the moment of some strong emotional trauma (a conditioned emotional response).

Breuer and Freud[1] revolutionized the concept of hysteria. Freud taught that every hysterical symptom is based on, or is symbolical of, some repressed sexual wish. Such wishes are repressed from consciousness because they run counter to the social and ethical standards imposed on the individual. Although buried in the unconscious, they are not inactive. The emotional tone of the wish is displaced and attaches itself to other ideas or reactions, which of themselves are not socially taboo. When this emotionality is shifted over to, or "converted" into, a physical symptom (such as blindness or paralysis), the condition is called "conversion hysteria."

Physiological Explanations

There is no satisfactory evidence concerning the physiology, anatomy, or organic pathology in hysteria. It is paradoxical that the physical symptoms, having no known basis, constitute the outstanding characteristic of hysteria. Physiological theories of hysteria have been advanced, but they never have had enough supporting evidence to warrant general acceptance. The hypothesis of Pavlov[6] has received attention in recent years, particularly in relation to experimental neurosis (see Chap. XXXII). Pavlov pointed out that hysteria might result from a "weakness" of the cerebral hemispheres of the brain. If the activity of the brain is inhibited, either through too intense stimulation or through neurological weakness, then the various physical complaints of the hysteric patient might be understood as forms of inadequate brain functioning.

Psychological Explanations

The common factor in the different psychological theories advanced in explanation of hysteria is the emphasis placed on dissociation. What is meant by *dissociation?* The term usually refers to a state of disturbed integration of conscious life in which thought systems or action systems separate themselves from the center of consciousness. The ability to do one thing while attending to something else is part of everyday experience. The typist whose fingers continue to fly while she is thinking or talking of something else, and the person who knits a sweater and reads a book at the same time, are examples of activities which are dissociated from the usual stream of awareness. Dissociations of this type are normal. More severe forms of dissociation may occur in the normal personality under the influence of a strong emotional shock. Under such circumstances, the person may be stunned and unaware of things going on around him, and so behave in an automatic fashion. In the normal person, such an episode is short-lived; he soon "finds himself." The dissociated state of the hysteric, on the other hand, is prolonged in duration and may be set off by simple, everyday occurrences.

Janet referred to these phenomena as retractions of the field of consciousness. He believed that in the hysteric certain elements of consciousness (an idea, an emotion, or a system of movements) separated themselves from consciousness and took on an independent existence of their own, apart from the rest of the personality. Consciousness was no longer able to control them when they had developed to this exaggerated degree of independence. The different types of symptoms which developed depended upon the particular idea or set of ideas that split off from normal consciousness and achieved this independent existence.

Freud recognized the importance of dissociation in hysteria, but was mainly interested in the causes of this dissociation and the dynamics of the specific symptoms that occurred. As mentioned previously, he held that hysterical symptoms represented the symbolic fulfillment of an inadequately repressed sexual wish. If the wish were completely repressed, its emotional tone would not be displaced and converted into these physical symptoms. Thus the tendency of the hysterical patient to cling to his symptoms and exploit them results from the fact that they satisfy some basic wish.

Explanations of Multiple Personality

The significance of histories of multiple personality has been questioned on the ground that suggestion from the investigator might be the cause of the appearance of the different personalities in hysteric persons who have a tendency to dissociation. The evidence indicating the genuine nature of multiple personality is as follows:[10]

About one hundred different investigators have reported more than one hundred such instances ranging over different centuries and different parts of the world. Most of the cases had never heard of other such persons. In all the various case histories there are many common elements. The essential question is how suggestion became so effective and dissociation so complete in these individuals. In multiple personality the secondary-personality organization may afford an escape from stress, and in this sense plays a protective role. The form of this role may be passively acquired through suggestion, past history, or a living example; or it may be formed actively as a synthesis of various emotions and thoughts that are broken off from the normal stream of consciousness.

Harriman[2] has described the experimental production during hypnosis of phenomena very similar to multiple personality. A trained hypnotic subject was put into deep trance. He was told that he should open his eyes, but that his hand and arm would not feel like part of him. He was then told that he would not remember any action of this hand and arm. Later he was given a paper and pencil, with which he produced cryptic automatic writing. He then went to sleep and was later awakened. When shown what he had written, he was unable to say what it meant. Following the induction of a light hypnotic trance, the subject was told that he fully understood the whole situation, although no specific reference to the writing was made. When he awakened, he translated or amplified the cryptic automatic writing. Harriman drew the parallel that there were three personalities involved: x2, in which the cryptic automatic writing was done; x3, the posthypnotic somnambulistic state, in which the subject knew nothing of the writing; and x1, the normal personality which returned after the second trance. Personalities x2 and x3 were dissociated states produced by the nature of the hypnotic suggestion in this experimental situation.

A satisfactory explanation of why some people, and not others, develop hysteria, dissociated states, or multiple personalities still awaits experimental proof.

Summary

Hysteria is one of the oldest recognized forms of abnormal psychology. It has been the subject of clinical observation, medical and psychological speculation and experimentation, and popular interest for centuries. Most authorities hold that hysteria is essentially a psychological problem. It occurs in individuals having a poorly organized personality, a tendency toward dissociation, and a suggestible nature. The psychological process of dissociation, as an escape from unpleasantness, is quite common. This one symptom does not, of itself, constitute hysteria. The hysteric patient is essentially a neurotic person whose chief symptoms are (*a*) physical complaints without recognizable organic basis, and (*b*) dissociated states which are deep and prolonged.

There seems to be no doubt but that multiple personalities do occur and that they are, in all probability, a special form of hysteria. They afford interesting material for psychological study and shed light on a rare, but important, variety of psychopathology.

REFERENCES

1. Breuer, J., and S. Freud, *Studies in Hysteria.* Nerv. Ment. Dis. Mono., 1936, #61, 241 pp.
2. Harriman, P. L., "The Experimental Induction of a Multiple Personality," *Psychiatry*, 1942, *5*, 179–186.
3. Janet, P., *The Major Symptoms of Hysteria* (2d ed.). New York, Macmillan, 1920.
4. Jung, C. G., *Psychological Types.* New York, Harcourt, 1923.
5. McInnes, R. G., "Observations on Heredity in Neurosis," *Proc. Roy. Soc. Med.*, 1937, *30*, 895–904.
6. Pavlov, I. P., *Conditioned Reflexes and Psychiatry.* New York, International Publishers, 1941.
7. Prince, M., *The Dissociation of a Personality.* New York, Longmans, 1920.
8. ——, *Clinical and Experimental Studies in Personality.* Cambridge, Mass., Sci.-Art, 1929.
9. Schilder, P., "The Concept of Hysteria," *Amer. Jour. Psychiat.*, 1939, *95*, 1389–1413.
10. Taylor, W. S., and M. F. Martin, "Multiple Personality," *Jour. Abn. Soc. Psychol.*, 1944, *39*, 281–300.

Chapter VIII

TRAUMATIC NEUROSES

IN ADDITION to the various forms of neurosis considered in the previous two chapters, there are several other varieties, identical or closely akin in symptoms, but whose provocation is related to physical injury or prolonged stress. To these, the name traumatic neurosis is applied. Traumatic neuroses occur both in peace and war, but the conditions peculiar to warfare markedly increase their frequency. The war situation does not produce forms of psychopathology which are essentially different from those of peace. However, certain varieties of neurotic symptoms assume particular importance and are called "acute war neuroses." The increased occurrence of these types of neuroses under combat conditions is particularly interesting in light of the fact that there is no corresponding increase in the rate of onset of any form of psychosis, such as manic-depressive psychosis or dementia praecox, during wartime either among the services or in civilian life. In other words, the physical and psychological stress of combat has a provocative significance for neurosis, but not for psychosis. Hence, a description and survey of the knowledge relevant to traumatic neuroses should provide greater understanding of the neuroses in general.

The American observations on war neuroses start with the publications of Horsthorne[6] and of DaCosta,[1] following the Civil War. At that time, observations and studies were made of such abnormal reactions to effort, such as undue palpitation of the heart, exhaustion, pain in the center of the chest, and breathlessness in the absence of any demonstrable organic defect of the heart or blood vessels. These symptoms have been variously called "soldier's heart," "effort syndrome," "disordered action of the heart," and "neurocirculatory asthenia."[2] These terms came into use during World War I, when a great deal of attention was given to the problem because of its frequency and seriousness. Of some 70,000 men in the British Army who had been under observation for cardiac disorder in 1914–18, only one sixth were found to be suffering from organic heart disease. In the remaining cases the major precipitating cause was usually found to be emotional strain, physical strain, or infection. Such factors brought out anxiety, anger, or guilt which was accentuated by the military experience.

World War I left as a heritage the term *shell shock*, which was applied to many of the neurotic war casualties. This name came from the fact that, at first, the cause of these psychological deviations was assumed to be actual concussion. It was believed that the concussion caused changes in the central nervous system; or that the atmospheric pressure changes, produced by the exploding shells and the carbon monoxide gas liberated, resulted in the psychological symptoms of cerebral concussion and carbon monoxide poisoning.[9] With prolonged observation, this interpretation was found incorrect. Identical symptoms occurred in soldiers far behind the front who were never exposed to gunfire; shell shock was rare among prisoners and wounded; the symptoms disappeared with suggestion or hypnosis; and the organic disorders that appeared did not fit in with any type of known neuropathology. The existence of sudden and dramatic improvements also argued against the presence of any basic organic pathology. Thus, the etiological factors were assumed to lie in the field of psychological trauma rather than organic pathology, and the term *traumatic neurosis* gradually supplanted the term *shell shock*.

When World War II began, the medical profession, as well as the general public, was much more alert to the possible psychological effect of military service and battle experience upon emotionally unstable individuals. World War I had shown the value of group tests in screening out many who were psychologically unfit. World War II saw the initiation of further advances in psychological testing and screening. The pressure of having to examine large numbers of individuals within a short period of time made it impossible to eliminate all of the potentially unfit or emotionally unstable individuals from induction into military service. The recognition, treatment, compensation, and rehabilitation of these "mistakes" constitute a serious problem, both during the war and in postwar periods. It is probably true that even the most perfect screening system would not have been able to eradicate the threat of war neurosis completely. Many soldiers who break down in combat are known to have been fairly well adjusted in civilian life and any potential neurosis could not have been detected by any available test or psychiatric interview at the time of induction into the military service.

However, many neurotic casualties of war show definite evidence of emotional instability in their previous personality make-up. The psychological situation in these cases is practically the same as it is in many other forms of neurosis. Unstable individuals who could not withstand the additional stress placed upon them by the war situation showed the same pattern of symptoms which they might have had under stress in civilian life; namely, anxiety, hysteria, neurasthenia. Because the acute phase of the condition came when such persons were in military service, they have been classified as suffering from traumatic or war neurosis.

War neuroses are not limited to those persons of previous emotional instability. Cases of acute war neurosis that had been adequately adjusted before the war were well described by Sargant and Slater.[12] They reported on military patients who had been through the evacuation at Dunkirk. Most of these men had shown a satisfactory adjustment to army life and most of them were of normal intelligence and personality. They had lived through the catastrophe of military defeat and the evacuation from Dunkirk, which had been marked by continuous physical exertion, bodily danger, loss of sleep, insufficient and irregular meals, recurrent bombardment, and the sight of comrades and civilians being killed around them. Their psychopathological symptoms were surprisingly uniform. They consisted of physical and mental exhaustion, revealed either through tension and anxiety or through listless apathy; neurological signs of a functional nature (coarse, irregular tremor, exaggerated reflexes, and so on); sleeplessness with terrifying, bad dreams; a feeling of inner unrest; and a tendency to be startled by the least noise (particularly the sound of airplanes).

A very characteristic symptom of the traumatic form of war neurosis is the repetitious catastrophic nightmare.[8,10] These dreams are usually a reenactment of some vivid situation and are so intense that sleep habits are severely disturbed, and the feelings of fear that are aroused are carried over upon awakening. Another common reaction that appears in exaggerated form and frequency is that of startle. This reaction is elicited by any loud or sudden noise, such as the slamming of a door. The patient's physiological response to the sound is usually tremor, sweating, dry mouth, dilated pupils, and palpitation; the psychological reaction may be one of panic, so that the patient screams, cries, and tries to escape by crawling under the bed or running from the room. In addition to these two outstanding symptoms (battle dreams and startle), there may be a personality change, so that the patient becomes irritable, intolerant, sullen, and morose.

In a few cases, there is a continuous feeling of guilt which is accompanied by emotional depression.

To avoid the unfortunate connotations of the term *neurosis*, the symptom picture of acute war neurosis is now usually called "combat fatigue." When other symptoms, such as those of conversion hysteria, neurasthenia, or obsessions are present, the name for the variety of neurosis should be used. For practical purposes, four general criteria for the diagnosis of acute war neurosis have been laid down, as follows: (*a*) a stable personality prior to the appearance of the traumatic emotional disturbance; (*b*) a combat experience of real intensity; (*c*) objective evidence of subjective anxiety (the patient sweats, trembles, flushes or pales, swallows frequently or smokes incessantly); (*d*) symptoms disappear (patient recovers) in a relatively short period of time.

The following history illustrates the pattern of symptoms that many of these cases show:

CASE 12: Corporal C was a physically healthy, athletic individual, twenty-two years of age. His childhood and early development were characterized by an outgoing and self-reliant attitude. He completed two years of high school and then voluntarily left school to take a job. He enlisted in the army when he saw he was going to be drafted and rather enjoyed the active, masculine atmosphere of army training. He was made a corporal after six months. He admits that in the original landing in North Africa he was very frightened, but led his men adequately through one sharp scrimmage before that phase of the campaign was completed. His unit was in continuous combat for six weeks during the early days of the campaign for Tunisia and he was involved in a withdrawal in the face of heavy enemy superiority. Many men in his unit were killed around him. He went for days with very little sleep and ate only emergency rations. During this phase of action, he felt an increasing irritability and restlessness, particularly when things quieted down for a while. After his unit was withdrawn from action, he became even more tense, could eat but little at a time, and his sleep was repeatedly disturbed by terrifying dreams of the battles he had lived through.

His particular squad had been reduced to six men, and when reinforcements came up he made every effort to conceal his increasing tenseness and nervousness. However, shortly afterward he made a violent scene when one of the new men accidently stumbled and discharged his rifle in the darkness. When, after a week of rest, his unit was ordered back into action, there was a reactivation of his old apprehensions but also a feeling of relief at getting away from inactivity. By the time he had been back in action three days — during which time he had had very little sleep — his squad was assigned to attack a machine-gun position and he and his closest friend were pinned down by the machine-gun fire. His friend, who was about fifteen feet away from him, was seriously wounded. His friend's screams of pain filled him with panic, but he tried to work his way over toward him. When he had crawled about half the distance, a direct hit killed his friend. Shortly thereafter, another shell came even nearer the patient. He remembers nothing of the succeeding three hours, and finally became fully conscious in an aid station.

He had been found wandering aimlessly about the battlefield crying and calling for his lost friend. In the aid station he was confused, could remember nothing that had happened, stared stupidly at the people around him, and repeated his friend's name questioningly. When a plane passed near the aid station, he suddenly changed from his apathetic stupor and ran screaming from the room until he was caught. He was given large doses of sedatives for three days but remained anxious and confused, so that he was evacuated to a rear-area hospital for further treatment. There, rest, medication, and open discussion of his experience with the medical officers brought about recovery.

The prognosis of recovery for true cases of acute war neurosis is favorable if suitable treatment is begun before the symptoms become habitual or "set."[3] The severe symptoms usually disappear after a short term of rest and therapy in which reassurance is given. This therapy must be started as soon as possible after the patient has been removed from the combat area. Many soldiers who suffer from an acute war neurosis are able to return to active duty, but early return to active combat is inadvisable.

The immediate treatment which is used in these cases is to provide prolonged rest. Anything from simple sedatives to a deep drug narcosis may be used. Of particular value seems to be a therapeutic method which has been called "narco-analysis."[5] This method consists of the induction of a drug narcosis, during which the patient is encouraged to talk about his battle experiences. Sometimes he does this spontaneously, but usually, because of existing amnesia, suggestions from the therapist are necessary to reinstate these earlier experiences. The patient is told that he is on a battlefield, under fire, plus whatever details are known of the traumatic situation. In some cases the patient may tell his experiences as a story, but many times he will act out the original situation with accompanying strong emotions of fear, anxiety, or anger, as the case may be.

Under the influence of the drug, there is a release of the intense, repressed emotions. This release is gradual, so that the patient becomes able to deal with his intense emotions in a more rational manner than before, and the catastrophic reactions that occurred previously drop out. There is gradual synthesis of the emotions and memories of the traumatic experience as these emotions are brought back into consciousness and reenacted, and with this synthesis there is recovery.

Background Factors

One interesting study of the neurotic constitution of two thousand neuropsychiatric military casualties in World War II was made by Slater[14] in an English emergency hospital between November 1939 and June 1941. He looked into the family histories of all these patients, reporting on positive histories. A positive family history was one in which one or more of the parents, brothers and sisters, or children had suffered from definite neurotic illness, psychosis, epilepsy, or from some form of psychopathy (such as drunkenness, chronic shiftlessness, or violent and brutal habits) which had entailed undesirable social consequences. Table 1 is drawn from Slater's figures and gives the percentage of positive family histories in certain relevant groups.

TABLE I. PERCENT OF POSITIVE FAMILY HISTORIES IN CERTAIN GROUPS OF NEUROPSYCHIATRIC CASUALTIES IN WORLD WAR II.*

Diagnosis	Number of Cases	Percent of Positive Family Histories Reported
Organic states (physical)	74	37.3
True head injury	87	32.1
Anxiety neurosis	710	56.7
Hysteria	392	50.8
Reactive depression	232	55.7

These figures indicate that a positive family history is found more frequently in patients suffering from neurosis than in patients with organic states or head injury, which confirms the figures reported for World War I. This tabulation does not separate out those suffering from acute war neurosis, in whom, presumably, the positive family history of nervousness would be lower.

The real significance of neurotic constitution should be considered in relation to the "threshold" for breakdown. The inadequate, unstable personality will break under slight provocation; and the more stable the constitution, the greater will be the resistance to shock or to the constant fatigue and stress of warfare. The question of neurotic constitution, therefore, comes to these points: How much can this individual stand before he breaks? If the person is completely free of any neurotic constitution, will any amount of stress cause a break? These are theoretical questions for which there is no answer. If neurotic constitution is a distinct predisposition, then those who do not have it will be free from all forms of neurosis, including "combat

* Slater, E., "The Neurotic Constitution," *Jour. Neurol. Psychiat.*, 1943, *6*, 5.

fatigue." If neurotic constitution means nothing more than a low degree of resistance to neurotic breakdown, then even the best adjusted person will succumb if the stress becomes great enough.

It is believed that the most active factor precipitating acute war neurosis is fear. Continued threat of serious injury and death, together with the sight of injured and dead companions, has a cumulative effect. Prolonged fear without hope of reprieve finally accomplishes what a single exposure will not. In addition, lack of proper food and water, irregular supplies, along with lack of opportunity for rest, play their part in wearing down the physical resistance of the soldier. Prolonged exposure to explosions, particularly when the soldier is in a position of enforced inactivity, is another factor facilitating the break. These positive factors occur against a background of a completely changed life routine. The soldier is separated from all his previous emotional attachments; his old habits of thought and action are completely disorganized; and the social values of his civilian life are no longer operating, or even considered. In other words, the majority of the sources of security in his past life are now absent. If his military training has not given him confidence in his leaders, complete efficiency in the use of his fighting tools, and a sense of pride in, and loyalty toward, his fellow soldiers to take the place of all former sources of security, the chances of a break are increased.

The explanations which have been offered to account for the psychology of war neuroses do not differ in any important way from those offered to explain neuroses in general. The orthodox psychoanalytic explanation that all neuroses are due to psychosexual disturbances is obviously inappropriate. This has been modified in different ways by several writers who have attempted to widen the basic explanatory concept so that it will cover the war neuroses. For example, Kardiner[8] held that the essence of the problem lay, not in a conflict between the individual and his instincts, but in the relation of the individual as a functioning being to his environment. According to this concept, a person who cannot cope successfully with his environment develops a feeling of helplessness which further inhibits him, and which makes the outer world seem thoroughly hostile. Hence, the soldier's attempt to defend himself against this apparently hostile world, without the aid of the organized, integrated, and orderly techniques which were previously available to him, constitutes the psychological basis of war neurosis, in this newer psychoanalytic sense.

An excellent summary of the complex problem of war neurosis has been stated as follows:

. . . it is evident that we must look within the individual for the most important factors in the etiology of war neurosis, but that heredity and environment may not be excluded. Heredity may not be excluded because the ability of the person to stand up under his conflicts, and work through them, may depend upon his constitutional stability: a bad environment, say, one which gives the individual insufficient rest, food, or continual emotional strain and tension, may temporarily also upset his usual stability and render him more susceptible to breaking down under conflicts which he might in time of less external strain be able to handle.*

Traumatic Neurosis in Civil Life

The term *traumatic neurosis* is frequently applied to any form of neurosis that develops shortly after a physical injury and in which a definite relationship between the two can be assumed. Huddleson[7] used the term *posttraumatic neurosis* in referring to cases of a "psychogenic or non-structural nervous disorder, shortly following a physical injury." There is frequently a period of a few weeks or months between the time of injury and the onset of the neurotic symptoms. This has been called the "meditation period." The complaints in such cases are in no way different from those of the varieties of neuroses already described. Hysterical symptoms and anxiety states are common. Many patients complain of headache, backache, and general weakness. Loss of function, as in paralysis, blindness, and deafness, may occur but it is somewhat less frequent. The following case is typical.

CASE 13: A forty-six-year-old man suffered a blow on the head from a falling ladder while in a public building, which resulted in a short period of unconsciousness. Upon physical examination there was no evidence of skull fracture, and a diagnosis of slight concussion was made. From this, he made an uneventful recovery. Three months after the accident he developed slight tremors of the hands, palpitation, headaches, and general nervousness. He claimed that he was unable to drive his car and could not work full time at his job. The physical examination was negative. Following an unsuccessful lawsuit for damages, there was a gradual diminution of symptoms.

When the complaints center around some specific injury, such as broken leg or sprained back, it is usually difficult to establish when the neurotic features started. In general, the neurosis is assumed to begin at the time when the health and physical fitness, which are expected to parallel tissue repair and restored organic function, fail to appear. Instead, a gradual falling off in efficiency occurs, usually about three

* Zabriskie, E. G., and A. L. Brush, "Psychoneurosis in Wartime," *Psychosom. Med.*, 1941, *3*, 305.

or four months after the injury. Most traumatic neuroses occur within six months after injury, but exceptional cases have been described after intervals of more than six months.

Many neuroses, following injury, are complicated by the psychological effects of the workmen's compensation laws. Since compensation is awarded for partial or complete impairment of working capacity, and since any neurosis developed after injury is legally held to be a disturbance of work capacity in the same sense as direct injury, a "subsidy for psychogenic illness" is created. While there are no accurate figures on the relative proportion of neurotic to nonneurotic complaints for which compensation is given, it has been estimated that 15 per cent of the applicants for compensation complain of essentially neurotic symptoms.

Many studies have shown that it is not the injury alone, but the assurance of remuneration, that prolongs the duration of disability. For this reason, it is believed best to have early, lump-sum settlement of all compensation claims. A suit hanging fire over months or even years encourages the litigant to prolong and exaggerate his complaints and to drift into habits of illness which make treatment difficult, if not impossible. Continued payments, as a pension, remove the incentive to improve, and for this reason a lump-sum payment is preferable.

What are the psychological factors acting in these cases?[13] At first glance, it would appear that the patients are merely exploiting and exaggerating their physical disability. If they can get paid for not working, why work? In certain cases, there may be such conscious motivation (malingering); but in others, the disturbance is more basic and not of conscious instigation. The desire for financial reimbursement may reinforce and perpetuate a traumatic neurosis, once established. Severe injuries, for which compensation awards are high, are less likely to give rise to traumatic neurosis than less severe injuries.

Among the background factors of this type of neurosis, the outstanding one is previous neurotic tendency or psychological maladjustment. The history of many posttraumatic neurotic patients shows that they were self-centered, had feelings of inferiority, had an inability to face difficulty with courage, and a tendency to seek refuge in excuses and illness.[4] In persons having such tendencies, any new stress or difficulty may precipitate a neurosis. None the less, there are some cases of traumatic neuroses in which the individual showed no previous evidence of neurosis. These are usually explained by saying that dissatisfaction with one's work or feelings of incompetence may be so strong that physical injury provides a welcome relief from an uncomfortable situation. A further background factor is the general social attitude that the employer should be held responsible for any accidents that occur. This shifting of responsibility may encourage the development of traumatic neurosis in certain cases.

Among the precipitating causes, after the accident, are mishandling by the examining physician, sympathy and solicitousness from friends and relatives, and fear of loss of security. The physician may alarm the patient unduly and make him feel that he has a very serious condition with little chance of recovery. The patient's fears and worries about himself become fixed by some incidental remark by the doctor, especially if his friends express great concern over his condition which reinforces his belief that he is terribly injured. He knows of other cases in which legal suit against a company resulted in a substantial award. He develops a sense of resentment against his employers because he has experienced pain and disablement and is anxious to get satisfaction. Because of his very real worries about his condition, he feels his source of livelihood may be permanently interfered with. While he is receiving compensation, he is financially secure, as well as a person of interest and attention. There is often little incentive provided to get him to resume his normal line of work.

Malingering

"Malingering" means the conscious feigning of illness or the intentional exaggeration of some actual physical complaint. In traumatic neurosis, in either soldiers or civilians, the question of whether or not the patient is a malingerer very frequently arises. Psychiatrists believe that true, conscious malingering is rare and that a careful clinician should have little difficulty in detecting most of these cases because the simulation is usually imperfect in some detail. For example, such symptoms as the physiological signs of anxiety are very difficult to imitate. There is more possibility that hysterical symptoms will be confused with malingering; but, again, if one has some psychological understanding of conversion symptoms, they are not too hard to distinguish from consciously feigned complaints. In differentiating between malingering and anxiety neuroses, it has been found that the malingerer is unlikely to describe previous symptoms and increasing feelings of fear in terms which are characteristic of one having a true anxiety state.

Malingering and mental disease are not mutually exclusive. Malingering in normal individuals is rare. It usually occurs in those of inferior psychological make-up. The attitude of the general public toward such behavior in war may be stated as follows:

> I am suffering from neurosis
> You should pull yourself together
> He is a coward and malingerer.[11]

The person who experiences neurotic feelings and reactions knows how uncontrollable they are; but when they occur in someone else, they seem to be intentionally assumed and the result of a lack of "will power" to overcome them.

Summary

Some psychopathologists find so little difference between traumatic neurosis and other forms of neuroses that they are disinclined to separate them as a special group. However, most investigators who have worked with cases of this type hold that they should be considered as a distinct subgroup within the neuroses in general because of the rather characteristic symptoms, motivation, and the course of recovery.

The basic characteristic of the traumatic neurosis is fixation on the traumatic event without displacement of either anxiety or guilt to other subjects, and without the accumulation of new neurotic features over a period of time, such as usually occurs in the other forms of neurosis.

The two main sources of traumatic neurosis are industrial accidents and battle casualties. Both groups constitute important social and economic problems because of the principle of compensation for prolonged disability.

REFERENCES

1. Da Costa, J. M., "On Irritable Heart: A Clinical Study of a Form of Functional Cardiac Disorder and Its Consequences," *Amer. Jour. Med. Sci.*, 1871, *61–62*, 2–52.
2. Dunn, W. H., "Emotional Factors in Neurocirculatory Asthenia," *Psychosom. Med.*, 1942, *4*, 333–354.
3. Grinker, R. R., and J. P. Spiegel, *Men Under Stress*. Philadelphia, Blakiston, 1945.
4. Hall, G. W., and R. P. Mackay, "The Post-traumatic Neuroses," *Jour. Amer. Med. Asso.*, 1934, *102*, 510–513.
5. Horsley, J. S., *Narco-analysis*. London, Oxford University Press, 1943.
6. Horsthorne, H., "On Heart Disease in the Army," *Amer. Jour. Med. Sci.*, 1864, *48*, 89–92.

7. Huddleson, J. H., *Accidents, Neuroses and Compensation*. Baltimore, Williams & Wilkins, 1932.

8. Kardiner, A., *The Traumatic Neuroses of War*. Psychosom. Med. Mono., 1941, *1*, #2 & 3.

9. Mott, F. W., "Effects of High Explosives upon the Central Nervous System," *Lancet*, 1916, *1*, 331–338.

10. Raines, G. N., and L. C. Kolb, "Combat Fatigue and War Neurosis," *U. S. Naval Med. Bull.*, 1943, *41*, 923–936.

11. Ross, T. A., *Lectures on War Neuroses*. Baltimore, Williams & Wilkins, 1941.

12. Sargant, W., and E. Slater, "Acute War Neuroses," *Lancet*, 1940, *2*, 1–2.

13. Schaller, W. F., and M. R. Somers, "Psychogenic Factors and Precipitation Point in the Post-traumatic Neuroses," *Jour. Amer. Med. Asso.*, 1929, *93*, 967–971.

14. Slater, E., "The Neurotic Constitution," *Jour. Neurol. Psychiat.*, 1943, *6*, 1–16.

15. Zabriskie, E. G., and A. L. Brush, "Psychoneuroses in Wartime," *Psychosom. Med.*, 1941, *3*, 295–329.

Chapter IX

EPILEPSY

EPILEPTIC seizures occur in both man and animals. They have been described and explanations offered for their occurrence in the literature of all ages. The explanation of the ancient Greeks was that the seizures were due to heredity or to some sort of brain damage, while the ancient Hebrew explanation was that the epileptic was possessed of an evil spirit, as is shown by the appeal of a father in Galilee to Christ.* Epilepsy is also known as the "falling sickness," the "sacred disease," "fits," "cerebral dysrhythmia," or "convulsions." Since epilepsy is of various types and causes, these manifold conditions are now classified in the medical literature as "convulsive states" or as "the epilepsies"[5] although psychologically all these states are known as epilepsy.

Anyone witnessing an epileptic seizure for the first time will be both startled and alarmed. The sudden onset of convulsions in a person who was a moment before in apparently perfect health is both appalling and mystifying. The different interpretations of the condition which have been made in ancient and medieval times and the social stigma which still attaches itself to the condition are more understandable when one has observed an attack. A *grand mal* seizure usually occurs somewhat as follows: The patient's face becomes blank, the eyes take on a fixed stare, the extremities stiffen. With a hoarse, weird cry, he falls to the floor forcibly. The rigid, tense muscular spasm gives way to a series of violent jerks, so that both sides of the body are involved in waves of contraction and relaxation. The jerks and twitches may last for several minutes. During the tense phase, respiration may be temporarily interfered with, so that the patient's face becomes blue.

* "And one of the multitude answered and said, Master, I have brought unto thee my son, which hath a dumb spirit. And wheresoever he taketh him, he teareth him: and he foameth and gnasheth with his teeth, and pineth away. . . . And they brought him unto Him; and when he saw Him; straightway the spirit tare him; and he fell on the ground, and wallowed foaming. And He asked his father, How long is it ago since this came unto him? And he said, of a child. And oft times it hath cast him into the fire, and into the waters, to destroy him." St. Mark, 9:17–21.

Frothy saliva appears on the lips. The jerking movements of the jaw often produce injuries to the tongue. There may be involuntary urination and defecation. From two to ten minutes after the beginning of the attack, the patient passes into a state of deep sleep or coma, which may last a variable length of time ranging from minutes to hours.

Case History

The following description illustrates the course of the life development of a typical epileptic girl:

CASE 14: Miss E, aged twenty-two, came from a home of American-born, Protestant parents of moderate financial means. The father died when she was eight years old and her mother had to take up daily work outside the home to support the four children. The mother was fairly strict with the children and had little time to show them affection. The first seizure occurred on an open street when she was thirteen, soon after menstruation started. She refused to let her mother take her to the doctor. Attacks occurred at rare intervals until she was seventeen years old, and then they became more frequent and severe. She finally went to see a doctor and the medication which he administered decreased the number of *grand mal* attacks to about one a month. However, she had daily slight attacks (*petit mal*). She never had any warning (aura) of either the *petit mal* or *grand mal* attacks. The frequency and severity of the seizures caused her to discontinue her education in the third year of high school and from that time on she seldom left the house. She had few girl friends in childhood and adolescence, spending a great deal of her time reading.

She wanted to go out with boys when she was sixteen years old but her mother would not let her. From the time she was eighteen she went out with boys occasionally and became fond of one boy in particular. Her desires for the future centered around being married and having a home of her own. She had never been very religious and did not feel that religion had influenced her attitudes or beliefs to any great extent, except that it at times cheered her up when she felt discouraged and depressed. These disconsolate moments occurred when she worried about her "spells" or about the fact that she could not get a job. Sometimes she felt that she did not care what happened to her and that she would be better off dead. She reported that at times she was irritable at home and became upset and annoyed at little things.

In general, this girl was shy and retiring, had few social contacts outside the home, and made little effort toward getting any vocational training or placement. She was extremely discouraged, feeling that her attacks made gainful employment unlikely. Since she had never given up the desire to carry on a normal life, the feeling of frustration gave her many "bad moments."*

* Modified from C. Landis, and M. M. Bolles, *The Personality and Sexuality of the Physically Handicapped Woman.* New York, Hoeber, 1942, 68–69.

Types of Seizures

The *grand mal* or generalized seizure described previously is the most severe form of epilepsy. The pattern of the seizure is by no means the same in all cases, or even in the same case at different times. The hoarse cry, frothing of saliva, involuntary urination and defecation may or may not be present in the *grand mal* attack. Constant features are the sudden complete loss of consciousness, the coma after the attack, and the slow return to consciousness, like one awakening from a deep sleep. The attacks may occur during the day, or at night (during sleep).

The *petit mal* attack is more frequent than the *grand mal*, both in the number of individuals so afflicted and in the number of attacks experienced by any one individual. These attacks consist of momentary lapses of consciousness, together with disturbances in expression and with momentary suspension of activity, which may be so brief as to be barely perceptible to the observer or which may last ten or twenty seconds. They are blank spots in the stream of consciousness and behavior, after which normal activity is resumed as though nothing had happened. In some, these attacks are more severe; the head may drop forward and slight twitchings of the muscles may occur. In other individuals a *petit mal* attack may on occasion develop into a generalized, *grand mal* attack. *Petit mal* attacks are relatively more common during adolescence. When present, they occur much more frequently than *grand mal* seizures, so that an individual may have from one to a hundred or more such "lapses" every day. So long as an individual has only *petit mal* attacks, there is little, if any, mental impairment.

The third type of attack is the *Jacksonian seizure*. This is characterized by a convulsion of some part of the body, usually an arm or a leg. There is no loss of consciousness during the attack, although there is a loss of voluntary control over the convulsing member of the body. Jacksonian attacks sometimes spread or change into generalized, *grand mal* seizures.

Psychic seizures (psychic equivalents, psychomotor seizures) are difficult to describe since the attack differs in its expression in each patient. The patient loses consciousness and memory for the attack, although he acts and even speaks as if more or less conscious. He may mumble incoherently, get up and walk, gesticulate, chew or grind his teeth, attempt to take off or put on his clothing. He may answer questions in a confused fashion. He may walk, sometimes for long distances. Usually, such an attack lasts only a few minutes, but it may go on for hours or even days. In such a prolonged attack the person may find himself in a new, strange place when he recovers consciousness. Some of these individuals act as though they were in an irritable, ugly intoxication and fight violently if restrained. Others have been known to commit crimes of violence during such a seizure. Since in any one person each successive attack is somewhat similar to its predecessor, measures can be taken to prevent possible injury to the patient or to others.

Some "behavior-problem" children are, in reality, suffering from psychic seizures. They are destructive, irritable, hostile, and assaultive. They have fits of temper, run away, or have spells of meanness; but between these episodes they display a good disposition and normal behavior. By no means all behavior-problem children suffer from psychic seizures. It is possible to distinguish such children from other behavior problems on the basis of their electroencephalograms (see below).

Somewhat more than one half of persons who have *grand mal* attacks have an *aura* or warning of the approaching seizure. (Aura is Latin for "wind," that is, the wind before the storm.) This initial symptom occurs from one to ten or fifteen seconds before the attack. Such a patient may be fortunate enough to have time between the aura and the seizure to lie down or to seek seclusion. The nature of the aura varies widely in different individuals. Sometimes peculiar sensations are felt in the pit of the stomach; other cases develop dizziness, or numbness and tingling of the feet or hands. Still other persons report peculiar sensations in their muscles, head, eyes, mouth, or throat. The particular kind of aura experienced seems to be characteristic of that individual. For many years the aura has been recognized as the beginning of the seizure, and not its cause. Neurosurgeons have shown that the aura can be experimentally produced by the direct stimulation of the brain cortex in certain appropriate areas.[10]

Another grouping of the types of epileptic seizures is based on the three general conditions under which they usually occur. Epileptic seizures may be associated (*a*) with organic injury of the brain; (*b*) with acute fever or intoxication; or (*c*) they may be idiopathic, meaning that they are not regularly associated with any known cause.

There is no lesion or injury of the brain that will inevitably produce epilepsy, and there is hardly any lesion or injury that has not "caused" epilepsy. In some persons having convulsive seizures, there is a demonstrable cerebral lesion, such as degeneration of brain tissue, tumorous growth, or scar tissue. In these cases the cerebral pathology may be termed the basic cause which, under certain conditions of stimulation, results in convulsive phenomena.

In certain cases of epilepsy which are without demonstrable cerebral lesion there is some other factor, such as very low blood sugar level, a bodily toxicity, or a cardiac insufficiency, which causes changes in the condition of the brain, thus producing convulsions. In the third group, the idiopathic condition, there is no known pathology of the brain (or of the brain physiology) to which the convulsions may be attributed. Hence, this latter group is referred to as "essential" or "true" epilepsy.

Facts and Figures

On the basis of public health surveys, rejection for military service, and similar sources, the incidence of epilepsy in the general population has been estimated to be about 5 per 1000 persons, which means that there are more than 600,000 people so afflicted in the United States. Only a small percentage of all epileptics are institutionalized. (Over 30,000 were resident in mental institutions and 2227 were first admitted to mental hospitals in 1942.) It is believed that convulsive seizures afflict men and women with equal frequency.

In a study of 1869 epileptics,[7] 60 per cent had only 1 type of seizure, 40 per cent had more than 1 type, and 2.5 per cent had 3 or more types. *Grand mal* had occurred in 90 per cent of the patients, *petit mal* in 45 per cent, and psychic seizures in 8 per cent. Two thirds of those having *petit mal* seizures developed *grand mal* later in life.

Of nearly 4,000,000 seizures recorded in one survey,[7] 71 per cent were *petit mal*, 26 per cent *grand mal*, and 3 per cent psychic seizures. Of patients having *grand mal*, the average annual number of seizures was 114; of those having *petit mal*, 573; and of those having psychic seizures, 217. Of 1567 patients who had *grand mal*, 25 per cent had less than 5 seizures a year, 50 per cent less than 15, 75 per cent less than 50, 2.2 per cent more than 1000 a year, and 0.4 per cent more than 5000. Generally speaking, as an epileptic grows older the attacks become less frequent, especially if they are of the *petit mal* type.

Most persons who have seizures, experience their first one either during the first two years of life or during adolescence. The age at onset and the causes of seizures are shown schematically in Fig. 1, which also gives some indication of the relative importance of factors which are thought to produce seizures.

Granting that the basic cause of epileptic seizures lies in some condition of the brain, what factors bring out or set off the convulsions? A distinction must be made between the factors which will produce convulsions in any human being, and those which will precipitate convulsions in persons predisposed or previously subject to seizures. Essentially anyone will have convulsions if given certain drugs, such as strychnine, absinthe, or metrazol. Convulsions may also be produced in anyone by direct electrical stimulation of the brain, a deficiency of

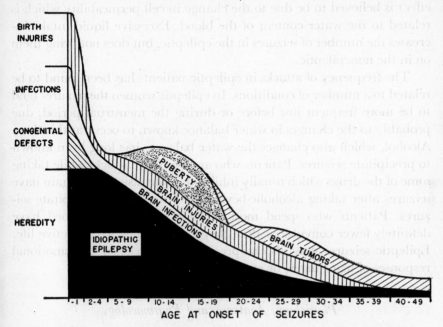

BIRTH INJURIES

INFECTIONS

CONGENITAL DEFECTS

HEREDITY

PUBERTY

BRAIN INJURIES

BRAIN INFECTIONS

IDIOPATHIC EPILEPSY

BRAIN TUMORS

-1 | 2-4 | 5-9 | 10-14 | 15-19 | 20-24 | 25-29 | 30-34 | 35-39 | 40-49

AGE AT ONSET OF SEIZURES

Fig. 1. Suggested causes of seizures which begin at various ages.
(Modified from Lennox[7])

sugar in the blood, or by heart block (which produces sudden inter-ference with the blood supply of the brain).

A wide range of factors may precipitate convulsions in persons who are subject to seizures, either because of brain injury or hereditary predisposition. Most of these factors change the permeability of the cell walls of the neurons of the brain. This permeability relates to the ability of the brain cells to absorb water, sugar, mineral salts, and oxygen from the blood stream and to excrete from the cell body into the blood stream carbon dioxide and other waste products. When there is an unbalanced relationship between the oxygen and carbon dioxide in or around the neurons of the brain cortex, there are periodic bursts of nerve impulses which manifest themselves as convulsions or as the lapses in *petit mal*. Forced breathing (hyperventilation leading to an oversupply of oxygen) is a way in which either *petit mal* or *grand mal* seizures may be set off.

For many years it has been known that the water balance of the body is related to the frequency of epileptic attacks. When a patient is relatively dehydrated, there are fewer seizures. Water deprivation has been used as a method of controlling the number of convulsions. This effect is believed to be due to the change in cell permeability which is related to the water content of the blood. Excessive liquid intake increases the number of seizures in the epileptic, but does not bring them on in the nonepileptic.

The frequency of attacks in epileptic patients has been found to be related to a number of conditions. In epileptic women the seizures tend to be more frequent just before or during the menstrual period, due probably to the changes in water balance known to occur at this time. Alcohol, which also changes the water balance, has long been known to precipitate seizures. Patients who are free from attacks while taking some of the drugs which usually inhibit the convulsions will again have seizures after taking alcoholic beverages. Fatigue may precipitate seizures. Patients who spend most of their time resting in bed have definitely fewer convulsions than they would if they led an active life. Epileptic seizures may also be precipitated as part of the emotional responses of fear, anger, or excitement.

Physiology, Anatomy, and Pharmacology

Berger[4] in 1929 demonstrated that the pulsating variations in electrical potential of the brain itself could be recorded from electrodes pasted to the scalp.[12] These electrodes are connected to suitable electronic amplification devices which amplify (magnify) about one million times the minute electrical changes of the brain which are picked up on the scalp. These amplified pulsations are led to a device which records the changes on a moving paper tape. These records are called "electroencephalograms" (EEG) or "brain waves." Figures 2 and 3 illustrate the way in which these electrodes are attached to the scalp and one of the types of apparatus which is used to make such records.

The EEG records obtained from persons afflicted with different types of epilepsy are distinct and furnish an objective basis for distinguishing between the varieties of seizures. Figure 4 illustrates certain types of EEG records. These records indicate the hereditary potentiality for seizures, focal points of brain damage or injury due to infection, tumor, and an underlying organic basis of disorder in certain behavior-problem children. The EEG is not infallible, but it clearly corresponds to the clinical symptoms nine times out of ten.

The evidence afforded by the brain-wave records indicates that convulsions are based on an abnormal pattern of discharge of nerve

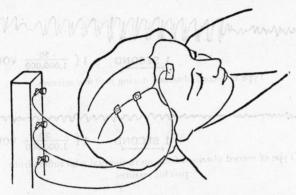

Fig. 2. Electrodes of metal foil are attached to the skin by means of collodion or adhesive tape in order that the minute electrical potential changes may be led to an electroencephalograph and recorded.[12]

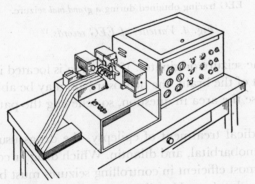

Fig. 3. One type of electroencephalographic recording apparatus.[12]

impulses by the brain. This discharge may involve only a limited and well-defined area, or it may involve, so far as we know, the entire cerebral cortex. It may start at one point and spread, involving more and more of the cortex. Hyperventilation will often produce abnormal EEG patterns, characteristic of some form of epilepsy, both in persons who have had seizures and in those who have never had a seizure.

In some cases the EEG, together with other methods of neurological investigation, indicates that there is a "trigger" area of the brain

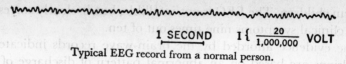

1 SECOND   1 { $\frac{20}{1,000,000}$ **VOLT**

Typical EEG record from a normal person.

1 SECOND   1 { $\frac{50}{1,000,000}$ **VOLT**

Type of record obtained during *petit mal* seizures.

1 SECOND   1 { $\frac{20}{1,000,000}$ **VOLT**

Type of record obtained from an individual who suffers from
psychic seizures

1 SECOND   1 { $\frac{20}{1,000,000}$ **VOLT**

EEG tracing obtained during a *grand mal* seizure.

Fig. 4. Varieties of EEG records.[12]

from which the seizure originates. If this area is located in a surgically accessible part of the brain, the neurosurgeon may be able to open the skull and excise the area in question, so relieving the patient of future convulsions.

In the medical treatment of epilepsy, the drugs usually used are bromides, phenobarbital, and dilantin. Which drug or combination of drugs will be most efficient in controlling seizures must be determined for each particular case. Usually some combination of drugs is more effective than the use of any particular one. It was formerly suggested that the prolonged administration of bromides to epileptics might have aggravated progressive mental deterioration in some cases. Investigations of this point have shown that deterioration was no more frequent among epileptics treated with bromides than it was among those who did not have that form of medication.[9]

Psychology

Certain characteristic personality traits, such as irritability, egotism, hypersensitivity, and emotional instability, have been said to characterize the epileptic. So much attention has been given to this pattern of personality that it is sometimes discussed as a distinct type comparable to the schizoid or cycloid types. Individuals who have never had seizures are sometimes described as having an *epileptoid* personality.

The question of the existence of epileptic personality is of importance if one looks to the psychological make-up for an explanation of the seizures, as is sometimes done in the case of idiopathic epilepsy where no known organic basis or cause has been found. The existence of the so-called epileptic personality traits without the occurrence of seizures has been sometimes called "latent epilepsy," implying that at some later time or under certain conditions the person may be subject to seizures.

Before it is justifiable to speak of an epileptoid personality, we must first make certain that such a pattern of psychological responses occurs frequently enough in true epileptics to justify our speaking of a specific personality type. Personality studies[1] show that not all, or even any large percentage, of epileptic patients have an epileptic personality, as it has been described. Some individuals do show the irritable explosiveness said to characterize the epileptoid personality, but there is not a sufficient number of them to make it typical of the condition.

There has been a great deal of argument as to whether the irritability, hypersensitivity, and emotional instability shown by some epileptic patients antedate the seizures or are the aftereffects of the seizures. A study[8] of 150 epileptic patients indicated that there was a definite correlation between the age at onset of seizures and the type of personality reactions manifested in adult life. Only when the seizures had begun early in life was the so-called epileptic personality found, and then not in all cases. In those patients who were said to have "normal" personalities, the onset of seizures usually was after adolescence. These findings bear evidence that the peculiarities that were developed came about as a result of the seizures or of other factors going with the seizures, since they were not present before the onset of epilepsy. The so-called epileptic traits are really psychological reactions of the individual to the fact that he is afflicted with epilepsy. When the disease develops early in life, there is less chance for the development of a normal personality. Epileptic personality traits are mental reactions which are encouraged and determined by the social deprivation and home protection to which the patient is subjected. Most epileptics, before the onset of seizures, seem to have the usual, average personality traits which are found in most human beings.

Although frequent convulsions may not affect the personality of different individuals the same way, the problems of adjusting to having seizures might be expected to have some effect on personality formation. The epileptic individual has serious social and psychological problems to face. The fear of having attacks in public with the resulting personal embarrassment may lead the person to avoid most social gatherings. He does not wish to be an object of pity or revulsion and, in attempting to prevent others from knowing of his condition, he avoids making friends or acquaintances. His notion of the way others react to him is not delusional in any sense; people do view the epileptic this way. It is highly unfortunate and unfair. Perhaps better education and mental hygiene will result in a more sympathetic understanding of the problems of the epileptic on the part of the general public.

The epileptic who is highly sensitive to withdrawal reactions in others has a very real personal problem to meet. If he withdraws socially and is unable to work out any vocational or avocational adjustment, a vicious cycle of maladjustment will be set up. He may gradually make less and less effort to help and improve himself. Then the evidence of lack of accomplishment may convince him that his life is empty and hopeless, and that he is inferior and incapable of anything worth while. His interests and activities become more and more circumscribed and he becomes increasingly sensitive to the reactions of others. He is aware of his failings but flies up in anger at even slight criticism. The pattern of egotism, hypersensitivity, and irritability shown by some of these cases is thus understandable.

Intellectual Deterioration

In the minds of many persons the idea exists that epilepsy is practically always accompanied by mental deterioration or insanity. There is generally believed to be a progressive loss of intellectual acuity, a slowing of mental associations, and a definite memory loss in most cases. Those connected with institutions for epileptics are impressed by the frequency of mental deterioration among the patients. It should be remembered, however, that the hospitalized epileptics represent only a small portion of the total number of persons so afflicted, and those who are without mental deterioration are less apt to be institutionalized.

The analysis of standard intelligence tests applied to many different groups of epileptic patients has shown consistently that their average intelligence is below normal; but for the most part, these reports have been based on the examination of institution populations which include many who are congenitally defective, in addition to being epileptic. Various investigators[2, 3, 13,] have reported that the IQ of groups of institutionalized epileptics averages between 65 and 92, in contrast to similar nonepileptic groups whose average IQ is 100. However, these figures include the test performances of cases in which there was probably gross cerebral damage, cases having true mental defect, cases in which the disease has interfered with the usual course of education, and cases that grew up in environments which provided little stimulation or encouragement for intellectual activity.

In evaluating the mental changes in epileptics, the best method is to determine whether there are progressive mental losses in the same case as the affliction continues and as the person grows older. Although there are no studies based on standard tests which have followed the same subjects over a long period of years, Lennox[7] has reported on the clinical observation of 1899 patients who had had convulsive seizures for a varying period of years. Figure 5 shows graphically his results.

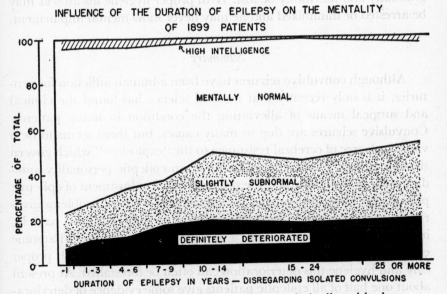

Fig. 5. *Influence of the duration of epilepsy on the intellectual level.*
(*Modified from Lennox[7]*)

The decrease in the number of mentally normal patients with the passage of years is evident. It is interesting to note, however, that almost one half of the patients showed no mental loss even after twenty-five years. Standardized psychological tests given to small groups of patients indicate that the mental loss is most apparent on tests involving memory (especially for recent events), attention, and language ability.

Some have held that mental deterioration is most apt to occur either in those cases with an early onset of seizure, or in those who have had frequent and severe attacks. That these relationships are very close has not been clearly established. Whenever the cause of the seizures is cerebral damage (such as birth injury) and this damage is of a progressive nature, a gradual loss in mental ability may be expected. From the amount of cerebral atrophy or damage found in the brain of many an epileptic patient, it is surprising that there is not more deterioration in mental ability in many instances than the record of the case indicates. However, as might be expected, organic damage and mental deterioration are more apt to be associated with *grand mal* than with *petit mal* seizures.

In general, the person who suffers from epileptic attacks should not assume that he has a condition in which all his mental abilities will gradually and inevitably be lost. With proper hygiene his attacks may be arrested or minimized and he may never show mental impairment.

Summary

Although convulsive seizures have been a human affliction for centuries, it is only recently that medical science has found the clinical and surgical means of alleviating the condition in many patients. Convulsive seizures are due to many causes, but there seems to be a varying degree of cerebral resistance to the "explosions" which govern the convulsion. There is no evidence of an epileptic personality antedating the seizures. Rather, the problems of life adjustment of epileptic patients are fairly similar and the adjustment to those problems gives rise to certain common behavior patterns in some patients; namely, irritability, seclusiveness, and a self-protective egotism. That some epileptics show marked mental deterioration is true, but with proper care and hygiene this deterioration can often be forestalled. At present about one half of all epileptic patients give some evidence of deterioration, and that deterioration varies from slight to profound.

REFERENCES

1. Doolittle, G. J., "The Epileptic Personality," *Psychiat. Quart.*, 1932, *6*, 89–96.
2. Fetterman, J., and M. R. Barnes, "Serial Studies of the Intelligence of Patients with Epilepsy," *Arch. Neurol. Psychiat.*, 1934, *32*, 797–801.

3. Fox, J. T., "The Response of Epileptic Children to Mental and Educational Tests," *Brit. Jour. Med. Psychol.*, 1924, *4*, 235–248.

4. Jasper, H. H., "Electroencephalography." Chapter XIV in W. Penfield and T. C. Erickson, *Epilepsy and Cerebral Localization*. Springfield, Ill., C. C. Thomas, 1941, 380–454.

5. Kanner, L., "The Names of the Falling Sickness," *Human Biol.*, 1930, *2*, 109–127.

6. Landis, C., and M. M. Bolles, *Personality and Sexuality of the Physically Handicapped Woman*. New York, Hoeber, 1942.

7. Lennox, W. G., *Science and Seizures*. New York, Harper, 1941.

8. Notkin, J., "Is There an Epileptic Personality Make-up?" *Arch. Neurol. Psychiat.*, 1928, *20*, 799–803.

9. Paskind, H. A., "The Absence of Deteriorating Effects of Bromides in Epilepsy," *Jour. Amer. Med. Asso.*, 1934, *103*, 100–103.

10. Penfield, W., and T. C. Erickson, *Epilepsy and Cerebral Localization*. Springfield, Ill., C. C. Thomas, 1941.

11. Pollock, H. M., "A Statistical Review of Convulsive Disorders in the United States," *Amer. Jour. Psychiat.*, 1931, *10*, 655–661.

12. Putnam, T. J., *Convulsive Seizures: How to Deal with Them*. Philadelphia, Lippincott, 1943.

13. Sullivan, E. B., and L. Gahagan, "On Intelligence of Epileptic Children," *Genet. Psychol. Mono.*, 1935, *17*, 309–376.

Chapter X

MENTAL DEFICIENCY

MENTAL deficiency is a true form of mental abnormality. This condition is also called "feeble-mindedness," "amentia," "oligophrenia," "weakness of mind," or "idiocy." Essentially, it is a condition in which there is a limited capacity for mental development, as a result of which the person is unable during childhood or at maturity to maintain himself without outside help and supervision. The definition or delimitation of mental deficiency or any one of its synonyms is not the same in different countries. For example, in England the factor of social competence is the most important criterion, whereas in most of the United States an essential criterion is the intellectual status as shown on an intelligence examination. In England the terms *idiot*, *imbecile*, and *moron*, or *simpleton*, are related to the self-sufficiency of the individual, while in America these terms are applied to certain ranges on the intelligence-quotient (IQ) scale.

There are different viewpoints which may be taken concerning the basic nature of feeble-mindedness. From the standpoint of education, we know that most children (or adults) reach certain standards of scholastic proficiency, a few are exceptionally intelligent, and a few are exceptionally dull. Standard intelligence tests have been well defined as measures of school aptitude. In this sense it may be said that the ament has little or no aptitude for school subjects. From a biological standpoint, the essential requirement of any living creature is its capacity for maintaining its own existence. Mental deficiency is, then, an incomplete mental development of such degree that the individual is incapable of adapting himself to the normal social environment in a fashion which will enable him to maintain his own existence independent of supervision, control, or external support. In England the legal definition (1927) states, "Mental defectiveness means a condition of arrested or incomplete development of mind existing before the age of eighteen years, whether arising from inherent causes or induced by disease or injury."[15] This legal definition is, in practice, the one accepted in most American courts, although some states add an educational qualification or proof in terms of an intelligence examination.

Facts and Figures

How many mental defectives are there in the United States? The answer to this question cannot be given in a simple figure for two principal reasons. First, mental deficiency exists in a continuum and the number of individuals who are classified as defective depends on where the dividing point between normal and defective is established. Since various investigators have used different figures on the IQ scale as the division points, it is necessary to state this point of reference whenever any comparisons are made. For example, 50, 60, 70, or 75, or some other point may have been used. Second, although mental deficiency is, in large part, an intellectual defect, if the individual is industrious, amiable, cooperative, and not too completely stupid he can, with supervision, get along in society and, hence, will be called "dull" or "stupid," but not "a mental defective."

During World War I the Army Alpha intelligence test was given to over a 1,500,000 drafted men.[21] Those who did poorly on the Alpha (over 400,000 men) were given the performance test, Beta; and, of these, over 80,000 were given individual intelligence tests. On the basis of these examinations, together with all other relevant information, 0.5 per cent of the white draftees were recommended for discharge because of mental inferiority; 0.6 per cent were recommended for assignment to labor battalions because of low-grade intelligence; and another 0.6 per cent were assigned to development battalions for the same reason. In brief, 1 man out of 200 drafted was so intellectually retarded that the army could make no use of him, and 12 out of 1000 were so retarded that labor or development battalion service was recommended. The percentage of those already in institutions and of those rejected by local draft boards must be added to the 0.5 per cent recommended for discharge. Hence, 1.4 per cent of the white male population of draft age were of such defective intelligence that they could not be utilized by the army. (The comparable figure for the Negro draft was 1.9 per cent.)

Since the mortality of defectives under age ten is several times that of normal children of the same age, there is a selective factor operating in any determination of the number of children who are feeble-minded. In a study of 6688 children in ordinary common schools Haggerty and Nash[8] reported that 1.15 per cent were feeble-minded (below 60 IQ) and 5.1 per cent were of borderline intelligence (IQ between 60 and 70). A 1931 summary of surveys[9] of the mental health of 52,514 school children conducted by the National Committee for Mental Hygiene in various parts of the United States between 1919 and 1924 indicated that 3.2 per cent were mentally defective and 3.7 per cent were borderline mental defectives.

The total American population of over 130 million persons includes between one and one half and two million mental defectives who are totally or almost totally dependent because of their defect. In addition, there are more than seven million persons who possess only borderline intellect, and who can care for themselves only under favorable circumstances and with some supervision and guidance. Approximately ninety thousand of these defectives are being cared for in institutions for the feeble-minded. How many more are in correctional institutions, almshouses, and the like, is impossible to ascertain.

Some doubt exists on the question of whether amentia occurs more frequently in the male than in the female sex. Many statistical surveys show that somewhat more males than females are institutionalized or diagnosed at clinics. Since this excess is not large, and since males are more difficult to care for and more apt to get into social conflicts, it is probable, though not certain, that amentia is equally frequent in males and females.

The report of the intelligence of the drafted men in World War I[21] with respect to national origin is of interest. Those born in Canada, Great Britain, and the Scandinavian and Teutonic countries had about the same distribution of intelligence scores as did the American-born white draft, while those born in Russia and Italy had three or more times as many of markedly defective intelligence as the American whites.

Varieties

Mental deficiency occurs in different forms and degrees. Usually, aments are classified according to the assumed or known cause, or on the basis of the degree of their intellectual defect. Another system of classification distinguishes between primary amentia and secondary amentia. "Primary amentia" is applied to all kinds of mental defect in which the cause is thought to be inherent, intrinsic, or endogenous; that is, hereditary. "Secondary amentia" refers to those cases which result from some adverse factor in the environment acting upon the individual at any stage of development from the time of conception to the end of adolescence. Since there is no involvement of the germ cells, secondary amentia is not transmissible from one generation to the next. These secondary cases constitute about 20 per cent of all feeble-minded of all ages.

From the viewpoint of school aptitude or intelligence-test results, the difference in intelligence on a combined battery of tests among 2030 school children in one small city was found[11] to distribute itself as follows:

Per Cent	Classification	IQ
1.2	Gifted	Above 140
15.3	Very superior	120–140
22.9	Superior	110–120
45.9	Normal	90–110
8.9	Dull or backward	80–90
4.0	Borderline	70–80
1.8	Aments	Below 70

Among the feeble-minded (IQ below 75) Tredgold[15] reports the mental levels as follows:

75 per cent	Moron	50–75 IQ
20	Imbecile	25–50 IQ
5	Idiot	Below 25 IQ

From the standpoint of abnormal psychology, the group whose IQ is between 75 and 85 (that is, borderline cases who can make their own way without too much help) may be disregarded. The stupid, dull group, with IQ's from 50 to 75, are usually classified as morons and do require care, supervision, and control for their own protection and for the protection of others. They also present a certain amount of psycho-pathology. They are subnormal in their ability to control, coordinate, and adapt their conduct. Their educational capacity varies widely; but, almost without exception, they are incapable of profiting from the usual common school curriculum and should be put in special un-graded classes for retarded children. Some morons are able to learn elementary reading, writing, and arithmetic, and to understand other simple items of scholastic knowledge; also some are capable of getting along in society if trained in some simple task and given sufficient supervision.*

Psychologically, it is advisable to distinguish between stable and unstable types of morons. Those who are stable are usually inoffen-sive, well behaved, fairly industrious persons who pursue their way of life comparatively unmoved by things going on around them. They

---

* See E. R. Wembridge, *Life Among the Low-Brows*, Boston, Houghton, 1931, for interesting examples.

are easily pleased and made happy by praise and by childish amusements. Neither their joy nor their sorrow is excessive or of long duration. They appreciate and return affection and have some conception of simple religious, moral, and social ideals; but their feelings regarding them are not very strong. Many of these stable morons, who are cheerful and obedient, get into difficulty because of their unthinking eagerness to do anything which is requested of them. They rush blithely into situations which intelligent individuals would hesitate to enter and, therefore, they become the causes, and sometimes the victims, of situations having serious consequences.

The threat to society which comes from the unstable moron is more direct and, of course, more severe. The combination of emotional instability and mental defect produces a class of maladjusted personalities which provides a seemingly inexhaustible reservoir of asocial and antisocial persons. Unstable morons, psychopathic personalities, and borderline or unhospitalized schizophrenics account for most of the real problems of modern society.

Imbeciles and idiots are low-grade defectives whose IQs are below 50. They are unable to care for themselves or to benefit from any ordinary educational procedure. Imbeciles have been defined as "persons in whose case there exists mental defectiveness which, though not amounting to idiocy, is yet so pronounced that they are incapable of managing themselves or their affairs, or, in the case of children, of being taught to do so."[15] There is a wide variation in the physical growth and development of imbeciles. Some are as grotesque as the worst of the idiots; others are as good looking and pleasant appearing as any normal individual. (See Plate 17, which is on page 466; Deborah Kallikak is a high-grade imbecile.) Older imbeciles usually have a vacuous or stupid expression, even though the face itself may be well formed. At the time of school age imbeciles are incapable of responding in any satisfactory way to the teaching of ordinary school subjects. They are unable to perform simple calculations (such as making change), to copy geometrical figures, or to recognize missing parts in pictures. Many of them can name the colors; understand and carry out simple commands; and say whether it is day or night, morning or afternoon. Some of them may learn to read or to spell a few of the two- or three-letter words, and to add and subtract numbers less than ten. A few can be taught to read and write simple sentences. Some of them are talkative, chattering in a childish way, but usually incapable of carrying on a conversation. They can be taught to dress and undress themselves under supervision and to understand and avoid many of the simple physical dangers of life. For example, an imbecile will understand that fire will burn him or that he may drown if he falls into a river. As a result of training, many imbeciles can be employed in such simple duties as scrubbing, sweeping, polishing, weeding garden paths, picking up stones in a field, collecting eggs, or helping in the laundry. These tasks they can do only under supervision. None of them contribute in any appreciable way toward the cost of their keep.

The idiot, by legal definition, is one characterized by mental defect of such degree that he is unable to guard himself against common physical dangers. A few of the high-grade idiots may learn to feed themselves or to connect some simple words with objects so that they can point to and name certain things, or make their wants known. However, many of them have to be fed and cared for like infants. Almost all of them are incapable of forming sentences. Motor and sensory defects are common. Many idiots have a grotesque, stunted, and misshapen appearance because of physical malformation. The lowest grade of idiocy may be born without even the sucking reflex. Many of this grade make sounds but never learn to speak, nor do they learn to walk. They show no power of reasoning nor of memory. Many of them do not seem to see or hear anything that goes on about them.

Special Pathological Types of Amentia

The special types of mental defect include microcephaly, phenyl-pyruvic oligophrenia, and certain other rare conditions. Both spastic paralysis with amentia, and cretinism present instances of mental defect which do not depend upon hereditary factors. This same lack of a familial determination is true for mongolism, except that this latter condition is usually attributed to a prenatal, but exogenous, injury of either the embryo or the germ plasm.

MONGOLISM

About 5 per cent of all of the feeble-minded are differentiated from the other varieties in that they have certain features which are characteristic of the Mongolian race. The eyes are slanted or almond-shaped. There is usually a fold of skin covering the inner corner of the eye. The head is small and round, the ears are malformed, the hands are stubby with an inturning of the little finger, which finger frequently has only one crease. The tongue is fissured crosswise. This abnormality is congenital in that it is present at birth. No one has ever observed any tendency for a child born normal to become a mongolian idiot, or even to grow more mongoloid with age. On the other hand, some infants who appear mongolian at birth later lose the physical marks of this condition and develop normally. Evidently, whatever circumstances produce this condition must occur before birth.

The resemblance among mongols is startling to anyone who visits an institution for defectives for the first time. They all look like

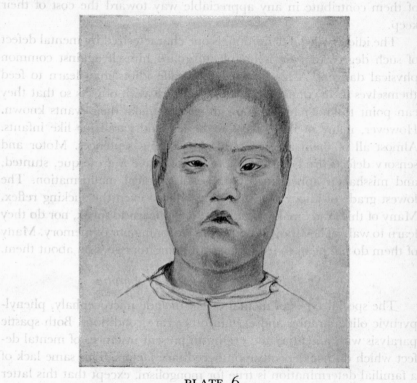

PLATE 6

MONGOLIAN IDIOT

brothers and sisters and have no resemblance to the family stock from which they come. This consistency in physical appearance and in mental level (high-grade idiots or low-grade imbeciles) leads one to expect some specific, uniform pathology. However, no significant difference from the pathological changes seen in other low-grade defectives has been found. In particular, there is no abnormality of the internal glands, central nervous system, or any other part of the body, that is typical of the mongol. His brain is usually underweight and poorly developed, but not in any way which would differentiate it from the brain of other mentally defective persons.

There is a tendency for mongolian idiots to have relatively older mothers and to be among the last-born children in larger families. Some have assumed, therefore, that the condition might be due to some nutritional, toxic, or hormone deficiency affecting the fertilized ovum during the first weeks of embryonic development. Various studies, particularly that of Brousseau,[4] have shown that the advanced age of the mother cannot be more than a contributing cause. Mongol children have been born to mothers as young as fifteen, and their births have been preceded and succeeded by the births of normal children in the same family.

The evidence in favor of a genetic basis is equally inconclusive. It has been reported that about one mongol in fifty has a similarly affected brother or sister; but mongolism usually occurs in families without any known case of mental defect for many preceding generations. In one study a family was reported in which there were ten mongols occurring in three succeeding generations. According to Tredgold, mongolism is probably due to a combination of factors, including defective heredity, uterine exhaustion, and some specific nutritional defect during gestation.

The mental characteristics of the mongol show many variations, but a mental age of seven years is regarded as their upper limit of intelligence. There is no specific form of sensory or motor disturbance. There often is marked sensitivity to heat and cold, while motor coordination and development are delayed and poor. Most mongols are unable to learn any tasks requiring complicated motor coordination. Generally, they are lively, restless, good-natured, and cheerful. Many mongols die in infancy of some respiratory infection, and very few survive beyond the age of twenty.

MICROCEPHALY

This classification is applied to mentally defective individuals whose skull at completion of growth is less than 17 inches at its greatest circumference. The head has a peculiar shape because of the failure in development of that part of the cranium above the eyebrows and the ears. Most microcephalics are either low-grade imbeciles or idiots. They constitute about 5 per cent of all defectives under the age of ten, or 0.5 per cent of all defectives at all ages. The condition has been erroneously attributed to either a premature union of the bones of the skull (leaving the brain with not enough space to grow and develop), or to atavistic reversion (evolutionary throwback). Actually, it is a gross mental defect which is associated with a primary physical malformation like other skeletal deformities of a congenital origin. Familial occurrence has been observed, but the present evidence for a genetic explanation of microcephaly is far from sufficient. Some reports have indicated that abnormalities of foetal environment may have either produced or accentuated this condition.

PLATE 7

MICROCEPHALIC IDIOT

There is no sensory or motor defect which is regularly associated with microcephaly. Usually, these individuals are restless, vivacious, given to imitation, but unable to continue any kind of activity for a very long period of time.

PHENYLPYRUVIC OLIGOPHRENIA

Among the metabolic disturbances which characterize special hereditary types of mental deficiency is phenylpyruvic oligophrenia. Phenylpyruvic acid is a chemical substance which results from an error in metabolism and its presence in the urine is the main diagnostic criterion for this type of mental deficiency. In one study of over 20,000 patients Jervis[12] found this error in metabolism in 161 instances. Genetically, this condition depends on the effect of a single recessive gene. Clinically, these cases show motor disturbances and pronounced intellectual defect of the imbecile or idiot level. They are of particular interest because they indicate the possibility of isolating other types of mental defect which are associated with, or depend upon, some specific organic dysfunction.

CRETINISM

Of the endocrine disorders which are found to be associated with mental deficiency, hypothyroidism (that is, cretinism), which is due to insufficient secretion of the thyroid gland, is the most frequent and

PLATE 8

CRETIN

most important variety. The condition may be either sporadic or endemic, meaning that it may occur in isolated instances without known antecedents, or it may occur rather commonly in certain population groups where there is a known deficiency of iodine in the water supply. It constitutes 3 to 5 per cent of all institutionalized defectives.

In sporadic or isolated cases of cretinism — the type most commonly encountered in America — it is unusual to see the gross deformities characteristic of the untreated condition, since today practically all of these patients have been subjected to intensive thyroid medication. There are many instances, however, in which this treatment succeeds only in removing the physical marks of the disease without affecting the mental condition. The discovery and use of thyroid treatment will be discussed more fully in Chap. XXIX.

The characteristic features of the fully developed condition of cretinism are arrested growth, large head, extremely short legs, flattened nose, thick lips, protruding tongue, and sallow, dry skin which is so loose as to appear much too large for the stunted body. The child usually appears normal at birth and is not recognized as abnormal before the sixth month. At that time it is apathetic and slow in movement, does not laugh or smile readily, and may be so lethargic as to refuse to nurse. Such children make little effort to sit up, to stand, or to walk until as late as the fourth or fifth year. Speech is delayed and may not appear until age seven or eight.

As the cretin becomes older his body is greatly dwarfed and many who are fifteen or twenty years old are no taller than 3 feet. The legs are short and extremely bowed; the hands and feet are stumpy and ill formed. Puberty is usually late and many of these patients remain sterile.

Mentally, the cretin is characterized by a defect extending to both intellect and emotional development. The intelligence level of most cretins is that of the idiot or low-grade imbecile; while others are somewhat more alert, although not reaching the level of a moron. As a group they are placid, harmless, good-natured, and affectionate. They are among the least troublesome of all defectives.

IDIOTS SAVANTS

There is an uncommon and rather unusual group of aments who have been termed *idiots savants*. The *idiot savant* is a mental defective with some special ability which is quite outstanding in comparison to his other defects; for example, an occasional imbecile may be able to paint pictures, play some musical instrument, give the day of the week for any past date, recite long columns of numbers, and so on. These cases are extremely rare and are probably of two kinds: (*a*) cases of simple dementia praecox whose history is not sufficiently known; and (*b*) feeble-minded patients whose one talent seems marked in the social group in which they live, but which on investigation proves to be very unimpressive.

SECONDARY AMENTIA

Apart from certain rare hereditary types of mental defect, the remaining special varieties of low-grade deficiency are secondary manifestations of gross brain damage caused by injury or infection before, during, or very shortly after birth. Usually, these cases of secondary mental deficiency occur in otherwise normal families. There is fairly clear evidence of the operation of some adequate *external* cause. The child's appearance and physical development, apart from the specific effects of some cerebral lesion, may not differ from those of the ordinary child. The most important conditions producing secondary amentia are spastic paralysis (birth injury), epilepsy, and syphilitic infection before birth (congenital syphilis). Each of these conditions is discussed in other chapters, as they usually occur without the complication of mental defect.

The frequency and significance of traumatic factors in the causation of mental deficiency have long been overestimated. Very few instances of mental defect are really due to the time-worn explanation, "He fell on his head when he was a small baby."

The mental defect in certain cases of spastic paralysis often appears greater than it really is because of the motor disturbance, and many of these children respond very well to training in spite of their physical handicap. However, there are in this category many low-grade defectives who present that state of absolute or complete idiocy in which humanity is reduced to its lowest possible expression.

Another variety of secondary amentia is one which may be simulated by the simple form of dementia praecox. In Chap. IV it was stated that the only way to differentiate certain cases of simple schizophrenia from feeble-mindedness was on the basis of the prepsychotic history. Since an adequate history is often not available, it is easy to understand why some of the simple dementia praecox patients become classified as cases of amentia.

The question of moral imbecility will be dealt with in the chapter on psychopathic personalities. This condition is not believed to be a true imbecility of intellect, but is considered a defective state involving other aspects of the mental life of the individual.

Causes

field of abnormal psychology has there been a greater contro-
y than that which has raged around the basic cause of feeble-
mindedness. The question of whether these conditions are due to
heredity or to environmental surroundings is one which has been
debated for the past hundred years. There is no question but that the
family stock of many feeble-minded patients is replete with other instances of feeble-mindedness, psychosis, neurosis, criminal behavior, or
pauperism. There are those who hold that the defect in intellect is
determined by hereditary predisposition and that the deplorable social
circumstances surrounding feeble-minded families grow out of the fact
that most of their members are stupid and unable to care for themselves adequately. There are others who argue just as vigorously that
the primary cause of feeble-mindedness is to be seen in the lamentable
environmental circumstances which involve the lack of economic opportunity, poor nutrition, and poor education. They maintain that if
these stupid persons had had adequate educational and social opportunities, they would be, at least, considerably brighter than they
are.

Clark[5] postulated, on theoretical grounds, that the intellectual defect of some feeble-minded persons is due to early emotional repression,
and that, if selected mental defectives were treated by psychoanalysis
to remove the emotional blocking, their intellectual development
would be greatly aided. This therapeutic procedure has been tried
with many aments, but there is no indication that there was any real
intellectual improvement achieved in any instances of true amentia.

Since these aments are, for the most part, defective from birth, the
basic cause must either be in the germ plasm or must affect the foetus
during gestation. There is some evidence to the effect that a foetus exposed to *overdoses* of X-ray irradiation may develop certain physical
anomalies, such as microcephaly. It has also been shown that deficiencies in nutrition, particularly lack of vitamins, may interfere with
normal development, and so become the cause of mental defect. Other
factors which may produce amentia during or soon after birth include
epileptiform convulsions, unusually poor nutrition, direct injury to the
brain, and infections such as meningitis, encephalitis, measles, and
syphilis.

Much investigation has been directed toward the point of whether
or not alcohol and drugs taken by parents are capable of producing
mental abnormalities in the offspring. The best available evidence at

present indicates that no mental defect results from either alcoholism or drug addiction in the mother or father.

In Chap. XVIII the evidence bearing on heredity as a cause of mental disorder and defect will be considered. The famous family lines that have been extensively studied, such as the Kallikak or the Juke families, certainly indicate that mental defect does run in some families. That too much stress has been placed at times on these instances, and that a fatalistic attitude toward the whole problem has often been engendered on the part of some, by this evidence, is true. However, the evidence should not be denied. Rather, it should be evaluated and dealt with in a positive way.

It is impossible to study, in an experimental way, human genetics over periods of many generations. It is possible, however, to conduct genetic studies with animals, running through many successive generations. Tryon[16] reported a study of selective breeding in rats, carried out over eighteen consecutive generations. He made use of an automatic maze and selected, in successive generations, for breeding purposes those rats that learned the maze most rapidly and those that learned it most slowly. There was an increasing difference in maze-learning ability with succeeding generations until, by the seventh generation, very little overlapping was found in the learning scores of the bright group and the dull group. After the seventh generation, practically no increase or decrease was obtained in either of the two groups. When the bright strain was then bred with the dull strain, their progeny showed a learning ability which was similar to that shown by the rats in the first generation. This finding indicated that genetic factors, rather than any extrinsic or chance conditions, operated to produce the brightness and dullness. It was also found that the bright animals had a significantly greater brain size, body weight, and fertility. The bright animals were better adjusted emotionally to the maze-learning situation than were the dull. The maze-learning ability appeared to be specific, since the bright and dull groups did about equally well on other learning and discrimination problems. Tryon explained his data on the hypothesis that inherited multiple factors determined the maze-learning ability. Although this evidence from animals must be considered with caution in its application to humans, it is suggestive for our understanding of the role of heredity in human amentia.

Pathology

Many low-grade defectives are physically malformed and show deviations in development. In an effort to find additional concomitants of this maldevelopment, various laboratory tests have been used. Most studies have failed to reveal any important or consistent difference in the blood chemistry or cell constituents of defectives and of normal controls. Since syphilis is known to produce mental defect, repeated investigations have been made of large groups of aments to see whether or not the Wassermann test would disclose the fact that idiots and imbeciles who were not known to have had syphilitic infection might react positively with this indicator of syphilis. In general, such positive Wassermann reactions as are found among the mental defectives do not represent an increase in the known incidence of congenital syphilis.[14]

The anatomy of the brain of the mental defective has been shown to include many anomalous conditions. It is impossible, at present, to assign any known cause of these anatomical deviations. In a few cases of both idiocy and imbecility, no gross anatomical changes have been found in the brain. The microscopic examination of the neurological structure of the brain of the mental defective does reveal a wide variety of deviations and defects in the development of cell structure. It is difficult to interpret these deviations, since we are still on unsure ground with respect to the relationship between neurological structure and psychological function. It is definite, however, that the imbecile or idiot shows deviations in structural development and that these deviations are of wide variety.

Psychology

The mentally defective are obviously inferior to the normal in certain general psychological functions. They show inferiorities in controlled attention, memory and simple ideation, and in the ability to grasp similarities, differences, and other relationships. Because of these deficiencies, their reasoning, judgment, imagination, and ability to learn are poor. They have difficulty in adjusting to new situations and show little or no originality.

Most of the usual techniques of research used for the study of sensation, perception, and mental organization are not appropriate for studying persons of very low intellectual level. These persons do not have the capacity for introspection, nor are they able to use or to understand language which is involved in the research. For this reason, much of the psychological description of amentia is based on general observation of groups of cases.

In regard to sensory acuity, there does not seem to be gross impairment except in some of the low-grade cases. Attention to stimuli or alertness may be of such low order that the moron or imbecile may appear to have a grave sensory defect, when but little exists. Observations of certain low-grade cases have indicated that they often do not respond to stimuli which are intensely unpleasant to the normal. They will chew quinine or smell strong ammonia fumes without giving any indication that it is unpleasant to them. Perception depends upon sensory representation in higher brain centers so that, even though sensory mechanisms are normal in the mental defective, their organized perceptions may be of a different order because of the defective brain structure.

In recent years there have been several applications of the testing procedures used with subhuman primates to groups of low-grade mental defectives. Several interesting findings have resulted. Aldrich and Doll[2] applied problem-solving tests involving the use of tools, similar to those used by Köhler with apes. The goal object was a ball or cookie placed in a cage which could be reached only by a hooked stick, two joined sticks, or a second stick procured by use of the first stick. The more difficult tasks were solved only by the superior portion of the group, whose mental levels were about three years. In comparing the performance of idiots and apes, the idiots displayed a comparatively greater learning facility, but there was a marked similarity between the two groups in the mode of attack and the type of solution employed. Preschool children, with approximately the same degree of mental development as the idiots, were superior in the development of language and in the ability to acquire new modes of response. All subjects showed the sudden drop in the learning curve that has been called "insight."

Harlow and Israel[10] tested mental defectives with mental ages of less than three years and catarrhine monkeys, by means of a delayed reaction test. They found that the defectives had no difficulty with delays of 15 seconds, and that in this aspect of immediate learning they were superior to the monkeys. With longer delays, there were no essential differences between the groups in learning ability. Gordon and Norman[7] employed puzzle boxes with increasingly complex lever systems with two hundred defectives. The great majority of the cases used the general trial-and-error method, as do anthropoid apes on similar tasks. Unlike normal adults, they were unable to form an immediate perceptual configuration of the whole problem. The grasping of spatiomechanical relationships of such complexity presented serious difficulties to the mentally defective.

These experimental investigations dealt primarily with the very low-grade defectives and, of course, did not describe the mental defectives as a group. The mental organization of high-grade mental defectives is much more similar to the normal. When morons are contrasted with normals, the differences found are considerably less.

In an interesting series of experiments, Werner[18, 19, 20,] and his collaborators have demonstrated differences between those who are mentally defective because of some brain injury and those in whom there is no such injury. Differences were found in the way in which each group organized their perceptual field and made use of abstractions in thinking and in animistic thinking. The brain-injured cases were more concrete in their thinking and problem solving. For example the brain-injured differentiated between animate and inanimate objects most frequently on the basis of use or human characteristics, while the familial-type defectives usually discriminated on the basis of spontaneous movement. Werner attributed these differences to either a disturbance in the primary schemes necessary to adequate perception, or to undue attraction which random stimuli exert on the brain-injured child.

With respect to personality traits other than intellectual ability, it has been pointed out that all degrees of aggressiveness and submissiveness occur among aments. There is evidence that the defectives are more suggestible than the normal.[1] In many cases of criminal offenses or petty thievery among the feeble-minded, it was found that they were passively led into antisocial behavior.

Morrison[13] described reactions of fear and anger occurring in very low-grade cases, but there was no possible comparison with the normal as to relative frequency of these reactions because of the protected environments in which these aments lived. In a study of fears of normal and defective children, Bolles[3] found that the reported sources of fear correlated more closely with mental age than with chronological age or IQ. The feeble-minded generally have been found to be lacking in the more complex emotions or sentiments, where intellectual factors necessarily play a role.

There is a difference in opinion as to the relative strength of instinctive drives in the feeble-minded. Some believe them to be weaker and others believe they are essentially as strong as in the normal. In some very low grades, the experiences of hunger and thirst seem to be diminished. Evidence of strong sex drive is usually lacking. Penrose[14] stated that, although sex development is physically normal in the majority of cases, sex desire apparently is lacking in idiots and low-grade imbeciles; and that the intensity of sexual desire seems to be roughly in proportion to the intellectual quotient.

Goddard,[6] who introduced intelligence testing to America, made the best and most comprehensive studies of the feeble-minded of his day. He summarized the practical psychology of the ament in what he called an "industrial classification," as follows:*

Mental Age	Industrial Classification	Grade	
Under			
1 year	Helpless	Low	
1 year	Feeds self	Middle	Idiot
2 years	Discriminates food from non-food	High	
3 years	No work; plays a little	Low	
4 years	Tries to help	Low	
5 years	Only simplest tasks	Middle	Imbecile
6 years	Tasks of short duration; washes dishes	High	
7 years	Little errands in the house; dusting	High	
8 years	Errands; light work; makes beds	Low	
9 years	Heavier work; scrubs; mends; lays bricks	Low	
10 years	Good institution helpers; routine work	Middle	Moron
11 years	Fairly complicated work with occasional oversight	High	
12 years	Uses machinery; cares for animals; cannot plan	High	

Goddard believed that three points are of major importance in dealing with and thinking about the problem of amentia. First, there are levels of intelligence or of psychological intellect, and the intelligence tests are indicators of these levels. Second, most cases of feeble-mindedness are hereditary, and this fact is of major importance in connection with social problems. Third, a person can never be trained to do intelligently any task, the doing of which requires intelligence of a higher level than that which he has attained. These three points, which may seem more or less self-evident, have not really entered into the everyday thinking of most people.

Summary

Amentia is primarily a deficit, a failure in development of intelligence or intellectual capacity. It is associated with physical malformation and brain anomalies. Over 75 per cent of mental defectives are cases of primary amentia — meaning that, except for heredity, there is no known cause. The remaining 25 per cent are attributable to injury, infection, endocrine disturbance, and the like. Mental defect occurs in all degrees from absolute, helpless idiocy to borderline normality. Special pathological varieties are cretinism, mongolism, microcephaly. There is no consistent or uniform pathology found among aments. Psychological studies have shown a fair amount of variability in factors other than intellect, but, in general, the deviations are closely related to the deficit in intelligence.

* Goddard, H. H., *Feeblemindedness: Its Causes and Consequences.* New York, Macmillan, 1914, 581.

REFERENCES

1. Ackerson, L., "Behavior Traits of Higher-Grade Mental Defectives," *Proc. Amer. Asso. Ment. Def.*, 1935, *40*, 435–443.
2. Aldrich, C. G., and E. A. Doll, "Problem Solving among Idiots: The Use of Implements," *Jour. Soc. Psychol.*, 1931, *2*, 306–336.
3. Bolles, M., M., "A Study of Fears in Abnormal Children." Unpublished Master's Essay, Columbia University Library, 1934.
4. Brousseau, K., *Mongolism.* Baltimore, Williams & Wilkins, 1928.
5. Clark, L. P., *The Nature and Treatment of Amentia.* Baltimore, Wood, 1933.
6. Goddard, H. H., *Feeblemindedness: Its Causes and Consequences.* New York, Macmillan, 1916.
7. Gordon, R. G., and R. M. Norman, "Some Psychological Experiments on Mental Defectives in Relation to the Perceptual Configurations Which May Underlie Speech," *Brit. Jour. Psychol.*, 1932, *23*, 20–41, 85–114.
8. Haggerty, M. E., and H. B. Nash, Mental Capacity of Children and Parental Occupation," *Jour. Educ. Psychol.*, 1924, *15*, 559–572.
9. Haines, T. H., "Mental Deficiency among Public School Children in the United States," *Proc. Addr. Amer. Asso. Stud. Feeblemind.*, 1931, *36*, 31–36.
10. Harlow, H. F., and R. H. Israel, "Comparative Behavior of Primates: IV. Delayed Reaction Tests on Subnormal Humans." *Jour. Comp. Psychol.*, 1932, *14*, 253–262.
11. Holley, C. E., *Mental Tests for School Use.* Univ. Ill. Bull. Educ. Res., 1920, No. 4.
12. Jervis, G. A., "A Contribution to the Study of the Influence of Heredity on Mental Deficiency. The Genetics of Phenylpyruvic Oligophrenia," *Proc. Amer. Asso. Ment. Def.*, 1939, *44*, 13–24.
13. Morrison, B. M., "A Study of the Major Emotions in Persons of Defective Intelligence," *Univ. Calif. Publ. Psychol.*, 1924, *3*, 73–145.
14. Penrose, L. S., *Mental Defect.* New York, Rinehart, 1934.
15. Tredgold, A. F., *Mental Deficiency* (6th ed.). Baltimore, Wood, 1937.
16. Tryon, R. C., "Genetic Differences in Maze-Learning Ability in Rats," *39th Yearbook*, Nat. Soc. Stud. Educ., 1940, *39* (I), 111–119.
17. Wembridge, E. R., *Life Among the Low-Brows.* Boston, Houghton, 1931.
18. Werner, H., "Perception of Spatial Relationship in Mentally Deficient Children," *Jour. Genet. Psychol.*, 1940, *57*, 93–100.
19. ———, and D. Carrison, "Animistic Thinking in Brain-Injured Mentally Retarded Children," *Jour. Abn. Soc. Psychol.*, 1944, *39*, 43–62.
20. ———, and A. A. Strauss, "Pathology of Figure-Background Relation in the Child," *Jour. Abn. Soc. Psychol.*, 1941, *36*, 236–248.
21. Yerkes, R. M., "Psychological Examining in the U. S. Army," *Memoirs* Nat. Acad. Sci., 1921, *15*, 7–877.

Chapter XI

MENTAL CHANGES AND DISORDERS OF OLD AGE

MANY different investigations have established the fact that the process of aging is associated with a true decline in both physical and mental abilities. There are large individual differences both in the time of life at which this decline becomes apparent and in the rate and amount of decline over a period of years. Most of these changes are regarded as "normal" since both the person in whom the changes occur and those about him have a fair amount of insight and understanding of the nature of the alterations. Even the behavior of the old man in his "second childhood" or of the old woman in her "dotage" is not regarded as abnormal, since it appears so regularly and has been accepted as part of the usual course of human life.

There are many diseases to which older people are subject which affect the mind and the behavior. Usually these diseases have a well-marked physical basis so that the mental symptoms are regarded as attendant and not too much stress is laid upon them. The general idea is that if the physical condition could be remedied, the mental symptoms would take care of themselves. There are two mentally abnormal or psychotic states which are prevalent after age sixty: namely, cerebral arteriosclerosis and senile dementia. Cerebral arteriosclerosis usually starts with a rather sudden onset of confusion, excitement, and other forms of psychotic behavior, following which there may or may not be a period of remission. This condition, in theory at any rate, is due to the "hardening of the arteries." Senile dementia has a more gradual onset, marked by an increased intellectual and emotional deterioration and exaggeration of all of the personality characteristics of the aged person.

Psychological Changes in Old Age

Even though the physical and mental changes which accompany aging are common to most old people, those changes are not always understood by the younger generations. These changes may or may not be forerunners of a true mental abnormality; in any event, a better knowledge of the changes should clarify certain sorts of behavior which are of interest to the student of abnormal psychology. Three lines of evidence concerning these changes are available — the experimental, the clinical, and the introspective.

EXPERIMENTAL FINDINGS

According to the extensive experimental studies of Miles[8,9] certain motor skills and reactions (such as reaching and grasping, or operating a pursuitmeter) reach their peak of efficiency in the twenties and then constantly and slowly decrease throughout the remainder of the life span. The decline in perceptual acuity which depends to a large degree on the anatomy of the sense organ receptors begins about age 30. For example, the average number of taste buds per papilla from birth to age 20 is 245. During maturity and early old age the average is 208, while it declines to 88 for the age period 74–85.

Learning of new material, if interest and motivation are sufficient, shows little decline until after age 45, but it does show a marked decline between 60 and 80. Scores on a standardized intelligence test given to comparable age groups show that the decline is slight in the twenties and thirties, somewhat steeper in the forties, fifties and sixties, and falls rather rapidly from seventy to ninety. However, an active mind, wide and varied interests, persistent endeavor, well-formed and practiced mental habits, plus the knowledge increment, will in individual cases tend to compensate in later age for the quickness in comprehension and action that typify early maturity. With respect to the pursuit of active interests, either in business or in play, older men are less sociable than younger men because they are less interested in the people who are associated with them.

From the experimental work three generalizations may be drawn: (a) There is a slow, constant decline in those abilities which depend directly on the anatomy and physiology of the organism. Psychological regression goes hand in hand with physiological regression. (b) There are wide individual differences in this regression and the way in which different individuals compensate it. An old man of superior ability will exceed a young man of average ability. (c) The more the behavior involves experience and considered judgment, the more resistant it is to regression.

CLINICAL DESCRIPTION

MacCurdy[7] has made a systematic presentation of the changes as they have been reported by many observers. We shall, for the most part, follow his descriptions.

The first of the outstanding personality characteristics of advancing age is *conservatism*. In so far as this character trait is associated with good judgment, which is the greatest asset of age, it is of real value. Conservatism facilitates the dispassionate and impartial weighing of evidence which is essential to all judgment and which is difficult to achieve when one is young and enthusiastic. On the other hand, it inhibits the formulation and execution of new ideas.

Two tendencies which are exaggerated in senile psychoses contribute to the establishment and maintenance of conservatism. The first is an indirect result of the slowing up of mental life, which always occurs to a greater or less extent as one grows older. This aspect is primarily a physical matter, but it has distinct psychological effects. It is more difficult to reason quickly and intelligently about new problems than it is to exercise judgment dependent on well-established habits. This difference between original thinking and habit becomes more marked when physical regression begins to show itself in the functions of the central nervous system. We all attend and are interested in activities in which we are proficient or which we can do easily, and we avoid tasks in which we expect to be incompetent. As senility approaches (and its advance is insidious but certain) one automatically restricts one's interests to the familiar routine and shuns new ideas and occupations. Thus, one becomes conservative and rationalizes it in many ways, rather than admit to oneself the evidence of one's growing incompetence.

The second factor is the idea of death, which is an inevitable development in old age. The greatest change which one can imagine is the change from living to not-living; hence, any change will be a painful reminder of the supreme one, which becomes an ever closer prospect. It is the old person who says, "Things are not what they used to be." Young people are confronted with change as are the old people, but the sight is rarely painful to them; for youth it usually means growth and development, not death.

A second characteristic of old age is *opinionativeness*. This trait is dependent on the same factors which favor conservatism, and is augmented by the tendency to irritability, which also grows out of the fear of change.

A third characteristic is *stinginess*, together with a fear of loss of property. Conservatism is nowhere better exhibited than in the investments of an old man, and the petty economies of the aged, even when wealthy, would be ludicrous were they not pathetic.

A fourth trait is *restlessness*. This characteristic is not always present.

If it becomes pronounced, it is usually associated with other changes that are definitely pathological. It is when the idea of death becomes increasingly conscious that physical restlessness appears. Mental restlessness is a more frequent phenomenon in old age. The desire to

PLATE 9

PERPLEXED SENILE DEMENTIA PATIENT

maintain contact with the world leads to pottering activity or a disorganized sort of intrusion into the affairs of others.

The most serious characteristic of senility is *selfishness* which appears in most personal relationships. Among younger people, selfishness is camouflaged, concealed, and rationalized. Its obsessive nature in the aged is usually masked and may not be recognized. Old people need affection and support from those whom they earlier loved to serve.

Hence, the aged person makes demands that are unfair and undesirable. If the parent is to be kept happy, his opinions and prejudices must be respected, no matter how old-fashioned. If selfishness appears in no other form, it comes to light in the attitude of grandparents toward discipline. It is easier to spoil children and win their love (for the moment at least) than to keep their ultimate welfare in mind. Hence, the grandparent, hungry for attention and affection, uses his authority to relax parental discipline, so making himself more popular with the third generation than are the children's parents. This is the simplest camouflage for selfishness to assume because it is so easily rationalized as kindness and true sympathy.

INTROSPECTIVE DESCRIPTION

A description of the subjective experience of advanced age may be taken from Paget.*

The old man, he says, wonders at his own existence, is bewildered at the feel of the pen in his hand, at the taste of his food; that he is alive when so many millions are dead or unborn; at a funeral is fascinated by someone's whisper or the contour of a face or some other irrelevancy; is smitten with momentary surprise that he is or that it is it; finds an apocalypse on looking in the glass; is oppressed by a sense of mystery that is very far from philosophic contemplation; and realizes that when others observe him thus, they reflect that there is no speculation — "No speculation in those eyes that thou dost glare with"; finds himself growing out "of the world, of life, of time"; feels it not unreasonable to consider the one, the all, the infinite, if his mind drifts that way. His mind wanders while he wonders whether heaven lies about him in his second infancy. . . . The old problems of politics and religion lose their charm and in place of pure art we turn to that of the street. He says we old are thus a sentimental lot and for the sake of economy live on our emotions, which cost nothing.

Senile Dementia and Cerebral Arteriosclerosis

These two forms of dementia are advanced or terminal states, resulting from the more ordinary changes of physiological and psychological regression. Senile dementia, generally speaking, is a dementia so severe that the person is disoriented, confused, and no longer able to care for himself adequately. The onset of the dementia is usually more sudden in cerebral arteriosclerosis, which depends on the "hardening" of the arteries of the brain. This hardening produces an interference with cerebral nutrition due to an arterial failure, either in the form of a small rupture of the blood vessels or in blockage or toxic

* Paget, S., quoted from G. S. Hall, *Senescence.* New York, Appleton-Century, 1923, 132–133.

processes in the vessels. The ways in which the psychological abnormalities show themselves in these dementias are somewhat more varied from person to person than they are in the other psychoses. The following case history of a senile dementia patient is fairly representative.

Case History

CASE 15: Mrs. S, aged sixty-eight, had a public-school education, was of average intelligence; married, no children; had no real marital difficulties; and had had no serious illnesses or operations during her life. She had an attack of influenza from which she did not seem to recover. Physically there were no outstanding symptoms, but she became mentally deranged. She became irrational, assaultive, and untidy, so that it was impossible to manage her at home. When brought to the hospital she was resistive and confused, she cried easily, and complained of many delusions concerning her health. She was incoherent, irrelevant, and rambling. She was disoriented as to time, place, and person, and her memory impairment was pronounced.

When asked what was the matter with her, she replied, "Injected you see, that spinal nerve which has to do with — what — hypnotize — I said they started so fact that. I remember my mother, grandmother and grandfather, they keep telling it to you till I find death. Gee, what she gave me that back. You have completely done that. Father had the same thing done to him that I have done to me. Uncle Abe was perfectly healthy, so that proves nothing was hereditary, that proves that, which the sick wards injected into my head, in my thinking head, in the head that does the controlling. Take me out, if you will take me out. I know didn't anybody put me in here. I'm talking about my life and health right now. My Aunt Hattie talked to me most. My mother is a very jealous person."

Her mental confusion gradually cleared up. Emotionally she remained very unstable, having frequent crying spells and complaining about small events or imaginary happenings. After six weeks in the hospital she returned to her home. Six months later her behavior again became such that home care was impossible. She was returned to the hospital, where she died after several months.

Facts and Figures

An outstanding fact concerning the structure of American population groups is the increasing median age of the people of our nation, with an associated increasing proportion of older persons. In 1820 the median age of the entire population was 16.7 years; in 1860, 19.4; in 1900, 22.9; and in 1940, 28.7. In 1860, 13 per cent of the population were aged over 45; in 1900, 18 per cent; in 1920, 21 per cent; and in 1940, 27 per cent. This increase is attributed to two major causes: (a) a declining birth rate so that there are fewer infants and children whose age would serve to keep the median age of the total population down; and (b) the greater absolute longevity of persons who have survived infancy. All of the medical progress of the past century has contributed to the length of life. The decrease in deaths due to smallpox, diphtheria, appendicitis, and tuberculosis allows more individuals to survive to the sixties and seventies. In 1850 only 2.6 per cent of the population were aged over 65, while in 1940 the percentage was 6.9.

Another source of the increased number of senile patients in mental hospitals comes from a real decrease in the number of "old people's homes," almshouses, county homes, and the like, where the aged members of the community were formerly cared for. Likewise, there is a continuing increase in the numbers of the urban population at the expense of the rural population. Urban population groups are less able than rural populations to provide home or family care for the aged. As a consequence of the greater number of those over age 50, fewer old people's homes, and less home care, there has been an enormous increase in the number of aged who are admitted to public mental hospitals.[10]

In 1942 there were more than 28,000 mental-hospital patients in the United States who were suffering from senile or arteriosclerotic dementia. During the same year, over 25,000 individuals aged over 60 were admitted for the first time to the mental hospitals, of whom more than 17,000 were diagnosed as senile dementia or cerebral arteriosclerosis. The annual death rate of these hospitalized seniles is about 500 per 1000. The ratio of men to women is 1.15 to 1.0 for senile dementia and 1.52 to 1.0 for cerebral arteriosclerosis. Among the first-admissions the ratio of urban to rural patients is 2.05 to 1.0 for senile dementia, and 2.47 to 1.0 for arteriosclerosis. Of patients in these categories in the state mental hospitals, 95 per cent are in dependent or marginal circumstances, while the educational achievement is high school or better in but 9 per cent of them.[6]

A comparison of the nationality of these patients shows that 53 per cent are native and 47 per cent foreign-born. The rate of first-admissions for senile dementia is 90 per cent higher, and for cerebral arteriosclerosis 190 per cent higher, among Negroes than among whites.

There is no directly pertinent information concerning the relative importance of nature and nurture among the dementias of the aged. The fact that such information is not available is not remarkable. By the time these old people become mental-hospital patients, their friends, and relatives are aged (or dead) and to a large extent information is not available concerning the family history. They themselves are, of course, unable to give adequate information. In the same way, it is impossible to secure very much material of an accurate or adequate nature concerning the previous health and physical constitution of such persons. When one compares the interest which is taken in children's problems by the medical, social, and psychological professions, the interest and care accorded to the aged is insignificant, amounting to neglect. Since the general attitude of society is that these persons have reached a hopeless, terminal life state, little has been done to give us much understanding of the factors which may facilitate or inhibit such states, even though they do represent a most important economic, social, and psychological problem.

Psychopathology of the Aged

Among the senile there are two fairly distinct forms of psychopathology. The first is the more or less gradual mental enfeeblement and deterioration which is characteristic of senile dementia; the second is the rapid and often sudden episodic type of deviation which may be followed by some degree of recovery and which is characteristic of cerebral arteriosclerosis and the toxic psychoses of old age.

Senile dementia represents the last stages of psychological regression accompanying physiological regression. There is a general imperception (that is, impaired registration of external impressions). This impairment is attributed to the clouding of consciousness and disorientation which, in turn, are thought to be related to the deterioration processes taking place in the cerebral cortex itself. In conversation there is repetition, dearth of ideas, many unimportant details, and falsification of memory. The changes in memory itself are usually quite marked. Paramnesia, in the sense of fabrication and falsification to fill the gaps in memory, is common. This falsification is not based on a conscious process of deception, but is related to the general disorientation and mental confusion which pervades the mental life of the individual. There is also a loss of memory for both immediate and past events, although the memory for past events tends to remain more accurate than that for recent. This type of memory loss was called by Ribot the "law of regression," in that recent memories disappear first, whereas childhood memories are the last to go.

The judgment of these patients is markedly impaired. There is a lack of insight into their own mental and physical condition. They express confused delusions and illusions of a temporary and transient nature. For example, an individual will be quite upset because of some fancied robbery and will talk about it for a day or so and then forget, or point out himself that it was only his imagination. There is a marked intolerance for any change in the routine of the life or care which such patients obtain, even though the change may be one which adds decidedly to their comfort and well-being. These patients are variable in their emotional expressions; they are unstable, irritable, indifferent, lack sympathy and, in general, show a marked deviation from the previous control of their emotional life. In the more severe episodes there may be periods of delirium marked by hallucinations, disorientation, profound clouding of consciousness, incoherence, restlessness, and destructiveness.

This entire process is a true dementia, in that it is progressive and irreversible. The rate of this process varies among individuals, but in extreme cases the terminal mental status is one of practically complete "idiocy."

The behavior and mental life of the arteriosclerotic or toxic case differs somewhat from that of the senile dement.[11] Usually, there is a relatively sudden onset, marked by headaches, insomnia, and mental confusion. Judgment usually is somewhat better than in the deteriorating senile; insight persists for some time, although it is gradually lost. Delusions of reference and infidelity are common. Patients are frequently depressed and emotionally unstable, laughing or weeping very easily. They are unable to make decisions, they are restless but easily fatigued, and they show a progressive forgetfulness. There may be intervals during which there is marked improvement or even apparent recovery from the acute symptoms, so that the patient is able to conduct himself with a fair degree of prudence. This form of dementia is a steplike loss, whereas the true senile dementia is a gradual decline. The steplike process may end in a terminal dementia as profound as that reached by the gradual decline.

Explanations of the Psychological Changes in Old Age

ORGANIC

Practically without exception the post-mortem examination of the senile brain shows marked destruction, alteration, or softening of one or another part. This deterioration is in many cases accompanied by a thickening and obstruction of the arteries of the brain. This arteriosclerotic process is one toward which much research has been directed.[12, 13] The process may involve many or all of the arteries of the body. Whether the process is a "normal" one, in the sense that the process of aging itself is normal, or whether it is due to pathological or infectious causes is a matter of dispute. No matter what the cause or where the tissue has ceased functioning, it has interfered with psychological integration. The confusion, disorientation, loss of memory and insight are thought to be explicable in terms of the organic loss. Interference with ordinary neural function by the destruction of brain tissue results in mental confusion and the release of many processes which were formerly held in check. After the immediate shock passes — a period of several weeks — there is a gradual reorganization of both physiological and psychological functions. The resultant behavior has been spoken of as a damaged organism doing the best it can with what functional parts remain.

The weakness of this organic explanation rests on the failure to establish any consistent relationship between the anatomical tissues involved and the psychopathology observed. One might reasonably expect to find that the psychological symptoms are related in some regular fashion to certain areas or, at least, to the gross amount of tissue which has become nonfunctional. No such relationship has been established.

PSYCHOBIOLOGICAL

The lack of correlation between organic tissue destruction and the psychological symptoms has led some psychiatrists to the viewpoint that the mental deviation is but an exaggeration of the personality characteristics or temperamental tendencies which marked the person before the onset of senility. They claim that many of these senile cases were rigid, constricted perfectionists during most of their adult lives. When the organic changes of old age occur, the rigidity of the habit systems is said to make it impossible for the individual to compensate for brain damage; therefore, the gross mental changes result. This explanation is open to dispute because so little is known about the prepsychotic personality of the senile patient. We must remember that his friends and relatives are themselves either aged or dead; also, that the history is usually given by the children or other younger individuals to whom he has always seemed relatively old and, therefore, rigid.

PSYCHOANALYTIC

The psychoanalyst[1] will hold that the fact of the organic damage to a senile brain is indisputable, but that from a psychological viewpoint the important question is the why — the dynamics — of the changes in mental life which occur. Although the details of the dynamics of senility are pretty speculative, in general it is held that the changes are essentially those of regression.[3] By "regression" is meant the return to infantile or childish habits and patterns of response. Freud has pointed out that there is a "repetition tendency" marking the psychology of the aged individual. Hamilton[5] has shown that when any animal (or human) is confronted with a persistently baffling situation, it usually falls back on its initial mode of response. When this repetition tendency occurs, it is a falling back upon modes of functioning characteristic of earlier periods of life, which were adequate at that time but which are now inappropriate. The physical disabilities, reduction in self-control (Ego-inhibition), and the environmental handicaps that confront the aging person constitute frustration, and the frustration brings out this repetition tendency.

Other analysts have claimed that the repetitive tendency and rigidity are a self-defense against anxiety. The rigidity is thought to be the expression of the refusal of the aged to admit the possibility of a change in their evaluation of their environment or any possible alteration in their life values. The relative weakening of the Ego and intellect gives rise to the psychotic outbreaks characteristic of the aged. It is only through the increase in intellectual efficiency and self-control that the aging individual can maintain his mental equilibrium. Any attempt to change from some level of adjustment already achieved, even though none too satisfactory, or to give up certain habitual forms of behavior in order to make some new readjustment to an untried situation, must increase the feeling of anxiety and will work against intellectual integration and efficiency. Hence, the individual regards changes as dangerous and is hostile and irritable toward them. The changing world is regarded with fear and suspicion. The solution of any problem or new demand for reorientation is thought of as a threat to self-control, which already is strained by the task of mastering the physical defects attendant on old age and by the basic fear of the end of life, which is felt by the aged to be imminent.

This explanation which in part depends on the theory of a return to childish modes of thought (narcissistic regression) has not been borne out by experimentation. Cameron[2] investigated in a comparative fashion the thought processes of normal adults, normal children, schizophrenic patients, and senile dements. He found that neither in senile dilapidation nor in schizophrenic disorganization was a language or ideational product obtained which was comparable to the material produced by normal children. In other words, the regressive process in senile dementia did not express itself in ideas or in verbal tendencies that were comparable to those shown by children. There was a change in the thought processes of senile patients, but the change was not in the direction of similarity to the thought processes of children, so that it was not truly a regression.

Summary

A most important change which is taking place in the population composition of America is the increasing median age which is associated with an increase in the portion of the population aged over fifty. In contrast to the extensive psychological knowledge, available and useful, regarding the first twenty years of life, very little is known concerning the last twenty (or more) years. There is an unquestionable increase in the number of older persons who require care in mental hospitals. Probably because the last years of life are regarded by many to be "useless" and the aged mental cases "hopeless," little is done to improve our understanding of older people and their particular problems.

It is reasonable to expect that systematic research will amplify our information concerning the psychological changes in advanced maturity. Such knowledge is necessary if we are to meet the very urgent problems raised by this population change, for which there is no known historical precedent.

REFERENCES

1. Atkin, S., "Discussion: Old Age and Aging; The Psychoanalytic Point of View," *Amer. Jour. Orthopsychiat.*, 1940, *10*, 79–84.
2. Cameron, N., "A Study of Thinking in Senile Deterioration and Schizophrenic Disorganization," *Amer. Jour. Psychol.*, 1938, *51*, 650–664.
3. Grotjahn, M., "Psychoanalytic Investigation of a Seventy-One-Year-Old Man with Senile Dementia," *Psychoanal. Quart.*, 1940, *9*, 80–97.
4. Hall, G. S., *Senescence*. New York, Appleton-Century, 1923, 132–133.
5. Hamilton, G. V., "Changes in Personality and Psychosexuality with Age." Chapter 16 in E. V. Cowdry, *Problems of Aging*. Baltimore, Williams & Wilkins, 1939, 459–482.
6. Landis, C., and J. D. Page, *Modern Society and Mental Disease*. New York, Rinehart, 1938.
7. MacCurdy, J. T., *The Psychology of Emotion*. New York, Harcourt, 1925, 179–181.
8. Miles, W. R., "Age and Human Ability," *Psychol. Rev.*, 1933, *40*, 99–123.
9. ———, "Psychological Aspects of Aging." Chapter 20 in E. V. Cowdry, *Problems of Aging*. Baltimore, Williams & Wilkins, 1939, 535–571.
10. Page J. D., and C. Landis, "Trends in Mental Disease, 1910–1940," *Jour. Abn. Soc. Psychol.*, 1943, *38*, 518–524.

11. Rothschild, D., "The Clinical Differentiation of Senile and Arteriosclerotic Psychoses," *Amer. Jour. Psychiat.*, 1941, *98*, 324–333.

12. ———, "Neuropathological Changes in Arteriosclerotic Psychoses and Their Psychiatric Significance," *Arch. Neurol. Psychiat.*, 1942, *48*, 417–436.

13. ———, and M. L. Sharp, "The Origin of Senile Psychoses: Neuropathologic Factors and Factors of a More Personal Nature," *Dis. Nerv. Syst.*, 1941, *2*, 49–54.

14. White, W. A., *Outline of Psychiatry* (12th ed.). New York, Nervous and Mental Disease Monographs, 1929.

Chapter XII

INVOLUTIONAL MELANCHOLIA, MIXED PSYCHOTIC STATES, AND PARANOIA

THE TWO major forms of mental disorder, dementia praecox and manic-depressive psychosis, are distinguished on the basis of psychological symptoms and clinical impression. Unfortunately, there is no reliable way in which to make a physical differentiation between the two diseases. There are many mentally disturbed patients whose psychological symptoms are similar to one or the other major disease but which do not fit clearly into either category. It is uncertain whether or not these variants are simply unclear psychological manifestations of the two major types of psychosis, or whether they are really different disorders both physically and psychologically. Any number of attempts have been made to classify adequately the patients who do not fit into these or other fairly well-established diagnostic groups. In spite of all of these attempts, there is no essential agreement among the authorities in the field, with the result that debate and controversy continue. Certain of these subvarieties of mental abnormality should be considered. Although no one of them comprises a large per cent of the total number of mental cases, these variations, when added together, amount to almost a fifth of the total number of cases entering our mental hospitals.

INVOLUTIONAL MELANCHOLIA

This disorder is a type of depression which is differentiated from other melancholic episodes on the basis of the fact that it commonly occurs in persons between the ages of forty-five and sixty who have had no history of any previous mental illness. It is marked by an increase in motor activity which ranges from restlessness to frenzied agitation. Psychologically speaking, the depression is just as acute as it is in any of the other varieties of depression, but in place of the motor retardation there is usually a marked motor agitation which does not occur in manic-depressive depression.

Case History

CASE 16: Mrs. I, age fifty-three, had a sudden onset of very noisy behavior and incoherent speech. She wailed that she had many illnesses, that she was eternally damned, that she had ruined both her children, and that her bowels were stopped up and would never move again. The noisy behavior and confusion continued for several weeks. She became obsessed with the idea that she was a bad woman, that the world would never forgive her. She seemed particularly afraid that cattle would attack her. She listened to all the health lectures on the radio and finally insisted that she had tuberculosis and refused to allow anyone to touch her. There was constant talk about ruining her children's lives, that it was all her fault, that she would never be forgiven, and that she should kill herself. The family physician insisted on hospitalization.

On admission to the hospital she was extremely restless, agitated, and markedly depressed. She kept wringing her hands and pacing the floor, emitting whining cries. She talked spontaneously in an agitated, apprehensive fashion, repeating the same thing over and over again. There was no intellectual deterioration or memory defect. She seemed well oriented and in good contact with her surroundings. Her rather monotonous monologue ran as follows: "There's nothing the matter with me; I'm all right. I'm only afraid of what will happen to Mary. Mary is all alone, she's my daughter. I must go out and take care of her, she's my child. Oh God, why must this happen, my bowels. I haven't moved my bowels for months. I take in food, but it sticks here. I have no opening at all. I have no bowels. I have no heart. I'm nothing. My poor Mary. What are you doing with Mary? You are keeping her in the cellar. You are going to torture me."

During the next five months there was little change in her condition. Frequently, her agitation was so great that she had to be kept in cold packs or continuous baths. She did not respond to psychotherapy. Electric convulsive therapy was initiated and after twelve treatments she became much less agitated and depressed and was cooperative for the first time, making a gradual recovery. She was finally discharged from the hospital, and although not completely in command of herself, both she and her husband felt that she would be able to get along at home.

This case illustrates several points which are peculiar to the disease. The agitation, deep depression, somatic delusions, and suicidal tendencies are quite characteristic. This agitated depression is in a sense superimposed on the normal personality so that it is sometimes difficult to understand what the individual was like before the onset of the depression. In these involutional cases, the observer gains the impression that the fundamental personality is not greatly changed or disturbed, but that it is carrying a load of depression and agitation; which load is only partially synthesized into the usual or normal character of the individual.

Facts and Figures

There are about 6000 cases of involutional melancholia resident in the mental hospitals of the entire United States, and between 4500 and 5000 such patients are admitted for the first time each year. Of every 100 of these patients under treatment in the United States, about 20 are discharged as improved during any one year. The average age at first-admission to the hospitals is 55 years for men and 52 for women.[10] The ratio of men to women among first-admissions is 0.45 to 1; while the ratio of urban to rural patients is 1.9 to 1.

The rate of admission of these patients to the mental hospitals of New York State increased between 1930 and 1940 from 5 to 13 per 100,000 of the general population of the state aged over 35. This increase was probably due to the greater number of older persons in the general population, so that there were more individuals alive who could succumb to this psychosis. The onset of the disease is commonly associated with physical illness, loss of employment, or family difficulties.

Brockhausen[1] studied the genetic history of 201 melancholic patients, finding that those cases which occurred during the involutional period showed clear evidence of having more than the expected number of relatives who had had the same illness. Patients whose psychosis did not occur during the involutional period did not have this "hereditary tainting."

History and Explanations of the Involutional Melancholia Concept

Involutional melancholia was distinguished by Kraepelin, who found that he had among his patients many cases of depression which occurred rather late in life and which were not clearly manic-depressive, depressed, or senile. He termed these cases *melancholia*, pointing out that this particular kind of depression is marked by anxiety, a feeling of unreality, and hypochondriacal or nihilistic delusions.

The absence of a satisfactory biological explanation of this type of mental disorder has led to psychological speculation concerning its dynamics. These interpretations are mainly descriptive, but they provide ways of thinking about this particular variety of abnormal psychology.

PSYCHOANALYTIC EXPLANATION

Many years ago, Freud[4] analyzed the psychological course of melancholia. His formulation, together with the amplifications of his followers, may be stated in simplified form as follows: In this illness, there is an injury to one's feelings of self-importance. The injury is so severe that all adult ambition and sexual interest are given up. With the loss of ambition and interest, there is a regression to childish impulses and a display of infantile characteristics. The self (Ego) permits the conscience (Superego) to torture it because of the regression. This becomes a real mental splitting so that the patient is unable to understand why his conscience is so tyrannical and torturing. Some patients will cry out, asking to know why they allow themselves to suffer as they do, and in the next breath will ask why they cried out.

This mental torture (psychic sadism) is transferred to various parts of the body. The patient suffers with peculiar intensity from imaginary ailments. On occasion, the torturing conscience forces the self to deny that the body exists, so that there are feelings of unreality and of depersonalization. In another sense the self bribes the conscience with suffering in order that it may not be tortured by ideas and reproaches which are more painful than the imaginary physical pain. According to the analysts, all this goes on in the mind of the involutional patient, and exhibits itself in the agitated depression and hypochondriacal delusions.

PSYCHOGENIC EXPLANATION

MacCurdy[11] developed an explanation of the psychological symptoms of involutional melancholia in psychogenic terms. He held that the melancholic reaction is essentially due to bad habits of thought and to maladjusted attitudes. He pointed out that the disorder, appearing in the declining years of life when physical disease is apt to be manifest or suspected, furnished a widespread impression that the menopause, with its unquestioned endocrine gland changes, is the basis for the melancholia. It is, however, more usual for the physical "change of life" to produce a mild neurosis than a marked psychosis.

Specific arguments must be advanced, therefore, in favor of its being essentially a psychological reaction. There usually is some definite precipitating incident which is of a psychological nature and to which the specific ideas and other symptoms seem to be related. The abnormal reactions derive their characteristics from three interrelated factors: (*a*) the nature of the situation from which relief is sought, (*b*) the occurrence of some disturbing event which precipitates the abnormal reaction, and (*c*) the goal to which the retreat or regression is directed.

At the time of involution any person realizes that he (or she) is past the peak of life and only increasing age and senility remain. Then, some unfortunate event occurs. He worries and becomes increasingly depressed because this worry is the nearest approach to a solution which his aging mind can make. He soon fears that his life is finished. Physically speaking, this is false, for many years of life may remain; but psychologically, the fear may be near to the truth. A man's fortune, for better or worse, is made. A woman's children have married, gone out of her life, and they no longer need her. The idea of "end of life" is emotionally ambivalent. It is desired (depression) and feared (agitation).

PSYCHOBIOLOGICAL EXPLANATION

Meyer and his collaborator, Muncie,[14] related this form of melancholia to "rigid personality." Muncie said that the rigidity of personality is compounded in no fixed proportion of many factors, such as obstinacy, aggressiveness, pride, sensitiveness, and a rigid code of personal ethics. This explanation would imply that the disease is an exaggeration of habit tendencies and patterns built up during a lifetime, which are affected by the many physiological changes of the involutional period. The rigid personality cannot alter to meet these changes; it breaks and the broken state constitutes the psychosis as we see it. In those cases in which the personality in the disease is so different from that seen previously, the explanation lies in the fact that either the individual repressed much of his rigidity or the physiological changes of involution were so marked as to overwhelm the normal personality.

Since involutional melancholia has its onset late in life; since the patients were usually "normal" before the psychosis; and finally, since most people go through this period of life without becoming psychotic, it has seemed worth while to many investigators to study the prepsychotic personality of these patients, hoping that from careful study one might be able to find what sort of person it is that will develop this particular set of symptoms.

Prepsychotic Personality

Titley[15] reported that in about half of the cases certain of the symptoms seem to be an exaggeration of personality tendencies which have marked much of the adult life of the individual; namely, obstinacy, parsimony, and perfectionism. In other cases the psychotic symptoms are in more or less contrast to the personality before the illness. Many are said to have been normal, pleasant, well-adjusted persons whose behavior in their psychosis is totally different from their previous personality.

The inquiry into the personality of the involutional patient whose symptoms are in line with his previous character shows that he was an inhibited person inclined to be serious, sensitive, frugal, lacking in humor, stubborn, reticent, of rigid moral code, and with a tendency toward depressive apprehension and worry. His adult existence was narrow and devoid of interests or diversions, and his behavior was often that of a worrisome, fidgety, fretful, or overanxious person. Such characteristics are said to grow out of the deeply rooted, lifelong feeling of insecurity. By the time the involutional period is reached, adjustment to new situations or frustrating circumstances is no longer possible. In a woman, the realization that her most highly valued biological function, that of childbearing, is now definitely lost may give her a feeling that her entire life has been a failure.

In other individuals, the psychosis seems to be an exaggeration of the ordinary characteristics of the involutional period of life of normal individuals. In the woman these symptoms are nervousness, excitability, fatiguability, depression, insomnia, failing memory, and vague, indefinite pains. In the man the usual symptoms are emotional instability with sudden, uncontrollable shifts in mood, sullen anxiety, a tendency to break into tears, an inability to concentrate, general apathy, and vague bodily complaints. In either sex, when such symptoms become acute and are complicated by fears, the psychotic state seems but an exaggeration of the normal reactions.

In general, studies of this sort have shown that there seem to be three varieties of involutional prepsychotic personalities. In the first, the involutional symptoms merely color and are superimposed upon preexisting abnormal mental states or severe personality deviations. In the second, the psychosis grows out of emotional maladjustments and physical complaints incidental to the involutional period. The third group consists of previously normal persons whose psychotic symptoms are not in accord with the expected changes in personality usually found as a person grows older.

Psychology[11]

The symptoms which present themselves prominently and consistently in this disease can be grouped psychologically, as follows: First, the patient's interest which has been directed toward his family, business, and social life is withdrawn and turned in on himself. He is concerned only with the insecurity of his own life, the afflictions of his body, or the unhealthy state of his soul. Second, this introversion is correlated with the rapid development of various ideas that are exaggerated or utterly false. He believes that he is about to die by disease or violence, that his property is gone, that the world is strangely altered, that his soul is lost, and that he is doomed to everlasting torment. Third, the mental processes suffer radical alteration, in that he entertains thoughts which are obviously absurd; he misinterprets the intentions of those about him; and, in general, substitutes uncritical imagination for rational judgment. Finally, his conduct alters; he abandons his former social adaptation and becomes surly, ungrateful, resentful, irritable, and brutal. These are not mere uncontrolled impulses but reflect a change of character, because when the unkindly act is completed there is no reaction of remorse nor a desire for forgiveness.

In order to understand these psychological events, they must be considered in relation to the age period of the individual who develops this psychosis; namely, the period between forty-five and sixty. The important motives of adult life, self-preservation, sex activities, and home or social functions, change at this age. Sex interest and potency wane. Social functions are no longer felt to be of real importance, so that the individual becomes more self-centered. This tendency to egotism is augmented by other factors. Generally speaking, we invest our emotional interests in social undertakings and home relationships that yield some return in emotional satisfaction, and if the return on the investment declines we become increasingly indifferent to it. The involutional period of life is full of such declines. The man in his fifties finds himself physically and mentally incapable of accomplishing the amount (or quality) of work that was easy for him some years before. Similar changes occur in his family life. His children are grown up and independent, hence becoming less attached to him. He has to realize that he is no longer the man that he once was and that he must cast his ambitions in a form compatible with his decreasing abilities.

In addition, worries and anxieties concerning money or property become prominent. This concern is not solely because of the intrinsic or buying value of money; but rather, and to a greater degree, because the possession of money attracts respect and establishes prestige, so necessary to bolster up the felt insecurity. The reverse is also true; poverty entails social degradation or social extinction. In this way, loss of property means loss of the usual social life; hence, delusions of poverty are closely allied with fears of death.

Another expression of the death-fear is the feeling of unreality common to all forms of depression. Things feel real to us in proportion to the amount of interest we take in them. They lose their meaning when we become indifferent to them. If our indifference is great, the whole world gets to be a shadowy, unreal place.

Due to egotism, the patient becomes not merely asocial; he is exclusively interested in himself and antisocial. The plainest evidence of this appears in his irritability and negativism. Such patients kick, scratch, and fight even when they are approached with the kindest intent. This positive interest in self is the basis for the hypochondriacal symptoms. When social and sex interests are intact, one can maintain the idea (true or false) of one's importance in the world. When this idea of importance in the world is gone, one's own body becomes a matter of supreme importance. One's interests are focused on the body. A decreased physical and mental energy is inevitable at this time of life. Coupled with this is the universal habit of exploiting physical disease as a means of gaining attention. These hypochondriacal symptoms may be due to misinterpretation of obscure visceral sensations set up by endocrine deficiency at this period of life, or they may rest on purely psychological motives.

Physiology and Neurology

Various investigators have attempted to show how the physiological and neurological changes which take place at the involutional period are associated with the mental symptoms of involutional melancholia. So far, no one has found real evidence of any special neurological change which is specifically associated with the disease. Also, no one has produced any clear evidence that there is any outstanding physiological change in these patients which is not found in the "sane" person going through the involutional period without these psychological abnormalities. From this, one may conclude that whatever the relationship is which may exist between the biological changes occurring at this time of life and the involutional mental symptoms, it must be a very complex one which depends upon the interaction of several of the different glandular and neurological systems.

The treatment of these patients with rather large doses of various hormones, which might be expected to replace those which are deficient at the involutional period, has brought about conflicting reports with respect to recovery from the mental abnormality. Some individuals have shown marked recovery following administration of one or nother glandular extract; while other patients, who seemed to be in a similar physiological and psychological status, failed to improve.[5]

The rather spectacular recoveries of patients with involutional melancholia, who have been treated with either electric convulsive therapy or with prefrontal lobotomy (surgical severing of the nerve tracts connecting the frontal lobes and the thalamus of the brain), lead to speculation concerning the possible neurological mechanisms which may be involved together with the endocrine dysfunctions. It is possible that either the electric shock or the severing of the fiber tracts in the brain interferes with a disordered pattern of organization which became fixed in the brain centers controlling emotional activity during physiological involution. The electrical or surgical shock to the nervous system might somehow disrupt these disordered patterns of neural control. This disruption might permit more normal and adequate functional interrelationships to be resumed as they existed before the onset of the period of involution. Such a hypothesis provides a possible explanation for recoveries brought about by electric convulsive therapy or prefrontal lobotomy.

MIXED PSYCHOTIC STATES

There are many psychotic patients who at times show elation or depression similar to that shown in the manic-depressive psychosis; at other times they exhibit apathy, inaccessibility, or stupor similar to schizophrenia; or again, they have periods of agitated depression. In other words, the outstanding symptoms change from time to time. In addition, there are many patients who seem to lack the particular combination of symptoms which would clearly identify them as suffering from any of the psychoses that have been described so far. Usually these patients have some of the symptoms of dementia praecox or manic-depressive psychosis, but they also have some one or two outstanding and atypical complaints which may indicate a variant psychopathological process or a clearly different disease. All these variations are lumped together as mixed psychotic states. Certain ones occur with sufficient frequency to warrant brief description.

BENIGN STUPOR

In certain persons, usually those of a cycloid temperament, there is a type of reaction which Hoch[7] studied and named the *benign stupor*. Stuporous states are characteristic of catatonia and are frequent in hysteria. The benign stupor is neither catatonic nor hysterical. It occurs usually after a period of mental depression which commonly had a fairly adequate basis in fact (such as death in the family or loss of job). The person becomes preoccupied, inaccessible, apathetic, and finally, stuporous. Such a person will lie in bed with a fixed gaze, mute and resistive to interference. After several weeks in this condition, he comes out of the stupor and in a few days regains contact with his surroundings. His normal mental health usually returns, although he may be somewhat excited and ecstatic for a week or so. He has little or no memory of the period of the stupor.

Psychologically, these individuals show a simple and complete regression. They abandon their adjustment to everyday existence and give themselves over to complete indifference, inactivity, and apathy. The idea uppermost in their thought seems to be a wish to die and a notion that they are psychologically dead. When the normal individual fails to achieve his wants, he tends to become bored. This benign stupor is similar to a very exaggerated boredom. After the patient, in fantasy, has been dead for a while, he then behaves as though he were reborn. His reactions on recovery are sometimes comparable to the ecstatic state marking the religious experience of conversion.

PERPLEXITY STATES[11]

Some patients show a marked restlessness and aimlessness of behavior. They appear dazed, dreamy, and apprehensive. They may remark, "Have I done something?" "Do people want something?" "I have damaged the building, haven't I?" To questions, they reply, "I don't know." "I feel mixed up." "I can't get it together." "I can't remember anything." "I don't know whether I am myself or not." The behavior of such a patient is not a depressive blankness, but rather the bewilderment of one who cannot understand what he sees, hears, or does. They are painfully distressed and disoriented concerning their perplexed, anxious condition.

In this state, the patient is unable to be certain whether the facts of the world about him are real, or whether his ideas, fancies, or dreams are real. Such an individual attempts to rationalize or make logical to himself the conflict between the ideas occurring in his fantasy and the facts of reality. The difficulty which he has in this process of rationalization leads to an overwhelming perplexity and the associated psychological distress.

SENSITIVE REFERENCE PSYCHOSIS

This particular variety of abnormality was differentiated and described by Kretschmer.[9] It occurs in persons who are of a mild, weak disposition, but possessed of a certain amount of self-assured ambition and obstinacy. They have very intense emotional reactions but keep the outward expression of such reactions under strict control. They are very self-conscious and given to self-criticism, which is based on a scrupulous code of ethics. They are serious-minded with unobtrusive manners.

In persons of this sort, the reverberations of some painful emotional experience cannot be forgotten, and yet cannot be expressed. In consequence, the emotional memories force themselves into consciousness time after time. They are tormented by self-reproach and moral scruples. Internally, they are at battle, driven by a constant reproach for their own felt inferiority. Such a person has a feeling that his humiliation must be known to everyone, and that people in the street turn around and look at him as he passes, smiling and making depreciating signs. He detects reference to himself in harmless, everyday conversation, in newspaper articles, or in things he hears from the radio. In some instances, this reaction seems to be first organized around the moral scruples which the person may have concerning a secret habit of masturbation. Every failure in sex repression re-creates the experience of a humiliating moral defeat. This gives rise to a combination of delusional ideas, general depression, nervousness, and imaginary or real physical ailments. The self-reproach and self-blame which mark the mental life of these individuals may be so strong that suicidal attempts result and hospitalization becomes necessary in order to protect them from themselves.

PARANOIA

Kraepelin[8] used the word "paranoia" to describe a condition marked by chronic, systematized, gradually developing delusions arising from internal causes without accompanying hallucinations and without the tendency to mental deterioration, remission, or recovery. The essential psychological abnormality in paranoia is delusion (false belief). In normal persons, delusions may occur at any time due to imperfect observation, misinformation, or faulty reasoning. This defect in intellectual performance is usually accompanied by a certain amount of emotion or affect which may facilitate or inhibit the intellectual operation itself. We tend to judge or believe in accordance with our wishes or emotions. If there is an undue amount of emotion in the judgment, prejudice results. There is no clear line which can be drawn between these strong prejudices or so-called delusions, and delusions which are morbid or abnormal. For example, most of us maintain false beliefs as to our own importance and the esteem given us by our fellow men. We very easily distort the meaning of remarks and attitudes of others. We are apt to give significance to actions or remarks which had no reference to ourselves. When we are aware of some personal weakness or have some feeling of guilt, we are unduly sensitive and inclined to interpret the remarks of others as accusatory or depreciatory of ourselves. When we have accomplished some act of which we are proud and for which we grant ourselves self-approval, we tend to interpret neutral remarks and events as adding to this approval.

The line between true belief and false belief, between fact and delusion, is in theory extraordinarily difficult to establish. In actual practice and in most instances, the consensus of any social group serves as a sufficient reference for the truth or falsity of the beliefs expressed by any member of the group. In an absolute sense, the majority may be wrong and deluded, while the individual who is deviant may be correct. Undoubtedly, almost every person is possessed of delusions in this sense of the term; that is, it is rare to find any person whose every belief is in accord with the majority of his social group. Only when the false beliefs endanger the health and safety of either the individual himself or his community, is the "deluded" person segregated. If such a deluded person is sent to a mental hospital and if there is no other evidence of mental abnormality, then he is said to be suffering from paranoia. Some of the most difficult and controversial issues in abnormal psychology and legal psychiatry (forensic medicine) revolve about the point of the degree of danger which is attendant upon the delusional system of such individuals.

Case History

CASE 17: Mr. P, aged twenty-four, was working as a riveter in a shipyard. He came to see a physician at the urging of the personnel manager of the company by which he was employed. He told the following story. He quit high school at the end of the second year because other members of his class had united to spread evil stories concerning him which caused the teachers to reprove him for things which he had not actually done. He left home and took a training course in metal work at a near-by city and was soon able to secure employment as a construction worker. In order to secure employment, it was necessary for him to join the union at whatever place he worked. Since employment in metal construction work is of a changing character, he had to change from one to another union membership. He was certain that this changing of membership caused the various unions to regard him with suspicion. Each union, he believed, regarded him as a spy for the other unions. He was sure that repeated attempts were made to injure him on the job, to introduce poison into his food, or to represent to his employers that he was an untrustworthy and worthless workman. In order to protect himself against this constant persecution and espionage, he moved repeatedly and unexpectedly without leaving any forwarding address. He ate at different restaurants and in different parts of the city, never going to the same place twice. He requested police protection and special protection by the company guards.

Investigation showed that, so far as his work relations were concerned, there was no basis of fact in any of his beliefs. He was considered to be a good workman. He had repeated verbal battles with his fellow workers, accusing them of making remarks about him, dropping tools which might injure him, and similar false statements. It was impossible for the physician to convince him of his good faith. He told this physician that undoubtedly the personnel manager had been instructed to send him to him by the leader of a union, of which he was not at that time a member. His story was one of systematic persecution, in which he was convinced that he had been singled out among the twenty thousand men working for his particular company to be the scapegoat for the difficulty between the unions. Shortly after consulting the physician, he was arrested and charged with an attempt to kill another workman who he claimed had been spreading untrue stories about him. The court committed him to a mental hospital.

Personal Experience

The story which the paranoid patient tells of himself does not differ greatly from that which is observed by others. The way in which these ideas circulate in the mind of such a patient is illustrated by the following extracts from a letter written by a woman paranoid patient.

During the fourteen years that I have lived here, I have led the life of a martyr which mocks of all comparison. It concerns the embezzlement of inherited money, and on account of this all imaginable evil and cunning was exercised, that I might be passed off as insane and so on, or that I should be made so, and that the necessary means of living, credit and honor should be taken from me. This inexcusable behavior by day and by night is carried on by the secret police and their aiders and abettors, female and male, young or old, poor or rich — all must assist; since it is for the police! The hounding was ordered in all houses and disticts of the town and no regard was had for an old widow full of years. Since I came to Munich, all my letters have been kept back, opened, and delivered without a stamp. Letters about inheritance were simply suppressed, so that I never could be present at the distribution like the other heirs. Every effort is made that I may not be seen and that I should not come into contact with anyone; indeed it is horrible and incredible that such abominable occurrences can happen, carried out by certain lawyers, who have embezzled my money; of course they have also a certain police jurisdiction at hand, which facilitates for them their infernal ongoings in order that it should not come to light; besides they are rich, with which one can close the mouth of many a crime. . . . When I arrived in Munich I found my house in the greatest disorder, although, before I left home, I left everything punctiliously in order. The furniture was covered with a layer of dirt and dust, the bed-clothes were thrown about anyhow, every drawer and cupboard was opened, although I had carefully locked up everything, closed the box of keys and taken it with me; in the kitchen the pretty mirror was in fragments. It went so far that I was forced to hesitate about eating anything, for after these rascally tricks people are capable of anything, whatever can be conceived horrible and mean.*

Facts and Figures

In 1942 there were admitted to all mental hospitals in the United States a total of 1726 persons who were diagnosed as paranoia or paranoid conditions, constituting 1.5 per cent of all first-admissions. There are more than 10,000 resident patients in the hospitals of the United States suffering from this condition. The ratio of hospitalized men to women patients is 0.6 to 1.0. As a group, these patients have a lower death rate in the hospitals than any other group of mental patients.[12] Most hospitalized paranoids are chronic patients in a healthy physical status who show only slight mental deterioration with the passage of years. Paranoid patients tend to have a better education and to come from a better socioeconomic group than do the other groups of patients. The average age for first-admission for paranoia is 49 years, which is exceeded only by involutional melancholia and the mental diseases of old age.[10] Because of the relatively small number of paranoid cases admitted to mental hospitals, it is impossible to be sure whether the condition occurs more frequently in one or another national, religious, or racial group.

In one study[13] of a group of 400 cases, there was a remarkable amount of marital maladjustment. Of the 268 married persons in the group, 122 had been divorced, plus 41 who had their marriages end in separation or annulment. Of those not married, 35 were sexually promiscuous and 40 were abnormally shy with members of the opposite sex. Approximately half of these 400 patients were said to have shown the same character traits in early life which they exhibited in marked degree after being admitted to the hospital. The traits which they had shown in childhood were described as marked seclusiveness, extreme shyness, inability to accept discipline, temper tantrums, and obsessive or compulsive behavior. The pedigree of 231 of the group was obtained and 58 individuals showed some familial taint, 44 were the direct descendants of persons who had suffered from nervous or mental disease (other than that characterized by paranoia),

* Kraepelin, E., *Manic-Depressive Insanity and Paranoia*, Edinburgh, Livingstone, 1921, 227–228.

while 8 had ancestors who were said to have been paranoid. These figures indicate that the role of heredity in paranoia is no greater or no less than it is assumed to be in dementia praecox.

History and Nature of Concept[14]

Heinroth in 1818 characterized paranoia as a disorder of intellect. In 1845 Griesinger used the term to cover the delusional states following attacks of either mania or melancholia; that is, he believed that the delusional formation was largely dependent upon emotional disturbance. Thus, there were two opposing opinions as to the nature of the paranoid state: one, that it was a disorder of intellect; and the other, that it had its origin in emotional disturbance. This controversy continued until Kraepelin in 1893 distinguished between paranoid dementia praecox and paranoia, as we now understand them. Paranoia, Kraepelin held, was a condition in which there was a growth of a delusional system which had a gradual onset, but which was marked by the permanence of the delusions and by the unfavorable prospects of recovery. He held that true paranoia developed from purely internal, but unknown causes. He further held that in paranoia there were no genuine hallucinations. He noted that paranoia and dementia praecox frequently had a common heredity. Irritable excitement and occasional rough and violent behavior appeared to be the most frequent prepsychotic characteristics. Some patients were said to have been distrustful, self-willed, to have had homosexual tendencies, and to have suffered from nocturnal enuresis.

Freud[3] and the psychoanalysts have held that paranoia is dependent upon homosexual fixation and the repression of homosexual tendencies. The rejection of these tendencies constitutes the basis of the delusional symptoms of the disease. Paranoid delusions of persecution are said to grow out of a thought process which runs as follows: "I must not love him; hence I hate him." But this conflict is not possible, so the paranoiac projects the feeling of hate, saying, "He hates me, which justifies my hating him." This, in turn, becomes, "I do not love him; I hate him because he persecutes me." In the delusions of jealousy the process is said to develop as follows: A man may be disappointed by something his wife has done, and so he goes to a tavern to get drunk, knowing that at the tavern he will meet other men. This meeting is the basic motivation. The thought then becomes, not, "I love a man," but, "She loves him." In consequence, he suspects his wife in relation to all men — men whom he himself had unconsciously sought to love. Another form of conflict underlying the megalomanic delusions is, "I love nothing and no one," which is equivalent to saying, "I love only myself." On this basis grow the delusions of grandeur which may be thought of as an overevaluation of one's own sexual importance.

It cannot be doubted that in some, but not all, cases of paranoia this conflict of ideas and wishes growing out of repressed homosexuality does play an important role. However, a great number of histories of paranoid patients do not reveal any information which would indicate that a homosexual component is the kernel of the delusional system. Probably, some persons suffering from homosexual conflicts develop paranoia or paranoid conditions. Most homosexuals do not, and many paranoid patients give no evidence of a repressed homosexual component.

Meyer holds that the paranoid condition applies to peculiar individuals, rather than to people who are actually ill. He recognizes the following grades in the development of paranoiac reactions:

(a) Uneasy, brooding, sensitive type, with an inability to correct notions and to make concessions;
(b) Appearance of dominant notions, suspicions, or ill balanced aims;
(c) False interpretations, with self-reference, and a tendency to systematization without or within;
(d) Retrospective or hallucinatory falsifications;
(e) Megalomanic developments or deterioration, or intercurrent acute episodes;
(f) At any period antisocial and dangerous reactions may result from the lack of adaptability and excessive assertion of the aberrant personality.*

It seems probable that most of the so-called paranoids are persons who develop delusions in conjunction with some mental disease. These delusions are developed and maintained in an attempt to rationalize the illness in a fashion which makes that ailment tolerable to the patient's own self-regard.

Neurology and Physiology

No one anatomical defect or deviation, no one physiological dysfunction, no one biochemical or bacteriological change has been found to be associated with the paranoid state. It is not uncommon for an individual who is suffering from some physical ailment (such as tuberculosis or rheumatism) to develop pronounced paranoid condi-

---

* Henderson, D. K., and R. D. Gillespie, *A Textbook of Psychiatry.* (5th ed.). New York, Oxford, 1940, 273.

tions. Quite frequently, a patient who is convalescing from influenza, pneumonia, or some other exhausting illness will have such a paranoid episode. It is as if the physical weakness attendant on the illness had released or made possible an exhibition of personality deviation which was beyond all self-control. For example, a dermatologist had pneumonia from which he made an uneventful recovery. When he returned to his office, he was possessed of ideas that his patients were trying to infect him with the very skin diseases which he was attempting to treat. He also believed that they were telling stories to his medical colleagues concerning his own professional incompetence. Realizing the abnormality of his mental condition, he sought aid. After several weeks of talking daily to the psychotherapist and of resting from all his professional duties, his delusions disappeared. He had full memory for the details of the psychotic episode, but had no understanding of why he had developed these peculiar ideas and delusions.

Certain drugs commonly produce delusions. The false interpretations and faulty judgments shown by the drunken man are examples. Different drugs bring forth different sorts of delusions. Whether the type of delusion is directly produced by the drugs, or whether the drugs only act to release latent personality possibilities, is unknown.

Psychology

Delusion is considered by Cameron[2] to be basically a disorder of interpretation. Misinterpretations and their results are discovered and realized by every normal person from childhood on. The continual interaction between personal attitudes and the attitudes of other persons, together with the modifications and corrections which are involved, results in adequate socialized behavior. Much of this interchange depends upon language. The use of language and the increasing store of experience make possible not only greatly increased opportunities for other and more complex misunderstandings, but also provide more frequent opportunities for the correction of misunderstanding. Thus, the normal person builds up a fairly comprehensive system for checking his ideas and beliefs before much damage is done or before there is much need for detailed explanation. Paranoid thinking creates a serious defect in the ability of the individual to alter his perspectives and, as a natural result, there is an accumulation of progressive misunderstandings.

The paranoiac, in falsely ascribing functions, attitudes, and intentions to other persons, does far more than merely project his thoughts upon them. He actually sets up hypothetical relationships (which are to him real) between other persons and himself, and organizes them into a pseudo community made up of true persons and imaginary phenomena. These imaginary functions are formed from the fragments of social behavior of other persons. The fragments are misunderstood by the paranoiac in his thinking.* The actual movements, remarks, and behavior of people about him become cues, signals, threats, and warnings within his pseudo community of plotters.

So long as the paranoiac's thinking is confined to fantasy, hurt feelings, wondering, and suspicious observations, he does not get into any real trouble. As soon as he acts on the basis of his thinking, he implicates others in the consequences of his act, which can no longer be controlled by himself as they were in fantasy. The addition of action to fantasy gives the false impression of a sudden onset of disordered thinking. Actually, the only difference has been that some action was substituted at some point for the fantasy which had been going on for a long time. As a final outcome, either his acts are detrimental to his surroundings and meet retaliation, or his fellows tolerate, ignore, or isolate him because his conduct is such that it cannot be incorporated in their own activities.

Chapter Summary

The different disorders in behavior and mental life considered in this chapter all have as a central point a defect of judgment or belief; that is, they involve *delusion* associated with other forms of psychological disorder. Involutional melancholia usually occurs in the sixth decade of life. It is an agitated depression accompanied by absurd delusions. There are several ways of describing this form of psychological disorder. The symptoms have been related to a rigid personality structure, to an exaggeration of maladjusted habits of thought existing over most of the adult life, to injured feelings of self-importance. Admittedly, these psychological theories are speculative. No adequate physiological or anatomical basis has so far been established. The condition of many such patients is benefited by either electric convulsive therapy or prefrontal lobotomy.

Mixed psychotic state is a descriptive phrase used to classify patients where the symptom picture is atypical, changeable, and mixed. In this group are the benign stupors, perplexity states, and

---

* The general argument of paranoid proof usually takes this form: "Didn't you say this?" "Didn't he say that?" "Didn't she do this?" "Didn't I tell you that?" — "Well, that certainly proves what I thought!" Each statement is true, but the conclusion is completely erroneous.

sensitive reference psychosis. These are all delusional states complicated by other psychotic symptoms.

Paranoia consists of chronic, systematized, delusional ideas which are well integrated with the rest of the mental life of the individual. Paranoia differs from the paranoid type of dementia praecox in that the delusions are well systematized, chronic, and usually unaccompanied by other evidence of psychopathology or dementia. The true paranoid is hospitalized only when his false ideas come into sharp conflict with the rights of others.

REFERENCES

1. Brockhausen, K., "Erbbiologische Untersuchungen über depressive Psychosen des Rückbildungsalters," *Allg. zeit. f. Psychiat.*, 1939, *112*, 179–183.
2. Cameron, N., "The Development of Paranoic Thinking," *Psychol. Rev.*, 1943, *50*, 219–233.
3. Freud, S., "Psychoanalytic Notes upon an Autobiographical Account of a Case of Paranoia (Dementia Paranoides). In S. Freud, *Collected Papers*. Vol. III. London, Hogarth, 1925, 387–470.
4. ———, "Mourning and Melancholia." In S. Freud, *Collected Papers*. Vol. IV. London, Hogarth, 1934, 152–170.
5. Hempill, R. E., and M. Reiss, "Investigations into the Significance of the Endocrines in Involutional Melancholia," *Jour. Ment. Sci.*, 1940, *86*, 1065–1077.
6. Henderson, D. K., and R. D. Gillespie, *A Textbook of Psychiatry* (5th ed.). New York, Oxford, 1940.
7. Hoch, A., *Benign Stupors; The Study of a New Manic-Depressive Reaction*. New York, Macmillan, 1921.
8. Kraepelin, E., *Manic-Depressive Insanity and Paranoia* (trans., R. M. Barclay). Edinburgh, Livingstone, 1921.
9. Kretschmer, E., *A Textbook of Medical Psychology* (trans., E. B. Strauss). London, Oxford, 1934.
10. Landis, C., and J. E. Farwell, "A Trend Analysis of Age at First-Admission, Age at Death, and Years of Residence for State Mental Hospitals, 1913–1941," *Jour. Abn. Soc. Psychol.*, 1944, *39*, 3–23.
11. MacCurdy, J. T., *The Psychology of Emotion*. New York, Harcourt, 1925.
12. Malzberg, B., "Mortality among Patients with Paranoia or Paranoid Conditions," *Human Biol.*, 1936, *8*, 601–606.
13. Miller, C. W., "The Paranoid Syndrome," *Arch. Neurol. Psychiat.*, 1941, *45*, 953–963.
14. Muncie, W., *Psychobiology and Psychiatry*. St. Louis, Mosby, 1939.
15. Titley, W. B., "Prepsychotic Personality of Patients with Involutional Melancholia," *Arch. Neurol. Psychiat.*, 1936. *36*, 19–33.

Chapter XIII

ALCOHOLISM AND ALCOHOLIC MENTAL DISEASE

IS HE crazy because he drinks or does he drink because he is crazy? This question is the essence of the problem of the complicated relationship between inebriety and psychopathology. With the question so posed, we have a fairly clear-cut issue from a psychological standpoint and one on which a good deal of direct evidence is obtainable.

The problems of inebriety as they are related to psychopathology have been treated by many writers during all of the centuries of recorded history. For example, Sebastian Franck in the year 1531 stated that:

Much has been tried against drinking among Germans but nothing has been achieved. The legislators have failed, although they have made promises . . . . [Drinking] is too deeply rooted and sin has become a habit. . . . I deem that no one will be able to eradicate it. . . . [Drink] opens all doors to vice. When the devil has caught us with wine, deprived us of sense and made fools of us, he uses us as his toys for his amusement and drives us from one evil to the other. . . . This man sings, that man weeps. One man wants to fight and the other one wishes to count the money he does not even have. One man becomes abusive, the other one meticulously polite. One man boasts and another one belittles himself. One man falls asleep, another one vomits.*

Most of the popular discussion which is found in the medical, sociological, and psychological literature of today is not too different from observations made and recorded four or five hundred years ago. Little of an observational nature has been added. Classifications which are more precise and, therefore, more useful for our purposes appear regularly.

Chronic Alcoholism, Alcoholic Addiction, and Alcoholic Psychoses

The excessive use of alcoholic beverages brings about a deviation from our accepted standards of normal behavior in some, but not all,

* Franck, S., quoted from E. M. Jellinek, "Classics of Alcoholic Literature," *Quart. Jour. Stud. Alc.*, 1941, 2, 392–395.

persons. It is considered abnormal when alcohol produces marked psychopathological symptoms. The symptoms which result from excessive use of alcohol are abnormal (in the sense in which we have used this word) since a sizable percentage of our general population at one time or another during their lives imbibe large quantities of alcoholic beverages and do not become either chronic users or true alcoholic addicts.

A distinction has been made between chronic alcoholism and alcoholic addiction, but it is not always possible to adhere to this distinction, nor is it always of any great importance to do so. In general, chronic alcoholism is defined as those recognizable physical and psychological changes following the prolonged use of alcoholic beverages. Alcoholic addiction is defined as an uncontrollable craving for alcohol. The outstanding criterion of the addiction is its obsessional nature. Either chronic alcoholism or addiction may exist alone or with the other.

Chronic alcoholism or addiction usually refers to a psychopathological state which is uncomplicated by any other form of neurosis or psychosis. Alcoholism may occur in conjunction with almost every type of mental disorder. These conditions are termed *symptomatic alcoholic states*, in that the alcoholism is regarded as a symptom of a more basic disorder which, if remedied, would at the same time correct the alcoholism. The excessive use of alcohol will complicate any form of psychosis or neurosis, adding unique features to each.

Causes of Alcoholic Addiction

Causes of addiction include personality, heredity, general constitution, psychotic or psychopathic tendencies, environmental factors, occupation, physiological tolerance, and the drinking customs of the community. There are many "reasons" given for alcoholic addiction but, for the most part, these reasons only state what the drinker hopes to achieve through the use of the beverage. Reasons such as escape, revolt, relief from tension, pleasure, realization of daydreams, social and gregarious tendencies, or inflation of the ego are commonly mentioned. These are all more or less abstract and superficial. For real understanding of the fundamental process of addiction, it is necessary to go much deeper both physiologically and psychologically.

Explanations of alcoholic addiction in terms of the physiology of the organism have stressed the effect produced by alcohol on metabolism, the accumulation of toxins which lead to a pathological "thirst" or craving, metabolic poisoning, allergic addiction, and possible thyroid disturbance. While these physiological changes afford some explanation of the process of habituation to alcohol, there is no satisfactory physiological evidence available to explain the factors which determine excessive drinking in the first place.

Personality Factors in Alcoholic Addiction

Many present-day explanations refer primarily to the personality of the individual as the basis of addiction. The importance of these personality factors is probably overemphasized. Personality is one of the determining agents of addiction, but it must be evaluated in combination with biological, physiological, and chemical evidence. There is no known unitary constellation of personality traits which leads, of necessity, to addiction. Social and cultural forces must act on any type of constitution and personality to bring about either addiction or abnormal drinking.

Psychological studies which have stressed the personality structure and function of alcoholics are exceedingly varied in nature and in scope. Psychometric studies, psychoanalytic formulations, collated clinical pictures, and statistical summaries have all been presented and all are of value. Certain factors must be kept in mind in evaluating personality studies of alcoholic individuals. In the first place, the reasons for drinking, special personality traits, and manifestations of drunkenness have to be kept apart in the reporting and in our evaluation of the reports. The interchanging of any one of these three factors leads to confusion and contradiction. Second, studies which have been made on individuals suffering from the alcoholic psychoses are not representative of the personality of the alcoholic addict. These psychotics are but a fraction, an unrepresentative fraction, of the total alcoholic population. In the third place, there are two quite different types of addicts — those whose addiction is incidental to social or occupational drinking over a long period of time, and those whose addiction is entrenched in the deeper layers of personality. These two groups must be kept separate in our thinking, since there is true psychological difference between them. Lastly, no psychological test, method, or procedure has been demonstrated to be of more than indicative value in dealing with alcoholics. Such persons are usually uncooperative, evasive, and unreliable when one tries to study them with the usual psychological and psychiatric methods.

Wittman,[9] making use of various methods, has studied the developmental and personality characteristics of chronic alcoholics and alcoholic addicts, excluding the alcoholic psychotics. She reported that in many of these persons the following characteristics may be found:

1. A domineering but idealized and beloved mother and a stern, autocratic father whom as a child the patient feared.

2. A marked degree of strict, unquestioning obedience demanded in family life, with but little personal freedom permitted.

3. Marked insecurity shown by an insistent feeling of need for religious security and a strong feeling of sin and guilt.

4. Marked interest in the opposite sex with many love affairs but poor marital adjustment.

5. Lack of self-consciousness with a particular ability to get along with and be socially acceptable to others.

6. Occasional depressions and periods of marked unhappiness.

7. A keyed-up emotional level; work done under high nervous tension.

Generally speaking, Wittman's studies have made an interesting contribution to our knowledge of the abnormal drinker as he describes or reveals himself after years of overindulgence in alcohol. Whether or not any of the fundamental traits of the prealcoholic period have been indicated in these studies is unknown. Furthermore, we have no way of knowing the degree to which they are specific to the alcoholic addict and not merely representative of the difficulties of any maladjusted person.

There is a wide divergence of opinion among psychoanalysts concerning the basic personality structure of the alcoholic addict.[3] This divergence probably comes from two major considerations: no individual analyst sees very many alcoholic patients in his lifetime, and alcoholics are among themselves a very heterogeneous pyschological group. Analysts have mentioned repressed homosexuality, oral eroticism, mother fixation, castration anxiety, and disguised suicidal tendencies as basic drives leading to alcoholism. Such mechanisms are used to explain a wide variety of both "normal" and pathological personality manifestations, so that little of positive differentiating value can be gained from these formulations.

Cimbal[2] made biographical records of the life history of hundreds of individual drinkers. From these records he formulated four groupings which have been of value in classifying the addict. In the first group there is a family history of degeneration in behavior and life adjustment in successive generations. Persons with such a history tend to become *decadent* drinkers in the same way as others become gamblers, adventurers, or narcotic addicts. In general, this group is recruited from families which have "gone to seed." A second group he termed *impassioned* drinkers. These individuals are psychologically and psychosexually immature and their striving for maturity leads to tensions and conflicts from which they seek relief through the development of alcoholic addiction. The third group is made up of the spineless, *stupid* drinkers who may be either of low intellect or of very submissive character. The fourth group he termed the *self-aggrandizing* drinker. This is a form of ambition without energy. Such individuals have a craving for power and ascendance in a very primitive, undeveloped form, characterized by weak will power. When more or less intoxicated, they feel important and at ease. A fifth group, according to Jellinek,[5] should be added to complete this descriptive classification of the true addicts, namely, the *poverty* drinker. Such persons are the "down-and-out Bowery Bums," unemployed, unemployable, without hope or ambition, whose sole gratification in existence is drunkenness.

As we have said, a major distinction must be made between true addicts so far discussed, and those individuals whose alcoholism is most probably an associated symptom of a psychosis or neurosis. Often it is difficult or even impossible to establish whether the alcoholism is merely another symptom of an already existing and developing psychosis, or whether the psychotic behavior is directly attributable to the chronic alcoholic state. Usually the deprivation from alcohol which results when such a person is hospitalized gives us the clue as to whether the condition is true addiction or symptomatic. If it is addiction, then the outstanding psychopathology tends to disappear on withdrawal of the alcohol.

Still another group might be termed *social* or *gregarious* drinkers. Here are classified the easygoing and rather unsophisticated individuals for whom drinking is a form of relaxation — the high-pressure salesman who uses drinking to promote business and falls a victim of his own methods; the social, compensating drinkers who are possessed of inferiority feelings of which they are more or less conscious, and who become chronic alcoholics while deliberately attempting to overcome a felt social inadequacy; and the occupational drinkers who are employed in breweries, distilleries, barrooms, and the like, where there is a constant exposure to alcoholic beverages to which they fall victim.

Role of Social Factors in Alcoholism

Social factors operating to create alcoholic addiction or chronic alcoholism have long been stressed by reformers and have received some attention from scientific investigators. Poverty is frequently blamed, but its effect has been greatly overrated since there is no evidence which would indicate any true correlation between poverty, as such, and the consumption of alcohol. Unemployment, long working hours, and inadequate opportunities for recreation and leisure have all been advertised as factors leading to chronic alcoholism. Undoubtedly, all of these factors enter into the picture, but it is most doubtful that they are of basic importance; rather, they are all indicators of a deeper difficulty.

The general attitude of the community toward alcohol is a major factor in determining the differences in frequency of alcoholism in men and in women. Different nations show a wide variation in the male-female ratio of inebriety. In the United States the ratio is approximately six men to one woman; in England, two to one; in Switzerland, twelve to one; and in Norway, twenty-three to one. This national variation, as well as the consistent and universal excess of men inebriates in contrast to women, can be attributed in part — though not entirely — to the prevailing attitude of the community. Much more tolerance, many more excuses, and much less condemnation are extended in American and western European cultures to men who drink to excess than to women. In most social groups a man may become drunken without any particular social stigma, but a woman who is known to drink to excess loses social standing and meets with very severe disapproval. The social attitude toward drinking among men has been termed by Myerson[8] *social ambivalence.* He pointed out how society on one hand praises drinking, including it in social and religious customs, and as a sign of good fellowship; and on the other hand regards with mixed contempt and amusement the drunken man. Society does not extend this ambivalent attitude to women — only contempt and scorn tempered but slightly with pity, expresses the attitude, conscious or unconscious, of our society toward the woman who is alcoholic. This is not intended to be a statement of morals, but a description of the basic attitude of present-day society.

Therapeutic Outcome

Alcoholics — chronic, addicted, or psychotic — are very difficult to cure by any method whether physical or psychological. The alcoholic, either with or without psychosis, usually makes a recovery or remission of sorts, but all investigators agree that the majority of recoveries are temporary. Of those individuals having received one or another variety of therapy for alcoholism, somewhere between 7 and 30 per cent remain total abstainers for as long as two years after treatment.

Alcoholic Psychoses

In addition to chronic alcoholics and the alcoholic addicts, there is a fairly large group (5054 with psychoses and 6283 without psychoses, among first-admissions to American mental hospitals in 1942) in which a definite psychopathology justifies the designation of alcoholic psychosis. Certain of these psychopathological states may be due to a direct effect of alcohol on the brain. Since only a small proportion of drinkers develop alcoholic psychoses, it is usually held that psychotic drinkers become psychotic because of some underlying factor, such as infection, injury, nutritional imbalance, or genetic predisposition. Most alcoholic psychotics are admitted for the first time to mental hospitals when they are between the ages of 30 and 60 years and have been drinking to excess for 15 to 20 years. It is estimated that there are between 9000 and 10,000 persons being treated in institutions of the United States for alcoholism at the present time, and of these, about half are suffering from an alcoholic psychosis. According to present expectancy, 3 of every 1000 children born alive will spend some part of their lives in a state hospital because of an alcoholic psychosis. Of every 100 such patients under treatment during any one year, 21 per cent will leave the hospital in an improved condition. If a group of such patients is followed over a period of years, it will be found that about 40 per cent of the group will still be in the hospital at the end of the first year, and that 6 per cent of those who have left the hospital will never be readmitted to a mental hospital. Of the original group, about 20 per cent will still be in the hospital at the end of 5 years, about 15 per cent at the end of 10 years, and about 12 per cent at the end of 15 years.

That there is a wide variation in the incidence of the alcoholic psychoses among the various national and racial groups as they come to the mental hospitals is shown by Table 2.[7]

TABLE 2. FIRST–ADMISSION RATES FOR ALCOHOLIC PSYCHOSIS OF THOSE BORN IN VARIOUS FOREIGN NATIONS AND AMERICAN BORN NEGROES PER 100,000 OF THE SAME NATIONALITY IN NEW YORK STATE HOSPITALS, 1929–1931.   (Not Standardized for Age)

Nationality	First-Admission Rate
Irish	25.6
Scandinavian	7.8
Italian	4.8
English	4.3
German	3.8
Jews of all nationalities	0.5
Negroes (American-born)	107.5

The reasons for this wide variation among those of different national or racial origin are a matter of debate. Social factors such as the attitude of the group toward alcoholic indulgence, differences in economic status which may favor or disfavor the admission to public institutions, and possible genetic variations in susceptibility have been put forward as explanations. The real answer must await a thoroughgoing survey directed at this particular point.

Prohibition

The effect of national prohibition on the mental health of the community offers evidence of the complicated nature of the alcohol problem.[6] It was believed that total prohibition would materially decrease the *number of alcoholic psychotics.* As Fig. 6 shows, it did. The average

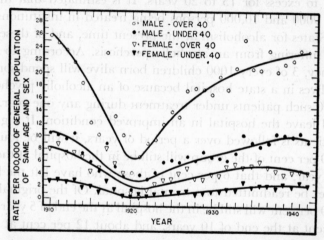

Fig. 6. The trend of the rate of first-admissions for alcoholic psychoses to all New York State mental hospitals, 1909–1942, for men and for women, aged 20 to 40 and 40 to 60 years.[6]

admission rate per 100,000 of the general population of the same age and sex for the years 1911–1915 was 23. During 1920–1924, the first years of prohibition when the law was best enforced, the average rate was 15. The rate gradually rose after 1926 until it leveled off to an average of 26 between 1935 and 1940. The temporary decrease was principally due to a sharp decline in the number of men aged forty to sixty who were diagnosed as suffering from alcoholic psychoses. Now, if there had been a true decrease in the number of psychotics, it should have shown itself, not only in the trend curve for the occurrence of alcoholic psychoses, but there should also be a dip in the curves representing all first-admissions, male, aged twenty to forty and aged forty to sixty, since the shortage of alcoholic psychotics should have decreased the total rate. As Fig. 7 indicates, this is not true. We can only

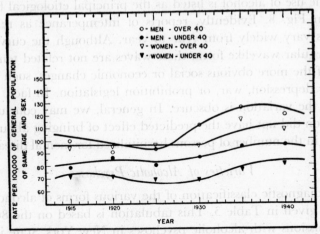

Fig. 7. *The trend of the rate of first-admissions for all mental diseases to all New York State mental hospitals, 1913–1943, for men and for women, aged 20 to 40 and 40 to 60 years.*

conclude that the rate of first-admissions to mental hospitals was not affected by prohibition. Probably the usual sort of psychotic persons, who were formerly admitted to the hospitals following an alcoholic

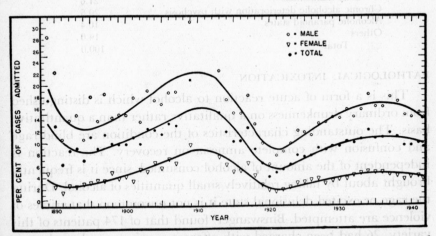

Fig. 8. *The trend of the percentage of patients admitted to all New York State mental hospitals, 1889–1943, male, female, and total, for whom it was stated that the intemperate use of alcohol was the principal "cause" or precipitating factor leading to hospitalization.*[6]

bout, came to the hospitals during the days of the enforcement of prohibition but without a history of recent alcoholism.

The trend between 1889 and 1943 of first-admission patients, in whom the use of alcohol is listed as the principal etiological factor, is shown in Fig. 8. Evidently, reports of intemperance as related to psychosis vary widely from year to year. Although the curve shows such a regular wavelike form, these waves are not related temporally to any of the more obvious social or economic changes, such as prosperity or depression, war, or prohibition legislation. In fact, the real cause of the variation is obscure. In general, we may conclude that prohibition did not have the predicted effect of bringing about a true decrease in the number of persons hospitalized for mental disease.

Varieties of Alcoholic Psychoses

The diagnostic classification of the various forms of alcoholic psychoses is given in Table 3. This tabulation is based on the 868 total first-admissions with alcoholic psychoses in New York State in 1939.

TABLE 3. PERCENTAGE DISTRIBUTION OF THE ALCOHOLIC PSYCHOSES IN FIRST-ADMISSION PATIENTS, NEW YORK STATE HOSPITALS, 1939

	Percentage of All Alcoholic Psychoses
Pathological intoxication	11.8
Delirium tremens	11.2
Korsakoff's psychosis	10.5
Alcoholic hallucinosis	21.6
Chronic alcoholic deterioration with psychosis	20.5
Alcoholic paranoid states	10.4
Others	14.0
Total	100.0

PATHOLOGICAL INTOXICATION

This is a form of acute reaction to alcohol which is distinguished from ordinary drunkenness on a qualitative rather than a quantitative basis. The outstanding characteristics of the condition are blind rage and confusion with complete amnesia on recovery. The reaction is independent of the amount of alcohol consumed, since it is frequently brought about by taking relatively small quantities of alcohol. During the rage or excited delusional state it is not uncommon that crimes of violence are attempted. Binswanger[1] found that of 174 patients of this variety, 26 had been charged with offenses or crimes, such as threats, manslaughter, attempted murder, arson, burglary, or sexual assault. The condition may occur in normal persons whose tolerance to alcohol is temporarily lowered by overfatigue, prolonged exposure to heat, or emotional stress; but it is more common in physically inferior and emotionally unstable persons with a permanent lack of resistance to alcohol.

This peculiarity of behavior may be illustrated by the case of a plumber who was usually regarded as eccentric but harmless. On occasion he would become depressed and grouchy. In such a mood he would go to a barroom and drink one or two glasses of whiskey. He would then suddenly beat his fist on the bar and declare that he could whip any man in the room, any man in town, any man in the world. He would shout that he was all-powerful, and if any bystander made a harmless gesture or remark he would misinterpret it as a contradiction and would become assaultive. He would throw bottles or glasses, and once in his rage he attempted suicide by slashing himself with broken glass. When the police arrived and took him to jail, he quickly fell into a deep sleep from which he awakened with no memory whatsoever of the entire episode.

DELIRIUM TREMENS

This disorder was described and named by Thomas Sutton in 1813. These patients, usually after a prolonged drinking bout, become anxious, restless, fearful, have headaches, vertigo, and often have convulsions. They are disturbed by visual hallucinations in which unpleasant objects are seen, which change in size, form, and color. These objects are usually fast-moving animals, such as white mice, dogs, insects, snakes, and even pink elephants. There is also spatial and temporal disorientation; the patients believe that the hospital is a tavern, palace, or church, or that they are living in some past time, or they mistake the doctors and nurses for childhood friends or school acquaintances. They are very suggestible. They can be induced to read from a blank piece of paper or interpret spots on the wall as pictures according to suggestions. Immediate memory and learning ability are greatly impaired, but remote memory does not seem to suffer.

This condition rarely lasts longer than four or five days, after which the excitement gives way to deep sleep. When the patient awakens, he feels rested and has but few symptoms, such as tremor and impaired memory remaining. Many of those who go through an attack of delirium tremens do not resume heavy drinking for two or three months because they are frightened, but most of them eventually return to their former habits. Since there is no immunity, they sooner or later return to the hospital with a new attack. Delirium tremens seems to develop mainly in those who are of healthy, normal family stock. They have an extraordinarily high tolerance for alcohol and can drink heavily for many years without any marked ill effects. Consequently, they believe they can continue to drink heavily with impunity. Their resistance is suddenly broken, often by the strain of disease or injury, and the violent reactions of delirium tremens follow. Formerly there was a rather high death rate, but modern medical treatment has reduced this to 4 or 5 per cent.

KORSAKOFF'S PSYCHOSIS

In this condition the chronic alcoholic seems to struggle to fill the gaps in his memory to an extent that his whole conduct and mode of expression are disordered by these efforts. The disorder was first described by the Russian psychiatrist, Korsakoff, in 1887. His description of the early states of the disease is as follows:

In the beginning it is difficult to notice any mental disturbance in conversation with this patient. He gives the impression of a person who has command of his mental capacity; he speaks with deliberation, draws the proper conclusions from given premises, plays chess or cards; in brief he comports himself as a mentally normal person. Only after a long conversation can one notice that the patient mixes up events and does not keep in mind things which happen around him. He does not, for instance, remember whether he has eaten or whether he has gotten up from bed. Sometimes the patient forgets immediately what has happened. One may have visited him and left him for a minute and on returning, he has not the least idea that one has been there before. Such patients may look at one and the same page for hours because what they have read does not remain in their memory. They may repeat the same thing twenty times without being aware of the repetition. . . . The patient does not remember persons with whom he is in continual contact. He does not remember his attending physician or the nurses, and assures one every time that it is the first meeting. It is remarkable, however, that these patients who forget everything that has just happened are usually able to recall events which happened before their illness. Everything that happens during the illness or shortly before it vanishes from their memory. This, however, is the rule in the more typical cases only. In others remote memory is also lost.*

Such patients tend increasingly to fill in gaps in their reminiscences with odd snatches from events which are occurring in their immediate surroundings. This tendency to bring together irrelevant and unconnected ideas and events is termed *confabulation* and is one of the most conspicuous features of the condition.

Many experimental studies[5] have been made on patients of this

---

* Korsakoff, S., quoted from E. M. Jellinek, *Alcoholic Addiction and Chronic Alcoholism.* New Haven, Yale University Press, 1942, 129.

type. The general conclusion is that the memory disturbance is more apparent than real. The apparent memory loss is usually attributed to the inability to form new associations. This inability makes it difficult to find relations between past and present experiences or to distinguish between them. The examination of the brains of persons who died in the course of Korsakoff's psychosis has revealed no gross organic damage such as might be expected to account for the marked symptoms.

ALCOHOLIC HALLUCINOSIS AND ALCOHOLIC PARANOID STATES

These two conditions constitute about 30 per cent of the alcoholic psychoses. So far as hallucinations and delusions are concerned, they are similar to those shown in schizophrenia and paranoia. However, they occur in inebriates only after many years of heavy drinking. It is possible that such persons possess the latent possibility of these psychoses which continued inebriety finally makes manifest. In the alcoholic paranoid states there are ideas of persecution; in alcoholic hallucinosis there is a rather sudden onset in which the main symptoms are auditory hallucinations. The voices which are heard are usually identified as coming from some definite person. At the beginning the voices make simple statements. Later they become reproachful and criticizing. In many instances the hallucinations are heard as conversations of a number of persons talking about the patient in the third person. Although visual hallucinations commonly occur, they play a smaller role in the psychopathology than the voices. Suicidal attempts and attempts at self-injury are often the result of directions received through the hallucinations.

CHRONIC ALCOHOLIC DETERIORATION

The continued use of excessive amounts of alcohol over a long period of time may produce a characteristic physical and mental disorder. Bleuler provided the following description of chronic alcoholic deterioration.

In the psychological field there is ethical degeneration, dulling of the finer sentiments, and brutality. This is the picture usually given, but it is not quite true. The originally decent alcoholic remains attached to his club and is very sympathetic with the misfortunes of his fellow men. He can become enthusiastic about ethical aims. He not only expresses himself with fine sentiments but may really experience them. If he is an artist he may create works which are expressions of fine sentiments, ethic and tact. Nevertheless the descriptions of his brutality and impulsive actions are not without foundation, for he does behave brutally in the presence of affects and under certain conditions. This is especially likely to occur at home, where he is subject to the overt or implied reproaches of the family; or at work, in which he cannot persist, or whenever a difference of opinion arises. The fact that these alcoholics, when the occasion arises, have at their disposal the most beautiful sentiments, and actually genuine ones, makes them especially dangerous, because they do not dissimulate these feelings.

The most important change of the affects and sentiments of the chronic alcoholics is their lability. With this is coupled a great affect tone to all experience which makes the affect master over the will and common sense. This lability of affect makes consistent goal-behavior impossible. Will power is markedly diminished. The euphoric attitude makes it possible to perceive misery as something good, or, at least, not very bad. The exaggerated ego reference forms the basis of the suspiciousness of the alcoholic. The memory is impaired. Much of the behavior is dependent on the oblique position of the alcoholic toward his surroundings. In spite of his aggressiveness it is easily seen that he is actually on the defensive in relation to those who do not indulge in alcohol. Orientation remains intact in the uncomplicated cases. Jealousy is a frequent manifestation. *

Summary

The material which has been presented in this chapter illustrates clearly how both opportunity and predisposition play differing roles in different persons who are alcoholic. There is good reason to believe that the various syndromes constituting the alcoholic conditions are closely allied to certain of the psychoses which depend in part on an hereditary basis. Pathological intoxication and delirium tremens seem to depend on an accentuation of constitutional and social conditions. In general, alcoholism can and does occur in all human groups and in all personality types. In some national groups and in some personality types it acts as an accentuating agent, in others as a more or less incidental social symptom.

The psychoanalytic explanations which have attempted to go deeper into personality structure than any other type of investigation have not shed too much light on the problem. This is due to the fact that relatively few alcoholics have been studied by the analytic method and also that there are widely divergent kinds of alcoholic persons.

In brief, there is no single explanation of alcoholism. Indeed, there is no systematic viewpoint which will include any large fraction of the alcoholic cases. If there is any human disorder which can be truly said to be of multiple etiology, it is alcoholism in all its diverse forms.

* Bleuler, E., quoted from E. M. Jellinek, *ibid.*, 146–147.

REFERENCES

1. Binswanger, H., "Klinische und charakterologische Untersuchungen an pathologisch Berauschten," *Zeit. f. ges. Neurol. Psychiat.*, 1935, *152*, 703–737.
2. Cimbal, W., "Trinkerfürsorge als Teil der Verwahrlostenfürsorge," *Allg. Zeit. Psychiat.*, 1926, *84*, 52–86.
3. Crowley, R. M., "Psychoanalytic Literature in Drug Addiction and Alcoholism," *Psychoanal. Rev.*, 1939, *26*, 37–54.
4. Franck, S., quoted from E. M. Jellinek, "Classics of Alcoholic Literature," *Quart. Jour. Stud. Alc.*, 1941, *2*, 391–395.
5. Jellinek, E. M., *Alcohol Addiction and Chronic Alcoholism.* New Haven, Yale University Press, 1942.
6. Landis, C., and J. F. Cushman, "The Relation of National Prohibition to Mental Disease," *Quart. Jour. Stud. Alc.*, 1945, *6*, 527–534.
7. ———, and J. D. Page, *Modern Society and Mental Disease.* New York, Rinehart, 1938.
8. Myerson, A., "Alcohol: A Study of Social Ambivalence," *Quart. Jour. Stud. Alc.*, 1940, *1*, 13–20.
9. Wittman, P., "Diagnosis and Analysis of Temperament for a Group of Alcoholics Compared with Controls," *Elgin Papers*, 1939, *3*, 94–99.

Chapter XIV

GENERAL PARESIS

GENERAL PARESIS is also called "general paralysis of the insane," "softening of the brain," "dementia paralytica," "cerebral syphilis," or "syphilitic meningoencephalitis," depending on the authority who is being followed or the symptoms which are being emphasized. The earliest descriptions of this condition were made by Willis in 1672 and by Haslam in 1798. Bayle in 1822 gave the first detailed observations of the relationship between the physical and mental symptoms, which makes up the separate, distinct disease as it is recognized today. Essentially, general paresis is a form of progressive motor paralysis accompanied by a peculiar form of mental deterioration.

Most psychopathologists cite general paresis as the outstanding example of a mental disorder whose true nature was clarified by experimental research methods. The symptoms, both physical and mental, are fairly clear-cut and not usually confused with those of other mental or physical diseases. There are laboratory tests (Wassermann, Kahn, colloidal gold) which confirm the diagnosis made on the basis of the physical and mental symptoms. The course of the physical and mental changes is relatively predictable. The cause is known, namely the invasion of the central nervous system by the spirocheta pallida (the organism which causes syphilis) with a consequent destruction of the tissue of the brain itself. Methods of treatment have been discovered, which are fairly adequate in a majority of the cases, and the action of the methods is understood.

The history[10] of the speculation concerning the nature of general paresis is most interesting. During the eighteenth and nineteenth centuries this condition was said by various investigators to be due to alcoholism, use of tobacco or coffee, or to moral excesses. These interpretations were based on the early observation that the disease occurs much more frequently in men than in women. Others said that it was an accompaniment of mental excitement and overwork or of outstanding intellect, since its occurrence was frequently observed among government officials, military officers, poets, and musicians. Others believed that differences in the climate had an influence, since it was rather infrequent in the south of France and Italy and much more common in northern Germany. Austin[1] in 1859 held that the disease was due to powerful impressions of a painful character which were inflicted upon the moral sense of the patient. Still other investigators held that the disease was due to sexual excesses, particularly to masturbation.

Esmarch and Jessen in 1857 proposed the idea that syphilis was the essential cause. This idea caused a great deal of controversy; but it was gradually accepted by the beginning of the twentieth century that there was a high degree of association between general paresis and syphilitic infection.

When Schaudinn and Hoffmann[8] in 1905 first identified the spirocheta pallida under the microscope, the way was clear for the understanding of the basic relationship. The final proof was provided in 1913 by Noguchi and Moore[7] who first demonstrated the presence of the spirochete in the brain tissue of the paretic patient. Since that time repeated investigations have amply verified that general paresis is a syphilitic infection of the central nervous system.

Facts and Figures

General paresis furnishes 9 per cent of the first-admission patients and 6 per cent of the resident patients of the mental hospitals of the United States. The first-admission rate is 36 per 100,000 of the general population aged 30 to 75 years. The average age at first-admission is 44 years for men and 42 for women. The ratio of male to female patients is 3.5 to 1.0; of urban to rural 2.9 to 1.0; of Negroes to whites 4.1 to 1.0; of Jews to non-Jews 0.6 to 1.0.

The first-admission rates for this disease have gradually declined during the past forty years. This decrease is due to better and more widespread medical treatment of primary syphilitic infection. One survey made in Denmark failed to find a single case of general paresis in a large sample of cases that had received adequate medical treatment during the initial stages of syphilitic infection.

Since 1920 there has been a marked increase in the rates of remission and recovery from this disease. Where formerly 80 to 90 per cent of paretics died within the first four years following onset, after a rapid dementia and physical deterioration, the picture is now reversed with only 5 to 10 per cent of treated patients dying during a corresponding period.

Case History

CASE 18: Mr. P, aged fifty-three, was a well-known attorney. He had been very successful in his profession and had enjoyed high and fast living. He knew all the best people, belonged to many clubs and political organizations. He had traveled extensively. He was noted for the fact that he was always very well dressed, usually appearing at court wearing striped trousers, a black cutaway coat and a flower in his buttonhole.

The first abnormal symptoms were noticeable about two years before he was admitted to the hospital. His wife said, on thinking it over, that the first unusual behavior which she could remember was that of certain peculiarities in dress. He had been very careful about all his color combinations but, about two years previous to coming to the hospital, he began wearing colored shirts with peculiar neckties and a different style hat of a rather conspicuous nature. Subsequently, he began drinking more heavily, became extremely egotistical and domineering, and began to start flirtations with waitresses and show girls whom he had previously scorned.

Two months previous to his entry into the hospital, he showed very bad lapses of memory. He would forget things that were said to him from day to day and ignore his courtroom appointments. He became very petty over small items and, at the same time, he would talk about buying automobiles, diamond necklaces, and mink coats for his many women friends. He seemed to lack interest in his work and neglected several cases in court to the extent that he was reprimanded by the judge. On the last such occasion he seemed to realize that something was wrong, and on the next day did not come to his office at all. He was found in a low-class barroom talking loudly and in a grandiose fashion, with his clothing mussed and dirty.

His wife and chauffeur were able to persuade him to get into his automobile, whereupon he was driven to the hospital. Although he resisted vigorously, he was admitted and on examination found to be suffering from general paresis. He was of dilapidated appearance, untidy and unkempt, and kept moving about in a mechanical, stilted fashion. He was disoriented for time and place, saying that he was in a hospital in a different city and giving the incorrect day and month. At times he merely responded to questioning with short sentences; at other times he was quite verbose and expansive, rambling a great deal in his speech. Occasionally, he would turn and walk out of the room in the middle of a sentence. All of his spontaneous remarks were either irritable or grandiose. He said that he made a million a year and had a billion stored away. He said that he was a famous lawyer, engineer, architect, musician, and scientist. He denied that he had ever been ill and said that he had been placed in the hospital under false pretenses by criminals who wished to get even with him, or by his business associates who wanted to get control of his riches. He had no insight into his own condition. When asked what schools he had attended, he recited, "Public school No. 3, 9, 15, 11, 27, St. Ann's, West Point, Oxford, Harvard, Paris, and the Medal of Honor."

During the first six weeks in the hospital his condition remained about the same. He would attempt to walk about the ward entirely nude except for his hat and a cigar. He tossed his clothing and toilet articles out the window. At the table he would mix all of the food on his plate into a stew and eat it rapidly with a large spoon. He would propose to the nurse on the ward three or four times a day, offering her a million dollars and three automobiles. He would ask for a pencil and paper and would write what he called telegrams to his friends, asking them to come and rescue him or to bring him food, whiskey, or money.

Fever therapy was instituted and after three weeks he was much improved. He was tidier, better natured, and talked more rationally. He remained cheerful and cooperative, was not nearly so grandiose, and seemed to realize that he was ill, although he had no insight into his previous condition or his present mental sickness. He slowly improved in physical and mental status; however, although quiet and cooperative, he never regained complete insight nor was his mentality at all comparable to what it had been before the onset of the illness.

Psychopathology

A *loss of judgment* is one of the first abnormalities to appear and one which continues with a varying degree of severity throughout the course of the illness. The paretics will not notice contradictions or unclearnesses in their own thinking or in the conversation of others. In doing problems they are distracted by the sound of the numbers $(9 \times 9 = 99)$ or will give any numerical answer that occurs to them. In reading, they often do not notice omissions or distortions, nor do they attempt to correct such errors. They will repeat the content of a story or an event in their life very incompletely with alterations and omissions, and without realization of the senselessness of what they have just said. They complacently bring forth some absurd plan, disposing of obvious objections in an irrational fashion. They will tell deluded stories and seem unable to pursue an ordered train of thought, so ending up with senseless conclusions which have no connection with either their original idea or with the surrounding circumstances. These patients gradually lose their grasp of common sense and everyday logic, as well as their ability to observe facts and to distinguish properly between their own imagination and actual occurrences. Mentally they seem to be in a sort of dream world in which their own ideas, wishes, fears, and everyday occurrences are mixed up, with no distinction between fact and fancy.

It is the *intellectual weakness* and *deterioration* which gives paresis its own particular mental quality. There is seldom a connected, delusional system of ideas which exists more than a month or so. Usually, the most diverse ideas and delusions get entangled with each other, without regard to obvious contradictions and discrepancies, so that the senseless and fantastic ideas of the paretic are carried far beyond the limits of probability or even possibility. The activity of their imagination seems to far outrun their powers of self-criticism, making the wealth and exuberance of their changing delusions enormous.

Disorders of *memory* are usually profound. They are as severe as in any form of dementia but show marked improvement if the patient responds successfully to treatment. The paretic forgets the more recent happenings. He may not remember what occurred to him yesterday, what letters he wrote last evening, or what the doctor told him this morning. As the general deterioration continues, the patient may seem fairly alert and intelligent but cannot remember what he did 15 minutes previously or whether he has ever seen his physician or nurse before, although he may have been in their care over a period of months. Memories of the more remote past are fairly well retained, although obvious fabrication sometimes enters into the account which the patient will give of his childhood.

The *loss of time relations* is quite marked. The paretic is unable to organize his everyday perceptions into any linked chain of memory images, so that he cannot measure the interval between events or arrange the past in definite periods of time. He cannot recall the sequence or interrelationships of occurrences. Time limits melt into each other and are blotted out. Although he may be able to give the year of his marriage and the age of his oldest child, he still may be unable to state how long he has been married or how long his child has been in school. He seems unable to make use of such items as the appearance of the ground, position of the sun, leaves on the trees, or temperature to orient himself in time. In spite of snow on the ground and heat in the radiators, he will say it is July when it is January.

A marked and often important mental change is *difficulty in calculating*. The patient may retain the ability to recite multiplication tables but cannot make use of them in doing simple calculations. He will make arithmetic errors when required to carry numbers in memory, as, for instance, in the subtraction of 15 from 73, he may give the answer of 68.

There is also a continuous and progressive *loss in the store of ideas*. This loss is more in the connections between ideas than in the single elements themselves. Occasionally, for short periods of time a patient will be able to give surprisingly correct answers regarding specific events, but will be unable to recall the connections between them. Very frequently the missing links between ideas and memories are filled in by pure imagination. This filling out is for the most part drawn from the environment and has only a superficial and temporary relationship to the immediate production. Such transient connections are quickly replaced by new ones which arise from the sense perception, thoughts, and moods of the patient. He is highly distractible, so that any accidental interruption diverts him to an entirely new train of aimless, confused thought. At other times a monotony of thought is marked; the patient will talk repetitiously about his few remaining ideas. He seems to have forgotten what he has just said or is unable to suppress those few ideas that come into his mind.

The patient's *disposition* is affected in much the same way as his intellect. In the earlier months he usually shows an increased excitability. He will be changeable, easily angered, sulky, emotionally excited

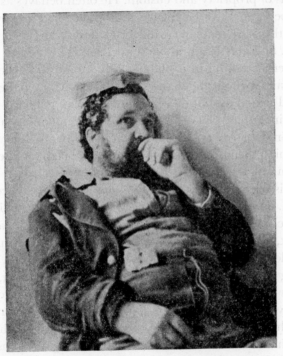

PLATE 10

ELATED PARETIC PATIENT[9]

at small events, will lose control of his temper or will have fits of crying and wailing with self-pity. There is a decrease in the deeper and finer feelings. He will be careless in the face of danger, lack foresight with respect to approaching difficulty, and be quickly reassured after severe misfortune. The pleasure which he once had in reading, art, or music, or the satisfaction of home life and friends, gives way to indifference and slovenliness. Abrupt alteration in emotions is common. In the midst of happiness there will be a sudden storm of tears, or in the middle of a depressed or depressing account of his illness he will respond, in a childish fashion of delight, to an unexpected joke or small gift.

These changes add up to an *alteration in character and personality*. In place of stability, independence, and clear thinking, there is a marked indecision, instability, and a foolish, headstrong waywardness. As voluntary activity is reduced, suggestibility increases. He is credulous and trustful, falling victim to the most obvious frauds and extortions.

In the behavior of the paretic there is an increasing disregard for the demands of propriety and custom. He often behaves as though intoxicated, being tactless, lacking in inhibitions, and grossly offensive, without in the least realizing what he is doing. He is careless of his appearance, and may be untidy and unclean. He will form friendships with strangers, boasting in a blatant fashion and discussing his most intimate affairs without the slightest inhibition. Many patients display an increased sexual excitability so that they may tell lewd stories in a loud voice in public places, seek doubtful companions and involve themselves in debauchery. They will eat greedily anything in the way of food, helping themselves from the plate of a neighbor and becoming angered if in any way restrained at the table.

As the disease progresses the *motor symptoms* become more and more pronounced. The disturbance of speech becomes quite obvious. Repetition of such test phrases as "Methodist Episcopal," "around the rugged rock," and "she picked thistles," is done in a slurred, often unintelligible fashion. In some there are mannerisms such as grimacing, dancing about, ceaseless rubbing and picking, grunting, smacking, chewing, or monotonous, long-continued sighing. Movements are clumsy, slow, and awkward. The patient cannot catch a rubber ball thrown to him. He has difficulty in buttoning his clothing. He is unable to thread a needle or to tie a knot. His gait is unsteady and shuffling. His features become flabby and expressionless while his voice is monotonous or tremulous. In his handwriting he leaves out syllables, crosses out words, makes mistakes in spelling, and repeats letters or phrases in an irrational fashion.

In brief, the most prominent psychological changes which take place in this disease are a peculiar loss of judgment, memory, and emotional stability, together with a progressive disturbance in motor control.

Inner Experience

As one might expect from the description of this process of dementia, no patient can give any adequate autobiographical report of his experience. During the illness the disorder of memory and of time linkage of experience prevents any recording of his experiences. Those patients who recover, either spontaneously or as a result of one or another variety of therapy, do not have very much recollection of their illness. They will give accounts of isolated events but have no connected memory of their hospital stay or of their own inner life or behavior. Frequently, those memories which they do have are in part erroneous. They mix together two or more events or add to actual occurrences fantastic and imaginary settings which to them are as real as any other part of their memories.

In general, it appears that the experience is a fantastic, dreamlike state which the person himself does not understand or evaluate while living through it. After recovery, his memory of the illness is fragmentary in the same way that a normal person will remember fragments of a long, involved dream which seems partly dream, partly real, but which he realizes to be dreamlike.

Relation between Physical and Mental Pathology

Since in this disease we know the cause, together with the nature and extent of the physical damage done to the central nervous system, it would seem that we should be able to correlate fairly closely the amount of destruction of brain tissue and the extent of the mental deviations. Unfortunately, no one, thus far, has been able to define in other than the most general terms the relationship between the brain pathology and psychopathology. Ignorance of this essential relationship is also true in epilepsy, senile states, brain tumors, and other organic brain conditions. In trying to establish such relationships, several general questions must be considered even though no satisfactory answers can be given.

Why does only a fraction of the population who contract primary syphilis develop general paresis? Among white males who have contracted primary syphilis, 8 per cent develop general paresis; among white females, 5 per cent; among Negro males, 2 per cent; and among female Negroes, 0.3 per cent. Again, it has been shown by many investigators that some racial or ethnic groups have little or no general paresis, while other racial groups run high percentages. For example, primary syphilitic infection is very common among American Indians and yet general paresis has never been observed in a full-blooded Indian, although it does occur among half breeds.[4] It is generally accepted that no evidence has been produced in favor of a specific susceptibility to general paresis bearing a relation to heredity. Various writers have advanced the hypothesis that general paresis may be due to some specific strain of spirochetes, offering in evidence the observation that two or more individuals infected by the same source subsequently developed general paresis. Still other investigators have pointed out that in many cases of paresis there is evidence of some head injury, frequently very mild, before the onset of the paretic symptoms. Finally, others have advanced claims that, from individual to individual, the various tissues of the human body may vary in resistance to disease. Hence, the paretic may be thought of as one whose brain tissue lacked high natural resistance to syphilis. There is no final or definite answer to the question of why one syphilitic becomes a paretic while another does not.

What relationship exists between the prepsychotic personality of the paretic and the course of his symptoms during the disease? This question has raised a great deal of controversy. There are some who say that the paretic state only exaggerates the prepsychotic personality, particularly if that personality was depressive, euphoric, schizoid, or neurotic. Other investigators believe that no constant relationship between prepsychotic personality and the diseased personality of the paretic has been demonstrated. (It is, of course, possible for a manic-depressive or a dementia praecox patient to develop general paresis, in which case the two diseases would complicate each other.) In the majority of cases the friends and relatives of the paretic patient insist on his essential normality before the onset of the first symptoms of general paresis.

In those cases in which recovery or marked improvement is obtained, how does the subsequent mental life of the person compare with his mental life before the disease? Most individuals who recover or improve are said to be somewhat blunted in intellect, emotional life, and in their general mental capacities. The degree of this blunting is thought to be related to both the amount and the location of the brain tissue which was destroyed. It seems that there is a general lowering or deterioration of mental function which may be very marked during the disease, and that as the individual recovers, a reorganization takes place so that there is but a slight diminution in most of the mental abilities.

Outcome of Treatment

Until the discovery of fever therapy, the prognosis of recovery or improvement in general paresis was very gloomy. Table 4 gives the present-day picture of the outcome of treatment.

TABLE 4. COMPARISON OF OUTCOME OF GENERAL PARESIS WITH RESPECT TO TREATMENT[5]

| | Percentage of patients in which there is | | |
Treatment	Complete Remission	Incomplete Remission	Death within 4 Years of Onset
None	3–5	5–15	80
Routine (arsphenamines and heavy metals)	3–5	15–25	60–70
Fever therapy	30–40	30–40	5–10

Explanations of Psychological Changes

The explanation advanced for the changes in character and personality which mark the acute phase of the paretic illness reflects the basic theory or philosophy of the authority who is being quoted. The psychoanalysts[2] have pointed out that the symptoms are essentially narcissistic. The brain is the central organ of ego function and when it is damaged by the infection the narcissistic equilibrium is disturbed. The euphoric mood, the periods of melancholia, and the essential disregard for reality are overt expressions of ego damage.

The psychobiologist[6] explains the behavior abnormalities as directly dependent on a permanent loss of brain substance. When such a loss occurs it is characterized by deviations in the personality assets of the individual, especially in memory, judgment, and language. These losses permit the outcropping of certain disturbing behavior tendencies previously kept in check by personal and social integration. When there is a complete recovery, it is not assumed that there was a true loss in personality assets, but rather that there was a loss of ability to make use of them.

Kraepelin[3] suggested that the psychic disturbances were dependent not only on immediate brain damage but also on interference with brain nutrition, since the blood vessels leading to the cortex are irritated and inflamed during the disease process. Hence, the mental deviations vary from person to person because of differences in nervous tissue destruction and in terms of interference with orderly nervous function resulting from disturbed brain metabolism. This hypothesis accounts for the dementia during the acute phase of the illness, as well as the apparent recovery of adequate mental function following treatment.

Summary

General paresis furnishes an example of the way in which scientific research methods can solve the essential problems of a mental disease. The solution of this problem also shows how new problems are raised which demand further research. The disease itself shows clearly the interdependence of physical damage and mental abnormalities. The relationship between the arrest of the progressive damage to brain tissue, the "healing" of the tissue, and the mental reconstruction is a most interesting psychological phenomenon. Systematic studies of this phenomenon promise valuable new information concerning the relationship of brain injury and psychological loss.

REFERENCES

1. Austin, T. J., *Practical Account of General Paresis.* London, Churchill, 1859.
2. Hollos, S., and S. Ferenczi, *Psychoanalysis and the Psychic Disorder of General Paresis.* New York, Nervous and Mental Disease Monograph, 1925, #42.
3. Kraepelin, E., *General Paresis.* New York, Nervous and Mental Disease Monograph, 1913, #14.
4. Landis, C., and J. D. Page, *Modern Society and Mental Disease.* New York, Rinehart, 1938.
5. Moore, J. E., *The Modern Treatment of Syphilis* (2d ed.). Springfield, Ill., C. C. Thomas, 1941.
6. Muncie, W., *Psychobiology and Psychiatry.* St. Louis, Mosby, 1939.
7. Noguchi, H., and J. W. Moore, "A Demonstration of the Treponema Pallidum in the Brain in Cases of General Paresis," *Jour. Exp. Med.,* 1913, *17,* 232–238.
8. Schaudinn, F. and E. Hoffmann, "Ueber Spirochaetenbefunde im Lymphdrüsensaft Syphilitischer," *Deutsche Med. Wchnschr.,* 1905, *31,* 711–714.
9. White, W. A., *Outline of Psychiatry* (12th ed.). New York, Nervous and Mental Disease Monograph, 1929.
10. Zilboorg, G., and G. W. Henry, *A History of Medical Psychology.* New York, Norton, 1941.

Chapter XV

ABNORMALITIES ASSOCIATED WITH
CERTAIN ORGANIC CHANGES OF THE BRAIN

THE INTEGRATION and coordination of the entire body depends upon the functional relationships existing between the central nervous system, the endocrine glands, and the blood stream. Most important in this integration is the functioning of the cerebral cortex of the brain. When the brain is injured, when it fails to develop properly, when toxic or infectious processes affect it, or when new growths or other structural changes take place we find abnormalities of behavior and mental life. The relation existing between these structural changes (pathology) and their attendant psychological disorders (psychopathology) constitutes the medical specialty of neurology.

The psychosomatic (mind-body) aspects of neurology are but partially understood. Many organic abnormalities are known — many functional abnormalities are known — but only in certain instances is the interrelationship between structure and function understood. There are conditions in which there is profound, widespread pathology, either in the form of damage or infection, where but little effect on either organized behavior or the mental life of the individual can be demonstrated. There are conditions where a very small, restricted structural damage brings about a disorganization of both behavior and mental life, which seems to change completely the personality of the individual. There are gross disorders in the mental life and behavior of the individual, with no regular or constantly occurring pathology which can be demonstrated by our present scientific methods. Because the history of medicine has so regularly demonstrated that abnormal function (either physical or mental) depends upon structural alteration or infection, the basic assumption of most contemporary scientists is that some brain pathology is the basis for the mental abnormality, even though the site and nature of the pathology may not at present be recognized or identified. Whether pathology can be brought about by maladjusted habits or emotions is regarded as debatable.

Other chapters deal with the psychopathology of epilepsy, general paresis, old age, and feeble-mindedness, all of which depend largely or wholly on organic brain pathology. In the present chapter, we will take up the psychopathology associated with brain tumors, paralysis agitans, spastic paralysis, and Huntington's chorea, all of which offer examples of organic pathology with attendant psychopathological changes.

Psychopathology in Cases of Brain Tumor

Tumors, either benign or malignant, are not uncommon in the central nervous system. Deviation in cell growth with consequent development of tumors may involve a wide variety of bodily tissues and may take place at various evolutionary stages through which the tissues pass during development.

From one series of over 31,000 autopsies done in general hospitals,[13] brain tumors were found in 1.7 per cent of the cases; while in another series of 13,000 autopsies, brain tumors were found in 2 per cent of the cases. In 1642 autopsies done in a mental hospital, 1.7 per cent were found to have had brain tumors. Brain tumors are more frequent in men than in women, the ratio being 4 to 3. They occur at all ages of life, but are more common between 30 and 50. They are not related to race, nationality, social, or economic circumstances. Mental disturbances are said to accompany brain tumor in 40 to 100 per cent of the cases.

GENERAL BEHAVIOR[4]

Psychological disturbance varies widely, depending upon the location of the tumor, the rapidity of its growth, and the state of its development. In the early stages, irritability, restlessness, and aggressive tendencies are fairly common. The patient may have vague feelings of discomfort or actual pains in his head. He may be tense, impatient, and subject to outbursts of anger or violence. As the tumorous growth increases, his restlessness may be succeeded by a general overactivity extending to an active delirium. Some patients become quite excited and destructive, for example, tearing up the bedclothes and tying fragments to the frame of the bed in a fantastic manner. This excitement is usually followed by a period of apathy in which unusual effort must be made in order to perform ordinary daily tasks. In the later stages of the illness, excited and apathetic periods may alternate. In excitement, the behavior resembles that seen in the manic states. At other times, the behavior may resemble that of a catatonic dementia praecox patient.

SPEECH

The variations in the disorders of speech which are frequently associated with brain tumors are determined by the location and extent of the tumor as well as by the prevailing mood or degree of mental disturbance. In the early stages, the patient may complain in an anxious or hysterical fashion, as though the illness were purely imaginary. It is often difficult then, to distinguish whether the complaints are genuine expressions of organic disability or faulty adjustment to personal problems. Somewhat later, there comes a lack of spontaneity, together with a monotonous and retarded quality, in both the tone and the manner of speaking. Such a patient must exert unusual effort in order to comprehend questions and to elaborate a response. The more complicated the question, the more laborious are the formulation and expression of the response. Within a few hours the same individual may pass from a mute condition into one where he answers questions quite adequately.

Aphasic disorders are present in about 10 per cent of brain-tumor cases. In some forms of aphasia the speech may deteriorate to little more than a jargon. For example, the speech of one aphasic patient was recorded as follows, when he was asked to identify certain objects:

[Nickel?] "25, ain't it?" [Key?] "25." [Purse?] "50." [Dollar bill?] "Dollar, ain't it? [Watch?] "50 cents." [Bottle?] "50 ain't it 50?" [Bill?] "50 — now ring a bell." [Memo book?] "50 cent piece." [Clock?] "Ah-ah-I don't know." When asked to repeat "Methodist Episcopal," he said, "Misty pel;" and to repeat "electric hippopotamus," he said, "Electric cohoes pocroes." *

MOOD

Much clinical attention has been paid to the emotional changes accompanying brain tumors. A peculiarity of humor or wit occurs in some frontal lobe tumor cases, as well as in certain patients following prefrontal lobectomy. (See Chap. XXVIII, p. 431.) This symptom is called *Witzelsucht* ("joking ailment") and consists of an ill-timed jocularity and facetiousness, occurring together with euphoria and lack of insight. A distinction is made between *Witzelsucht* and *Galgenhumor* (gallows humor), which bravely jokes in the face of death. Wilson cited the example of a gently bred woman who, when he hinted at the nature of her brain ailment, slapped him playfully on the arm, and

* Henry, G. W., "Mental Phenomena Observed in Cases of Brain Tumor," *Amer. Jour. Psychiat.*, 1932, *12*, 427.

said, "Go on, silly! My head hasn't got anything in it." Her tumor lay in the right lateral ventricle.

States of anxiety, apprehension, depression, euphoria, or indifference go with brain pathology. Some clinicians believe that the mood of the patient is determined largely by the type of personality which existed before the onset of the illness. However, there are so many individual variations that it is difficult to draw any general conclusion on this point. These mood changes do not seem to take place in any orderly sequence, so far as any single patient is concerned; nor are they regularly related to the location or type of the tumor. In the early stages, the patient loses initiative and courage; later, he becomes impatient, peevish, and irritable; and as the disease progresses, he tends to be more seriously concerned about himself, acting as though contemplating some terrible fate. As his symptoms become more distressing, he is seldom at peace and can no longer attend to his work, becoming more and more hopeless in his outlook. In the final stages, most patients seem to become less sensitive to pain, less capable of appreciating the seriousness of their illness, to have less insight, and to lose contact with the reality surrounding them. They are no longer concerned about their illness, social conventions, or responsibilities. They may laugh and joke in a hilarious, unrestrained manner. They may become careless in their personal appearance and indifferent in their manners and personal care. Other patients become so deeply depressed that they contemplate suicide and make impulsive attempts at self-destruction.

HALLUCINATIONS

Those hallucinations which accompany the progressive growth of a brain tumor are not thought to be different in any psychological way from those which occur in dementia praecox or alcoholism. At some time during the course of the illness about half of the brain-tumor cases have hallucinations. More than 50 per cent of them have hallucinations of the visual type, while about 30 per cent have hallucinations of the auditory type. They may be experienced at any time during the course of the illness. A large proportion of the visual hallucinations consist of flashes of light, vividly colored lights or objects, or contrasting black darkness and dazzling light. Animals of all kinds and sizes and in all degrees of activity are reported. The auditory hallucinations include voices, singing, ringing bells, buzzing, roaring, crackling, and occasionally meaningful sentences or entire conversations.

ORIENTATION

Ordinary orientation of time, place, and person depends upon a constant reference to the external world represented through incoming sensory stimulation. When there is an interference with any of the incoming sensory material, the individual is bound to be disoriented. As a rule, the orientation for time becomes defective first, then the patient is unable to identify his surroundings, and finally he fails to recognize even his own relatives. Not uncommonly, the patient returns mentally to an earlier period in his life. He may give correctly a former address, or he may seem to have returned to the scenes of his childhood. In the more severe forms, he may not be able to find his way about his own house, or even to locate himself properly in his own bed. He will wander about aimlessly, becoming lost in his own living room. He may be unable to dress himself, trying to get his feet through the arms of his shirt. He will rarely have any conception of the date or time of day.

INSIGHT

The degree of insight varies in different persons, and in the same individual at different stages of his illness. The lack of insight may be expressed in general behavior, facial expression, or emotional attitude, as well as in speech. At least half of the patients, at some time during their illness, recognize that they are seriously ill. They may make some vague reference to their head being out of order, while others complain of confusion and memory disorders. As long as the patient maintains contact with reality or is kept alert by pain, he usually localizes his illness in his head and often complains bitterly of both failing mental ability and physical strength. One patient protested to his physician, saying, "I've really got something," while another patient, who had been considered delusional because he insisted that he had a cancer in his brain, was actually found at autopsy to have a brain tumor.

Paralysis Agitans[13]

The cause of this disorder, which is also called "shaking palsy" or "Parkinson's disease," is unknown in the majority of cases. Certain cases follow epidemic encephalitis (sleeping sickness), others follow carbon monoxide poisoning, and still others are thought to depend on some hereditary predisposition. The disorder depends on a destructive process damaging certain portions of the basal ganglia of the brain. James Parkinson in 1817 provided an account of the symptoms of the disease, which is still valid. His description, in part, is as follows: "Involuntary tremulous motion, with lessened muscular power, in parts not in action and even when supported; with a propensity to bend the trunk forwards, and to pass from a walking to a running pace; the senses and intellects being uninjured."

It is estimated that paralysis agitans constitutes some 0.2 to 0.7 per cent of neurological cases. It is found in all countries. It occurs in all economic or social groups. It occurs slightly more frequently among men than among women, the ratio being about 10 to 7. The most frequent age at onset is between 50 and 60, the onset being rare before age 40 or after age 70. Exciting or precipitating factors to which the affliction has been attributed are, emotional upset, worry, overwork, exposure. At the beginning of the illness, there is a general slowness and stiffness of movement, a rigidity of posture, an infrequent blinking of the eyes, and a characteristic position taken by the hands when the person is at rest. As the disorder develops, there is added an increasing trembling of one or both of the hands and arms, so that the hands, unless clasped, are in a constant tremor. The patient complains of awkwardness in all of the finely coordinated manipulations common to everyday life, such as holding a pen, shaving, or buttoning.

As the affliction progresses, the tremor, which is composed of rhythmically alternating contractions of the muscle groups of the hands and arms, becomes more marked. The smaller the muscle mass, the more prone it is to tremor, so that the tongue, lips, and larynx become involved. The range of action is small and its rate usually is between three to four oscillations a second. The tremor of the tongue, lips, and larynx brings on what has been described as "murmuring an eternal litany." The tremor of the hands is present during rest but disappears during purposeful movement, particularly during its initial phases. A firm handclasp will stop the shaking but it will return after ten or fifteen seconds, even though the clasp itself may not be relaxed.

The facial expression is described as masklike; the features are "starched," or described as a "reptilian stare." There is little or no play of expression, such as one sees in ordinary existence. Slowness of movement is a counterpart of the muscular rigidity. These individuals move in a deliberate fashion. For all of the acts of daily life, they are slow in getting started. The inertia is such as to bring purposeful activity almost to a standstill.

MENTAL SYMPTOMS

Although there is a marked tremor of small muscle groups accompanied by rigidity of the larger body movements, the mental life of the patients is not greatly altered. They complain of aches, pains, feelings of stiffness, dragging, tightening, which are related to the muscular rigidity. Aubrun[1] made use of different psychological procedures to study the mental changes in a group of these patients. He concluded that the motor symptoms brought about indifference, decrease in ability to concentrate, and in intellect in general. Whether these changes are more pronounced than are to be expected from persons of equal chronological age is yet to be established. On the basis of clinical observation, it is known that they can and do think clearly if enough stimulation and encouragement are provided. It is as if the mental life of the individual were surrounded by a cage made up of his own tremors and rigidity. In brief, in this condition there is a physical handicap based on brain damage, which results in little or no true psychopathology.

Spastic Paralysis

Spastic paralysis* (infantile cerebral palsy, Little's disease, birth-injury palsy, cerebral diplegia, hereditary spastic diplegia) is a gross form of motor disability due to organic brain changes which exists from birth or shortly thereafter and affects the entire life span.[11] The cause and extent of the brain damage in most cases is unclear or unknown. Sachs separated these cases into three groups: (*a*) prenatal, in which the cause is difficult to determine; (*b*) true birth palsy, in which the injury is acquired during labor; and (*c*) the acute or acquired palsy, in which there is thought to have been some infectious agent or brain injury during the early years of life.

Spasticity (the leading symptom) is a condition of rigidity of the muscles, associated with inadequate voluntary control. There are wide differences in the variety and degree of spasticity. In some instances, only one side of the body or one limb is affected; while in extreme cases, all members of the body as well as the organs of speech may be involved. In nearly one third of the cases the afflicted individual is born prematurely. The symptoms are usually not observable until the child is several weeks or months old. Several months after birth, there may be noticeable inability to sit up or to hold up the head, together with difficulty in swallowing. Speech is almost always delayed and

---

* This section is drawn from C. Landis and M. M. Bolles, *The Personality and Sexuality of the Physically Handicapped Woman.* New York, Hoeber, 1942, 38–47.

imperfect in the severe cases. Growth and development are markedly retarded, although improvement in the control of muscular co-ordination up to the age of twelve is common.

In general, the picture is one of gross motor disability existing from an early age. The motor skills acquired by the normal individual in the first few years of life are delayed, and are achieved by the spastic only after years of training and practice. The extent of impairment and the amount of improvement vary considerably. Phelps[10] stated that there are between 40 and 50 cases per 100,000 of the general population, and of these cases, about 30 per cent are mentally retarded. Whether the mental retardation evidenced in some cases is due to feeble-mindedness per se, or to interference with the usual mechanisms of expression and lack of schooling, it is impossible to say.

With such a grave physical handicap, it might reasonably be expected that the course of personality development would show some deviation, which would be accentuated by the psychological problems of adjustment which the individual must face. Most handicapped persons have several fields of activity in which they can compete adequately with normal people of their own age; but the patient with spastic paralysis, particularly the more extreme type, in which all limbs as well as the speech mechanism are involved, lives in a world in which any adequate motor response is difficult or impossible. Social relationships constitute an additional source of difficulty for the spastic child. Children can understand why another child uses crutches, or walks with a limp, but cannot understand the chaotic, jerky inco-ordination of the spastic youngster.

Some insight into the psychology of these individuals can be gained from such autobiographical accounts as Carlson's *Born That Way*, Hoopes' *Out of the Running*, or Hoskins' *The Broken String*.* Hoskins re-ported that adolescents with spastic paralysis may not be consciously aware of their limitations unless they are continually brought to their attention. She felt that a materialistic view of existence would produce unhappiness and maladjustment in these patients, while they could achieve satisfaction and contentment by turning to religion.

In order to understand more clearly the effects of spastic paralysis on the personality development, Landis and Bolles made a psycho-logical study of twenty-five women who were so afflicted. No one of the group studied was completely handicapped. Rather, the type of

---

* Carlson, E. R., *Born That Way*. New York, Day, 1941.
  Hoopes, C. G., *Out of the Running*, Springfield, Ill., C. C. Thomas, 1939.
  Hoskins, F. H., "The Broken String," *Train. School Bull.*, 1939, *36*, 41–48, 67–74,

case that is more or less in social competition with healthy persons was chosen for investigation.

A major hypothesis of present-day psychological theory maintains that the course of the psychosexual development of the individual is a most important element in the development and structure of the total personality. Hence, this phase of growth and experience in spastic patients was compared by Landis and Bolles, with that of physically and mentally normal women. No differences were found between spastics and normals with respect to the physiology of sex function. Fewer of these patients than of the physically normal women reported that they had masturbated. Ten of these twenty-five girls had never had dates with boys. This is a much higher proportion than was found in physically normal girls of similar ages. The lack of heterosexual orientation in some cases seemed to be related to shyness, which made the girls hold back or avoid contacts with boys. Girls who were not shy had many dates and social contacts with boys, even though they were severely handicapped.

In spite of the limited autoerotic practices and heterosexual contacts of the spastics, no evidence was obtained which would indicate that homosexual attachments had been substituted as a sexual outlet. Actually, there was little or no evidence of homoerotic experience. Immaturity on the part of many of them was the most outstanding psychosexual characteristic. However, they were not all immature; but as a group they were more likely to be immature than were the physically normal women.

There were some individuals in this survey who were acutely unhappy. Twelve of them reported that they had at some time wished they had never been born. In spite of this apparent dissatisfaction with their lives, eighteen of the twenty-five said that they would rather relive their lives than stop living, if such a choice had to be made. Various writers have pointed out that individuals with spastic paralysis have difficulty in controlling their emotional expressions and reactions, just as they lack control of other forms of coordinated motor activity. Despite the wide difference in the degree of handicap within this group, no real differences in emotional control or expression were found.

The following is a composite picture which Landis and Bolles drew up to represent the personality of the twenty-five spastics which they studied.:

CASE 19: Miss S was twenty-five years old when interviewed. Her parents had realized before she was a year old that she was not developing normally and had taken her to their family physician. He told them that they would have to wait at least two years more before he could tell them what could or should be done to help her, and that in the meantime they should care for her and treat her just as though she were a "normal" child. . . . As she grew older she did learn to walk alone but her gait was very uneven, and she fell frequently. For this reason she stayed indoors by herself more than most children do. When she was eight years old she started to school. Being with other children brought her first acute realization that she was different, and could not do the things that they did. She was anxious to join in their games, but held back because she was shy. She tried very hard to do well in her schoolwork for the next few years, so that in this regard at least she could keep up with the other children; but even when she knew her lessons perfectly she became so agitated and confused when the teacher called on her that her performance was poor. . . .

She became used to the limitation of her activities by her handicap, so that she took it for granted. She actively resented the way that people looked at her in the street, and became very much annoyed when little children imitated her. She felt that her parents had been wrong in not encouraging her to do things for herself. She had a few girl friends of her own age, but did not enjoy being in large groups, because they made her "nervous." She had her first date with a boy when she was eighteen, and this was a very casual relationship. . . .

She was very anxious to get a job so that she could help contribute to the family's budget, as she felt that they had done much for her and given up much because of her. In her late teens she began to get discouraged, feeling that her condition would never improve. There had been very definite improvement when she first went to school, but now there was no further progress. . . . Sometimes she became acutely discouraged and depressed. These feelings were apt to come when she wondered about what would happen to her in the future, and how she would get along if her parents died.

Her social life was very limited, but she derived a great deal of pleasure from the few friends she did have. She said that she would like to have more friends, but had actually made little effort to go out and meet new people. After she was twenty years old, her mother encouraged her in going out, although she had previously prevented her from forming close friendships with girls by making her stay at home much of the time. She felt that if her mother had encouraged her to go around with other children, she would have been able to get along with them better. She was more at ease when she was with people who were also physically handicapped than with physically normal people. . . .

When she first started to look for a job, she thought that it was very unfair that employers should discriminate against her because she was handicapped, and felt that she could have carried out the work adequately and should have been given a chance. However, her efforts to gain employment were rather haphazard. Her desires for the future were not clearly formulated. She thought that she might like to marry if the opportunity presented itself, but she had never been really fond of any one particular boy. She was still closely tied to her family in thought and feeling although at times she actively resented and reacted against them.

This composite history illustrates two major points: first, that in spite of spastic paralysis existing from birth, such persons do not differ from normals in many aspects of personality development; and second, those differences in emotional attachment and maturity which are observed seem to be logical consequences of the environmental forces surrounding the individual.

Huntington's Chorea

This disease is of particular interest to the student of psychopathology, since there is consistency in the following characteristics: (a) definite hereditary component; (b) onset relatively late in life with mental and physical abnormalities which develop without any detectable symptoms previous to the onset; (c) undetermined brain pathology; and (d) a progressive and marked mental deterioration. Choreas are disorders which are distinguished by persistent rhythmical or jerky muscular movements. Saint Vitus's dance (Sydenham's chorea) is the commonest and best known. Huntington's chorea is a rare affliction. The beginning symptoms usually appear between thirty-five and forty years of age. It is marked by jerky twitching movements, an increasing irritability, shyness, and a terminal dementia.

Although this condition was recognized in the early years of the nineteenth century, it remained for Huntington[7] in 1872 to provide the first clear description and differentiation. He said that there were "three marked peculiarities in this disease: (1) Its hereditary nature. (2) A tendency to insanity and suicide. (3) Its manifesting itself as a grave disease only in adult life." Concerning its hereditary nature, he pointed out that "whenever either or both the parents have shown manifestations of the disease, and more especially when these manifestations have been of a serious nature, one or more of the offspring almost invariably suffer from the disease, if they live to adult age. But if by any chance these children go through life without it, the thread is broken, and the grandchildren and great grandchildren of the original shakers may rest assured that they are free of the disease." Huntington based his description on the observations of his grandfather, his father, and himself, all of whom had been physicians in the same locality on Long Island and who had observed several generations within certain family groups who exhibited this disease picture.

Huntington's chorea has subsequently been reported from all parts of the world, in all races, and in all colors. It accounts for about 0.2 per cent of the first-admissions to American mental hospitals. For the most part, affected families are found in rural communities and are of the lower middle economic class. In one collection[3] of 962 cases (521 men, 441 women), there were enumerated 5 legislators, 1 judge, 2 university professors, 2 ministers, 1 eminent surgeon, 3 authors, 2 inventors, and 2 organizers of public institutions. The average age at onset of the disease is 37.5 years. A very few cases have been recorded where the onset was before age 20 or after age 60.

Once started, the disease never stops; temporary remission or amelioration seldom, if ever, interrupts its course. The progress of the dementia is slow in some cases and rapid in others. The average length of life after onset is from 10 to 15 years, although the range is from 1 to 35 years.

Vessie[12] reported on the appearance of this affliction through twelve consecutive generations, tracing it from three individuals who came to America from England in 1630. Of interest is the role which certain of these choreic persons played during the period from 1647 to 1697 when in colonial Connecticut the legislators, ministers, and judges let the hangman settle their belief in witchcraft. The description of the behavior of certain of the witches who were condemned, together with our knowledge of the reappearance of chorea in many succeeding generations of their families, seems conclusive evidence that at least in part the suspicion of witchcraft was based on the chorea shown by these individuals. "It was believed that the weaving motions, jerking backward and forward of the head, peculiar grimacing and twitching, puckering of the lips, squirming shoulders, spasmodic movements of the chest and diaphragm, and the involuntary jerking of the hands, arms, feet and legs, represented the suffering of Christ during crucifixion; and that this affliction was a curse inherited by these sad choreics from their forefathers for having dared to derisively pantomime the Saviour."*

Vessie concluded that Huntington's chorea is transmitted directly and manifested persistently from generation to generation with no disposition to revoke or alter the nature of the heritage. Other investigators have shown that from one fourth to one half of the children in any affected family develop the disease. It is impossible to foretell which of the children in any family will be affected and which will escape.

CASE HISTORY

CASE 20: H. C., aged forty-three years, was born in New York State. His paternal grandfather had six children, three sons and three daughters;

---

*Vessie, P. R., "On the Transmission of Huntington's Chorea for 300 Years: the Bures Family Group," *Jour. Nerv. Ment. Dis.*, 1932, 76, 563.

of these, two sons and one daughter were afflicted with Huntington's chorea. The patient has no brothers and but one sister, who was afflicted in the same manner as himself. The sister developed the disease at age thirty-five. His father was accidentally killed at age thirty, dying before the age at which the affliction appears in this family. His mother died from the effects of a fall.

At thirty-five years of age, the patient developed irregular, involuntary movements of the legs. His gait became hesitating and staggering; it gave him no inconvenience, but it annoyed him, because people imagined him drunk. He first noticed it himself in coming down hill, which was only accomplished with great difficulty. At thirty-seven years of age, the same involuntary movements developed in the arms. Three years later, the head and trunk became involved.

When forty-three years old, the patient had choreic movements of the whole body, every muscle being involved in these involuntary movements. The head was constantly turned from side to side, and the arms (especially the left), were continually in motion. All the movements were very much increased when the patient knew he was being watched, or when he attempted to speak or walk. When he walked, he bent his legs but slightly, planting one foot firmly on the ground and resting it a moment before lifting up the other foot. There was no motion during sleep. When sitting, he would grasp the side of the chair to steady and rest himself. He had no pain whatever, and was unconscious of the movements unless his attention was directed to them. He was able to control voluntarily the movements to some extent, but could not stop them entirely. For example, he could steady his hand enough to write his name in a jerky manner.

His memory was fairly good, and he seemed to be intelligent. There were no delusions or evidence of deterioration. Subsequently, he did deteriorate and became quite demented before his death.

PSYCHOPATHOLOGY[13]

The case history illustrates the way in which the motor disorder develops. In the earlier states of the disease, voluntary action is usually unimpeded, so that habitual and ordinarily coordinated movements are carried through successfully; while the involuntary choreic action starts in again as soon as the voluntary act is completed.

Gradual, progressive, unremitting mental deterioration occurs in many, but not all, of these patients. Usually the earliest symptoms are emotional rather than intellectual. The patient appears irritable, easily excited, quick tempered, curt, and shows deviations from the usual self-control which marked his personality. For example, one such patient became intolerable at her home because of her continuous nagging. Others are cranky and eccentric or indulge in faultfinding. Still others show disorders in judgment, becoming grandiose and behaving in a very superior fashion. These early manifestations are usually unaccompanied by any insight, ideas of illness, or of personal responsibility. In certain families, suicide is quite common; in others, the faulty control is shown by excessive use of alcohol or drugs, promiscuous sexuality, or destructive violence.

As the disease progresses, the intellect becomes more involved, with memory showing progressive deterioration. Both recognition and recall are disturbed, and there is increasing inattention and imperception. If one asks such a patient to give the names of as many flowers or vegetables as he can remember, he will proceed somewhat as follows, with long pauses between: "Carrots . . . potatoes . . . turnips . . . potatoes . . . carrots . . ." In the earlier stages, there is merely a restric-

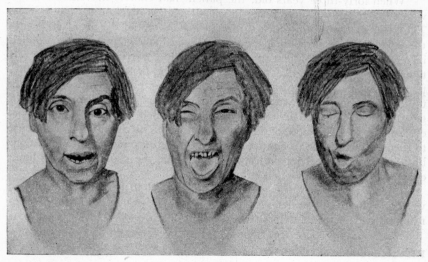

PLATE II

FACIAL CONTORTIONS IN HUNTINGTON'S CHOREA

tion of interest in the world, but with time, this progressive mental disorganization shows itself in disorientation, intellectual slowing, incoherence, and poverty of ideas. Some patients are able to read and converse a little until the end of their lives; in others dementia becomes profound and complete.

NEUROPATHOLOGY

Since this disease shows itself in a fairly clear-cut form, both as to symptoms and development, one should expect a uniform pathology somewhere in the nervous system. A great many neuropathological studies have been made of the brains of patients who died of this disease. Pfeiffer,[9] reviewing both his own work and that of others, concluded, "It is obvious that the only agreement which exists among investigators is that an organic change in the brain occurs. . . . It may be stated that the pathology of chronic degenerative chorea consists not only in a degenerative process in the nervous elements of the cortex, but of the thalamus and corpus striatum."

Other than the fact that the disease runs in families and that the symptoms and course of the affliction are relatively constant from case to case, all else in the way of explanation is at present speculative.

Summary

The four conditions which have been discussed in this chapter are all believed, on the basis of good evidence, to be basically organic in nature. They illustrate certain relationships which must be considered in any attempt to relate mental pathology to physical pathology. In no one of these conditions has sufficient evidence been obtained to indicate that the varying combinations of attendant personality deviations are referable in more than a very general fashion to the particular localization of the organic brain damage. On the other hand, there is much evidence that the psychopathology of these conditions does depend, in part, on some given neuropathology and, in part, to faulty habits, emotional trauma, and the like. Special training in motor coordination does alleviate some of the difficulties in spastic paralysis.

Marked psychological changes are usually associated with brain tumors, where we are dealing with the growth of new tissue that replaces and destroys the normal neural tissue of the brain. The organic brain damage in paralysis agitans is limited to the midbrain areas and generally is not accompanied by psychological changes other than those directly attributable to the motor disturbance. In spastic paralysis there are organic lesions which may be located in various midbrain areas or, less frequently, in other parts of the brain. A third of these spastic patients are mentally defective; the remainder manage to develop normal intellect and personality within the limits set up by the handicap itself. Finally, in Huntington's chorea we find varying combinations of organic brain changes in conjunction with marked motor and mental involvements. Unfortunately, not enough information is available in order to put forth a satisfactory hypothesis to account for the psychological and physiological relationships in these syndromes as well as many other conditions which are associated with brain damage.

REFERENCES

1. Aubrun, W., *L'état mental des Parkinsoniens*. Paris, Baillière, 1937.
2. Carlson, E. R., *Born That Way*. New York, Day, 1941.
3. Davenport, C. B., and E. B. Muncey, "Huntington's Chorea in Relation to Heredity and Eugenics," *Amer. Jour. Insan.*, 1916, *73*, 195–222.
4. Henry, G. W., "Mental Phenomena Observed in Cases of Brain Tumor," *Amer. Jour. Psychiat.*, 1932, *12*, 415–470.
5. Hoopes, C. G., *Out of the Running*. Springfield, Ill., C. C. Thomas, 1939.
6. Hoskins, F. H., "The Broken String," *Train. School Bull.*, 1939, *36*, 41–48, 67–74.
7. Huntington, G., "On Chorea," *Medical and Surgical Reporter*, 1872, *26*, 317–321.
8. Landis, C., and M. M. Bolles, *Personality and Sexuality of the Physically Handicapped Woman*. New York, Hoeber, 1942.
9. Pfeiffer, J. A. F., "A Contribution to the Pathology of Chronic Progressive Chorea," *Brain*, 1913, *35*, 276–289.
10. Phelps, W. M., "Motor Handicaps and Retardation," *Proc. Amer. Asso. Ment. Def.*, 1938, *43*, 26–31.
11. Sachs, B., and L. Hausman, *Nervous and Mental Disorders from Birth through Adolescence*. New York, Hoeber, 1926.
12. Vessie, P. R., "On the Transmission of Huntington's Chorea for 300 Years: the Bures Family Group," *Jour. Nerv. Ment. Dis.*, 1932, *76*, 553–573.
13. Wilson, S. A. K., *Neurology* (Vol. II). Baltimore, Williams & Wilkins, 1940.

Chapter XVI

PSYCHOPATHOLOGY ASSOCIATED WITH PHYSICAL DISEASE AND WITH CHILDBIRTH

CERTAIN psychological concomitants of ordinary illness or of childbirth are considered within the range of normality. The tendency to be irritable, morose, cranky, nervous, demanding, anxious, and full of self-pity is part of the normal reaction to illness. The study of the interrelationship between these psychological states and physical disorders constitutes an approach which is called "psychosomatic medicine." The art and science of medicine is largely devoted to the diagnosis and treatment of physical ailments, while the psychological deviations often receive very little attention and, occasionally, are completely neglected. This attitude is attributable to the fact that most sick people are, on recovery from their physical ailment, expected to lose their psychological symptoms. Hence, treatment of the physical ailment in most instances may be relied upon to relieve the mental complaints. There are many exceptions to this general rule. Some patients are so emotionally disturbed that the process of physical recovery is markedly interfered with. The physical ailment in certain cases may even be secondary to mental derangement or emotional disturbance, for example, the development of stomach ulcers as the result of self-medication which in turn has been due to anxiety growing out of the desire to escape responsibility by being sick. In still other patients it will often be impossible to tell whether the ailment is primarily physical or mental; hence, both aspects of the ailment must be carefully studied. This approach is not new but it has been at times neglected.

Psychologically speaking, there are four different ways in which psychopathology may be associated with physical ailments. First, the physical aspects of the disease or its secondary toxic effects may be directly responsible for psychopathological symptoms. Second, the existence of the disease produces secondary changes in the life of a person by the introduction of new problems in adjustment, limitation of the range of activities and interests, or the release of fears of invalidism, dependence, and death. Third, physical disease and personality reaction may be associated with particular types of physical constitution. It is altogether possible that certain physical constitutions may be susceptible to special types of physical illness which are associated with certain psychological patterns of response. Finally, psychological phenomena, such as fear, tension, and worry, with their correlated physiological substructure, may contribute largely to the formation of physical symptoms (such as gastrointestinal complaints, rheumatism, allergy).

Of more direct interest to the psychologist are the mental or temperamental states which have been thought to be related to certain well-defined and rather common ailments. The grouchy ill-humor of the choleric temperament has long been said to be associated with liver disorders; irritable pessimism with dyspepsia; and euphoric optimism and a sanguine temperament with respiratory complaints such as pulmonary tuberculosis. In order to deal adequately with all of the mental peculiarities which are said to accompany one or another of the physical diseases, it would be necessary to go through all of the ailments known to mankind. Such thoroughness is, for a variety of reasons, not in keeping with this presentation of abnormal psychology. We shall, therefore, confine ourselves to a consideration of the mental deviations which are associated with cardiac disease, pulmonary tuberculosis, peptic ulcer, and childbirth.

Cardiac Disease

Rheumatic heart disease is one of the most important causes of chronic heart trouble in an adult. The severe disability which sometimes follows rheumatic fever is of particular psychological interest since it may continue through many years of a person's life. The cause of rheumatic fever is unknown and not all rheumatic conditions result in cardiac impairment. When rheumatic fever does affect the heart, the valves of the heart are permanently damaged. The actual cardiac symptoms depend upon the degree to which the heart is able to compensate for the damage to the valves. Such persons may live for many years with adequate medical attention and self-care.

Many studies[5,6,9] have been made of the mental correlates of cardiac disease. Some of them were case reports of seriously ill adults who appeared to be either neurotic or psychotic during the acute phase of their illness. The main neurotic symptoms observed by psychiatric and psychoanalytic investigators in chronic cardiac patients included claustrophobia (fear of closed places), exaggerated dependence on parents, generalized emotional disturbance, anxiety, guilt feelings, and even panic.

The cardiologists (heart specialists) usually differentiate between organic heart disease with associated mental symptoms and the so-called cardiac neurosis. The personal life history of the patient before the onset of the cardiac symptoms affords the basis for differentiation. If the patient had neurotic or psychotic tendencies previously, then the psychological picture going with the organic disability is usually interpreted as the result of basic personality tendencies brought out by the illness. Although some psychiatrists claim that the cardiac disease itself is the cause of the psychopathologic state, the majority believe that the psychological changes in cardiac patients are no more than the uncovering or release of those tendencies which have been dormant in the personality.

Several investigators have emphasized that many patients with cardiac disease are not truly aware of the seriousness of their condition. Such patients minimize their symptoms and keep on with their usual activities against the advice of their physicians. Cases have been reported in which serious organic heart disease occurred with no definite correlation between the seriousness of the disability and the subjective experience which might have been expected to accompany the illness. Other investigators have found little evidence of any real emotional or social difficulty which could be directly attributed to the cardiac disease itself; rather, the psychic disturbances which occurred were ascribed to the recognition of the handicap by the friends and relatives and not by the patient.

The consensus of more recent studies of cardiac and cardiovascular disorders in patients suffering from nervous or mental disease is that the cardiac condition is not the cause of the mental disorder but that the psychic and organic components should be regarded as interdependent. When a neurosis or psychosis develops during or following cardiac disease the mental disorder is thought to be precipitated (rather than caused) by a generalized decrease in physical resistance.

Landis and Bolles[13] made a study of twenty-five women suffering from chronic cardiac disease of differing degrees of severity. They found that these patients gave evidence of being either very well adjusted to their environment or very poorly adjusted with but few intermediate cases. No special physical or psychological concomitants were observed in those persons who were extremely depressed or hopeless. When the cardiac patients were compared to other types of physically handicapped women, more of the former reported feelings of fear without explicable cause, conflict between their parents, and day-dreams about romantic relationships and situations. The basic personality structure of this particular group of cardiac cases was, in general, very similar to that found in other groups of handicapped persons. The most outstanding trait found in all of the handicapped was their emotional infantilism and immaturity. Whether this immaturity was due to the deprivation of normal patterns of experience and expression because of the chronic nature of the disease, or whether it was a reaction to the social circumstances surrounding a handi-capped individual was impossible to determine.

The personality development of a chronic cardiac patient may be illustrated by the following case history:

CASE 21: Miss D, aged twenty, came from an Irish Catholic home. She described her parents as quiet and easygoing and as never having used strict discipline with their children. Her first attack of rheumatic fever came when she was six years old, and since then there had been recurrent attacks practically every spring and fall. These illnesses required protracted care and treatment in hospitals and convalescent homes. When interviewed she said that the two preceding years constituted the longest time that she had been home continuously since she was six. She felt completely well at the time of the interview and said optimistically (?) that there was not anything that she could not do.

She had never had any close girl friends at any period of her life. She used to play with children before she started going away to convalescent homes; but later, in order to avoid embarrassing questions, she shunned acquaintances. She did not like demonstrations of affection and could not bear to have others (including members of her family) put their arms around her. She had never been out with a boy and did not think that she would be interested in having a date.

She spent her time either sitting idly at home or going for walks by herself, not caring for reading or motion pictures. Her mother did not allow her to help with the housework. When asked what her greatest desire for the future was, she said, "Nothing. I don't know because I don't look to the future." She felt that having been sick so much of the time and being in and out of hospitals had made her indifferent to what happened to her.

Although she said she disliked "hanging around home" she had never made any effort to form friendships or develop outside interests. Her attitude did not result from an overly strong attachment to the parents. Rather it was a very deeply rooted habit of invalidism which did not change even when there was a definite improvement in her physical condition.[13]

The apparently identical twin sister of Miss D had also had severe rheumatic heart disease and had spent a great deal of her early life in convalescent homes. This twin, however, stopped going to the cardiac clinic because she felt that she was getting no help from it. She could not be induced to give information about herself because she did not want to have anything to do with doctors. She was spending most of her time in search of a job so that she could be independent of her family. In spite of the similarity in the nature of the handicap, early history, and family background of these twins, the difference in the form of their rebellion to authority calls attention to the individuality of such patients. Other surveys of the attitudes and character traits of cardiac patients have shown this same point; namely, that the individuality of the person is more important than his heart disease so far as the personality development is concerned.

Pulmonary Tuberculosis

The psychopathology of the tuberculous patient is usually found to be more variable and complicated, since the average life span after the onset of the disease is greater than that of the cardiac patient. Consequently, there is more time for a tuberculous patient to develop a variety of psychological reactions and complex character deviations. Out of the multitude of possible personality changes it will be sufficient to consider four of the main psychosomatic relationships: the effect of tuberculosis on the mental life of the otherwise normal person; the relationship between tuberculosis and mental disease; the effect of emotion and stress on the onset and outcome of tuberculosis; and the question of euphoria in the chronic pulmonary tuberculosis (spes phthisica*). There is a wide divergence of opinion and much contradiction among the reports dealing with the psychology of the tuberculous patient. There is also a sharp difference between the observations published at the beginning of this century and present-day clinical accounts. Whether this difference is due to a true change in the psychology of the tuberculous patient as a result of better medical care; to the difference in social circumstances brought about by the progress in medical treatment; or whether it is due to a greater psychological sophistication on the part of physicians, is difficult to say.

EFFECT OF TUBERCULOSIS ON THE MENTAL LIFE OF THE OTHERWISE NORMAL PERSON

Here the most controversial claims of investigators range from the statements that tuberculosis occurs only in neurotic or psychotic persons, to the theory that tuberculosis has essentially no effect on or

* Pronounced "space tiz-e-ka."

relationship to the personality of the patient. Munro[16] stated that the disease had a specific influence on the individual, going so far as to state that "there is no disease in which the mental and moral characteristics of the patient are so profoundly modified and with which psychoneuroses are so constantly associated as chronic pulmonary tuberculosis." He claimed that there was a definite relationship between the severity of the disease and the degree of mental abnormality, since he interpreted the psychopathology as the result of a prolonged intoxication set up by the *tuberculosis bacillus*. Knopf,[12] on the other hand, defended the tuberculous patient against the claim that the disease leads to mental abnormality. According to his observations, tuberculosis occurred only as might be expected on the basis of chance in patients who were clearly psychotic or neurotic before the onset of the disease. Banister,[2] after surveying a fairly large group of tuberculous patients, reported that he had found no mental disorders which were the direct consequence of tuberculosis. Mental abnormalities which did arise in these patients were considered by him to be expressions of maladjustments such as occurred in any nontuberculous individual.

In a survey of 100 consecutive cases of tuberculosis examined in his office, Breuer[3] found no psychopathological factors in 63 cases, a neurosis secondary to tuberculosis in 3 cases (exaggerated anxiety), and psychic factors of a neurotic variety in the life history of 34 cases. These psychic factors he classified as: effects of undesirable parental home, 8; marital difficulties, 10; occupational difficulties, 3; constitutional or health difficulties, 9; and psychoses, 4. He stated, "Maladjustments in the work-life, the social life, and emotional life easily produce upsets which undermine the resistance-maintaining way of living. Therefore, it is not surprising that psychic disturbances, such as long-continued mental conflict, excessive fatigue, or emotional situations from which there is no escape, result in tuberculosis."

In Eyre's[8] study of 755 tuberculous patients there were 87 who had been classified by the medical staffs as troublemakers, despondent, "nuts," or "crazy." Her study of these 87 indicated that their abnormalities of behavior might be completely explained by the disturbance in personal relationships, financial burdens, social segregation, and the long duration of the disease. She concluded that the deviations could not be considered as essentially psychotic or neurotic of themselves.

No conclusive evidence is available to prove that tuberculosis has ever been precipitated by psychological stress, or that it is the development of a tuberculous condition which brings about a neurosis or a psychosis without the preexistence of latent or overt tendencies to a neurotic or psychotic condition. That the tuberculous patient is fearful, anxious, or even panic-stricken is not an expression of true psychopathology — rather, it indicates the fear that any person has when confronted with a situation which may soon cause his death.

EFFECT OF EMOTION AND STRESS ON TUBERCULOSIS

The mental attitudes of tuberculous patients have been investigated by use of both psychiatric and psychometric approaches. Strecker[18] and his coworkers made a psychiatric study of a group of seventy-five patients selected at random from various economic, social, cultural, and age levels. They found these patients to be neither particularly introverted nor extroverted before the onset of the disease. When the patients first learned that they had tuberculosis their reactions were diverse — some were reasonable, some anxious, some very depressed, some rebellious; some were suicidal, some accepted it as God's will, and some were relieved because they no longer had to work while feeling ill. The predominating mood of these patients was either depressed or fatalistic (making the best of it). After they knew the nature of their illness, only a few ever had periods of elation or euphoria.

The treatment of pulmonary tuberculosis emphasizes rest and inactivity, allowing the patient weeks and months with little to do. With so much idle time it might be expected that the fantasy life of these patients would be very rich. Actually, it has been found to be neither deep nor complicated but of a simple, compensatory nature. It does not in any way resemble the tendency to fantastic daydreaming which is typical of the psychotic patient.

The most persistent and consistent emotional state which various investigators have identified in tuberculous patients is apprehensive anxiety or fear. Some of these fears are specifically directed, others are generalized. Many of the patients are fearful of their reception by their friends and families after their return from the hospital. Each patient knew one or two stories of the cold reception accorded to some one whose disease process had been arrested. For the most part the stories conformed to type and the following are examples:

"Just as he was about to go home, he received a telegram from his brother telling him not to stop in on his way home, as they were afraid for the children." "The day upon which she was to be discharged, her sister wrote her offering to pay her board somewhere else, but telling her not to come home." These stories distress the patients and are kept in mind. They serve to further the idea that tuberculous patients are a people apart. One of the patients, a young economics teacher in a university, remarked that he would leave the hospital within the next week and would immediately go West, not stopping to see his friends, even though he wanted to visit them very much. He said, "I would like to have dinner with some of them, but I fear that they would be careful with the dishes I had used and I could not stand that." Another man who was socially prominent said: "I could never go home again. My wife comes to see me and does not even shake hands with me. My aunt stopped coming to our house when she heard I had t. b." Another person remarked: "Just now I hate society and wonder if it will shun me when I get out." A Jewish boy said: "If you have t. b. people will shun you. They do not know what they are afraid of, but they are afraid. I have lost my dearest friends. Even my adopted brother has dropped me, and we were very close during childhood." One attractive girl who had studied nursing and was an "arrested case" felt that she could not go back to her home town again as people would be apt to avoid her. She said: "That would kill me." Some of the patients kept their whereabouts secret and did not intend to tell any one of their illness. Some intended to start anew in another locality. Several patients bewailed the fact that there was not some place to which recovered patients might emigrate, since there no one would slight them or ask questions. *

Psychologists have given standardized, as well as specially prepared, tests to tuberculous and normal control groups. The Bernreuter Personality Inventory indicated that the tuberculous patients were more emotionally unstable than the general population, that they were more introverted, had less self-confidence, but were more sociable. The Bell Adjustment Inventory showed that both tuberculous men and women had a greater maladjustment score than normal comparison groups. The particular items giving the higher maladjustment scores were related to the disease and its effect on the patient's home and social relationships. A modification of Jasper's Depression-Elation scale showed that the tuberculous patients were somewhat more depressed than were the normal control subjects, but that there was a great deal of overlap in scores between the two groups.[17]

From both the psychiatric and psychometric investigations it is apparent that the disease itself does not alter the basic personality structure of the individual with respect to emotion, attitude, or intellect, except for the fear and anxiety directly related to the illness and its outcome. Tuberculous patients have been shown by all investigators to be in need of reassurance and encouragement, since most of them are depressed and anxious because of their weakened physical state and the social effects of their hospitalization.

* Strecker, E. A., F. J. Braceland, and B. Gordon, "Mental Attitudes of Tuberculous Patients," *Ment. Hyg.*, 1938, 22, 538-539.

RELATIONSHIP BETWEEN TUBERCULOSIS AND MENTAL DISEASE

It is a well-known fact, borne out by statistical reports from many countries and from many different periods of time, that mental hospital patients, particularly those suffering from dementia praecox, show a high death rate from tuberculosis. This observation has created a great deal of speculation and investigation concerning the possibility of some cause and effect relationship or association between mental disease and tuberculosis. These investigations range all of the way from opinionated recountals of hospital superintendents to actual psychiatric studies of large groups of tuberculous patients. It has been found that about 10 per cent of dementia praecox patients have tuberculosis while only 3 or 4 per cent of other mental patients have this disease, no matter what their mental disorder may be. An explanation which has been advanced for this association is that the dementia praecox patient is inactive, given to shallow breathing, and leads a vegetative sort of existence. This lack of activity might possibly make the patient more susceptible to tuberculous infection or lower his resistance to an old, inactive lesion.

In a study of 308 tuberculous twin families including 308 tuberculous-twin index cases and their co-twins, as well as 930 brothers and sisters and 688 parents of patients, Kallmann and Reisner[10] established that in any family group the chance of developing tuberculosis increased proportionally to the degree of blood relationship to an active tuberculosis case. The occurrence of tuberculosis in both twins was ascertained in 87 per cent of identical pairs and in 26 per cent of fraternal pairs, while the tuberculosis rate of the brothers and sisters was found to be 26 per cent, that of half-brothers and half-sisters 12 per cent, and that of parents 17 per cent. Under conditions of ordinary exposure to possible infection, these relationships were shown to be independent of age, sex, race, degree of exposure to other tuberculous patients, or any special environmental factors. These findings, which contribute the best available evidence today, indicated that whether or not any person will develop overt tuberculosis under ordinary conditions of exposure depends on the bodily resistance of that person as determined by what is called a "multifactorial genetic mechanism." The fact that fatal tuberculosis does occur more frequently in mental patients who are suffering from dementia praecox than would be expected by chance was also shown by Kallmann and Reisner to rest on genetic phenomena. In all probability certain nonspecific genetic factors involved in both tuberculosis and dementia praecox act to lessen an individual's resistance to either disease, although the diseases themselves are not genetically related. All of this may be summarized by the statement that tuberculosis and the mental disease, dementia praecox, do have a close biological association but that there is little evidence that the mental reactions going with either ailment have a causal relationship to the other disease. Anxiety about one's tuberculosis does not lead to the mental symptoms of dementia praecox, nor the hallucinations of a schizophrenic patient to tuberculosis.

SPES PHTHISICA

A mental exaltation or euphoria which has been said to occur in tuberculous patients is called "spes phthisica" and has been commented on in the medical literature since the middle of the seventeenth century. Estimates of the incidence of this euphoria have varied from 1 per cent to 75 per cent of all tuberculous cases. Indeed, Clouston in the 1860's held that 3 per cent of all cases of consumption developed what he called "phthisical insanity" which he interpreted as a type of manic-euphoria of a truly psychotic origin.

The existence and nature of spes phthisica are questionable. There is no evidence that when this sort of euphoria is observed it is directly referable to the type or extent of the disease. Most investigators who have made a special point of studying this symptom are inclined to believe that it is not a true euphoria or optimism but an overcompensatory reaction in an attempt to bring relief from internal anguish. It is a disguise for fear. It is a way of reassuring physicians, nurses, friends, and relatives in a painful situation in which the patient himself is basically depressed and despondent. Still another explanation is that spes phthisica is a form of dissociation in which the patient, in his anxiety based on the knowledge of his disease and its consequences, pushes this knowledge completely out of his mind and forces himself to believe that he will soon be out and around. Some writers have stated that the occurrence of this symptom is most common in the terminal stage of the illness. They claim that the disease produces such a general toxic condition by this time that the brain itself is affected, as it would be by any toxin (for example, alcohol which weakens critical self-judgment).

Probably there is no true spes phthisica in the sense that a unique mental state is set up by tuberculosis; rather, there are certain patients whose overcompensation for their very real fear is misinterpreted by uncritical observers.

Peptic Ulcer

Peptic ulcers include ulcers of the stomach and the duodenum. They present very interesting medical and psychological problems. The basic cause of peptic ulcer is unknown. From a physiological standpoint such ulcers are attributed to the assault of the normal acid-pepsin of the stomach on the gastroduodenal tissue and to the failure of the tissues to defend themselves against the action. They have been shown to follow infectious diseases, traumatic head injury, nutritional deficiencies or disturbances, and exposure to certain chemical substances such as lead or chromium as they are used in industry. They also may be found to be associated with emotional stress, fear, anxiety, or tension. Their treatment may be either surgical, medical, dietetic, or psychological, or some combination of these. The interesting question concerning peptic ulcers from the psychological standpoint is its relationship to the general emotional adjustment of the individual.

In a psychiatric and medical study of eighty cases of peptic ulcer, Draper[7] tabulated certain of his psychological findings as follows:

Psychological Mechanisms	No. of Positive Cases	No. of Negative Cases
Inner sense of insecurity based on actual or supposed physical inferiority	63	12
Mother fixation	76	2
Jealousy and aggression	50	27
Fear and guilt concerning sex	31	32
Compensatory striving	41	32

(The totals do not add up to 80 in each instance because of incomplete information.)

Whether or not similar psychological investigations of eighty patients showing physical complaints other than peptic ulcer would bring out the same variety and number of psychopathological symptoms is unknown, but that there is a marked tendency for peptic ulcer to be associated with psychopathological personality traits is shown by Draper's report.

In a study of 208 cases of duodenal ulcer Morrison and Feldman[15] reported that most of the patients were not psychologically well adjusted, partly because of constant annoyance with diets, but mainly because of pain or discomfort from the gastrointestinal region. Lack of rest explained much of their inability to meet situations, while loss of self-confidence and failure to perform a satisfactory day's work were contributing factors. Many of the patients were discouraged over recurrences of the ulcer after supposed cures. Because of restricted activity and diet some patients became more and more introverted; others were very keen and alert, giving the impression that they were overcompensating for their restricted life by doing certain things exceedingly well.

The personality and emotional reactions of a group of unselected patients suffering from peptic ulcer were studied in detail by Mittelmann, Wolff, and Scharf.[14] They found that the personalities of these patients were of various types and that the incidents precipitating the emotional reactions were numerous. Reactions of intense anxiety, insecurity, resentment, guilt, and frustration occurred in all individuals studied. Such reactions led to compensation through an effort to bolster their self-esteem by a show of independence, self-sufficiency, and perfectionism. The personality disturbances were of such long duration that the peptic ulcer of itself seemed only incidental to the major emotional conflicts. The onset of the ulcer symptoms and the occurrence of some unusually severe emotional reaction frequently took place at the same time. The situations which were associated with the gastric symptoms were not necessarily dramatic or of a critical nature, but they had important effects upon the patient because they occurred when he was already in an emotionally disturbed condition. In experimental situations it was possible to induce emotional crises which precipitated gastric symptoms at times when the patient had been free of such symptoms. On the other hand, when an experimentally disturbed patient was systematically reassured, a feeling of emotional security was created which often led to a prompt remission of the gastric symptoms.

The association and interrelation of emotional states and gastric function were well described by Wolf and Wolff[19, 20] who made an intensive study of a single case which may be summarized as follows:

CASE 22: Tom was aged fifty-six when this study was made. At the age of nine his esophagus had been occluded by drinking scalding-hot clam chowder. Ever since that age he had fed himself through a fistulous opening which had been made through the abdominal wall and the wall of the stomach. A collar of gastric mucosa, derived from the lining of the stomach, extended around this fistula making it ideal for direct observation. Tom was in excellent health, rarely having any digestive complaints. He was shy, sensitive, proud, stubborn, and slightly suspicious. He was funloving but very conscientious. It was possible to take advantage of the fistula and of the collar of gastric mucosa to study the effect of emotion and of changes in everyday mood upon the stomach itself.

Emotionally charged situations were not experimentally produced, but advantage was taken of the spontaneously occurring life situations, problems, and conflicts in order to make the observations. On one occasion Tom suddenly experienced intense fear when an irate doctor entered the experimental room in search of an important hospital record which had been lost. Tom feared that he had mislaid it and might lose his job as a consequence. There was a prompt and decided pallor occurring in the gastric mucosa and a fall in the rate of the acid production of the stomach. A minute later the doctor found his paper and left the room, whereupon the gastric mucosa regained its former color and the acid secretion resumed. Sadness, dejection, and feelings of self-reproach were accompanied in this subject by a taciturnity, lack of energy, slowness of movement, and by a pallor of the gastric mucosa. Even the stomach's normal response to ingestion of food was inhibited when he was depressed. On another occasion a member of the hospital staff entered the experimental room to discharge the subject from a job which he had been doing for this doctor after hours in order to earn extra money. The doctor complained that he was slow, ineffective, and that he charged too much. Tom had taken a good deal of pride in his conscientious attitude toward his duties and resented the charges. When fired, he accepted the situation, but he quickly showed a reddened and engorged mucosa. Acid production accelerated sharply and vigorous gastric contractions began.

When Tom's stomach was engorged and turgid, which occurred whenever he was anxious, hostile, or resentful, he complained of heart burn and abdominal pain. At such times it was possible to demonstrate experimentally that the tissues in the stomach wall were more sensitive to pain; and susceptibility of the mucosa to injury which resulted in slight bleeding was found to be greatly enhanced. Vigorous contractions of the stomach itself produced bleeding points around the exposed collar of mucosa. Ordinarily, these small bleeding points were quickly covered with mucous and healed uneventfully in twenty-four hours or less. The failure of any of these lesions to persist to form a peptic ulcer was due to the effective protection afforded by the secreted mucous. If efforts were made to wipe away the protective mucous so that the bleeding point was repeatedly subject to the action of fresh gastric juice, an area of erosion was set up which took longer to heal.

Emotional conflict, in which anxiety, hostility, or resentment occurred, induced in the stomach profound increases in motility, secretion, and engorgement of the tissues. It was thought that the reason that Tom never acquired a true peptic ulcer was due to the fact that his emotional conflicts were relatively transitory. He was not the sort of person who harbored grudges or maintained emotional stress for long periods of time.*

Since the emotional reactions were clearly followed by bleeding points, it has been inferred that such emotionally charged situations may be directly involved in the genesis of peptic ulcer. That one person develops ulcers while another does not, seems to depend upon whether or not the individual is emotionally upset for long periods of time and

* Wolff, H. G., "Emotions and Gastric Function," *Science*, 1943, *98*, 481–484.

whether the protective mechanism of mucous secretion is adequate in its functioning to allow for healing when small erosions do take place.

A very interesting experiment which illustrated the effect of group psychotherapy on peptic ulcer cases was carried on by Chappell and Stevenson.[4] They divided 52 peptic ulcer cases into two groups. In an experimental group of 32, daily instruction was given for seven weeks concerning the nature of worry and tension, and training in methods of self-suggestion which would lead to emotional control. The second group of 20 patients received medical treatment but no psychotherapy for a period of six weeks. At the end of three weeks 31 of the 32 experimental subjects were free from gastric symptoms, and 26 of them remained symptom-free for differing lengths of time after the end of the treatment. (Ten were symptom-free and on ordinary diets three years after the therapy.) All of the 20 patients in the second group lost their symptoms in response to diet and medication, but within two weeks after the return to a normal diet there was a recurrence of symptoms in 18 of the 20. The results indicated clearly the significance of psychological training, not only in the amelioration of symptoms, but also in keeping the patient in good health after the completion of the training.

It seems, in view of these experimental and clinical observations, that the peptic ulcer patient tends to overreact physiologically and anatomically to the events of everyday life. The effect of the ulcer is to cause pain, discomfort, and a restriction of diet and activity. All these factors cooperate in making the overresponsive individual even more irritable, anxious, and depressed. Many of the ulcer patients show a remarkable and lasting benefit from mental hygiene measures, psychological reeducation, and any kind of psychotherapy promoting emotional stability and self-control. In general, the personality of the peptic ulcer patient is of a reactive nature responding directly to emotional events, particularly those which can be directly related to his actual physical disability.

Mental Abnormalities Associated with Childbirth

Following childbirth a certain per cent of mothers develop acute mental disorders (the estimated percentage varies from 0.1 to 3 per cent). These disorders are usually transitory and episodic in nature and do not constitute specific psychopathological abnormalities which associated themselves only with childbirth or lactation. They are "symptomatic" psychotic episodes precipitated by the physiological and psychological trauma attendant on childbirth and the various following circumstances.

The most common psychopathological occurrence is a delirious excitement and a clouding of consciousness which usually start suddenly. When such a delirium occurs it usually appears during the first or second week following childbirth. It is of varying intensity and often intermingled with other mental abnormalities, such as mania, depression, anxiety, panic, confusion, sudden aversion to relatives, hallucinations, and disorders of speech. If this delirious period does not end in death, it may be followed by (*a*) quick recovery, (*b*) a manic phase and more gradual recovery, (*c*) a depressed phase with immediate recovery or a very prolonged depression, or (*d*) a schizophrenic psychosis with the usual course. In all probability the pregnancy and childbirth act to precipitate one of the common varieties of psychosis in which the delirium is the leading initial symptom. The following case history typifies the events which occur in patients of this variety:

CASE 23: Mrs. Z, age thirty-five, had been admitted to the mental hospital from a general hospital three weeks after the birth of her second child.

Her family history indicated that an aunt had died in a mental hospital, that her older sister had had tuberculosis, and that two other sisters were high-strung and unstable. Her husband said that she was an energetic person, overenthusiastic in her interests. She was inclined to be of a suspicious nature and, although fairly happy during her pregnancy, she did not take too much interest in the anticipated child.

On the third day after childbirth she became very irritable and noisy. She said that her sister was not her sister; she heard voices of unknown guests and of two little girls. She prayed to an imaginary man not to chop down the tree which he was about to do. She said, "Somebody almost robbed me of my baby. I have got to solve all the problems of the universe. I speak to my husband, my soul's husband." This disoriented condition continued for three weeks, although as time went by she became somewhat quieter and exhibited periods of mutism.

When transferred to the mental hospital she still acted only in accordance with the orders which she said were unknown voices which came to her by radio waves. She would sing and mutter to herself. She was restless and slept only in short intervals. She objected violently to being called by her married name and denied that she had ever had a baby. After three months she gradually improved. She returned to her home and children, making a satisfactory adjustment.

The age of onset in this condition ranges from 17 to 45 with an average between 25 and 30. Some observers have reported that it is more frequent in women of Jewish descent than in any other national, racial, or religious group. There is general agreement that mental episodes of this variety occur most frequently in women whose familial ancestry includes more than the usual number of relatives who have had some form of mental disorder.

Anderson[1] made a comparative study of the personality and psy-

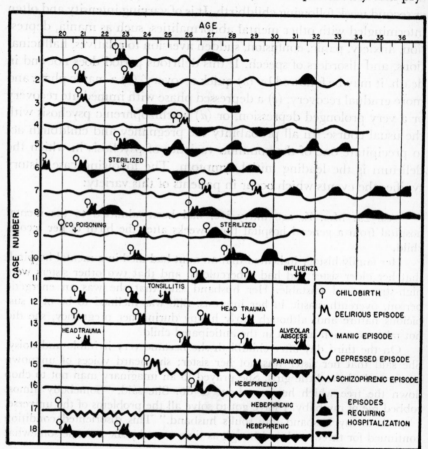

Fig. 9. Diagram of the relation of childbirth, illness, or injury to the onset of a psychotic episode.[11]

chosexuality of 50 cases of married mothers in whom childbirth was followed by psychosis, and of 50 comparable psychotic cases in the same hospital (same age and social status) in whom childbirth had not been followed by a psychosis. The two groups were quite comparable with respect to their psychopathological symptoms. Between the two groups, he found no difference in the premarital sex life, no evidence of differences in degree or variety of shyness, and no significant variations with respect to the adequacy of sex adjustment in marriage. In fact, there was about the same degree of marital happiness or unhappiness in each group.

The relationship between childbirth and psychopathological episodes of varying sorts has been brought out very clearly by the study of Karnosh and Hope.[11] Figure 9 demonstrates in schematic fashion how childbirth, in the same way as influenza, tonsillitis, or head injury, may act to produce psychopathological episodes of differing severity and kinds which may or may not require care in a mental hospital.

These representations of portions of the life of eighteen "susceptible" women show that childbirth sometimes, though not always, precipitates a psychotic episode. According to Karnosh and Hope, whether or not such an episode occurs apparently depends, not only upon the biological and physiological status of the patient, but also upon situational and social factors which may add to the psychological burden.

Summary

In this chapter it has been pointed out that mental symptoms, varying in degree and kind, occur in connection with common physical diseases and following childbirth. It has been emphasized that these psychopathological episodes are associated with occurrences which in most persons do not lead to unusual complications or abnormal behavior. These symptoms do not appear with any degree of regularity, but they are by no means infrequent. Their occurrence in such different chronic diseases as rheumatic heart trouble, tuberculosis, and peptic ulcer illustrates the need for considering the entire personality of the patient and not merely the physical symptoms. As one famous physician said, "Tis not the man's stomach that is sick, 'tis the entire man." No one of these psychopathological complications has ever been shown conclusively to be related directly to any particular aspect of the physical disease itself. Instead, it is assumed that the physical disability either precipitates or accentuates certain preexisting phenomena of the personality structure and emotional life of the affected person.

REFERENCES

1. Anderson, E. W., "A Study of the Sexual Life in Psychoses Associated with Childbirth," *Jour. Ment. Sci.*, 1933, *79*, 137–149.
2. Banister, H., "Some Psychological Observations on Adult Male Tuberculous Patients," *Lancet*, 1930, *218*, 784–786.

3. Breuer, M. J., "The Psychic Element in the Aetiology of Tuberculosis," *Amer. Rev. Tuberc.*, 1935, *31*, 233–239.

4. Chappell, M. N., and T. I. Stevenson, "Group Psychological Training in Some Organic Conditions," *Ment. Hyg.*, 1936, *20*, 588–597.

5. Conner, L. A., "The Psychic Factor in Cardiac Disorders," *Jour. Amer. Med. Asso.*, 1930, *94*, 447–452.

6. Coombs, C. F., "Mental Disorders in Cardiac Disease," *Jour. Ment. Sci.*, 1928, *74*, 250–259.

7. Draper, G., "The Emotion Component of the Ulcer Susceptible Constitution," *Ann. Int. Med.*, 1942, *16*, 633–658.

8. Eyre, M. B., "The Role of Emotion in Tuberculosis," *Amer. Rev. Tuberc.*, 1933, *27*, 315–329.

9. Hoedemaker, E. D., "Psychologic Aspects of Heart Disease," *Ann. Int. Med.*, 1942, *17*, 486–495.

10. Kallmann, F. J., and D. Reisner, "Twin Studies on the Significance of Genetic Factors in Tuberculosis," *Amer. Rev. Tuberc.*, 1943, *47*, 549–574.

11. Karnosh, L. J., and J. M. Hope, "Puerperal Psychoses and Their Sequelae," *Amer. Jour. Psychiat.*, 1937, *94*, 537–550.

12. Knopf, S. A., "Psychology, Psychopathology and Psychotherapy in Tuberculosis in Civil and Military Life," *Military Surgeon*, 1925, *56*, 308–331.

13. Landis, C., and M. M. Bolles, *Personality and Sexuality of the Physically Handicapped Woman*. New York, Hoeber, 1942.

14. Mittelmann, B., H. G. Wolff, and M. P. Scharf, "Emotions and Gastroduodenal Function: Experimenta Studies on Patients with Gastritis, Duodenitis, and Peptic Ulcer," *Psychosom. Med.*, 1942, *4*, 5–61.

15. Morrison, S., and M. Feldman, "Psychosomatic Correlations of Duodenal Ulcer," *Jour. Amer. Med. Asso.*, 1942, *120*, 738–740.

16. Munro, D. G. M., *The Psychopathology of Tuberculosis*. London, Oxford University Press, 1926.

17. Skobel, S., "A Study of Euphoria in Tuberculosis." Unpublished Master's Essay, Columbia University Library, 1935.

18. Strecker, E. A., F. J. Braceland, and B. Gordon, "Mental Attitudes of Tuberculous Patients," *Ment. Hyg.*, 1938, *22*, 529–543.

19. Wolf, S., and H. G. Wolff, *Human Gastric Function*. New York, Oxford, 1943.

20. Wolff, H. G., "Emotions and Gastric Function," *Science*, 1943, *98*, 481–484.

Chapter XVII

PSYCHOPATHIC PERSONALITIES

THE VARIETIES of abnormal persons so far discussed have included the neurotics, the feeble-minded, the psychotics, those with psychosomatic complaints, and certain behavior problems. There remain those individuals without physical or mental disease, but whose behavior is socially disturbing or unduly characterized by jealousy, ill-balanced enthusiasms, embitterment, fanaticism, or sexual deviations. These remaining are usually called "psychopathic personalities." Equivalent names for this category are constitutional inferiority, constitutional psychopathic inferiority, psychopath, constitutional psychopathic state, moral imbecile, constitutional defective, defective delinquent, neurotic constitution. The term *psychopathic personality* is a general classification used to describe all those deviants who cannot, for any of a variety of reasons, be placed in the other accepted categories.

This is at the same time the broadest and the narrowest category of classification of abnormal persons. It is broad in two senses. It includes many different types of deviants and it is, at times, used to describe persons who cannot be diagnosed more precisely because of a lack of specific information. It is a narrow classification since it should be used only after all other possibilities of descriptive diagnosis have been excluded.

Generally speaking, the psychopathic personality is a maladjusted individual whose abnormality is limited or circumscribed within part of his total personality. The focus of abnormality may be compensated for, or rationalized, but the compensation or rationalization frequently causes as much or more trouble than the basic deviation itself ever did.

Deviant Types[5]

Psychopathic personalities are most heterogeneous and are usually placed in this group since they differ from the normal in their mental life and behavior without being clearly psychotic, neurotic, mentally defective, or psychosomatic patients, per se. Hence, when anyone wishes to subdivide these psychopaths into further subclassifications or special types, it is fairly easy to do so; but since the individual cases are so different, it is difficult to make any type precise, distinct, or clearly defined. The types or varieties to be considered are illustrative, but by no means inclusive, of all of this variegated group.

Eccentrics are marked by a lack of inner unity and consistency in their own mental lives. They may show eccentricities in expression, bearing, dress, and speech, as well as in their motives and their thinking. Within the range of normal individuals, there are many who show slight eccentricities, striking habits, and peculiarities; some who exaggerate their enunciation, lay special emphasis on certain food or clothing, and so forth. Because of this similarity, it is not possible to call all eccentrics "psychopaths," and certainly all psychopaths are not eccentric. In the character of the eccentric psychopath there is an essential *weakness* which shows itself in various forms of motivation, anxiety, ill-humor, depression, or hysterical tendencies. All of these expressions of inner weakness or insecurity find expression or compensation in forms of oddness, peculiarity, or originality which serve to mask the inner feeling so far as they are personally concerned. Some of these eccentrics have a marked aversion to some definite person, for example, a brother or a stepmother, regarding this person as the source of their unhappiness. Others show impulsive weaknesses, psychosexual infantilism, avoidance of the opposite sex, peculiar ascetic ideas concerning the relationship of the sexes, or some variety of sexual abnormality.

Vagrants are those who are unable to take up any fixed abode, and who seemingly prefer the hardships which they endure to the greater comforts which could be obtained by a moderate amount of occupational stability. Most vagrants (nonpsychopathics) are either (a) the occupational migrants whose work, for example, farm labor or lumbering, is seasonal; (b) those who must keep on the move because of a criminal record; (c) those whose health seems better with regular change of climate; or (d) those who are frank psychotics. The vagrant who is classed as a psychopathic personality is one who is overwhelmed by the desire to move on, and one in which no other easily recognizable explanation can be given for his behavior.

Many of these psychopathic vagrants are willing workers, following some skilled or semiskilled trade. They will seek employment, do excellent work, and then, after several months, leave the job and move on to some distant city or village where they will repeat the cycle. They can give no good account of their desire to move on except that they are overwhelmed by a wish to be somewhere else, that "somewhere" being none too definite in their own minds. Since many persons with criminal records and many who are more or less psychotic move about in a similar aimless fashion, these psychopathic vagrants meet with trouble at the hands of both local police and social agencies. Although innocent of law infringement, they are charged with crimes and have difficulty in proving their innocence.

Troublemakers (or cranks) are in many instances suffering from paranoia or paranoid dementia praecox. So long as they are not brought to a mental institution the community regards them as troublemakers whose ill nature must be put up with. Their socially undesirable beliefs (either good or bad, true or false) are fairly systematically worked out. Some of these persons are particularly quarrelsome and inclined to take legal action on little or no basis. They show a lack of the usual feeling and sentiment; a lack of the quality of mercy. They do not understand other people; they have few if any true friends. Their troublemaking grows out of their own dominating egocentricity, their lack of human understanding, and their craving for prestige, plus an opposition to their environment, all of which adds up to a gross deviation in self-reference and paranoid ideas.

To assure themselves of their own essential importance they seize upon the events and conversations of everyday life, from which they select items which they combine into systematic ideas of personal affront and insult which must be met by combat. Their own ideas are sacred and must not be questioned. Some of these individuals have a superficial vivacity and humor which enable them to make good initial impressions that may continue if one meets them but occasionally. Where they are associated with others, either in the family or on the job, their crankiness is a source of continual discord.

Like the troublemakers, most *fanatics* are paranoids who have not expressed their maladjustment in a fashion which would lead to mental hospitalization. Fanatics may be either active or passive. The active fanatics identify themselves completely with an overvalued idea which may of itself be quite reasonable (fighting against alcohol), or quite unreasonable (closing of all hospitals). It is all the same to them whether the case is reasonable or not. The idea is fought for in such an inconsiderate, one-sided manner that the fanatic frequently hurts the cause more than he helps. With complete lack of judgment the fanatic charges his opponent with impure motives, untruth, immorality, and dishonesty. He insults his adversary in the most uninhibited manner and is greatly surprised when his own words are reechoed. This only serves for an immediate strengthening of his conviction that he is waging a battle against scoundrels and blockheads. These zealots are excitable, irritable, and yet predominantly cool. They are overly self-reliant, frequently suspicious and jealous, very ambitious for prestige, and lacking in humor.

The passive fanatic has been called the "natural man," the queer fellow, the stranger to reality. Such persons are highly egocentric, desirous of prestige, filled with resentment, and truly eccentric. No matter what the nature of their overvalued ideas, they usually remain harmless either as leaders or followers, at least until they are driven to battle by inexpedient law and prosecution. This may lead them to consider it their duty to devote themselves to demonstration and action. In this group are found the dreamers, the founders and followers of new or strange religious cults.

Senseless criminals commit offenses, murder, assault, arson, theft, when neither they themselves nor anyone else can see any reason or justification for the act. Generally speaking, their criminal conduct is of an aggressive, self-assertive nature. In the history of most such criminals one finds evidence of uncontrolled aggressive outbursts before the age of eighteen. They recognize their difficulties and inability to control their own explosive, aggressive tendencies. They constitute types of partially dissociated personality in which the dissociation is not completely incoordinate or unconscious. Their conduct disorder is more serious in its effects than the dissociation of the hysteric, and yet not so disorganized as that of the psychotic.

One such individual wrote of himself: "I cannot explain anything as my actions have certainly been inexcusable. The irony of returning to this sort of life [prison] after tasting the sweets of real living makes me grit my teeth in an agony of despair which is indescribable. . . . The difference between my thoughts and deeds must strike any intelligent person that I am a madman, utterly and irredeemably insane. Perhaps I am at times. I cannot account for the diversity of my thoughts and actions."*

Such individuals are difficult to please, are intolerant of routine, imperious, bad losers, petulant, egotistical, and emotionally immature. The impulsive, furious act seems to be a symbol of a person in rebellion against organized society. It is an overwhelming of their social inhibitions (Superego) by their blind, unconscious impulses (Id). Some

* Henderson, D. K., *Psychopathic States*. New York, Norton, 1939, 64.

psychological maladjustment appears to set up a state of tension which eventually crystallizes into violence which is followed by relief.

The particular peculiarity of the *explosive psychopath* is his exaggerated tendency to respond to unpleasant events and other stimuli by an explosionlike burst of temper. This tension rapidly reaches a peak of excitement which almost as suddenly subsides. This uncomfortable trait is similar to the impulsiveness which forms part of the character of the senseless criminal. The aggressive act may take the form of suicide which is, in many instances, an impulsive response to frustrating circumstances. The act is consistent with such a person's life pattern of turbulent, impulsive outbreaks whenever difficulties arise. Suicide is the final stroke of a rebel who has been in constant warfare with himself and with society. The man who, on account of a headache associated with a family quarrel, reached for his pistol, saying that a long sleep — preferably in a graveyard — was the only thing that would cure him and his trouble, illustrates the point.

The *depressive psychopath* is characterized by a constant gloomy feeling pervading all his life experience. He is serious, overconscientious, and unable to throw off the effects of the events of everyday existence. He is a genuine pessimist who sees the future dark and dangerous before him. Overestimating the darkness of the future, he underestimates himself. To escape from himself and from reality, he may resort to suicide. The suicidal act is his method of preventing himself from committing forbidden acts; an atonement for forbidden acts; or, an attempt to find security and peace of mind through an act of final escape.

Suicides[2] are by no means limited to these two varieties of psychopathic personality or to persons who are mentally or physically sick. In all probability, any person may think of committing suicide if a certain life situation appears unusually desperate and the proper means for suicide happen to be available; that is, suicide is attempted only as a result of a peculiar and complex combination of circumstances.

Moral defectives[7] or moral imbeciles constitute a group recognized and defined (1927) by English law as, "Persons in whose case there exists mental defectiveness coupled with strongly vicious or criminal propensities, and who require care, supervision, and control for the protection of others." This essential and uncomplicated moral defect, though rare, does occur and is a real and permanent type of mental defect.

These persons profit by training in the ordinary school subjects, may be nimble-witted, good conversationalists, plausible in argument, and well equipped to explain their own conduct. In spite of this, they are incapable of adapting themselves satisfactorily to their social environment. They are unable to foresee actions in their true values, are unable to form sound judgments, to take long views, to make prudent plans, to forego an immediate but transient gain for the sake of a greater and permanent advantage. They seem truly incapable of experiencing any emotion concerning the rightness or wrongness of an act, or of profiting from experience. Personal ethics are purely theoretical to them. They are selfish, showing not the slightest regard for the rights or feelings of others; they are devoid of affection, gratitude, shame, or remorse. They are vain and conceited, but without self-respect.

Pathological liars[3] indulge in falsification which is entirely disproportionate to any discernible end. Usually such liars are not otherwise physically or mentally ill. Such lying rarely centers about a single event, but manifests itself over a period of years or even a lifetime. It is a trait rather than an episode. It sometimes takes the form of accusation either of the self or of some other person. It frequently develops into swindling. Pathological lying is a frequent element in juvenile delinquency, but only a small proportion of delinquents can be called "pathological liars." An example of a pathological liar was a carpenter, aged thirty-five, who presented himself at the district attorney's office and stated that in a fit of jealousy he had shot and killed a man. He gave a detailed and convincing account of his actions. Police investigation showed that his story was completely untrue. He acted as though astonished when told that the man he claimed to have killed was still alive. Further investigation disclosed that he had never met the man, who was in reality a well-known politician.

Psychological studies of pathological liars have shown that their range of ideas is wide; their range of interests is wider than would be expected on the basis of their education; their perceptions are better than average; they are quick-witted; they exhibit faultiness in the development of the concepts and judgments. Their judgment (except self-judgment) is sharp and clear. They show a lack of self-criticism combined with an abnormal egocentric trend of thought that biases their judgments concerning themselves. Their thought processes are logical but there is a marked lack in ethical discernment. The pathological liar never faces openly the question of whether or not his lies may be seen through.

Sexual Psychopathology

There are many varieties and degrees of sexual deviations. The varieties are both simple and complicated; complicated in form of expression, complicated by neurosis, by psychosis, by stupidity, or by physical anomaly or disease. The varieties are attributed to many causes. Some forms are considered natural, some perverse, and some criminal. This presentation is limited to brief description and comment on the possible basis of the deviation. Actually, little is known in any exact form, and present-day social and legal regulation prevents acquisition of much of the knowledge that is necessary for either understanding or control.

Masturbation, generally speaking, is a normal phenomenon. It is a phase of sexual development through which most human beings pass, and which usually drops out during late adolescence. Where masturbation continues to be the main sex outlet in adult life, it is often found to be associated with other psychopathological symptoms. Fear of the opposite sex, a mother (or father) fixation, or a hopeless shyness binds such a person to masturbation which continues both as a sex outlet and as a form of sexual fantasy.

Psychosexual infantilism[6] occurs when the organization or expression of sexuality remains more or less incomplete, or when the infantile or childish expressions (or lack of expression) persist into adult life. This state is frequently found in those of an underdeveloped (hypoplastic) body build. It is essentially either an arrested development of sexuality or, at the best, a very slow and retarded growth. Such individuals are not necessarily otherwise deviant, but this sort of immaturity causes social and psychological trouble, even if the other features of their mental and physical development are fairly normal. Their developmental failure in sexuality is often misinterpreted, ridiculed, or not recognized either by themselves or by others so creating maladjusted attitudes.

Narcissism is an exaggerated form of self-regard or self-love; the state of being in love with one's own Ego, with outspoken and overt erotic attraction to one's own body. The extreme narcissist takes himself (or herself) as his sexual goal and sexual object. The psychopathic narcissist collects photographs of himself in the nude; dresses or ornaments himself fantastically before the mirror. Narcissists are reserved, tender, delicate, or cold individuals who love solitude and are literally self-sufficient.

Transvestites gain erotic satisfaction from wearing the clothing of the opposite sex. They are not necessarily homosexual, although some of them are.

Pedophilia, gerontophilia, and zoophilia are abnormalities in the preference of the object for sex outlet. The pedophile seeks a child or young adolescent as a sex object; the gerontophile, an elderly person; and a zoophile, an animal. The preference of each of these types is based on a complicated emotional fixation related to feelings of personal insecurity, shyness, inadequacy, and, perhaps, of incest desire. These abnormalities are subject to criminal prosecution.

Fetishism refers to a sex emotional fixation on some unusual object which in itself may give rise to erotic feeling or satisfaction, or it may be a necessary associate for a   otherwise normal sex outlet. The objects vary from love symbols (ribbons, rings, locks of hair) to abnormal forms of erotic and sexual fetishism in which the sexual partner disappears entirely from the symbol and the symbol itself becomes the adequate sex object. Clothing, shoes, furs, handkerchiefs, and the like, may become sex objects of themselves. In other forms of fetishism the sex partner must be clad in a certain way, must bear only a special odor, or the bed must have only certain decorations before sex-excitement can be established. Probably, fetishism is a form of conditioned emotional response.

Exhibitionism means the public display of the genital regions with the conscious purpose of sexual satisfaction. It occurs more frequently in men than in women, and more frequently in old men than in young men. The exhibitionistic psychopath usually is bashful and defiant, has an exaggerated childish sense of shame, together with a general deterioration of emotional control.

Sadism and masochism are methods of securing sexual satisfaction through the infliction and endurance, respectively, of pain or torture. These terms have been widely used and broadened in meaning by the psychoanalysts. The analysts point out that sadistic torture and masochistic suffering are not limited to the physical preparation for, and accomplishment of, the sex act, but constitute basic attitudes which reach deeply into the individual mental life. In the psychopath, evidence is frequently found of either or both of these tendencies. This may or may not reach the level of criminality in any one individual, but many crimes which are called "psychopathic" are sadistic or masochistic in nature.

Satyriasis and nymphomania are exaggerations of the normal heterosexual impulse in the male and female, respectively. Such persons are possessed by an almost constant sex urge; they are the sexual athletes.

Constant desire keeps pace with their sexual capacity and activity. In the unstable male psychopath, this desire may lead to various abnormalities in behavior, or to sex crimes if adequate outlet cannot otherwise be accomplished. In the female, prostitution, either paid or unpaid and without regard to disease or possible conception, may occur.

Homosexuality is only incidentally associated with psychopathic personality. The homosexual is attracted to members of his (or her) own sex in the same emotional fashion and degree that the normal individual is attracted to members of the opposite sex. As a form of sex outlet, overt homosexuality occurs one or more times in the life of 20 to 35 per cent of the white male population, and in 15 to 30 per cent of the white female population. The number of persons who have had or are having homosexual relations varies widely, depending on social, economic, and educational circumstances, as well as opportunity. The fact that such a large percentage of the population has had homosexual experience does not mean that the practice is overly common. Like masturbation, most homosexual experience occurs during late adolescence or early adult life and is but a passing phase — a form of sex experimentation — in certain persons who pass on to heterosexual orientation without any particular psychological trauma. If, at a later period of life, heterosexual relations are not possible for any of a variety of reasons, some individuals may resume homosexual practices.

There are some persons who are both homosexual and heterosexual in their behavior for long periods of time or for most of their lives. Other individuals are exclusively homosexual for all or for most of their adult life. This latter group is relatively small and includes individuals whose behavior, dress, and attitude are those of an *invert*, a male who acts or dresses like a woman, or a female who acts or dresses like a man. These inverts are usually the persons who are called "homos," and against whom society directs scorn and punishment.

Overt homosexuality is not limited to one sex, or to any social, economic, racial, educational, or cultural group. Its true origin is unknown. Heredity, constitution, parental overprotection during childhood, sexual trauma during adolescence, endocrine imbalance, homosexual practice and fixation during adolescence are among the explanations advanced. The wide variety of persons and practices precludes any single explanatory principle. In many instances the simplest explanation is in terms of a fixation of a conditioned emotional response. During adolescence society throws many barriers between the sexes while approving of close friendships between members of the same sex. Homoerotic attachments and some overt homosexual experience may occur. Certain individuals become emotionally fixed at this level and find themselves unable to become heterosexually oriented. Others are able, with varying degrees of difficulty, to break the original conditioned fixation, more or less completely. In most instances the fixation and breaking of the fixation are socially or psychologically determined; otherwise stated, in a majority of cases there is no conclusive evidence of an anatomical or physiological basis for homosexuality.

Psychological Description and Explanation[4,5]

Are there some common underlying psychological elements in these groups of psychopathic personalities, or is it really a mixture of widely different types? Experts in dealing with such cases agree that the psychopath should and can be differentiated from other diagnostic groups; but as to what really constitutes the psychopath, there is a wide diversity of opinion and explanation. Many investigators have been impressed by the number of blood relatives of psychopaths who were mental deviants; in other words, the bad heredity. Others have been impressed by the "constitutional inferiority" — the defective, dysplastic, physically unfit, or unhealthy body. But bad heredity and constitutional inferiority of themselves do not constitute psychopathy. Hence, recourse is had to psychological concepts for description and explanation.

Kraepelin divided psychopaths into the excitable, the unstable, the impulsive, the eccentric, and the quarrelsome. Sheetz described the psychopath as superficial, impractical, incapable of clear or precise concepts, unable to grasp the finer meanings of moral issues, weak-willed, poor planners, lacking in foresight and self-control, childish in judgment, selfish, self-centered, unreliable, and, because of a marvelous lack of common sense, dangerous.

Sullivan emphasized three prominent characteristics: (a) Psychopaths show in certain isolated fields an inability to profit by experience, with a complete inability to grasp what society expects of them in certain situations. (b) They have marked feelings of inadequacy or defect, so that they develop a great talent at compensation and rationalization. (c) They show inability to use foresight to control their immediate gratification. They can think ahead, but when they go into action they are governed by immediate satisfactions.

Another recent formulation[1] divides the psychopaths into three overlapping groups: the vulnerable personalities, the unusual personalities, and the sociopathic personalities. The vulnerable personalities are the potentially unstable persons who have only a small margin of reserve and who, when caught by circumstances, are liable to develop neurotic, psychotic, or psychopathic reactions. The type of reaction will depend on the circumstances. These are the persons who do "break" under tension or maladjustment. They recover when the circumstances are altered. Therapy is usually successful if the environmental circumstances can be made easy and kept favorable for the patient.

The unusual personalities are not necessarily unstable or socially undesirable; for example, a well-adjusted homosexual or an eccentric inventor. On the other hand, if they are schizoid, cycloid, hysterical, explosive, or obsessional, then emotional maladjustment and social conflicts are apt to occur. Their life history is a story of one escapade after another.

The sociopathic personalities are asocial and antisocial. They may be either predominantly inadequate or predominantly aggressive. Those who are inadequate are usually characterized as having constitutional psychopathic inferiority. They are weak, unstable, and complaining. Therapy consists of constant care, supervision, and "babying." The predominantly aggressive may be either fanatics or criminals, depending on whether their aggression is directed toward the betterment (?) of society or toward the deliberate flaunting of social rules and laws. No form of therapy has been effective with the antisocial psychopath.

Summary

In spite of all efforts to bring some understanding and systematic viewpoint to bear on this group of abnormal persons, we find that little more than direct descriptions of individual cases is possible. These persons are not mentally defective or insane in the usual sense of the terms. Their behavior is unusual, asocial, or antisocial. The individual, himself, may or may not realize that his behavior is inadequate, but he will offer little more than rationalizations in explanation. Therapy can be directed only to the immediate problem. Therefore, it is only in very exceptional cases that any real, lasting benefit has been reported as resulting from any form of therapy.

REFERENCES

1. Curran, D., and P. Mallinson, "Psychopathic Personality," *Jour. Ment. Sci.*, 1944, *90*, 266–286.

2. Dublin, L. I., and B. Bunzel, *To Be or Not To Be*. New York, Smith and Haas, 1933.

3. Healy, W., and M. T. Healy, *Pathological Lying, Accusation and Swindling*. Boston, Little, 1915.

4. Henderson, D. K., *Psychopathic States*. New York, Norton, 1939.

5. Kahn, E., *Psychopathic Personalities*. New Haven, Yale University Press, 1931.

6. Landis, C., *et al.*, *Sex in Development*. New York, Hoeber, 1940.

7. Tredgold, A. F., *Mental Deficiency* (6th ed.). Baltimore, Wood, 1937.

Chapter XVIII

HEREDITY

IN THE preceding chapters we have taken up first, the psychological concepts of abnormality, and next, the description and "explanation" of certain of the common or illustrative forms of abnormal behavior. We have dealt with general types, rather than specific forms of abnormality. In no sense has more than a small sample of the immense variety of forms which human abnormality of behavior and mental life can take, been covered. Recall for a moment the varieties of abnormality which have been taken up, and note that some of these varieties are clearly disease processes in the usual medical sense; others are legal concepts; others are precipitated by personal actions or outside agents; others are associated with natural developmental or degenerative processes; others arise from the basic personality structure; and still others do not fall clearly into any of these classifications. The descriptions and elucidations have been given in terms of psychological or medical concepts, wherever possible.

So far, there has been presented the gross picture of the abnormality as it occurs and as it is seen by others or experienced by the individual. Given briefly, wherever possible, have been various findings and theories which have been advanced to explain the conditions, without implying that a final explanation was at hand, which would be agreed upon by practically all authorities working in this field. The reader may quite legitimately be puzzled, by this time, by the lack of any satisfactory or comprehensive scheme of explanation. He may feel that many of the explanations are pretty flimsy and that the statement has been made too often that the essential nature or cause of the disability is unknown. To meet this objection, wherever possible, this and the succeeding two chapters are devoted to the consideration of the problems of basic explanation in terms of heredity, culture, environment or development.

What are the relative roles of heredity and environment in determining human behavior? This question constitutes one of the most controversial fields in both the biological and social sciences. Time after time leaders of thought, well qualified to express themselves in this particular controversy, have pointed out that there can be no solution to the problem so long as it is posed as though heredity and environment were completely independent entities. Actually, heredity cannot exist without environment, or environment without heredity.

All animate existence is dependent upon heredity. No individual organism exists save through a process of hereditary transmission. This particular process varies somewhat in its detail and complexity among various living organisms, but the essential scheme remains the same. From this point, authorities proceed to indicate the evidence and logical deductions which have convinced them that all forms of human abnormality are strictly governed by the laws and forms of organic inheritance. Certain of these authorities hold to what one may call a theory of mechanistic evolution. According to this concept, all variations are mechanically and inevitably produced, and no circumstance or human action can change the rigid predetermination of the course of existence. Abnormality is merely the name given to one form of mechanically determined variation. Others hold to a theory of "emergent" evolution, in which emphasis is placed on the fact that new forms and new variations do occur in a fashion which is essentially unpredictable. New forms are continually occurring or emerging, so that new types of human abnormality may be the result of the emergent evolutionary processes.

In contrast to the hereditary or genetic point of view, there is a sociological or behavioristic viewpoint which claims that all forms of human nature, both normal and abnormal, are due to environmental, social, or educational circumstances in the life of each particular individual. The similarity in final form among individuals results from similarity in these circumstances. These writers believe that heredity operates only in the determination of the general form and physique; for example, white, Negro, tall, short, blond, brunette; but after these basic qualities have been laid down at the instant of conception, all remaining variation during the life of any individual is determined by such factors as nutrition, education, social pressure, and so on. Watson probably made the most extreme statement of this viewpoint, as follows: "Give me a dozen healthy infants, well formed, and my own specified world to bring them up in and I'll guarantee to take any one at random and train him to become any type of specialist I might select — doctor, lawyer, artist, merchant-chief and, yes, even beggarman and thief, regardless of his talents, penchants, tendencies, abilities, vocations, and race of his ancestors."*

A more constructive and illuminating viewpoint lies between that of the strict geneticist and the overzealous environmentalist.[23] Here the claims and explanations, the facts and theories, the phenomena and speculations of both schools are appraised and coordinated, with an eye to the use of the best from the two approaches. This may be called the "developmental approach." By development, in this sense, is meant the reciprocal effect of heredity and environment in the determination of the constitution, the behavior, and the mental life of each being.

In the present chapter, then, we will consider the facts, the laws, and the speculations concerning the role played by heredity in the determination of any individual, particularly the abnormal individual.

Heredity

Every human being originates by the union of an ovum and a spermatozoon. The fusion of these two cells into a single cell takes place at the instant of conception. In the nucleus of both the ovum and

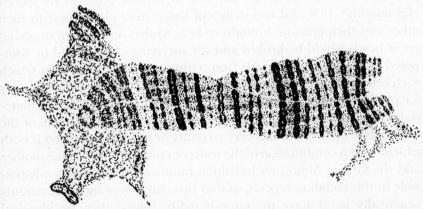

Fig. 10. Drawing of the salivary chromosomes of drosophila melanogaster.[2]

spermatozoon are minute microscopic, threadlike structures which are known as "chromosomes." As Figure 10 shows, each chromosome has banded areas which are related to the parts which are called "genes." The genes are the carriers of the individual characteristics which determine the fundamental physical and mental differences among in-

* Watson, J. B., *Behaviorism.* New York, Norton, 1930, 82.

dividuals. The entire heredity of any individual, all that the individual obtains from his ancestry, is present at the moment of conception. After the fusion of the ovum and spermatozoon has taken place, the fertilized cell begins dividing. This process of division always consists of the cell dividing itself into two, each new cell receiving half of the nucleus and the same number of chromosomes and genes as the original cell had. As this process of cell division goes forward, cells take on certain specialized functions, namely skin cells, brain cells, and muscle cells, but in every case the nucleus of the cell carries the same number of chromosomes and, presumably, the same gene construction. In this sense, every single cell of the body is merely a specialized modification of the single fertilized cell which started the life of that particular individual.

Both the ovum and spermatozoon carry a complete set of chromosomes. At the time of fertilization, the chromosomes from the spermatozoon take up a position in a paired relationship to the chromosomes of the ovum. In this way, half of any individual's heredity comes from the mother and half from the father. Which half of the genes will be obtained from which parent is dependent on a process in which there is a large element of chance, since certain of the genes of one chromosome are shoved out at the expense of certain genes in its paired chromosome. It is as if two strings of beads were placed next to each other and then pressure brought to bear so that one of each opposing set of beads would be broken and the surviving chain would be composed of the unbroken beads from either set. This process, in which each cell originally contained all of the materials which were necessary for producing an individual — the mother supplying all of the materials for producing an individual of one type and the father all of the materials necessary for another — results in an individual who is both a blend and a combination of the traits or character of both the mother and the father. Almost an indefinite number of combinations is possible in this blending process, so that two children of the same parents practically never have the same heredity (unless they are identical twins, who develop from one fertilized ovum). The child receives from the parents the gene combination of his chromosomes, and, so far as we know at present, the physical inheritance is entirely determined by the chromosomal structure of each particular individual. *Heredity is that which is passed (either physical or mental) from parent to child through the chromosomes and the genes.* The genetic constitution of the cell is acted upon continuously by the environment from the moment of conception. The result of the action of the genetic component and all the given environmental occurrences sets up the constitution of each particular individual. In this sense, then, the term *constitution* is reserved for *the resultant of the interaction between heredity and environment.*

The existence of hybrids demonstrates the importance of heredity.[22] If a donkey and a mare are mated, the offspring is a mule, even though the environment during pregnancy and shortly after birth is entirely that of the species of the mother, that is, the horse. On the other hand, some environmental conditions during foetal life do affect the offspring. It has been demonstrated that one can irradiate the developing embryo with X-rays, or one can cool the body of the mother markedly for a short period of time early in pregnancy, and the offspring will show pronounced physical deviations from those which would be found if neither X-ray nor cooling had been used. (Such offspring biologists call "monsters.") Hence it is evident that environmental factors, even during the earliest stages of life, are capable of interfering drastically with the normal development of the individual. Fortunately, true human hybrids or monsters occur but rarely.

It is important to realize that oversimplified ideas concerning the independent effects of heredity or environment are no longer tenable. One can no longer postulate that the development of an individual is an unfolding process in which his inherited characteristics determine his entire constitution, or, that development is a molding process in which the environment does the work and the individual is practically passive. Actually, the problem concerns itself with the relative effect of maturation versus growth-through-use.

By *maturation* is meant the sort of development which occurs any time during the life of the individual and which does not depend directly upon uses, function, or characteristic activity of the organism or any part of the organism. Growth-through-use means, as the phrase implies, the sort of development which takes place in habit formation after exercise, and through learning or thinking. These are separate and distinct developmental processes, as has been experimentally demonstrated.

The phenomenon of maturation is not necessarily due to an increase in size or function of the organism. Rather, it accompanies the process of cell differentiation. Very shortly after conception and during the early stages of cell multiplication, certain cells tend to assume specialized functions, while some tend to grow more rapidly and to develop in more complicated patterns of relationship than do others.

This process has been the subject of a vast amount of research in the science of embryology. The determining factors of this differentiation in function and rate of growth are complicated, but many of them have been experimentally worked out, so that we may accept them as factual.

Growth-through-use or exercise is the normal, common-sense view of development that we apply in our everyday thinking. One's muscles become stronger through exercise; by practice one is able to read more rapidly; through the acquisition of skill one can knit more rapidly. Many of us never consider the possibility that this sort of development is related to either heredity or maturation. It has been taken for granted that we have inherited the anatomy of the arms and hands, while the process of knitting is regarded as an acquired ability based on adequate muscular coordination. That this is not entirely true is apparent when one considers the knitting done by a small child. The arms, hands, and fingers, the muscles and nerves are all present and, as we know, quite highly functional; and yet, the process of learning to knit is very slow and clumsy in the six-year-old, whereas, when the same process is started at age twelve or fourteen, it is much more rapidly acquired. We have, here, evidence of the interaction between maturation and growth in normal development. Experimentation has shown that maturation does not necessarily cease when use begins. Each forward step in maturation supplies the individual with the basis for new activity and for new learning.

General Observations

Heredity, inheritance, and genetics are not usually advanced as explanatory concepts in psychology or in any of the social sciences. Somehow, the notion has spread abroad that any evidence concerning the action of hereditary factors in human affairs makes those affairs hopeless and justifies adopting a fatalistic attitude. This has gone so far that in much which is written concerning mental hygiene, man has been assumed to be free of all of the genetic laws which have been found to govern the predisposition and preformation of all other forms of living organisms. It is true that the earlier applications of genetic principles which were based on simple Mendelian laws were rather inexact and unfruitful in abnormal psychology. Since the earlier applications were found wanting, many social scientists have continued to reject genetic concepts, even though the flood of new discoveries has completely changed our knowledge of genetic principles.

Modern human genetics has demonstrated that the factors involved in mental disorders may be either specific or nonspecific* in predisposing any one person to some form of psychopathology. The genetic factors may be related to either the *predisposition* (which provides the basis for and tendency toward a particular form of deviation) or to *preformation* (which concerns the gradual development in the direction of a particular deviation). A third mechanism acting in the organization of any mental disorder is that of *provocation* (precipitating cause) which refers to its beginning, activation, precipitation, and actual manifestation as we see it in its complete form. The relationship existing between these three factors is complicated and varies among the different abnormalities. The following presentation of the role which heredity plays in abnormal psychology is made without reference to Mendelian laws or to many of the principles which the geneticist believes necessary for the complete explanation and understanding of heredity. Anyone interested in the more exact mechanics of the action of heredity can find the relevant material in any of the more recent books in the field of genetics.

Methods of Investigation of Heredity in Psychopathology

There are three methods by which the contribution of heredity to psychopathology can be investigated. These are (*a*) the pedigree or family-history method, (*b*) the contingency method of statistical prediction of association, and (*c*) the twin-study method.

PEDIGREE OR FAMILY-HISTORY METHOD

The most obvious method for the study of the possible inheritance of abnormal conditions is the family history. If one can look into the genealogy of any particular abnormal individual, it should be theoretically possible to find how frequently the same or similar varieties of abnormality have been exhibited in past generations. The most clearcut examples of this type of research are found in the family-history studies of Huntington's chorea, where the presence of the disorder has been traced back for twelve generations and three hundred years. Similar studies have been made of feeble-minded individuals, notably the Kallikak family and the Juke family.

Certain very real criticisms and difficulties are attached to the

* "Specific factor" means some distinct, definite result will occur, for example, blue eyes or Huntington's chorea; "nonspecific factor" means a general resistance or lack of resistance which will facilitate or inhibit the appearance of some condition, for example, physical strength or tuberculosis.

pedigree studies of abnormal persons. In the first place, most of the diseases or abnormalities, which we regard today as more or less unitary manifestations, are rather recent concepts in the history of human thought. Feeble-mindedness and epilepsy are the only two conditions which have been known in the same general way for any considerable period of our past history. Manic-depressive insanity, dementia praecox, or the psychoneuroses are based on concepts which have been developed in the last fifty or sixty years. If we attempt to trace dementia praecox back through generations previous to 1900, we must have access to very good case records which will allow us to make a classification entirely on the basis of described symptoms. This is usually an impossible condition of investigation, since satisfactory histories are seldom available. Records which do exist were, very frequently, taken in a different conceptual scheme, with emphasis placed on events and symptoms which are now considered unimportant or irrelevant.

A second difficulty grows out of the fact that mental abnormality has been (and still is) regarded by most people as a disgrace to the family in which it occurs. Hence, many families do anything in their power to conceal the occurrence of mental illness. In particular, they do not inform their children or grandchildren that certain members of the family have had one or another form of psychopathological disturbance. Furthermore, many of these queer relatives are never brought to the attention of public authorities, since they are cared for at home; hence, there is no public record of the abnormality.

Another difficulty in the pedigree method relates to the different standards of abnormality which have prevailed in different communities in times past. For example, an individual who today would be said to be suffering from either simple or hebephrenic dementia praecox, might very easily have been thought to be feeble-minded or to have been gifted in piety, if his hallucinations were interpreted as the voices of God and the angels. The entire group of symptoms having to do with depression, anxiety, guilt feelings, and the like, were lumped together under the single category of melancholia. Burton's[3] classical book, *The Anatomy of Melancholy* (1621), illustrates the tremendous variety of depressive features which were grouped under one heading, and which would make family history studies most difficult to analyze, since here were thrown together many different symptom pictures as we understand them today.

At the best, then, one can only deal with the histories of certain families, in which the abnormality was fairly constant and clear and

PLATE 12

FRANCIS GALTON (1822–1911)

of such a nature that it could not be concealed from the general public. These histories are "minimum" histories, in that many ancestors and offspring who were free from the particular condition broke away from the family and are lost from the records.

In spite of all of these difficulties, human beings have been convinced throughout the ages that certain *abnormalities run in families*. On this one point, popular belief and common sense are clear and definite, and frequently at odds with scientific theories or clinical evidence.

CONTINGENCY OR STATISTICAL METHOD

In 1869 Galton[5] first pointed out and made use of both the statistical method and the twin method in the analysis of the heredity of psychopathological persons. Essentially, the contingency method tests whether two variables are associated. In this case the specific problem is whether certain traits or abnormalities occur more frequently in some families than would be expected by chance. For example, the school achievement of siblings correlates more highly than the school achievement of unrelated persons; the occurrence of catatonic states in child and parent correlates more highly than the occurrence in un-related persons in two succeeding generations. This method has the advantage of making use of large samples of the general population who are alive and measurable at any one time. Today, the contingency method is used mainly as an auxiliary procedure with either the pedigree or twin-study method.

TWIN-STUDY METHOD

The most difficult method to use in the investigation of human heredity, but at the same time, the most precise, is the twin method. In the United States identical twins occur about three times out of a thousand births, while nonidentical twins occur about nine times out of a thousand. Identical twins result from a division of a single fertilized ovum at a very early stage in development. Since all cells derived from the same fertilized ovum have exactly the same make-up of chromosomes and genes, the two individuals coming from this single fertilized ovum are exactly alike in their heredity. They are always of the same sex, similar in appearance, have similar fingerprints, and have many other physical and mental similarities. Since they are of identical heredity, any difference which develops between them must be due to some difference in the effect of environment or in the differential rate of growth or maturation. Nonidentical twins are derived from two different ova fertilized by two different spermatozoa. Genetically, they are no more alike than any other two siblings. The fact that they are conceived and born at the same time does not make their heredity similar, although their environment both before and after birth has a greater similarity than that of other siblings.

Since identical twins have identical heredity, they form ideal material on which to base investigation of psychopathological conditions. Identical twins reared apart form a more crucial group for experimental purposes than any other that can be obtained. In this last instance, we have two individuals with exactly the same heredity, who are subjected to different environments, different nutrition, different training, different social attitudes. Then, if we compare the variety of psychopathology which occurs in one twin with the presence or absence of psychopathology in the other, we have a practically certain answer to the question of the importance of heredity in the formation of the abnormal condition.

The discussion of the biological principles of heredity and of the methods of investigation of human heredity which we have just given has been expressed in simple terms. We have not taken up the nature of the Mendelian laws of heredity, the necessary statistical corrections, the effect of unit characters and of multifactorial influences, and so on. These are all of great importance in the final answers which the geneticist uses to confirm or deny the effect of heredity in psychopathology. It is enough to point out those relationships which seem to have a fair degree of certainty and those in which a great deal of question still remains, without going too far into the details of the evidence.

Heredity in Specific Forms of Abnormality

We must remind ourselves again of the exceedingly complicated nature of human heredity and of the even more uncertain knowledge concerning the true disorder in many of the psychopathological states. Actually, the clearest records of human heredity in morbid conditions have been obtained in studies which have to do with skin disease and abnormalities of the eyes. In either state the tissue or organ involved is on the outside of the body where it can be easily studied, treated, measured, or experimented upon. When we contrast this to ear diseases, we at once recognize the difficulties encountered, since the essential mechanism of the ear is deeply imbedded in hard bone, making it extremely difficult to study even after death. The brain is the primary structure in which the basis of abnormality of behavior or mental life rests. Only under exceptional surgical conditions is the brain ever exposed for direct study. Hence, our evidence concerning the interrelationship between hereditary, anatomical, and physiological disorders of the brain itself, and their attendant abnormal mental states must rest on indirect evidence.

The following tabulation summarizes the present-day evidence with respect to the predisposing role of heredity in specific conditions:

1. Conditions which are predominantly or completely due to genetic factors: Huntington's chorea, idiopathic epilepsy, dementia praecox, manic-depressive psychosis, mental deficiency (idiopathic, but not all special forms).

2. Conditions in which both environmental (development and aging as natural processes) and genetic factors play a part: primary behavior disorders in children, involutional melancholia, senile psychoses, psychoneuroses, anxiety states, hysteria, neurasthenia, tuberculosis.

3. Conditions which are due predominantly or completely to environmental factors and where heredity plays very little or no direct part: general paresis, neurosis following trauma, reactive depressions, symptomatic psychoses due to intoxication (including some forms of alcoholism).

EPILEPSY

It will be recalled that the central symptom in this condition is the convulsive seizure. These seizures can be the result of organic injury or infection of the brain or its coverings, of toxic influences, or idiopathic conditions. When the family histories of the idiopathic epileptics are studied, we find good evidence that epilepsy is more apt to occur among their blood relatives than among the blood relatives of nonepileptic persons. The actual incidence reported varies according to the different types of patients included in the various studies. Convulsive reactions occur in 18 per cent of the members of the immediate families of epileptics and in but 1.3 per cent of the relatives of nonepileptics.[8,19] Migraine, alcoholism, and other nervous and mental conditions have been found to run in the same families that have epileptic members.

A further line of supporting evidence for the hereditary component in epilepsy comes from the studies of twins.[15] When one of a pair of identical twins has any type of epileptic seizure, the other twin, in two out of three cases, also has seizures; while in nonidentical twins only 3 out of 100 of the twin partners have seizures.[4] Among nonidentical twins having idiopathic seizures, 24 per cent of twin partners were also found to have seizures.

In many of the older studies of the heredity of convulsive states the finding of such a predisposition was itself so vague that no adequate understanding of the condition was reached. Recent electroencephalographic studies[10] have put this assumption of a genetic predisposition on a firmer basis. One study showed abnormal brain waves in 46 per cent (17 out of 37) of the relatives of idiopathic epileptics. These relatives were supposedly normal; at least, up to that time they had shown no convulsions. Another investigation[9] of 138 relatives of 76 epileptics indicated that 54 per cent showed some abnormality of brain waves, as compared to 6 per cent of the relatives of a control group of normal subjects. In 94 per cent of the epileptic cases, at least one of the parents had abnormal records. Another group of investigators[20] found that in 45 per cent of the cases of idiopathic epilepsy, at least one member of the family had abnormal brain waves. These findings show that abnormal brain waves are an indication of cerebral dysfunction which has the possibility of giving rise to convulsive seizures, and that this potentiality runs in certain families.

GENERAL PARESIS

A common mistake, made not only by the general public but by scientists and medical men as well, is to say that syphilis may be hereditary (rather than congenital). There is no evidence that syphilis affects the germ plasm or that it infects the foetus before birth. It is possible for the infant to become infected with syphilis at the time of birth, or from the mother at a very early age. This, of course, is not hereditary transmission but an example of infection or contagion.

There is one possibility where heredity might play a role in general paresis. It is estimated that general paresis occurs in not more than one out of twenty to thirty cases of untreated primary syphilitic infection. What evidence is there, then, that this one case out of twenty has an inherited lack of resistance to syphilitic invasion of the central nervous system? On the basis of a rather small group of identical twins, one of whom had developed general paresis, one investigator[11] concluded that there was a somewhat higher incidence of general paresis in the co-twin than one would have expected by chance. This study has been criticized, but it remains the only pertinent evidence. In our present state of knowledge there is no conclusive evidence concerning the heredity of a susceptibility to general paresis.

ALCOHOLIC PSYCHOSES

The chronic alcoholics, the alcohol addicts, and the alcoholics with psychosis constitute a very heterogeneous group. Generally speaking, when one lumps together all varieties of alcoholism, one finds evidence that alcoholism occurs in the blood relatives of alcoholics much more frequently than one would expect by chance. Is this sufficient to conclude that heredity determines susceptibility to alcohol and its effects? Or, does alcohol have some effect on the germ plasm and, hence, are the children of alcoholics apt to deviate in one way or another? In answer to the first question, Pohlisch[13] found that the children and grandchildren of alcoholics admitted to mental hospitals did not succumb to alcoholic addiction themselves to any greater extent than one would find in a random population. This statement has to be qualified by pointing out that Pohlisch limited his conclusion to alcoholic patients who were not suffering from some other form of mental disorder, such as dementia praecox or epilepsy. If the alcoholic patient comes from a family in which there is some psychopathological disorder in addition to the alcoholism, then the same per cent of the offspring will show the mental deviation that one would find in the particular defective stock of which he is a member.

A very extensive research study[1] carried out on some five or six hundred generations of white mice indicated that the exposure to alcohol throughout all of these generations seemed eventually to lead to an increase in the number of physical mutations. However, no effects were found until after several hundred generations of animals had been so treated. If it is possible to generalize from this work on mice to the human race, then we would have to have a rather high degree of exposure to the effects of alcohol for all members of the community, over several hundred generations, before any physical anomalies would show themselves. There is no evidence, other than this, which would indicate that alcohol may damage or affect the germ plasm.

MENTAL DISEASES OF OLD AGE

Despite the fact that senile dementia is a major public health problem, we have no reliable evidence indicating whether or not heredity has any effect upon the development of this condition. It is true that death from arteriosclerosis (not necessarily cerebral) does seem to run in many families. Since arteriosclerosis is a terminal condition reached only by those who have survived all other hazards of life, it is impossible to say whether this evidence is significant or not.

NEUROLOGICAL DISEASES

There is the widest sort of difference among the various neurological diseases with respect to heredity. Some conditions, such as Huntington's chorea, show clear and undeniable evidence of heredity. Others show a combination of hereditary vulnerability to certain infections which are effective only in the more susceptible cases. At the other extreme we have diseases, such as poliomyelitis, which operate seemingly without respect to any known hereditary factor of resistance or susceptibility.

FEEBLE-MINDEDNESS

Like epilepsy, feeble-mindedness may arise from a variety of conditions. If we consider, at present, the heredity of only the idiopathic aments, the findings are markedly similar to those of epilepsy. The famous family histories of the Kallikaks, the Jukes, the Namms, and the like, have illustrated beyond doubt that in certain families low-grade mentality was marked, persistent, and undeniable in many succeeding generations. In all probability, these histories covered exceptional family situations occurring in exceptional cultural circumstances. Only under extraordinary conditions do imbeciles or idiots reproduce (many of them are sterile). Hence, most of the new cases of amentia must come either from parents who are of moronic or upper imbecile level, or from parents of normal intellect who have amentia in their family history. The present theory is that mental deficiency is brought about by the interaction of many factors operating together in the heredity of the individual (multifactorial inheritance).[12] Feeblemindedness, in general, turns out to be made up of a collection of biological deviants in whom the leading symptom is a defect in intelligence and intellect. Earlier workers attempted to show that feeblemindedness was due to some unit character in inheritance, but today it is thought that such instances are the exception rather than the rule.

PSYCHONEUROSES AND PSYCHOPATHIC PERSONALITIES

In previous chapters, a distinction was made between the various forms of psychoneuroses and of psychopathic personalities. This distinction was made because we wished to present and explain the respective deviations as forms of abnormal psychology. When we consider the possible role of heredity in these conditions, it is advisable to change the basis of distinction. Furthermore, all the evidence of the particular relationship of heredity to these conditions is tentative and speculative, in contrast to the material available for the other psychopathological states. If one puts together all persons who show marked symptoms of some variety of either psychoneurosis or psychopathic personality, it is possible to redivide this total into two major groupings. The first, we may call the "psychologically and constitutionally inadequate." These are individuals who suffer from simple anxieties, phobias, hysterical manifestations, weak will, indecisiveness. Some authorities have held that in these inadequate individuals there is a multifactorial genetic mechanism basic to the inadequacy. If this is true, the psychological abnormalities are the result of a variable hereditary defect which shows itself in an inadequate constitution responding in an inadequate way to environmental circumstances.

In contrast to the inadequate group, the second group is made up of individuals who resemble schizophrenics, manic-depressives, and certain of the epileptic patients, so that we may speak of neurotic or psychopathic persons having schizoid, cycloid, or epileptoid tendencies. These individuals possibly come from schizophrenic, manic-depressive, or epileptic family strains. In them the hereditary predisposition to the disease process has not completely expressed itself in the physical constitution and personality make-up of the individual.

The hereditary tainting in psychopathic personalities is commonly stated to be greater than that of any other of the mental disabilities. When one remembers that the group of psychopathic personalities is made up not only of mental hospital patients exhibiting various forms of social and emotional maladjustment, but also of criminals, fanatics, suicides, and eccentrics in general, it is not surprising that the family-history investigation has shown so many deviants and defectives in the blood relationship.

Further speculation concerning the genetic basis of both psychopathic personalities or the psychoneuroses is not warranted; but it is apparent that genetic factors play some role in these conditions.

DEMENTIA PRAECOX

Twelve per cent of the first-admissions, and half of the resident population of mental hospitals, suffer from dementia praecox. Since this is the largest group of mentally disordered persons, the operation of heredity in the group has been, and should be, intensively investigated.

The varieties of dementia praecox patients, the hebephrenic, catatonic, paranoid, and simple forms, complicate the interpretation of results of genetic studies dealing with these individuals. Kallmann[6] made a study of the blood relatives of 1087 dementia praecox patients, involving 13,851 individuals. He found that when he divided the patients into the clinical subgroups, there were biologically distinct differences between the hebephrenics and catatonics, on the one hand, and the paranoid and simple, on the other. The differences between these two groups show themselves in a variety of ways. The catatonic-hebephrenic group have a much lower marriage and fertility rate and a significantly greater number of relatives who have had the same mental condition. It is as if this group constituted the nucleus of a biological deviation, while the paranoid and simple schizophrenics and certain schizoid types of psychopathic personality are on the periphery of the central group. From the study of the descendants of the entire group of schizophrenic patients, without respect to diagnosis, he found that when both of the parents were schizophrenic, 86 per cent of the children were likewise schizophrenic; when one parent was schizophrenic and the other schizoid, 24 per cent; when one parent was schizoid and one was normal, 15 per cent; and when both parents were free of schizophrenia themselves but had the disease somewhere in their ancestry, 9 per cent. This is in contrast to the basic figure on which all investigators agree, namely, that 0.85 per cent of the general population may be expected to develop schizophrenia. In another study,[7] the same investigator reported that in identical twin pairs, where one twin was suffering from the disease, 82 per cent of the co-twins had the same condition; in nonidentical pairs, the per cent was 12.5, and in siblings it was 11.5. Since Kallmann's conclusions are based on the analysis of a large and unselected number of schizo-phrenic families and twin pairs, and since they are in essential agree-ment with most of the better investigations in the same field, it seems fair to conclude that heredity is one of the important predisposing factors for the development of schizophrenia.

Additional evidence concerning the relative importance of hered-ity and of childhood home background, as causative factors for schizo-phrenia, is given in the findings of Kallmann[6] with respect to the half-brothers and half-sisters of schizophrenic patients. In those instances where the common parent of the half-brother or half-sister and the original patient was schizophrenic, there were 5 out of 21 in-stances in which the half-brother or half-sister was also schizophrenic, which is almost the same figure as that found among ordinary siblings. In those cases where the half-brothers and half-sisters were not related to a schizophrenic patient through a common schizo-phrenic parent, only 1 case out of 58 showed schizophrenia, which rate is much closer to the normal chance expectancy. This bit of evidence indicates that the inherited predisposition must be present for the development of the disease, even when the childhood home environment is relatively unfavorable.

Dr. Franz Kallmann has provided the following history of identical twins who were reared apart and who both developed dementia praecox.

CASES 24, 25: Miss Anna T. and Miss Emma T. were born in 1894, the only children of a poor farmer who was described as pleasant, although emotionally unstable. Their mother developed a psychosis immediately following the birth of the twins, and died of pulmonary tuberculosis when the twins were nine months old. Because of the mother's mental state, a paternal aunt took them into her home when they were only a few weeks old, and kept them for about two years. They were about the same weight at birth and equally strong and healthy as babies. In childhood and as adults, they were physically so much alike that they were frequently mis-taken for each other. Neither had any serious illness or accident throughout childhood. Anna has always been slightly taller and heavier. At present she is $\frac{1}{4}$ inch taller and weighs 2 or 3 pounds more than Emma.

Shortly after the twins' second birthday, the father remarried and moved to a farm in the middle west. He took Anna with him while Emma remained with the aunt, who treated her like her own child although she had three older children of her own. The twins liked their foster mothers fairly well and were easy to handle as children. They did not see each other between age two and age fourteen, and after that only a few times, and never for more than a few days. Anna grew up on a rather isolated farm without the companionship of other children. Emma grew up in a moderate sized town in New York State, in a family with other children. The family was of relatively better social and economic standing than the one in which her sister was raised.

Anna finished the eighth grade in a country school near the farm and afterward worked as a domestic, taking a sewing and dressmaking course in the evening. Emma completed high school at eighteen, taught in country schools for several years, and at twenty-two opened a stationery store in one of the suburbs of New York City. Although there was this definite difference in schooling, both twins developed average intelligence, but were said to be rather shy and reserved. They were both active in church work, fond of outdoor life, and very musical, although only Emma took music lessons. Neither became actively interested in the other sex, although both were described as attractive.

A definite change in personality was observed in both twins at about their twenty-fourth birthday. The development of active psychotic symptoms was more rapid and noticeable in Emma, who was living in, and adjusting to, urban surroundings; while Anna was able to take refuge on her father's farm for a while.

During the first months of her twenty-fourth year, Emma stopped working in the store, became untidy in her dress, and secluded herself for days in her room. She began to talk at length about mental science, hypnosis, and thought transference. She believed that people were talking about her, so that she developed delusions of a persecutory nature. She was admitted to a New York State mental hospital at age twenty-six. At that time she was described as careless in her appearance, apathetic, delusional, and actively hallucinated. Her psychosis progressed rapidly, and for the past twenty years she has been in a chronic advanced stage of mental deterioration.

Anna gave up her last housekeeping job during the summer of her twenty-fourth year and remained idle on her father's farm until her admission to a midwestern state hospital five years later. During these five years she was described as irritable, suspicious, sarcastic and seclusive. She had visual as well as auditory hallucinations, frequently striking at something in the air and complaining about snakes. She expressed delusions of a sexual, religious and persecutory nature. On admission to the mental hospital, she was noisy, abusive and assaultive; she barked like a dog, tore her clothing, and believed that there were snakes all about her. Her psychosis remained in this active state for several years, and then progressed into a chronic advanced stage of mental deterioration comparable to that of Emma. Both twins are still resident in mental hospitals.

We have here two identical twins who were separated at the age of two years. They showed very similar schizophrenic psychoses at twenty-four, which led to an advanced state of mental deterioration in both of them. This process developed despite wide differences in their environmental, social, and educational histories.

In order to clarify, by contrast, the relative roles of the hereditary predisposing factor of physical constitution and of environment, we cite the following histories:

CASES 26, 27: Two nonidentical twin girls were exposed to the same, extremely unfavorable, childhood experiences. They were only two years old when they were abandoned by their alcoholic and probably psychotic mother. They were brought up together in various charity homes and orphanages. At about age ten they were returned to their father who was a brutal, shiftless drunkard. They were badly mistreated by their step-mother who finally deserted them, declaring that they were equally un-manageable and mentally retarded children. At the age of thirteen they were both sexually assaulted by the father and were then sent to an institu-tion. Shortly afterwards, an acute and definitely deteriorating dementia praecox process manifested itself in the physically inferior and less mature of the twins. The other twin, who was five inches taller and almost thirty pounds heavier at age fourteen, continued to develop normally, seemingly unaffected by her almost unbelievably bad childhood environment, the sexual assault of her father, and the psychosis of her twin sister. In this case, it would seem that the stronger girl was protected from the disease either by a lack of a specific inherited predisposition, or because of her stronger physical constitution in comparison to her psychotic co-twin.*

MANIC-DEPRESSIVE PSYCHOSIS

The manic-depressive psychosis, second only to dementia praecox as a form of major mental disability, has also been extensively investi-gated from the genetic viewpoint.

Various investigators have shown that 0.44 per cent of the general population develop manic-depressive psychosis. Among the close rela-tives of manic-depressives, the expectancy rate runs much higher than this figure. It has been estimated that, of the children of manic-depressive patients, from 10 to 24 per cent develop the disease. Schulz[17] reported that about 15 per cent of manic-depressive patients had at least one parent who was suffering, or had suffered, from the same disease. Rüdin[16] found manic-depressive psychosis in 7.4 per cent of the siblings of patients whose parents were free from this disorder, and

* This history is quoted in shortened form from F. J. Kallmann and S. E. Barrera, "The Heredoconstitutional Mechanisms of Predisposition and Resistance to Schizo-phrenia." Amer. Jour. Psychiat., 1942, 98, 549.

23.8 per cent in the siblings of patients, one of whose parents was or had been a manic-depressive case. Only 1.4 per cent of the half-brothers and half-sisters of manic-depressive patients may be expected to have the same condition. In a study of 23 pairs of identical twins, Rosanoff[14] found that in 16 pairs (70 per cent of the pairs) both members were affected by manic-depressive psychosis; while in the remaining 7 pairs, only one member was affected.

The best evidence, at present, indicates that the inheritance of the basic genetic factor for dementia praecox depends on either a unit genetic character or a very small number of unit characters; whereas manic-depressive psychosis seems to be based upon several, or even many, genetic factors which must operate together to produce this predisposition.[18] When this multifactorial condition does obtain, the disease appears more clearly and regularly than is true in dementia praecox. One may assume that, if the hereditary mechanism of manic-depressive psychosis is present, it is more or less completely dominant in its effect. Therefore, it is more apt to lead to overt expression of the psychosis in the life history of the individual than is the predisposing mechanism of dementia praecox.

To illustrate the role of heredity in manic-depressive psychosis, Dr. Franz Kallmann has provided the following history of a pair of identical twins who were reared apart:

CASES 28, 29: Mrs. Mary R. and Mrs. Molly N. were born in 1889 on an upstate New York farm of English-Dutch descent. There was no history of mental abnormality in the mother's family, but many instances of personality deviation were present on the father's side (moodiness, phobias, depressions, dipsomania, and one suicide). These identical twins were the youngest of ten children. Their delivery was normal, weight at birth being 4 pounds, 6 ounces each. During a normal early childhood, they were mistaken, each for the other, by even their parents and siblings. There were no accidents or serious childhood diseases, so that they developed normally, seeming to be equally strong and healthy and having the same habits and friends in childhood.

These twins lived together until the age of eight and were considered inseparable. Illness of the parents made the removal of the twins from the farm advisable. Molly refused to leave but Mary was taken to live with an older married sister in another town. She remained there for several years, and then was taken into the home of an elderly, childless couple who practically adopted her. At age ten their mother died, and at fourteen, their father. Mary returned to the farm only once or twice for a very brief visit before the death of her parents, and following the death of her father saw her twin sister only on very rare occasions.

Molly remained on the farm of her parents until her marriage to a farmer at age twenty, when she moved to another farm. She had two children and adjusted without difficulty to the quiet, frugal, laborious life on a prosperous but secluded farm, which she rarely left.

Mary graduated from high school, took normal-school training, and taught in various schools until her marriage at age forty-seven to a retired engineer. She was active in politics and church matters. She traveled extensively and spent four years as a missionary in China. Her marriage was childless and unhappy, ending in divorce within a few years.

Despite the twins' separation at age eight, their mental and physical development showed no significant differences when they were seen at age fifty-two. Both were rather strong and heavy set. Neither smoked nor drank. Mary was quite outspoken in her opposition to smoking and drinking. Both were of the same height, while Molly's usual weight exceeded that of Mary by 20 pounds. Neither had had a serious illness, accident, or operation.

At age thirty-seven Mary developed her first psychotic episode while teaching in a missionary school in China. She attributed this to "sunstroke." She was overactive, irritable, fault-finding, and talked about various things at the same time and without interruption. For several weeks she was so restless that she neither ate nor slept. Following this excitement, she became moody, worried, and indifferent, so that she had to be sent home to the United States where she made a gradual recovery. She has had four episodes of comparable intensity and duration between 1937 and 1942, while minor spells occurred every few months, lasting only a week or so.

Molly had her first psychotic attack at age thirty-seven, without apparent provocation. She has been hospitalized only twice. Following several minor depressive episodes, which were distributed over more than three years, each lasting one or two weeks, her most severe manic attack developed at age forty-three. She suddenly became voluble and "talked more in an hour than she ordinarily did in a week." She showed expansive interests, greatly increased activities, and a marked flight of ideas. She visited neighbors that she had never talked to before, neglected her household and farm, and wandered aimlessly about the countryside. When admitted to the hospital, she was restless, aggressive, and uncooperative, but after a few days, she began to quiet down. She was discharged in a much improved condition and readily resumed her responsibilities at home. She has gotten along fairly well ever since, except for short depressive periods.

We have here typical manic-depressive psychoses occurring in identical twins who had been separated at age eight. They were very much alike as to personality and outlook on life in spite of their separation. Their mental disorder was of much the same nature, although the first episode occurred in the one while she was a missionary in China, and in the other during the same year while she was a farm wife in New York State.

Summary

It has been shown that in some of the mental disorders, heredity plays little or no role, in others an intermediate role, and in still others, it seems to be an extremely important predisposing or determining factor. An attempt has been made to classify the extent to which the various specific forms of abnormality may be related to hereditary predisposition, constitutional preformation, or environmental provocation. This analysis provides a better degree of comprehension and understanding of the importance of heredity in abnormal psychology.

Mental disease runs in families. This simple statement has been part of common knowledge for centuries and is one to which very few ever take exception. Mental abnormality does not occur in all families. Mental abnormality does not occur in every branch of certain families in which mental deviations are prevalent. Abnormality will occur in one member of a family in which such a condition has not been observed in any other member for several generations past. The question of isolated instances of abnormality, in which there is no indication that the abnormality had any basis in the known family history, must be mentioned; for example, sometimes a feeble-minded child is born into a family in which all living members are of a normal intelligence and in which no feeble-mindedness has been manifested during several generations past. Such isolated instances may be due to a variety of circumstances. They may be due to the occurrence of a biological mutation, that is, a new biological deviation occurring in a hitherto clear heredity. They may be due to malnutrition. They may be due to actual physical injury. They may be due to a toxic condition, such as lead poisoning, or they may be due to a variety of other obscure causes of a genetic or nongenetic nature. Most instances may come under the heading of provocation in the scheme which we have mentioned previously.

All available evidence indicates that each form of psychopathology must be separately studied before the correct role of heredity as a predisposing or preformative factor can be clearly understood.

REFERENCES

1. Bluhm, A., "Darf die Erblichkeit der Alcoholschäden als bewiesen gelten," *Zeit. f. Sex.-wiss. u. Sex.-pol.*, 1931, *28*, 145–151.
2. Bridges, C. B., "Salivary Chromosome Maps," *Jour. Heredity*, 1935, *26*, 60–64.
3. Burton, R., *The Anatomy of Melancholy* (ed. by F. Dell and P. Jordan-Smith). New York, Rinehart, 1927.
4. Conrad, K., "Die Bedeutung der Erbanlage bei der Epilepsie: Untersuchung an 253 Zwillungspaaren," *Deutsche Zeitschr. f. Nervenh.*, 1936, *139*, 76–79.

5. Galton, F., *Hereditary Genius*. London, Macmillan, 1869.

6. Kallmann, F. J., *The Genetics of Schizophrenia*. New York, Augustin, 1938.

7. ——, and S. E. Barrera, "The Heredoconstitutional Mechanisms of Predisposition and Resistance to Schizophrenia," *Amer. Jour. Psychiat.*, 1942, *98*, 544–550.

8. Lennox, W. G., and S. Cobb, "The Non-institutionalized Epileptic: A Preliminary Report," *Proc. Asso. Res. Nerv. Ment. Dis.*, 1931, 7, 358–372.

9. ——, E. L. Gibbs, and F. A. Gibbs, "The Inheritance of Epilepsy as Revealed by the Electroencephalograph," *Jour. Amer. Med. Asso.*, 1939, *113*, 1002–1003.

10. Löwenbach, H., "The Electroencephalogram in Healthy Relatives of Epileptics: Constitutional Elements in 'Idiopathic Epilepsy,'" *Johns Hopkins Hosp. Bull.*, 1939, *65*, 125–137.

11. Luxenburger, H., "Kurzer Abriss der psychiatrischen Erblehre und Erbgesundheitspflege," In E. Bleuler, *Lehrbuch der Psychiatrie* (6th ed.). Berlin, Springer, 1937, 130–178.

12. Penrose, L. S., *Mental Defect*. New York, Rinehart, 1934.

13. Pohlisch, K., *Soziale und persönliche Bedingungen des chronischen Alkoholismus*. Leipzig, Thieme, 1933.

14. Rosanoff, A. J., L. M. Handy, and I. R. Plesset, "The Etiology of Manic-Depressive Syndromes with Special Reference to Their Occurrence in Twins. *Amer. Jour. Psychiat.*, 1935, *91*, 725–762.

15. ——, ——, and I. A. Rosanoff, "Etiology of Epilepsy with Special Reference to Its Occurrence in Twins," *Arch. Neurol. Psychiat.*, 1934, *31*. 1165–1193.

16. Rüdin, E., "Über Vererbung geistiger Störungen," *Zeit. f. ges. Neurol. Psychiat.*, 1923, *81*, 459–496.

17. Schulz, B., "Übersicht über auslesefreie Untersuchungen in der Verwandtschaft Manisch-Depressiver," *Zeit. psychische Hyg.*, 1937, *10*, 39–60.

18. Slater, E., "Zur Erbpathologie des manisch-depressiven Irreseins: Die Eltern und Kinder von Manisch-Depressiven," *Zeit. f. ges. Neurol. Psychiat.*, 1938, *163*, 1–47.

19. Stein, C., "Hereditary Factors in Epilepsy: Comparative Study of 1000 Institutionalized Epileptics and 1115 Non-epileptic Controls," *Amer. Jour. Psychiat.*, 1933, *12*, 989–1037.

20. Strauss, H., W. E. Rahm, and S. E. Barrera, "Electroencephalographic Studies in Relatives of Epileptics," *Proc. Soc. Exp. Biol. Med.*, 1939, *42*, 207–212.

21. Watson, J. B., *Behaviorism*. New York, Norton, 1930.

22. Woodworth, R. S., *Psychology* (4th ed.). New York, Holt, 1940.

23. ——, *Heredity and Environment*. New York, Soc. Sci. Res. Council Bull., #47, 1941.

Chapter XIX

CULTURAL AND SOCIOLOGICAL FACTORS

MAN IS a social being and a large portion of man's necessary life adjustments grow out of his being a member of a social group. Social existence makes certain demands and creates certain problems for the individual; social forms and customs prescribe the way in which these problems must be handled to avoid conflict with the society. These attitudes, beliefs, and habits of thought and action of any individual are greatly influenced by the social and cultural environment in which he grows and develops. The environment is continually changing, and the changes continually require new adjustments. One is punished, encouraged, instructed, and led to imitate other individuals. One's ideas of what is good, desirable, and valuable are slowly and continually developed through the processes of social intercourse.

Anthropology and sociology have made valuable contributions to our understanding of the factors which enter into, and pattern, human reactions. Culture has been defined by the anthropologists as the sum total of the attitudes, ideas, and behavior shared and transmitted by the members of a society, together with the material results of such behavior. Soon after a child is born, he is exposed to certain attitudes and ideas that make up the culture into which he was born. Later, he becomes part of many other groups which form his cultural environment and collectively influence his attitudes and behavior. These cultural influences are not a fixed mold in which each personality is cast. Different individuals will respond differently to the same cultural influences, and not all individuals in the group will have exactly the same cultural influences exerted upon them.

There are certain powerful factors in a given culture which affect all individuals. Under this category come language, customs, and group ideas. These forces influence the formation of the personality of each individual within that group and make for such cultural similarities as do exist. There are aspects of any culture which pertain only

276

to certain groups of people. The customs and standards of conduct are different for the male and the female, or for different occupational groups in which the person is either born, placed, or which he selects for himself. Within one culture these groups may have a characteristic set of living conditions which will influence the behavior and attitudes of the members. In addition to these cultural subdivisions, there are changing social conditions within the whole culture which have their reflection in personality formation because they change the pattern of life of all individuals in that culture. Under this heading come war, famine, economic depression, or great plagues which sweep over a large portion of a population.

Sociological and anthropological studies have, in several ways, added to our understanding of human behavior. Some studies are concerned with such things as the contrasting of different types of cultures to show that many of the factors which were thought to be basic to human nature (that is, instinctive and unlearned) are actually a product of the particular circumstances that surrounded the developing individual. When our knowledge is restricted to the forms of our own culture, we have no way of knowing which aspects of our psychology are fundamental and which are a product of our particular environment and culture. By comparing different cultures, anthropologists have shown that only certain broad human needs are universal, and that even these may be expressed and satisfied in widely different ways. Even the universal drives of hunger, sex, and the avoidance of pain have no constant pattern of expression. There are cultural groups in which prolonged, voluntary fasting, celibacy, and self-torture have a definite place and are considered socially desirable goals.

To illustrate the way in which different cultures influence (exagerate or diminish) the personality traits of individuals, several reports made by cultural anthropologists may be considered. Fortune[7] has reported on the natives of Dobu, an island in Melanesia. He stated that fear and distrust, akin to paranoia, pervade the entire group. Many of the beliefs and practices of the natives are based on a fundamental attitude of distrust of others in the group. They put a premium on ill-will and treachery and accept this form of social relationship as natural. The seed for planting is so strongly defended that one member of the family would not dare use the seed of another member of the same family. Each person is occupied with taking care of his own seed and full of fear that someone else, by witchcraft or trickery, will take it away from him. They fear being poisoned. The wife cooking the dinner in the pot does not leave it for a moment lest someone poison it. The social form of thanking a person is the phrase, "If you should poison me, how would I repay you?" This culture, which from our viewpoint seems so paranoid, may be contrasted with that of the Zuni Indians in New Mexico, as described by Benedict.[2]

Zuni culture is based on mutual cooperation and mutual owner-ship of property. The strong competitive spirit found in the Dobus is nonexistent, and the striving for protection of personal rights is absent. Excesses of any type are looked down upon and personal violence and treachery are very rare. The goals and standards of conduct are highly formalized, and no one wishes to stand out as being different or having more than his neighbor.

Wide differences among cultures in sex customs of primitive people have been reported by Malinowski,[12] Mead,[13] and others. The formal repression of sexual play in childhood, which we insist upon, is absent in some of the Southwest Pacific island cultures which have been studied. There are certain forms of sex play which are acceptable, and other forms which are forbidden in each culture. Incest, particularly a mother-son relationship, is said to be universally taboo; but the open acceptance, condoning, disapproval, or virtual taboo on all other relationships varies from culture to culture.

The studies in social anthropology have done more than show the variability of human behavior and relationships. They have enhanced our knowledge of the relation between specific cultural forces and the formation of personality. Although much of this work is speculative, it suggests interesting interpretations of human behavior, both normal and abnormal.

Kardiner[10] has worked out, in part factually and in part by specu-lation, the relationship between the various cultural institutions and the personality reactions of the individuals living in those cultures. He distinguishes between primary and secondary institutions. The pri-mary institutions are those which create the basic and inescapable problems of adaptation. Among them are family organization, sub-sistence economy, sex taboos, and the discipline systems, such as the care, feeding, and training of children. These institutions shape any person's basic personality structure through a conditioning process which is most effective during the early formative years. The adapta-tion to primary institutions sets up secondary institutions, examples of which are techniques of thinking, attitudes toward objects, security systems, and systems of beliefs and ideals, such as rituals, folk tales, and taboos.

The primary and secondary institutions in the culture will determine what the individual values, strives toward, is ashamed of, and fears; the ways in which hunger, grief, or pleasure are shown; and the way in which the sexual drive is satisfied. The way in which an individual views himself and others around him is patterned largely by the secondary institutions of the culture to which he belongs. Both by conscious and unconscious imitation, he acquires these forms because he is a member of society, raised in a particular type of family constellation, and conditioned to certain disciplines.

Certain of the problems of abnormal psychology are better understood since it has been shown that the repressions which are imposed in different cultures are not the same. All cultures have their repressions, but the nature of these repressions depends upon the external physical environment (food and shelter needs) and upon the primary institutions of that culture. Frustrations of different types exist. In one culture there may be frustration of the need for food, of the need for protection and security in childhood, or of sexual satisfaction. The pattern of frustrations will partly determine the worries, problems, and anxieties which exist in the individual. Different cultures seem to have different ways of handling anxiety and different methods of resolving frustration, although there is still a division of opinion of authorities concerning the basic nature of anxiety as it relates to frustration. Freud taught that repression and anxiety were the same in all cultures; that they were biologically determined; and that the outward form or particular customs of a culture did little save modify the way in which the symptoms were exhibited. Another viewpoint is that only when the particular cultural frustrations are unearthed can the anxieties that exist in that culture be understood. It would follow from this theory that there may be fundamental differences in the nature of anxiety among different cultures. Since no good evidence is available to show which idea is correct, the point remains speculative.

The general impression gained from anthropological data would indicate that the content of the symptoms of mental abnormality or disease may vary among different cultures. The problem then arises as to whether more than the content is affected by culture; that is, whether the mental disease itself is influenced by the characteristics of the culture.

Mental Disease (Abnormality) in Different Cultures

The crucial test of whether cultural influences produce definite variations in psychopathology lies in whether there is a difference in incidence of certain mental disorders in different cultures. Unfortunately, there are no clear-cut statistics that can be presented on this point and speculation must rest on fragmentary bits of evidence, many of which have been collected by people who were not psychiatrically or psychologically trained. Heated arguments developed from the statement made by some anthropologists that neuroses do not occur in "primitive" cultures and are manifested in these groups only when there is increasing contact with the repressions and disciplines of our Western civilization.[15] This notion was accepted by those who held that infantile and childhood sex repression is the cause of all neuroses. If the culture did not impose these early sex repressions, there should be no neuroses. A more careful study of these so-called primitive cultures failed, however, to substantiate this contention. Neurotic forms of behavior do seem to occur in primitive cultures, although they are said to be somewhat different in the form of the symptoms when compared to neuroses of our culture. Nevertheless, the behavior of some primitive individuals is such that we must call it "neurotic." That neurotic behavior is more frequently recognized in those primitive cultures which have increased contact with our civilization may be true. This does not mean, however, that it is the conflict between the institutions of the two cultures which has been responsible for the abnormal behavior. It may also be that when our ideas, institutions, and values are taken over by other cultural groups, the symptom complexes shown are more similar to the symptom complexes that occur in our culture. Therefore, abnormality can be recognized, where previously it was not, because the observer did not have sufficient understanding of the pattern of the different culture. As the mental abnormality takes forms that fit more into our categories of neurotic and psychotic behavior, the observer gets the impression that the incidence of abnormality is increasing. Abnormal behavior may have existed in these same individuals and may have been missed merely because of a lack of understanding of what constituted deviation in that culture.

The present data on the incidence of mental disease in "primitive" cultures[1] are very meager and unsatisfactory because of many uncontrolled factors, such as sex and age composition of the group, and the questionable acceptability and availability of mental hospitals. Some figures have been reported, but they are based on so few cases and such inconsistent concepts about mental disorders that they shed little or no light on the problem.

Although no reliable statistical data are available on the incidence of different types of mental disease, there are many ethnological observations suggesting that certain forms of mental abnormality may be more frequent in one culture than in another. This is true, especially, of hysteria. Reactions of the hysterical type have been described in essentially every cultural group; but in some cultures they are said to be very frequent, in others very rare. For example, in studies made of many different tribes and cultures living under conditions of privation and physical discomfort in Arctic regions, hysterical reactions have been reported to be very common. Convulsive seizures, either epileptic or hysterical, have been seen in cultural groups from all parts of the world. Periods of intense excitement also have been widely observed, but whether or not these are manic episodes of a manic-depressive syndrome is not known. On the other hand, there are some conditions which are thought to stem directly from specific cultural factors, and so are limited to certain cultures having these factors. Under this heading come the conditions termed *amok* and *lattah*. It is said that running amok, as it occurs in Malay, can be understood only in terms of the Malayan culture. The pattern of destructive behavior is not truly comparable to the form of homicidal or destructive fury as it is seen in other cultures. It is viewed and treated by the natives in a way which is different from the way in which we would view it.

One form of aberrant reaction upon which we can compare different cultures is suicide.[4] On this topic, at least, we do not have to worry about differences in terminology; the person either took his own life or he did not. In order to evaluate the psychological significance of suicide, we must consider the social and cultural conditions surrounding the individual and the attitude of that culture toward suicide. There is definite evidence that cultural patterns influence the incidence of suicide. In some cultures it is common, as, for example, among the Navajos; in others it is rare or even completely absent, as among the Zunis. There are certain primitive cultures which have set ways and conditions of committing suicide. The psychological attitude leading to suicide apparently depends, in part, upon the accepted cultural belief of the nature of the afterlife. Suicide may be a legitimate way of revenging oneself upon another person, of clearing one's honor, or of expiating some breaking of cultural taboos. Malinowski[12] describes an incident in the Trobriand Islands, showing the cultural determinant of a suicide. A man had sexual relations with a girl who was, to him, sexually taboo. The community looked down upon this relationship but no steps were taken to punish him until an offended rival, who was supposed to marry the girl, denounced him publicly. Then, he had no choice about his actions. The next day he donned ceremonial robes, went through the traditional form of blaming his rival for this act, and killed himself. The Japanese practice of hara-kiri, when in disgrace or when wishing to disgrace an enemy, is an additional example of suicide as an act occurring from, and determined by, cultural forms. Necessarily, it has a different psychological significance from suicide in our culture.

Mental Disease in Our Culture

In anthropological terms, our own culture is a patriarchal society with legal monogamy. The mother is responsible for the care and raising of the children, while the father is the economic provider and frequently the principal disciplinarian of the child. Actual hunger (food deprivation for long periods) is rare. Save for accident, war, and disease, life itself is seldom endangered. Sexual play in childhood is tabooed and the child is made to feel that such practice is very bad and shameful. Formal education of the child is carried on into the teens. Only by the late teens or early twenties does the individual become self-supporting and socially independent of his family. Throughout childhood and adolescence he is indoctrinated with standards of what is right and wrong to do. The fact that people he knows and respects may do things that he has been told are wrong will puzzle and worry him. He has been given a code of behavior involving respect for the rights of others, but he is part of a culture in which the competitive spirit is strong and where successful rivalry with others meets marked approval. The approved pattern of behavior depends on both the sex and the age of the individual. Many of the ways in which the individual feels, thinks, and behaves depend upon the particular religious, economic, educational, or vocational subgroups to which he belongs.

In analyzing the effect of different social factors upon the development of various mental diseases, it is advisable to compare different subgroups within one culture. We cannot be sure, of course, that these relationships will hold in other cultures. This possibility can only be evaluated when similar data are available to make the same comparisons. Therefore, all of the statements with respect to such relationships should be read with a mental note attached, I.O.C. — In Our Culture —, a point which Dollard[3] explicitly made in another connection.

AGE

One comparison that can be easily made within the subgroups in our culture is that based on age differences in the population. Landis and Page[11] have pointed out that the most important single determining fact that we can know about mental disease is the age of the patient or the age distribution of a group of patients. If these data are avail-

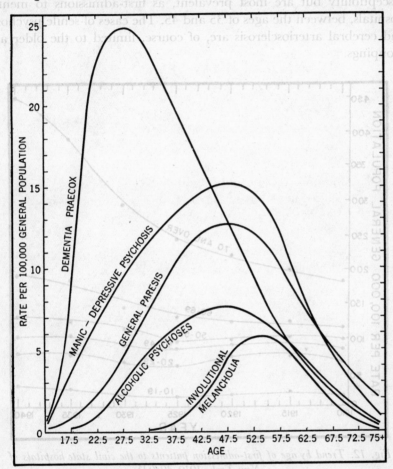

Fig. 11. Number of first-admissions to state mental hospitals in the United States, during 1933, by age and psychosis; expressed as rates per 100,000 of the corresponding general population of 1933.[11]

able, one can make fairly accurate estimates of the frequency of the different diagnostic types of mental disease, the relative proportion of males to females, and the number of cases that can be expected to improve. As Fig. 11 shows, most of the mental diseases have a characteristic age distribution. In some diseases this age span is relatively broad, but each has what might be called the "age of maximum susceptibility." For example, the age group between 25 and 30 is most susceptible to dementia praecox and very few individuals develop it before age 18 or after age 50. Manic-depressive psychosis, general paresis, and alcoholic psychoses have a broader span of age-susceptibility but are most prevalent, as first-admissions to mental hospitals, between the ages of 35 and 45. The cases of senile psychosis and cerebral arteriosclerosis are, of course, limited to the older age groupings.

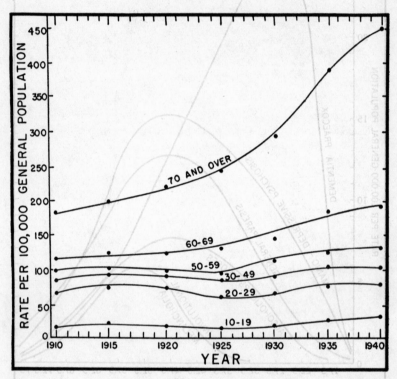

Fig. 12. Trend by age of first-admission patients to the civil state hospitals of New York, 1910–1940.[14]

Although youth and adolescence are usually regarded as periods of great emotional stress and strain, the incidence of mental disease at these ages is much lower than at the older ages (Fig. 12). Actually, the probability of developing a mental disease which will lead to hospitalization increases with age. To be specific, only 22 per 100,000 individuals between the ages 15 to 19 were first-admitted to the mental hospitals of the United States (1933), as compared with 66 for the age group 30 to 34; 82 for the age group 45 to 49; 114 for the age group 65 to 69; and 226 for the age group of 70 years and over. A marked acceleration in the tendency to break down with a mental disease takes place at the transition period between maturity and senility, namely, about age 50.

Age and incidence of the onset of mental disease may be causally related in several ways. There are differences in the stresses and strains placed upon the individual by society at particular periods of his life. At certain ages he is expected to adjust to a new pattern of living because he is forced to accept or renounce important duties and responsibilities. When he first reaches adult status or when he is finally retired or sees retirement near at hand, there are real problems of adjustment. In an individual with a limited ability to adjust a breakdown may occur.

Another possibility is that certain of these mental disorders depend upon the process of biological maturation. Such abnormal phenomena cannot appear unless the person has matured to a definite point. In this sense they are a real product of aging and not a product of the specific experiences that preceded their appearance. Maturation in certain diseases we know to be the truer explanation, as, for example, in Huntington's chorea where the person may show no physical or mental pathology until the age of 35 or 40. Since it is possible for maturation to bring out this type of pathology, it is conceivable that other forms of psychopathology may also be related to maturation.

Even though we cannot reach a definite conclusion as to why age and incidence of mental disease are related, the important point to keep in mind is that most varieties of psychopathology bear a constant relationship to age. Unfortunately, these constancies are available only in data obtained from American and European hospitals. The incidence or rates of mental disease in primitive cultures are not available or comparable.

EDUCATION AND ECONOMIC STATUS

With the information provided by our mental-hospital systems it has been difficult to evaluate any differences which may exist between the educational levels of mental patients and the general population. It is definite, however, that the percentage of illiteracy is higher for first-admission mental patients than it is for the general population. Other differences appear when the various diagnostic groups of mental patients are compared in regard to educational status. In general, patients diagnosed as having paranoia, psychoneurosis, involutional melancholia, or psychopathic personality have had more years in school than have patients who develop the organic psychoses (alcoholic psychoses, cerebral arteriosclerosis, and senile dementia).[11]

Various inquiries have been made of the relation between economic status and mental disease.[8] The first-admissions to certain Illinois State mental hospitals from the city of Chicago for 1922–1934 were studied in relation to the sociological conditions of housing; that is, the cost of rent and type of building. Where the rent was under $50 a month, there was a probability of 1 out of 18 white men, and 1 out of 20 white women being admitted to mental hospitals sometime during their life; as compared to 1 out of 21, and 1 out of 22, respectively, in the higher rent districts. These differences do not permit us to conclude, however, that the general living conditions directly influence the production of mental disease. They merely indicate that families who can pay higher rents can also afford to take care of their older relatives at home, so that they have a lower hospitalization rate, particularly for senile psychosis and cerebral arteriosclerosis.

Faris and Dunham[6] analyzed the first-admission incidence of mental disorders in Chicago and in Providence. They found that the incidence of hospitalized mental disease was higher in those districts in which poverty, unemployment, juvenile delinquency, criminality, and suicide were higher. They suggested that the same factors gave rise to mental disease as gave rise to these other forms of social deviation. After dividing the entire urban area into separate sociological areas, they found that the incidence of mental disease was higher near the center of the city and decreased toward the periphery. There were differences in the distribution of the various forms of mental disorder. The majority of schizophrenics were encountered in the socially disorganized areas at or near the center of the city and the highest rates were found where islands of one racial group lived among members of other racial groups, for example, a Negro city block within a predominantly Jewish area. A greater incidence of general paresis was observed in areas where vice was prevalent. Senile psychosis and cerebral arteriosclerosis came more frequently from the rooming-house areas of the city. Manic-depressive psychosis occurred only sporadically and was not characteristic of any specific area, though there was some tendency for it to be more frequent in areas having a higher cultural and economic level.

The evidence from this and other such sociological surveys indicates that the incidence of mental disease is highest among single male individuals living alone in the low-rent areas of a city. This finding does not mean, of course, that low economic status or isolation from family contacts is the cause of their mental disorder. It is more probable that their poor living conditions are the effect, rather than the cause, of the prolonged maladjustment. Mental abnormality which is developing into a psychosis tends more and more to incapacitate the person vocationally and financially, so that his economic level decreases. One investigation of families with an accumulation of schizophrenia in several successive generations revealed a progressive and uninterrupted decline in social status.[9]

RURAL-URBAN RATE

The statistical reports for America and other countries show that the incidence of hospitalized mental disease is much higher for urban than for rural communities. This holds true for both sexes and for all diagnoses. In certain diagnostic categories the difference between urban and rural rates is wider than in others. For example, alcoholic psychoses, general paresis, and psychopathic personality are at least three times more prevalent in the urban than in the rural population.

These marked differences might suggest that the "mad pace of the city" produces mental breakdown. A moment's consideration discloses the inadequacy of such a conclusion. In the first place, the housing conditions in the city, close neighbors, and similar factors, prevent a person who is mentally disturbed from being kept at home even if there is room for him. Second, city dwellers use and trust hospitals for all sorts of illness far more than do rural dwellers. Clinics and hospital facilities of various types are popular and easily available in the city, whereas many rural inhabitants avoid going to a hospital as long as possible. Third, the larger size of the family unit in rural areas favors home care, since there is more apt to be someone to take care of those who are mentally disordered, while in the city this is not so true. A further factor is that living in the country is a safer environment for the abnormal person who becomes confused and wanders about. Such behavior in the city may lead to accidents, and it certainly leads to the attention of the police who will taken any person potentially dangerous to himself or others to a hospital. Since the rural environment is simpler and makes fewer demands, many mentally disturbed persons are able to adjust to life on a farm or in a village without becoming sufficiently conspicuous to require commitment to a mental hospital.

From the figures that are available on actual number of urban and rural persons who are mentally abnormal, irrespective of whether hospitalized or not, it has been found that the rates for the rural areas closely approximate the urban areas. The Swedish census (1930) showed a rate of 45.4 per 10,000 of the general population in rural areas and 45.1 in urban areas.[11]

NATIONALITY

Upon first inspection the differences in the rates of hospitalized mental disease between foreign-born and native-born Americans are as startling as the differences between rural and urban groups. The uncorrected figures indicate that mental disease is twice as prevalent among foreign-born whites as among native whites. When these rates are corrected so that they are directly comparable for the age and urban or rural environment, then the foreign-born rate is but 8 per cent higher than the native-born. If the rates were to be further corrected to allow for the fact that the foreign-born group is predominantly made up of unmarried men of low economic status, in which group we know that the incidence of mental disease is increased, then the 8 per cent difference would probably disappear. Hence, it is apparent that no sweeping statement as to the prevalence of mental disease in the foreign-born can be made.

Less complex is the finding that migratory groups have a higher incidence of mental disease than those living at home. Inability to adjust is a prime mark of abnormality and should be expected to express itself in higher figures for mental disorders among migrants, since it is mainly such abnormal persons who move from one place to another or frequently shift localities of home or employment.

The greater incidence of mental disease among migratory individuals has been used by some writers to explain why the rate of mental hospitalization for Negroes in the North is higher than for whites. But the fact that the first-admission rate in thirty-seven of the forty-eight states (1933) was higher for Negroes than for the native white population shows that migration is not the sole reason. The Negro rates are especially high for general paresis and alcoholic psychoses, and are also increased for cerebral arteriosclerosis, dementia praecox, and senile dementia. This excess in the hospitalization rates for Negroes may largely be ascribed to the lack of home care which, in turn, rests in part on a lack of economic opportunity and security. Another consequence of the lower economic level of Negroes is the decrease in the quality of the treatment for syphilis and other organic diseases.

WAR AND ECONOMIC DEPRESSION

Analysis of admission rates to mental hospitals indicates that war, economic depression, and unemployment have not led to an increase in the rates of hospitalized mental disease. This seems surprising if we consider the amount of mental stress, insecurity, and emotional upset which are associated with these conditions. Landis and Page[11] have shown that the first-admissions to the state mental hospitals in New York, Massachusetts, and Illinois gave no evidence that the last depression had any effect on hospitalization for mental disease. (See Fig. 7, page 189). The trend of incidence rate for the different types of mental disease remained relatively constant under the changing conditions of World Wars I and II. It seems that economic depression and unemployment may be reflected in a temporary impairment of the general psychological adjustment of certain groups and in the intensification of everyday worries of many individuals, but they do not make them candidates for a mental hospital.

The suicide rate[4] has been shown to follow the business cycle. When business conditions are good the rate is low, and when economic times are bad the rate increases. It is evident, however, that it is not low economic status itself that leads to suicide, but the shattering of social and economic circumstances accompanying a change from a previously more satisfactory economic status.

Unemployment has been found to have certain psychological correlates. Lazarsfeld and others[5,16] made a clinical study of unemployed people and spoke of three basic attitudes fostered by unemployment: the unbroken, the distressed, and the broken. In the first group were those whose personality adjustment was not fundamentally disturbed. They were not resigned to their lowered standard of living and continued to struggle against it. The second group, the distressed, included those who were fundamentally disturbed but not completely discouraged. They fluctuated markedly between acts of aggression or rage, and despair, resignation, and attempts to escape. The broken individuals had given up hope and interest in life to such an extent that they were completely apathetic and without ambition. The psychological problems were found, of course, to be related to the duration of unemployment. Prolonged unemployment was usually followed by emotional instability, anxiety, and the development of a state in which the person lost confidence in himself and felt inferior, helpless, and afraid of the future. The problem was not so much one of low financial level with marked deprivation of the basic essentials of life, as it was a reaction to loss of something that the person had had before and a forced change from the status he had formerly held.

Summary

The various cultural and social categories that have been discussed are clearly related to both the incidence and the distribution of mental disease in our culture. Socioeconomic and cultural factors do influence the rates of hospitalization for mental disease, even if they have no direct relationship to the primary causes of the psychopathology involved. They require careful analysis whenever comparative figures are available for different cultural groups. The relation between these general cultural factors and the individual's development will be considered in the next chapter, which deals more specifically with individual reactions. It may be borne in mind that many of the social institutions, repressions, and anxieties which seem "natural" to us are actually a product of our culture and may not be found in other cultural groups, especially in those of a more primitive structure.

REFERENCES

1. Beaglehole, E., "Culture and Psychosis in New Zealand," *Jour. Polynesian Soc.*, 1939, *48*, 144–155.
2. Benedict, R., *Patterns of Culture*. Boston, Houghton, 1934.
3. Dollard, J., *Criteria for the Life History*. New Haven, Yale University Press, 1936.
4. Dublin, L. I., and B. Bunzel, *To Be or Not To Be*. New York, Smith and Haas, 1933.
5. Eisenberg, P., and P. F. Lazarsfeld, "The Psychological Effects of Unemployment," *Psychol. Bull.*, 1938, *35*, 358–390.
6. Faris, R. E. L., and H. Dunham, *Mental Disorders in Urban Areas*. Chicago, University of Chicago Press, 1939.
7. Fortune, R. F., *The Sorcerers of Dobu*. New York, Dutton, 1932.
8. Jaffe, A. J., and E. Shanas, "Economic Differential in the Probability of Insanity," *Amer. Jour. Sociol.*, 1939, *44*, 534–539.
9. Kallmann, F. J., *The Genetics of Schizophrenia*, New York, Augustin, 1938, 31–34.
10. Kardiner, A., *The Individual and his Society*. New York, Columbia University Press, 1939.
11. Landis, C., and J. D. Page, *Modern Society and Mental Disease*, New York, Rinehart, 1938.

12. Malinowski, B., *Sex and Repression in Savage Society*. New York, Harcourt, 1927.
13. Mead, M., *Coming of Age in Samoa*. New York, Morrow, 1928.
14. Page, J. D., and C. Landis, "Trends in Mental Disease, 1910–1940," *Jour. Abn. Soc. Psychol.*, 1943, *38*, 518–524.
15. Seligman, C. G., "Temperament, Conflict and Psychosis in a Stone-Age Population," *Brit. Jour. Med. Psychol.*, 1929, *9*, 187–202.
16. Zawadzki, B., and P. F. Lazarsfeld, "The Psychological Consequences of Unemployment," *Jour. Soc. Psychol.*, 1935, *6*, 224–251.

Chapter XX

DEVELOPMENT

WHEN our attention is focused on the life development of the individual, it becomes immediately obvious that we are dealing with the interrelated factors of both nature and nurture. To speak of one as though it could exist without the other is inaccurate and artificial. Every stage of development is a product of the interaction of structural, physiological, and environmental factors, each affecting, and being affected by, the others. The process of growth is a continuous one and any one stage evolves from the preceding stages. To understand the personality reactions of the individual, we must go back to reconstruct the course of his development.

Adolph Meyer has done much to emphasize the developmental study of the personality. He has stressed the importance of viewing behavior and mental disorders in their proper perspective, with all the events that led up to them. In order to understand the significance of any disorder, one must discover the antecedent events that make the later reactions understandable, and, in fact, necessary results. Without an understanding of the life history in which the symptoms occur, they cannot be truly evaluated. The psychobiological approach to the life history includes investigation of early habit formation, various psychological functions, possible constitutional deficiencies, and the anatomical and physiological components that may enter into the personality reaction types.

G. W. Allport[1] has recently systematized and brought together a great deal of the information that is available on personality development. He believes that the essence of personality is *individuality*, so that recognition and study of the person as a unique, concrete organization are the main problems of the psychology of personality. A single life history,[2] when fully studied, shows an orderly and necessary process of growth, each stage being the necessary result of what has gone before. Allport includes differentiation, integration, maturation, and learning as different aspects of growth. He adds another which he feels is necessary to provide an understanding of the dynamics of the mature personality. This principle he calls the "functional autonomy of motives," and he uses it to explain the ultimate uniqueness of personality.

Dynamic psychology . . . regards adult motives as infinitely varied, and as self-sustaining, *contemporary* systems, growing out of antecedent systems, but functionally independent of them. Just as the child gradually repudiates his dependence on his parents, develops a will of his own, becomes self-active and self-determining, and outlives his parents, so it is with motives. Each motive has a definite point of origin which may lie in the hypothetical instincts, or, more likely, in the organic tensions and diffuse irritability [of the infant]. . . . Theoretically all adult purposes can be traced back to these seed-forms in infancy. But as the individual matures the bond is broken. The tie is historical, not functional. *

This view is a marked departure from the earlier concept of instincts or motives as predetermined, purposive patterns of reaction continuing from infancy and going along with the individual like his shadow, influencing contemporary reactions but not influenced by them. Instead, one motive is viewed as growing out of a previous motive, and finally reaching the point where it exists independently of this earlier motive. In other words, it comes to be functionally autonomous.

Outline of Development

EARLY BACKGROUND

At the moment of conception, the genetic endowment of the individual is established. This consists of *potentialities* for certain types of development. Whether or not these tendencies reach expression will depend upon conditions outside of, and within the organism. Strictly speaking, one does not inherit blue eyes, but one inherits the capacity to develop blue eyes. This capacity will be realized whenever developmental conditions are adequate. Thus, the range of potential development is genetically determined, but environmental conditions determine which specific forms will develop out of this range.

The environment of the foetus is much more constant than the complex human environment after birth. Nevertheless, there are various conditions which may influence foetal development. Nutrition, abnormal pressure, toxins, X-rays, or severe temperature changes may affect the developing organism. There is even evidence of the capacity

* Allport, G. W., *Personality: A Psychological Interpretation.* New York, Holt, 1937, 194.

for learning (in the limited sense) before birth. Conditioned responses have been established in foetal animals and humans.

The first responses of the infant after birth consist of (*a*) diffuse, random movements involving the body, head, and extremities; and (*b*) smaller patterns of reaction, such as breathing, swallowing, sucking, grasping, and the like. These action patterns are more marked following external stimulation by sound or touch or when the infant is hungry.[6] They may be modified or integrated into new patterns of reaction; the mass actions become specialized into adaptive movements, the smaller patterns of reaction become integrated into larger patterns that appear only under specific conditions of stimulation. In general, the early periods of growth include the building up of adaptive responses through conditioning and integration. The responses that can be acquired depend not only upon environmental stimulation, but also upon the state of maturation of muscles and of the nervous system. For example, control of the sphincter muscles necessary for voluntary bowel and bladder control is possible only after the nervous system has sufficiently matured. No matter how much training is given, some finer patterns of motor coordination require that the maturation of the nervous system shall have progressed to the proper extent. The process of growth is based on both environmental influences and the structural or physiological condition of the organism.

The human infant with its diffuse, poorly integrated patterns of response is rather helpless when we compare it to certain animals, such as the calf or colt, which are able to run around quite adeptly very shortly after birth. Much of their adaptive equipment seems to be prefabricated. The outstanding characteristic of the human infant is a wide range for potential development. This potentiality includes the capacity for modification of behavior and for high and complex levels of integration of response, and for a development based on both maturation and growth by learning.

The first five years of life are a period of rapid development of many different types. The child acquires many new motor skills and new patterns of response to his environment. With the development of verbal ability, he is able to communicate his likes and dislikes. He comes in contact with restraints in his environment, imposed either by the parents or by others around him. Cultural influences and social pressures are brought to bear on him. He is not allowed free expression of his needs and desires, but must learn to conform. This learning is frequently associated with evidence of psychological strain in the child. For example, a period of negativism frequently occurs at the age of two or three years. This attitude has been interpreted as a product of frustration resulting from the child's inability to handle his environment according to his own desires. Even in infancy, there may be disorganizing factors present. Ribble[11] has observed infant behavior from the point of view of determining what experiences may distort fundamental behavior patterns and thereby modify the orderly course of development. She[10] claims that there is a need for frequent sucking periods which are neither limited nor interrupted. The periods are needed even apart from the matter of food intake. There is also said to be a need for long and uninterrupted periods of consistent "psychological mothering." By this, Ribble means holding, rocking, and other types of sensory stimulation. These attentions seem necessary until the child acquires speech and voluntary control of his body. Absence of this mothering has been found to be associated with privation reactions which may develop into emotional disorders in later childhood.

Even in the first year of life, temperamental variations can be observed. Individual differences among babies with respect to being attentive or inattentive to people, and differences in the amount of laughing and crying have been studied.[3,14] Although there are no complete follow-up studies that show whether these early patterns continue into temperamental characteristics in adult life, it has been found that there is individual consistency, of a limited sort, in these early years. Shirley[13] reported certain consistencies in regard to adaptability, timidity, and aggressiveness based on observations for a two-year period beginning at the time of birth.

The course of early development also depends upon the physical health of the child. A sickly, frail baby may be slow in reaching certain types of motor control and mastery.

The home situation and the parent-child relationship involve many factors which influence psychological development. The feeling of security and of being loved and wanted is indispensable for the well-being of the child. Levy[8] has shown how behavior disorders in childhood may frequently be traced back to what he has called "primary affect hunger." Absence of love and affection does not produce one single type of deviant behavior. Rather, a child may feel insecure and manifest this insecurity in extreme timidity, in fear of being out of sight of the mother, or in being disobedient, defiant, delinquent, and using every possible means of getting attention.

Deficiencies in the family organization or in the quality of the home will also produce feelings of insecurity in the child. Among the unfavorable factors are broken homes which result when one parent is dead or the parents are living apart. Privation because of an extremely low economic level of the home or exposure to frightening or unusual behavior on the part of mentally abnormal, alcoholic, or morally delinquent parents may exert unfavorable influences on the course of development of the child. Feelings of insecurity have been related to an interference with a healthy course of development, either by maternal overprotection, oversolicitousness, and domination, or by marked inconsistencies in handling and discipline. Maternal behavior of this sort is frequently tied up with a basic hostility toward the child or with a general emotional maladjustment.

The sex component in psychological development starts long before physiological sex maturity. The role of infantile sexuality in the first year of life has been emphasized by Freud. Whether it is actually that early or not is debatable, but it is clear that the roots (or seed-forms) of sexuality are found in the early childhood years. This does not mean that the infantile or childish sexuality can be identified with, or directly traced to adult sexuality. The child experiences satisfaction in the manipulation and stimulation of his own body in many different ways; one of these ways may be stimulation of the genital regions. Such early childish self-stimulation seems allied with adolescent or adult autoerotic practice, but due to both physical and psychological maturation the real significance of the activity varies at different periods in life development.

As part of learning about things and people around him, the child becomes interested in the physical differences between boys and girls. The exact age at which such curiosity occurs varies with the amount of contact or play he has with members of the opposite sex. Sex exploration and play among children are frequent occurrences, but they are emotionally upsetting only when the parents make them into traumatic situations.

During the early years of life, the child's relationship to the parents is one of dependence and strong emotional attachments. The parents set the standards of what is good, bad, shameful or desirable, and thus represent the forces of authority and discipline. The child seeks to win love, approval, and attention from the parents. When he starts to go to school the number of social influences acting upon him suddenly increases. The teacher takes over certain roles that the parents previously held. The rapid expansion of new activities and experiences, as well as competitive contacts with children of his own age, require new adjustments and readjustments on his part. He is no longer the center of interest and attention, as he was at home. He has to learn to get along under these new conditions.

ADOLESCENCE

The emotional attachments of the child broaden in scope as he grows older and his circle of friends increases. Preceding and during the time of adolescence, he is most interested in, and concerned with, members of his own sex. For several years after the time of physiological adolescence, he or she may remain shy with respect to the opposite sex. Probably because, in our culture, childhood and adolescent heterosexual play is taboo while close friendship with others of one's own sex is approved, homoerotic attachments appear to be part of the normal course of development at this time of life. The gradual weakening of the taboo permits freer expression of attraction to members of the opposite sex, and emotional attachments to members of the same sex become less and less strong. The process of heterosexual orientation is a step by step development, in which several factors play important roles. First, there is a gradual decrease in emotional dependence on the parents, which is associated with a growing self-independence. Where intense emotional attachment to the parents exists, heterosexual orientation may be long delayed in appearing, or even fail to appear. Self-independence is reached only after the individual has outgrown his childhood need for security and protection. A second factor is physiological maturation which is an important component in the psychobiological development of heterosexuality. The importance of this process is shown by certain persons who have a hormone deficiency and therefore, fail or are grossly retarded in anatomical genital development. In such cases the normal attraction to the opposite sex may never develop. The third factor depends on the relaxing of the taboo against close friendships between boys and girls, so that the boy or girl learns to feel more at ease in the presence of the other. The cultural approval of friendships between the sexes and of courtship facilitates heterosexual emotional attachments.

The period of adolescence is commonly called one of great stress and strain.[5] Certainly, it is a time at which new demands, new ideals, new goals, new experiences, and new emotional attachments occur. The new situations and relationships require new personal adjustments. In light of all these new phenomena, it is not unusual that we find personality changes at adolescence. The way in which the individual meets these changing conditions will be influenced both by the course of development up to that point, and by the particular constellation of factors that are effective at that time. Actually, the course of development merely becomes more complex in this expanding universe of adolescence, and only in exceptional instances is it a period of really great upheaval and trauma.

ADULT LIFE ADJUSTMENT

The curves for both mental and physical growth level off during the teens, but this does not mean that the adult status is a static one. No more inches may be added to the stature nor years to the mental age, but the processes of psychological growth and adjustment continue. The direction of growth and the problems for adjustment change.

In vocational choice, abilities, interests, and opportunities all play a role. If a person likes his work or his profession, he derives satisfaction and a feeling of security and accomplishment. In some instances of vocational maladjustment, the source of the difficulty may be in environmental obstacles which prevent any opportunity for accomplishment; or, circumstances may have forced a person into an ill-advised choice of occupation. But in most cases, problems of maladjustment stem from personality difficulties inherent in the individual himself, and many of the inherent difficulties can be traced back to the course of his development. He may be resentful of criticism, bear a chronic grouch toward those in authority over him, or feel that he is being abused or persecuted without justification. Very often, these reactions cannot be understood in terms of the particular vocational situation alone, but depend on the individual's whole personality structure.

Training for a vocation and its effect on life is directly comparable to many other kinds of training which are necessary for different types of adult adjustment. For example, adjustment to marriage depends on the growth and development of many factors which originate in earlier experiences and attitudes: emotional ties to the parents, relationships with members of the opposite sex during and after adolescence, and the general ability to adjust oneself to the needs and demands of a new situation. The difficulties that face a person who expects sustained romance, excitement, and glamour in marriage, and who cannot accept settling down to the level of everyday living are common knowledge.[9] Marital maladjustment frequently occurs in individuals who have developed an exaggerated evaluation of love and marriage, or who are unable to establish a deep and stable attachment to one person.

The desire to have children and to make a home for them, as well as for oneself, is part of adult maturity. The kind of marriage partner and parent that one becomes seems, very frequently, to be related to the kind of parents and home life that one had. It has been said that there is a pendulum tendency in successive generations of parents as regards discipline. Those who had very strict parents tend to swing to the opposite extreme in handling their children; similarly, those who had very little or no discipline from their own parents will, in turn, be very strict disciplinarians with their own children. Certainly, there are many instances in which parents try to avoid or to correct some unpleasantness in their child's life that they had experienced in their own.

Whether or not a person will make a good parent is not a chance occurrence, but is related to the degree of his or her adjustment to other life relationships. Many behavior-problem children come from homes in which one or both of the parents are unhappy and maladjusted. In some of these cases the mother, dissatisfied with her husband, turns her entire affection on the child, weighing him down with her love and attention, and centering all her interests, ambitions, and desires on him. Under these conditions, she interferes with his normal development of independence and, thus, does him more harm than good.

By the time a person is an adult, he has developed a consistent habit system, a general philosophy, a style of life. The particular style depends upon the basic constitutional make-up and the environmental factors that have characterized his development. The interaction between these factors is complex; the nature of the physical constitution in adult life depends not solely on inherited tendencies and immediate environmental circumstances, but also on those conditions surrounding development, such as nutrition, habit formation, exercise, injury, or disease. To explain the way Mr. Grouch is acting, we may refer to the fact that he has a stomach ache, that his hormone level is low, that he did not sleep well last night, or that his mother rejected him as a child so that he still feels insecure and has to demonstrate his own importance. No single item will tell the story. Unfortunately, we have to know a lot about Grouch's general reaction tendencies, and the entire course of development of these tendencies, before we can understand him psychologically or help him in his life adjustment.

Abilities, motives, and physiological conditions vary with age. The motives influencing conduct show a process of growth and change, just as the body does. Motives appearing later in life may derive from earlier ones, but they gradually achieve independence in their own right.

Factors Bearing on Individual Deviation

So far, a few of the factors that enter into the development of the adult personality have been described. Physical maturation, emotional ties to the family, feelings of security, and the achievement of personal independence have been considered. Deviation in any one of these factors disturbs the normal course and rate of development, as well as the final form and level of development that will be reached. Some individuals never attain a mature adult status and much of their maladjustment can be understood when viewed as childish, immature reactions appearing where adult reactions are necessary.[7] In the field of psychosexual development, the person may remain so immature that he is self-centered, narcissistic, capable only of self-love, and unable to form strong emotional attachments to any other individual. In marriage, such individuals seek a reduplication of their own childhood home, demanding attention and protection without making any personal contribution to the marriage. In the case of a man, he may marry someone who reminds him of his mother and expect her to fill the same role for him that his mother did. If it is a woman, she may approach marriage as a refuge and source of protection, looking for a sturdy oak on which to lean, a father and not a husband. Of course, such attitudes prevent a mutually satisfactory adjustment in marriage.

Physical immaturity itself presents a difficult problem of adjustment. The child or adolescent whose growth is physically retarded is at a disadvantage in a group of children of his own age. If he is not physically able to participate in their games and other activities, he may feel isolated or inferior and tend to stay by himself or develop socially undesirable methods of compensation for these feelings. In extreme cases a pattern of social withdrawal and seclusiveness may develop, which is later difficult, or even impossible, to overcome. Just as physical inferiority may be conducive to maladjustment, so may mental retardation (even of a relatively mild degree) produce psychological deviation. The child who is intellectually unable to keep up with his class or who feels incompetent in activities based on mental ability, has a tendency to develop into a behavior problem at school or at home. It is frequently noted by teachers that when a child begins to have difficulty in school work because of limited intellectual capacity, he becomes a social problem in the classroom and shows defiant, or even delinquent, behavior.

The varieties of reaction to frustration constitute an important aspect of personality development.[12] Frustration itself is meaningful only when considered as a psychological problem in terms of the individual, his needs, and his response patterns. Frustration comes from the interaction between the individual and the outside world. In the first two years of life, frustration is usually limited to interference with bodily or physiological needs. In subsequent years, the sources of frustration become more complex, involving not only lack of gratification of physical needs, but also of the more complex personality needs, such as security, affection, prestige, and self-esteem. Some of the frustrations imposed upon the individual are culturally determined. Others, of a more individual character, are determined by the course of personal experience. Physical handicap, failure in a job, loss of prestige, lack of affection and attention by a loved one, or the death of a loved one may constitute a frustration. In some instances, it is apparent that frustration is the result of the fact that the individual set too high a standard or goal for his own performance.

Frustration is a universal human experience which gets special attention in the field of abnormal psychology because it is a very prominent neurotic complaint. There are individual differences in the source of frustration, and, more particularly, in the type of reaction to frustration or in the ability to adjust to frustration. The individual who sets goals far beyond his level of achievement seeks certain disappointment. The reaction to the discrepancy between what one is and what one wants to be may be very strong and can be understood only when we consider what far-flung goals had been set. The establishment and failure to reach these impossible goals is a neurotic tendency. The feelings of failure and worthlessness, which, to the outside observer, seem completely unjustified and nonunderstandable, are but a phase of neurotic maladjustment.

Deviations occur in the type of response to frustration. The usual resolution of frustration takes place by compromise or substitution of another type of satisfaction for the one that is denied. Neurotic patients frequently lack the ability to make this form of adjustment and tend to overreact to, and become preoccupied with, their failures. Their overreaction is apt to take the form of loss in self-confidence and of consequent feelings of worthlessness and incompetence.

A common result of frustration is aggression, which has been found to be directly related to the amount of frustration.[4] The way in which aggression is expressed, whether as direct or indirect injury to another person, as aggression turned against some innocuous object, or inwardly against oneself, depends upon the particular personality structure. In many psychopathic personalities, the reaction to even mild forms of frustration may be overt aggression against persons or objects. In such overreactions, the destructive behavior appears to an outside observer as having insufficient cause. Such psychopaths seem to lack the capacity for inhibiting overt aggression. They fail to anticipate or disregard consequent punishment or other unpleasantness.

Another psychological problem that enters into personality development is that of internal personal conflicts. Needs, wants, urges, wishes, desires, ideals, morals, and practical necessity are frequently incompatible. The person may have two desires or ambitions which are mutually exclusive; he may have a sex urge which is denied expression because of his training and moral code, or his standards of conduct may themselves be in opposition to the temptations of a specific situation. The sources of such conflict are found in all the factors that influence development: the interaction of basic biological needs, of cultural patterns, of codes and rules imposed by the parents and teachers, as well as the attitudes, values, and motives that are unique for each individual. Sometimes the sources of conflict are conscious; sometimes they are unconscious. The concept of conflict between unconscious desires and the demands of reality or the conscience constitutes one of Freud's major contributions to psychological knowledge.

Conflict, like frustration, is practically a universal human experience, but it seems to play an exaggerated role in the life of the neurotic. The average person resolves a situation one way or another and forgets about it. The neurotic is unable to evolve a satisfactory solution for his conflicts. He dallies endlessly (consciously or unconsciously) over two or more possible courses of action, or perseverates over whether the correct course has been chosen. The normal person is impatient with these neurotic conflicts, feeling that the person should make up his mind and forget about it. The coexistence of opposing elements in the personality marks the maladjusted person. Although no one has perfect integration in this sense, in the normal person the opposing tendencies are usually worked out or compromised in some way. Where the conflicts remain unresolved, and indecision, worry, and tension persist, they form a powerful potential source for neurotic behavior, with or without true neurosis.

In addition to the problems of adjustment and maladjustment arising from the ordinary gradual course of development, it does happen that the usual development is redirected and partially repatterned by some important or abrupt change requiring new attitudes and feelings. These events may range from the birth of another child in the family to the loss of a loved parent, failure in school, or physical injury. Such sudden alterations (reorientations) are more significant in childhood and adolescence than they are in adult life. In one sense, these events are the chance factors in development. A knowledge of the personality before their occurrence might have enabled one to predict with relative certainty how a person would react if such an event occurred, but one could never predict with certainty that the event would occur.

The histories of many psychiatric patients indicate that acute mental symptoms appeared in a situation causing conflict and worry or after some emotionally traumatic episode. It is frequently stated by untrained observers that such events were the cause of the symptoms. Breakdowns are attributed to any one of such conditions as overwork, unrequited love, or poor health. As pointed out previously, such events do not, of and by themselves, produce real mental pathology; they merely bring about the release and demonstration of personality deviations already possible. If the individual's adjustment has been poor, any added strain will have an unbalancing effect. In a fairly well-adjusted individual, only intense strain is capable of precipitating psychopathology. In some instances, if this strain is relieved, the person will soon be able to adjust adequately again. In other cases, the precipitated psychopathology continues in an irreversible fashion. The ability to recover following relief of tension is found rather frequently in the war neuroses, in which soldiers break down under trying battle conditions, although they have shown little or no previous neurotic tendency. Once removed from the battle situation, most of them improve rapidly. Even if there is some evidence of previous inadequate adjustment, the acute symptoms are attributable to the stress of the immediate situation, which rose above the individual's tolerance level. In cases of this type, therapy of the "change of scene" or "trip to the country" variety may relieve the immediate stress and gradually cure the acute symptoms. However, if the difficulty is more deep-seated and based on fundamental personality structure defects, superficial measures cannot produce any lasting effect.

Even in those mental disorders which have a constitutional basis, the occurrence of frustration, conflict, or other circumstances taxing the adjustive powers will bring out the overt expression of certain constitutional weaknesses or deficiencies in resistance. They release forms of reaction that are latent within the personality. A low level of physical or mental resistance or a marked physiological change, such as accompanies childbirth, may act in a similar way. Because certain problems of adjustment and certain physiological changes are characteristic of different periods in human-life development, mental symptoms tend to be similar at the same general age span in different individuals. In this sense they are products of aging. In some conditions it appears that the morbid process itself goes through a period of maturation before it reaches frank expression. In these cases, slight inadequacies of adjustment or inappropriate reactions become more and more marked and a psychosis gradually develops with but little relationship to any environmental or experiential factors in the life history. Such a development accounts for conditions appearing characteristically at certain age levels, in that the process of maturation of the mental disorder requires a relatively constant amount of time.

Summary

Although this chapter has stressed the joint, interrelated action of constitution and environment in the development of the individual, for the purpose of summarizing it may be clearer to mention their contributions separately. Constitutional factors determine how much frustration, trauma, and environmental stress the person can withstand (in other words, his psychological resistance) and what the specific type of deviation will be if he does break down. Evaluation of adult personality reactions must include, not only an analysis of the person's physical and mental endowment, but also an account of his past experiences and of the effective present needs, tensions, and motives. The content and particular form of his mental deviation (at least, in certain of the diagnostic categories), the fact of whether or not he breaks down, and the particular time at which he breaks down will be determined by his life experiences, past and present.

The factors of cultural and social taboo and approval operate largely to color or to give a particular content to the morbid process. A deluded American Indian complains of the Great Bear, while a Russian's feelings are directed against the Stakhanovites. Certain social conditions favor hospitalization for mental disease: immigration, divorce, living in a city, hazardous occupations. Other factors mitigate against hospitalization: large family units, rural or village life, simple uncomplicated work.

We have, then, some persons whose genetic and physical constitutions provide them with adequate resistance to any sort of real psychological breakdown. We have others of weak resistance. Many developmental histories show clearly that persons of apparently high resistance go through practically any type of life situation without breaking. Other histories demonstrate that in persons of varying degrees of inadequate resistance, the circumstances of early life and childhood either strengthened or weakened the potential resistance. The problems of both mental hygiene and psychotherapy are essentially related to the understanding of the social, cultural, and developmental factors which favor or inhibit the potentialities of resistance which an individual may have to the various forms of mental deviation.

REFERENCES

1. Allport, G. W., *Personality: A Psychological Interpretation*. New York, Holt, 1937.
2. ———, *The Use of Personal Documents in Psychological Science*. New York, Soc. Sci. Res. Council Bull., #49, 1942.
3. Bühler, C., "The Social Behavior of the Child," in C. Murchison, *Handbook of Child Psychology*. Worcester, Clark University Press, 1931, 392–431.
4. Dollard, J., N. E. Miller, L. W. Doob, O. H. Mower, and R. R. Sears, *Frustration and Aggression*. New Haven, Yale University Press, 1939.
5. Hollingworth, L. S., *The Psychology of Adolescence*. New York, Appleton-Century, 1928.
6. Irwin, O., "The Amount and Nature of Activities of New-Born Infants under Constant Eternal Stimulating Conditions during the First Ten Days of Life. *Genet. Psychol. Mono.*, 1930, *8*, 1–92.
7. Landis, C., *et. al.*, *Sex in Development*. New York, Hoeber, 1940.
8. Levy, D., "Primary Affect Hunger," *Amer. Jour. Psychiat.*, 1937, *94*, 643–652.
9. Levy, J., and R. Munroe, *The Happy Family*. New York, Knopf, 1938.
10. Ribble, M. A., "The Significance of Infantile Sucking for the Psychic Development of the Individual," *Jour. Nerv. Ment. Dis.*, 1939, *90*, 455–463.
11. ———, *The Rights of Infants: Early Psychological Needs and Their Satisfaction*. New York, Columbia University Press, 1943.
12. Rosenzweig, S., "A General Outline of Frustration," *Char. and Pers.*, 1938, *7*, 151–160.
13. Shirley, M., *The First Two Years of Life*. Minneapolis, University of Minnesota Press, Vol. I, 1931, Vol. II, 1933, Vol. III, 1933.
14. Washburn, R. W., "A Study of the Smiling and Laughing of Infants in the First Year of Life," *Genet. Psychol. Mono.*, 1929, *6*, 397–537.

Chapter XXI

DISORDERS OF SENSATION, PERCEPTION, AND ACTION

IN THE preceding chapters, pictures of different sorts of abnormal behavior and experience have been given, followed by a discussion of the basic explanatory concepts which guide present-day thinking in abnormal psychology. It is plain that only rarely do isolated symptoms appear. Almost always each item in any disorder (physical or mental) exists, along with other symptoms, in a complicated relationship to other structures and functions which themselves may be either orderly or disordered. Since it is impossible to hold in mind all of the interrelationships at one time, we customarily break down the complex pictures; we oversimplify things; we endeavor to group together in our thinking those features which seem to belong together, and so present a generalization which has some value in holding diverse facts in mind.

In Chaps. XXI–XXVII which follow, the disorders of behavior and mental life will be classed and examined in light of the conventional divisions of the field of psychology; namely, perception, memory, volition. It will be apparent that these conventional divisions are often not too appropriate for describing the phenomena of abnormal psychology. Even so, it is best to follow this system of presentation for two reasons: (a) it brings the material in line with normal psychology, and (b) most of the psychological experiments have been conducted and reported in these terms. Until such time as a more adequate system of classification of psychological phenomena is formulated, and until the facts now arranged in the older classifications are translated into some new system, the conventional system, admittedly not too satisfactory, is preferable to hypothetical innovations.

The three most obvious ways in which we recognize abnormality in another person are, first, he does not seem to see, hear, or feel things the way most of us do; second, his behavior (motor responses) is different from that of the usual person; and third, his speech (the way he expresses himself) is different from that which we would expect from one of his age and education. We will take up each variety of psychopathological process without particular reference to the disorder or disease in which it occurs. It must be remembered that these disorders of relatively simple functions rarely, if ever, occur alone. They usually are parts of a complex whole which can be more easily understood if one has a good working knowledge of its components.

Sensation and Perception

By *sensation* is meant that form of experience, aroused from outside the nervous system, which cannot be further analyzed by introspection, that is, an element of consciousness. *Perception* is the awareness of external objects on the basis of sensation; the integration of sensory experience with previously acquired knowledge. The description of disorders of sensation and perception simplifies some of the phenomena of psychopathology. In some instances this simplification adds to clarification, in others it fails to do so.

Among the disorders of cutaneous sensation are those which have a direct organic basis; those which are indirectly organic; and those for which no organic basis can be found. An example of the first variety is the loss of skin sensitivity after the sensory nerve serving the area has been cut; of the second variety, a drug addict's illusion of bugs crawling under the skin; and of the third variety, the "glove anesthesia" in hysteria, where the loss of sensation does not correspond to any defined sensory nerve distribution.

An interesting and baffling variety of *paresthesia* (false or distorted sensation) may follow sensory nerve injury or limb amputation.[7] Occasionally, after nerve injury due to a bullet wound or the crushing of tissue, the patients suffer from a type of pain which they describe as "burning," "mustard red-hot," or as "red-hot file rasping the skin." Such pain is termed *causalgia* and is usually related to the hand, arm, foot, or leg. It follows injury to a nerve trunk in the upper arm or leg, and is comparable to the tingling sensation of the fingers following a blow on the elbow. The skin of the affected part often becomes mottled and glossy. The temperature of the painful area may be several degrees lower or higher than that of the corresponding area of the opposite limb. The pain is so continuous and intense that the patient is unable to sleep without sedatives, can eat but little, and cannot bear the slightest manipulation of the affected limb. Medical examination usually shows that the injured nerve trunk has not regenerated properly, probably due to scar tissue. Treatment consists of the injection along the nerve trunk of some drug, such as novocaine, which often brings immediate relief.

Sometimes, following the amputation of a limb, the patient will complain of intense sensory experiences which seem to come from the missing member. This phenomenon is termed *phantom limb*. One individual said it felt as though his fingers were clenched over his thumb, his wrist was flexed, and the fist pressed toward the shoulder and held there; another said that it felt as though a wire which ran down the center of the missing arm was attached to the fingers and was pulling the fingers up through the arm. Phantom limb, as well as causalgia, is reported to respond well to the removal of scar tissue and the freeing of the nerve ending at the stump, or to the injection of novocaine.

The generally accepted explanation of these conditions rests on the hypothesis that sustained or excessive irritation of sensory nerves initiates nervous activity of portions of the central nervous system. This nervous activity, in turn, leads to secondary changes, such as local skin conditions, which reinstate the subjective pain. Thus, a vicious circle arrangement results. The interference with the circle by surgery or drug injection stops the pain, at least temporarily.

The decrease in auditory sensitivity which occurs in progressive deafness is, of itself, almost always on an organic basis. It is due to degeneration of the auditory nerve or of the auditory mechanism of the inner ear. Progressive deafness frequently has attendant psychopathological symptoms, among which are anxiety, depression, or paranoid states. Such progressive changes are not difficult to understand. In everyday speech we lower our voices when we do not wish others to hear what we are talking about. We have all had the experience of being left out of conversations which had some personal reference. With the loss of auditory acuity, these muted conversations will increase, and this increase will be attributed to personal motives. These motives, of course, have no basis in fact. Depending on the personality of the individual, he will become increasingly anxious, depressed, or paranoid. When these reaction tendencies and their relation to the handicap of growing deafness are properly handled and explained, intelligent and stable persons are usually able to adjust to the circumstances. However, in a maladjusted and emotionally unstable person with little psychological insight to start with, a severe mental illness may be precipitated.

Disorders in the sensations of hunger occur quite frequently in psychiatric patients. Diminution or absence of hunger or appetite (*anorexia*) is a fairly common occurrence in the depressed or hysterical patient. Neurotic and depressed patients complain that food no longer has any taste, while the schizophrenic insists that he tastes poison in his food. Such disorders in taste and in hunger furnish a basis for a distaste for food, even when the patient is obviously starving and in need of a substantial diet. This anorexia may be so acute that even tube feeding results in nausea.

Some patients have abnormally intense hunger sensations (*bulimia*). This symptom occurs in paresis, epilepsy, and in certain forms of feeble-mindedness. Such individuals eat enormous quantities of food and complain that they are always hungry. Craving for unusual foods (*parorexia*) is found in vitamin deficiencies, particularly in those associated with alcoholism and pellagra.

Imperception is a condition in which stimulation and sensation fail to arouse their usually associated images, ideas, or responses, so that experience has little or no meaning. It produces a strange feeling of vagueness and uncertainty which is called "clouded consciousness." For example, patients who suffer from word-blindness say that the printed characters on the page have lost their meaning, although they may be seen clearly enough and even spelled out. Other patients report that objects seem to have lost their visual meanings (object-blindness), so that they are not recognized unless they are carefully handled or otherwise studied. Still other patients complain that they have been deprived of the ability to perceive depth or the third dimension, so that the world seems flat to them. In psychic deafness sounds lose their meanings. This disorder may manifest itself either as specific word-deafness, where spoken words become sounds without meaning, or as the inability to apprehend melodies. Another form of imperception is *astereognosis*, the loss of the ability to recognize objects by cutaneous or kinesthetic sensation, that is, by feeling them. Practically all of these symptoms are related to organic brain disturbances.

Imperception may arise in several different fashions. For example, if an individual is distracted by great pain or anxiety, there will be an interference with attention. This interference will deprive the primary sensations of their usual associated meanings and ideas, so resulting in imperception. If there is a progressive brain damage, or a toxic condition which is interfering with brain functioning, then the usual connections between ideas, memories, and sensations will be interrupted and imperception will result. The same effect may take place in a splitting or fragmentation of consciousness when the usual ideas and memories do not become associated with sensation. Similarly, a patient will experience imperception when he is occupied with his own compulsions or hallucinations, and hence inattentive.

Some persons have the tendency to experience visual color whenever they hear certain sounds or certain melodies. This arousing of a sensory experience in a modality which is different from that of the primary stimulus is termed *synesthesia*.[11] Colored hearing, colored taste, musical pressures, and tonal temperatures have been reported. Investigation of this experience in the same individuals over widely spaced periods of time has shown that the synesthetic association remains practically constant. A great deal of experimental work has been done with persons who report synesthetic experience, but its real basis is still unknown. It has been variously attributed to some pathological condition, to a physiological anomaly in which the wrong nerve structures or patterns have become connected, or to a conditioned response type of learning.

The changes in sensory threshold for all varieties of stimulation in neuropsychiatric patients have been the subject of extensive investigations. In psychotics this variability is usually related to imperception or to lack of attention. The report[10] that there was a definite increase in the auditory threshold of the schizophrenic during reverie was not confirmed.[1] The variability, the decreases, and occasional increases in thresholds which are found in certain groups of neurotic patients have generally been attributed to hysterical components in their personality structure.

Psychotic patients tend to be more fixed or rigid than normal persons in their perceiving of almost any kind of material which is presented to them. When they see ambiguous figures* in one way, they are often unable to shift to a second interpretation. Mental completion of incompletely drawn pictures is difficult for them. Most psychotics seem to require a greater amount of sensory material before the sensation actually becomes a perception, or to change from one perception to another.[3]

Organic brain damage is frequently associated with a variety of disturbances in pattern perception. Sometimes a patient is able to read only when he follows the outline of the letters with his finger. Other patients cannot perceive words or letters which are momentarily exposed to them, although they are clearly perceptible to normal individuals. Slowness in pattern perception is also a common symptom in cases of cerebral injury. There is no systematic way in which the

---

* An ambiguous figure or drawing is one which can be seen by most people in either of two ways.

differences in sensation and perception are related to the different kinds of psychosis, neurosis, or organic brain injury, although most cases show a decrease in acuitv, a rigidity of organization, and a slowness of pattern perception.

ILLUSION

By *illusion* is meant the inexact or inaccurate perception of some actual object or situation. A passive illusion is a normal phenomenon and may be experienced by everyone. Such illusions are determined by the nature of our sense organs and by the environment about us. An example is the apparent convergence of parallel lines at the horizon. Active illusions are due to a conscious expectation based on habit, suggestion, attitude, or unconscious motivation. The mirage of a boat seen by shipwrecked sailors, the report of good health by the advanced paretic, a patient calling the nurse by his mother's name, all are instances of active illusions. It is often difficult to differentiate between this type of illusion and hallucination. However, in general, active illusions occur in many cases of physical or mental illness, particularly when the patients are delirious or disoriented. It is as if the primary sensations had lost part of their meaning (imperception) and were given a new sort of meaning emotionally related to the general mental trend of the moment.

HALLUCINATION

While an illusion is a false interpretation of some actual object or stimulation, hallucination is a perception without any known external stimulation. Hallucinations may occur in any single sense field or in several sense fields at the same time. One may have an hallucination of an angel and the angel may be seen, heard, and felt to touch one during the experience. Hallucinations are generally, although not invariably, related to abnormal conditions. They may be experienced by otherwise normal individuals during periods of great fatigue or intense emotional excitement, or due to the effect of drugs, alcohol, drowsiness, or the like. In the normal person such hallucinatory experiences are always transient and are understood by the person who has experienced them as unusual and unreal, once the phenomenon has ceased.

Hallucinations are usually classified according to the sense modality in which they occur. Auditory hallucinations are the most frequent variety. The patient hears noises, tones, voices, meaningless words, meaningful words, sentences, or messages which seem to originate within his head, within his body, outside himself but near to him, or at a distance from him. He may hear "attack and defense" voices which alternately accuse and defend him. He may experience a "soundless voice" or "thoughts-out-loud." He may complain of "double thought," during which he hears his own thoughts spoken aloud by another voice. These experiences may occur at regular or irregular intervals, or they may go on continuously over long periods of time. Some schizophrenic patients report that their hearing of voices has been practically continuous over a period of years.

Visual hallucinations may be stationary, moving, variable, transient, large, small, colored, achromatic, and of any form or description. The patient may see angels, the Devil, insects, a printed page, snakes, animals.

Hallucinations of taste and smell frequently occur together and are usually disagreeable. For example, the patient will complain that his food tastes and smells of arsenic, of poisoned gas, or filth. Hallucinations of pain are described as pinpricks, stabs, electric shocks; or the patient may make up a word to describe these pain experiences.

The patient may insist that he has been, or is, moving about the room or building. He may say that he is floating in space over his bed. He may ascribe this movement to angels or devils that are supporting him or chasing him through space.

Verbal hallucinations which involve the speech mechanism may also occur. If they are weak, the patient may think he is speaking when he is not, and mutism may result. If they are intense, the patient may actually speak involuntarily, "the escape of thought."

The experience of hallucination is, of course, personal and subjective, but it has in most instances a profound influence on all other mental functions. Hallucinations cannot be resisted. No effort of will on the part of the patient can control or halt the experience. They *compel* attention. Sometimes the patient may recognize the unreality of the hallucination; at other times he will be unable to differentiate between external reality and his hallucinatory experience. Since the experience does compel attention and cannot be controlled, it is often mistaken for true perception and the individual will maintain its reality against all other testimony and evidence. The hallucinations are usually disagreeable or indifferent, although, on occasion, they may be agreeable. Since they are believed and since they have emotional tone, they are bound to influence the behavior of the person. Often the voices will be immediately obeyed. Strange and bizarre acts may be carried out at the instruction of these voices. Also, a patient may remain mute because he hears his own thoughts spoken and he can only wonder at the deafness or stupidity of those about him who do not hear his remarks.

Lang,[5, 6] himself a schizophrenic patient for more than eight years, has written a subjective description of hallucinations as he experienced them. His first hallucinatory experience consisted of hearing a voice speaking in a soothing monotone from a point slightly above his ear. It uttered only a sentence or two at a time and claimed to originate from God. Another type of auditory hallucination described by Lang was one which seemed to arise from actual human beings. For example, on one occasion he was playing bridge. He heard his partner bid three clubs, so he bid to take him out since he had only a weak hand in clubs himself. He secured the bid, but when his partner's hand was laid down he noticed that his partner had only two small clubs in his hand. He asked his partner why he had made such a bid. His partner denied bidding and the other two men at the table supported him. Actually, he had declared an entirely different bid at the time Lang heard him bidding three clubs. Hence, there was the blocking of a real stimulus and the substitution of an hallucinatory one. Hallucinations of this variety could not be distinguished from the actual speech of the person who seemed to be talking. Only subsequently could Lang check to find out what had really happened. Such checks were of little value to him, for the hallucination was the actual experience so far as he was concerned.

Lang's visual hallucinations were sometimes simple and sometimes complicated moving forms. In the simple forms there were flashes of light, the appearance of the picture of some individual projected on the wall, and so on. Usually his visual hallucinations were combined with auditory experiences. On one occasion he was walking down the street near the end of a streetcar line. He saw, about half a block ahead of him, a streetcar heading toward the end of the line. The car had every appearance of an actual car. It was tridimensional, opaque except for the windows, and it had passengers and a crew. He distinctly heard the rumble of the car wheels. When he reached the end of the street and the end of the streetcar line where the car should have been standing, there was no car and actually no car had passed. On another occasion he had a very unusual kinesthetic hallucination. He had walked to the end of the dock with the idea of attempting suicide by drowning. He poised on the edge of the pier, then tensed and jumped off, feeling himself falling through the air. As he fell, he looked to see how close he was getting to the water and found that he had actually never jumped and was still standing solidly on the pier.

Lang pointed out that the hallucinations constituted aspects of conscious experience which were real to him. They appeared as organized experience. His conscious self did not anticipate them or initiate them. He, himself, had nothing more to do with the voices than he had to do with a conversation which he might have overheard. The hallucinations appeared spontaneously. They did not grow out of fantasy which was related to his consciousness; they often did not even correlate in any way with the configuration of the conscious field which existed at the time they occurred. He was unable to produce stimulations or experiences similar to those presented by the hallucinations. Lang claimed that he had tried to do this on numerous occasions but had never succeeded in producing hallucinations voluntarily.

Part of the peculiarity of the behavior and mental outlook of the psychotic patient can be understood if one considers the compelling nature of hallucinatory experience. When hallucinations continue over a period of time, the patient is apt to form delusional systems. He will believe himself to be the Son of God, a sinner sentenced to everlasting hell, a prophet, or a famous figure in history, in an attempt to rationalize these strange experiences. The influence of hallucination upon the mental life of an individual is so unique that it should never be underestimated.

Since hallucinations exert such an important and potent force in abnormal behavior, it is not surprising to find a great deal of both experiment and theory concerning their nature. Of particular interest are Penfield's[9] observations made during brain operations. When he stimulated directly the surface of the brain, the patient reported organized hallucinatory experiences. Upon stimulation, one patient said, "I don't feel normal. I don't know whether it is one of my dreams or not. A familiar sight danced into my mind and away again. Three or four things danced before my memory. They went too fast. I can't quite remember who they were. I think I saw the same scene before." Another patient, on stimulation, said, "I hear people coming in. I hear music now, a funny little piece." The music was identified by the patient as something similar to the theme song of a children's program which she had heard on the radio.

Most modern investigators believe that hallucination is a centrally initiated process which depends on some organic brain process. Older theories attributed hallucinatory experiences to incorrect perception, synesthesia, imperception, or to outer stimulation. Careful experimental studies of hallucinations, together with the work of the brain surgeons, have led to the acceptance of the notion that hallucinations are somehow directly related to the activity of the brain itself.

Equally significant is the content of hallucinations, concerning which there has been endless speculation. For instance, if a childless woman has an hallucination of many babies, such an hallucinatory experience has been interpreted as a projection of her emotional wishes. But when the same woman first sees a single pencil or a chair, and then suddenly sees a row of pencils or a row of chairs, it would not seem likely that emotional factors were responsible for the multiplicity. Any object, event, or idea may have emotional significance. A patient with a crippled arm saw in his hallucinations persons around him who were also crippled, while a blind patient saw heads with empty eye sockets. That a particular object should appear, in hallucination, connected with some emotional need, seems no more significant than the fact that our perception of actual objects may be modified in meaning by the conditions under which we see these objects.

The relationship of hallucinations to dreams is obvious. We all tend to be moved by events which occur in our dreams. We often awake to find that we have been crying, laughing, or sweating. Since the dream phenomena occurred during sleep, they are usually considered unreal; only under exceptional circumstances do they modify our everyday existence. Drug experiments have shown that the mescal hallucinations which appear when a person is awake and the mescal dreams which occur when he is asleep are very similar as to form, content, and spatial and temporal relationships.

Extensive experimental investigations of hallucination have been carried out with drugs, especially mescaline and hasheesh. In mescal hallucinations, Klüver[4] found three consistent tendencies: (a) certain constant forms, of which lattices, spirals, fretwork, and arabesques seemed to be outstanding; (b) alterations in the number, size, and shape of the figures seen; and (c) changes in the spatial and temporal relations of the material. For example, one subject who had taken mescal stated that he saw a fretwork before his eyes; that his arms, hands, and fingers turned into fretwork; that he became identical with the fretwork. Every object in the room and the walls changed into fretwork, becoming identical with him. All ideas changed into glass fretwork which he saw, thought, felt, tasted, and smelled.

On the basis of experimental evidence, Klüver concluded that hallucinations produced in mescaline intoxication are very close, and possibly the same in form and content to the hallucinations of schizophrenics. Other psychotic features of the mescal state resemble those seen in the schizophrenic syndrome. The biochemical processes involved are not understood, but the similarity in the total picture of the two conditions is most striking.

Reflex Action

It is customary to think of motor behavior as built up of more or less simple reflex response units. A simple reflex has been defined as the response of a single effector unit to the stimulation of a single receptor unit when these are linked together in a simple reflex arc. This concept is a convenient abstraction but, in all probability, a single reflex arc never functions alone. Physiologists and neurologists have found through practical experience that certain of the simple reflexes are indicative of disturbances of more complicated functions. In general, reflex disturbances indicate either that the immediate neural connections underlying the response are not functioning properly, or that they are being interfered with by the dysfunction of some higher nervous center.

Such reflex disorders are exemplified in the disturbances of the pupillary, patellar, or the Babinski reflexes. Ordinarily, the size of the pupil of the eye changes when one looks from near objects to far objects and vice versa, or when the illumination falling upon the retina is increased or decreased. In some types of brain injury or brain infection it is found that the size of the pupil alters for distance accommodation but not for changes in illumination. In other types of cortical lesion the size of the pupils will change in response to altered illumination, but will not respond to accommodation, that is shifting of vision to a different distance.

The patellar reflex (knee jerk) is elicited by a sharp tap just below the kneecap, causing the lower leg and foot to kick forward vigorously. Absence of this response is taken as an indicator of damage to the lower part of the spinal cord, such as one finds in various forms of paralysis, meningitis, or certain toxic conditions. The Babinski response is brought out by drawing a finger rapidly across the sole of the foot from the heel to the great toe. Ordinarily, this stimulation is followed by a contraction of all of the toes. If a lesion exists in the motor centers or pathways from the brain down through the spinal cord, there will be an extension, rather than a contraction, of the great toe and a flaring of the other toes.

Motor Disorders

Motor disorders may show themselves as absence of response, decrease in response, exaggeration of response, or disorder of response. The various forms of paralysis are examples of absence of motor response. True paralysis is due to some interference with the motor nerves, nerve tracts, or nerve centers with resultant loss of function, just as a telephone ceases to function when the wires are cut. "Functional" paralysis occurs in hysteria, where the patient loses the use of a limb with no damage to either the nerves or the muscles. The "miraculous" cures which are seen at religious revivals or shrines, or as the result of hypnosis or some newly invented form of therapy are usually cases that would be classified as hysterical paralyses.

Decreased motor responsiveness is exemplified by the functional muscular weakness of the neurotic, the retardation of the depressed patient, or by the posttraumatic disability of the compensation case who has suffered some industrial accident.

There are many forms of exaggerated motor function, for example, manic excitement, tremors, spasms, convulsions, chorea, athetosis, and tics. *Chorea* is a state of spasmodic muscular twitchings which are involuntary, irregular, and jerky. The condition is usually accompanied by moods of irritability and depression, and occasionally by some mental impairment. The most frequent variety is Sydenham's chorea (St. Vitus's dance) which occurs in childhood and affects girls more frequently than boys. In *athetosis* there is a constant, recurring series of tentaclelike movements of the hands and feet. This continual slow change in position is usually attributed to some brain injury in infancy and is frequently associated with mental defect. Quick, sudden spasms, similar in form to involuntary movements, and without known organic basis, are spoken of as *tics*. They consist of a spasmodic twitching in a coordinated fashion of some part of the face, a movement of the head and shoulders, or sometimes the arms. Any or all of these parts of the body may be included in the pattern. Regardless of whether or not such a tic occurs on a compulsive or organic basis, it is characterized by the fact that the individual is unable to inhibit it. Some tics are preceded by a strong desire to carry out the particular grimace or twitch, and its performance is said to lead to a feeling of relief. Others are thought to be remnants of outgrown habits, symbols of repressed ideas, or conversion expressions of some emotional conflict.

APRAXIA

Apraxia is the loss of ability to perform some skilled act in the absence of either motor or sensory paralysis.[8] In motor apraxia the person knows what is to be done but cannot accomplish it, despite voluntary attempts to do so. This disorder is found in certain lesions of the motor area of the brain, by which the normal course of the nerve impulses is either totally or partially blocked. Such a patient, when asked to touch his nose, may grasp his ear; or, when asked to thread a needle, will make clumsy and helpless movements with his hands.

In sensory or ideational apraxia the patient does not know what is to be done because the sensory cues to action are missing. When lighting a cigar, he may put both the cigar and the match in his mouth; or when he attempts to dress himself, he puts his arms into the legs of his underwear and cannot proceed further; or, if requested to get up from his chair and walk about the room, he merely looks puzzled. He seems unable to comprehend the meaning of such requests, although he may be capable of repeating the order and even of explaining it. However, he cannot make the connection between his explanation and the actual performance of the act.

DISORDERS OF WRITING

A great deal of attention has been given to the analysis of the handwriting of mentally abnormal persons. The change in writing which accompanies any psychotic or deterioration process is usually marked and, to an extent, characteristic of the disorder. With advancing age the writing becomes quavering, small, and formal. The writing of the paretic sprawls, is full of misspellings, and is quite irregular. The manic patient writes with a sweeping, flourishing manner, while the same person in a depression will write with a small, compressed, limited style. The writing of the schizophrenic is a mixture of writing, printing, pictures, and symbols which seem to have little connection and meaning. In fact, the writing often resembles the scribbling of a small child.

A peculiar disturbance of writing which is found in some children and which continues into their adult life is mirror writing. It consists in the tendency to write either from right to left, or both right to left and upside down. The cause and explanation for either type are not clear, but it is assumed that some disturbance of space perception is involved.

CATALEPSY AND CATATONIA

In catalepsy there is a total suspension of sensation and voluntary motion. The muscles are rigid, the pulse and respiration are slow, the body is cold and pale, and the person appears unconscious. Such a condition may last from a few minutes to several days, and is seen especially in certain organic brain lesions or infections. It was at one time described as a common hysterical symptom and even considered by Charcot to be a leading feature of hysteria.

Catatonia and the catatonic state give the name to one of the forms of dementia praecox. The catatonic patient may assume either of two response patterns, rigidity or waxy flexibility. In the rigid, negativistic form the patient holds himself in a fixed, stiff position for hours or days on end. His jaws may be so tightly clamped together that it is necessary to feed him by means of a tube passed through the nose. He usually is mute and does not respond to strong or even painful stimulation. If an arm or leg is forcibly held in some new position, it will spring back to the original position the instant the force is relieved. In the waxy flexibility state the patient sits or reclines in an immobile fashion, but his position can easily be changed or molded by the observer. After such a change, the patient will maintain the new position as though he were actually made of wax. All the time, he appears to be so wrapped up by his own thoughts that he cannot be bothered by anything that goes on around him or is done to him. However, when he goes to sleep the catatonic responses disappear and his posture and changes of posture during sleep will be similar to those found in the normal individual.

Following recovery from such a catatonic attack, many patients report that they were overwhelmed or "smothered" by ideas and hallucinations which entirely occupied their conscious attention. They may remember some things which occurred, but only in a fragmentary fashion. They usually know that they were unable to speak or unwilling to speak because of this intense preoccupation. Somewhat similar pathological conditions have been produced in animals with drugs. For example, bulbocapnine brings about waxy flexibility in cats and monkeys, while mescal produces a rigid and apparently hallucinated state in monkeys and dogs.

Summary

Although sensation, perception, and motor response are the simplest terms to which one may reduce psychological experience, even this simplicity fails in many aspects of psychopathology to bring about an adequate explanation. In some instances a better understanding of abnormality is gained from a study of the way in which these simple processes modify behavior. It is still a debatable point, however, whether the simple processes themselves are disordered or whether they are representative of a disorder extending throughout the entire organism. In general, the importance of the disorders of sensation and perception in the behavior and mental life of the abnormal individual is well established and accepted as a basic reference point. Disordered motor responses may be either organic or functional in nature, but they usually are symptoms rather than causes of psychopathology.

REFERENCES

1. Bartlett, M. R., *The Auditory Threshold in Reverie*. Arch. Psychol., #182, 1935, *27*, 42 pp.
2. Frey, H., A. B. Stokes, and I. R. Ewing, "Discussion on the Psychological Aspects of Deafness," *Proc. Roy. Soc. Med.*, 1940–41, *34*, 309–320.
3. Goldstein, K., *The Organism*. New York, American Book, 1939.
4. Klüver, H., "Mechanisms of Hallucinations." Chapter 10 in: *Studies in Personality*, contributed in honor of L. M. Terman. New York, McGraw-Hill, 1942, 175–207.
5. Lang, J., "The Other Side of Hallucinations, I," *Amer. Jour. Psychiat.*, 1938, *94*, 1089–1097.
6. ———, "The Other Side of Hallucinations, II," *Amer. Jour. Psychiat.*, 1939, *96*, 423–430.
7. Livingston, W. K., *Pain Mechanisms*. New York, Macmillan, 1943.
8. Nielson, J. M., *Agnosia, Apraxia, Aphasia*. Los Angeles, Los Angeles Neurological Society, 1936.
9. Penfield, W., "The Cerebral Cortex in Man: I. The Cerebral Cortex and Consciousness," *Arch. Neurol. Psychiat.*, 1938, *40*, 415–442.
10. Travis, L. E., "A Test for Distinguishing between Schizophrenoses and Psychoneuroses," *Jour. Abn. Soc. Psychol.*, 1924, *19*, 283–298.
11. Wheeler, R. H., *The Synaesthesia of a Blind Subject*. University of Oregon Publ. #5, 1920, *1*, 61 pp.

Chapter XXII

DISORDERS OF SPEECH

SPEECH is at once a distinguishing human characteristic and the most certain indicator of the normality or abnormality of the mental life of our fellow men. It is itself subject to many disorders and abnormalities. We will consider in this chapter three of these disorders: stuttering, aphasia, and some of the abnormalities which occur in the psychoses.

Stuttering

Although not all authorities would agree that stuttering and stammering are the same, we will assume that they are and that the two words can be used interchangeably. Stuttering (or stammering) is a disorder in the rhythm of verbal expression.

There is no accurate census of the number of stutterers, but it is estimated that there are at least two million in the general population of the United States. Surveys of school children indicate that from 1 to 5 per cent of the school population show this disability.[11] Boys outnumber girls in ratios varying from 2 to 1, to 10 to 1. The ratio changes with age, so that among older groups there is a far greater preponderance of male to female stutterers. Not only are boys more apt to stutter, but they are also more likely to persist in this defect throughout their lives. Many theories have been suggested to explain this difference in sex ratio. Except for the marked association of stuttering with left-handedness and the excess of left-handed males over left-handed females, there are no relevant data available to explain this disproportion.

Stuttering occurs more frequently among the mentally defective than among those of normal intellectual ability. According to Travis, stutterers in the ordinary public-school classes show the same distribution of IQ's as the nonstutterers, although stutterers are retarded from one to two years in school progress. About 85 per cent of stuttering individuals began their stuttering before the age of eight.

321

SYMPTOMS OF STUTTERING[11]

In normal speech there is a mobilization and organization in proper temporal sequence of a series of complex motor responses. Any disturbance in the temporal order will disrupt the whole performance. Speech is, in this sense, an expression of a dynamic and kinetic rhythm. The major characteristic of stuttering is a disorganization in the temporal forward-moving process of speech and a disintegration among the various speech apparatus movements. Some elements function out of temporal phase with other elements so that the organization is defective.

In stuttering there is frequently found to be an abdominal inspiration and thoracic expiration at one time. Because of this, they tend to neutralize each other so that no air moves through the larynx. In normal speech there exists an independence between the movements of the breathing mechanism and those of the larynx; in stuttering there is a marked tendency for the larynx to move synchronously with the abdomen or the thorax or both. Inspiration may continue for as long as 10 seconds while a stutterer is attempting to speak. During this long inspiration the larynx may be in a tonic spasm or show abrupt vertical movements. Spasms of the speech mechanism muscles may be short or exceedingly long. Tremors in certain of the speech muscles during stuttering or in muscles not related to speech may occur and interfere with the rhythmical organization. The average stutterer holds his tones during speaking three times as long as does the normal speaker. In normal speech there is usually a gradual building up in the amplitude of the tone, while in the stutterer's speech there is an abrupt initiation of tone. One of the most obvious signs of stuttering is a repetition of sounds. There is no real difference between the repeating and the blocking, the repetition being a marked prolongation of the blocking phase. Many stutterers block when attempting to speak, so that they are unable to produce the sound for an appreciable length of time. There is a good deal of variation among stutterers and in the same individual from time to time. These symptoms are all primary, in that they affect the speech itself in a more or less mechanical fashion.

INFLUENCE OF STUTTERING ON PERSONALITY

Johnson,[8] himself a stutterer, has made excellent studies of the personality of stutterers. In one investigation of 80 stutterers (61 men, 19 women) who were of better than average intelligence, he inquired particularly into their personality make-up and the effect which stuttering had upon their personality. He obtained from each a family history and an autobiography. He gave all subjects several specialized questionnaires, together with personal interviews, in order to bring out facts concerning their attitude toward life and the way in which their handicap had affected it.

He found that most stutterers think of their speaking disability in one or more of the following ways: (*a*) a handicap, either general or specific; (*b*) a mark of inferiority; (*c*) a way to talk, inconvenient at times but not an important reason for worry or shame; or (*d*) an advantage with respect to certain kinds of adaptation. The immediate reaction of the stutterer to his stuttering depends on the setting in which it occurs. The two major influences on his personal attitude to his disability are the training and general treatment which he received from his parents and at school. If either the parents or the school-teachers force the stutterer to do a great deal of oral recitation, public speaking, or other activity in which his speech difficulty is a major interference, he is likely to become more fearful, tense, nervous, and maladjusted. If he is allowed to go on at his own pace, doing as much oral recitation as he thinks he can, with some degree of encouragement, he is not apt to acquire a sense of inferiority and maladjustment.

Many stutterers compensate for their disability by taking up athletics, some form of music, or a hobby in which they can excel and in which their speech difficulty is no handicap. Most of them have no trouble when they sing or play a musical instrument. However, some are unable to sing, particularly in a solo part, or under emotional circumstances. One of Johnson's cases reported "finger hesitation" when playing the piano. He said:

"This is a hesitation in the finger action caused by the fact that the right kind of nerve energy doesn't get to the muscles of the fingers. In playing the piano I will sometimes have this difficulty, especially if I am working on a new piece that I have to analyze. It bothers me much more if I am tired and fidgety, or feeling blue. . . . These periods of hesitation don't come all the time, but when they do come they come all at once. . . . I will place my fingers over the proper keys; I will know exactly what I want to play, but yet I am unable to press down the keys. The nervous tension that comes over me at this time is impossible to describe."*

The material which Johnson obtained from a mental hygiene questionnaire showed that the stutterers, as a group, were more similar in their emotional and social adjustments to normal individuals than

* Johnson, W., "Influence of Stuttering on Personality," *Univer. of Iowa Studies in Child Welfare*, 1932, 5, 41-42.

they were to neurotic persons. This was true both for the number and severity of the personality problems of stutterers, although it was found that their problems tended to become more exaggerated as they grew older, particularly if the stuttering was severe. Over half of their personality problems were attributed to the frustrating and humiliating consequences of the stuttering itself.

Stutterers reported fantasies which were classed as (a) success-normal speech, (b) revenge, (c) anxiety, and (d) despair. The success-normal speech fantasy was the most common. In their reported day-dreams the stutterers indicated that they were normally sociable, considerate individuals. Their apparent introversion frequently appeared to be a frustrated extroversion. The most common wish expressed by stutterers was that they might be cured of their stuttering.

From the standpoint of mental hygiene and personality development, Johnson emphasized the point that the stutterer should be regarded neither as a psychiatric patient nor as a laboratory subject, but as a human being who has many problems, one of which is the manner in which he speaks. How important this latter problem will be depends upon the part which stuttering plays in the stutterer's life, upon the definition which the individual gives to his disability, and upon the general life situation in which he finds himself.

In his autobiography, entitled *Because I Stutter*, Johnson[7] provided additional data illustrating the effect of stuttering on personality development and life adjustments. Johnson began stuttering at the age of five, for no apparent reason. The handicap persisted during the remainder of his life. There was nothing in his family history, birth, childhood illness, or social circumstances which was extraordinary or could in any way be thought to be responsible for the condition. His father explained his stuttering by telling him that he was "thinking ahead of his speech" and that he would "grow out of it." His mother said that his stuttering was "a kind of nervousness." Others told him that he stuttered because he was afraid that he would stutter which, he says, was a reversal of the true situation. An older brother was fond of the notion that he stuttered because he really wanted to. This, Johnson said, was not true. (Everyday observation of stutterers brings one to the conclusion that stuttering occurs whether the stutterer wants to have difficulty, does not want to, or does not care one way or the other.) Johnson consciously directed his interests toward scholarship, athletics, writing, and good fellowship. These activities reassured him, so that, even though his speech was defective, he could express himself more accurately and adequately than most of his fellows.

When nineteen, he went to a "stuttering school." Here he was taught to speak slowly, to keep his voice flowing, to hit consonants lightly, and to glide over words. He was taught to keep calm and to adopt a public-be-damned attitude. He was encouraged to carry on physical exercise and breathing practice. While at the school he did not stutter very much, especially when he spoke in a drawling monotone. However, after three months of diligent work, he returned home stuttering just as much as ever. The failure of the method and his own previous inability to overcome his difficulty under ordinary circumstances came as a tremendous blow to his hopes and aspirations. Later, he went to a university where he took part in the research program on speech pathology. He shifted from right-handedness to left-handedness This shift helped, but did not cure the stuttering.

He also underwent psychoanalysis in order to discover factors which might have been responsible for the stuttering. This analysis showed no evidence of any severe psychopathic tendency which might explain the defect. It did show that as a stuttering individual he had reacted to a glib society rather vehemently, and that because of his stuttering he had developed certain fears and ideas of a paranoid nature. The analysis seemed to clear up these particular symptoms, but the stuttering continued.

THEORIES OF THE NATURE OF STUTTERING

There are many theories concerning the essential nature of stuttering, some of which are flatly contradictory. There is the theory of absent or weak visualization; the theory of auditory amnesia and recall; the conditioned response theory; the theory of fear and self-consciousness; the theory of neural conflict between the brain cortex and lower nervous centers; the psychoanalytic theory of oral eroticism, oral fixation, and fear of revealing unconscious material; the theory of cerebral dominance and cortical gradients, and others. Each of these theories has had its vigorous proponents and those who held that it was completely wrong. "Cures" and "failures" have been recorded in terms of every theory. Particular theories have given rise to different types of reeducation. Most of these have been built around rules of breathing, enunciation, and continuity of sound production. In one sense, all such efforts are equally futile. So long as confidence lasts and the new way of speaking is still a novelty, one method is about as effective as any other. The moment, however, confidence breaks down and the novelty of the new way of speaking wears off, one is as useless as the other.

Both Appelt[1] and Coriat[2] have presented an interpretation of stuttering in terms of the psychoanalytic theory. They hold that in all stutterers there is a conflict between the Ego (self) and the oral libido (sexuality associated with the mouth). They believe that therapeutic efforts should be concentrated on the oral libido and its consequent character traits, and not on neurotic anxieties or fears. In the analytic process, the Ego is said to become educated and to accustom itself to recognize expressions of the oral libido. These expressions are held to be contrary to the ideals of the Ego on which the Ego had become fixed. They presumably led to a repetition of the old processes of repression. According to this theory, stuttering is a form of unconscious, compulsive repetition whose object it is to retain infantile pleasure. Although this psychoanalytic explanation tells us something of the possible character formation of the stutterer, it does not offer any very clear road toward a successful therapy which may remove the essential difficulty; nor have many stutterers been relieved of their stuttering by psychoanalysis.

The theory that stuttering is related to the cerebral dominance of one or the other brain hemisphere was originated by Orton and developed by Travis.[11] More experimental findings and relevant facts bearing on the nature of the basic difficulty were assembled by Travis than by any of the other workers in the field of speech pathology. It has long been known that the left hemisphere of the brain integrates and controls the movements of the right side of the body, and the right hemisphere, those of the left side of the body. The action of the speech mechanism involves both sides of the body simultaneously. One brain hemisphere must lead the other in the coordination and temporal, rhythmic ordering of speech movements, or blockage and disorganization will result. In right-handed persons the left hemisphere dominates and leads in coordination. If the person was originally left-handed and has been trained to the right hand, there may be conflict and disorganization in the brain control of speech. Or, if the person were originally ambidextrous (those who use the right and the left hand equally well), no essential brain dominance would occur. This hypothesis attributes stuttering to the fact that one or the other brain hemisphere, which should follow, tends to act simultaneously with the dominant hemisphere which should lead. The result will be cerebral blocking leading to stuttering.

In a fair number of stutterers who have shifted from right- to left-handedness (or vice versa), a marked improvement or even complete cure of stuttering has taken place. The theory of cerebral dominance is supported by recent work in electroencephalography.[3,9] According to these findings, stutterers show a marked tendency to synchronization of brain potentials from both hemispheres, so that their hemispheric excitability is different from that of nonstutterers.

To repeat, all the known methods of treatment have produced both successes and failures, and even the work on cerebral dominance has not been entirely successful. It may be concluded, therefore, that not all stuttering is of the same origin or nature, even though it exhibits itself in the same types of laryngeal spasm. Probably many stutterers have reversed or conflicting cerebral dominance; in some, the symptoms are a form of hysterical conversion; in others, a kind of conditioned response mechanism; and in still others, the stuttering is but one manifestation of a neurotic personality. Therefore, each case must be investigated individually and treated in terms of the most probable basic difficulty.

Aphasia

Aphasia is a disorder in the use of language. It is not a disease but a symptom or a symptom complex. There is no more difficult subject to understand in the realm of either psychology or neurology than that of aphasia. Many outstanding neurologists, physiologists, and psychologists have studied aphasic patients and presented theories to explain the peculiarities of this abnormality. There is the widest sort of disagreement among these authorities concerning both the actual phenomena which have been observed and the interpretation which may be placed upon them. Wilson[12] has synthesized the viewpoints of the neurologists, physiologists, and psychologists in a fashion which will be followed in this presentation.

During the thirty or forty years following 1870, most investigators of the problem of aphasia included in their reports a diagram which represented in schematic form either the anatomy, the physiology, or the psychology of the relationship between the disordered elements. Each of these diagrams had value, in that it represented a scheme which could be used to explain certain cases, but no diagram offered a satisfactory explanation for any considerable number of patients.

The term *aphasia* itself is not too satisfactory. It means loss of ability to speak. The term *dysphasia* would be more accurate since, usually, there is not a total loss but a disorder of speaking. J. Hughlings Jackson[6] pointed out many years ago that the aphasic patient "speaks badly with what of his brain is left." By this, he meant that aphasia is not merely a loss, but also a representation of what the individual can do with the damaged tissue which remains. Hence, we should bear in mind that aphasics are not easily comparable, since we are dealing not only with differing amounts of loss and different parts of the cortex, but also with different degrees of efficiency of the remaining functional tissues.

Distinction should be made between aphasia, as an abnormality of speech, and certain other abnormali ies which are closely associated with it. *Alexia* refers to a disturbance in the ability to read; *agraphia*, to a disturbance in the ability to write; *amusia*, to a disturbance in the ability to appreciate or produce music; *agnosia*, to a loss of the ability to recognize persons, objects, sounds, or sights (sensory aphasia); and *apraxia*, to a loss of the ability to perform skilled or coordinated movements when no paralysis, as such, is present.

The physiological disorganization in any of the forms of aphasia may take on quite varied aspects. It may be that the sensory elements are missing, so that a condition called "sensory aphasia" results. Here, the patient is unable to comprehend the meaning of the sounds, although there is every evidence that there is no true deafness. In motor aphasia he is able to produce sounds, but cannot form them into meaningful speech. In transcortical sensory aphasia the patient can read aloud, write spontaneously, or repeat successfully, but he gives no evidence of understanding what he has done or said. In transcortical motor aphasia the patient cannot speak spontaneously, but he can repeat what he is told to say.

ANATOMICAL CONSIDERATIONS

One way to approach the problem of aphasia, viewed either as a disorder of speech or as a symptom complex which involves the entire organism, is to try to determine the area in which damage or dysfunction is present in the brain. The assumption here is that some fairly close relationship exists between brain structure and the production of speech. Henschen[5] collected and analyzed the reports of 1337 cases in which both a clinical description of aphasia and an autopsy study of the brain had been made. Certain factors reappeared with some degree of regularity. Most of the cases showed some damage to the left cerebral hemisphere if the patient was right-handed, or to the right hemisphere if he was left-handed. In a majority of cases of motor aphasia (inability to speak even though language is comprehended) there was an involvement of Broca's area of the cortex. However, the correlation between the specific area of anatomical damage and the variety of speech disorder was not perfect.

The relationship between the extent of cerebral tissue damaged or disturbed and the severity of the aphasia is not consistent. Generally speaking, the larger the amount of tissue involved, the more severe the aphasia. However, there are many pronounced cases in which the pathology was found to be limited to a very small area; indeed, instances have been reported in which no damage could be located at the time of autopsy. In general, then, some forms of aphasia seem to be specifically located, while in other forms no localized defect can be demonstrated.

PHYSIOLOGICAL CONSIDERATIONS

Long before a child begins to speak his ears have been accustomed to sounds, including the sounds of words. He has received both the auditory and kinesthetic sensations produced by his own crying or babbling. The child hears hundreds of words and makes hundreds of sounds before speech, as such, occurs. The impression of this sensory material is retained in some fashion and later utilized in the physiological organization of speech. For example, a case was reported of a little boy, aged six, who had never uttered a single vocal sound and who was regarded as dumb. One day, upon breaking one of his favorite toys, he suddenly said, "What a pity!" and thereafter progressed rapidly in speaking.[12] In such a case one can believe that maturation must have taken place within the nervous system without any overt activity of the usual trial-and-error method used by children in learning to speak.

The spoken word and the written word are movements; while, on the sensory side, a seen word is no more than a seen object and a heard word is no more than a heard sound. Before a child can write a single letter correctly, he will scribble with a pencil and say that it is writing. And if, to us, it is an unintelligible scrawl, it is physiologically identified with an intelligible scrawl. The child's laryngeal noises may be unintelligible, but they do not differ essentially from the laryngeal noises which we call "words." Accordingly, all of these sounds and movements must be considered in the study of the physiology of motion and sensation, and the physiological organization for motion and sensation should be the focus of the disorder of aphasia. All of this is to say that in aphasia there is no essential loss of the physiological elements. The loss or disintegration is in the organization of the elements. There is a vast difference between the performance of the patient suffering from a paralyzed right arm and the patient suffering from agraphia.

PSYCHOLOGICAL CONSIDERATIONS

Hughlings Jackson pointed out that there was a fundamental difference between interjectional (emotional) use and propositional (intellectual) use of words as symbols of thought. There are aphasics who have full consciousness of the meanings and intellectual use of words, phrases, or objects. There are other aphasics in whom the perception of single words seems normal, and yet further examination discloses a true defect in the consciousness of the meaning of phrases and sentences. In ordinary aphasia there is usually little damage to emotional or interjectional speech, while intellectual or propositional speech is apt to be severely damaged. There is a great deal of evidence that this distinction is a true one, psychologically speaking. The child who said, "What a pity!"; the mute motor aphasic who, seeing a Zeppelin disappear in flames, exclaimed, "Hallelujah!"; the patient who will repeat one word or one phrase — such observations are common in the clinical histories of aphasia. Some patients may swear with a great deal of fluency and yet be totally unable to use the same words in an intellectual or propositional sentence.

Wilson gave some interesting descriptions which illustrate Jackson's point. For example, one patient was unable to repeat any number when requested or to use numbers correctly in a sentence, but when shown the figure "1" in print he suddenly began to count and counted rapidly past 20 until he was told to stop. Some aphasics can sing what they cannot say. Others can recite poetry but are incapable of putting words together to answer an ordinary question. In another instance the Lord's Prayer was repeated, while volitional speech was almost entirely lost. These examples demonstrate the fact that in many cases of aphasia there has been no destruction or loss of memories or images, but only a loss of the ability to arouse or to use these memories or images.

Still another psychological aspect of aphasia is the seeming inability to complete an idea or proposition which has been started. For example, a patient was shown a paper knife. She said, "That's a knife . . . a knife . . . what you cut the sign . . . the iron . . . it's for iron . . . walker. . . ." Shown a pencil she said, "That's a bensha . . . what you press . . . what you say you fire in the nent . . . scratch in the lead work . . . what you wish is your neck . . . nick a nick. . . ." Such remarks reveal not only a constructional or ungrammatical defect, but a start at a proposition with an inability to complete that proposition. For instance, when she said, "That's a bensha," and then, "What you press," apparently she was attempting to use the correct word and to specify a correct usage but was unable to complete the proposition.

Following an intensive study of a group of aphasic patients, Head[4] questioned that the usual anatomical and physiological classifications reflect the true nature of aphasia. He classified the phenomena into verbal, syntactical, nominal, and semantic defects. According to his system, verbal-defect cases show a disturbance in the perception of word meanings. The patient may know what he wants to say or write but he cannot find the proper words. Even after saying a word spontaneously, he is unable to repeat the word at command. In syntactical defect, the trouble is not with individual words, but with their arrangement and meaning in groups or extended discourse. The patient may be able to speak and to make his wants known, but he speaks in a jumble of brief phrases. When he attempts to read, his ideas become so confused and misarranged that the meaning is lost. In nominal defect, words are spoken correctly and in a coherent fashion. The disturbance appears in the inability to associate names with objects. The patient is able to describe an object but not to give its name. Recitation of the alphabet is possible, but the use of single letters is faulty. In semantic defect, there is a disturbance of the meanings of larger groups of words or ideas. Although expression may be adequate, the sentences are often short and jerky. Use of names for objects is normal, but there is a lack of understanding of sentences and paragraphs as a whole. Such a patient may look at a picture and be able to pick out and name the various details. However, he cannot perceive the meaning of the entire picture.

From the psychological point of view, Head's formulation furnishes a framework in which the language defects can be classified. These classifications are not limited to aphasia, as such, since similar deviations in language appear not only in neurological or psychiatric patients, but also in healthy persons of normal intellect.

RECOVERY

In aphasic conditions the outcome depends largely upon the type and severity of the symptoms. If they are not widespread and are pronounced only for several days or weeks, a fair or complete recovery may take place. If aphasia occurs in a young child or during early adult life and is not too severe, reeducation is possible. The patient may soon learn again to speak correctly and to replace the words and phrases which have been lost. In elderly individuals, if the damage has been severe, there is not too much chance for improvement.

Speech Disorders in Psychotic Conditions

Disorders of speech occur in general paresis, senile disorders, manic-depressive psychosis, dementia praecox, and to a lesser extent in other mental diseases. Paretic speech is caused by a weakness and incoordination of the muscles involved in articulation. It is drawling, tremulous, scanning, and inarticulate due to omission, reduplication, or interchange of syllables. For example, to the standard test phrase, "Around the rugged rock," the paretic may say, "Rounds rug-ock." Such omissions and slurring of syllables, together with a drawling and tremulous production, are distinctive. Paretic speech is different from the slurred speech of the intoxicated person or from the speech of the true paralytic, where there is an actual loss of ability to speak due to paralysis of the lips, tongue, or larynx. The speech of the paretic patient becomes normal if the disease is cured.

The senile patient starts to tell of an occurrence or a conversation, but will be sidetracked by an associated idea which, in turn, will suggest another idea, and that another, and so on. In this process, fabrication and pseudoreminiscences fill many of the gaps in the long, involved description. If allowed to continue, such an individual will eventually complete his story, even though the ramifications and fabricated embellishments may stretch the simple, half-minute incident to a few hours of rambling conversation. Frequently, senile speech is marked by childish phrases, grammatical mistakes, and substitution of words. However, the enunciation remains clear and the ideas themselves are connected so that the end point of a story is achieved.

In manic-depressive patients the speech production reflects the general mental picture. In one study, phonographic recordings were made of an interview with forty patients.[10] A systematic analysis of these records forms the basis of Table 5.

TABLE 5. ANALYSIS OF SPEECH OF 40 MANIC–DEPRESSIVE PATIENTS.*

	Depression	Mania
Articulatory movements	Lax	Vigorous
Pitch range	Narrow	Wide
Pitch changes	Step-wise; infrequent	Gliding; frequent
Emphatic accents	Absent or rare	Frequent
Pauses	Hesitating	Accented
Resonance	Nasal	Oral
Level of style	Colloquial	Elevated
Syntactic elaboration	Meager	Rich
Syntactic techniques	Limited	Diversified
Initiation of response	Slow	Quick
Length of response	Short	Long

* Modified from S. Newman, and V. G. Mather, "Analysis of Spoken Language of Patients with Affective Disorders," *Amer. Jour. Psychiat.*, 1938, *94*, 941.

As the tabulation indicates, in the depressed condition emphatic accents are absent or rare, the speech tempo is slow, hesitating pauses are frequent, there is meager elaboration, and slowness exists in the initiation of response. In the manic phase, there is emphatic accenting, wide pitch range, elevated style, rich, diversified elaboration, and quick response. The manic patient passes rapidly from one topic to another and rarely completes any one of the topics in the succession of speech. He rambles in his conversation without obvious logical connections between ideas or without reaching any particular goal in his story.

The language of the schizophrenic is the most bizarre and distorted of all of the speech disturbances. These patients seem to give up the conventions of ordinary communication and to change to a fashion which seems more fitting to their thought processes. This new style leads to the formation of condensations, neologisms, word salads, and stereotypes. A study of the language production of a group of schizophrenic patients, made by Woods,[13] provides examples and some general principles.

The transference of certain like qualities from one experience to another is accomplished, in normal language, by the expedient of allusions, similes, or metaphors. The uncritical employment of language by the schizophrenic allows him to make use of vague and farfetched metaphors in his speech. Both internal feelings and conflicts, as well as events in the outside world, may be commented on metaphorically by the schizophrenic. A patient described, as follows, her reluctance to sit on a bench, under the shade of a tree, from which a highway was visible:

"Well, I don't know. It seemed I went through a big decision and I look out of the window on the tennis court and I watch the tennis game and then Dorothy and Mrs. Trukken wanted me to sit on the court." [What was wrong about that?] "Well, I don't know. It seemed to have a meaning." [What did it mean?] "It meant freedom." [What did?] "Well, I don't know. If I had gone on with them and faced the sunshine it meant that." [Why?] "Well, if I had faced that way my back would have been toward this institution and there was an open road that way." *

In the use of the metaphor, the schizophrenic neglects to inform the listener that he is using a metaphor; indeed, it sometimes seems that he is unaware of the fact himself. Sometimes the patient will use phrases like "just as" or "as though," but more frequently these are

* Woods, W. L., "Language Study in Schizophrenia," *Jour. Nerv. Ment. Dis.*, 1938, 87, 305.

omitted. Generally, the metaphor becomes eccentric, consonant with what appears to be carelessness and lack of precision. Part of the eccentricity is due to the strange subjective nature of the material to be depicted — somatic sensation, emotional conflict — which apparently requires neologisms and unusual metaphorical formulations.

Another characteristic of schizophrenic language is a poverty of precise, crystallized thought. For example, a patient said, "It seemed like, as though somebody wanted me to go ahead and to do something. After that they didn't seem to do anything so much until a little later on again, why, it just seemed like as though they knew what I was doing all the time." This patient had no answers for insistent or logical questions, and so used the most available material in a vague sort of way. Another example of this same poverty is shown by a florid style where many words are used without really saying anything. When a patient was asked to explain the proverb, "Let sleeping dogs lie," he said, "It would be normal to any object that was seemingly comfortable to let it remain uncomfortable and if there was something to be appreciably gained it would be better to let it continue." Such speech is given plausibility by being cast in a casual language structure which meets the formal requirements of conversation. In contrast to this deceptive semblance to concrete ideation, there is really much vagueness and many empty phrases and platitudes. Such speech is rendered possible by the retention of language habits and facility. At times this poverty leads to eccentric speech, mannerisms, inexact words, neologisms, all of which develop into a style which is stiff, rigid, short, condensed, and stereotyped.

A final oddity in schizophrenic speech is the way in which they slip from one idea into another. For example, one patient said, "They just want to laugh is all." [About you?] "No, about milk bottles." [What does that mean?] "Oh, pure food." As the patients become more deteriorated, they use more inexact approximations in which one idea is confused with another. For instance, "It's two thousand pounds across my stomach." "A dictionary is too many miles long." The general tendency is for the thinking to get into a category which is inexact instead of precise and to show a lack of direction. In this type of thinking it is easy to make a rapid passage from one idea to another on the basis of like qualities, even though these similarities may be very superficial. Due to a pronounced deficiency in conceptual thinking, the patient can change easily in his thought processes without any permanence or reference to logical associations.

In brief, then, the speech of the dementia praecox patient seems bizarre to the listener because of its poverty in precise thought. It is characterized by different degrees of egocentricity and marked by metaphors which are not understandable, as such, by the listener, but which represent a very unstable private language which the patient uses to describe his thoughts and feelings, lacking ordinary words.

Summary

Stuttering is the result of disorganization in the temporal rhythmic process of speech. It is probably related in some fashion to the lack of functional dominance of one cerebral hemisphere over the other. It does not, of itself, constitute either a neurosis or other form of psychopathology. It is a distinct social handicap and one which affects the developing personality, depending upon the circumstances of life in which the stutterer finds himself. There is no uniformly successful method of treatment. Each case must be investigated and treatment determined in terms of the probable basic organic difficulty and the personality structure of the individual.

Aphasia is a disorder of language. It may be considered from the standpoint of anatomy, physiology, or psychology. No uniform anatomical localization has been found for any particular variety of aphasic disturbance, although certain general tendencies exist. When aphasia occurs, the physiological elements of speech production are not actually lost, but they disintegrate in their organization and co-operation. There have been many attempts — none too successful — to formulate the nature of the psychological disturbance in aphasia. Evidently, aphasic cases vary considerably, not only in the extent and nature of the disorder, but also in the form and regularity of the individual process of deterioration. There is a basic and consistent distinction between emotional and intellectual speech, so that either form of expression may be disordered without involving the other.

The disturbances of speech in the various forms of mental disease are, generally speaking, distinctive to each disease. The most peculiar speech disorders occur in dementia praecox. Here, the listener is baffled because of the lack of precise, crystallized thought. The patients are inexact and indefinite in their expressions, make use of metaphors, and create many neologisms. Basically, these tendencies grow out of the disruption of the patient's thought processes and his attempts to describe his very unusual sensations and ideas with a meager and inexact vocabulary.

In general paresis the speech disturbances are in part due to a weakness and incoordination of the muscles involved in articulation.

REFERENCES

1. Appelt, A., *The Real Cause of Stammering and its Permanent Cure* (2d ed.). London, Methuen, 1920.

2. Coriat, I. H., *Stammering: A Psychoanalytic Interpretation*. Nerv. Ment. Dis. Mono., #47, 1928.

3. Douglass, L. C., "A Study of Bilaterally Recorded Electroencephalograms of Adult Stutterers," *Jour. Exp. Psychol.*, 1943, *32*, 247–265.

4. Head, H., *Aphasia and Kindred Disorders of Speech*, Vol. I. London, Cambridge University Press, 1926.

5. Henschen, S. E., "Clinical and Anatomical Contributions on Brain Pathology." (Abstract and comment by W. F. Schaller). *Arch. Neurol. Psychiat.*, 1925, *13*, 226–249.

6. Jackson, J. H., *Selected Writings of John Hughlings Jackson* (ed., J. J. Taylor) Vol. II. London, Hodder, 1932.

7. Johnson, W., *Because I Stutter*. New York, Appleton-Century, 1930.

8. ———, "The Influence of Stuttering on the Personality," *Univ. Iowa. Stud. Child Welf.*, 1932, *5*, 1–140.

9. Knott, J. R., and T. D. Tjossem, "Bilateral Electroencephalograms from Normal Speakers and Stutterers," *Jour. Exp. Psychol.*, 1943, *32*, 357–362.

10. Newman, S., and V. G. Mather, "Analysis of Spoken Language of Patients with Affective Disorders," *Amer. Jour. Psychiat.*, 1938, *94*, 913–942.

11. Travis, L. E., *Speech Pathology*. New York, Appleton-Century, 1931.

12. Wilson, S. A. K., *Aphasia*. London, Kegan Paul, 1926.

13. Woods, W. L., "Language Study in Schizophrenia," *Jour. Nerv. Ment. Dis.*, 1938, *87*, 290–316.

Chapter XXIII

AMNESIA

IN 1881 Ribot wrote, "Materials for the study of the diseases of memory are abundant. They are scattered through books of medicine, works on mental disorders, and the writings of many psychologists. They may, with some little trouble, be brought together, and we have then at hand all the facts needed to facilitate investigation. The difficulty lies in classifying them; in giving each case its proper interpretation; in learning its true bearing upon the mechanism of memory. In this respect, facts collected at random are very unequal in value; the most extraordinary are not the most constructive; the most curious are not the best sources of light."* This statement is still true. The disorders of memory are of an extraordinarily wide variety. The way in which the disorders are described or explained depends largely upon the viewpoint and training of the observer.

The classical laboratory methods of investigating learning and forgetting, which all possible factors save those under consideration are carefully controlled, have shown many interesting facts and relationships. The clinical description of memory disorders which are attendant on various mental diseases, either organic or functional, usually bears little relation to the carefully controlled experimental studies. This statement does not mean that either the controlled methods or the clinical descriptions are wrong. The implication here is that each procedure has its place and application in the more general problems involved.

Some Definitions and Concepts

The term *amnesia* means loss of memory which may be either general or partial. This loss may involve, to a varying degree, all ideas and actions, or it may be limited to some special class or group of memories, such as numbers, names, certain events, special fields of sensation,

* Ribot, T., *Diseases of Memory*. (English trans. 5th ed.), London, Kegan, Paul, 1906, 69.

or special motor functions. The term *anterograde amnesia* refers to defaults in memory which are thought to be due to inattention or imperception. Hence, the event is not remembered because it was not adequately perceived in the first place. Or, there has been interference with its adequate fixation in the nervous system due to some neural disturbance. *Retrograde amnesia* involves loss of memory in the usual sense of forgetting previously acquired ideas or actions. The "Law of Regression" (Ribot) states that retrograde amnesia descends progressively from the unstable to the stable memories, that is, recent events are forgotten before remote events, and ideas before actions. *Retroactive amnesia* is a special case of retrograde amnesia. Here the memory loss extends backward for a certain limited period before the occurrence of the shock or injury which disturbed the memory process. *Hypermnesia* refers to exaggerated memory which may be either general or partial. It is said that certain occasions, usually of an emotional nature, lead to an abnormal fixation of many small and irrelevant details which took place on some particular occasion. *Paramnesia* means falsification or illusions of memory. There may be simple fabrication in which an idea or image is wrongly placed in the past; illusions of recognition (*déjà vu*) in which there is a feeling of familiarity attached to some new perception, so that it is incorrectly referred to past experience; or the falsification may be retrospective, in the sense that there is a misinterpretation of the past under the influence of a delusion or the suggestive power of an idea.

The phenomena of amnesia are so diverse in their manifestations that there is no single concept or system of concepts which serves as a perfect framework of explanation. Traditionally, psychology has regarded memory as a process of associative retention, recall, and recognition. Sensory impressions arouse associated meanings and lead to perceptions which are somehow retained and later used in recall or in recognition. This system, because of its simplicity, has been used in most experimental studies of amnesia.

Another way of classifying memory disorders is to divide them into organic, functional, or malingering manifestations. When brain injury occurs, there may be a memory loss. This loss may be diffuse or localized, systematic or unsystematic. It is as if a small wheel in a calculating machine had lost one or two cogs. Depending on where the wheel is located, the answers obtained when the machine is operated will be wrong only if this particular wheel enters into the computation mechanism. In certain problems no defect in the answer will occur, and in others a very gross defect will result. Essentially, this concept implies that memory depends on some sort of anatomical brain localization which can be destroyed or disturbed.

In the functional disturbances of memory, of which hysteria provides some of our best examples, there is no known organic disturbance; and yet specific and generalized, systematic and unsystematic, memory disorders may occur. Many of the functional amnesias are said to be due to dissociation or to repression associated with emotional trauma. The memory disorders of malingering are, of course, conscious fakery.

The various nervous and mental diseases are distinguished by certain peculiar memory defects and disturbances. In earlier chapters, disturbances have been described which are characteristic of the senile person, the dementia praecox patient, the alcoholic. In addition, there are special neurological conditions, such as Pick's disease, in which very specific memory disturbances occur. In fact, it is difficult to find any single explanatory system which would fit all the memory disorders found in these particular psychopathological conditions.

Experimental Investigations of Memory Disorder

Memory is an important element contributing to the general efficiency of mental performance. On this basis the general mental efficiency of demented and defective patients has been investigated and the various elements entering into their general efficiency have been compared. Work with mental patients generally shows that memory ability suffers more than vocabulary usage or ability to calculate, but suffers less than the ability to handle abstract ideas or concepts.

Assuming that retention depends upon impression and the formation of associations, investigators have studied both the process of impression and association formation in various psychopathological conditions marked by disturbances in memory. In some patients it has been established that there is a defect in the ability to form associations. They require a longer time than normals to learn new material and do not retain it so long. In Korsakoff's syndrome, the essence of the disturbance is the inability to form new impressions, that is, a loss at the fixation stage of memory. In general paresis and senile psychosis it has been reported that, although retention and formation of associations (apprehension) are both involved, the impairment is greater in the formation of association.

Studies of recognition and recall indicate that these two aspects of memory are frequently disturbed in psychotic patients. The disturbance bears no direct relationship to the type of psychosis, but is related to the individual and his own particular process of deterioration. Studies[18] of the memory disorder following electric convulsive therapy have shown that immediately following the period of unconsciousness brought about by the shock, there is a complete loss of both recall and retention of paired-associates, as measured by relearning time. Strangely enough, recognition is not too badly disturbed. These patients maintain that they have never previously seen nor heard of the test material. Nevertheless, they are able to select out of a number of choices those items which they had previously learned, demonstrating that recognition is still functioning though ordinary recall has disappeared. Fortunately, the memory disorder following this form of therapy is a transient one. Several days after the treatments are discontinued the patient recovers most of his ordinary memory efficiency, although there may still remain a specific loss for material learned just before or just after shock.

Hunt[8] has summarized the experimental studies of memory defect in the following way: (1) The performance of psychotics on memory tests in scales of intelligence are less efficient, comparatively, than their performances on the vocabulary tests. (2) Impression suffers more than retention. (3) Impression appears to be most affected in psychotic cases involving known neural damage. (4) The psychotic's inefficiency is evident in tests of both recall and recognition. Differential loss has been found in isolated cases, but is not definitely established. (5) The psychotic's success in committing to memory is apparently reduced relatively more than the normal's by the presentation of meaningless material. (6) The psychotic's fund of available information is reduced. The reduction is apparently greatest when organic damage is involved, and information recently acquired tends to be the first to be lost.

Clinical Observations of Amnesia

Gillespie[6] has formulated the problem of amnesia as it occurs in psychopathological individuals, using the concepts of Hughlings Jackson and of Bartlett as his basis. He assumes that remembering is a mental activity of the highest functional level of the organism. Bartlett said, "Remembering is not the re-excitation of innumerable fixed, lifeless and fragmentary traces. It is an imaginative reconstruction, or construction, built out of the relation of our attitude towards a whole active mass of organized past reactions or experience."* Such recon-

* Bartlett, F. C.: *Remembering*. London, Cambridge University Press, 1932, 213.

structions Bartlett called "schemata." By this, he meant that memories (or remembering) do not occur as isolated fragments, but as part of a moving pattern of experience. The moving patterns or schemata are determined, not only by the immediate stimulation and environment, but also by food seeking, sleeping, fear, anger, and so on. In this determination there goes on at all times an unconscious analysis giving differing weights to different elements, so that some details stand out clearly in images and others do not. In general, we use words to communicate these more outstanding images from one person to another. The words and images which are first used to break up the schemata tend to become automatized. In pathological conditions, therefore, the ability to use words may be fully retained when no remembering in either the true or the mechanical sense is possible.

To the traditional concepts of registration, retention, and recall Gillespie added other elements which are disturbed in certain of the psychopathological conditions. These factors and the conditions in which they appear are summarized in Table 6.

TABLE 6. RELATION OF MEMORY ELEMENTS TO THE PSYCHOPATHOLOGICAL CONDITIONS WHERE THEY ARE DISORDERED.*

Factors in Remembering	Conditions in Which These Factors Are Interfered with or Appear in Isolation
Registration	Acute organic reaction type (delirium); manic excitement (inattention); hysteria (global inattention)
Retention	Organic reaction type in general
Recall (simple)	Organic reaction type (severe degree)
Recall (voluntary)	Psychogenic conditions, e.g., hysteria; certain forms of organic reaction type, e.g., trauma to the head; Korsakoff's syndrome; epilepsy
Time sense	Various psychoses with depersonalization; Korsakoff's syndrome (amnesic symptom-complex)
Pastness	Epilepsy (*dèja vû*); anesthetic states
Personal Identity (awareness of)	Hysteria; depersonalization in various psychoses

REGISTRATION

Defects in registration are mostly due to failure of attention as it occurs in acute mania or in febrile delirium. Another variety of failure of registration is seen in some hysterical patients. They may show either a concentric limitation in the visual field or a selectivity in auditory perception. This selectivity is more apparent than real, since it has been demonstrated during hypnosis that such patients really do see and hear events which they claim never to have experienced

* Gillespie, R. D., "Amnesia," *Arch. Neurol. Psychiat.*, 1937, *37*, 750–751.

RETENTION

If memory depends essentially upon the retention of traces or memory images, then defective retention should be a frequent and fundamental disorder of memory. As a matter of fact, there is a loss of retention in most of the organic conditions but not in any simple fashion. For example, it has been shown that patients suffering from Korsakoff's syndrome seem incapable of recalling events that happened 5 minutes before. However, when they partially recover, they may recollect events which they did not seem to note at the time of their occurrence. In the same way visual impressions that were apparently not retained during the acute phase of the disorder may be recognized later. In cases of concussion it has been reported that the patient will repeatedly ask the same question, seeming to fail in his retention of the idea which is conveyed in the answer. After recovery from the acute phase he may or may not regain the memory of the particular question and answer. For example, Cason[4] reported that after a head injury which occurred during skating he repeatedly asked, "Is there much swelling?" although he was reassured several times that there was none. On later recovery of conscious memory he had no memory (retention) of either the questioning or the answer.

RECALL

Two processes of differing complexity are involved here — simple mechanical or sensorimotor recall, and recall involving voluntary effort. That recall of the voluntary or most complex type should fail first is to be expected, since it involves the greatest amount of integration. The process of deterioration in recall, as shown (temporarily) in fatigue or (permanently) in senility, may be taken as an indication that this voluntary type fails long before the simple mechanical type. For example, one may be unable to remember a person's proper name and yet will clearly recognize him.

Various organic conditions, among them epilepsy, have supplied evidence that there is a failure of recall while retention remains relatively unaffected. When such patients can be induced to make an effort at remembering, they usually recall much more than any ordinary, routine test indicates. In the recovery process following successful treatment of general paresis, the improvement in immediate recall is quite marked and serves as an indicator of the restoration of an dordere mental state after a period of dementia.[13]

When patients are being anesthetized or given certain drugs, they are often able to carry on a conversation, to answer questions, and to ask questions in a fairly intelligent fashion, without any subsequent remembering or recognition of the conversation after recovery from the effect of the anesthetic or the drug. This is a deficiency in recall, since during later hypnosis such conversations can occasionally be recalled.

TIME ORDERING OF EXPERIENCE

In all of our mental life we attach to our experience a sense of time. This is not a "clock" time, but a private time which links or fixes the experience in its proper sequence. It is not just an appreciation of duration, but it is a sense of continuing activity and relationship which gives a background of total integration to experience.

In Korsakoff's syndrome there is a defect in the time ordering. The patient is unable to place his experience correctly in the past. For example, when such a case was given a cigar and then asked about it 15 minutes later, he replied, "I *have* had a cigar, but that was last week"; or when another patient was asked, "How long have we been talking?", he would answer anything from five minutes to two weeks, although he was able to remember the entire content of the conversation.

PASTNESS

Gillespie suggests that there exists, as an independent function, a feeling of pastness. The existence of this, he says, may be demonstrated by two kinds of experience — the feeling of *déjà vu* associated with some epileptic attacks, and the experience which some persons have of having dreamed a dream which, although not recollected, is thought to have been dreamed previously. The feeling of recapitulation of something that had happened previously is distinct and apparently independent of the content of the dream, or at least of any conscious recollection of such content. This feeling of pastness seems, therefore, to be a separate memory experience which can be disturbed.

PERSONAL IDENTITY

Instances of amnesia for all personal data are not at all uncommon. We frequently read newspaper reports and see the published photograph of some person who is at a hospital and for whom the police are seeking personal data, because the individual cannot remember who he is or anything concerning his past life. An example of this sort is as follows:

CASE 30: A man, apparently about twenty-five, was brought to the hospital by the police, having been found wandering in a London street, unable to say who he was or where he came from. He looked somewhat pale and anxious and answered all questions readily and to the point, but all that he could remember [about himself] was a Latin motto and the face of a rather stern-looking man with a stubby moustache. He spoke in an educated fashion but could give no account of where he had been brought up, or indeed of anything up to the moment, a few hours before, when he had found himself in the street. With reassurance and persistent persuasion, his memory of the journey that had brought him to London was, bit by bit, brought back, till suddenly one night, at about 3 A.M., everything he had forgotten was remembered. It was then learned that he had come from a northern town, that he was in business with his father, with whom he had quarreled, principally on account of his drinking habits, and that his sudden journey to London had begun on the evening of the day of the quarrel, just after he had seen his fiancée to her home. He had had some notion of going over to the Continent, but when he reached Victoria Station he found that he had insufficient money. It then dawned on him that he was behaving foolishly. He suddenly felt confused, could not think and could not even give his name to a policeman whom he approached after he began to feel "mixed up" in his head. In this instance, the complex actuating first the fugue and then the loss of memory was apparent. The "stern-looking man" turned out to be his father. The Latin motto was that of the university of his native city. A reconciliation was effected in the hospital, and the patient went home to his father's house, apparently well.*

This history illustrates an instance of almost complete loss of memory for the events of life and for even the simplest personal data, together with the retention of two isolated factors, one of which was closely related to the precipitating situation. It also shows that the condition can be suddenly brought about by an acute emotional experience and that there may be a sudden recall of all of the missing data, including personal identity. Most of these cases are classified as hysterical, but some of them turn out to be true psychotics or plain malingerers. Among the psychotic cases are dementia praecox, manic-depressive, organic diseases of the brain, and carbon monoxide poisoning.

In a series of 63 cases studied by Abeles and Schilder,[1] in which there was a loss of personal identity, it was found that some unpleasant social conflict, either financial or familial, was usually the immediate precipitating cause of the amnesia. The duration varied from 3 hours to several months. In addition to the loss of personal identity, there was usually poor and inadequate general knowledge, information, and

* Gillespie, R. D., "Amnesia," *Arch. Neurol. Psychiat.*, 1937, *37*, 755-756.

memory for past events. The ability to retain new information during the amnesia was often, but not regularly, preserved. Most patients seemed puzzled and perplexed. Over two thirds of them recovered spontaneously; the recovery of the others was assisted by hypnosis, persuasion, automatic writing, or association with dream material. Psychological analysis going beyond the superficial conflict which precipitated the amnesia often disclosed deeper motives. In general, the conflicts of actual life were met by a rather infantile type of reaction. The amnesia was frequently an attempt to escape from punishment, particularly from self-blame or self-punishment, by wiping out one's own personality. Amnesia is often a giving-in to a stronger force, and may be either conscious or unconscious in nature. One patient became amnesic after having been robbed of money which he needed for the family. On the whole, amnesia of personal identity is a weak attempt of a weak personality to escape conflicts which are chiefly those of actual life. It is often the fear of being punished by the family, by the father or the mother, or by someone who stands emotionally in the place of the father or mother, which leads to this kind of escape which does not harm the person too much.

A similar formulation of clinical observations has been related by Gillespie to cases of lost identity based on organic or psychotic conditions, with only passing reference to neurotic states. Many amnesias occurring in psychotic patients seem basically different from those so far described. They must be considered in a different light, even though many of the essential elements in their general picture are the same.

Faulty Reproduction

REPRESSION

In an attempt to explain many forms of psychopathology, including functional amnesic disorders, the psychoanalysts have made use of the concept of repression.[15] The essence of repression lies in an active process of rejecting and keeping something out of consciousness. Usually, it is a technique for preventing either consummation or conscious recognition of the existence of some basic instinctive impulses which will cause pain or unpleasantness if admitted into consciousness. The process consists of an automatic and unconscious rejection of the idea or image, accompanied by a loss of effectiveness of the idea or impulse in initiating action.

According to Freud,[5] repressed impulses have certain well-defined characteristics. They are not represented in their true form in consciousness, and they develop in the unconscious in a more luxuriant fashion than they would if they were conscious, so that they give the illusion of greater strength than they actually possess. Furthermore, repression is highly specific to each idea and substitute idea and is very mobile; it does not occur once and only once, but demands a constant expenditure of energy. The degree of repression varies with the strength of the repressed impulse.

Essentially, repression is a method of resolving a conflict between two mutually incompatible tendencies. Its existence as an active process can be determined only if the presence of two or more conflicting tendencies can be verified. The process of repression involves the blockage of one or the other tendency from consciousness. This blockage is shown first by the discovery of the existence of some emotional tendency as a potential source of action, and second, by a known lack of relevant conscious associations.

Sears[17] surveyed the evidence, both clinical and experimental, which might indicate that amnesia is basically a process of repression, in the sense in which this concept has just been stated. He concluded that experimental evidence related to the repression hypothesis was neither plentiful nor too convincing. Most of the experimental studies had been directed at the establishment of the primary conditions under which repression was believed to occur, and then an objective test was made of the recall process to determine whether or not repression or the indications of repression had occurred. Almost invariably, the experiments failed in one way or another to demonstrate either the truth or falsity of the hypothesis. In the same way, Sears found that the clinical reports which had been made or which could be interpreted in the light of this repression hypothesis were not very much more satisfactory than the experimental evidence. Clear-cut cases of either retrograde or anterograde amnesia which are of psychic origin and which demonstrate repression, and only repression, are rare. Usually these functional or emotional cases of amnesia are associated with such psychosomatic complications as injury, fever, or asphyxiation.

The amnesias set up by suggestion during hypnosis seem, on first thought, to be examples of true psychogenic repression. It is possible to hypnotize a subject and suggest or emphasize some emotional complex, and then the subject may be told that he will not remember anything about the emotional incident when the hypnosis is over. Unfortunately, we do not know enough about the nature of the hypnotic process itself. We cannot be sure, for instance, whether, following the seance, the amnesia due to suggestion is a true amnesia, in the sense of a phenomenon which may be related to a head injury, or whether the forgetting is part of the hypnosis itself and belongs to an entirely different realm of events. The problem is illustrated by the analogy of a headache following either a head injury or a disappointment in love; both are headaches, but quite different in their origin.

The psychoanalytic theory of repression has been used to explain partial amnesias or forgettings. As a rule, however, the difference between a specific or limited amnesia and the complete personal amnesia in which the individual loses his personal identity, has not been sufficiently emphasized. E. Jones,[11] in a study of an amnesic, hysterical patient, showed that the various hysterical symptoms were based on forgotten or repressed traumatic memories. In addition, the patient had experienced a series of partial or limited amnesias. Hence, Jones believed that the complete loss of personal identity in this case was built up on an extensive series of partial amnesias which had not been converted into other hysterical symptoms related to bodily symptoms. If Jones's notion concerning the nature of total amnesia were true, then it might be possible that the startling completeness of the classical instances of total amnesia may have been due to incomplete study or inexact reporting. Actually, in all of the more recent reports of amnesic cases which were investigated as thoroughly as possible, the alleged syndrome of complete amnesia was found to be far from complete and often rather spotty in nature. Also, many of these spots were found to be more or less transient.

DISSOCIATION

Another way of classifying different types of amnesia is to distinguish between mere forgetting, which is due to the passage of time, and amnesia of the pathological variety, in which whole blocks of experience are missing from the mental life of the individual. Janet proposed the idea that the second type involves a state of dissociation. According to this theory which has been of value in explaining certain aspects of disorders of memory, amnesias are of emotional origin and belong to what he called "hysterical somnambulistic states." His description of this sort of somnambulism was as follows: "What then, exactly, is a somnambulist? Popular observation has answered long ago: it is an individual who thinks and acts while he is asleep. Without a doubt that answer is not very clear, for we don't know very well what sleep is. That answer means only that the person spoken of thinks and acts in an odd way, different from that of other people, and

that at the same time that person is in some way like a person asleep." *
The ideas and actions of the somnambulist were called by Janet
"monoideic" or "polyideic," depending on whether they seemed to
revolve around one idea or several ideas. When some emotional occurrence brings undue stress to bear on a somnambulistic individual,
there is a tendency for these systems of ideas to drop out of the normally integrated mental life. In the somnambulistic state itself, all of
the person's behavior and mental life is governed by, and revolves
around, either the monoideic or polyideic system. A somnambulistic
condition, involving the entire personality, is termed a *fugue*. In a
fugue, the individual wanders away without later having any memory
of this period of his life. It is really remarkable that during these fugue
states a person is able to travel and to conduct his ordinary life without
appearing particularly abnormal to those with whom he comes in
contact. Sometimes, such a person is said to have behaved as though
preoccupied or dreamy, but usually his behavior is not peculiar enough
to cause anyone to suspect that there is anything wrong with him.

The notion of dissociation in relation to amnesia was further developed by Morton Prince.[14] His theory and description of cases was
given in Chap. VII in connection with the phenomena of hysteria. His
point in connection with amnesia was that normal memory is essentially identified with the conscious state of the individual and is
limited by this conscious state, while hysterical (or neurotic) amnesias
are associated with co-conscious or subconscious states. This is in
contrast to the Freudian idea that memories are held out of consciousness by repression and dwell in the unconscious.

There is no really relevant experimental literature on the relation
of dissociation and amnesia. These states can be produced in hypnosis,
but we know too little about hypnosis itself to be sure of the meaning
of results obtained by such experiments. The chief value of concepts
relating to repression or dissociation is in their descriptive power. They
present a picture of a type of disorder, and emphasize the fact that
memory loss is not an isolated function but part of a general disability
of the entire mental life of such an individual.

Organic Amnesias

KORSAKOFF'S SYNDROME

There are several varieties of amnesia which are specific to certain
disease processes to such an extent that they are a leading symptom

* Janet, P., *The Major Symptoms of Hysteria.* New York, Macmillan, 1907, 24.

used in making the diagnosis of the particular disease. In Korsakoff's syndrome which follows organic brain damage, usually associated with chronic alcoholism, there is a specific memory disability which is of psychological interest. Such patients have deficient retention for recent events, with a tendency to falsify and fill in their conversation with confabulations revealing gross disorientation for time, place, and person. Memory for remote events is usually satisfactory, but the organization of recent material is completely lacking.

Although the objective facts are clear, many different explanations have been advanced.[10] Some have held that there is a disturbance of thinking, especially in the orientation of thought, so that the patient cannot find the proper memory at the proper time, even though there is no true memory loss. Others claim that the disturbance is not due to loss of orientation, but to a loss in the time sense or temporal signs of the memories. Other investigators suggest that the patient is able to grasp and retain only simple relations, while the whole situation and background are foggy or unorganized. Still others believe that the memory loss is only an apparent one and actually represents a special memory organization which resembles that seen in dreams. It is therefore said to be characterized by symbolization, distortion, condensation, and elimination of disagreeable memories, with the addition of other elements which transform the memory material in terms of wish fulfillment. Finally, another group concluded that it was impossible to explain the Korsakoff's syndrome in terms of a pure memory loss, or even to maintain that the memory disturbance was essential in the psychopathological picture. They held that the whole emotionality and personality of the individual was disturbed. Since his urges and emotions are no longer driving forces, he lacks spontaneity and awaits external impulses, being no longer able to do anything on his own. Thus, all of these investigators agree that there is a defect in memory, but they interpret the cause and significance of the defect in different ways.

PICK'S DISEASE

Pick's disease is a form of presenile dementia and organic deterioration in which there is a more or less definite and circumscribed location of cortical atrophy. This dementing process leads first to a breaking down of the more complicated social adjustments, and cultural and ethical standards, while memory remains intact. As the disease progresses, memory, as such, becomes impaired in a peculiar way. The material of memory is still preserved, even in cases that have progressed a long way in their dementia, but they are unable to use memory as an intellectual tool. Such patients become childlike, wander about, often get lost, tell poor jokes, and keep repeating the same stories over and over. They are able to recall details rather exactly, but cannot use their memory in their adjustment to everyday life.[12]

A careful study was made of the psychological deviations of such a case by Goldstein and Katz.[7] In this patient they found that most of the tests of simple, direct memory gave no evidence of disturbance. If the memory was in any way complicated, either by relationship to time or to space, it became ineffective. For example, this patient was able to find her way from her room through the corridors and stairs of the hospital to the workroom where she had been sewing. If she was disturbed or detoured on her pathway, she became confused. While she was knitting she would follow a pattern fairly accurately, but if interrupted and asked to show how she was doing the work she would get completely lost and be unable to demonstrate what she had been doing. If asked to reproduce the drawing of a straight line, a circle, and a square, she could copy them correctly; but if a minute later she was asked to reproduce what she had just drawn she was unable to do so. Instead, she would make a square with a horizontal and a vertical line bisecting it, which she said was "a window of a church." In general, then, the memory disturbance in Pick's disease is a distortion of relationships, so that the memory images are somehow no longer connected properly in time and space with the mental life of the individual.

ALZHEIMER'S DISEASE

Another variety of presenile dementia is called "Alzheimer's disease." These patients retain memory for remote events fairly well.[3] Any events which were outstanding or had some emotional coloring are especially easily and elaborately recalled. The main defect is in immediate memory and recall. For example, when asked to remember a series of five or six words or letters, the patient may be able to repeat only two or three after a 30-second delay. He may complain, "It got away," or "I can't keep all those." However, when the series of material to be memorized was dwelt upon very intensely with a good deal of overlearning, it will be held in mind and reproduced several days or weeks later. The defect here is in the loss of immediate retention which is out of proportion to the accompanying deterioration in other intellectual functions.

Korsakoff's syndrome, Pick's disease, and Alzheimer's disease are similar in that they all show a memory defect. However, the character of the memory disorder in all three is quite distinct. This distinction occurs in the relationship existing between memory and the remainder of the intellectual organization of the patient. In all three there is a loss in simple, apparent memory. In Korsakoff's syndrome this loss is related to the association among the ideas themselves and leads to a fabrication of material to supply the missing links. In Pick's disease, the memory disorder pertains to failures of orientation in time and space, or to some variety of a figure-ground relationship. In Alzheimer's disease, there is a constriction or narrowing of the ability to perform mental activity in several fields at the same time. The result is a loss in fixation which can be compensated for by a high degree of attention.

Summary

As Ribot pointed out, the confusion encountered in the studies of diseases of memory lies, not in the facts of memory loss, but in the interpretation of those facts in the mind of the observer. The more that any particular patient or group of patients is studied with respect to amnesias, the more one finds that there is never (or, at least, very rarely) a true, undeniably complete amnesia. Rather, there is a breaking down of relationships existing between memory and other mental functions. The ways in which these disjunctions take place cause the disordered memory to seem quite different; whereas, in reality it is often only the relationship which is altered and not the memory itself. It is true that memory loss, per se, can and does occur, but such losses are of themselves not nearly so important as the disturbances in the relationships between memory dysfunctions and other simultaneously occurring mental disabilities.

REFERENCES

1. Abeles, M., and P. Schilder, "Psychogenic Loss of Personal Identity," *Arch. Neurol. Psychiat.*, 1935, *34*, 587–604.
2. Bartlett, F. C., *Remembering*. London, Cambridge University Press, 1932.
3. Boyd, D. A., "A Contribution to the Psychopathology of Alzheimer's Disease," *Amer. Jour. Psychiat.*, 1936–37, *93*, 155–175.
4. Cason, H., "A Case of Anterograde Amnesia," *Jour. Abn. Soc. Psychol.*, 1935–36, *30*, 107–110.
5. Freud, S., "Repression," in *Collected Papers of Sigmund Freud*, Vol. IV. London, Hogarth, 1925, 84–97.
6. Gillespie, R. D., "Amnesia." *Arch. Neurol. Psychiat.*, 1937, *37*, 748–764.

7. Goldstein, K., and S. E. Katz, "The Psychopathology of Pick's Disease," *Arch. Neurol. Psychiat.*, 1937, *38*, 473–490.

8. Hunt, J. McV., "Psychological Experiments with Disordered Persons," *Psychol. Bull.*, 1936, *33*, 1–58.

9. Janet, P., *The Major Symptoms of Hysteria*. New York, Macmillan, 1907.

10. Jellinek, E. M., *Alcohol Addiction and Chronic Alcoholism*. New Haven, Yale University Press, 1942, 127–133.

11. Jones, E., "Remarks on a Case of Complete Autopsychic Amnesia," *Jour. Abn. Psychol.*, 1909, *4*, 218–235.

12. Kahn, E., and L. J. Thompson, "Concerning Pick's Disease," *Amer. Jour. Psychiat.*, 1933–34, *13*, 937–946.

13. Landis, C., and J. Rechetnick, "Changes in Psychological Functions in Paresis," I., *Psychiat. Quart.*, 1934, *8*, 693–698.

14. Prince, M., *The Unconscious* (2d ed.). New York, Macmillan, 1929.

15. Rapaport, D., *Emotions and Memory*. Baltimore, Williams & Wilkins, 1942, Chap. VII, 183–236.

16. Ribot, T., *Diseases of Memory* (5th ed.). London, Kegan Paul, 1906.

17. Sears, R. R., "Functional Abnormalities of Memory with Special Reference to Amnesia," *Psychol. Bull.*, 1936, *33*, 229–274.

18. Zubin, J., and S. E. Barrera, "Effect of Electric Convulsive Therapy on Memory," *Proc. Soc. Exp. Biol. Med.*, 1941, *48*, 596–597.

Chapter XXIV

DISORDERED EMOTION: DESCRIPTION

IT WILL be recalled that the distinction between normal and abnormal is one between behavior which is usual or easily comprehended and behavior which is unusual or strange. This distinction presents certain difficulties when one considers the disorders of emotion. There is a tendency to call any or all varieties of strong emotion "abnormal," and to regard them as unusual or incomprehensible. This has come from the common literary usage of the word "emotion," which implies that it is unusual. Everyone knows that feeling and emotional expressions form part of everyday life and that most emotions and feelings are normal, while but few are unusual. In attempting to differentiate between feelings and expressions which are normal and those which are abnormal, it is possible to set up certain criteria. These criteria are not necessarily discrete or all inclusive; they overlap each other and do not always apply to the same particular experience or behavior.

1. *Usualness or Predictability.* If the feeling or expression is that which is usual to the situation or to the individual, or if it is the sort of a reaction which we would predict ahead of time, we call it "normal"; otherwise, "abnormal."

2. *Relevance or Appropriateness.* If the feeling or expression is relevant and appropriate and of the same variety which is shown by most individuals of the same cultural and social group, we call it "normal"; otherwise, "abnormal."

3. *Personal Reference.* If the feeling or expression is that which either the observer or the patient thinks should be appropriate because of the personal relationship between the patient and some other person, it is called "normal"; if not, "abnormal."

4. *Duration.* Most emotional reactions are governed in their duration by the intensity and vividness of the experience. If, after a very serious accident, the participant very quickly and completely recovers from his emotional shock, it is unusual. If, after a death in the family, the bereaved mourns deeply for a period of years, the emotional reaction is called "abnormal." In either instance the emotional reaction deviated in duration from the length

of time during which most individuals experience emotion after some appropriate stimulus.

5. *Possible Injury to Self or Others.* If the intensity of the emotional expression is such that the individual may injure himself or others, we consider it abnormal, even though the stimulation may have been most provocative. The concept of emotion so strong that it cannot be controlled is used in the law when, after some very provocative incident, one person kills or injures another and then pleads temporary insanity.

In general psychology much experimentation and discussion have been devoted to the problems of how emotions or emotional reactions may be recognized; how they may be measured; and how they may be compared. There are always two aspects to emotional reactions: first, the expression or behavior which any observer may see; and second, the personal feeling which only the experiencing person knows and can communicate to others, usually by descriptive words. Only a low degree of correlation has been found between personal feeling and the outward expression of emotion as judged by observers. This has been true in studies of normal individuals and, as we shall see later, is even more true in studies of the abnormal. This low correlation between expression and feeling complicates both the description and experimental approach to the problem of emotional abnormalities.

Some persons conceal much of the expression of their feelings, while others give vent to an exaggerated display of emotional reactions with but little appropriate feeling, hoping to deceive the observer. There are wide differences in the meanings and usages of the descriptive adjectives and nouns which are used to express feelings and experiences. There is a continually developing, new terminology which shifts quite rapidly. It is in the form of slang and colloquial expressions which are used for a month or a year and then are no longer regarded as appropriate or sufficiently descriptive. All of this grows out of the fact that a fundamental distinction is made between intellectual experience and emotional experience. To intellectual experience we assign definite words and measurable and comparable standards. For emotional experience we have no such definite words, measures, or comparisons.

In the present chapter disordered emotion as it is shown in the major psychoses, in the neuroses, and in psychopathic personalities will be described.

Mania

Elation, distractibility, overactivity, and volatile expressiveness are the chief emotional symptoms marking manic reactions. These symptoms are shown in the excited phase of many sorts of psychosis, but are seen in their clearest form in the manic phase of the manic-depressive psychosis.

One intelligent and well-educated patient described his elation as follows:

The exhilarated condition is essentially creative and synthetical and has as its characteristic a desire for composition. . . . It is characterized by an abnormal desire on my part for starting enterprises, a strong feeling of power for accomplishing and an abnormal adequacy, together with a craving for command. All of this usually culminates, in spite of various side schemes and ambitions, in an intense desire for intellectual activity and organization. . . . I think I perceive an almost mathematical unity and interdependence in all things. . . . Were the restless activity of this powerful mental delirium not so ineffably wearying, and its individual points of light not so ephemeral, its ecstatic pleasure would be comparable to that of the old Greek Gods. . . . The only sane state of mind which I know at all comparable to this exhilarated condition is that of a person deeply in love. . . . In my experience with the disease I am, when exhilarated . . . embarrassed . . . by the very intensity and generosity of my feelings, whose essence is kindliness and good-will towards men. But this benevolence is no longer administered according to the dictates of reasoning sympathy; it has rather become an exaggerated, insane beneficence or an all embracing widely extravagant munificence. The original sympathetic desire for the sharing of joy, happiness and well-being has run mad.*

Such elation consists of several psychopathological changes. First, there is a lifting or abolition of inhibition. The manic feels that somehow his ideas and desires are no longer subject to the customary restraints and taboos of everyday life. Next, there seems to be a lack of the normal compulsion for logical thought. The elated patient feels that his inspiration is of such a high order that the usual plodding necessity of logic and reason can be transcended, so that the ordinary logical checks on thought are no longer important or necessary. Third, the manic may give expression to his usually repressed desires, wishes, and instincts in a fashion which is often crudely unconventional.

Looking into the content of normal elation provides a greater understanding of the abnormal exhibitions of mania.

In our daily lives the greatest happiness seems to come from the prospect of achievement of cherished ambitions, whether these be concerned with one's career or with one's love affairs. When we analyze such emotions we see that contentment with actual achievement is a less violent affair. Further,

* MacCurdy, J. T., *The Psychology of Emotion.* New York, Harcourt, 1925, 298–299.

we must recognize that situations which produce the purest joy are never purely altruistic. They come nearest to this in the case of parents elated over the progress of their children, or of lovers similarly overjoyed with the triumph of fiancé or partner. The egoistic component of this situation is discernible in the identification which characterizes genuine love. . . . [Elated] happiness comes from the vision of success in some undertaking which will indirectly benefit others.*

When compared with this normal elation, the manic differs chiefly in that his form of expression is derived principally from repressed wishes to which the patient gives vent in an unconventional form of sublimation. We understand the normal elation because it is related to ordinary and obvious life experience; but the elation of the manic surprises us because it fails to show such a relationship.

As to the basic cause of this difference between normal and abnormal elation, we may assume that there is a defect in personality function which results in emotional, as well as intellectual, disintegration. This disintegration is shown by uninhibited and disordered emotional expressiveness. Many individuals with manic tendencies are unusually excitable and overreact to slight stimulation throughout their lives; that is, they always show a cycloid temperament. When such individuals get into situations which are difficult or intolerable for them, they cannot maintain a state of affective integration. Therefore, minor circumstances may precipitate an explosion which we call "mania."

Next to elation comes distractibility as an outstanding characteristic of mania. This distractibility concerns feeling, as well as thought. A patient is said to be "distraught," which means that his emotional reactions are disordered and disconnected. One patient gave the following description of this condition:

I feel that when I am exhilarated, my mind occupies itself, for the most part with its own affairs. . . . It is, as a rule, too busy and too much in a hurry to stop and to make minute, rational and detailed account in [the] passing of external objects. Its tendency is towards flightiness. . . . Ideas move so rapidly that grief follows inspiration, joy, anger and ambition in a fashion which is to me connected but illogical. . . . Naturally the more exhilarated I become the more difficult it is for me to reason to myself. . . . During the heat of my conversation I am momentarily carried away and believe my own stories. I am not, however, sufficiently carried away to prevent my taking account afterwards and to separate the truth from the falsehood and to experience regret for the latter. . . . During my worst and

* MacCurdy, J. T., *ibid.*, 185

most severe exhilaration I have a tendency to become very emotional, hysterical and even at times to break down and cry.*

To understand how distraction disturbs clarity of feeling and thought, we have only to turn to our own daily experience. The desire to be understood makes our normal thought and feeling coherent and intelligible. When in everyday life we are concentrating on something and become excited, we tend to be incoherent and can be understood only with difficulty. If we answer a question in an irrelevant fashion because we are concentrating our attention on some other problem, we are said to be "absentminded." The thoughts of a manic patient, who is self-absorbed and in an ecstatic mood, consequently appear illogical and unintelligible.

Coupled with the symptoms of elation and distractibility are overactivity and the volatile nature of emotional expressiveness. Such individuals do not smile or laugh softly. They scream with pleasure or sob with joy over some phrase in their conversation which seems totally trite to the normal individual. This overexpressiveness is but another manifestation of the manic's elation and distractibility. The lack of inhibitions, the absence of logic, and the crude, unconventional emotional demonstration are the basis of the volatile expression of emotion, just as they are the basis for elation and distraction.

Another type of exaggerated good feeling is associated with the grandiose delusions which characterize the expansive general paretic patient. These patients have a pervasive mood of euphoria which exhibits itself in boastfulness. It is not uncommon for them to present checks for a million dollars to strangers or to tell fantastic stories of unlimited wealth to anyone who will listen to them. They are motivated by practically the same psychological mechanisms which are at work in the manic patient, but they usually do not display the other manic symptoms to such an extent. The paretic's lack of inhibitions and his tendency to distractibility, elation, and overexpressiveness are somewhat mitigated by the progressive destruction of brain tissue which blunts his ingenuity of thought and emotion.

Depression

Very few people go through life without periods of despondency, "the blues," or prolonged sadness. Such transient periods cannot be regarded as unhealthy or abnormal, even though the individual who is experiencing the depression may lack the psychological insight neces-

* MacCurdy, J. T., *ibid.*, 301–303.

sary to understand his own experience. Depressive moods are considered abnormal only when they continue over long periods of time, when they completely interfere with the life of the individual, when they are unmotivated, or when they lead to suicidal attempts. A distinction is made between different kinds of pathological depression; namely, the depressive phase of manic-depressive psychosis, reactive neurosis, involutional melancholia, and a wide variety of anxiety states which include feelings of depression.

DEPRESSED PHASE OF THE MANIC-DEPRESSIVE PSYCHOSIS

This particular state is characterized by sadness, hopelessness, mental retardation, and feelings of inadequacy and unreality.

The sadness is almost synonymous with depression itself. There is a lack of desire and ambition, together with a feeling of lethargy. It may include the grief of Alexander the Great who wept because there were no more worlds to conquer. Sadness is not necessarily related to the loss of someone who had been beloved. It is often identified with the loss of the feeling of personal ambition and worthiness. This loss leads to hopelessness which easily associates itself with a feeling of unreality. Human hope is maintained and supported by our desires and imagination of the future. The loss of this vital interest affects the future first, since dissatisfaction with present and past achievements is usually compensated for by an imagination of future desires and potential accomplishments. If this active interest becomes exhausted, we are no longer able to gloss over the minor difficulties of everyday life. We commonly put together all of our hopes in some form of personal faith ("The substance of things hoped for, the evidence of things not seen"). If sadness and hopelessness pervade mental life, they often involve a feeling of unreality which may or may not be accompanied by insight. Unreality is felt because interest is lacking, and things or events are real in direct proportion to our interest in them. The feeling of unreality may lead to the development of actual delusions. A depressed patient may insist that the sun has ceased to shine or that his heart has been removed. He may be so bereft of any attachment to things in the outside world that there is no longer a distinction between the reality of himself and the reality of his surroundings.

With the progress of the depression a retardation becomes more evident, ". . . a sorrowfulness so weighing down the mind that there is no good it likes to do. It has attached to it as its inseparable comrade a distress and weariness of soul, and a sluggishness in all good works, which plunges the whole man into lazy languor, and works in him a constant bitterness. And out of this vehement woe springs silence and a flagging of the voice, because the soul is so absorbed and taken up with its own indolent dejection, that it has no energy for utterance, but is cramped and hampered and imprisoned in its own confused bewilderment, and has not a word to say."* This retardation is related to a deficiency in mental energy which, in turn, comes out of the person's sadness and hopelessness.

Simple retardation is by no means a rare occurrence in everyday life. It requires an effort to think or move actively when we are fatigued or sad as a result of some recent frustrating experience. We can think keenly and rapidly when we are engaged in solving some welcome problem, but distasteful exercises are slow. Temporary incompetence in our mental processes often follows an unexpected emotional blocking produced by some very unpleasant experience or anticipation. Such a sudden inhibition is a miniature depression with a miniature retardation.

Most depressed patients complain of either mental or physical inadequacy. This complaint is based on the realization that their energies and interests have been diminished to such a degree as to constitute a feeling of utter impotence.

All of these symptoms of sadness, hopelessness, unreality, retardation, and inadequacy seem to have a common characteristic; namely, a lack of mental energy or a deficiency in the drive or motivation for everyday existence. If this deficiency can be filled in, the psychopathological symptoms will disappear. The core of the depression is a felt lack of a motive for existence, and of this lack the patient is most keenly aware. Psychologically speaking, some emotional idea or complex may have become so powerful that total repression of all ideas is inevitable if the person is to escape the consequences of this internal conflict. Since the conflict itself is unconscious, the patient does not realize the overwhelming nature of the repressed idea. This mechanism is similar to the effect of guilty conscience in normal life. Both the ordinary feeling of guilt or dejection in a depressive psychosis is characterized by a conviction of sin and a benumbing lethargy. All this provokes mental promises of future good deeds and thoughts, since the true cause of his sorrow is unknown to the depressed patient.

REACTIVE NEUROSIS (DEPRESSION)

In the reactive type of depression, the patient worries excessively over some real trouble that happened in the recent past. The worry is

* St. John of Damascus, quoted from J. T. MacCurdy, *ibid.*, 343.

accompanied by a feeling of hopelessness and sorrow, but usually there is no clear evidence of mental retardation or feelings of inadequacy and unreality. Instead of a crushed hopelessness, there is an actual overt display of emotion in which tears and wailing are prominent. Usually the excessive grief is attached to some occurrence, such as a death in the family, which is a normal excitant of grief. The distinction between normal grief and reactive depression is largely determined by the duration and by the vigor of the emotional display. The patient's mind is filled with exaggerated emotion and attention directed toward the precipitating, distressing event. The event itself is real, but the response of the patient is so intense and prolonged that it is definitely in discord with the facts.

Such a depression is often the result of unsuccessful compromises which an ambitious person is forced to make because of circumstances over which he has no control. The compromise forces a retreat which is, in part, prevented by an obsessive preoccupation with some painful and frustrating situation. This obsessional mechanism serves to camouflage the feeling of failure in accomplishing a certain level of aspiration, and is followed by a partial regression in which rationalization plays a delaying role.

INVOLUTIONAL MELANCHOLIA

In Chap. XII it was pointed out that involutional melancholia is differentiated from other forms of depression as a syndrome marked by overactivity ranging from restlessness to frenzied agitation. As a rule, such agitated states do not seem to depend on any logical, factual basis. The involutional patient attaches his depression to some totally irrelevant or imaginary cause, while the agitation grows out of the fear of old age and death.

Confusion or Perplexity

Many psychotic patients experience a state of perplexity or confused emotionality. They seem bewildered and complain that there seems to be a "mist" or "wall of snow" which is interposed between them and reality. Such individuals are restless and apprehensive in an aimless fashion and act as though they were dazed or dreamy. They speak slowly with initial difficulty. They may repeatedly ask, "Have I done something?" When asked what they have done, they will say, "I don't know, I feel all mixed up. I don't know what I am talking about. Everything is mixed. Am I happy or am I sad? I don't feel the same for two minutes." This subjective perplexity engages the patient most of the time. His expression and his introspection indicate that he is neither deeply depressed nor elated; rather, he is puzzled and disoriented to varying degrees. When asked where he is, what time it is, who he is, and so on, the patient will either say he does not know, or he will go on talking about something else as if the question had not been asked. At times, he may find himself and be quite accurate in his orientation for several days, but relapses are common.

The disorders of feeling evident in these cases add to our difficulty in explaining them. The patient is peculiarly distressed by his unsuccessful efforts to control his thoughts and to understand them. His experience is similar to that of a tired person who has been roused from sleep and attempts to decide whether he is actually awake or still dreaming. In fact, perplexity acts much in the same way as depression to bring about a retardation of thought and feeling. Some patients explain the distress to themselves as a feeling of guilt, saying that it is a result of wickedness or of sin and that they are ashamed. This explanation on the basis of a false idea differs from that offered by the depressive patient who will say, "I am an evil man," while the perplexed patient will say, "They say that I am an evil man."

One way of trying to understand these confused states is to relate the thought and feeling process to our everyday distinction between reality and nonreality; for example, the contrast between wakefulness and dreams during sleep. As we turn our attention to our inner thoughts, either in dreams or in fantasy, they tend to become "real." A drowsy person is inclined to think that his dreams are real, but when he awakens thoroughly, he checks himself, grasps his surroundings accurately, and recognizes that his dreams were unreal. The perplexed patient attempts this but cannot achieve a consistent feeling of reality. Instead, he remains in painful confusion because he can neither affirm nor deny the truth of his thoughts.

Another variety of emotional confusion which follows certain brain lesions is that which has been termed *pathological forced laughing and crying*.[8] Such patients lose control over their emotional expressions so that laughter or crying starts as a result of very slight stimulation. The stimulus for the outburst may be either adequate or inadequate, appropriate or inappropriate. One patient cried whenever she was spoken to or when anyone sat beside her. Another was forced to walk about the hospital with his gazed fixed on the floor, for if he met anyone's gaze, he was immediately overcome by gales of laughter which would last four or five minutes. Many intelligent patients of this kind are conscious of the insufficiency of the stimulus and are painfully aware of the incongruity of their behavior. Such a patient will laugh against his will although his mood is not gay, and this will greatly distress him. Others will indicate by gestures of impatience and denial how much they are annoyed and ashamed of their tears. In brief, the outward expression of the emotion may or may not correspond with the patient's real feelings.

Apathy

An emotional dullness that may amount to a complete loss of affective experience is termed *apathy*. Apathetic persons have no real joy in life, no human feelings. To them, nothing matters; everything seems the same; they feel no grief and no gaiety; their hearts are not in what they say; their emotionality is flat and indifferent.

The analysis of this apathetic condition, particularly as it appears in dementia praecox, discloses a disappearance of delicacy of feeling. Such a patient no longer has any regard for his surroundings, nor does he suit his behavior to the situation. He is untidy, dirty, unwashed, unkempt, and exhibits no feeling of disgust or shame. He becomes insensitive to bodily discomfort. He may assume and hold uncomfortable positions; he may burn himself with a cigarette; he may glare at the noonday sun; he may not chase away flies that settle on his eyelids. He is without sympathy and equally indifferent to the misfortunes or good fortunes of others. He may grievously injure other patients because of some trifling event, or receive the visits of his friends and relatives without any sign of greeting or emotion. All the higher moral sentiments seem to have disappeared. A great many of the criminally insane who have been convicted of heinous crimes show gross lack of moral and ethical ideals and little appreciation of the seriousness of their act. The most outstanding characteristic of such emotional dullness is the apparent extreme uniformity of apathetic feelings or moods. It is not too hard to comprehend the emotional abnormalities of mania or depression, but it is difficult to understand the psychology of apathy. There are various psychotic conditions which may give rise to an apathetic state.

The dementia praecox patient,[5] whose account of his inner life was cited in Chap. IV, provides some information about schizophrenic apathy. He maintained that his loss of emotionality was considerably less than it may have seemed to the observer. According to his account, external stimuli still produce emotional experience in the schizophrenic. Foods provide pleasant feelings. Attitudes toward relatives may be of high affective content and emotional interest may extend to many activities going on around the patient. Schizophrenic apathy is apparently due to two major factors: (*a*) the patient is so preoccupied with his hallucinatory experience that he blocks or represses outward evidence of affective response in order to favor the ideas which have taken possession of him; and (*b*) the hallucinations are so closely coupled with his affect that they give rise to silly and inappropriate expressions. For example, "A thought-out-loud [hallucination] stating 'Let's make Johnny feel happy' penetrates the conscious field. Immediately my affective tone shifts from one of indifference to one of pleasure. Then a thought-out-loud will state: 'Let's make Johnny feel sad.' Immediately the affective state shifts to one of sadness." * Evidently, hallucinations determine the observable emotional expression. However, without introspective information provided by the patient it is very difficult to appraise the lack of emotionality.

Another type of emotional dulling or apathy is seen in neurotic cases, as well as in certain toxic or exhaustive states. A personal description of this type of lack of feeling, which is of a different variety from that shown by the schizophrenic, has been given as follows:

I still continue to suffer constantly; I have not a moment of comfort and no human sensations. Surrounded by all that can render life happy and agreeable, still to me the faculty of enjoyment and of feeling is wanting — both have become physical impossibilities. In everything, even in the most tender caresses of my children, I find only bitterness. I cover them with kisses, but there is something between their lips and mine; and this horrid something is between me and all the enjoyments of life. My existence is incomplete. The functions and acts of ordinary life, it is true, still remain to me, but in every one of them there is something wanting — to wit, the feeling which is proper to them and the pleasure which follows them. . . . Music has lost all charm for me, I used to love it dearly. My daughter plays very well, but for me it is mere noise. That lively interest which a year ago made me hear a delicious concert in the smallest air their fingers played — that thrill, that general vibration which made me shed such tender tears — all that exists no more.†

Some of these patients complain that there is a splitting away of emotions from their thinking. The relative importance of thought and feeling becomes confused. Almost everything occurs in the same "flat" manner. It is as if the differences between important and unimportant events and experiences had been washed out and nothing remained to which any special importance could be attached. The proverb, "The

* Lang, J., "The Other Side of the Affective Aspects of Schizophrenia," *Psychiatry,* 1939, *2*, 198.

† Johnson, H. K., "The Symptom of Loss of Feelings," *Amer. Jour. Psychiat.*, 1935, *91*, 1327–1328.

salt has lost its savor," suggests that such experience does happen in many individuals under not too abnormal circumstances.

Neurotic apathy and the emotional dulling in exhaustion states is understandable in at least two ways. First, there may be true fatigue, so that real imperception results. The patient actually does not perceive or grasp the full meaning of things which occur around him, and so fails to react in the usual way. Second, the person may be so preoccupied with his own phobias and anxieties that the events of everyday life become relatively banal and unimportant to him. In other words, a repressed emotional complex may effectively hold out of mind the import of newer events.

Anxiety

The term *anxiety* includes the vague fears, worries, guilt feelings, security seeking, apprehension, and various needs for reassurance. The experience itself is one which every human has had for greater or shorter periods of time and in varying degrees of intensity. It is an experience easily recognized by oneself, and "understandable" when described to another. The distinction between normal anxiety and morbid anxiety is based on two criteria: (*a*) disproportion between the external stimulus and the response; and (*b*) disharmony between bodily and mental manifestations.

The following is an instance of morbid anxiety:

CASE 31: A single woman, aged thirty, was jilted by her fiancé. Some six months after this event the patient began to worry excessively and consulted fortunetellers and astrologists concerning her worries and her blighted love affair. When the predictions of the fortunetellers did not materialize, her apprehension increased so that on the advice of her physician she was admitted to a hospital. On admission she appeared anxious and worried. She was constantly wringing her hands, groaning, and sighing. She had little to say, but when she did speak she repeated such statements as, "Oh, do something for me. Something awful is going to happen. I can't sleep. My heart skips beats. I am so worried I can't think. I am sinful. I don't know what is going to happen to me." This acute anxiety continued for three months, but with persuasion and suggestive therapy she regained insight and was able to resume her former work.

Essentially, this condition of anxiety neurosis, as well as other forms of anxiety, is marked by an increase of a general fearful and irritable tension, a hypersensitiveness to noise, lights, or other stimuli, and changeable or vague physical complaints.[4] Attacks of anxiety and its psychosomatic equivalents commonly take the form of cardiac disturbances, difficulty in breathing, perspiration, dizziness, tremor, or stammering. The fears are often related either to physical disabilities, such as heart failure and suffocation, or to normal culpability. Freud's original theory was that any anxiety neurosis could be explained by a lack in sexual outlet and sexual gratification. According to present psychoanalytic concepts, anxiety is due to an increase in sensory attention and motor tension, called "anxiety preparedness." This state leads to the development of anxious feelings and to a repetition of some old traumatic experience, not unlike the conditioned fear response. The original traumatic experience tends to push itself from the unconscious in such fashion that the emotional responses paralyze the capacity for adjustment to immediate situations. As a rule, such anxiety is directed against mental images of a dangerous nature, which in the neurosis come partially or fully into consciousness.

Some investigators have made use of hypnosis to establish anxiety symptoms in normal individuals. During an hypnotic trance, suggestions were given with the intention to precipitate a mental conflict between motives or desires following the trance. Even when any suggestion of anxiety was avoided, the artificially created conflict was found to lead in most normal individuals to a report of anxiety, together with varying physical complaints. Anxiety and conflict could be removed by subsequent rehypnotization and the suggestion that the conflict no longer existed. In a similar fashion, psychotherapists have used hypnosis to clarify the basic nature of some conflict which they assumed to be the cause of an anxiety neurosis. In some cases excellent and seemingly permanent results have been reported. Such a favorable outcome, however, cannot be regularly counted on.

Acute Fear or Phobia

Acute fear or phobia differs from anxiety in that it is always directed toward some object, person, or idea. It is distinguished from normal apprehension in that it is related to events or experiences which would not set up a really fearful reaction in the ordinary individual. Another characteristic of abnormal fear (phobia) is that the person is unable to give a reasonable explanation for his experience.

The development of fear attitudes has been the point of a great deal of research, particularly with normal, growing children.[2] One study dealt with the response of children and adults of differing ages to a live snake. Up to the age of two, children displayed no fear of snakes. Between the ages of three and three and a half there was a cautious response, so that the children paid close attention to the snake's movements and seemed somewhat on their guard when approaching it. Definite fear of snakes showed itself only after the age of four. Adults were much more pronounced in this fear reaction than were children. Tests of college students indicated that they were more frequently afraid of snakes than were small children. No sex difference was found in the extent of this fear of live snakes, which constitutes an interesting example of an attitude of fear or phobia developing progressively in the normal child from year to year in a particular culture. In other cultures (such as India) this type of fear does not exist. Actually, the attitude of most Occidentals toward a harmless, live snake is very similar to, or identical with, the reaction of patients who have phobias. An unreasonable and unreasoning emotional response is directed toward some object or event without rational explanation.

A distinction [7] has been made between specific fears and general fear, or panophobia. In the latter condition, a terror exists that is not directed toward any particular object or event, and may spread quickly from one stimulus to another. More common are the special fears or phobias which are characterized by an exaggerated reaction to some particular stimulus. There are long lists of technical words used to describe the various phobias; for example, "agoraphobia," fear of open places; "claustrophobia," fear of closed places; "thanatophobia," fear of death; "zoophobia," fear of animals.

Various explanations have been offered for these phobias. In some instances the phobia seems directly related to some exaggeration of fear or fright in early childhood. There may have been a punishment, social taboo, or religious instruction which the individual no longer remembers. Possibly the affect derived from this experience has persisted and extended, attaching itself to associated events or ideas in adult life. Another explanation holds that many phobias bear a logical or symbolical relation to some repressed complex. They are developed only when events occur in everyday life which are in some way related to repressed material. Some psychoanalysts go even further with the theory that phobia is not an expression of fear but of sexual prohibition. It is considered a substitute or a displacement of the affect that is associated with sexuality and compensates for repressed childhood experiences, trends, or desires.

In the understanding and treatment of phobias the general problem is one of correctly establishing the relationship between the frightening experience with which the fear had been primarily associated and the events which led to further frustrations in the adult life of the individual. The patient's objective is to make the correct association and, in conversation and his own thinking, to review the original fear-inciting experience until it is fully in his consciousness. If he is able to do this he has a fair chance to recover from this particular phobia. In other cases of phobia it may be possible for the individual, either by his own volition or through compulsion by others, to establish systematic daily contact with the fear incitant. In response to this procedure certain phobias will lose their vigor and become unimportant.

Anger and Irritation

Whether or not anger and irritability are normal or abnormal depends chiefly upon the intensity and appropriateness of a given feeling and reaction. All varieties of anger and irritation may occur in abnormal patients, although such reactions are rarely the cardinal symptom of any one of the mental disorders, except in the case of certain forms of psychopathic personality.

The outbursts of anger and irritation which are seen in manic-depressive and involutional patients are often of a self-protective nature. When our own self-regard indicates to us our shortcomings, we frequently tend to evade the issue by searching for similar or worse shortcomings in others. Usually, this process is hampered by a more or less complete recognition that the behavior of others in this respect is none of our business. The psychotic patient has no such inhibitions and, consequently, tends to justify or correct the defects in his own system of ideas by discovering faults in others. When he fails in his attempt to force such attentions and ideas upon his surroundings, or when people intimate that his self-reproach has no good basis in fact, he becomes irritable because he vaguely feels that their attitude implies some criticism of himself.

Exaggerated rage and anger are commonly spoken of as *furor.* Such attacks occur in dementia praecox, epilepsy, senility, and in some other organic brain disorders. Schizophrenic furor is usually associated with a crisis in the hallucinatory system of the patient. For example, voices may have been telling him for weeks that he is divine, and finally the voices tell him that he must prove his divinity by purging the world of sin. In attempting to carry out such a purge, he will give vent to a display of anger and fury which may lead to serious injuries to himself and others. Similar attacks occur in some epileptic patients, either as a postseizure phenomenon or as psychic equivalents of a seizure. These attacks consist of a temporary display of senseless rage and fury from which most patients recover with a total amnesia of the event. Milder outbreaks are seen in senile and other organic brain conditions where the furor states seem to be due to damage or deterioration of brain tissue.

A good deal of observation and investigation has been centered around the hypothesis that chronic irritation and anxiety are produced by frustration and emotional conflict in the everyday life of a neurotic person. Some have held that neurosis itself is a result of frustration and conflict. When we remember that no human being ever lives through any period of his life without either internal or external frustration or conflict, and when we think of the number of normal individuals in contrast to the number of neurotics, we must conclude that frustration and conflict alone are not sufficient to set up a neurosis under ordinary circumstances. It is also true that the neurotic's anxiety and irritation have not been found to differ essentially, except in degree and duration, from the anxiety and irritation shown by the normal individual. The difference is in the response to the feeling — what the patient does about his feelings — rather than in the feeling itself. Frustration and conflict are unquestionably able to precipitate overt displays of anxiety and irritation. Ordinarily, however, they do not produce a true neurosis unless there is a constitutional lack of integration and resistance in the frustrated individual.

Persistent anger[3] continuing over very long periods of time is shown mainly by that type of psychopathic personality that has been called "troublemaker" or "quarrelsome psychopath." Such persons are oversensitive, basically weak and egocentric, rigid and unable to relax. Their inner tension expresses itself in irritable quarreling which serves as a tool to satisfy ambition and intensified desire for prestige. Their righteous attitude easily leads to nagging, faultfinding, dogmatic contradiction, and a tendency to depreciate others. These psychopaths not only will not, but cannot allow themselves to be influenced or convinced. As a result, they develop a feeling of almost constant irritation which exhibits itself in angry outbursts at the slightest provocation.

Love

It is apparent from previous chapters that disturbed love and sex emotion are intimately involved in the psychopathology of both neurosis and psychosis. The entire system of Freudian psychoanalysis has been erected on the theory that repression, suppression, and deviation in love (libido) can be found in every neurotic. The effects of social customs, child education, and personal relationships profoundly influence the ways in which these basic instincts and feelings can manifest themselves. Many systematic investigations have shown that there is in practically every psychotic or neurotic patient some disorder or deviation in sex and love feelings.

Of all the expressions of emotion, love is guarded by the most rigid set of taboos and social customs. Here, there is less opportunity for deviation in expression than in any other sort of emotion. No really maladjusted individual is capable of dealing with this rigidity. Furthermore, the rigidity itself may set up the maladjustment. In our society many of the expressions of love are associated with ideas of sin, blame, and other religious or ethical concepts. These scruples add to the troubles which any individual has in adjusting his inner life to the circumstances of everyday existence. Whenever a person is weak, sick, has formed bad habits of social adjustment, is unintelligent, or immature, is placed under personal stress, or meets any of the usual difficulties of life, he will be unable to cope effectively with the complications of an existence which is subjected to very rigid and exacting cultural restraints. Regardless of whether sexual maladjustment is considered a cause or an effect of these difficulties, it is to be expected that neurotic or psychotic individuals will be more frequently disturbed with respect to love and sex than to any other aspect of their emotional life.

Abnormal self-love is spoken of as *narcissism*. It is considered infantile in nature, in that most persons live through and outgrow it. When it is present in the adult, it constitutes either a fixation or a regression in development. Such persons are interested only in themselves — are in love with themselves. On the sexual side, gratification is obtained through masturbation. Many psychotic patients show an exaggeration of masturbatory activity and little or no interest in adult heterosexuality. They endlessly adorn themselves, sometimes with fantastic garments or odd coiffures, and often seem so disinterested in others that they find complete satisfaction in their own being. The narcissistic behavior of some of these patients evidently results from a developmental failure, a fixation, or sexual immaturity. In others it seems to be due to a true regression to an infantile state, and may be taken as an indication that these patients have lost their previously strong emotional attachments to their spouse, children, or parents.

There is little or no exact knowledge available about the nature, variability, and distribution of sex outlets which are found in the normal human population. Until we have more information about the normal range and variation of sex feeling and expression, we shall not be able either to understand fully or to appraise correctly what seem to be evident abnormalities in mental deviants. It is quite possible that sex in its broadest sense does serve as the dynamic biological and psychological force of human existence. It is also possible that what is commonly considered as an abnormality of this driving force is not truly abnormal at all. Rather, the behavior came to our attention because the individual was suffering from some other deviation which either released normal inhibition or facilitated expression of some unusual form of sexuality.

Summary

In many instances the most marked deviation from normal behavior shown by psychiatric patients is in the realm of emotion. Excellent descriptions and explanations of the psychopathology of this phase of mental life are available. It is possible to gain much knowledge, insight, and understanding of the psychopathology of emotion, and from this to understand many forms of unusual behavior which are otherwise puzzling. For emotional disorders we have better descriptive material available than for practically any other phase of abnormal psychology.

REFERENCES

1. Johnson, H. K., "The Symptom of Loss of Feelings," *Amer. Jour. Psychiat.*, 1935, *91*, 1327–1341.

2. Jones, M. C., "The Conditioning of Children's Emotion," Chapter 3 in C. Murchison, (ed.), *A Handbook of Child Psychology*. Worcester, Clark University Press, 1931, 71–93.

3. Kahn, E., *Psychopathic Personalities*. New Haven, Yale University Press, 1931.

4. Kubie, L. S., "A Physiological Approch to the Concept of Anxiety," *Psychosom. Med.*, 1941, *3*, 263–276.

5. Lang, J., "The Other Side of the Affective Aspects of Schizophrenia," *Psychiatry*, 1939, *2*, 195–202.

6. MacCurdy, J. T., *The Psychology of Emotion*. New York, Harcourt, 1925.

7. Sidis, B., *The Causation and Treatment of Psychopathic Diseases*. Boston, Badger, 1916.

8. Wilson, S. A. K., *Modern Problems in Neurology*. Baltimore, Wood, 1929.

Chapter XXV

DISORDERED EMOTION: EXPERIMENTAL FINDINGS

IT IS EVIDENT, from the previous chapter, that our understanding of the types of emotional deviation is always based on two kinds of evidence — the psychological and the physiological. Affect and emotion are evidenced by how we *feel* about something and by overt expressions that others can observe. The "feel" evidence is subjective; that is, a personal experience which can be known by others only if described or communicated by the person who had the experience. The physiological, behavioristic, or objective evidence can be seen or otherwise perceived. As a rule, it can be made more or less quantitative through the use of some measuring instrument, such as an indicator of change in blood pressure or respiration.

This distinction between subjective and objective evidence is not always clear. Many who have written on this subject have not held to this distinction, since there is no generally accepted theory, hypothesis, or formulation which covers affective phenomena. The old argument of, "I see a bear — run — feel fear," versus, "I see a bear — feel fear — run," is still undecided.

Psychology

The psychological viewpoint holds that feeling and emotion constitute that part of the mental life of an individual which is marked by *pleasantness* or *unpleasantness*. Such personal experience is known to others, only when they ask directly or indirectly, "How do you feel about it?" and receive an expressive and intelligible reply.

Direct questions concerning affective experience in abnormal individuals are often particularly difficult to phrase so that the person can answer, and the answer obtained is sometimes difficult to understand. There is frequently such a wide deviation between the behavior and the report of how the patient feels that the discrepancy itself can be considered evidence of psychopathology. For example, a dilapidated paretic patient may say that he feels fine, that there is nothing wrong with him, or that he could lift the corner of a building with one hand. Another real difficulty may arise from the problem of understanding the words which an abnormal individual uses to describe his feelings. The schizophrenic patient makes up words because none of the ordinary terms — such as fear, awe, or curiosity — describe the particular feelings which he has. Other patients will ask, "Do you mean how I feel about it now, or how I felt about it before I got sick?" They imply that there is a difference between the feeling of fear or anger when they are sick, in contrast to those feelings when they were well. Many psychotic patients will elaborate in a romantic way descriptions of emotional experiences for which there is no evidence other than that which might have occurred in their fantasy life. It will frequently happen, therefore, that they contradict themselves in describing their feelings and experiences on successive occasions. In spite of this lack of reliability, direct questioning is still the most productive form of getting information about subjective emotional experience.

EVIDENCE FROM INTERVIEWS

Several studies have made use of a standardized type of interview in which both normal and abnormal individuals were asked the same questions in a conversational fashion while the replies were taken verbatim.[13] If the individual being interviewed is not too disturbed, is fairly intelligent, and is cooperative, a fair degree of reliability can be obtained in the answers which pertain to emotional experience. It has also been found true that a good deal of information can be obtained concerning emotional events which occurred in the childhood or adolescent years of life, although one cannot always be sure whether these reports are fact or fancy. In general, the statements made by mental patients about their emotional life bear out the descriptions which were given for the various types of emotional experience in the previous chapter. During the convalescence from an acute phase of a psychosis, answers to questions are apt to be both confused and confusing. The patient may not remember why he was angry, why he was depressed, or exactly how his feelings then were different from his feelings now. It seems as if he is trying to describe what happened to him and how he felt about it, in much the same way that a normal individual might try to describe the terror or rage which took place in a nightmare.

QUESTIONNAIRES

The usefulness of the questionnaire method in collecting information on emotional life has been the subject of many investigations. Essentially, the questionnaire poses a list of more or less simple questions which are supposed to be answered by a choice of "Yes — No — ?" They further assume that the individuals answering the questions understand the ideas and words, and are cooperating by reporting as truthfully as possible. Expected individual inaccuracies are usually compensated for by taking large groups of patients suffering from the same type of mental disorder, in the hope that the errors may cancel each other and leave apparent the major trends. From the standpoint of abnormal psychology, such investigations emphasize consistency rather than truthfulness of report. That is, if any considerable number of patients will answer the questions in the same way, it is of more interest than whether that report is either true or false. Such consistency is evidence of an association between the particular mental disorder being investigated and the way in which the patients feel about certain questions.[12]

One such investigation[15] studied the reports concerning fear, anger, and the occurrence of physical disease in childhood in groups of normal persons and psychiatric patients. No real correlation was obtained between an individual's fearfulness or ill temper and his general mental health. Those persons, either normal or abnormal, who tended to be fearful also tended to be ill-tempered. In another study[19] which concerned itself with the religious attitude of various groups of psychiatric patients, no significant differences in responses were found between normals, schizophrenics, manic-depressives, or psychoneurotics. Practically all of them tended to report the more conventional attitudes of their own particular faith without any indication that the mental abnormality had particularly altered their religious attitudes.

Many workers have made use of the Bernreuter Personality Inventory. This is a questionnaire that can be scored for different personality traits, one of which is neurotic tendency. Landis and Katz[18] found that about three fourths of the answers which neurotic patients gave on the Bernreuter were verified by the previous history of the patient. The greatest source of disagreement in the answers lay in a contradiction between the patient's own opinion of himself and his past record. The score on the test did not prove to be an adequate measure of neurotic tendency so far as its correlation with the hospital record was concerned. The score, when high, was usually found to be indicative of poorly adjusted or neurotic personality. When the score was low, no conclusion could be drawn concerning the emotional adjustment of the individual.

Benton[2] studied the questions on a specially devised personality schedule which was designed to bring out evidence of emotional differences between normal and abnormal persons. Since their interpretations did not differ significantly on any of the test items, the information obtained by this questionnaire procedure was considered by him to be about as reliable and varied for the abnormal as for the normal person.

In general the questionnaire method has proved inadequate as a direct measure of normality or abnormality in dealing with an individual case. It may be used advantageously for a preliminary interview from which one goes on to a more detailed and thorough study of the individual. When used in this way it often indicates where some of the emotional difficulties of the individual may be located. In applying the questionnaire type of approach to large numbers of cases, it is usually possible to detect two thirds to three fourths of the abnormal individuals in such a group if the test has been properly designed. It is essential that these questionnaires be specifically devised for the particular group one wishes to investigate and that the questions be phrased to bring out the special information one wishes to obtain. Unlike intelligence tests which can be obtained ready-made for almost any situation, the personality questionnaire must be custom tailored.

HYPNOTIC EXPERIMENTS

During the past hundred years many attempts have been made to study the emotional life of both normal and abnormal individuals through the use of hypnosis. It has been assumed that in a deep trance information might be obtained concerning either the emotional state of the hypnotized individual at some particular time, or concerning his response to some specific set of circumstances which apparently produced an emotional reaction in him. That this goal can be accomplished in certain persons has been demonstrated time after time. Unfortunately, not all human beings are hypnotizable, nor are all of those who are hypnotizable capable of being put into a deep enough trance so that emotional factors may be investigated. Probably not more than 10 to 20 per cent of human beings can actually be studied in this way.

Whenever deep trance can be induced, many interesting findings concerning emotional experience may be expected.[7] One can ask a person in such a trance to live through again the experience of some previous emotional event which has been repressed or forgotten. One can establish in the mind of the deeply hypnotized person a suggestion that he has been involved in some acute emotional shock, and have the subsequent behavior of the patient indicate that the suggestion has been accepted and that he is reacting as if the suggestion were true. One can lead such hypnotized individuals to portray all of the appropriate symptoms of an acute neurosis or hysterical condition. Such demonstrations have been done repeatedly by competent investigators, so that the reality of the experiment can no longer be questioned.

In addition to the fact that a deep trance can be induced in only a few individuals, there is the further difficulty that little is known about the nature of the hypnotic trance itself. Whether or not hypnosis is a state of exaggerated suggestibility, a modified sleep state, an evidence of hysterical personality, or just what it is, either psychologically or physiologically, is still an open question. Until the nature of both hypnosis and emotion are more clearly understood, experiments of this kind cannot be too helpful in the analysis of the basic psychological mechanisms operating in emotional deviations.

AUTOBIOGRAPHY

Whenever it was possible in previous chapters, examples have been given of the way in which emotional responses are reported by mental patients. One of the most enlightening presentations of this sort was that of Leonard[21] in his autobiography entitled, *The Locomotive God*, which was cited in Chap. VI. The use of such personal documents as explanatory material in abnormal psychology, particularly with relation to emotion and personality, is not common. It has been thought that mental patients lack so much in self-understanding and are so completely at the mercy of their distorted emotions, that it is usual to minimize the value of their autobiographical reports. Since it is possible to guard against fraud, errors in memory, rationalization, and the like, we may gain much knowledge from the experience of those who have lived through psychotic and neurotic episodes. As Allport[1] has pointed out, the use of such autobiographical material anchors our knowledge in the bedrock of human experience and can meet the critical tests of science; namely, understanding, prediction, and control. Considerable progress in our knowledge of emotional disorders may be expected to result from the future development of this method.

PSYCHOANALYSIS AND THE PROBLEM OF EMOTION

Psychoanalysis, as a method, has made it possible to probe deeply into the nature of emotional mechanisms in both normal and abnormal persons. For the most part, analytical reports are clinical observations which were made during therapeutic sessions, together with speculative explanations advanced to explain the observations. These explanations usually center around the development of unconscious wishes and desires, and around the ways in which the analyzee either conceals or explains his behavior and thoughts which, for one reason or another, he cannot easily tolerate; that is, the mechanisms of self-deceit. There exists a very considerable literature which has been directed toward the experimental verification of many of the psychoanalytic concepts. Sears[24] recently surveyed these studies as they related to emotional factors.

The concept of infantile sexuality, which forms the basis of many of our emotional attitudes and affective experiences, is well supported by investigations which have been carried out with children and adolescents. Sexual practices in childhood have been shown to be exceedingly common and seem to be associated with the same kind of guilt feeling as is found among adults in comparable conditions.

Freud's theory of an Oedipus relationship (namely, that the child is in love with the parent of the opposite sex which situation patterns most of his later emotional tendencies) has not been universally verified by either experimental or sociological investigations. There are many diverse patterns of family life, and each of them seems to constitute a learning situation for the child and a potential source for his emotional attitudes, but not in the comparatively rigid sense which Freud postulated. In other words, Freud apparently underestimated the wide variety of family relationships in the establishment of early emotional patterns, and possibly overestimated the fantasies related to him by his neurotic patients.

The way in which an emotional tendency, repressed into the unconscious, may show itself in the conscious life of a person is called a "mental mechanism," as was explained in Chap. II. Experimental investigation of these mental mechanisms has not added appreciably to our understanding of the psychology of emotion. The descriptive categories used are so intimately dependent on strong emotions, motives, and language or verbal report that they do not lend themselves to our usual methods of laboratory research. Strong emotion may be generated in animals, and nonemotional language (expressions, gestures) may be studied in man; but an experimental combination has not as yet been worked out with human beings at the present time. Such objective experimentation based on certain of the psychoanalytic concepts would represent a very promising field for future development in the understanding of emotional attitudes and their deviations.

Physiology and Neurology

When we turn to the more objective aspects of emotional disturbances, there are several major questions which immediately present themselves. Is there any part of the central nervous system which, when injured or altered in function, changes affective experience and expression? Will affective experience and expression be changed by alteration in the function of, or by injury to, any one or a combination of the endocrine glands, or by injury to another of the organic systems, such as the digestive or respiratory organs? What is the effect of affective experience on endocrine or brain functions? What do the tests of physiological function, such as blood pressure, metabolism, or brain waves show concerning disturbances in affective experience and expression? In reviewing the evidence relevant to these questions, it should be borne in mind that the emotional display of the abnormal person differs in both its quantity and quality from that of the normal person, and that such differences are often the basis for a judgment of abnormality.

ROLE OF THE NERVOUS SYSTEM

Frontal Lobes of the Cerebral Cortex.[5] A surgical technique called "prefrontal lobotomy" is used in the treatment of certain psychiatric patients. It consists of severing the nervous tracts between the frontal lobes and the thalamus. It usually produces profound emotional changes. There is a quickening of emotional life so that depressed patients lose their "psychic pain." They react more vigorously and abruptly. Some manic patients who were operated on during an excited state calmed down immediately thereafter. All of these changes in temperament and emotionality are said to take place without any measurable intellectual deviation, either in a negative or positive way. The psychological results of this operation will be considered in more detail in Chap. XXVIII.

Temporal Lobes. Klüver and Bucy[10] removed both temporal lobes in monkeys and observed very marked changes in their emotional and personality structure. Following the operation the animals were tame and friendly and seemed to know no fear. They were also extremely hypersexed, having prolonged periods of sexual excitement.

Hypothalamus. The role of the hypothalamus in emotional experience and expression has long been a matter of clinical observation and neurological experimentation.[9] The hypothalamus constitutes part of the midbrain which is the center of many of the basic biological controls of bodily function. Here one finds the nuclei which regulate body temperature, water balance, respiration, various metabolic functions, and certain interrelationships among endocrine functions. In addition, a lesion in this area may result in pathological forced laughing and crying. Direct experimental stimulation of the hypothalamic region produces rage reactions in cats.

Evidently emotional expression is organized in certain portions of the hypothalamus. If this area is disturbed or directly stimulated, a variety of emotional displays may be produced. There is, however, no evidence to indicate that damage or stimulation to this area produces a subjective emotional experience or feelings of pleasantness or unpleasantness. Lashley has summarized the evidence to this point as follows:

> The supposed evidence that the thalamus adds the affective or emotional character to sensations breaks down completely when subjected to critical analysis. The affective changes resulting from thalamic lesion are restricted to a small group of [visceral] sensations and cannot be interpreted as a general change in affectivity. . . . The pathological changes following thalamic lesions are primarily in the character of the sensations, in intensity, duration, localization, and are therefore not relevant to the problem of affect. . . . The only part of the thalamic theory of emotion which has factual support is the localization of motor centers for emotional expression within the hypothalamus. *

Autonomic Nervous System. This division of the nervous system is constituted by a nerve-net which connects the vegetative organs of the body and the central nervous system. It functions in the control of glandular secretions, sweating, heart rate, breathing, digestion, elimination, and sex responses. It is divided into two anatomic divisions: the sympathetic and the parasympathetic. Generally speaking, the activity of the sympathetic division is balanced against or antagonistic to that of the parasympathetic. For example, the heart rate is slowed by nervous excitation reaching it over the parasympathetic system, while it is accelerated by excitation from the sympathetic system.

Stimuli which bring about emotional reactions usually act through

---

* Lashley, K. S., "The Thalamus and Emotion," *Psychol. Rev.*, 1938, *45*, 60.

nervous impulses going out over the autonomic nervous system. According to an hypothesis put forth some years ago by Eppinger and Hess,[4] the depressed type of emotional deviation was attributed to an increase in function of the parasympathetic division, while the excited reactions were due to overfunctioning of the sympathetic division. Much clinical experimentation has been done in an attempt to find whether melancholia and mania are in any way related to continuous dysfunction or irritation of one or the other divisions of the autonomic nervous system. There is still no evidence at hand which would really substantiate this hypothesis. It may be true that depressed and excited patients show certain respective changes in the balance of their autonomic nervous systems, but such changes cannot be assumed to be the basic cause of their emotional deviations. Rather, they may act as a channel by which the deviations are at least partially maintained.

THE ENDOCRINE GLANDS

These are the glands of internal secretion which secrete their chemical products directly into the blood stream. They have been shown to be most important in the regulation and maintenance of internal integration and coordination of organic bodily functions. To a great extent they work together with, and supplement the activity of, the autonomic nervous system.

Thyroid Gland. Either an increase or a decrease in the function of the thyroid gland is followed by a change in the emotional status of the individual. If the secretion of the gland is absent or markedly deficient, the result in the child will be the condition known as "cretinism" (see Chap. X), and in the adult a syndrome called "myxedema." These individuals are sluggish, apathetic, and seemingly defective in emotionality.

Where there is an exaggeration of thyroid function (such as the various forms of goiter), the person tends to be nervous, irritable, apprehensive, and, in general, emotionally unstable. If part of the diseased gland is removed, the emotional instability disappears. A similar emotional condition can be brought about by overdoses of thyroid extract. The symptoms apparently constitute a true deviation in emotional experience and expression. The person feels apprehensive, vaguely unhappy, irritable, and anxious. This feeling is often reinforced by the perception of an increased heart rate and respiration. However, such an apprehensive state is not identical with the subjective experiences of an anxiety neurosis or a reactive depression. The symptoms may be quite similar, but it is impossible to explain all acute anxiety conditions as instances of thyroid dysfunction.

Adrenal Glands. These glands secrete adrenalin into the blood stream, which increases the tremor of voluntary muscle, causes a relaxation of smooth muscle, counteracts fatigue, alters blood distribution and blood pressure, relaxes the bronchioles, causes the liver to release sugar (glycogen), and stimulates the spleen to release red blood corpuscles into the blood stream. These physiological changes brought about by adrenalin are emergency reactions which are thought to prepare the individual to meet a situation demanding quick and prolonged discharge of energy. The reactions themselves do not produce a specific pattern for any one of the emotional states, but they furnish a background for emotional responses.

Several investigators[16] studied the direct effect of adrenalin injection into normal and abnormal adults. In many instances they observed merely the resultant physiological disturbance, which seemed devoid of emotional experience. Other cases reported what is termed a *cold emotion.* That is to say, they had an experience which they felt was somehow emotional in nature, although no situation justifying the experience was at hand. A few individuals reported definite emotional experiences subsequent to the injection of the adrenalin. Sometimes the feeling was so clearly that of anxiety, apprehension, fear, or anger that the subject could detect no difference between ordinary and artificially produced emotional experience.

The Gonads. The gonads or sex glands are known to be directly related to sexual desire and sex feelings. In one psychological study of several male castrates it was found that there was a gradual, but definite, loss in sex desire and potency. Administration of male sex hormone led to a reestablishment of sex desire and sex outlet.[26] This was shown, not only by the overt report and behavior of the individuals, but was confirmed by dreams and other material brought out by the psychoanalytic method. Comparable studies made on women have not been reported, but there is every reason to believe that similar findings would be obtained. There is no good evidence that the administration of large doses of male or female sex hormones leads to any particular change in the sex life or emotionality of the normal person.

The various deviations in sexuality which occur in psychotic and neurotic states have not been found to be directly related to the hormone balance or to the secretion of the gonads. These deviations are only in rare instances related to gonadal dysfunction.

Pituitary Gland. This gland, located at the base of the brain in close approximation to the hypothalamus, is the controlling or master gland of internal secretion. Its secretion and function are essential in maintaining the activities and interrelationships of all the other endocrine glands. Pituitary dysfunction leads to a disturbance in both the emotional life and in the general personality of the individual. These changes in emotionality are not thought to be specific to the gland itself, but rather are the result of a disturbed balance among the other glands. Any deficiency in pituitary function involves inadequate development of the gonads, and hence produces sexual immaturity. Hyperfunction of the gland has a variety of effects. Some of them are irritability and apprehensiveness, duplicating the symptoms shown by goiterous patients.

General. There is ample clinical and experimental evidence demonstrating that either hypofunction or hyperfunction of the glands of internal secretion produces emotional disorders. However, there is no evidence that the major emotional disturbances shown in the psychotic or neurotic patient are (save in the rarest instances) to be attributed to either a dysfunction of any one kind of gland or to a disturbance in the functional balance among the glands. It is possible that future investigation will demonstrate a basic relationship between such conditions as manic-depressive psychosis or involutional melancholia and certain glands of internal secretion. There is a good deal of suggestive evidence that such a relationship may exist. However, the methods now available have not demonstrated the nature of any specific relationship.

ORGANIC SYSTEMS OF THE BODY

In Chap. XVI the psychopathology associated with such common physical diseases as tuberculosis was considered. The possible relationship which may exist between the pathology of some organic system and a deviation in experience or expression of emotion deserves further attention. We all know that when we are frightened or angry we have an increase in heart rate and in breathing. On the other hand, if a person is short of breath, as in asthma, his emotional experience is not one of anger, but of fearful anxiety due to a feeling of suffocation. In the study of the lining of the stomach (gastric mucosa) Wolf and Wolff[28] have shown that the emotional events of everyday life produce visible and pronounced changes in both the blood supply and the surface of the lining itself. Marked and prolonged emotional disturbance may set up small gastric ulcers. In fact, most disturbances of bodily organs are accompanied by emotional reactions which are considered more or less normal. For example, any person suffering from angina or intestinal cramps is expected to be irritable and apprehensive. Only if his irritation or apprehensiveness continues over long periods of time and in the absence of any additional stimulation would his emotional disturbance be called "abnormal."

There is no particular emotional reaction which is specific to any of the organic systems. The ancient observation that affections above the diaphragm are accompanied by euphoria, while those below the diaphragm are accompanied by anxious irritation is occasionally, but not consistently, true. There is no evidence that the organic disturbance must precede the feeling, although often it may do so. The relationship may be in either direction.

PHYSICAL INDICATORS OR MEASURES OF EMOTIONALITY

Certain psychopathologists have urged, on theoretical grounds, that unconscious motives or wishes reveal themselves in some symbolic fashion which involves interference with the orderly function of some one or more of the bodily organs. If this theory is correct, appropriate indicators of such function should show some relationship to one or another mental mechanism. This would be particularly true in regard to the mechanism of *conversion*, since hysterical symptoms are said to express themselves in the malfunctioning of various organs. Even before this theory was advanced, many attempts had been made to determine whether or not disturbed emotional states persisting over a period of time did bring about disordered bodily functions. In light of this theory it is of interest to review briefly the various psychosomatic test findings which have been obtained in emotionally disturbed persons.

Cardiovascular Indicators. These indicators are changes in blood pressure, changes in blood volume, changes in pulse rate, and changes in the electrical response of the heart itself. It is common knowledge that in everyday life, as well as under experimental conditions, pronounced emotional disturbance is attended by changes in all of these cardiovascular indicators. Therefore, it is surprising to find that the profound emotional displays observed in either mania, depression, or anxiety are not consistently reflected by any of these indicators. The pulse rate and blood pressure of the depressed patient are usually found to be somewhat below normal. However, these individuals tend to be very quiet and sedentary, so that the response may only be a reflection of the lack of physical activity. Many manic patients show symptoms of cardiac failure, but this finding is usually interpreted in terms of overactivity and fatigue. In fact, no mental disorder can be properly identified by merely comparing the results obtained with the aid of any one of the cardiovascular indicators before and during a given illness. Without observing the total behavior of a mental patient, it is impossible to tell what the particular emotional content of his psychosis might be.

Respiration. Studies of the breathing curve have been made in practically all groups of psychopathological patients.[3] Generally speaking, the depressed patient shows a shallow type of breathing; the anxious patient, an irregular breathing curve; and the excited patient, a well-marked curve indicating considerable respiratory activity. Since respiration is directly related to verbal expression, a fairly close relationship might be expected to exist between the verbal expressions of disordered emotional experience and the breathing curves. For example, the curve of anxious patients is frequently distinguished by records of sighs, gasps, periods of shallow breathing, and other irregularities. In a sense, it is as if the patient in his anxiety were whispering to himself, and this whispering is reflected in the breathing curve. Unfortunately, no type of curve is directly related to any particular variety of emotional experience, even in normal individuals who exhibit usual and well-defined emotional reactions. If one knows a patient and is familiar with the nature of his emotional troubles, it is sometimes easy to "explain" the characteristics of his breathing curve in terms of possible associations between its irregularities and the particular mental state. However, if one has only a tracing of the respiration and no other knowledge of the patient's symptoms, the diagnosis of the mental state on the basis of such a tracing would be but little better than chance. By examining the electrical record of the activity of the heart, it is possible to diagnose with a great deal of exactitude any cardiac dysfunctions which produce an abnormal record. Some day we may be able to reach the same goal in regard to the breathing curve, but so far it has not been possible.

Blood Chemistry. As mentioned previously, increased activity of the sympathetic division of the autonomic nervous system or of the adrenal glands acts to release sugar into the blood stream. If emotional excitement increases blood sugar, we should be able to measure, after a fashion, the degree of emotional excitement in terms of the level of blood sugar. Whitehorn[27] reported the findings of a blood-sugar study of 958 psychotic patients, 32 of whom were extremely excited at the time the blood sample was obtained. According to his observations, emotional excitement rarely, if ever, produced a rise in the blood-sugar level. High values of blood sugar were found in a very few of the younger patients. High values did occur among older patients, especially in those suffering from somatic disease in addition to their mental disorder. The range of variation in the blood-sugar level of the mental patients did not exceed that of normal individuals of the same age distribution. Other investigators[22] studied the pH (acid-base ratio) of the blood and other bodily fluids in psychotic and in normal individuals. Again, no constant deviation marked any of the clinical varieties of emotional disturbance.

Basal Metabolic Rate. The metabolic rate is an expression of the way in which the body utilizes sugar and eliminates carbon dioxide. It is markedly increased in hyperthyroid conditions and decreased in hypothyroidism. A marked increase in basal metabolism accompanies and follows physical exercise. The rate is at its basal level after sleeping and fasting for eight or ten hours. Since depressed patients are inactive and manic patients extremely overactive, the two contrasting states should be expected to be distinguished by a definite difference in the respective metabolic rates. Actually, there is but little difference in the basal rate in the two states.

Everything that has been said about the basal metabolic rate, respiration, blood chemistry, and cardiovascular reactions is part of a general psychosomatic picture. Evidently, the pathological emotional disturbances do not find the same psychosomatic resonance and organic expression characterizing the normal individual who is emotionally excited. This observation has led to the theory that abnormal emotional experience depends on some dysfunction of the brain itself. The results of prefrontal lobotomy operations apparently support this viewpoint.

Electroencephalogram. The electroencephalographic record of apathetic schizophrenic patients and certain (but not all) depressed patients reveals slow electrical waves of the order of one or two cycles per second, in addition to all of the more rapid wave forms seen in normal individuals. So far, no one has been able to establish any direct relationship between emotional experience or expression and the brain-wave picture. Brain waves have been taken directly by placing an electrode on to the base of the hypothalamus via the upper nasal passage. In this procedure the slow waves from the hypothalamus, thought to be associated with emotional experience, have been found to precede the slow waves obtained from the brain cortex by a few thousandths of a second. Hence, they have been interpreted as "the cortical signal of some conscious correlate of the emotional response."[6]

Apart from this observation, electrical changes as they show themselves in the electroencephalogram are not thought to be indicators or measures of emotional response.

Conditioned Responses. Conditioned responses were established in schizophrenics by Shipley,[25] Mays,[23] and others. They were found difficult to change in these patients, although they may easily be altered in normal individuals and in other varieties of mental patients. This "stickiness" of response in the schizophrenic (particularly the catatonic and hebephrenic types) has been reported by other investigators in regard to certain other physiological indicators as well. It possibly constitutes a clue to the emotional disorganization of some psychiatric patients. Once an emotional pattern of response is established, it seems to be somehow maintained in the organism in a constant fashion and does not disappear when the emergency situation is ended. It may be possible that future research on this point will give us more information about the way in which emotional responses are maintained over long periods of time without any of the expected changes in bodily function.

The Psychogalvanic Reflex. If the human body is connected directly to a sensitive galvanometer, or connected together with a Wheatstone bridge, a small battery, and a galvanometer, changes in the electrical potential of the body, or of the electrical resistance of the body, respectively, may be measured. If, while the body is so connected, a sharp, sudden stimulus occurs, such as a loud sound or a pinprick, there will be a deflection of the galvanometer showing that the electrical potential or the resistance of the body has rapidly changed. This change is called the "psychogalvanic reflex." It was first discovered in the 1870's but systematic investigation of the phenomenon was started by Veraguth in 1904.[14]

Veraguth's findings came to the attention of Jung, who was soon convinced that the reflex was a valid indicator, and even a measure of emotion. Since in Jung's psychoanalytic theory an emotion was the core of a complex, the psychogalvanic method was expected by him to be useful in locating hidden or repressed emotional complexes in pathological mental conditions.

Several of Jung's colleagues investigated this hypothesis and their reports, although conflicting, led others to take up similar investigations.[8] Most of these investigations have been made on schizophrenic and hysterical patients.[11] In general, psychogalvanic reactivity is decreased and the electrical resistance of the body increased in catatonia and in the manic-depressive psychosis. In other forms of dementia praecox, in hysteria, in the neuroses, in alcoholic conditions, and in amentia the findings of different investigators have been so contradictory that it may be concluded that this electrical phenomenon bears no regular relation to the psychopathology or to the emotional disorder. The uniformity of results in catatonia and manic-depressive psychosis is probably to be explained in terms of the raised threshold of attention or preoccupation of the patient. In any event, there is no evidence of relationship between these electrical measurements and the emotional life of the patient.

Landis and Hunt[17] in 1935 reported a study which was directed specifically at the conscious correlates of this reflex. With both normal persons and psychiatric patients they used a wide variety of stimuli, including part of Jung's diagnostic word association list. They obtained careful and adequate introspections following each stimulus. There was clear and unmistakable evidence that the psychogalvanic reflex might occur after any one of a very wide variety of stimuli or situations. The reflex was found to follow any word in the diagnostic word-association list, regardless of whether or not that word was accompanied by any other complex indicator. It has a tendency to occur more frequently when either tension or startle was reported as the conscious correlate. It sometimes occurred *spontaneously;* that is, with no known stimulus or consciously reported mental concomitant. Although the reflex seemed a fairly adequate indicator of the change of direction of mental activity, it was not a perfect or direct measure of these changes. So far as the findings obtained from psychiatric patients could be compared with those of the normals, there was a tendency for the type of conscious state reported to be associated with the particular psychopathology of the individual. In a very general way the psychogalvanic reflex was found to be an indicator of emotional reactions of the sudden or startling variety, of changes in the direction of mental activity, and of activity of the autonomic nervous system.

Summary

The clarification of the basic factors involved in the psychopathology of emotion is a problem of both psychology and physiology. Various methods of studying the subjective nature of emotion have been devised and many of them have added distinctly to our understanding. Interviews, autobiographies, and psychoanalytic methods provide basic material from which further experiments may proceed. The questionnaire method, if tailored to the specific problem under investigation, is productive. In brief, the methods of experimental psychology, when properly applied to these problems, have been fruitful.

The experimental physiology of emotion, normal or abnormal, has brought out many interesting facts. It has been difficult, however, to place these observations in an integrated whole which can be directly related to either clinical material or the findings of experimental psychology. The general impression at present is that all of the facts and observations are true and relevant but that not enough is known which will form a pattern into which the facts may be fitted.

REFERENCES

1. Allport, G. W., *The Use of Personal Documents in Psychological Science*. New York, Soc. Sci. Res. Council Bull. #49, 1942.
2. Benton, A. L., "The Interpretation of Questionnaire Items in a Personality Schedule," *Arch. Psychol.*, 1935, *28*, #190.
3. Dunbar, H. F., *Emotions and Bodily Changes* (2d ed.). New York, Columbia University Press, 1943.
4. Eppinger, H., and L. Hess, *Vagotonia*. New York, Nervous and Mental Disease Monograph, #20, 1917.
5. Freeman, W., and J. W. Watts, *Psychosurgery*. Springfield, Ill., C. C. Thomas, 1942.
6. Hoagland, H., D. E. Cameron, M. A. Rubin, and J. J. Tegelberg, "Emotion in Man as Tested by the Delta Index of the Electroencephalogram: II. Simultaneous Records from the Cortex and from a Region near the Hypothalamus," *Jour. Gen. Psychol.*, 1938, *19*, 247–261.
7. Huston, P. E., D. Shakow, and M. H. Erickson, "A Study of Hypnotically Induced Complexes by Means of the Luria Technique," *Jour. Gen. Psychol.*, 1934, *11*, 65–97.
8. Jung, C. G., *Studies in Word-Association*. London, Heinemann, 1918.
9. Kennedy, F., "Medical Syndromes of the Hypothalamus," *Proc. Asso. Res. Nerv. Ment. Dis.*, 1940, *20*, 864–874.
10. Klüver, H., and P. C. Bucy, "An Analysis of Certain Effects of Bilateral Temporal Lobectomy in the Rhesus Monkey, with Special Reference to 'Psychic Blindness'," *Jour. Psychol.*, 1938, *5*, 33–54.
11. Landis, C., "Psychiatry and the 'Psychogalvanic Reflex'," *Psychiat. Quart.* 1932, *6*, 262–272.
12. ———, "Questionnaires and the Study of Personality," *Jour. Nerv. Ment. Dis.*, 1936, *83*, 125–134.
13. ———, et al., *Sex in Development*. New York, Hoeber, 1940.
14. ———, and H. N. DeWick, "The Electrical Phenomena of the Skin (Psychogalvanic Reflex)," *Psychol. Bull.*, 1929, *26*, 64–119.
15. ———, S. Ferrall, and J. D. Page, "Fear, Anger and Disease," *Amer. Jour. Psychol.*, 1936, *48*, 585–597.

16. ――――, and W. A. Hunt, "Adrenalin and Emotion," *Psychol. Rev.*, 1932, *39*, 467–485.

17. ――――, and ――――, "The Conscious Correlate of the Galvanic Skin Response," *Jour. Exp. Psychol.*, 1935, *18*, 505–529.

18. ――――, and S. E. Katz, "The Validity of Certain Questions which Purport to Measure Neurotic Tendencies," *Jour. Appl. Psychol.*, 1934, *18*, 343–356.

19. ――――, and E. P. Wunderlich, "Religious Attitudes of Psychopathic Patients," *Jour. Abn. Soc. Psychol.*, 1936, *30*, 508–512.

20. Lashley, K. S., "The Thalamus and Emotion," *Psychol. Rev.*, 1938, *45*, 42–61.

21. Leonard, W. E., *The Locomotive God*. New York, Appleton-Century, 1927.

22. McFarland, R. A., and H. Goldstein, "The Biochemistry of Manic-Depressive Psychosis," *Amer. Jour. Psychiat.*, 1939, *96*, 21–58.

23. Mays, L. L., "Studies of Catatonia," V, *Psychiat. Quart.*, 1934, *8*, 728–735.

24. Sears, R. R., *Survey of Objective Studies of Psychoanalytic Concepts*. New York, Soc. Sci. Res. Council Bull., #51, 1943.

25. Shipley, W. C., "Studies of Catatonia," VI, *Psychiat. Quart.*, 1934, *8*, 736–744.

26. Tauber, E. S., and G. E. Daniels, "Sex Hormones and Psychic Conflict: A Case Report," *Psychosom. Med.*, 1941, *3*, 72–86.

27. Whitehorn, J. C., "The Blood Sugar in Relation to Emotional Reactions," *Amer. Jour. Psychiat.*, 1934, *13*, 987–1005.

28. Wolf, S. and H. G. Wolff, *Human Gastric Function*. New York, Oxford, 1943.

Chapter XXVI

DISORDERS OF VOLITION

THAT PHASE of human mental life and behavior, which in everyday conversation is called "will," is commonly omitted from general psychology. This omission grows out of the fact that the term *will* and all of its dependent concepts are involved in complex questions, such as "freedom of the will," "intent and responsibility," or "will power," which have specific meanings in the law and in philosophy. Psychologists usually avoid these issues, since not much gain could come from entering into this controversial field. However, if one continues to accept a common-sense view of psychopathology, then a consideration of disorders of volition and will must be included. Certainly, in everyday life we always speak and act as though everyone (including ourselves) has some sort of mental process which we all call "will." This phenomenon is related to the behavior which we speak of as *voluntary*, in contrast to *involuntary* or "unwilled" behavior.

Disorders of will and volition are an outstanding characteristic of abnormal behavior and mentality. Unfortunately, there is but little experimental literature bearing directly upon the measurement of voluntary and involuntary behavior, or bearing upon the will as it enters into the mental life of any individual. Most mental patients complain at one time or another that they are "forced" to do things against their will; that there is some inner compulsion which is beyond their self-control. Other patients complain of a lack of will power; of an inability to make up their minds even when they desire to do so. In the same fashion the friends and relatives of a neurotic or psychotic patient usually have the idea that the patient could get well if he wanted to; that his mental peculiarities are somehow due to a lack of will power.

That individuals differ in the degree of volition, just as they do in intelligence or emotion, goes without saying. Some are determined, strong-willed, and decisive; while others are spineless, indecisive, and very suggestible. Just what the limits of variation in voluntary behavior are has not been determined. There is no scale of volition comparable to intelligence tests. Nevertheless, the gross deficits in voluntary behavior which occur in psychopathological persons are obvious, and these deficits in degree or quality provide certain distinctive elements in the classification of mental disorders. The following aphorism illustrates the role of will impairment: "The patient says, 'I cannot'; his family says, 'He will not'; while the truth is, 'He cannot will'."

Disregarding all of the philosophical speculation concerning the nature of will, the major difficulty with the psychological formulation of the problem of the psychopathology of volition lies in the fact that there is so little relevant experimental material to serve as an anchorage in fact. There are a few experiments which deal with the level of aspiration (willful ambition), interrupted activity, and perseveration or persistence, in which normal and abnormal persons have been compared. The results, though interesting, do not shed too much light on the central problem.

An additional difficulty comes from the fact that many psychopathologists are convinced that clinical descriptions, oriented in terms of disorders of volition, are essentially meaningless. They point out that therapy directed toward rehabilitation of "will power" is unsuccessful. They also point to the long history of human thought which attributed mental abnormality to disorders of will, and to therapy which was based on punishment — a l of which led nowhere. For reasons such as these, there is but little modern clinical literature which deals with disorders of volition. A psychological formulation of the problem of volition was made by the German psychologist, Ach, and his principles were applied to psychopathology by Bostroem. Our presentation will, in the main, follow Ach[1] and Bostroem.[3]

Components of the Will Process

Ach, on the basis of his extensive investigations of volition, analyzed the phenomenon into three major components — *will-act, voluntary action*, and *motivation*. These three components together constitute a *determining tendency*. (See Fig. 13.) By will-act is meant the moment of decis on in the mind of the individual, at which instant the thought process is experienced as a subjective feeling which may be described by the phrase, "I now really will." Voluntary action is the actual carrying out of the activity, until the goal is attained which was decided upon in the will-act. Motivation refers to all of those factors which are felt or comprehended as causes of a given action. Factors of motivation may be overtly conscious, partly conscious, or truly subconscious. In

any case, they lead to the decision and, hence, to voluntary activity.
The entire process of motivation, decision, and volitional activity
constitutes a determining tendency. Such a tendency grows out of the
motivation; is released by the will-act; and continues to operate with
or without the awareness of the person until the goal is reached. Only
if some insurmountable obstacle happens to block the entire determining tendency, does the need for a new decision and a new line of voluntary activity arise, thus leading to a new determining tendency.

We will consider the disorders of will-act, voluntary activity,
motivation, and determining tendency as they occur in different

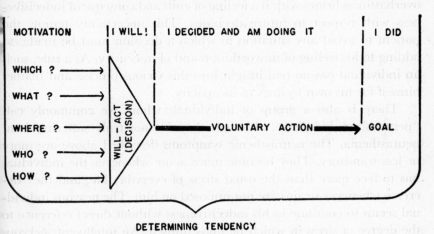

Fig. 13. *Schematic diagram of the voluntary process.*

psychopathological conditions, together with clinical descriptions and
such experimental evidence as is available. It should be borne in mind
that pure will pathology, unaccompanied by other morbid psychological disturbances, does not exist; any more than pure disturbance of
intellect or emotion exists.

Disorders of Will-Act (Decision)

That it is easier to "make up our minds" when we are wide-awake
and in good spirits is obvious. It becomes difficult to make decisions
when we are ill, fatigued, or frustrated. We usually say that a person
has good self-control and self-discipline when he is able to make decisions in spite of physical limitations due to illness or fatigue.

An example of a disorder in will-act is found in neurasthenia. Here
the patient is possessed by a feeling of fatigue and, with it, indecision.
He is unable to concentrate his attention on anything for more than

a very short period of time. Realizing that it has become more difficult for him to make decisions, he attempts to compensate for the difficulty with an increased effort and tension. Since this effort cannot be sustained, he will be more irritable and impulsive with respect to the decisions which he has to make. This overcompensation, extra attention, irritability, and impulsiveness add to the initial fatigue which the patient experiences. They have a cumulative effect and set up a greater and greater level of abnormal fatigue which finally results in a more or less complete incapacitation. These circumstances force the patient to substitute quick decisions for accurate, considered judgment. The overhastiness brings with it a feeling of guilt and consequent indecisiveness with respect to future decisions. This uncertainty tempts the patient to avoid any situation in which a decision must be made, so adding to his feeling of unworthiness and of insecurity. As a rule, such an individual has no real insight into this vicious process and blames himself for his own feelings of incapacity.

There is also a group of individuals whom we commonly call "nervous" or indecisive, although they are not truly suffering from neurasthenia. The neurasthenic symptoms described above are more or less transitory. They become more acute whenever the individual has to face more than the usual stress of everyday life, and they decrease whenever strains are not imposed on him. The nervous individual seems to continue in his indecisiveness without direct reference to the degree of stress in which he finds himself. An intelligent, nervous person often succeeds by substituting for his indecisiveness a feeling of social coercion or consciousness of duty which he attributes to outside sources without making it a part of his own self-consciousness. Such persons can concentrate only with difficulty and are continually fatigued, never knowing their own desires. They are unable to finish actions which they have started, unless they are forced to do so. They are characterized, not only by this volitional weakness, but by restlessness, mannerisms, and the like, which are expressions of their inner indecisiveness. According to Lindworsky,[7] who has made experimental studies of these nervous individuals, their deficiency is not so much in the will-act as in their motivation. If the situation itself exerts compulsion, they are able to make the decision and to carry through the voluntary activity regardless of the presence or absence of any intrinsic worthwhileness which the action may have.

On occasions when we are sad or depressed, we find it difficult to make decisions. There will be a lack of spontaneity in all mental processes which include voluntary processes and, particularly, will-acts. In pronounced depressions, it has been suggested by some investigators that it is the will-act which is the most affected element in voluntary activity. This opinion is based on the observation that once certain depressed patients have made a decision voluntary action is carried out, even though in a very slow fashion. Patients who are in, or near, a stuporous depression show a complete lack of voluntary action because of their apparent inability to make decisions which will lead to any type of activity. That they are definitely lacking in decisiveness is demonstrated by the lack of the spontaneous expressions associated with automatized behavior. In such a depressive stupor the mere task of getting up and dressing, which is usually done automatically, will require tremendous effort. The patient intends and desires to arise and go about the day's activity. He will reproach himself for failing to do so, but he is incapable of making the decision which will lead to the voluntary action.

In sharp contrast to the difficulty which the depressed or fatigued individual has in making decisions, is the rapid capacity for will-acts as seen in the euphoric or manic patient. The manic is characterized by a high level of optimism with respect to both his own capacities and to his ability to react to any situation which may present itself. He neither realizes difficulties which may arise nor exhibits inhibitions or countermotives. If such mechanisms operate, they are not important enough to influence his decisions. In fact, every manic feels that the success of any activity which he has decided upon is assured from the very beginning. He makes rapid decisions because he does not entertain any ideas of consequences, difficulty, or distrust. He readily shifts his activity from one process to another and, in so doing, revokes decisions and replaces them with new ones. Seemingly, there is no consistent and sustained motivation, but only a generalized state of directed voluntary activity, depending upon a momentary will-act, which can be readily upset or substituted by another will-act. While the decision itself may be altered in nature, there is no evidence of any real pathology in this part of the voluntary process. The patient never suffers from any difficulty in handling momentary wishes, strivings, or ambitions, but proceeds directly to a decision in each instance, even though the new decision runs contrary to those previously made. The result will be a lack of coordination and cooperation among the various parts of the will process, particularly with regard to the general combined process, that is, the determining tendency.

An apparent absence of the will-act is seen in tics, obsessional rituals (hand washing), and the like. The patient has a felt "need" for the activity which he describes as forced upon him. The motivation leads directly to action — either voluntary or involuntary without a decision. The patient reports that the process has motivation, action, and a goal but lacks any necessity for decision on his part.

Disorders of Voluntary Action

An example of a disorder in voluntary action, apparently uncomplicated by disturbance of either will-act or motivation, is found in the accounts given by certain persons who attempted suicide.[2] Due to feelings of dejection and hopelessness, they were overpowered by self-destructive intentions which carried on as an underlying theme of voluntary action in spite of all other tendencies, decisions, or basic motivation. Such persons state that they acted as though they were happy and well contented. They suppressed the usual expressive movements related to their sadness and dejection. They carried out the role of an actor without the advantage of an actor's training. Their expressive movements, the content of their thoughts, and, consequently, their entire life seemed to them to be artificial. This may be explained by assuming that there was an abnormally intense, powerful, and continuing voluntary action or stream of voluntary activity which carried on until such an individual arrived at the point where there was the physical opportunity for the execution of his plan. No difficult decision was involved in the selection of either the method or the time of the suicide when the attempt was made. The voluntary action usually carried the individual to the opportunity without any attendant necessity of decision.

Another variety of disturbance in voluntary action is shown in the outbursts of excitement seen in various groups of psychotic patients, particularly those in whom there is some brain damage. In a state of excitement certain psychotic patients display a stream of voluntarily directed activity in which there seems to be no element of decision or adequate motivation. When such a patient comes out of a depression or stupor, he may show tremendous excitement associated with destructive tendencies, and then will relapse into his former stuporous state. During the excitement his activity seems well directed and coordinated. He cannot easily be diverted from his goal and anyone who attempts to divert him is opposed and may even suffer physical injury.

Disorders of Motivation

In certain patients who are in a catatonic stupor there is an exalted thought process found in conjunction with inadequate emotionality and with some facial expression and occasional gestures, but with few other movements. Here, the patient is overpowered by pathologically determined "motives" which follow each other in close succession and are never really transformed into either decision or voluntary activity. Thus, despite the profusion of thought, the intensity of motives precludes any actual voluntary activity. This process may go so far that the patient is completely inattentive and, hence, appears to be totally self-engrossed or almost unconscious. Such patients will later report that their thoughts came so rapidly and intensely that it was as if they were living in a vivid dream. They seem to have witnessed the experience without themselves taking part in it. Whenever these catatonic patients act under the influence of certain motives, they behave in a very distractible and changeable fashion which is extremely difficult to comprehend.

The way in which motives are shaped and transformed into voluntary action is commonly referred to as the "basis of judgments of value." There is variation in the values of different persons, and this variation accounts in great part for the differences in tastes and customs among people. So long as the variations in values continue to be accepted by most members of the community, no particular problems present themselves. However, when any considerable variation in values, either social or moral, does arise in a community, it may lead to real difficulties. The majority of normal persons in our civilization tend to accept as desirable values our customs with respect to security, opportunity for work and personal advancement, religious freedom, freedom to choose an occupation, standards of honor, pride and honesty, social status, and, in a larger sense, good manners. Such values are usually taken for granted and are maintained without too much difficulty. The normal person will subordinate his momentary desires for what seems to him to be ultimately a greater good or a greater value. If a person is not feeble-minded or demented, he is expected by us to fit into a general set of values which the community holds. We also assume that if any individual of average intelligence does not conform with these values, he is capable of being educated to meet the standards if his attention is properly directed.

Certain psychopathic personalities show a deviation in their motives and, consequently, in value judgments. Such individuals are marked by an inability to apply themselves to routine or continuous work; an inability to judge right from wrong in the same terms that most members of the community use; an inability to fit into the standards, values, and motives which actuate their fellows. They are easily discouraged, frequently change occupations, fall easily in and out of love, neglect their children, friends, and relatives, change religious affiliation without good reason, and show other similar character vacillations. These defects may be attributed to a deficiency in motive formation, since they can make decisions and carry through voluntary activity. The direction of the activity varies and is claimed by some investigators to have no fixed relationship to the rest of the personality structure or mental life of the individual. In short, these individuals are characterized by a basic and usually permanent defect in value formation. The same is true for the moral imbecile, whose motives are either absent or so completely inverted that he cannot properly distinguish right from wrong and, consequently, cannot be trusted to form adequate value judgments.

Disorders of the Determining Tendency

Decision, voluntary action, and motivation together form the mental experience and behavior called "determining tendency," which is volition in action. If an individual cannot be aroused to take part in any voluntary action — that is, if he shows no determining tendencies — he is said to be suffering from *aboulia*. This state occurs in schizophrenia and in other forms of mental deterioration.

There are two groups of factors involved in the establishment of a determining tendency: (*a*) the internal processes, and (*b*) external events which occur during the process and which either facilitate or inhibit the tendency. Once a specific task is undertaken and a specific determining tendency is set in action, a person may be (1) fully prepared for any other events — facilitating or inhibiting — which may occur; (2) he may be only partly prepared; or (3) he may be totally unprepared. Lack of flexibility in the determining tendency is spoken of as *mental rigidity*. If the motives are set and the voluntary activity is relatively intense, the individual is said to be showing "a high degree of concentration" on the task before him, or to be "unyielding in his determination." In many persons suffering from organic brain damage, this inflexibility is so strong that it may lead to automatic behavior. Milder degrees of determination are responsible for one-sidedness in thinking and action. Such conditions are found in the paranoid patient who treats all situations in light of some particular over-evaluated motive of his own. A similar mechanism may operate in either the epileptic or the compulsive neurotic patient.

Inflexibility may be thought of as a form of compulsion in which the determining tendency has become so pronounced that it overwhelms most of the individual's mental life. Schizophrenic compulsion appears to be related to hallucinatory experiences of the patient. In some cases of chronic alcoholism the compulsion grows out of an habitual response which has been favored by the use of alcohol as an escape mechanism. In the obsessive neurotic, particularly, certain activities may become so compulsory that the person develops feelings of powerlessness of will, of being overcome, or of a lack of personal responsibility with respect to the outcome of his own action. The usual reaction of a compulsive patient is one of perplexity — he cannot give an explanation which is satisfactory to himself. He may attempt to account for his action through some sort of rationalization, attributing the compulsion to the Devil, Divine influence, or bad childhood habits. Such individuals become fearful that their compulsions will lead them to injure either themselves or someone else. Therefore, they set up defense actions in the form of continually repeated acts which are ceremonies or symbols serving to block momentarily the overwhelming compulsion of their determining tendency.

A specialized form of compulsion is perseveration. It consists in the tendency to reproduce previously used phrases, ideas, images, or previously executed acts which are irrelevant to the situation at hand instead of those which are relevant. Abnormal perseveration occurs whenever adequate performance is for some reason impossible. If such a blockage develops, it sometimes happens that the speech or motor action immediately preceding is repeated over and over again, much as a phonograph record repeats when the needle continues going round in the same groove. It is as if the will action, unable to continue in a forward direction, slides into the previously traversed path. A similar mechanism takes place in a speaker who repeats some sentence or expression when he becomes fatigued or when some question is raised for which he cannot, or does not want to, give a ready answer. Perseveration is clearly seen in some forms of aphasia. It appears in the aphasic when some action is required which is impossible for him to perform.

From the point of view of disturbances of volition, perseveration occurs when the determining tendencies for a given task are overcome, blocked, or diverted in some fashion by inhibiting events or ideas. The perseverating individual desires to respond (there is a tendency toward a genuine decision); he desires to carry out the required act (there is a tendency to voluntary action); but the act does not succeed because it lacks either the motivation or the favoring circumstances. Hence, the previously executed activity continues in a repetitive, secondary fashion. The continuing behavior is carried on automatically in the form which is most readily available, but without a new determining tendency.

Perseveration effects are not necessarily associated with any morbid process or with any particular character trait. They may occur whenever an attempt to do something new is blocked. If a person has the capacity for appreciating the consequences of his own determining tendency and persists toward his goal despite blockage or deviation, we say that he is determined. When there is a lack of elasticity and adaptiveness with respect to other inhibiting and facilitating factors, determination becomes inflexibility.

The action of many drugs (alcohol, cocaine, or opium) weakens voluntary activity, particularly with respect to the determining tendency. The addict can make decisions, has motives, and can carry through voluntary action though each element is reduced in strength. Hence, the determining tendencies of the addict become more and more inadequate.

Peculiarities of Volition in Different Mental Disorders

DEMENTIA PRAECOX

The earlier manifestations of a developing schizophrenic psychosis include disorders of volition. Decisions become so difficult and motivations are so defective that voluntary action takes on an automatic character. Such patients lack spontaneity and energy and are preoccupied with their own thoughts and feelings to the exclusion of external events. They can carry out in an orderly fashion certain activities demanding voluntary cooperation, if direction and initiative are supplied from without. They can apply themselves quite effectively and persistently to a given problem if properly directed from the outside. In the more advanced stages of the disease, however, very few patients can be aroused to spontaneous activity even if the stimulation is both intense and painful. Most schizophrenics follow orders, but seem to lack any of the self-motivation which ordinarily carries through volitional activity of everyday life.

The stuporous behavior of a catatonic patient is an exception to what has just been said. In such a stupor there seems to be a counterbalancing of motives, so that no decisions or voluntary activities result. These patients appear completely blocked by their conflicting motives. They either resist all sorts of stimulation from the outside (negativism), or they totally comply with outside stimulation without taking part in it (waxy flexibility).

When schizophrenic patients are subjected to experimental procedures involving interrupted activity, they have been found to respond to the interruptions somewhat differently than do normals.[10] The normal person will resume about three fourths of interrupted tasks, but the schizophrenic will resume less than one half of such interrupted activity. In addition, the patients often spontaneously interrupt their actions, and even those who finally complete a given task do so only after repeated interruptions of their own making. This finding indicates that their determining tendency is not nearly so strong as that of the normal person with respect to the attaining of a goal. Further evidence for this explanation may be seen in the observation that certain of the patients easily lose the thread of their thoughts and wander off from the point at issue with little or no reason for the diversion.

Experiments on the level of aspiration exhibited by dementia praecox patients have shown that their "ambition" differs from that of the normal person. Most patients tend to lower their level of predicted success after a failure and raise it after they have been successful. The paranoid patient is inclined to hold fixedly to a high level of aspiration regardless of failure. These level-of-aspiration experiments are essentially related to motivation and agree with the clinical observations of the motivational defects of such patients.

MANIC-DEPRESSIVE PSYCHOSIS

The disorders of volition shown by both the manic and the depressed patients have already been commented upon. The increased facility with which decisions are made and changed during manic excitement is peculiar to this disorder, just as the inability to carry through voluntary action is peculiar to depression. The clinical picture of the manic is characterized by an apparent increase in will-acts and by rapid decisions. His decisions are scarcely ever motivated by deliberation and are not affected by inhibitions. Self-control plays little or no role, so that the more elaborate types of volitional activity cannot be effective in controlling either instinctive or habitual behavior. In contrast to the experimental findings on level of aspiration in schizophrenic patients, it was found that in depressed patients neither success nor failure tended to change their rather low level of aspiration as indicated by their own prediction of achievement on the next task.[4] Manic patients were affected by failure and tended to be variable in predicting the degree of success which would attend the next task to be attempted.

GENERAL PARESIS

In the initial stages of general paresis, the developing changes in judgment and sense of values indicate a disorder of motive formation. As a result, the decisions which are made on a false or inaccurate evaluation of the situation (imperception) lead to incorrect or non-adjustive determining tendencies. As the disease progresses the perceptions and thought processes on which a decision must be based become more and more inaccurate, so that active decisions for correctly motivated behavior are finally totally absent.

Voluntary activity of the habitual variety, which does not depend upon new decisions, is not markedly affected in the earlier stages of the disease process; but when general motor disabilities begin to appear, they usually involve a disturbance in habitual volitional activity.

The following are examples of the ways in which volitional defects show themselves in general paresis. Before there is any true motor paralysis, the patients exhibit a number of incorrectly executed motor acts. They will put on their coats without their vests, or put on two neckties but forget a collar. When requested to flex their fingers, they will extend them; or when requested to make a kicking movement forward, they kick backward. Such incorrect movements are usually accompanied by movements of other parts of the body, thus resembling the incoordination shown by a growing child. These errors have been attributed to the fact that the patient has only a vague awareness of his awkwardness. Any incipient movements which are started carry through without correction because the patient cannot command sufficient voluntary attention or motivation to correct or inhibit the inappropriate response. Many of these patients give the impression of happy indifference to the world around them. This state of euphoria apparently grows out of the disorders in both emotion and volition. The paretic does not seem concerned about the possible unhappy consequences of his statements or his actions. The intellectual deterioration, the disorders in the ability to generalize, the emotional instability, all act to disrupt the course of voluntary action. Paresis serves as an illustration of the interdependence of mental functions, in that all such factors are disordered together with volition.

OLD AGE

In old age, even if the habitual behavior in everyday tasks is well preserved, there usually is a marked decline in the number of decisions which are made and acted upon. This decline is associated with both a deterioration in intellectual ability and the tendency to avoid decisions. As a result, old people find it difficult to start new types of activity or to overcome unexpected obstacles. The inability to make decisions may be accompanied by either stubbornness or undue suggestibility. Stubbornness grows out of the tendency to stick to those types of behavior which are habitual and, hence, more convenient than an attempt to develop new attitudes. If there is no adequate habitual response to use, the old person may be unduly suggestible, since it is easier to follow a suggestion than it is to make a decision. Any apparent increase in will activity which may occur in the aged is, generally speaking, not a real increase, but the result of a shift from one habitual response to another because of restlessness and changing motivation.

MENTAL DEFICIENCY

In idiocy or the lower grades of imbecility there is little or no development of volition. Any of the higher voluntary activities requires the participation of a fair degree of intellect. High-grade imbeciles and morons show a very wide variety of manifestations of volitional deficit and disorder.[5] This variability is due to both the differences in intellectual level and the differences in types of amentia. Occasionally, unusual motor ability or particular skills will conceal most of the volitional deficiency. Habit training is about as much as can be accomplished in the imbecile, since there is too little intelligence to support adequate will-acts or decisions.

In an experiment using the method of interrupted activities, the performance of moron children was compared with that of normal children. The mental defectives were found to resume their initial interrupted activity in practically every instance, while the normals would resume the activity in less than 75 per cent of the tasks.[8, 9] If a substitute task was interpolated after the interrupted task, the feeble-minded children would still resume 95 per cent of the interrupted activity, but the normals only 30 per cent. If the substitute activity was placed as closely as possible to the interrupted activity — for example, if the children were told to draw pictures of animals on red paper and, following interruption, were told to draw the animal on green paper — the feeble-minded had a record of 80 per cent resumption of the interrupted activity, while the normals showed very little tendency toward resuming their activity. Evidently, once a decision has been made by a moron either upon his own initiative or that of others, his voluntary action carries on in spite of interruption. This tendency is in contrast to the behavior of the normal child who requires a new will-act or a reinforcement of an old one before carrying on after interrupted activity.

Another series of experiments was designed to determine the working ability of different groups of children under conditions of forced activity, and under free working conditions. Again the results obtained in mentally retarded and in normal children differed considerably. Normal children did about three fourths as well under free working conditions as they did under forced conditions; while the retarded children worked only about 10 per cent as well under free conditions as under forced activity. This finding implies that the normal individual possesses normal will functions and, hence, can continue work freely upon his own inner motivation. However, will capacity and inner motivation are either absent or defective in the mentally retarded individual, accounting for part of his low level of performance.

EPILEPSY

Certain clinical observers have claimed (without experimental verification) that the epileptic inflexibility in thought and behavior can be related to the patients' inability to adjust their decisions to new circumstances. Some epileptic patients during a psychic seizure or a furor are unable to shift a line of voluntary action or a determining tendency which has been set in progress. They cannot readjust this tendency even when new circumstances arise which demand reconsideration. Attempts at diverting such patients, particularly when they are excited, are futile. No new decision can be made until the voluntary act already in progress has been completed to their own satisfaction.

ORGANIC CONDITIONS

It is possible that the disturbance in memory characterizing Korsakoff's syndrome may be directly connected with a disturbance of the will process. These patients show an inability to free themselves from a particular line of thought or activity which is operative. They are incapable of making new associations and new decisions with respect to subject matter which comes up in the course of their activity. If the attendant stimulation is intense enough, they attempt to realign their thinking and behavior, so that part of the falsification of memory is a filling in of material based on faulty decisions and incorrect motivation.

Volitional inflexibility and perseveration occur in patients suffering from organic brain pathology. This is associated with other disturbances, such as aphasia, apraxia, and amnesia. States of clouded consciousness, which are a symptom of brain injury or epilepsy, are also marked by perseveration. This symptom does not seem to be related to any definite localization of brain injury, but to a general disturbance in the organization of thought which occurs when any part of the brain is involved.

Summary

The present theories on disorders of will are largely based on clinical observation, while little experimental evidence is available to verify or evaluate the reported observations. An outstanding defect shown by many groups of mentally abnormal persons is their inability to respond voluntarily, as does a normal individual. This disorder of volition is very widely diversified in the way in which it appears in both the mental life and the behavior of the patients.

The analysis of volition into will-act, voluntary activity, and motivation — the three components making up a determining tendency — can be directly applied in psychopathology. Examples of defects in each of these components and in the entire determining tendency have been presented in connection with different mental conditions. A consideration of the psychopathology of volition as it is exhibited in the different varieties of mental disease sheds additional light on the problems involved.

Most of the experimental work which has bearing on volition has been done with schizophrenic patients or mentally defective children. It may be expected that experimental investigation of the complex disorders of volition in other varieties of mental disease will contribute interesting and valuable information to the understanding of abnormal psychology.

REFERENCES

1. Ach, N., "Analyse des Willens," *Handbuch der biologischen Arbeitsmethoden*, Abt. VI, Teil E, Berlin, Urban und Schwarzenberg, 1935.
2. Anon., "Ex-suicide," *Harper's Magazine*, 1932 (Sept.), *165*, 426–435.
3. Bostroem, A., "Störungen des Wollens," in O. Bumke, *Handbuch der Geisteskrankheiten*, Band II, Teil II, 1–90, Berlin, Springer, 1928.
4. Escalona, S. K., "The Effect of Success and Failure upon the Level of Aspiration and Behavior in Manic-Depressive Psychoses," *Univ. Iowa. Stud. Child Welfare*, 1940, *16*, 197–302.

5. Gottschaldt, K., "Der Aufbau des kindlichen Handelns," *Beih. z. Zsch. f. angew. Psychol.*, No. 68, 1933.

6. Hausmann, M. F., "A Test to Evaluate Some Personality Traits," *Jour. General Psychol.*, 1933, *9*, 179–189.

7. Lindworsky, J., "Die Willensdefekte vom Standpunkt der Normalpsychologie," *Ber. d. I. heilpäd. Kong.*, 1923, 45–61.

8. Rethlingshafer, D., "Measures of Tendency-to-Continue: I. Behavior of Feebleminded and Normal Subjects Following Interruption of Activities," *Jour. Genet. Psychol.*, 1941, *59*, 109–124.

9. ———, "Measures of Tendency-to-Continue: II. Comparison of Feebleminded and Normal Subjects when Interrupted under Different Conditions, *Jour. Genet. Psychol.*, 1941, *59*, 125–138.

10. Rickers-Ovsiankina, M., "Studies on the Personality Structure of Schizophrenic Individuals: II. Reaction to Interrupted Tasks," *Jour. General Psychol.*, 1937, *16*, 179–196.

Chapter XXVII

INTELLECTUAL DETERIORATION AND DISORGANIZATION

THE INTERFERENCE with intellectual efficiency in every form of mental disease, whether a psychosis or a neurosis, is unquestioned. This loss of mental ability is called "deterioration" or "dementia." The term *dementia* is sometimes applied to those conditions which show a progressive and irrevocable change associated with organic brain damage, while the term *deterioration* is usually applied to those cases which show progressive mental loss without assumption as to the cause or permanency of the change. In the following discussion the terms *dementia*, *deterioration*, and *psychological deficit* are used interchangeably without reference to the basis of the mental loss.

Measurement of Mental Deterioration

Mental deterioration varies in degree from barely perceptible changes to gross defects in all phases of conscious life. In order to determine both the quality and the quantity of mental deterioration, the obvious and desirable procedure would be to compare an individual's present performance with the scores he made prior to the onset of the illness on similar psychological tests. In the great majority of cases, there are no previous test results available, so that we must be satisfied with "next bests," most of which are none too adequate, but are all that are available.

Since standardized intelligence tests are among the best tools of a clinical psychologist they are regularly used both with individual patients and with the various groups and subgroups of abnormal persons. This testing has provided a mass of comparative information concerning the performance of the abnormal and the normal. In order to work out an evaluation of the group or individual scores, abnormal subjects are compared to the test norms or, in some investigations, to matched control groups. The results from different studies are not always in agreement because of variations in such factors as the number of cases, age, and type of patients available for study, the inclusion of uncooperative cases, and standards of diagnosis used.

Hunt and Cofer[12] have brought together in a systematic way the results of the various studies of the general intelligence of psychiatric patients. They concluded that the mental-age scores reported (from the Stanford-Binet, Yerkes Point Scale, and Bellevue Wechsler) cannot be interpreted as establishing absolute limits, although the relation among scores in the different diagnostic groups is of interest. In general, the results for these groups may be arranged from the greatest to the least psychological deficit (allowing for considerable overlap between the groups) as follows: senile dementia, general paresis, hebephrenic schizophrenia, chronic alcoholic dementia, catatonic and paranoid forms of schizophrenia, paranoia, psychopathic personality, manic-depressive psychosis, and psychoneurosis.

These comparisons between the varieties of mental abnormality supply interesting information concerning the general problem of deterioration, but they do not afford very much knowledge of the nature of that deterioration. Many demented patients are uncooperative and the question often arises as to whether the test results are truly representative of the patient's ability. For example, Roe and Shakow[17] went over the Binet test results of 827 patients suffering from different types of mental disease and, of these, one third of the tests were considered unrepresentative of the patients' mental ability.

A further difficulty lies in the fact that many studies of deterioration have used as an independent criterion psychiatrists' ratings of deterioration as a basis of determining the accuracy of the test results. This rating is not very satisfactory since the standards used vary widely among different psychiatrists. One will give most weight to social behavior and personal habit patterns; another, to the emotional life; and still another, to the patient's general alertness and responsiveness.

In order to meet these and other problems raised by the comparative use of tests, clinical psychologists have tried to find characteristics in the immediate test performance (that is, tests given during the mental illness) which would be indicative of both mental deterioration and the original level of mental ability.

"SCATTER" AS A MEASURE OF DETERIORATION

The range of successful performance on the subtests at the different mental-age levels on the Binet test has been called "scatter." The amount of scatter was believed (for a while, at least) to be an index of deterioration. The "spottiness" or irregularity of the test performance was assumed to be characteristic of deterioration. The results of many of the older investigators indicated that psychotic patients (both of the functional and organic types) showed wider scatter than did normal children. However, Kendig and Richmond[13] found that the scatter is little or no greater among psychotics than it is among normal adults. Harris and Shakow[11] established the fact that mental-age level correlates with the amount of scatter and that when this factor is held constant, the difference in scatter between normal and abnormal adults disappears. These findings indicate that scatter is not an adequate measure of deterioration.

The emphasis on scatter in the performance of psychotic patients was part of the general theory which held that dementia is a pattern of isolated defects in specific functions. This view has been supplanted by the idea of impairment in the general performance of the patient, as evidenced in a wide range of test situations. It is still believed that certain functions are less impaired than others or, in other words, are more resistant to the process of deterioration, and that the differential effect of impairment may form a basis for measuring deterioration.

THE BABCOCK METHOD AND THE SHIPLEY METHOD

Babcock[2] utilized the observation that the vocabulary (ability to use or define words) remains relatively unaffected when other performances are impaired. She took the vocabulary levels on standardized tests as approximations of the subjects' previous levels of intelligence. The difference between these levels and the general performance levels on a battery of tests, including measures of the speed of response in the use of old associations, recognition tests, and new learning material, she termed an *index of mental efficiency*. The wider the discrepancy between vocabulary and performance level on these other tests, the greater is the amount of mental deterioration. This index is, in effect, a ratio between the stable, remaining functions and the unstable, disorganized functions. Application of this battery of tests has shown that general paresis, cerebral arteriosclerosis, and epilepsy have a low mental efficiency. Schizophrenics also show a loss in mental efficiency, but this is somewhat less than that found in the organic psychoses.

A difficulty arises when one attempts to be too precise or to put too much weight on this index. This difficulty springs from the fact that the vocabulary function is not a simple one and that it also deteriorates. As Capps[7] demonstrated in epileptic patients, and

Ackelsberg[1] in senile dementia, all measures of vocabulary function show a consistent and progressive reduction in score associated with increased degrees of mental deterioration. In addition to the fact that vocabulary test level is not too adequate as an index of former mental level, the assumption that vocabulary really is less affected than other psychological functions has been criticized. For example, it has been suggested that the deteriorated patient's apparently superior performance on a vocabulary test may be due to the fact that vocabulary is an untimed test and a prolonged performance is given an acceptable score, whereas in other tests the requirements are stricter.

Shipley[19] devised a method for measuring intellectual impairment which consists in a comparison of the performances on a vocabulary test and on a test of the ability to grasp abstract relationships. The abstraction test requires the subject to infer a general principle from a series of items, and from this to deduce the specific answer. The degree of mental impairment is measured in terms of the ratio of the abstraction score (a rapidly disintegrating function) to the vocabulary score (a relatively stable function). This ratio, or *conceptual quotient*, is taken as a measure of the degree of mental impairment.

Both the Babcock method and the Shipley method are distinct advances in the field of experimental abnormal psychology. Neither is perfect nor appropriate for the study of every type of case. For example, they should be applied only if the previous level of intelligence of the patient has been near average, if there is no language handicap, if the dementia is not too extensive, and if the patient is less than sixty.

Only recently has there been available a standardized test measure of adult intelligence. Wechsler[24] included a wide range in age groups, with subjects as old as sixty to seventy years, in standardizing this test. This provides a better standard of performance at each age level than was previously available. Wechsler's scoring of his test indicates that certain abilities decline more slowly with age than others. The tests which hold up well as one grows older are information, comprehension, object assembly, picture completion, and vocabulary. Tests which do not hold up are digits forward and backward, arithmetic reasoning, digit-symbol test, picture arrangement, block design, and similarities. Wechsler has suggested that the difference in these two groups of tests can be used as a measure of deterioration — a rough measure — but one which has clinical value.

Passing from the general problem of measuring deterioration, we may next turn our attention to the varieties of deterioration and disorganization shown by patients with different types of mental disease.

Patterns of Mental Deterioration

MENTAL DETERIORATION IN OLD AGE

If we live long enough, we are bound to develop both physical and mental deterioration. These gradual losses in intellectual ability that accompany increased age are termed *normal mental deterioration.* At seventy, practically every individual will show general and specific quantitative losses in those abilities which he had when he was twenty. Most of these changes occur so gradually that neither the aged person himself nor those around him realize that they have been taking place. When the loss of mental efficiency is pronounced, the condition is called "senility." When these intellectual changes are accompanied by gross changes in personality and emotional life the condition is called "senile dementia."

MENTAL DETERIORATION IN PSYCHOSES OF KNOWN ORGANIC ORIGIN

The decline in mental efficiency in normal old people is qualitatively similar to that found in most organic brain disease. When gross organic brain disease occurs in the aged (such as cerebral arteriosclerosis), it is impossible to distinguish between the components due to the aging process and those derived from the arteriosclerotic lesions. In general, the psychopathological changes in the psychoses with a known organic basis have a more rapid onset and course than do the ordinary senile symptoms. As deterioration in the different diagnostic groups becomes extreme, the psychological picture grows more and more alike. It is in the early stages of the deterioration process that differential losses may be seen most clearly. For example, immediate memory is particularly disturbed in the alcoholic psychoses, while this type of memory functions fairly well when only certain areas of the brain are damaged or destroyed, as in Pick's disease. In general, psychological tests of deteriorated patients with generalized organic brain involvement show the following characteristics: relatively superior vocabulary scores involving word usage, as compared with scores on tests of conceptual thinking and any tests requiring new adjustments and associations or rapid shifts in attitude.

The psychological performance of patients with toxic psychoses or with severe postconcussion syndrome is characterized by confusion and disorientation. In addition to being incapable of any complex level of function, the patients show gross disturbance in simple perception. In the acute stages they offer little opportunity for psychological study because they usually are so incapacitated that there are not enough intellectual assets left with which to work. When they recover from this acute state, they almost always regain their previous level of mental function. Traumatic injury to the brain, in some cases, may be followed by a gradual destruction of brain tissue and accompanying mental deterioration. Here, the psychological picture duplicates that encountered in other types of progressive brain disease, but it is not part of the original concussion syndrome.

Brain damage caused either by injury or tumorous growth is frequently attended by sudden intellectual changes which are usually followed by gradual improvement in performance as reorganization and compensation for the defect take place. The extent and, to some degree, the location of the brain damage determine how much impairment will persist. The decrease in intellectual level of persons undergoing surgical extirpation of brain areas is variable. Many individual cases have been described in which the mental-age level after operation seemed unimpaired, even though some types of psychological performance tests showed that there was impairment in other mental functions. Rylander[18] found a reduction in mental age when brain-operated cases were matched with normal control cases in the testing. The reduction was greater when large areas of the frontal lobes were excised than when only small areas were removed.

MENTAL DETERIORATION IN DEMENTIA PRAECOX

For years the problem of functional deterioration, as seen in dementia praecox, has stimulated research investigators so that there is an abundance of data available on the subject. It is known that the dementias attendant on organic brain changes are in some respects similar to, and in other respects quite different from, both the deterioration and the disorganization found in dementia praecox. In most schizophrenic cases, conceptual thinking and the ability to retain new impressions are impaired. The schizophrenic performance is poor on tests requiring interpretation of fables, the detection of absurdities, and general social comprehension. Tests requiring practical judgment and directional control of thought are frequently failed.

There are various factors which influence the psychological performance of schizophrenics. They are responsive to their environment only in a superficial way, never becoming involved with it in any real sense. Both the association test and the Rorschach procedure reflect the frequency of unusual and individual responses, indicating something of the degree of this isolation. The patient's lack of adaptiveness and his inadequacy in the manipulation of environmental situations are brought out by the superficial, undirected nature of the tasks which he chooses, his nonresumption of tasks which are interrupted, and his apparent inability to accept substitute modes of activity. Even when the composite scores of intellectual function indicate little or no disturbance, the psychosis does interfere with the balance among mental functions, the ability to form concepts, and the ability to analyze situations of a practical, social nature.

In the course of schizophrenic deterioration, the first apparent loss is the inability to function mentally as rapidly as before the onset of the illness. This deficiency is, in part, attributable to a general weakening in volition. Later, disturbances in conceptual thinking, associative thinking, immediate recall, and speed of movement in self-initiated activities appear. The last functions to be affected are vocabulary, the recall of overlearned material of long standing, and the capacity for simple organization. Actually, in many cases there is little or no evidence of a true loss; rather, it is a disorganization of mind. In contrast, the deterioration of senility shows speed of reaction, motility, and immediate memory to be first affected, while conceptual thinking and recall of old material are relatively resistant to the deterioration process.

The distinction between the phenomena of deterioration in senile patients and the disorganization of schizophrenic patients is shown clearly in the process of generalization and concept formation.[6] Changes in generalizing ability occur in dementia praecox, and, although not so regularly, in other psychotic states. Schizophrenics may show disturbance in these higher functions even when little or no mental impairment is found in other types of tests. This disorder in generalization warrants special attention.

Experimental Studies of Ability to Think Abstractly

The distinction between concrete and abstract is one that has existed in philosophical discussion for centuries. The use of these philosophical terms has taken on special meaning in the psychological study of psychiatric cases.

The process of generalization — the ability to think abstractly — is one which matures gradually in the child. It has been repeatedly shown that the ability to see differences matures before the ability to see similarities. On the revised Stanford-Binet[21] scale of intelligence, it is expected that a six-year-old child should be able to state the difference between a bird and a dog, or between wood and glass. At the age of eight he should be able to state in what way bread and meat, or a window and a door, are alike. At age eleven he should be able to generalize the similarity among a sparrow, a cow, and a snake. The average adult is expected to know the essential difference between work and play, or between ability and achievement; while the superior adult should be able to derive the essential similarity between melting and burning, or between an egg and a seed. The responses of both mentally retarded children and deteriorated patients usually refer to differences rather than similarities, no matter what instructions are given.

The analysis of intelligence-test results furnished the first objective indication that generalizing ability is impaired in schizophrenics. In an item analysis of the Stanford-Binet performance of two hundred dementia praecox patients, Wentworth[26] showed that they had their greatest difficulty in tests based on ideational judgment, the ability to generalize, and the understanding of motives underlying social acts. Other tests given by Rawlings[16] to a group of paranoid dementia praecox patients revealed that there was an impairment of the processes of comparison, abstraction, and generalization. The nature of their failures was seen in the tendency to deal with the concrete rather than the abstract when the latter was indicated.

From careful observation of brain-injury cases, Gelb and Goldstein[8] developed a systematic explanation of the changes that appear following such injury. Instead of emphasizing isolated bits of behavior or characteristics of performance, a better understanding has been shown by them to come from viewing the changes as due to an impairment in abstract behavior and thinking. This impairment is a basic change involving all capacity levels of the total personality, which they demonstrated by the use of many different types of test material. According to Gelb and Goldstein, the concrete attitude is one in which the individual is reacting to the immediate stimulus, situation, or object, and is controlled by his immediate sense impressions. In the abstract attitude, he goes beyond the specific aspects of sense impressions and responds to the individual thing as representative of a category or class. He is no longer tied to the immediate object, but reacts to it in a representational way. The abstract attitude is necessary if the person is to be able to assume a mental set voluntarily, to shift voluntarily from one aspect of the situation to another, to generalize or abstract common properties of various objects, and to respond in terms of several aspects of a situation at the same time. Goldstein[9] has emphasized that there is a fundamental change in the boundaries between figure and ground when the abstract attitude is impaired. The boundary between the two may be vague and inversion may occur; that is, reversal of the normal figure-ground pattern, so that the ground enters into attention more than the figure.

Numerous tests have been developed to determine whether a patient is responding in a concrete or an abstract manner.[25] Among the more productive of these tests are those which require the patient to sort objects that are placed before him. Objects of different use, form, material, and color are included in the group. The patient is required to "put those together that seem to belong together." The way in which he classifies the objects indicates the particular aspect of his response to them. If he groups them on the basis of some general category, this is taken as an indication that he considers the objects as representative of a class and, thus, is capable of assuming an abstract attitude. If he brings together only those objects which are very nearly or perfectly identical, or which belong together only in reference to some specific use or concrete situation, he evidently is more impressed by their specific attributes than by their representational meaning. To illustrate[5] the generalizing type of response, a person might form a category of "tools" in which a hammer, a screw driver, and a saw of different sizes were included. The specific type would be shown by the person who selected only one hammer and one nail, and included no more in his group because, in his thinking, one hammer would be sufficient to drive the nail into the wall. Another example of this specific attitude was shown by a patient who, instead of putting a pipe, cigar, cigarettes, matchbox, and single matches together as "smoking materials," picked only the cigar and one match and said, "After I have my dinner I smoke a cigar and I use a match to light it." He could not see the basis for the broader type of grouping, even when the examiner demonstrated it to him. The procedure of h ving the patient form groups is supplemented by requiring him to interpret or name groups of objects, such as "tools" or "all red" in accordance with general categories determined by the examiner.

These sorting tests have many advantages in the psychological examination of patients. They can be adjusted to the interests and levels of knowledge of any person to be tested. In testing children, it is possible, for example, to employ objects that are familiar to them, and still to maintain the general principles of the testing procedure. Because the actual objects are placed before the patient, his interest and cooperation may often be obtained despite his unwillingness to respond to other types of testing. The number of variables included in the test objects can be controlled, so that the task set may be made either easy or difficult at will.

These sorting-test procedures have been[4, 27] applied to schizophrenic patients whose performance indicated that they were responding on a more concrete level of performance than were normals. Such patients not only are unable to assume the abstract attitude required of them, but also see odd and peculiar relationships between the objects. Frequently they verbalize some reason for this formation of a group, showing that they are really responding to the task set before them, but in a way different from that in which the normal would respond. Sometimes their basis of sorting is not understandable, either from the objects put together or from their verbalizations of why they group them that way. These peculiar types of sorting have not been found in a group of feeble-minded subjects of roughly the same mental age, although they too are incapable of abstract types of performance.

Vigotsky[23] has devised a complex and difficult form of sorting test to study the development of conceptual thinking. Twenty-two wooden blocks, varying in color, shape, height, size, and in the particular nonsense syllable printed on the block, are presented to the subject who is required to arrange them into groups that are, in some way, alike. The groupings can be varied from simple to complex. His study of schizophrenics has demonstrated that the most important change in their thought processes is a disturbance or impairment in the function of concept formation. Their performance on this sorting test indicated, he said, that there has been a transition to the more "primitive" forms of thought.

Hanfmann and Kasanin[10] have applied Vigotsky's method to a large number of schizophrenics. They report that there is a definite reduction in conceptual thinking, in the sense of an inability to grasp the idea of classification according to certain principles. Many patients used principles of classification different from those adopted by the average person. For example, one schizophrenic put the most heterogeneous blocks together, stating that they belonged together because they were all policemen or all little people, although they were really very dissimilar. Schizophrenics showed endless hesitancy and vacillation among various aspects of the test material, because they were unable to restrict their attention to one principle of the given material and to neglect the others. As a group, they exhibited tremendous variability compared to the performance of organic cases. The latter performed at a lower level of success than either the normal controls or schizophrenics. They never understood the task as a classification nor did they concern themselves with the totality of groupings. They did not show the vacillation found in schizophrenics but usually responded directly to one or another aspect of the material.

Rashkis, *et al.,*[15] devised a method of demonstrating these differences in attitude and ability using verbal material which demonstrated that the schizophrenic loss of ability to abstract is not a regression to a childish mode of thought, but a true disorganization, or at least a new method of performing abstractly.

In order to see whether the performance of either the brain-injured or psychotic patients represented a regression to an earlier type of response, several studies have been made of the performance of normal children on sorting tests. Thompson[22] found that children who were nine to eleven years of age were usually able to form groupings which involved abstraction and to state the generalization which they had used; but children of six to eight years were more apt to bring them together in concrete situations (for example, "I use a fork and a spoon to eat with."). In general, the ability to generalize or to use abstract concepts develops with age and begins to show itself between the ages of seven and nine in normal children. The disorganization in the process of generalization observed in the brain-injured and psychotic patients is similar to, but qualitatively different from, the performance of the younger children, just as the childish behavior of the senile dement is similar to, though qualitatively different from, the behavior of a child.

This point is further borne out by the work of Strauss and Werner[2f] who investigated the disorders of the conceptual thought processes in mentally retarded children who had suffered brain injury, and in ordinary idiopathic aments. They used three different test situations which involved the relation between objects, or the relation between objects and a pictorial situation. The brain-injured children selected more objects in the grouping procedures than did the idiopathic cases (who were matched with them in age and IQ), but uncommon responses were more frequent. The principle of selection used by the brain injured tended to rest on unusual, accidental, or apparently insignificant details. In the test involving the selection of objects to go with a pictorial situation, they produced highly concrete groups of relationships. Even when mental age was kept approximately constant, the brain-injured children showed differences from the normal and feeble-minded children in their strong reaction to unessential details of the objects and situations.

The disorders of simple verbal logic in schizophrenia and senile dementia were investigated by Cameron[6] in relation to the way in which logical thought develops in the normal child. The starting point for his studies was the question of whether or not the disorganized logic of psychotic patients regresses to a form characteristic of the child. In other words, is there a true regression in psychotic thinking and reasoning? He presented his subjects with fragments of sentences which they were asked to complete. For example, "I am in the hospital because . . ." Typical of the normal child's response was, "I was sick," or "I have a broken leg." The senile's responses were, "I hurt myself," or "I fell down just before I came here." Schizophrenics replied, "I wasn't working," "I will be twenty-eight in October," "I love life," or "Because of Egyptian methods."

Further analysis disclosed that some senile patients were evasive, uncertain, or self-critical in their answers. In general their responses were much more precise and direct and far less peculiar than those of schizophrenics, which differed in both logic and form. Schizophrenics threw two or three unrelated elements together where only one element was needed, and showed an extreme vagueness in their answers that was never found in either of the other groups. The logical forms of their responses were sufficiently different from those used by the children to suggest that schizophrenic thought was a true disorganization and not a reversion to an earlier form. While the senile responses offer only mild distortions on the basis of disorientation and simple circumstantiality, schizophrenics employed inexact substitute terms and phrases, and their answers were distorted by the presence of contradictory elements and personal preoccupations.

Another test that reveals disorganization in schizophrenic thought processes is the interpretation of proverbs. Benjamin[3] selected 14 proverbs which he asked 169 schizophrenic patients to explain. Examples of the sort of explanations obtained are as follows: Explain, "When the cat is away, the mice will play." One patient said, "As applied to what? Just gives the mice more liberty." Another stated, "The last supper of Jesus, all those that kissed the novita." Still another, "That means feline absence and rodential job which has its sources in the nature of the Savior." There was a marked tendency to literalness in the approach of some patients to this task. For instance, in explaining "Ingratitude, thy name is woman," a schizophrenic said, "Gratitude is a virtue, ingratitude is a vice." Most patients were unable to shift from the abstract to the literal, as was required, and gave an even more abstract response. In general, they tend to stay within the literal meaning of a problem when it is worded concretely, and remain with the abstract meaning when it is worded abstractly.

There is general agreement that young children, mental defectives, and brain-injured persons fail in tests of abstract intelligence, in performance tests requiring generalization, and in their use and understanding of abstract terms. The schizophrenic also performs on a lower and different level of abstraction from the normal. Although many of his verbal productions include vague, abstract terms, these abstract terms are not used by him in the same way the normal person uses them but seem to carry a very concrete connotation. His generalizations are made in too broad, too involved, too personal terms, and they are expressed in a distorted language structure.

General Observations and Interpretations of Dementia

Since the phenomena of deterioration and disorganization exhibited by organic and schizophrenic cases are rather similar, one might ask why so much effort has been spent in attempts to distinguish between the organic and "functional" types of dementia. One of the reasons has been our inability to demonstrate any definite structural basis for the functional dementia of schizophrenia. In addition, this form of impairment is variable and has other distinctive peculiarities. For instance, an apparently hopelessly demented patient may show an abrupt and often quite remarkable improvement in his mental capacities. In other words, his deterioration process is reversible, and, in all probability, he is not really so incapacitated and out of contact with the world as he appears.

Although the final stages of true dementia are distinguished by gross impairment of all psychological functions, there is evidence that not all abilities decrease in efficiency at the same rate. Several general principles seem to hold true for the course of progressive deterioration. The higher, more complex, and less organized mental processes are affected before the lower and more automatic ones. This tendency is demonstrated by the fact that many patients do poorly on tests requiring abstract intelligence although they may still be competent on simpler psychological test . General impressionability is decreased (otherwise stated, imperception increases), so that memory for recent events fails first because of inadequate registration. Strongly fixed, habitual responses are not affected so much as others. Also, the more recently acquired forms of reaction are lost before those formed earlier in life. The use and understanding of language may be only slightly influenced when other performances are markedly disturbed.

In general, complex mental functions, requiring extensive integration of many types of ability for successful performance, are affected in the course of deterioration before the simple, primary functions.

Goldstein[9] held that mental disintegration follows a consistent pattern. Categorical or abstract behavior suffers first and more severely than simpler forms of behavior. Tasks requiring representational behavior or imaginary elements are failed, while manipulations of concrete and tangible material are adequately done. Many patients are unable to shift their attention at will from one aspect of a situation to another. Voluntary performances are particularly affected, even when activities, directly or, so to speak, passively determined by the stimulus, remain relatively intact. Also, those performances which are important in maintaining the whole individual are less apt to be impaired than other functions.

In spite of the presence of defects, the responses of a deteriorated person (except for isolated periods of chaotic or catastrophic behavior) show adequate order or patterning, although this order is different from the normal. Such a state of order is achieved in several ways. A lack of "self-perception of the defect" is combined with a preference for situations which can be coped with adequately. The patient's tendency to stick to performances in which he feels at ease and competent expresses itself in the continued repetition of simple acts. Such persons are said to show "stereotyped" behavior. Careful and extensive psychological testing may be necessary to discover the impairment. The patient may be able to cover up actual defects through solving certain tasks in an unusual manner, or he may attempt to avoid the testing situation by some excuse as soon as he feels that he is going to fail.

The nature of some of the phenomena in the cortically injured has led Lashley[14] to postulate a disturbance in the general excitability level of the brain, in addition to the localized lesion. Every nervous function would then depend upon both a specific pattern of nervous organization and the level of nonspecific excitation or general vigilance of the rest of the brain. Thus, a lowered level of general excitability may explain why reactions or memories are slowed or less readily available without actually being lost. Although special intensive training may restore a specific memory trace, it cannot restore completely the general level of excitability of the system.

Lashley has called attention to the importance of motivation in these cases. A passive or hopeless attitude on the part of certain patients keeps them from making the most of their abilities and exaggerates the apparent extent of their defect. Lashley described an interesting incident in which a patient who was unable to learn the alphabet after nine hundred repetitions, accomplished the task in ten trials after having been bet one hundred cigarettes on his performance. Thus, it seems that many outside psychological factors may enter into the performance level of the mentally impaired patient.

In general, dementia is not characterized by defects which are isolated and restricted, but extends to many phases of function. Not all functions are equally disturbed. The type of the disturbance depends on the nature of the lesions and the general level of excitability of the brain. On the whole, the higher levels of integration are disturbed before the lower levels, and the later acquired mental functions before those acquired earlier. The greatest resistance to disintegration and disorganization is offered by functions which are established at an early period, subjected to frequent and intensive use, and basic to the maintenance of the individual.

Summary

There are various degrees and kinds of intellectual impairment found in different forms of psychopathology. In most cases it is impossible to make an accurate estimate of the patient's mental efficiency prior to his illness. Therefore, indirect measures in terms of scatter, of the difference between vocabulary efficiency and other mental performances, and of the ability to see abstract relationships are used to estimate the amount of deficit. No one of these methods is wholly satisfactory, but each provides some information of value. Under some circumstances, the relative stability of the vocabulary in comparison to other tests is a good index of deterioration.

There are differences in the patterns of deterioration distinguishing organic psychoses, senile dementia, and dementia praecox. In the first two conditions there are real, irrevocable losses, while in dementia praecox there is a disorganization (or reorganization) rather than a true loss.

Sorting tests, proverb interpretation, and reasoning tests reveal certain features of the dementia seen in schizophrenia. These patients are unable to assume an abstract attitude toward such material, reacting only to the direct concrete aspects of the situation. They are also unable to interpret proverbs when the task requires shifting from the abstract to the concrete or from the concrete to the abstract form of thought. Although their performance is often described as a form of mental regression, this regression is not a return to childish modes of thought. Rather, it is regression to a different variety of intellectual process.

In many patients, psychological deficit is compensated for in a variety of ways. These compensatory mechanisms include avoidance of situations which cannot be adequately met, substitution of methods which they can use for ones which they may fail, rationalization of failure in terms which provide self-reassurance and which may or may not conceal the difficulty from others, or by increased motivation.

REFERENCES

1. Ackelsberg, S. B., "Vocabulary and Mental Deterioration in Senile Dementia," *Jour. Abn. Soc. Psychol.*, 1944, *39*, 393–406.
2. Babcock, H., "An Experiment in the Measurement of Mental Deterioration," *Arch. Psychol.*, 1930, *18*, #117.
3. Benjamin, J. D., "A Method for Distinguishing and Evaluating Formal Thinking Disorders in Schizophrenia," in J. S. Kasinin, *Language and Thought in Schizophrenia*. Berkeley, University of California Press, 1944, 65–88.
4. Bolles, M. M., "The Basis of Pertinence," *Arch. Psychol.*, 1937, *30*, #212.
5. ———, and K. Goldstein, "A Study of the Impairment of 'Abstract Behavior' in Schizophrenic Patients," *Psychiat. Quart.*, 1938, *12*, 42–66.
6. Cameron, N., "A Study of Thinking in Senile Deterioration and Schizophrenic Disorganization," *Amer. Jour. Psychol.*, 1938, *51*, 650–664.
7. Capps, H. M., "Vocabulary Changes in Mental Deterioration." *Arch. Psychol.*, 1939, *34*, #242.
8. Gelb, A., and K. Goldstein, *Psychologische Analysen hirnpathologischer Fälle*. Leipzig, Barth, 1920.
9. Goldstein, K., *The Organism*. New York, American Book, 1939.
10. Hanfmann, E., and J. Kasanin, "A Method for the Study of Concept Formation," *Jour. Psychol.*, 1937, *3*, 521–540.
11. Harris, A. J., and D. Shakow, "Scatter on the Stanford-Binet in Schizophrenic, Normal, and Delinquent Adults," *Jour. Abn. Soc. Psychol.*, 1938, *33*, 100–111.
12. Hunt, J. M., and C. N. Cofer, "Psychological Deficit." Chapter 32 in J. M. Hunt, *Personality and the Behavior Disorders*. New York, Ronald, 1944, 990–993.
13. Kendig, I., and W. V. Richmond, *Psychological Studies in Dementia Praecox*. Ann Arbor, Edwards Bros., 1940.
14. Lashley, K. S., "Factors Limiting Recovery after Central Nervous Lesions," *Jour. Nerv. Ment. Dis.*, 1938, *88*, 733–755.
15. Rashkis, H., J. F. Cushman, and C. Landis, "A New Method for Studying Disorders of Conceptual Thinking," *Jour. Abn. Soc. Psychol.*, 1946, *41*, 70–74.

16. Rawlings, E., "Intellectual Status of Patients with Paranoid Dementia Praecox: Its Relation to the Organic Brain Changes." *Arch. Neurol. Psychiat.*, 1921, *5*, 283–295.

17. Roe, A., and D. Shakow "Intelligence in Mental Disorder," *Annals N. Y., Acad. Sci.*, 1942, *42*, 361–490.

18. Rylander, G., *Personality Changes after Operations on the Frontal Lobes.* London, Oxford University Press, 1939.

19. Shipley, W. C., "A Self-administering Scale for Measuring Intellectual Impairment and Deterioration," *Jour. Psychol.*, 1940, *9*, 371–377.

20. Strauss, W. C., and H. Werner, "Disorders of Conceptual Thinking in the Brain-Injured Child," *Jour. Nerv. Ment. Dis.*, 1942, *96*, 153–172.

21. Terman, L. M., and M. A. Merrill, *Measuring Intelligence.* Boston, Houghton, 1937.

22. Thompson, J., "The Ability of Children of Different Grade Levels to Generalize on Sorting Tests," *Jour. Psychol.*, 1941, *11*, 119–126.

23. Vigotsky, L. S., "Thought in Schizophrenia," *Arch. Neurol. Psychiat.*, 1934, *31*, 1063–1077.

24. Wechsler, D., *The Measurement of Adult Intelligence* (3d ed.). Baltimore, Williams & Wilkins, 1944.

25. Weigl, E., "On the Psychology of the So-called Process of Abstraction," *Jour. Abn. Soc. Psychol.*, 1941, *36*, 3–33.

26. Wentworth, M. M., "Two Hundred Cases of Dementia Praecox Tested by the Stanford Revision," *Jour. Abn. Soc. Psychol.*, 1924, *18*, 378–384.

27. Zubin, J., and J. Thompson, *Sorting Tests in Relation to Drug Therapy in Schizophrenia.* New York, Psychiatric Institute and Hospital, 1941.

Chapter XXVIII

THE ROLE OF THE BRAIN IN PSYCHOPATHOLOGY

IT IS POSSIBLE to deal with the entire field of abnormal psychology with no more than a passing reference to the central nervous system or to the brain. For instance, Freud's entire system of psychoanalysis is built up without reference to the activity of the brain or the central nervous system. Notwithstanding the fact that psychopathology can be described without a neurological basis, a working knowledge of the brain and its functions provides a sound and reliable background for the study of the phenomena of abnormal psychology. One must know what the brain, as an organ, can do and what it cannot do, in order to think accurately about these problems. It is more than theoretically possible that many of the disorders, which are at present thought of as psychological, will be found to be based on actual organic lesions or dysfunctions of the brain or of the central nervous system. We need only remember the story of general paresis or of paralysis agitans, both of which were for many years believed to be devoid of any essential neurological foundation, to demonstrate this point.

Until 1800 the functions of the brain, as we conceive of them today, were almost completely ignored by the medical men and other scientists of the time. Oddly enough, it was Gall, the inventor of the discredited system of phrenology, who was responsible for the notion that the activities of the mind depend upon the substance of the brain and are, indeed, localized in the brain. This idea had been mentioned by various writers from the time of the early Greeks. It had never been taken seriously, however, until Gall performed his anatomical dissections and made many dogmatic statements which led physiologists and anatomists to investigate the possible truth in what he said. He was wrong on many points, but he was right often enough to stimulate systematic work of others in the field.

The idea of the body-mind relationship during the Middle Ages was that the soul, as the principle of life, was distributed to various parts of the body, and that, together with the crude substances from these parts, it activated the body by three kinds of "spirits." The liver concocted from food the natural spirits; the heart was the center of the vital spirits; while the brain manufactured the animal spirits. These spirits were thought to be distributed to the body by means of the blood vessels and the nerves.

In contrast to these speculations, it was known from the time of Aristotle that cutting or injury of the brain substance itself was not attended by pain or any other sensation. It was also known that stimulation of much of the brain is accompanied by neither a change in consciousness nor in motor activity. Injury to, or removal of, parts of the brain had been shown to lead to a marked change in the behavior and conscious life. If some disease process affected the brain, its supporting tissues, or its blood supply, there was also known to be a deterioration in both behavior and conscious mental life.

All of these facts and relationships have been known for centuries, but only during the past hundred years have they led to real experimental studies of the relationship existing between the brain and the mind or our conscious mental life. Only recently have we begun to understand very much in a positive way about the functions of the brain as an organ of the body.

The Evolution of the Brain

All animals, including man, respond to environmental changes through special organs, the effectors. Of the effectors, muscles are the most important, although cilia and glands are also instruments of action. That effectors may operate in a coordinated fashion is made possible by some system of interconnection.[9] In those forms of animal life where the individual is composed of more than one cell, there is a beginning of the specialization of function, some cells acting as contracting units, others as digestive units and so on. In the larger organisms where there is an increase in the number of cells, there appear units which have the specialized function of connecting the outer skin surfaces to underlying muscles, so serving as simple triggers by which the muscles are excited to activity. These units are the *receptor neurons* which are the most primitive type of nervous tissue. They first appear in animal forms, such as the sponge, but are representative of the basic pattern of the sensory equipment of all higher forms, including man. In man, the sensitive area for odor reception contains cells which differ from those of this primitive form only in that they terminate in a nerve center instead of a muscle.

In the more complex of lower animal forms, these receptors connect with numerous deep-seated nerve cells whose branches join, constituting a *nerve-net* that spreads throughout most of the animal's body. Such nerve-nets are, primarily, conducting systems which transmit impulses from receptors in one part of the body to muscles in distant parts of the organism. Usually, these nets are so undifferentiated that the impulses spread in all directions. In higher animal forms there evolves a *polarization* of conduction which limits the direction of transmission so that the impulses can pass only in one way.

Passing from the simpler animal forms to the more complicated, one finds the appearance of groups of nervous elements (localized nerve-nets). These groups unite and so provide a more adequate means of interconnection and communication. This development of nerve-cell grouping is a gradual one and is accompanied by further specialization of polarization, facilitating a more definite point-to-point conduction. This process of specialization involves the development of different kinds of nerve cells — the receptors, effectors, and connectors. The receptors usually connect some point on the external surface with the central groupings of nervous tissue. The effectors extend from this central grouping to some point on a muscle or gland. The connectors primarily serve as a means of connection or communication between many receptor and many effector cells. The growth, differentiation, and specialization of these connector cells constitute the pattern of development of the central nervous system and of the brain itself.

The specialization of function, particularly of the receptors in the head end of the developing organism, led to the greater development of connecting nervous mechanisms at that end of the organism. There has been a gradual development and specialization of function of the nerve mass of this head end, which culminates in that exceedingly complex organ, the brain. The differences in the possibilities of reaction and adaptation which exist between any two animal forms depend largely upon the possibilities for interconnection within the brain and nervous system. In the evolution of the nervous system and brain, the more primitive elements still remain even when a new organization appears. There is a superstructure of new and more complicated controlling and connecting mechanisms, so that we have in the evolutionary series a conservation of the old with the addition of new or progressive elements from time to time. The conservative, fixed behavior patterns control the lower animal forms, while in mammals the progressive, plastic, modifiable patterns predominate.

The obvious dominance of the brain in the adjustment of human behavior and the uncertainty which obscures most of the details of its operation lead to the consideration of certain of the classical ideas which have dominated thinking and research in the field of neurology, particularly as they are related to psychopathology.

Localization versus Mass Action

To explain the operation of the brain in the coordination of behavior and its relation to mental reactions, various schemes have been proposed. Usually, these schemes have implied that the brain either works as a unit (mass action) or that its various parts have specific functions (localization).

Flourens (1842) was one of the first to hold that intelligent behavior is an indivisible function depending upon the activity of the entire brain. He said: "The cerebral hemispheres are the sole organs for the perceptions and volitions . . . [which] have the same distribution in the hemispheres; the faculties of perceiving, understanding, and willing constitute a single function which is essentially unitary. . . . Excitation of one point in the nervous system involves all others; there is community of reaction, of changes, of energy. Unity is the great principle which rules, is universal, dominates all. The nervous system forms a single unified system." *

Goltz (1881) held essentially the same viewpoint as Flourens, contending that intelligence cannot be dissociated into subordinate functions which have separate localization in the brain. He explained the dementia produced in dogs by removal of portions of the brain as a generalized deficit function not to be attributed to any specific sensory defect. He held that the essential element in dementia is a general defect in attention and not a loss of any special system of sensations or ideas. After brain injury an animal is not able to attend exclusively to any one group of stimuli and so is unable to integrate responses to stimuli intelligently. By this, Goltz implied that intellect is dependent upon the functioning of all parts of the brain, a functioning which is qualitatively the same, but varies in quantity.

In contrast to this mass action or dynamic theory was the localization hypothesis of Munk (1909). Briefly, Munk's theory was that there are a number of primary sensory spheres — visual, auditory, olfactory, — in which are stored and elaborated images and ideas associated with each particular mode of sensation. Intelligence or intellect is

* Lashley, K. S., *Brain Mechanisms and Intelligence*. Chicago, University of Chicago Press, 1929, 4.

conceived of as the aggregate of all of these products of the particular sensory spheres brought together by the many interconnections among them. Munk said: "I considered the whole cerebral cortex, the aggregate of all the sensory spheres, to be the seat of the intelligence, which I defined as the combination and product of all the ideas arising from the sense perceptions."* The elaborate interconnection between the sensory spheres provides for the most complex integration. According to this theory, the complex processes of memory which involve the coordination of many diverse sensory and motor processes are individually localized in different parts of the cortex and hence incapable of inclusion within a single or definite area.

Most neurologists and psychologists have taken the viewpoint originally formulated by Gall; namely, that the brain is the organ of the mind and that the various characteristics of personality are localized in specific parts of the brain. This notion of specific localization of mental function originally met with considerable opposition. However, medicine had long stressed the importance of localization, by which is meant that there is some structure or area of the body in which normal functions or diseased conditions can be found. This notion that psychological functions are somehow localized in the brain gained its momentum largely from Fritsch and H tzig.[6] During the Franco-Prussian War of 1870, they were afforded the opportunity of directly stimulating the brain of a soldier, part of whose skull had been blown away by a bullet. They succeeded in producing isolated movements of various muscle groups by electrical stimulation applied directly to the surface of the brain. Later, it was shown that removal or damage to these stimulable areas was followed by disorders of motion in the same parts of the body. Hence, by analogy, it was concluded that psychological functions depend for their existence on the activity of well-defined centers of the cerebral cortex.

The experimental work on localization was made possible by David Ferrier's (1876) introduction of induction currents for electrical stimulation of the brain. Sherrington has stated this viewpoint as follows:

The brain excited at certain points evokes motor acts, or bits of motor acts, e.g. of a limb, of one side of the face, etc. The phrase went that at this part or that part of the brain this or that movement of the arm, or of the face, was "represented." It might perhaps have been expected that these movements of the body so easily provoked by the application of electricity to this or that point of . . . the brain, would be just the stereotyped

* Lashley, K. S., *ibid.*, 6.

"reflex" movements which can be excited . . . from the skin and spinal cord. Instances of such reflexes are, for example in cat and dog, the rhythmic scratching with the hind-foot which grooms the hairy coat, or the twitch of the ear when irritated as by a fly, or the shaking of water from the wetted coat, or standing or walking. But no. These movements are not evoked by stimulation of the brain. They are reflex, but not, it would seem, "represented" in the cortex. . . . They seem rather fragments of motor behaviour which, if we could elicit the whole train, would bear the character of . . . the fringe of a composite act whose focal part occupies the attention. . . . But it cannot be said that anything closely resembling the performance of a deliberate act, such as one of those which in sequence occupy our attention and make up what counts as our "doing" for the waking day, has ever been evoked by electricity or any other artificial means from any part of the brain. Thus, no "word" or even an exclamation or a laugh or groan has ever been elicited, although "centres representing" speech have been, on other grounds, identified. . . . Further, it has been found that the several senses, sight, hearing, smell, are "localized" in certain areas of the brain. This was called sensory localization.*

The experimental evidence for and against localization or mass action still remains, while new evidence for either hypothesis appears from time to time. Since no conclusion is justified, the more specific evidence on one phase of the problem may next be considered.

Aphasia and Broca's Area

The jump from brain localization of control of simple, specific cutaneous sensation or muscular movement to brain localization of complicated psychological functions is a tremendous one. In spite of the distance, it has been made repeatedly by both neurologists and psychologists. The earlier theories of the relationship between certain brain areas and speech disorders (aphasia) are an excellent example.

In the 1840's, Flourens had held that the brain acted as a unitary organ and that there was no real evidence of cerebral localization. Broca,[7] in 1861, reported on the neurological damage which he found on examination of the brains of three patients who had suffered from aphasia before their deaths. He had observed the speech difficulties or losses, sensory and motor disturbances, and other mental symptoms before the death of these patients. On the basis of a post-morten examination of their brains, he reported that in the second and third convolution of the frontal lobe of the left hemisphere there was definite evidence of organic brain damage. On this basis, he concluded that speech, as such, is localized in this area. His theory was somewhat modified by subsequent workers who found that in certain aphasic

* Sherrington, C. S., *Man on His Nature*. New York, Macmillan, 1942, 237–238.

cases the brain damage was not only in the frontal convolutions, but also in the first and second convolutions of the temporal lobe. This area of the frontal and temporal lobes of the brain came to be called "Broca's area," and for more than forty years it was the accepted belief that speech was dependent upon the integrity of Broca's area.

In 1906, Marie[7] startled the medical world with a series of papers dealing with the question of aphasia in its relation to Broca's area. He reexamined two of the original brains on which Broca had based his conclusions and, with the newer techniques of histological examination available, demonstrated that the brains were not damaged in the manner that Broca had reported. In one case the loss of tissue included not only Broca's area, but other areas as well; while in the second case there was no definite lesion in Broca's area, but a generalized atrophy of the entire brain.

Between the time of Broca and that of Marie, many neurologists speculated on the probable interconnecting pathways in the brain, damage to which was responsible for various forms of psychopathology. Their systems usually consisted of drawing diagrams of the path which the nervous impulses were thought to traverse in various psychological functions, and indicating where the breaks in the paths occurred which gave rise to each variety of psychopathology. Head has called this "the era of diagram makers." Marie's findings threw all of this speculative diagram making into chaos. Today, it is considered more important to investigate aphasia in terms of psychological changes than it is to try to give it a neurological basis. That there is a neurological foundation for speech disorder is not questioned, but its specific nature is unknown.

Contributions of J. Hughlings Jackson[8]

The excellent clinical observations of Jackson, published between 1861 and 1909, which bore on the relationship between brain injury or damage and psychopathology, furnished a starting point for modern experimental work on many forms of mental disorder, including aphasia.

Jackson pointed out that the evolutionary process of the development of the nervous system is a change from the most to the least organized. Putting it otherwise, the course of development is from lowest centers, comparatively well organized at birth, up to the highest centers which are continually being organized throughout life. The evolution of brain function is a passage from the most automatic to the most voluntary. The highest centers of the brain, which are the climax of nervous evolution, and which make up the organ of mind — or physical basis of consciousness — are the least organized, the most complex, and the most voluntary.

Devolution is a developmental process in reverse; it is a "taking to pieces" in the order from the least organized, the most complex, and most voluntary, toward the most organized, most simple, and most automatic. Devolution is always partial in that only parts of areas of the brain are involved. The partial devolution gives rise to negative and positive symptoms in every case. Disease does not *cause* the symptoms of mental disease in a positive sense. Disease only *releases* negative mental symptoms attributable to the devolution. All of the elaborate mental symptoms — illusions, hallucinations, delusions, and extravagant conduct — are the outcome of activity of nervous elements untouched by any pathological process. They arise from the activity of the more automatic, well-organized levels of brain function which remain and which are functioning in an uncontrolled or uninhibited fashion. The most absurd thoughts and ideas, the most extravagant actions in mentally disturbed patients, are the survivals of mental states which characterized their earlier individual development or evolution, but which are normally held in a checked or balanced system. It is no wonder that a demented man believes in his hallucinations; they are his perceptions. His delusions are not caused by disease, but are the outcome of activity of what is left of him; of what disease has spared. His brain is functioning as best it can with that which is present and active.

As an example, Jackson explained that an epileptic convulsion depends on a sudden and excessive discharge or liberation of energy at some point in the cortex. Certain cells at this point gradually attain a very high tension or instability and suddenly liberate a large quantity of energy. Not only do such highly unstable cells discharge by downward lines toward the parts of the body which they especially represent, but they also discharge sidewise by cross connections. In so doing, they overcome the resistance of healthy, comparatively stable, collateral nervous arrangements which then also discharge downward. Thus, partly from the primary discharge, and much more from the secondary discharges of healthy nervous arrangements, there is an enormous energy liberation toward the periphery. To illustrate, suppose that a Navy Board consists of twenty-four members, each one of whom governs the whole of the Navy through control over middle and lower officials. If any one of the twenty-four members gives up his duties, the whole Navy administration will be only very slightly defective throughout, since there is compensation by greater activity of some of the remaining twenty-three members. This is analogous to destruction of some small area of the cerebral cortex. It is well known that a small part of the highest brain centers may be destroyed without any striking symptoms, compensation being practically perfect. But the situation analogous to the epileptic fit, or mania, is when one of the twenty-four highest Navy officials becomes demented. Then, by issuing foolish orders to lower officials, "discharging downwards" he produces widespread and yet slight disturbance in the Navy. But by wrongly advising his colleagues, "discharging collaterally," he leads them to discharge downward, issuing foolish orders to lower officials. Thus, by a multiplication of foolish orders, the whole Navy is severely and uniformly convulsed. The officials who, in the case of loss of one of their colleagues, work more to compensate for that loss, are compelled, when one becomes demented, to cooperate in his excess.

In the explanation of mental disease, Jackson said that in every insanity there is either some disease which is destructive of nervous elements, or some undiscovered pathological process which causes the loss of functions. He pointed out that some of the symptoms of mental diseases are thought of as devolution processes, as reversals of evolution. In the light of such natural experiments caused by accident or disease, one may comprehend something of the relation of psychology to the anatomy and physiology of the higher brain centers.

The main ideas which may be gained from Jackson are that the disturbances in consciousness are related to brain disorders and that there are certain psychological symptoms by which brain disorders may be recognized. There is no disorder of the brain without a psychological loss. What appears to be new and different is merely the release of negative, or more automatic, lower functions. Applying these concepts to the psychological symptoms which one sees in schizophrenia[16] indicates that the symptoms result from a partial interference with the orderly processes of inhibition exercised by normal consciousness, so leading to the bizarre and fragmentary type of consciousness which is shown by the patient. It is as if certain parts of his brain no longer function. As a result, the more automatic activity of lower centers finds expression and the normal integrated patterning of the mental life is lost.

Functions of Different Portions of the Brain

Having surveyed the general principles of brain function, the losses or phenomena resulting from operations on the different lobes of the brain may be described. The newer techniques of brain surgery and of psychological experimentation have added considerably to our knowledge of the psychological events which are, in part, dependent on certain general areas or lobes of the brain. The location of the lobes of the brain is shown in Fig. 14.

FRONTAL LOBES

The surgical severing of the nerve tracts connecting the frontal lobes and the thalamus has marked psychological effects, particularly in relation to self-consciousness. This operation was originated by

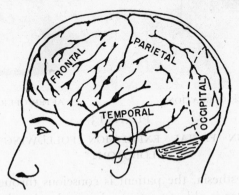

Fig. 14. The location of the lobes of the cerebral cortex.

Moniz in Portugal and developed in America by Freeman and Watts.[4] The use of this surgical technique with mental patients produces some astonishing results, particularly a reduction of the self-conscious emotional reactions and a loss of "psychic pain." Intellect, as measured by the standard intelligence tests, is usually unchanged after the operation. In many instances the use which is made of intelligence in social and personal relationships is somewhat diminished. As a consequence, some patients become indolent and exhibit a marked lack of social tact.

After recovery from the operation, many of the patients who had been totally disabled were able to return to the occupations which they had followed before their illness. Old people, so depressed that their lives had become a burden to them, were markedly improved because of the serenity of disposition which followed the operation. The best results were obtained in involutional melancholia, fair results in dementia praecox, and poor results in alcoholism. (See Plate 13.)

The mental changes which take place during and following the operation are psychologically interesting. Since the surgery is done

BEFORE OPERATION   AFTER OPERATION

PLATE 13

ALTERATION IN FACIAL EXPRESSION FOLLOWING PREFRONTAL
LOBOTOMY[5]

under local anesthesia, the patient is conscious throughout the procedure and hence is able to report adequately. An abrupt change in
the mental state takes place only after the incision of the fourth brain
quadrant, irrespective of which of the four quadrants is sectioned last.
(See Fig. 15.) Even after three quadrants have been cut, the patient
remains oriented, can carry out intellectual problems of considerable
complexity, and, although quieter, shows about the same degree of
anxiety and distress as he did before the operation was started. Immediately upon severing the fourth quadrant, the patient becomes unresponsive, disoriented, and confused, and no longer exhibits any
anxiety. Some patients are more lively and engage the doctor in
animated and sometimes humorous conversations, or they may sing
or say their prayers. But they are unable to recall anything concerning
their immediate surroundings and, while the skin is being sutured, they
may deny that they have been operated upon. During the first few days
following the operation, they remain somewhat confused and disoriented. After a week they regain orientation. Beginning with the
second week, the confusion usually clears up so completely that the
patient is able to return to his home.

Patients who have undergone this operation are different from
their prepsychotic selves, although sometimes the difference is not

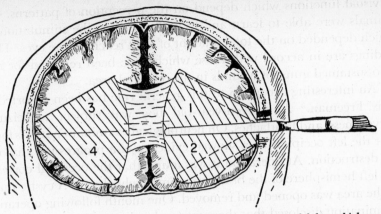

Fig. 15. Diagram indicating the four quadrants of the frontal lobes which are severed in prefrontal lobotomy. (After Freeman and Watts[5])

immediately recognizable. They are apt to be somewhat more indolent; they are often outspoken, saying the first thing that comes into their heads rather than waiting to think what response the remark will produce in others. They are aware that they are hasty, undiplomatic, and tactless, and often are sorry and apologetic. The emotional reactions are brisk, but shallow and short-lived. They laugh more and are of quicker temper. There is an absence of the brooding melancholia, the hurt feelings, the pouting, and the grim silences which marked them before the operation.

Freeman and Watts have emphasized that any mentally sick individual is characterized by self-conscious ideas and egotism so that interest in the outside world is more or less restricted while personal emotional experiences largely dominate his behavior. Along with such morbid preoccupation, he may or may not have insight into the falsity of his ideas. He is unable to control his thoughts and so becomes fixated on these abnormal ideas. The effect of the operation is to break up this fixation. As one patient expressed it, "The sensation has moved from the center of my attention to the periphery."

OCCIPITAL LOBES

The complete surgical removal of the occipital lobes results in permanent pattern blindness, although visual ability to distinguish daylight from dark still remains. In man this operation is performed only when destructive tumorous conditions make it absolutely necessary. Working with monkeys, Klüver[10] has shown that the removal of the cortex of the occipital lobes results in complete and permanent loss of visual functions which depend on the perception of patterns. The animals were able to learn and to perform tasks, the stimulation for which depended on the total amount of light reaching the eyes. These findings are in accord with those which have been reported for men who sustained gunshot wounds in the occipital area.

An interesting exception to this general rule has been reported by Ellis Freeman.[3] An eleven-year-old boy was subject to seizures, nervousness, and headaches. On neurological examination it was found that the left occipital area showed evidence of a progressive anatomical destruction. At operation it was found that the occipital cortex of the left hemisphere of the brain was completely absent. A cystic tumor in the area was opened and removed. One month following operation, examination disclosed that there was no loss in pattern or color vision, nor was there any constriction in the visual field for either eye. Careful examination showed that the boy had normal vision for the entire field of each eye, but with the normal brain mechanism for the left half of each retina absent. Since his brain damage was due to a very early injury, visual function, in this case, had been taken over by some other part of the brain.

TEMPORAL LOBES

The influence of Broca's work was such that for many years the temporal lobes were believed to be connected in some way with speech and with audition, although direct stimulation of these areas failed to produce any response in either man or animals. Klüver and Bucy[11] investigated the functions of this area by the bilateral removal of the temporal lobes in monkeys. They found most pronounced changes in behavior and "personality" following bilateral removal, but no change following unilateral removal.

The monkeys exhibited the following symptoms: (1) forms of behavior which seem to be indicative of "psychic blindness"; (2) strong oral tendencies in examining available objects (licking, biting gently, chewing, touching with the lips, "smelling"); (3) a strong tendency to attend and react to every visual stimulus; (4) marked changes in emotional behavior or absence of emotional reactions in the sense that the motor and vocal reactions generally associated with anger and fear are not exhibited, and (5) an increase in sexual activity. . . . Differential reactions to visual stimuli established preoperatively were seriously disturbed after bilateral temporal lobectomy, but it was possible to reestablish the response through training. The ability to "generalize" in responding to visual stimuli did not seem to be impaired. *

* Klüver, H. and P. C. Bucy, "Preliminary Analysis of the Functions of the Temporal Lobes in Monkeys," *Arch. Neurol. Psychiat.*, 1939, 42, 1000.

Several of these changes are quite unusual and have been made the basis of extensive study. Psychic blindness is a symptom which is seen in an organic brain condition known as "Pick's disease." Individuals having this symptom will approach any object without hesitation, but are unable to recognize what the object is on the basis of vision alone. Recognition takes place only by means of taste, smell, touch, or sound. In monkeys, if a succession of pieces of food and of nails was presented at regular intervals, the animal would pick up both the food and the nails until it ceased to react to both. The food was eaten while the nails were discarded after examination by mouth. After such a test, there might be several hundred nails on the bottom of the cage, which the monkey would continuously pick up and reexamine, even though they had all been rejected only a few minutes previously. In a normal monkey the nails were consistently rejected and the food consistently accepted on the basis of visual evidence alone.

The strong tendency of the experimental animals to attend and react to every stimulus seemed compulsory, irresistible, or forced. They appeared compelled to react to objects, events, and changes in their environment. This visual attention and inspection was not confined to objects within reach, but was set off by almost any kind of object, near or far. They did not seem to discriminate between significant and insignificant elements in the entire situation but reacted indifferently to a speck of dirt, a dot on a necktie, a whiff of smoke, a snake, a nail, a bit of sawdust, no matter whether the object was important, unimportant, dangerous, or indifferent.

The profound changes in emotional behavior, specifically, the almost complete absence of expressive emotional reactions which are normally associated with anger and fear, were most outstanding. The operated animal showed no fear of anything. Snakes, larger animals, human beings, and other animate objects which constituted a threat to the safety of the animal, were reacted to with indifference. In some animals the expressions of emotion (chattering and facial expressions) were lost completely; in others, expressiveness reappeared after several months. The increase in sexual activity was most marked and diverse. The animals were hypersexed, not only when with other animals, but when alone. All forms of overt sexual responses were exhibited and continued over long periods of time. These manifestations of hypersexuality had no counterpart in the normal monkey, and did not appear in monkeys in which only one temporal lobe had been removed.

An outstanding characteristic of the postoperative changes was the way in which the relation between the monkey and his environment was affected. A monkey which approached every object to examine it by taste or smell could not survive longer than a few hours if turned loose in a region with a plentiful supply of natural enemies. A monkey deprived of its frontal lobes, its parietal lobes, or even its occipital lobes, might conceivably exist in the wild under natural conditions, but it is inconceivable that it would exist long if deprived of its temporal lobes.

No other known brain operation brings about such marked changes in behavior as this bilateral removal of the temporal lobes. Other than the psychic blindness in Pick's disease and the behavior of certain children who have suffered from encephalitis, it bears little relationship to human psychopathology. (Some postencephalitic children seem compelled to touch and examine every object about them without uttering a word during the process.)

PARIETAL LOBES

That portion of the parietal lobe just adjacent to the frontal lobe is called the "postcentral sensory area." (See Fig. 14.) Direct electrical or chemical stimulation of this area in the human results in reports of cutaneous or kinesthetic sensory experience (tingling, shooting pain, itching) in specific areas on the opposite side of the body from the stimulated cortex.

If portions of the postcentral sensory area are surgically removed there is a loss or disturbance of sensation in that part of the body for which the area had been the primary sensory center. Lesions made near the border of the occipital area cause disturbance in form perception. Direct electrical stimulation of the parietal areas was found by Penfield[19] to produce visual and auditory hallucinations in certain patients. (Chap. XXI.)

The Neurological Basis of Consciousness

The difficulties encountered in attempting to translate the psychological facts of consciousness into neurological terms, or to give the neurological basis for any psychological functions, are clear. We know that certain simple sensory and motor functions are fairly well localized in the brain. We know that there is little or no evidence that psychological functions such as speech, imagination, memory, are localized in any particular area. Returning to the mass-action hypothesis and considering consciousness as the total functional expression of mental life, it is of interest to study the relationship which exists between brain function and consciousness in general.

Some psychologists have advanced the theory that consciousness depends on motor activity. For example, thought has been said to be "subvocal speech." In other words, one thinks with one's muscles. It has been demonstrated that consciousness is clearer and more effective when muscular tension is at a fairly high level. There is no evidence, however, that consciousness, as such, is solely dependent on motor activity or a reflection of the degree of motor activity. Individuals with complete motor paralysis due to spinal cord injury show no essential disorder in consciousness. The marked motor disability existing both in paralysis agitans and in spastic paralysis is not accompanied by a disordered consciousness. Consequently, as far as psychopathology is concerned, a motor theory of consciousness does not add anything to our understanding of the problem.

Pavlov[17] held, on the basis of experimental studies, that the ability to form a conditioned response is a criterion of consciousness and depends on the brain cortex. Subsequent research by other investigators has necessitated a revision of this point of view. Conditioned responses have been established in decerebrate dogs where only the spinal cord was functioning,[21] and in cats who were under deep anesthesia.[22] From this it may be concluded that consciousness, *defined as conditionability*, occurs even when the cerebral cortex is not functioning. Practically all modern evidence indicates that the cortex is necessary for the processes of consciousness, and hence, conditioning is not a necessary criterion of consciousness.

During many neurosurgical operations on the brain, Penfield[19] demonstrated that direct cortical stimulation would induce complex and organized sensory and motor phenomena. On the basis of this evidence, together with the clinical manifestations of epilepsy, he formulated an interesting theory of the neurological basis of consciousness.[18] He called attention to the aura preceding the motor convulsion in epilepsy. This aura is frequently of a nature which indicates that it originated in the thalamic centers having to do with autonomic responses. It is possible that some thalamic center sets off the motor discharge or explosion seen in the seizure, which is accompanied by a loss of consciousness. Hence, consciousness depends on certain unspecified functional connections between the thalamus and the cerebral cortex, in which the thalamus is the primary area. He supported this reasoning by the evidence that lesions in this region are frequently accompanied by severe disturbances in consciousness, plus the fact that the hypothalamus is known to be related to the control of sleep. Of course, he did not consider this region as the most important center for consciousness, since he recognized that all parts of the brain may contribute to consciousness under normal conditions.

That consciousness is consistently and permanently lost when the left anterior cerebral artery is blocked has been demonstrated by Dandy.[2] There does not seem to be any other blood vessel serving the brain for which this is true, which implies that the region supplied by this artery is basic to consciousness. Alford[1] pointed out that an area in the left base of the brain (served by the left anterior cerebral artery) was basic for consciousness. His evidence for this was the clinical observation that disturbances in consciousness do not occur when tumors are located in the right cerebral cortex or when the right hemisphere of the brain is surgically removed. This same observation has been made with regard to the upper portions of the left cortex, leaving only the left base of the brain as a possible seat of consciousness. (The argument that, if one section of the brain can be removed without the loss of consciousness, it, therefore, cannot be the seat of consciousness, is not completely conclusive because it is known that one part of the cortex can take over the functions of another.)

There is, as the foregoing indicates, not too much specific information available as to exact relationships which may exist between consciousness in general and any large portion of the brain except the left base and its connections with the hypothalamus. It has been fairly common for psychologists to assume that behavior, at least in its more simple forms, is a matter of reflexes. Usually this has been further simplified to the stimulus-response formula, in which behavior is described in terms of the stimulus and the response, with a good deal of speculation interposed as to the way in which the brain forms the connections and the integrations necessary between stimulus and response. Lashley[15] has experimentally demonstrated the inadequacy of both the chain-reflex and the stimulus-response formulae as adequate explanations of consciousness. At the same time, he refuted the neurological doctrine which emphasized a cerebral localization of psychological functions.

The facts of psychopathology and of brain function remain. The relationship between these two orders of events affords ground for endless speculation. Head once wrote, "Round and round like a stage army moves the procession; the clinical appearances are identical, but each fresh group of observers views them with new eyes and with different preconceptions."*

* Head, H., *Aphasia and Kindred Disorders of Speech*, Vol. I. London, Cambridge University Press, 1926, 84.

Summary

Behavior and mental life depend on the orderly functioning of the entire central nervous system. Without a brain there is no adaptive existence; and the better the organization of the nervous system, the more adaptive is the life of the organism. Injury or destruction of brain tissue leads to psychological changes, either in an actual loss or in a release of functions which are less adaptive. The evolutionary development of the nervous system shows throughout a one-to-one relationship between the complexity of the nervous system and the potentialities of adjustive behavior.

It has been experimentally demonstrated that visual stimulation is represented in the occipital lobes, and that cutaneous and kinesthetic sensation are primarily localized in the sensory area of the parietal lobe. Direct stimulation of the precentral convolution of the frontal lobe leads consistently to simple motor responses. Beyond these observations there are but very few accepted facts relating to cerebral localization. The cutting of the nerve tracts connecting the frontal lobes and the hypothalamus results in a relief of psychic pain and a diminution of self-consciousness. Stimulation of the parietal lobe may produce hallucinations. Bilateral removal of the temporal lobes in monkeys causes a profound change in the "personality" of the animal. Removal of occipital lobe tissue is usually followed by partial to complete blinding, depending on the amount of tissue removed. Consciousness is greatly disturbed or irretrievably lost when the areas constituting the base of the left cerebral hemisphere are damaged.

The exact relationship between brain anatomy, neural function, and psychological phenomena is speculative. Knowledge of brain anatomy is almost completely based on the study of dead material which must be stained so that it can be studied microscopically. That many artifacts grow out of this method — the only one available — is unquestioned. Functional neurophysiology has provided many excellent studies of simple structures. Behavior studies of animals in which brain lesions have been made provide further informative material. Clinical observation and psychological experimentation of the psychological changes in humans with brain damage provide still more information. The difficulty has been, and still is, in finding a key by which one may translate the observations of anatomy, physiology, and psychology into the same common language.

REFERENCES

1. Alford, L. B., "Localization of Consciousness and Emotion," *Amer. Jour. Psychiat.*, 1933, *12*, 789–799.
2. Dandy, W. E., "Changes in Our Conception of the Localization of Certain Functions of the Brain," *Amer. Jour. Physiol.*, 1930, *93*, 643.
3. Freeman, E., "Absence of the Left Occipital Lobe without Impairment of Vision," *Amer. Jour. Psychol.*, 1931, *43*, 503–505.
4. Freeman, W., and J. W. Watts, *Psychosurgery*. Springfield, Ill., C. C. Thomas, 1942.
5. ———, and ———, "Prefrontal Lobotomy," *Bull. N. Y. Acad. Med.*, 1942, *18*, 794–812.
6. Fritsch, G., and E. Hitzig, "Über die elektrische Erregbarkeit des Grosshirns," *Arch. Anat. Physiol.*, 1870, 300–332.
7. Head, H., *Aphasia and Kindred Disorders of Speech*, Vol. I. London, Cambridge University Press, 1926.
8. Jackson, J. H., *Selected Writings of John Hughlings Jackson*, Vol. II. (ed., J. J. Taylor). London, Hodder, 1932.
9. Jennings, H. S., *Biological Basis of Human Nature*. New York, Norton, 1930.
10. Klüver, H., "An Analysis of the Effects of the Removal of the Occipital Lobes in Monkeys," *Jour. Psychol.*, 1936, *2*, 49–61.
11. ———, and P. C. Bucy, "An Analysis of Certain Effects of Bilateral Temporal Lobectomy in the Rhesus Monkey, with Special Reference to "Psychic Blindness'," *Jour. Psychol.*, 1938, *5*, 33–54.
12. ———, and ———, "Preliminary Analysis of Functions of the Temporal Lobes in Monkeys," *Arch. Neurol. Psychiat.*, 1939, *42*, 979–1000.
13. Lashley, K. S., *Brain Mechanisms and Intelligence*. Chicago, University of Chicago Press, 1929.
14. ———, "Basic Neural Mechanisms in Behavior," *Psychol. Rev.*, 1930, *37*, 1–24.
15. ———, "Functional Determinants of Cerebral Localization," *Arch. Neurol. Psychiat.*, 1937, *38*, 371–387.
16. Levin, M., "On the Causation of Mental Symptoms," *Jour. Ment. Sci.*, 1936, *82*, 1–27.
17. Pavlov, I. P., *Lectures on Conditioned Reflexes*. New York, International Publishers, 1928.
18. Penfield, W., "The Cerebral Cortex in Man: I. The Cerebral Cortex and Consciousness," *Arch. Neurol. Psychiat.*, 1938, *40*, 417–442.
19. ———, and T. C. Erickson, *Epilepsy and Cerebral Localization*. Springfield, Ill., C. C. Thomas, 1941.
20. Sherrington, C. S., *Man on his Nature*. New York, Macmillan, 1941.
21. Shurrager, P. S., and E. Culler, "Phenomena Allied to Conditioning in the Spinal Dog," *Amer. Jour. Physiol.*, 1930, *123*, 186–187.
22. Sterling, K., and J. G. Miller, "Conditioning under Anesthesia" *Amer. Jour. Psychol.*, 1941, *54*, 92–101.

Chapter XXIX

THE INTERNAL ENVIRONMENT

CLAUDE BERNARD, the great French physiologist, suggested in his lectures in 1859–1860 that we live in two environments. The first is the general environment which is practically the same for all living organisms. It includes the weather, geography, the presence or absence of other members of the same species, and various other conditions related to the external environment as it surrounds the whole of each organism. A second environment, the internal environment, is constituted by the factors in which the living elements of each particular individual find their optimal habitat. Essentially, they consist of all the circulating fluids of the organism, that is, the blood, plasma, and lymph. This internal environment provides the vehicle for carrying nourishment to cells in all parts of the body and for removing from these cells their refuse for excretion. It is kept remarkably constant so that the interior of the organism is free from most external changes and stresses. As Bernard said, "It is the fixity of the [internal environment] which is the condition of free and independent life . . . [and] all the vital mechanisms, however varied they may be, have only one object, that of preserving constant the conditions of life in the internal environment." *

The two main regulating systems of the organism are the central nervous system (the brain) and the circulatory system comprised of the blood and lymph supplies. The study of the ways in which the human body is regulated and kept functional through the blood supply includes contributions from many of the specialized sciences. Physiology, pathology, biochemistry, bacteriology, immunology, pharmacology, and internal medicine all contribute to our knowledge of the nature of the internal environment.

The physiologist, Cannon,[1] emphasized certain of the broader implications which grew out of investigations of the internal environ-

* Bernard, C., quoted from W. B. Cannon, *The Wisdom of the Body.* New York, Norton, 1932, 38.

ment. The human body is made up of remarkably unstable (responsive) material. We have visual experience when the eye is stimulated by such minute energy values as 2.2 to 5.7×10^{-10} ergs,[7] while we hear when the eardrum is moved as little as 4.5×10^{-10} centimeters.[23] This visual sensitivity is in the range of 5 to 7 quanta of light energy,[7] while the auditory sensation results when the movement of the eardrum is less than 2 per cent of the diameter of a molecule of hydrogen.[23] The nose is sensitive to the odor of vanillin to the extent of 1 part by weight in 10 million parts of air, and to mercaptan to the extent of one twenty-third of a billionth of a gram in a liter of air.[1] These extraordinary sensitivities are far beyond any physical or chemical testing or measurement equipment which human beings have so far devised. Such instabilities make possible the extreme range of differential reactions which any human being can make.

In contrast to the extreme instability and sensitivity of the parts of the living organism, the organism itself is held at a remarkable degree of constancy both physically and chemically. The body temperature is maintained at a relatively constant figure no matter whether the external temperature is 40 degrees below zero or 130 degrees above zero. In flying, unless altitudes of more than 10,000 feet are reached, the amount of oxygen carried in the blood remains unaffected in most individuals. The material we include in our diet varies tremendously in regard to acidity or alkalinity, but acidity and alkalinity of the blood are retained at a very constant level. In fact, if this acid-base ratio is but slightly changed, death results.

The way in which coordinated physiological processes maintain a stabilized internal environment has been spoken of by Cannon as *homeostasis*, meaning a relatively constant condition which may vary to some extent. In studying such psychopathological phenomena as the increased output of energy in the manic state,[13] the prolonged rigidity in catatonia, or visual and auditory hallucinations, we are faced with two possibilities. These changes may take place either in the range permitted by ordinary homeostasis, or they may accompany the establishment of a new range of homeostasis.

Much fundamental biological research is still necessary to determine the types of psychopathology which can develop without alteration in the ordinary homeostasis of the human body, and those types involving the setting up of an entirely new interrelationship of controls. In spite of almost a century of experimental biological work in relation to psychopathological states, the available knowledge is still rather limited in regard to most of them. Unless we understand the physiology of these conditions, we can have no real insight into the psychological mechanisms.

Although our information about the relationship between internal environment and psychopathology is only fragmentary, certain of the more illustrative examples of research which have shed light on the problems of abnormal psychology will be presented in this chapter.

The Role of the Thyroid Gland

The long and interesting story of the relationship between the function of the thyroid gland and the emotional and intellectual life of the individual has involved many scientific disciplines, but the final picture has not become too complex. In the chapter on mental deficiency it was stated that cretinism is due to early failure in the functional development of the thyroid gland. It was pointed out that disturbances in the glandular function during adult life lead to the psychopathological syndrome of myxedema when there is a thyroid deficiency, and to Graves' disease if the thyroid supply is excessive.

The thyroid gland, an H-shaped structure lying across the larynx, secretes thyroxin directly into the blood stream. If its secretion is either deficient or excessive, the psychopathological conditions mentioned above result. The enlargement of the gland, commonly known as *goiter*, has been recognized for centuries. However, the relationship between the glandular disorders and psychopathological symptoms was not understood until late in the nineteenth century.

In 1873 Sir William Gull[6] described the cases of five women whose puffy faces, bulky forms, and general lethargy indicated the presence of a common disorder, which he called a "cretinoid state" and said might be related to a defective thyroid gland. Following the introduction of surgical antisepsis by Lister in the late 1870's, attempts were made to treat goiter by surgical removal of the thyroid gland. The original procedure disregarded the parathyroid glands which are embedded in the thyroid, and their loss usually was fatal. Removal of part of the gland was found to result in a mental and physical retardation which is now recognized as myxedema. Schiff was the first to transplant a piece of living thyroid tissue into the body of an animal whose thyroid gland had been removed. The animal continued to live, so proving that death following thyroid removal was due to thyroid deficiency. His finding was confirmed by von Eiselsberg with thyroid grafting in man. When these grafts had been slowly absorbed, the symptoms of thyroid deficiency reappeared. Next, it was found possible to make watery thyroid-gland extracts which could be injected into the body. As long as the injections were continued, the distressing symptoms of thyroid dysfunction did not occur. A further development was to administer the dried extract to the gland by mouth and to control the more obvious symptoms. This last fact was first reported by Fox in 1892.[8]

Following these findings, Kocher and Wagner-Jauregg attempted systematic treatment of cretinism with thyroid extract. They obtained favorable results even when the feeding was started late in life. In general, it was found that the earlier the recognition of the cretinous syndrome and the application of thyroid therapy, the more satisfactory was the outcome.

In 1937, Lewis[12] reported on seventy-nine cases who had been given thyroid therapy for a cretinous condition over a period of years. He found that the psychological test results indicated that it was possible for some cretins to become mentally normal. The IQ's of the cretins treated ranged from 13 to 116. The relation of the intellectual level to the treatment received indicated that the promptness and continuity of treatment were not alone decisive in determining whether and to what extent the child would remain retarded. There were a few who had attained normal intelligence despite inadequate treatment. Some had low intelligence although they had been treated regularly from the time of the first appearance of their symptoms. As a rule, however, there was a rough correspondence between the adequacy of specific treatment and the intellectual level attained. Other factors influencing psychological attainment were seen in the state of development at which the symptoms of thyroid deficiency appeared, in the degree of this deficiency, the heredity of the child as indicated by the intellectual level of his family, birth injury, and special education.

Evidently, thyroid deficiency and replacement therapy play a significant role in cretinism. Of equal importance in this connection is the fact that cretinism is a mental condition, with a new range of homeostasis explainable in terms of a basic deficiency in the internal environment.

Fever and General Paresis

Following the observation of remissions in certain psychotic patients who had recovered after an illness in which there was a marked fever, Wagner-Jauregg[22] proposed in 1887 to produce fever artificially for the treatment of general paresis. He first used Koch's tuberculin and found that the treated paretics had a higher rate of remissions than the untreated cases. In 1912 he abandoned tuberculin in favor of typhoid vaccine which also produced fever but did not increase the effectiveness of the procedure.

In 1917[21] he inoculated nine paretics with blood from a patient who was suffering from malaria. Six of them responded favorably and

PLATE 14

JULIUS WAGNER-JAUREGG
(1857–1940)

three of these six were still actively at work four years after the treatment. In 1922 he reported that out of two hundred cases of general paresis he had treated, fifty had improved or recovered sufficiently to have resumed their former occupations.

A survey of twenty years use of malaria with paretic patients in one hospital was made by Nicole.[17] The results are shown graphically in Fig. 16. From this figure, which is representative of the findings of many other investigators, it will be seen that, although malaria treatment is not uniformly successful, there is a vast difference between the number of deaths of patients who are treated when compared to those who are untreated.

The hypothesis which led Wagner-Jauregg to the development of fever therapy for paresis was that the natural response of the body to

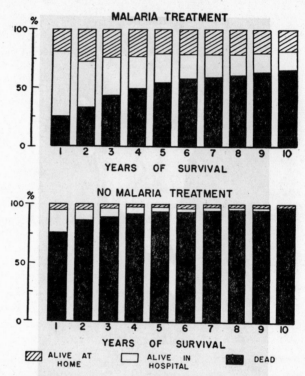

Fig. 16. *Effect of malaria treatment compared to no malaria treatment in general paresis. (From Nicole[17])*

the invasion of an infectious disease is an increase in temperature. This increase in temperature stimulates certain of the chemical reactions within the body so that the disease-resisting processes are increased in active efficiency. It is considered possible that an increased temperature of itself may be unfavorable to the infectious agent. There is still a certain amount of dispute concerning the mechanism by which the fever acts to stop the disease process in general paresis, although it has been established that it is the fever and not the malaria which is the effective agent. The procedure of raising the body temperature as a therapeutic measure has been applied to many diseases other than general paresis and is effective in some of them. However, it does not seem to be beneficial in any form of mental disease except general paresis.

Focal Infection and the Psychoses

In 1921, Cotton[3] reported that the elimination of "focal infections" in both psychotic and neurotic patients led to a marked amelioration in many instances. His theory was based on the observation, confirmed by many investigators, that a variety of streptococcal infections do, on occasion, localize at some point in the body without giving rise to pain symptoms. At the point of their localization they form a focus of infection which throws toxic substances into the blood stream and possibly produces, among other things, certain psychopathological reactions.

According to Cotton, many psychiatric patients have either infected teeth, tonsils, and sinuses, or infections in the gastrointestinal tract, the colon, and the genitourinary system. Most of these infections had been found by him in the teeth and tonsils. His contention was that through the removal of all infected teeth and tonsils as well as other foci of infection, the rate of remission from mental disease, as represented by the ratio of the average number of patients discharged to the number admitted, had increased from 43 per cent to 80 per cent. This report created a great deal of interest as it was in line with the best medical knowledge of the time.

In an attempt to evaluate the effectiveness of the elimination of sites of focal infection as a remedial measure in psychiatric cases, 120 patients were selected as an experimental group by Kopeloff and Kirby.[11] Sixty-two of them served as controls and 58 as the experimental group. They were carefully matched as to age, type of mental disease, duration of psychosis, prognosis, and sex. The outcome of this comparison is given in Table 7. Of all the operated cases, 38 per cent

TABLE 7. THE PRESENCE AND REMOVAL OF FOCI OF INFECTION AS THEY INFLUENCE THE CLINICAL OUTCOME OF DEMENTIA PRAECOX AND MANIC–DEPRESSIVE PSYCHOSIS.[11]

Group	Focal Infection Removed	Number of Cases	Per Cent Benefited	Per Cent Unimproved
Dementia praecox	Yes	33	18	82
	No	32	25	75
Manic-depressive	Yes	20	75	25
	No	25	72	28
Infected teeth and infected tonsils	Yes	37	41	59
	No	27	33	67
Infected teeth and noninfected tonsils	Yes	10	33	67
	No	23	52	48
Other sites of infection	Yes	19	21	79
	No	22	50	50

were classed as benefited and 62 per cent as unimproved. Of all the control cases, 47 per cent improved without surgery whereas 54 per cent were unimproved. Among those who had infected teeth and tonsils, 41 per cent of the operated cases improved as did 33 per cent of those who had not been operated upon. Of those who had infected teeth and noninfected tonsils, 33 per cent of the operated cases improved and 52 per cent of the nonoperated. Since none of these comparative data for operated and unoperated groups provided a statistically significant difference, the investigators concluded that "on the whole, then, the operated group appears to have improved no more by the elimination of focal infection than the control group which received no operative procedure."* In spite of this negative finding which has been confirmed by subsequent investigators, it is considered desirable for every mental patient to have possible focal infections treated, since their elimination may improve the general state of physical health. That toxic psychoses occur is well known, as is the fact that toxic states may precipitate a psychosis. However, dementia praecox and manic-depressive psychosis are not cured by the removal of focal infections.

Shock Therapy

For many years it had been known that severe physical shock or injury (and occasionally severe psychological crisis) seemed to agitate some psychiatric patients to such an extent that they were shaken out of their psychosis. In the early 1930's Sakel,[18] a Viennese physician, was investigating the effect of overdoses of insulin on morphine addiction. He attempted in this manner to upset the balance of the autonomic nervous system, and actually observed favorable results in certain addicts. This finding led him to formulate an interesting hypothesis. In the normal functioning of the nervous system certain pathways were believed by Sakel to be laid down and followed by the nervous impulses in the ordinary behavior and mental life of the individual. If some toxin or excitant hormone is thrown into the blood stream and reaches the nerve cells of the brain, there may be either (a) a blocking of ordinary pathways, particularly those which have been most recently established by activity, and consequently an exhibition of more primitive responses; or (b) a diversion of impulses into new pathways which may give rise to odd and bizarre types of

* Kopeloff, N., and G. H. Kirby, "Focal Infection and Mental Disease," *Amer. Jour. Psychiat.*, 1923, 3, 163.

esponse. According to this theory, insulin coma would either relieve the blocking of the pathways or give opportunity for the new, incorrect pathways to disappear and permit the establishment of correct connections. Insulin in overdoses acts to reduce the amount of sugar circulating within the blood and thereby withdraws sugar from the tissues of the body including the brain. Withdrawal of sugar has an anesthetic effect upon brain function, so that the patient in insulin shock acts as though he were deeply anesthetized. The shock is overcome by comparatively large amounts of sugar, given either directly into the blood stream or by mouth.

Since schizophrenics exhibit odd and bizarre behavior, Sakel thought it worth while to submit them to temporary insulin shock with the hope of altering their behavior. He found, as have many others since, that this procedure produced a beneficial effect in a considerable number of schizophrenic patients. The method led in some instances to a complete remission or cure.

About the same time that Sakel was doing his early experiments with insulin, Meduna[14] began the administration of metrazol to produce convulsions in schizophrenic patients. The theory had persisted in medical literature for many years that it was exceedingly rare to encounter dementia praecox and epilepsy in the same individual. The general conclusion had been that epileptic convulsions protect the individual from the development of schizophrenic symptoms. Metrazol, which is a chemical closely allied to camphor, was known to produce convulsions in animals, and unconsciousness with violent seizures in humans. On this basis Meduna worked out a therapeutic procedure which brought about amelioration and remission of symptoms in many schizophrenics following a series of convulsions induced by metrazol.

Somewhat later (1938), Cerletti and Bini[2] developed another method to bring about the convulsive seizures which were occasionally observed in insulin shock and were considered the main therapeutic agent in metrazol shock. They made use of ordinary alternating electrical current to produce shock and convulsions, first in animals and subsequently in psychiatric cases. Today all three methods, insulin, metrazol, and electric shock, are applied to mental patients with varying degrees of success depending on a variety of factors.

The earlier and highly optimistic reports concerning the remission rates following shock therapy have not been completely borne out through succeeding years of experience. Insulin shock seems most effective in milder schizophrenic attacks. Metrazol is used when schizophrenics do not respond to insulin. Electric shock apparently gives the most satisfactory results in depressions and in involutional cases.

There is at present no factual physiological or anatomical explanation for the therapeutic effect observed in a certain number of psychiatric cases. Some believe that the shock, no matter how induced, stimulates the autonomic nervous system. As a result, the regulating mechanisms of the body become more efficient and act to restore normal healthy function which is absent in psychotic individuals. Others hold that the effect of shock is to throw into action certain specialized blood cells which are known to operate both as agents of repair and as scavengers in infectious or toxic conditions. Still others claim that shock therapy causes actual damage to the brain tissue. The repair of this damage may lead to a restoration of normal function and to a disappearance of malfunction which has been responsible for the psychotic mechanisms.

Some psychiatrists have postulated that shock therapy is effective for psychological reasons and that it does not depend upon any physiological changes. Their theory is that the shock is regarded by the patient as a form of punishment which is gratifying to his masochistic tendencies and hence of therapeutic value. Actually, little credence can be given to this viewpoint since it is known that in both insulin and electric shock the unconscious state occurs without fear or apprehension. Although convulsive seizures are unpleasant for others to witness, they are not really part of the conscious experience of the individual who is receiving the therapy. It may be said, therefore, that the fundamental basis of the relationship between psychopathology and shock treatment is still unknown. However, the problem, as such, is an extremely interesting one because it represents an instance in which an induced change in homeostasis produces a change in psychological manifestations.

Dilantin and Epilepsy

The discovery by Merritt and Putnam[15] of the use of dilantin for the control or alleviation of seizures in epilepsy is an excellent example of a systematically planned procedure which ended in a positive finding. It had been known for many years that bromides and phenobarbital were relatively effective in limiting the number and severity of seizures in epilepsy. It was also known that many of the same drugs which inhibited or facilitated seizures in animals were effective in human beings. On the basis of this knowledge, Merritt and Putnam worked out a standard procedure for inducing convulsions in cats. They applied an alternating electrical current for a fixed period of time, during which a known amount of electrical energy was used. With this standardized method they systematically tried out a large number of drugs known to inhibit seizures and a series of entirely new drugs. Their objective was to find a chemical substance which combined the highest anticonvulsive effect with the least narcotic action. The drugs were tested by determining the convulsive threshold of the animal immediately before their administration, and again after an interval of from two-and-a-half to four hours, in order to allow for absorption of the drug. The tests were extended to a total of sixty-seven different drugs.

In this array, dilantin (sodium diphenyl hydantoinate) was found to be especially effective in protecting animals from electrically induced seizures and at the same time it had little narcotic or sedative effect. Since it was well tolerated by cats, dogs, and rats in large single doses as well as in long-continued daily doses, it was considered safe to be used with epileptic patients.

Two hundred patients were given the substance over a varying length of time. Of the 118 patients who were subject to frequent *grand mal* attacks, 58 per cent were completely relieved and an additional 27 per cent showed a marked reduction in the number of attacks; in the remainder there was little or no improvement. In a group of 74 patients with frequent *petit mal* attacks, complete relief was obtained in 35 per cent and a marked reduction in 49 per cent; in the remaining 16 per cent there was only slight or no improvement. In 6 patients suffering from psychomotor equivalent attacks, complete relief was obtained in 4 and very marked improvement in the other 2. In a subsequent study of 39 patients subject to such psychomotor equivalents (either alone or associated with *grand mal*), 62 per cent were found to be completely relieved and 23 per cent greatly improved. Out of 267 epileptic patients included in a later report,[16] a total of 227 had responded favorably to dilantin treatment, in that their seizures were either completely controlled or markedly reduced over a period varying from two months to two years.

This discovery constitutes an outstanding example of the application of the scientific method to a well-defined problem in the field of psychopathology. The new treatment was based on the combined contributions of pharmacology, biochemistry, and neurophysiology applied to a challenging problem.

The Use of Vitamins in Psychopathological States

One of the most promising and most rapidly developing fields of research with special implications in psychopathology is concerned with the discovery and use of vitamins. In 1920, no one of the four vitamins then known had been chemically identified or synthesized. By 1940, the identification and synthesis of vitamins A, C, D, E, K, P, and of more than a dozen of the B vitamins was an accomplished fact. It is known now that the vitamin B complex contains certainly two, and probably more, fractions whose deficiency may produce a variety of psychological states. These substances are niacin (which has also been called "nicotinic acid" or the "p-p factor") and thiamin (B_1).

That pellagra is usually accompanied by a definite psychosis has been known for many years. The three leading symptoms of this disease are dermatitis, diarrhea, and dementia. The acute manifestations may be fatal within a few months, but many cases become chronic and linger for several years. The disease is old in the history of medicine, has been found in all countries and races, and has been the topic of medical investigation and speculation for many years. Until recently, the leading explanatory theories were that the disorder occurred when corn was a principal item of the diet, and that it was due either to some toxin in one of the cereals used or to a generally unbalanced diet.

In 1937, Elvehjem et al.[4] demonstrated that niacin (nicotinic acid) cures black tongue in dogs, a canine disease which is analogous to pellagra in human beings. The same investigators also succeeded in isolating and chemically identifying the niacin itself.

The following year, Spies and his collaborators[19] showed that pellagra cases responded in a dramatic fashion to niacin. All the psychotic symptoms of sixty critical pellagra patients disappeared within 10 hours to 6 days following the administration of this vitamin. The mental symptoms of these sixty cases were of the severe and acute type. Many of the patients were violent and acutely hallucinated; others were deeply depressed. Shortly after the beginning of niacin therapy, the agitated patients became calm; the depressed, cheerful; and legally speaking, the insane became sane. "After recovery these patients often had an excellent memory of their actions, ideas, and of their surroundings during the psychotic period. They were usually completely adjusted after treatment, except for some perplexity about the cause of their actions during the psychosis. 'What made me act that way?' and 'Was I crazy?' are questions that are frequently asked at this time. In most cases improvement was abrupt, occurring sometimes overnight." *

After relief from their acute psychosis, thirty of the original patients were kept free from mental symptoms by continued use of the vitamin and without any essential change in their previous environment. Twenty of the remaining patients failed to maintain their recovery when they returned to their homes and no longer received the vitamin. The other ten patients were lost sight of after leaving the hospital.

As a check on the nature of the mental change produced, the investigators withdrew the administration of the vitamin in certain patients without their knowledge and substituted for it another medication of similar appearance. The usual result was that the patients who had responded favorably to vitamin therapy returned to their previous psychotic state within a week.

Hoping that niacin might be beneficial to nonpellagrous psychoses, it was administered to a wide variety of other types of psychiatric cases. In no instance did the administration of even large amounts of the vitamin produce a satisfactory effect.

In a subsequent study, Frostig and Spies[5] investigated the initial nervous and mental symptoms associated with the onset of a mild pellagrous condition. They found a striking uniformity of mental symptoms which varied in intensity but showed no connection with any single type of personality deviation or with the usual environmental stresses, conflicts, or other factors entering into neuroses. Many of the patients appeared to have anxiety states with depressive features. The outstanding features were psychosensory and psychomotor disturbances, emotional instability with marked anxiety, increased fatiguability, insomnia, and headaches. When niacin was administered, the symptoms rapidly diminished in intensity and gradually disappeared entirely.

The psychopathology of dietary thiamin deficiency was experimentally studied and well described by Williams et al.[24] Six physically active women, recovered mental patients, were chosen on the basis of their voluntary cooperation, lack of physical defects, absence of any history of abnormal nutrition, and quiescence of previous mental illness. They were put on a special diet composed of white flour, sugar, tapioca, cornstarch, polished rice, white raisins, egg white, cottage cheese, butter, tea, and cocoa. This diet is rich in carbohydrates but contains very little thiamin. The period of restricted diet

* Spies, T. D., C. D. Aring, J. Gelperin, and W. B. Bean, "The Mental Symptoms of Pellagra. Their Relief with Nicotinic Acid," *Amer. Jour. Med. Sci.*, 1938, *196*, 467.

was extended to 88 days. The onset of symptoms varied in time of appearance. In general, the more active subjects were affected first. The shortest time for the appearance of definite evidence of nutritional deficiency was 12 days, the longest 48 days.

The symptoms ultimately noted by all subjects were depressive mood, generalized physical weakness, dizziness, backache, muscular soreness, insomnia, nausea, loss of appetite, and vomiting. Less regular features were general apathy, difficulty in thought and memory, fear of lights, headaches, sensations of heat and cold, fatigue of the eye muscles, and a reawakening of psychotic trends which had previously been quiescent.

After 88 days a subcutaneous injection of thiamin was given while the special diet was continued. Subjective improvement was observed within a few hours after the injection. During the succeeding 18 days, regular thiamin injections were combined with the restricted diet. In this period all manifestations of the previous vitamin deficiency disappeared.

The investigators emphasized the neurasthenialike nature of the syndrome induced by the restriction of thiamin in the diet. In fact, they claimed that the symptoms of neurasthenia are practically identical with the symptoms of thiamin deprivation. It was not (and should not be) implied, of course, that all patients diagnosed as neurasthenic are suffering from thiamin deficiency. This kind of thiamin deficiency is probably very rare, but it should be considered as a possible etiological factor in all cases exhibiting neurasthenic symptoms.

It has been recognized for some years that certain forms of alcoholic psychoses offer symptoms which closely resemble those of pellagra. In a series of investigations since 1936, Jolliffe[9] and his coworkers have been able to show that this pellagralike accompaniment of chronic alcoholism is associated with a vitamin B deficiency. Many chronic alcoholics who are daily imbibing large quantities of alcoholic beverages seem to obtain sufficient energy from the alcohol which is substituted for the carbohydrates in a normal diet. They eat little or nothing, subsisting almost entirely on alcoholic beverages. Since these beverages contain no vitamins, the drinker develops an acute vitamin deficiency which is held by various investigators to be the basis of alcoholic hallucinosis, delirium tremens,[10] and even Korsakoff's disease. The restoration of vitamin B in large quantities to the diet has been reported to have a curative effect on the acute psychotic symptoms of many alcoholic addicts.

Another recent study made by a group of English investigators[20] was devoted to the effect of vitamins B and C upon the mental status of senile patients. As was to be expected, such vitamin treatment was not found adequate to stop the biologically inevitable development of senility, and did not affect the basic mental reactions associated with the physiological aspects of aging. However, it seemed to have a beneficial effect, in certain cases to a striking degree, upon various symptoms of senile dementia. Some of the patients became more coherent and intelligent in their conversation; others were either less depressed or less excited; others showed a decrease in aimless activity and became brighter, more friendly, and more sociable; others became more cleanly; while still others began to recognize their relatives and nurses and were able to care for themselves more adequately. Tests of psychomotor speed and coordination showed increases in the scores of the treated group, as compared with a series of patients who received medication other than the vitamins. In view of these findings it may be expected that the administration of large doses of vitamins to all aging persons might alleviate the course and nature of psychopathological phenomena attendant on senility.

Comment

These examples of both old and new contributions to our understanding of the abnormal psychology of the individual indicates that almost every therapeutic advance in psychopathology has been greatly enhanced by the application of the findings of the basic sciences to the problems of the internal environment and bodily homeostasis. If future progress in the therapy of the mental disorders is to be predicted on the basis of past experience, it seems safe to expect that the final solution of many of the major problems of psychopathology will come from the biological sciences.

It is true that the discovery of a biological basis for one or another psychopathological state does not clarify the psychology of the event. For example, the fact that some psychotic patient is suffering from a lack of niacin does not explain why he exhibits a mania rather than a depression. Nor do we gain much insight into the mental mechanisms if we find that a psychosis has been cured by niacin. It is essential to realize, however, that psychological research can lead to important biological discoveries if it is carried out in cooperation with the other basic sciences. In this light, psychological investigation may be expected to be of particular value in directing attention toward those biological mechanisms which are basically changed in certain of the mental disorders.

The relationship between psychopathology and variation in internal environment stands out as one of the greatest opportunities for promoting a better understanding of abnormal psychology. Our knowledge of this aspect of human life is still far from complete, but it is sufficient to indicate some basic correlations and to suggest other possible relations. One way of formulating these relationships is as follows:

1. Certain mental disorders are known to be characterized by unusual (abnormal) homeostasis, such as cretinism, myxedema, and Graves' disease, which are based on thyroid dysfunction.

2. Certain changes in homeostasis can be induced experimentally in any normal person and can be shown consistently to result in psychopathological states; for example, the psychoses attendant on vitamin deprivation or oxygen lack at high altitudes.

3. Certain mental diseases are considerably improved or completely cured by induced changes in homeostasis; for example, insulin shock therapy in schizophrenia.

These formulations support the belief that a close correlation exists between psychopathology and physiological homeostasis. It seems imperative, therefore, to investigate every psychopathological state with the objective of clarifying whether or not a change in homeostasis may be involved. The fact that no physiological changes have been found in many neurotic or psychotic conditions may mean either (a) that no change exists, or (b) that no adequate measures or indicators of such changes are now available. To repeat, many of the major therapeutic advances in neuropsychiatry have come from investigations of particular changes in the internal environment. It is safe to predict, therefore, that much of the future progress will come from the same source.

Summary

The internal environment consists of the totality of circulating fluids of the body. These circulatory systems, together with the central nervous system, act to regulate the life adjustment of the organism. The tissues of the body are extremely sensitive (unstable) to stimulation. The internal environment is held very constant through an elaborate integrative mechanism which is called the "process of homeostasis."

Defective development or dysfunction of the thyroid gland produces cretinism, myxedema, or Graves' disease. The first two syndromes are alleviated by the administration of thyroid extract, the third by surgical removal of part of the gland.

General paresis, which formerly was a rapidly deteriorating process with terminal dementia and early death, is now usually arrested by one or another fever therapy. Both thyroid medication and fever treatment were, in part, the discoveries of Wagner-Jauregg.

Earlier reports that the symptomatology of the major psychoses could be materially influenced by removal of sites of focal infection have not been substantiated. The introduction of insulin coma, metrazol seizures, or electrically induced convulsions has been found to be beneficial in a fair number of psychotic states, particularly in acute schizophrenic and depressive conditions.

The discovery of the effectiveness of dilantin in the control of epileptic seizures is an outstanding example of a well-conceived research project which solved an important therapeutic problem. The finding that mental disorders can be produced by vitamin deficiency and alleviated by the use of either thiamin or niacin shed light upon the mystery which surrounded various forms of mental disease. Further advances in this field may be expected.

Although the beneficial effect of some drug, hormone, or vitamin does not explain the nature of the actual psychopathological phenomena involved, it is true that psychological studies have served and should continue to serve as indicators of profitable points for research on the biology of mental disorder.

REFERENCES

1. Cannon, W. B., *The Wisdom of the Body*. New York, Norton, 1932.
2. Cerletti, U., and L. Bini, quoted from L. Kalinowski, "Electric Convulsion Therapy in Schizophrenia," *Lancet*, 1939, *2*, 1232–1233.
3. Cotton, H. A., *The Defective, Delinquent and Insane*. Princeton, Princeton University Press, 1921.
4. Elvehjem, C. A., R. J. Madden, F. M. Strong, and D. W. Woolley, "The Isolation and Identification of the Anti-black Tongue Factor," *Jour. Biol. Chem.*, 1938, *123*, 137–149.
5. Frostig, J. P., and T. D. Spies, "The Initial Nervous Syndrome of Pellagra and Associated Deficiency Diseases," *Amer. Jour. Med. Sci.*, 1940, *199*, 268–274.
6. Gull, W. W., "On a Cretinoid State Supervening in Adult Life in Women." Reprinted in T. D. Ackland, *The Published Writings of William Withey Gull*. London, New Sydenham Society, 1894, 313–321.
7. Hecht, S., "Energy Relations in Vision," in H. Klüver, *Visual Mechanisms*. Lancaster, J. Cattell Press, 1942, 19–20.

8. Hoskins, R. G., *Endocrinology: The Glands and Their Function*. New York, Norton, 1941.

9. Jolliffe, N., "Vitamin Deficiencies in Chronic Alcoholism." Chapter III in E. M. Jellinek, *Alcohol Addiction and Chronic Alcoholism*. New Haven, Yale University Press, 1942, 173–240.

10. Kiene, H. E., R. J. Streitwieser, and H. Miller, "The Role of Vitamin B_1 in Delirium Tremens," *Jour. Amer. Med. Asso.*, 1940, *114*, 2191–2194.

11. Kopeloff, N., and G. H. Kirby, "Focal Infection and Mental Disease," *Amer. Jour. Psychiat.*, 1923, *3*, 149–192.

12. Lewis, A., "A Study of Cretinism in London," *Lancet*, 1937, *1*, 1505–1509; *2*, 5–9.

13. McFarland, R. A., and H. Goldstein, "The Biochemistry of Manic-Depressive Psychosis," *Amer. Jour. Psychiat.*, 1939, *96*, 21–58.

14. von Meduna, L., "The Significance of the Convulsive Reaction during the Insulin and the Cardiazol Therapy of Schizophrenia," *Jour. Nerv. Ment. Dis.*, 1938, *87*, 133–139.

15. Merritt, H. H., and T. J. Putnam, "Sodium diphenyl hydantoinate (dilantin sodium) in the Treatment of Convulsive Seizures." *Jour. Amer. Med. Asso.*, 1938, *111*, 1068–1073.

16. ———, and ———, "Further Experiences with the Use of Sodium Diphenyl Hydantoinate in the Treatment of Convulsive Disorders," *Amer. Jour. Psychiat.*, 1940, *96*, 1023–1027.

17. Nicole, J., "Malaria in Neuro-Syphilis, 1923–1943." *Jour. Ment. Sci.*, 1943, *89*, 381–389.

18. Sakel, M., *The Pharmacological Shock Treatment of Schizophrenia*. New York, Nervous Mental Disease Monograph, #62, 1938.

19. Spies, T. D., C. D. Aring, J. Gelperin, and W. B. Bean, "The Mental Symptoms of Pellagra: Their Relief with Nicotinic Acid," *Amer. Jour. Med. Sci.*, 1938, *196*, 461–475.

20. Stephenson, W., C. Penton, and V. Korenchevsky, "Some Effects of Vitamins B and C on Senile Patients," *Brit. Med. Jour.*, 1941, *2*, 839–844.

21. Wagner-Jauregg, J., "The Treatment of General Paresis by Inoculation of Malaria," *Jour. Nerv. Ment. Dis.*, 1922, *55*, 369–375.

22. ———, "Message," in W. M. Simpson, and W. Bierman, *Fever Therapy*. New York, Hoeber, 1937, 2–4.

23. Wilksa, A., quoted from E. G. Boring, *Sensation and Perception in the History of Experimental Psychology*. New York, Appleton-Century, 1942, 339.

24. Williams, R. D., H. L. Mason, R. M. Wilder, and B. F. Smith, "Observations on Induced Thiamin (Vitamin B_1) Deficiency in Man," *Arch. Int. Med.*, 1940, *66*, 785–799.

Chapter XXX

EDUCATION

EDUCATION has been defined as the development of abilities, attitudes, or forms of behavior, and the acquisition of knowledge, as a result of teaching and training. It is apparent that the methods of education and reeducation are related in many ways to abnormal psychology. In a broad sense, any form of mental hygiene is a form of directed education, while much of psychotherapy is specialized reeducation. Abnormal conditions in which educational methods are of importance include feeble-mindedness and those states of maladjustment which either grow out of some irremediable handicap or are clearly due to the formation and persistence of nonadjustive habits. Manic-depressive psychosis, dementia praecox, and paranoia are among the conditions in which only a limited profit can be expected from the use of ordinary methods of education and reeducation.

Special educational programs directed toward the training and possible improvement of the feeble-minded have engaged the interest of many persons during the past two centuries. The development of specialized techniques for the education and rehabilitation of behavior-problem children, of delinquent children, and of physically handicapped children has occupied the center of the stage in child psychiatry for the past twenty-five years. Real progress and sound accomplishment have come from this work. World Wars I and II have directed attention to educational procedures in the rehabilitation of war casualties, both physical and neuropsychiatric. Although much of this reeducation has been designed to meet particular problems, the findings have shed light on the nature and therapy of traumatic neuroses.

Education and the Feeble-minded

If it were possible to find a human being who had somehow survived from infancy without contact with other humans, one might be able to determine the attitudes, traits, and mental processes that are native and those which are due to social imitation and education. One might also investigate the relative efficiency of different educational methods if several such persons were available. However, most of the accounts of wild children, wolf children, and savage orphans are folklore and very few instances of real scientific and educational research on such persons exist.

In September, 1799, the "Wild Boy of Aveyron" was captured in the Caune Woods in France.[7] As far as his early history could be recon-

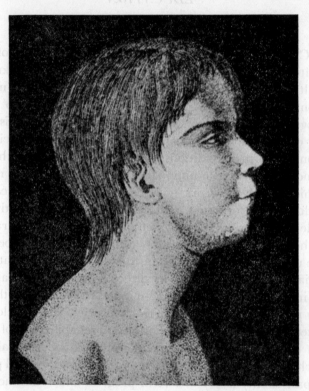

PLATE 15

THE WILD BOY OF AVEYRON

structed, he had been abandoned in this forest when he was five or six years old. He had been seen "naked and fleeing the approach of men" several years before he was captured. His age was estimated to be twelve when he was apprehended. His capture aroused great public curiosity, so that he was brought to Paris where he was visited by many doctors and scholars who wanted to see man in his savage state. Instead of a Noble Savage they saw "A degraded being, human only in shape; a dirty, scarred, inarticulate creature who trotted and grunted like the beasts of the fields, ate with apparent pleasure the most filthy refuse, was apparently incapable of attention or even of elementary perceptions such as heat or cold, and spent his time apathetically rocking himself backwards and forwards like the animals at the zoo."*

The boy was examined by Pinel, the leading specialist in France, who pronounced him an incurable idiot. Itard, a young medical man, "fired with the notion that science, particularly medical science, was all-powerful, and perhaps believing that his older colleague was too conservative in applying his own principle of the curability of mental disease, came to the conclusion that the boy's condition was curable."† Itard thought that the boy's state resulted from his lack of education and any opportunity to imitate and be influenced by human society. Since he had been greatly impressed by the philosophers Condillac and Locke, Itard saw this boy's mind as a *tabula rasa* (a blank page) upon which the experience which develops the normal mind had not yet written. He undertook with great patience and ingenuity to supply the mental and moral education that the boy had never had. His educational program included the following aims: interest in social life, increased sensibility to stimulation, a wider range of ideas and mental processes, and the use of speech.

Victor, the name Itard gave the Wild Boy, was a most unpromising subject. His eyes were unsteady and expressionless, and his hearing was equally unresponsive to the loudest sounds or the most touching music. A uniform guttural grunt was the only sound that he made. He showed equal indifference to the odor of perfume and the fetid odor of filth. He seemed destitute of memory, of judgment, and the ability to imitate. He was incapable of grasping the idea of climbing upon a chair to get food that was placed outside his normal reach. He made no attempt at communication by expressive movements. He managed to escape on several occasions, so that he had to be watched or kept in a locked room. His gait was either a trot or gallop, and he had "an obstinate habit" of smelling at any object that was given him. He showed neither interest nor affection toward those around him.

His sensitivity to cold and heat was very much below normal. When glowing embers rolled onto the hearth, he would pick them up with his bare fingers and replace them upon the fire without any particular haste. He was several times observed to pick potatoes out

* Itard, J–M–G., *The Wild Boy of Aveyron* (trans., G. and M. Humphrey). New York, Appleton-Century, 1932, vi-vii.
    † Itard, J–M–G., *ibid.*, vii.

of boiling water with his fingers and consume them while they were boiling hot. When Itard undertook to "prepare the senses to receive keener impressions," the stimulus of heat was applied in all possible ways. The boy was clothed, put in a warm bed, and given hot baths. After some time he showed himself responsive to temperature differences by testing the bath water with his hand and refusing to enter the tub if the water was only lukewarm. Similarly, he came to view his clothes as a means of keeping warm. Itard also used electric shocks and other forms of sensory stimulation to "increase his sensitivity." Gradually, his senses of taste, touch, and temperature improved, but there was no rapid improvement of responsiveness to sight or hearing.

Since Victor showed no interest in the usual toys and games that children of his age enjoyed, an attempt was made to develop those few interests he had, such as walks in the fields. He did not care for any sweets or highly seasoned food, but displayed obvious signs of joy when he was taken on trips to town or supplied with large quantities of his favorite foods.

In an attempt to "exercise the intellectual faculties," Itard tried out many ingenious ways of putting obstacles between Victor and his desires. These obstacles were expected to bring into play the boy's attention, memory, judgment, and sensory impressions. One of the most interesting experiments was based on his tendency to orderliness. He had been observed to place objects of furniture back in their original positions when they were displaced and to restore pictures to their former places on the walls. Itard hung objects on the wall with a drawing of each object placed above it and left them there for some time. As soon as an object was removed, Victor would return it to its proper position. Even when the order was changed, he returned all the objects to their correct positions. In the beginning, this activity was based solely on a memory factor of position. However, when the number of drawings and the frequency of their transposition were increased, the boy finally resorted to inspection of the drawing in placing the objects.

This observation led Itard to try a more complicated matching procedure. He pasted paper figures upon a board; one figure was a red circle, another a blue triangle, and the third a black square. Similar models of cardboard were made and placed over the figures pasted upon the board. When they were removed, Victor was able to replace them without difficulty. Shifts in the order of the figures indicated that he was using a process of comparison. Some days later Itard changed the board; this time he used the original figures, but all were of the same color so that the only difference was in the shape of the figures. Finally he added another change in which form was held constant and only color varied. Under all these circumstances, the boy was able to perform adequately.

The next task consisted of controlled variation of color and form. In one experiment, a long parallelogram was used with the square and, in a second experiment, a grayish-blue with a sky-blue. After some mistakes the boy mastered both problems. Itard proceeded to add new and more difficult complications until these exercises "finished by fatiguing his attention and his docility." Violent motions of impatience and rage appeared, and Victor threw the figures on the ground with vexation and made for his bed in a fury. When Itard persisted over several days in forcing him to try to do these tasks, the boy's fits of anger increased in violence. He became so destructive that he bit the sheets, blankets, and mantelpiece, scattered the ashes and andirons over the floor, and ended by falling into convulsions like those of epilepsy. These attacks became more frequent and were apt to appear at the slightest opposition or even without determining cause, so that Itard gave up this type of testing procedure.

It is worth noting that in these tests, Itard employed in a rudimentary fashion the methods which over a century later were called the "sorting-test" method, the method of "equivalent stimuli," and the introduction of an experimental conditioned neurosis.

The changes in the boy that Itard accomplished in nine months of work were startling. Victor's life changed from an unresponsive, animal existence to one in which he could compare, discern, and judge, and "apply the faculties of his understanding to the objects related to his instruction." At the end of two years of training he was no longer a Wild Boy but a clean, affectionate child. He responded to certain written words and understood much that was said to him. Itard continued working with Victor for four years, but during this subsequent period he suffered many disappointments over his pupil. In spite of the most careful attention and teaching, the boy never became a normal human being. He never learned to make more than a few sounds that had communicative significance.

In summing up the results of his training program, Itard admitted that only a very limited effect had been produced by the most intensive methods of education. These limitations were attributed by him to the almost complete "apathy" of Victor's organs of hearing and sight. This apathy, he said, was permanent. The improvements that were obtained were disappointing in terms of the standard of normality, but they were considerable in terms of the Wild Boy's state at the time of his capture. His senses of taste, sight, and touch had become much more differentiated, his relations to objects and people were more complex, and he could express his wants and follow simple orders. He had grown to be responsive to affection and attention from others, and learned to be ashamed of mistakes and outbursts. The absence of contact with other people and the usual course of experience in childhood had led to behavior patterns which were changed by Itard's intensive training program. However, the improvement was so limited that his mental status could not be attributed solely to the deficiencies of his early environment. He could not be taught to be a normal human being and Pinel had been correct in classifying him as feeble-minded.

PLATE 16

HENRY H. GODDARD (1866–

The particular importance of Itard's experiment centered around the fact that Victor could not proceed beyond a certain level of accomplishment in spite of patient, ingenious, skillful tutoring. There was a definite limit to his potential development. At the same time, the amount of change that was brought about, especially during the first two years of Itard's training, served as an indication of the way in which education and interaction with other human beings affect perception, discrimination, and behavioral patterns in general.

The case of the Wild Boy illustrated the point that mental defectives were, within limits, trainable. This observation stimulated Séguin, who was Itard's pupil, to develop more adequate training methods. He formulated a systematic training procedure for the feeble-minded based on what he called the "physiological" method. He incorporated these ideas in his lectures and gradually succeeded in stimulating interest in the problem of educating mentally retarded children. It was not until many years later, however, that these and other principles were put in actual use in special classes and schools for mental defectives.

The next long step forward in clarifying the value of education for the feeble-minded was made by Goddard.[5] In order to illustrate his contribution, the history and ancestry of a girl to whom he gave the pseudonym, Deborah Kallikak, may be considered. In 1898, at the age of eight, Deborah entered the Training School of Vineland, New Jersey. She had been born in an almshouse. Her mother had afterward married, not the father of Deborah, but the prospective father of another child; she later divorced him and married another man who was the father of some of her other children. She had been led into these marriages by well-meaning people who thought that it would be unfortunate for a child to be born illegitimately. On admission to the Training School, Deborah was disobedient, excitable, nervous, noisy, careless, obstinate, and destructive. She understood commands, knew the colors and a few letters, could not read or count, was able to carry wood and fill a kettle, could throw a ball but could not catch one, and could see and hear well.

After being in the Training School for fourteen years, she was at age twenty-two, cheerful, active, affectionate, and fairly good tempered. She learned new manual tasks quickly but required a half hour or twenty-four repetitions to memorize four lines of poetry. Her behavior demanded close supervision. She was quick and observing; did good work in wood carving in kindergarten, and was excellent in mimicry. She was a poor reader, poor at numbers, poor at spelling, but excellent at sewing. She had the mental age of a nine-year-old child. In other words, she was a high grade imbecile. While at the Training School she had been carefully guarded, and persistently trained, but very little was accomplished in the direction of raising general intel-

1912   1940

PLATE 17

DEBORAH KALLIKAK

ligence or mental ability. She would have been unable to maintain herself outside of the school because of her defective intelligence.

The great-great-grandfather of this girl was Martin Kallikak, Sr. He was of good family. During the Revolutionary War, he joined one of the numerous military companies. At one of the taverns frequented by the militia he met a feeble-minded girl by whom he became the father of a feeble-minded son. This child was given by its mother the full name of the father, and thus handed down to posterity the father's name and something of the mother's mental capacity. The illegitimate son was Martin Kallikak, Jr., from whom Goddard traced 480 descendants. Of these, there was conclusive proof that 143 were feeble-minded while only 46 were known to be normal. Evidence as to the mental status of the remainder was not available or was insufficient for forming an opinion.

Martin Kallikak, Sr., on leaving the Revolutionary Army, married a respectable girl of good family, and this union led to another line of descent of very different character. There were 496 direct descendants and all of them were described as normal people.

Here we have the history of six generations of two different family lines descended from a common ancestor. As might be expected, the interpretation of this family history, which is a record of a unique natural experiment, has met considerable criticism. It has been stated that the material was based on the surmises and opinions of ill-trained investigators who estimated the mental and physical states of both the dead and the living. Actually, this was not true. The investigators were well trained and really interviewed all the living members of the family. Regarding the persons who were dead, interviews were arranged with people who had personally known them. If conclusive evidence could not be obtained, the person in question was entered as undetermined. In fact, a study of the report as published in 1912 leaves one impressed with the scientific care and exactitude which were employed in this investigation. Whatever the criticism, Goddard did establish the fact that this variety of mental deficiency was a familial trait which persisted unaltered through several generations.

The second part of Goddard's[6] contribution consisted in the development of a new educational policy for the feeble-minded. From the days of Itard, efforts had been made to provide for them the usual formal education, with the emphasis on reading, writing, and computation as a means of increasing their defective mental capacity. Special training, designed to stimulate sensory and perceptual acuity, had also been stressed. Goddard rejected this procedure and showed that it had never been effective with true mental defectives. In place, he substituted manual training; training in the simpler arts and crafts which were within the scope of the ability of an ament. He emphasized the point that *a feeble-minded person can be trained but not mentally improved.*

The third part of Goddard's contribution was constituted by the development and application of the intelligence-test method which had first been introduced by Binet and Simon in France in 1908. Goddard translated, revised, and standardized the Binet test for American use. He was the one who recognized for the first time its great value as a method of diagnosing and evaluating the presence or absence of mental defect. The tremendous development of the mental-test method needs no further comment here, save to point out that it took the entire group of mental defectives out of the realm of uncertain diagnosis and formed a sound basis for segregation, care, training, and guidance.

Goddard demonstrated three major points with the utmost clarity — the familial nature of endogenous feeble-mindedness, the most profitable method of education for the mentally defective, and the use of intelligence tests to establish the presence and degree of amentia.

The more recent trends in the education of the feeble-minded have been summarized by Abel and Kinder.[1] As the ament grows older, the differences between his mental capacity and that of the normal child show themselves more clearly. Idiocy is recognized in infancy or in preschool years, so that those of the lowest grade of intellect are brought to the institutions early in life. As a rule, their condition leaves very little doubt in anyone's mind. The first two or three years of school attendance, that is, age groups 6 to 8, usually serve to disclose the defectives of the imbecile level. Their lack of intellectual ability becomes plainly apparent only when they are required to get along in ordinary school situations. A third group with an IQ between 60 and 80 is generally recognizable at the time of adolescence, when their school difficulties are complicated by the need of social and emotional adjustments necessary for adult self-independence. These high-grade defectives could be diagnosed by intelligence tests at an early age, but usually they are not examined before they run into social complications. The educational problems of each of these three groups are quite different.

With the lower grade idiots, very little can be achieved in the way of training, apart from some habit-training in self-care. Imbeciles are, within limits, trainable in simple tasks. Morons show a wide variation in their adaptability to training and this variation depends, only in part, on the IQ level. It is largely determined by personality and emotional traits.

One of the most promising educational objectives consists in training mental defectives to seek help and advice in the solution of their social, vocational, and personal problems. The normal person knows enough to seek assistance and advice when real problems confront him. Those of low intellect do not realize when they are faced with a real problem, nor do they know where to seek help, or how to distinguish between sound guidance and unfair exploitation. Conversely, social workers, psychologists, and psychiatrists who are expected to advise the mentally retarded must have a sound appreciation of the effects of limited mental ability and of the community resources available for helping these persons.

A further point, so far as education is concerned, turns on the distinction between those who are mentally deficient because of accident, injury, or illness — the exogenous cases — and those of essential or familial defect — the endogenous. The exogenous defectives are limited in their capability to perform mental abstractions or to function on a synthetic level. Their mental abilities are different and, as a result, their capability for training is different from that of the endogenous cases.

THE CONSTANCY OF THE INTELLIGENCE QUOTIENT

A basic assumption dating from Goddard's work is that the IQ is relatively constant and that special, intensive, educational procedures will not markedly alter it. This belief is founded on many experimental surveys, as well as on practical experience growing out of educational work with mental defectives. Several years ago a group of investigators at the Iowa Child Welfare Station called this assumption of constancy into question. They reported marked increases in IQ when retarded children were placed in foster homes where they were given special care and training.[9,10] In another investigation they showed that nursery-school children (tested upon entering nursery school and at the end of the school year) had an average increase of 7 points in IQ with the range of change varying from a gain of 45 points to a loss of 35.[11] The general implication of these Iowa studies would be that the IQ is an unstable measure of intelligence, and that intelligence can be considerably altered by special opportunity and training.

Woodworth[13] carefully evaluated these and other studies relating to the constancy of the IQ. He concluded that the Iowa studies confirm the existence of relatively small changes in IQ obtained from tests taken at intervals of time, but that their results do not indicate that the IQ is a totally unstable measure. It has always been incorrect to view an IQ as an absolute value. It should be realized that a certain amount of variation is to be expected and that in individual cases the amount of change may be comparatively great. In certain mentally retarded children it can be expected that exceptional instances of deprivation, illness, and the like will lead to an IQ which may be later increased to the normal range by training and opportunity. Woodworth said, "If the average change amounts to 5 points up or down, changes of 10 points will be common enough, changes of 15 points, will occur once or twice in a hundred cases, and even changes of 20 points may be expected occasionally. The still larger changes sometimes reported are based mostly on initial tests at a very early age which admittedly have little predictive value. These variations do not destroy the fact that the IQ is on the whole a relatively stable measure."* The content of teaching should be fitted to the child's capacities. Individualization of education is an important part of the philosophy of modern education. It has been recognized that an intellectually gifted child is out of place in a classroom of children of average intelligence. The methods of instruction required by ordinary children do not suit the educational needs of the exceptional child and may result in his becoming bored with the classroom procedures and so fail to stimulate him to the functional levels of which he is capable. The other side of that picture is shown by the subnormal child who has great difficulty in keeping up with average children of his age and, therefore, fails to profit from the methods of instruction appropriate to them. A child, who is out of his depth intellectually, tends to develop behavior disorders in class and may become a "problem child." If he is placed in a class of children of about the same level of intelligence, his antisocial behavior may disappear.

Although child-guidance and mental-hygiene clinics have made teachers more aware of the broad aspects of personality development, there are real differences between the objectives of the practical classroom teacher and the clinic worker dealing with problem cases. Wickman[12] made an interesting comparative study of teachers' attitudes and mental-hygiene clinic workers' attitudes toward children's behavior. The teachers were asked to rate the behavior problems that they considered most serious and to rank the relative seriousness of different types of behavior problems. They rated immoralities, dishonesties, and transgressions against authority as more serious than violations in orderliness in the classroom and application to schoolwork. The latter were rated as more serious than extravagant, aggressive personality and behavior traits which were, in turn, considered more serious than withdrawing, seclusive personality traits. When a group of mental-hygiene clinicians evaluated the different

---

* Woodworth, R. S., *Heredity and Environment,* New York, Soc. Sci. Res. Coun. Bull., 1941, #47, 82–83.

school problems, they rated the withdrawing type of personality as a more serious problem than any of the others, placing transgressions against authority and disorderliness in the classroom as the lowest in importance. The teachers' values were related to the immediate effects of behavior upon the social situation in the classroom rather than to their ultimate significance for the child's possible future personality development. Compliant, submissive, dependent behavior was more desirable to the teachers than aggressive, experimental, and independent behavior. The clinicians viewed unsocial behavior as having the most serious implications for later personality maldevelopment. The solitary, dependent child caused no trouble in the classroom and fitted the standards of behavior that the teachers wanted. In Wickman's opinion, these habits of withdrawal and dependency were encouraged and viewed as socially desirable by teachers who failed to realize that they might be symptoms of a basic underlying maladjustment, more serious than the aggressive, outgoing types of behavior.

Most schoolteachers have been sensitized to the problems of abnormal psychology and to the more commonly accepted procedures used in psychotherapy and mental hygiene. It still remains true that the majority of children respond to the ordinary school curriculum and pedagogical methods in a satisfactory fashion. They become good citizens and are normal people in the usual sense of the phrase. The abnormal child (either mentally defective or emotionally maladjusted) poses a problem for which there is no uniform solution. He must be viewed and treated as an individual case if an attempt to help him through educational methods is to be successful.

Education and Delinquency

A portion of those classified by society as delinquent or criminal are also psychopathic. Others are mentally defective; still others are the product of inadequate or improper education and training. All are abnormal in the sense that their behavior is surprising, unusual, and difficult to understand.

Sheldon and Eleanor Glueck[3] traced the criminal careers of youthful delinquents who had come before an outstanding juvenile court and had been treated at a leading child-guidance clinic. They investigated the records of a thousand boys who had been referred by the court for clinical examination. The average age was thirteen to fifteen. The social background of these cases was very poor and a large proportion gave evidence of unfavorable home conditions. poor heredity, low moral standards, and family criminality. Sixty-two per cent had very inferior homes and 70 per cent came from homes of unsound discipline. Seventy-five per cent of the families contained other criminals and about 90 per cent came from broken or poorly supervised homes. The offenses for which these boys had come in conflict with authority were larceny in about one half of the cases, burglary in one fourth, stubbornness in one tenth, and truancy in one tenth. About 88 per cent of the juvenile delinquents continued misconduct during a five-year period after their official treatment, and almost 80 per cent were recidivists. Of these, 70 per cent committed serious offenses and 33 per cent were arrested four or more times. There was but slight association between the nature of the juvenile delinquencies of the group and the kind of offenses for which they were later brought to court. The general implication was that the clinic and the court do not prevent the further development of delinquent careers. Neither agency can be depended on as a cure for delinquency or for the prevention of its development into criminality. The social problem that these boys presented was not solved by any of the reeducational methods that the court or clinic used. In fact, this juvenile-delinquent group had an appreciably higher proportion of recidivists during the five-year period than was found among the ex-inmates of a Massachusetts' reformatory for a similar period.

In another series of studies the Gluecks[4] followed for fifteen years the careers of 510 offenders who had been sent to a Massachusetts' reformatory after having been through the court and clinic. Of this group, 439 were still alive at the end of the fifteen years. More than one half of them were directly interviewed, while indirect evidence obtained from employers and families provided information concerning the remainder of the group. Over the years, the extent of their criminal conduct showed some tendency to decrease. At the end of the first five-year period, 20 per cent were nondelinquent, at the end of ten years 30 per cent were nondelinquent, and at the end of fifteen years 42 per cent were nondelinquent. Further evidence of improvement was found in the relative increase of minor offenses over major offenses. Minor offenses made up 29 per cent of the offenses in the first period, as compared with 32 per cent in the second period, and 39 per cent in the third. Most of those who, for one reason or another, "went straight" did so during and after the first five years, with a decrease in the rate of rehabilitations as time went by. On the whole, the study revealed the ineffectiveness of our attempts to rehabilitate delinquents who start a criminal career early in life. If the prevention of recurrent criminal offenses is regarded as the chief aim of punishment, all present methods of handling such persons fail miserably. It is possible that the use of indeterminate sentences with release of certain groups of prisoners when they reach certain stages in their mental development might help the situation. In general, both the current procedures of dealing with criminal and delinquent careers have been found to be discouraging in outcome and in hope for general improvement in social conditions. Changes in social policies seem necessary. According to the Gluecks, the fundamental attack upon the problems of antisocial behavior depends upon raising the socioeconomic status of the underprivileged.

For the most part, social evaluations of special educational and institutional methods are descriptive. They survey the outcome of "treatment" or "education" provided by some social institution and serve as a basis for theoretical speculation on the changes that revisions of the social institution might produce. One of the few studies in this field that makes use of a direct experimental approach is that of Moreno.[8] Much of his published material is speculative and theoretical, but certain results of the applications of his principles in specific social organizations are of definite interest. Moreno worked at the New York State Training School for Girls, an institution of five hundred to six hundred delinquent girls. They are sent to this school by courts from every part of the state, providing a cross section of ethnic and social groups. They live in a closed community, in which the unit of physical organization is a cottage under the supervision of a house mother. Moreno studied the social organization of this closed community and analyzed and described the psychological components which lead to the formation of specific social groups by the girls themselves. The difference from other social communities is that the unit here is not the natural family but an official cottage group or an unofficial, self-determined subgroup to which the girl belongs.

Moreno developed sociometric tests for evaluating, in this community, both the distribution of emotional attachments, likes and dislikes, friendships and enmities, and the position of each individual and group in relation to emotional patterns. The criterion of his testing procedure was the likes and dislikes of one girl for the other members of the community in respect to living together with them in the same cottage. Each girl was asked to name five girls, in order of choice, with whom she preferred to live. This question was not introduced as a theoretical problem but as a plan for the reorganization of living arrangements. The intention was to make the situation real and to have an actual criterion (that of living together) in working out the scales of preference or dislike. The spontaneous choices made by a girl were assumed to reveal the number of attractions and repulsions to which she was exposed in a group activity. Supplementary interviews brought out further information on the nature of these attractions and repulsions. Subsequently, each girl was encouraged, as part of her educational program, to act out in a "play" a standard life situation improvised to portray her own difficulties. Her part, as she developed it, was taken as a source of information on her character, intelligence, conduct, and psychological position in the group.

This educational procedure placed the emphasis on the immediate forces and personal interactions, rather than upon the investigation of past habits and patterns of reaction. The cross currents of emotion among individuals provided various concepts of psychological interest. For example, the volume of a girl's "emotional expansiveness" was rated on the basis of the number of acquaintances that she had had at any one time. There were marked individual differences in this respect, just as there were in the number of people to whom a girl was attracted. The position of any girl in the group was evaluated by relating both her own attractiveness and repulsions to the number of individuals by whom she was attracted and rejected. A desirable social grouping, with the relatively highest educational potentialities, was found to depend upon the attitudes of the girls toward each other and toward their house mother.

Through analysis of both the structure of the social groups and the individual attractions and repulsions, it was possible to determine the sources of conflict and friction and to make an attempt at removing or accentuating them, as seemed educationally desirable. In a training school of this type, the number of runaways may be taken as an indicator of the extent to which the community functions as a psychologically satisfactory home for its members. Following the introduction of Moreno's procedure in the study of delinquent girls, the number of runaways at this institution showed a remarkable decrease, apparently due to the improved educational method.

This procedure of individual study, with an emphasis on the emotional attachments of each person, might very well be worked out and applied to other problem groups, for example, prison populations, mental-hospital groups, schools for problem children, or orphanages. Such a method might reasonably be expected to make good educational procedures more effective.

Education of Postencephalitic Children

A particularly difficult group to handle, both theoretically and educationally, consists of persons who have suffered from encephalitis lethargica during childhood. Postencephalitic behavior disorders in children consist of restlessness, overactivity, uncontrolled aggressiveness, disobedience, truancy, and sexual offenses. Some of these deviations may be attributable to poor training during convalescence, but in most cases the behavior disorder is a result of inadequate emotional control and hyperactivity which cause overreactions to a wide range of stimuli.

A group of forty-eight postencephalitic children, together with a group of fourteen "problem" children who had not had encephalitis, were the subjects of a special educational program at the Pennsylvania Hospital under the direction of Bond and Appel.[2] These children were admitted to the hospital school where the buildings, schedule of activities, and staff of teachers and nurses had been specially selected for such a plan of remedial education. Although intensive medical observation had been part of the original plan, the educational considerations were found to be of primary importance. Planned schoolwork and play were organized in such a way as to exercise the most favorable effect upon the conduct of these children. A peculiarity of the behavior of encephalitic children was seen in their intense emotional reactions to their families. Therefore, all members of the institutional staff were explicitly directed to maintain an impersonal and patient attitude toward the children. A direct attack upon the behavior disorders was attempted with methods planned to develop more wholesome attitudes and more constructive behavior on the part of the children. Nothing very new or different was tried, but the best methods of education that had been developed both in theory and practice were integrated into the training system. Schedules of the child's time were carefully worked out so that he had a regular routine to follow. Outlets for strenuous activity were provided, in order to enable the child to express his overactivity without restraint at planned times and under certain conditions. In general, praise and reward were used rather than punishment. With these children it was found that systematic deprivation or explanation was of educational value where dogmatic discipline or physical punishment only increased the destructive behavior. In extreme cases, isolation from the group and isolation within the group (other children were instructed not to speak to the disobedient child) were the most severe forms of control used. Distraction and diversion by teachers and nurses were frequently able to avert oncoming temper tantrums or fights between children.

Of the forty-eight postencephalitic children, all but two showed improvement; and of the fourteen nonencephalitic problem cases, all but one improved. These results indicated that the children were able to learn by experience and to adjust to institutional life when their care and education were handled by a staff that understood their individual personality needs. Of twenty postencephalitic children sent home, 35 per cent made a good adjustment at home (exclusive of six cases who were feeble-minded). These figures show that planned education in a controlled environment may be beneficial to a certain proportion of postencephalitic children. The results deserve attention since practically all cases of this sort had been reported by previous investigators to be almost completely refractory in their response either to ordinary home or school instruction or to special institutional training.

The Role of Education in Rehabilitation

Rehabilitation involves the reestablishment of some person as nearly as possible to a former way and station in life. The soldier with a traumatic neurosis or combat fatigue, the woman who has long been hospitalized with some disabling mental or physical disease, the child who has been crippled by infantile paralysis, all must be rehabilitated. It is always the individual who must be considered, in relation to his assets, liabilities, and general life situation. Education itself plays a minor role, and in some instances it does not enter the picture at all. Most persons who are endeavoring to reestablish themselves ask only a fair chance and a bit of good-natured tolerance on the part of the community until they find a proper niche for themselves.

Education plays a significant part in the rehabilitation of those relatively few cases who have sustained physical injury and consequent handicap, or who had definite neurotic tendencies before some trauma that considerably intensified the previous state of maladjustment. Special consideration is given to war casualties and very systematic efforts are made to reeducate them. Because of the widely different types of injury involved, the educational procedures used differ greatly, although certain general principles apply.

Physical therapy, which includes massage, manipulation, stimulation, and specialized exercises, is especially beneficial for those who are partially paralyzed. As soon as some degree of motor control or substitute activity for the lost function is established, varying forms of active occupational therapy have been found to be more effective than routine, monotonous exercises. Every attempt should be made to make him feel that his efforts are worth while. He wants to be praised for his successes, but an oversympathetic attitude is to be avoided. If the standards set for his achievements are too low, he will make little or no effort to advance toward a possible goal. It has been found that giving the patient some objective measure of his improvement will stimulate his interest and his belief in his ability to improve.

Hence, the primary aims of rehabilitation are: (1) to reeducate the incapacitated individual for some type of work appropriate to his physical and mental ability, so that he will be able to be self-supporting and to return to a normal and independent life; (2) to make even a seriously handicapped person an integral part of the social structure of the group to which he belongs; and (3) to fortify in a physically or mentally improved patient a sense of accomplishment and personal importance, so that he will realize that in spite of his handicap he still has powers and abilities which he can employ in a worth-while fashion.

Summary

The most notable contribution of formal education in the field of abnormal psychology has been connected with the development of the concept of general intelligence. Individuals differ in their ability to profit from education and, therefore, require different types and methods of education which should be devised appropriately. Special educational programs have been developed for those who have particular abilities and disabilities, physical handicaps, and various forms of social deviation. The actual limits of potential development can be reached only when the educational programs are specially adapted to individual needs.

In general, if education is to be effective it must provide stimulation, encouragement, and a feeling of achievement and satisfaction. Frustration and fear of failure may prevent development of potentialities in both the child and the adult. Educational methods alone cannot be expected to solve all the problems of abnormal psychology. No one has yet advanced an educational system which would prevent the development of manic-depressive psychosis or cure general paresis. What education can do is to contribute to the full development of the individual's abilities and assets, and to aid in the management of his social adjustment. It is also able to provide methods and techniques of retraining and rehabilitation for persons who are physically or socially deviant.

REFERENCES

1. Abel, T. M., and E. F. Kinder, *The Subnormal Adolescent Girl*. New York, Columbia University Press, 1942.
2. Bond, E. D., and K. E. Appel, *The Treatment of Behavior Disorders Following Encephalitis: An Experiment in Reeducation*. New York, Commonwealth Fund, 1931.
3. Glueck, S., and E. T. Glueck, *One Thousand Juvenile Delinquents* (2d ed.). Cambridge, Harvard University Press, 1934.
4. ——, and ——, *Criminal Careers in Retrospect*. New York, Commonwealth Fund, 1943.
5. Goddard, H. H., *The Kallikak Family*. New York, Macmillan, 1913.
6. ——, *Psychology of the Normal and Subnormal*. New York, Dodd, Mead, 1919.
7. Itard, J–M–G., *The Wild Boy of Aveyron* (trans., G. and M. Humphrey). New York, Appleton-Century, 1932.
8. Moreno, J. L., *Who Shall Survive?* New York, Nervous and Mental Disease Monograph, 1934.
9. Skeels, H. M., "Mental Development of Children in Foster Homes," *Jour. Consult. Psychol.*, 1938, *2*, 33–43.
10. Skodak, M., "Children in Foster Homes: A Study of Mental Development," *Univ. Iowa Stud. Child Welf.*, 1939, *16*, 1–156.
11. Wellman, B. L., "Iowa Studies on the Effects of Schooling," *Yearbook Nat. Soc. Stud. Educ.*, 1940, *39* (II), 377–399.
12. Wickman, E. K., *Children's Behavior and Teachers' Attitudes*. New York, Commonwealth Fund, 1928.
13. Woodworth, R. S., *Heredity and Environment*. New York, Soc. Sci. Res. Council Bull. #47, 1941.

Chapter XXXI

THE LAW AND MENTAL ABNORMALITY

THE LEGAL status of both the mentally diseased and the mentally defective is a complicated, technical subject, but one well worth the attention of the student of psychology because it represents the position of these individuals in our society. The sprinkling of Latin phrases and formal legal verbiage are at first confusing. Nevertheless, the history of the law as it bears on the concept of legal insanity gives the student a new and different understanding of general attitudes and popular assumptions regarding mental disorder. Laws concerning the insane are a distillate of tradition and precedents, combined with prevailing feelings and beliefs. Thus, the court records provide a picture of social attitudes toward mental disorder that reflects earlier periods as well as the present day.

In discussing the legal status of the mentally diseased, it is necessary to modify certain concepts and terms that we have so far employed. There is no point in debating the relative merits of the psychological viewpoint in contrast to the legal; rather, one should try to appreciate the nature of definite differences in viewpoints. So far as insanity is concerned, the law is primarily interested in (*a*) responsibility (punishability or liability) for crimes, and (*b*) mental competency with regard to wills and contracts. It has long been recognized that mental disease may change a person's legal status so that he cannot be held responsible. It follows that the law is concerned only with those mental conditions which affect responsibility and thus produce incompetency. Psychology and psychiatry differentiate patterns and types of mental illness with different degrees of disturbance in function. The law merely places people into one of two groups, sane or insane. The imaginary line separating the two is established by so-called tests of responsibility and competency. A person is "legally insane" only if he fails those tests which have been formulated by the courts.

The vocabulary of legal decisions on mental abnormality often sounds antiquated to the psychologist. For example, the term *lunatic* rarely, if ever, appears in present-day psychological literature unless it is surrounded by quotation marks, and even the term *insane* is generally replaced by such expressions as "mentally ill" or "mentally disordered." One of the favorite legal phrases, "the knowledge of right and wrong," seems to belong to religion or ethics rather than to psychology. However, the vocabulary, the definitions, and the concepts of the law must be accepted as they are used, if one wants to understand legal practices. The terms grew from judiciary proceedings and not from medicine or psychology, and the same term may have a quite different connotation in the different systems.

It cannot be said that the legal attitude toward mental abnormality influences or determines the present psychological viewpoint. The reverse is true, to some extent, although it is the abnormal psychology of a century or more ago, rather than present-day interpretations, that is back of many legal formulations. The legal viewpoint is not significantly different from the popular concept of mental disease. The man on the street thinks in terms of a sharp division between sane and insane and is not concerned with the amount or nature of the psychological deviation. When someone in his family is acting queerly, he asks, "Tell me, Doctor, is she sane or insane?" Habits of thought change very slowly in this respect. Although many physicians and psychologists have worked toward the popular acceptance of the pathological nature of mental diseases, the average person still believes that insanity is a disgrace or, at least, an unmentionable subject. If one of the members of his family develops a mental disease, he is inclined to think that his whole family is stigmatized.

There are certain legal decisions that are classics in the field of medical jurisprudence, which have established basic principles from which subsequent decisions and even modern practices have developed. Only by referring back to these early cases are the present-day legal concepts understandable, because legal forms are based strongly upon precedent. Reliance on precedent produces an inertia in the law that is desirable in some respects. However, in the field of mental abnormality it results in a neglect of the more recent knowledge of these conditions. Thus, present legal concepts and terms are still influenced by psychological theories and beliefs that were common one or two centuries past.

It is true that legal recognition of insanity can be traced back to the Roman law which held that persons of unsound mind were incapable of all juristic acts. Our present legal standards, however, tie up more closely with the English Common Law. It is back to this period that we turn for many of the interpretations used today. The English Common Law was developed out of hundreds of years of tradition and custom in England and has influenced, in turn, legal practices in the whole Anglo-Saxon world.

Tort and Contract

Starting with the principle of tort (offenses such as assault and battery, libel, and negligence), we find that in the early period of the fifteenth century, insanity was not regarded as an excuse for such offenses. The insane individual was held liable for damages and injury to the property or body of another person. The theory behind this practice was that in such offenses, compensation should be given to the injured person for damage done, regardless of whether or not damage has been *intended*. In other words, intent was not the point at issue. For example, if an excited, agitated patient broke or damaged someone's property without reason, he was accountable in court for the extent of this damage. The present English interpretation is that the person is not guilty of a tort when he is incapable of wrongful intention or incapable of understanding the nature and consequences of the act which he is doing. American law on the subject of torts is that the insane person is responsible for damage done as far as civil action is concerned, but he is not responsible where intention is held to be a necessary element in the liability. This means that in cases of libel or slander, where intention is important, the insane patient would not be held responsible. If, however, he destroyed the property of someone else, he would be financially accountable.

The history of the relation between insanity and contract is a more complicated one. In ancient English law, mental incompetency prevented the formation of all contracts.[1] It was assumed that formation of contracts depended upon the consent of both parties. The lunatic was not capable of giving his consent and, therefore, could form no contract. This principle was reversed in the famous decision on Beverley's case in 1603, in which a lunatic was held liable for a contract which he had made. This change can be understood only when the whole social and economic pattern of the times is taken into consideration. The seventeenth and eighteenth centuries marked the beginning of a great commercial expansion. It was generally believed that if the contracts of a mentally incompetent person were not upheld, trade and commerce would be hindered. The security and stability of contracts would have been disturbed if no one could have been certain that a contract he signed would be valid, because the cosigner might have turned out to be mentally incompetent. It has been suggested that this decision may have grown out of the belief popular at the time that mental disease was a visitation from God. Having viewed mental disease in these terms, the court might have reasoned, "Why should we relieve a person of obligation, if God has seen fit to place this particular condition upon him?" The principle of Beverley's case, that "no man can stultify himself by pleading his own incapacity," actually was a revival of an ancient law rarely used. It provided a precedent for cases as late as the middle of the nineteenth century, although there were a few conflicting decisions.

In 1843, the famous case of Molton *v.* Camroux[1] gave a new turn to the problem of an insane person's responsibility for contracts which he had signed. In this instance, an action was brought by the administrators of the estate of a lunatic who had died without making a will, to recover money paid by him to an insurance company for two annuities. The man was of unsound mind at the time of purchase, but the company was not aware of this fact. The court decided that the money could not be recovered, stating that mental incompetency was not a defense in contractual cases except when the defendant's state of mind was known at the time of the transaction and advantage had been taken of it. In this case, the transaction itself was a fair one, and no advantage had been taken of the man. English law in general has maintained the interpretation that the contracts of the insane are void unless the lunatic has derived benefit and the other party has suffered. For example, if the lunatic has received services from another person under a contractual agreement, he must pay for them as the contract demands. This fits both into Common Law and the rule of equity, that no one is to be enriched at the expense of another.

A different reason for the voiding of contracts signed by lunatics was given by the United States Supreme Court in 1872 in the case of Dexter *v.* Hall.[2] Here, the defendant claimed title to some property, but the title depended upon the validity of a power of attorney. The plaintiff maintained that the maker of the contract was mentally incompetent at the time of execution of the power of attorney. The Supreme Court said, "The fundamental idea of a contract is that it requires the assent of two minds. But a lunatic, or a person *non compos mentis,* has nothing which the law recognizes as a mind, and it would seem, therefore, upon principle, that he cannot make a contract which may have any efficacy as such." *

* Green, M. D., "Public Policies Underlying the Law of Mental Incompetency," *Michigan Law Rev.,* 1940, *38,* 1202.

This reference to a lack of mind has been replaced in present legal proceedings by the concept of degree of capacity for understanding. The *understanding test*, as usually employed, is related to whether or not the person is capable of understanding the nature and effect of the particular act. Actually, the decisions of the courts do not always follow this standard closely. In some cases it has been supplemented by the *insane-delusions test*. If the contract can be shown to be materially affected or motivated, either by an insane delusion or by lack of understanding, it may be declared void. The legal definition of an insane delusion is, "A belief which is the spontaneous product of a diseased mind which comes into existence without reason or evidence to support it, and which is adhered to against reason and against the evidence." *

The decisions on the subject of mental incompetency have been summarized by Green.[4] He showed that frequently an inarticulate or unexpressed standard is used. Even though certain tests of competency may be quoted, the decision rests upon principles which cannot be verbalized simply. The decision is often based on a constellation of factors rather than on any one particular fact. Commonly, the constellation is that of fraud and undue influence, with mental incompetency. Different types of evidence are fitted together and are all weighed in the final decision, even though the amount of evidence on any one line would not have been sufficient to warrant the decision. As Green says, this is one of the rare instances in which the law adds an "almost" to an "almost" in coming to the final result.

Testamentary Capacity

In all legal proceedings except wills, the individual is considered sane until proved otherwise. In wills, the classic words of the document, "being of sound and disposing mind and memory," place the fact of mental competency in the foreground as a requirement in making the will. In general, if the testator (a person who leaves a will in force at his death) can be shown to have been mentally incompetent at the time the will was drawn, the will is not accepted at probate. The standards of mental competency on this point have not been very strict, and it has been said that it requires less mental capacity to make a will than to make a contract. Even when the ability to transact ordinary business affairs is lacking, a will made in this state may be sustained. The courts have held that, in order to make a will, a person

* Green, M. D., "Judicial Tests of Mental Incompetency," *Missouri Law Rev.*, 1941, *6*, 156.

must have the capacity for understanding the nature and extent of his property. He must know who his natural objects of bounty are, and how he wants to dispose of his property. Even if he had been adjudged insane, the will may be upheld if there was no evidence of insane delusions in the disposition he made of his property. In other words, if he followed the general form that most people use in making a will, leaving his money to his natural heirs, his will is apt to be upheld by the court. If the form of legacies is bizarre and eccentric, it will be taken as corroborative evidence that the disposition of his property was motivated by insane delusions when other lines of evidence of mental incompetency are submitted. As long as the contractual agreement or the division of property under the will is fair, that is, if it follows the usual pattern of such instruments in that community and fits popular opinion of what is just and right, the will or contract may be allowed to stand, even though the maker was incompetent at the time of making the instrument.[5] A judgment based on a constellation of factors or the popular notion of fairness in such a case is a turn away from usual legal precedence. No other (or few other) cases would have the same constellation of factors, so that each case is judged principally on its own merits rather than on its resemblance to earlier cases.

Crime

The early records show that insanity was used as a defense against criminal charges in England as early as the beginning of the fourteenth century, but the references are only of a fragmentary sort. The first outstanding writers on this aspect of criminal law were Coke and Hale in the seventeenth century. Coke[8] pointed out that "no felony or murder can be committed without a felonious intent or purpose," and that the lunatic, because he is lacking in mind and reason, cannot have a felonious intent. Hale[8] followed the same line of argument but distinguished between total insanity, in which there could be no criminal intent, and partial insanity, in which criminal intent was possible. This distinction established the point that not everyone with a mental disease should be considered irresponsible for his criminal acts. The amount or degree of mental disorder which might relieve one from responsibility became a crucial question, and many different standards have been formulated. Hale suggested a standard which was later spoken of as the *Child-of-Fourteen-Years Test*. He said, "Such a person as labouring under melancholy distempers hath yet ordinarily as great understanding, as ordinarily a child of fourteen years hath, is such a person as may be guilty of treason, or felony."* Paraphrasing this statement, the standard for total insanity was "melancholy distempers with less understanding than a child of fourteen," and the standard for partial insanity, "melancholy distempers with the understanding of a child of fourteen." The vagueness of such a standard is obvious.

Among the other tests of criminal responsibility that have been used are the *Twenty-Pence Test*[7] and the *Wild-Beast Test.*[7] Regarding the former test, Fitzherbert said, "And he who shall be said to be a sot, an idiot from his birth, is such a person who cannot account or number twenty pence nor can tell who was his mother or father, nor how old he is, etc., so as it may appear that he hath no understanding of reason, what shall be for his profit, or what for his loss. But if he hath such understanding that he shall know and understand his letters and read by telling or information of another mind, then it seemeth he is not a sot nor a natural idiot."† This test, to our present-day concepts, seems to apply more to mental deficiency than to insanity, but it was a classical standard in the history of criminal law and was used in many cases involving insanity. The Wild-Beast Test was handed down in a decision in 1724. It was stated that in order to be held not guilty for a crime, "It must be a man that is totally deprived of his understanding and memory, and doth not know what he is doing, no more than an infant, than a brute, or a wild beast, such a one is never the object of punishment."‡

Another famous decision, given in the Hadfield case[8] in 1800, introduced a new concept into criminal law, involving the *existence of delusion* as a test of responsibility. The defendant in this case was an army officer who had been discharged from the army because of insanity. He had the delusion that he should sacrifice himself for the world's salvation. In order to accomplish this sacrifice, which he felt was divinely inspired, he attempted to shoot King George III. In a brilliant and jury-confusing speech, the defense attorney was able to get a decision that the defendant was not responsible for his act. Later decisions did not use the presence of delusion as a test of irresponsibility in itself, but only as it had bearing on other tests. In the early part of the nineteenth century, the *Good and Evil Test* for mental responsibility was formulated. Its main principle was that "those who are under a natural disability of distinguishing between good and evil, as infants

---

* Weihofen, H., *Insanity as a Defense in Criminal Law.* New York, Commonwealth Fund, 1933, 19.

† Michael, J., and H. Wechsler, *Criminal Law and Its Administration.* Chicago, Foundation Press, 1940, 807–808.

‡ Michael, J., and H. Wechsler, *ibid.,* 809.

under the age of discretion, idiots, and lunatics, are not punishable by any criminal prosecution whatever." * It is interesting to note that this test referred to a knowledge of good and evil as abstract ideas.

The most famous case concerning criminal responsibility in the insane was that which led to the formulation of the *Right and Wrong Test*. M'Naughten's case of 1843[8] was one of great popular interest at the time and had great influence on all later decisions. Daniel M'Naughten shot and killed the private secretary of Sir Robert Peel, with the idea that the secretary was Peel. M'Naughten had the delusion that he was being persecuted by his enemies, one of whom he thought was Peel. He was found not guilty on the grounds of insanity. Because the murdered man was of public importance, a great deal of attention was aroused by the case and it was brought up in the House of Lords for debate. This led to a request for the opinion of fifteen eminent judges of England on the law governing such cases; that is, the existing laws of insanity at that time. Specific questions were posed concerning the responsibility of those claiming insanity as a defense to crime. The judges' answers to these questions came under two general headings: The first consensus of the judges was that, "The jury ought to be told in all cases that . . . to establish a defense on the ground of insanity, it must be clearly proved that, at the time of committing the act, the party accused was labouring under such a defect of reason, from disease of the mind, as not to know the nature and quality of the act he was doing, or if he did know it that he did not know he was doing what was wrong."† The important point here was that the knowledge of right and wrong should apply to the specific act with which the defendant is charged and not to some general sense of right and wrong. The Good and Evil Test, previously mentioned, referred to the abstract relationship.

The second part of the judicial consensus was, "Where a person labours under partial delusions only and is not in other respects insane . . . he must be considered in the same situation as to responsibility as if the facts with respect to which the delusion exists were real." ‡ For instance, if an insane person killed a man because of the delusion that the man was about to kill him, he would not be he'd responsible; but if he killed him because he thought the man was talking behind his back, he would be responsible. This has been termed the *Mistake of Fact Test*. This standard has been referred to at times by a few states

* Weihofen, H., *ibid*, 19–20.
† Weihofen, H., *ibid.*, 28.
‡ Weihofen, H., *ibid.*, 28–29.

in this country, and both judges and medical men have pointed out that it works hardship in some cases.

The courts generally agree today that the Right and Wrong Test is the standard to be applied. It is the sole test of responsibility in England and is upheld by all of the states in this country except New Hampshire. However, seventeen states have an additional test; that is, the test of *Irresistible Impulse*.[8] According to this test, a person is not criminally responsible for an act committed under the uncontrollable impulse resulting from mental disease, which overwhelms reason, conscience, and judgment. This standard is of American origin. Since it dates back further than the time of the formulation of the M'Naughten case, it cannot be considered a new trend in legal practice.

The principal point of discussion in many legal decisions concerning insanity is the standard for drawing the line between sanity and insanity in order to determine whether the person is responsible for his acts. A review of the cases shows, however, that no hard and fast rule has been applied. All the standards contain a large subjective element. Green[5] claims that most cases have actually been decided according to an inarticulate behavioristic standard. Even though a subjective standard may be mentioned, the outcome of most cases seems to have depended upon consideration of a wide constellation of factors, so that a just decision was reached in most cases.

Concepts of responsibility for criminal offenses have also shown certain changes. Weihofen[8] has summarized several different trends in the treatment of the plea of insanity in criminal law in this country. In the first place, there has been a tendency to demand less proof to entitle a defendant to acquittal on the basis of insanity. Second, there has been a trend toward resorting to legislation to get improved legal handling of insanity cases, instead of leaving the principles involved up to the judiciary. The procedure for trying such cases has been changed in several states. For example, the Briggs Law of Massachusetts provides for impartial, routine mental examination before trial of all persons accused of crime. The result has been that insane and irresponsible offenders are sorted out and prolonged criminal trials where insanity is an issue are avoided. The procedure involved has been amended several times and now provides that the State Department of Mental Health shall report to the court and the defendant's counsel concerning the defendant's mental condition and whether or not the Department considers he should be tried on the criminal charge. If declared sane and brought to trial, he is still permitted to enter the plea of insanity with recourse to the usual processes of summoning expert testimony. This procedure eliminates the haphazard system of leaving the recognition of mental unsoundness to laymen and provides for an examination made by a neutral, unbiased expert agency. The argument leveled so frequently against expert testimony is thus avoided and the state is saved the expense of long and expensive criminal trials. In spite of certain difficulties in legal procedure entailed in the administration of this law, it constitutes the most advanced type of legislation on the subject.

Massachusetts is not the only state with such an improved procedure, but it has gone further along this line than most of the other states. New York City provides for a preliminary mental examination of criminals, but the clinic making the examination is attached to the police department rather than to the courts. California, Colorado, Louisiana, and Maryland have made legislative provision that the issue of mental unsoundness is to be tried separately from other issues.

The judicial procedure in New Hampshire is sufficiently different from that in the other states to warrant consideration. Since 1871, the courts of this state have rejected all legal tests of insanity. "All symptoms and all tests of mental disease are purely matters of fact to be determined by the jury."[8] The question of whether or not a mental disease was present is determined on the basis of the testimony of experts. The function of the jury is to decide whether the defendant's criminal action was a product of his mental disease. If the criminal act was a product of that mental disease, he should be acquitted. The main question for the jury in such cases is whether or not the accused was of such disordered mind that he was incapable of guilty intent. In other words, the jury is asked to decide upon the motivation of the criminal act.

All of these tests of responsibility are legal and not medical concepts. They have been formulated by judges as instructions to juries who were about to decide the question of whether the accused was guilty or not guilty because of insanity. The tests have about them a seeming common-sense logic and objectivity and are certainly more easily comprehended than the descriptions and dynamics of mental action provided by the psychopathologists, even though the latter may be much nearer correct.

Present-Day Status of Legal Insanity

According to the laws of most countries and states, the insane are not responsible for their acts; they cannot commit crimes or torts, marry, make wills, sign binding contracts, be witnesses in court, or bring actions in court. There are still some differences among countries, and even among states in the United States as to the legal status of the insane. The presence of mental disease in a medical or psychological sense does not of itself negate responsibility and liability. Only when the condition is sufficiently obvious to meet certain standards or legal tests is the person considered legally insane and then forgiven his acts. No borderline or region of uncertainty is recognized; in the eyes of the law, the person is either responsible, or irresponsible because of insane mind.

In this country, contracts signed by mentally disordered individuals are viewed as voidable rather than void per se. The standard of mental competence is one of understanding the nature and consequences of the transaction. If the contract is fair and follows the pattern of similar transactions, the court tends to uphold it. If it is unfair and produces hardship, the fact of mental incompetency will be given more weight and the contract voided. Thus, there is an unexpressed, natural standard, by which the customs and traditions of the community are taken into consideration.

In determining criminal responsibility, the line is drawn on the basis of the Right and Wrong Test established in relation to the famous M'Naughten case in England.

Another principle of Common Law still operative is that an insane person shall not be executed for a crime even though he was sane at the time of commission. The principle upon which this practice is based was stated in some of the very early cases at Common Law as, "Such a person cannot be an example to others." It has been the rule that the person to be executed must be capable of understanding the nature and purpose of the punishment he is to be given. In the United States, if a person becomes insane after the commission of a crime, he is committed to a mental hospital (usually one for the criminally insane). Upon regaining his sanity, he is brought back to stand trial, or to undergo the punishment that was imposed at a trial.

The basic legal procedure employed in determining any question of responsibility is that of trial by jury. There have been many criticisms of this practice of using laymen's opinions and decisions on a subject as complex and specialized as is the analysis of an individual's mental status. It has been pointed out that no one would consider asking a layman to decide whether or not a person had a cancer or tuberculosis, but we still insist on making him the judge of the question of responsibility dependent on the presence or absence of mental disease. The New York Court of Appeals in 1896 ruled, "It is generally safer to take the judgment of unskilled jurors than the opinions of hired and generally biased experts."[8] In recent years there has been a trend to view the problem from two different angles. The qualified psychiatrist is now expected to evaluate the mental status of the defendant and to give this information to the jury. The jury's task is to decide whether or not the person was responsible for his act in the light of the expert opinion, which is a legal question and not a medical one.

The position of the psychiatrist as an expert witness in court has been, and often still is, an unhappy one, because there has been much misunderstanding. The psychiatrist and the court use different standards in sizing up a mental patient and apply different definitions to the term *insanity*. Popular opinion has been definitely prejudiced because some psychiatrist may testify on one side of a case and equally good authority may testify on the opposing side. Zilboorg formulated the difference between law and medicine as follows: "The law's battle cry: 'Justice must be done,' is mistaken by the psychiatrists as: 'Ill or well, the criminal must die.' Psychiatry's battle cry: 'Treat, do not beat the ill,' is mistaken by the jurist as: 'Guilty or not, let us treat him.' "* As a rule, expert testimony on sanity is now treated with more respect than it formerly was. The medical profession has set up standards and examinations which must be met before a physician can call himself a qualified expert. Another reason is the use of a clearer definition by most courts as to the role of the expert and of the jury. However, the final judgment of responsibility is made by the jury in most states of this country. It is a generally recognized legal procedure to hold that a well-trained specialist should evaluate the *mental status* of the defendant, rather than a jury of his peers. The double standard of usage — legal versus medical — of the concept of insanity is not socially desirable. The fault of the usage in the court lies mainly with the medical expert rather than with the law.[9]

Psychological Theory and Legal Practice

The history of legal insanity reflects many of the views of mental disease that existed in centuries past. Some of them have been outdated and dropped from legal phraseology, but others have survived to the present day. Even while the general direction of legal decisions has remained the same, the theory behind the decisions has changed.

* Zilboorg, G., "Misconceptions of Legal Insanity," *Amer. Jour. Orthopsychiat.*, 1939, 9, 543.

For example, in regard to contracts made by the insane, the early Common Law held them void because contract depended on the meeting of two minds and the lunatic had no mind. Later, the reason given for voiding such contracts was that contract depended upon *consent* and the lunatic did not have free consent. Today, judges speak in terms of the mentally disturbed person's degree of understanding in regard to the specific transaction. Thus, the shift in theory has been from viewing insanity as complete debilitation, existing on an all-or-none basis, to determining the quality of disturbance as it affects some specific situation. The direction of the legal decision as to validity of contract has not shifted.

In criminal law, present-day procedure still follows the formula of Right and Wrong, given in the M'Naughten case. The legal opinion in this case reflected the knowledge and beliefs held by fifteen eminent English judges one hundred years ago. Their formulation of the Right and Wrong Test was greatly influenced by years of precedent and, especially, by the writings of Lord Hale (seventeenth century) who believed in witchcraft, demon possession, and the influence of the moon on insanity.

The point at issue when insanity is pleaded as a defense for crime is whether or not the individual was responsible. Responsibility in the legal sense is linked with liability to punishment. If the man was not responsible, he is not punishable. Jacoby[6] has emphasized that all legal statutes recognize guilt as the prerequisite of punishment. Guilt, in this sense, is akin to intention, a direct connection between willing and acting. If the act occurred by the free will or choice of the doer, he is responsible; if mental disease prevented him from being a free agent, then he is not responsible for his acts.

In this viewpoint, the choice between right and wrong is made by "reason," one of the faculties of the mind which was so highly respected in the philosophy of the nineteenth century. The lunatic was forgiven his misdeeds because he had lost his reason. Today, psychologists do not conceive of reason as an independent power which acts separately from other mental operations. Reasoning power, as now conceived, concerns processes of deductive and inductive thinking. Crimes of the insane are viewed, not as the result of defects in reasoning power, but as uninhibited emotional response. It is not reason which keeps us from committing murder if we have the impulse to do so, but a complex integration of mental processes in which a large element is our identification with the person toward whom our hostility is directed. When this identification is absent, the impulse may break through, but it is not a matter of reason, or the lack of it, which permits its appearance.[9] Other factors involved are strictly situational. In one set of circumstances murder will take place, in another, it will not. The operation of reason is affected by emotional processes which, in turn, have been influenced by the surrounding circumstances.

The psychological and legal viewpoints also differ on the question of the imaginary line between sanity and insanity. The psychologist sees many transitional forms or borderline states between satisfactory adjustment and gross maladjustment. The law asks that a definite line be drawn between the two. Another difference between psychiatric practice and legal procedure is that the latter gives credence to the concept of insane delusions in a person otherwise sane. To the psychiatrist, the presence of one real delusion indicates definite mental disorder or unsound mind, while this is not true of the legal definition. The psychiatrist believes that a delusion occurs only when the whole person is mentally disordered; hence, it is impossible for him to say that a person is sane, but is suffering from an insane delusion.

The basic legal concept of criminal responsibility, that is, the question of whether the defendant was so mentally unsound as to lack knowledge that his act was wrong, is another point of dissension between psychology and law. In the first place, it is extremely difficult, if not impossible, to reconstruct and appraise what was going through the defendant's mind (his stream of consciousness) at the time of the crime. Even if such an appraisal is attempted, and some sort of a reconstruction is made, the question remains as to what is meant by the phrase, "*Know the act was wrong.*" Anything from simple perception to deep moral appreciation could be implied. Mere awareness that the act was wrong; that one has been told not to do it; that one will or may be punished; so much "knowledge" is probably present in most instances where a plea of insanity is made as a defense. More important, of course, is moral or ethical understanding as the point at issue. On this line of argument one might expect that the socially underprivileged person who has never received proper moral, ethical, or character education should be forgiven his crimes because he never had the opportunity to develop normal moral or ethical standards. Although this concept does not entirely conflict with the present legal practice, a psychologist could reasonably argue for legal irresponsibility due to a lack of educational opportunity. Actually, at law, the lack of knowledge that the act was wrong must stem from severe mental confusion, stupidity, or insanity in order to free the defendant from responsibility. The legal interpretations still follow the theory that any person not insane has a choice between right and wrong, while the insane patient does not have this choice.

If, at times, legal formulations and procedures seem archaic in terms of present-day knowledge of abnormal psychology, it should be remembered that the law has not been ineffective in its major aims; namely, (a) the protection of society from the action of potentially dangerous individuals, (b) the protection of the insane individual from his own abnormal conduct, (c) protection of the insane person from being taken advantage of by others because of his mental disorder, and (d) the protection of the interests of the dependents or heirs of the insane person by the precedents and procedures governing wills.

Summary

In general, the law is built upon traditions and social mores and as those change, legal forms also change. Although this process may be slow, incorporation of new standards does take place. The broad public policies of the law are the protection and security of the group and of the individual. Evidently, the laws regarding both criminal responsibility and mental incompetency on contracts and wills are colored by this general policy of giving protection and security to the individual and to the group.

The mentally abnormal individual does not fit into the society in which he lives. The rules, regulations, and responsibilities which control the group may make demands upon him which he is not able to meet. For this reason, special legal consideration is granted him for his own protection and the protection of society. Legal recognition of insanity as a cause for suspension of certain rights, privileges, and liabilities to punishment has existed since the time of early Roman law, but the ideology behind these exemptions has undergone many changes in connection with the beliefs concerning the nature of mental disease. The legal procedures and forms have also changed, although they still show a great deal of variation among different countries and states.

In general, the law operates as though there were a sharp line of demarcation between sane and insane. The legal point at issue is one of *responsibility* as regards criminal offenses, and of mental *competency* or degree of understanding in civil actions. The history of the laws regarding mental disease shows that many different standards have been used by the courts in cases involving mentally diseased persons. These standards usually have been formulations and instructions given by judges to juries on cases in which mental disease was used as a defense or as a reason for breaking some will or contract. These instructions frequently rest upon antiquated beliefs as to the nature of mental disease because legal procedure rests upon precedent.

Several encouraging trends have developed in recent years which have improved the legal handling of mentally ill persons. Expert testimony is now given more weight in the court, and those who give expert testimony have had to meet more adequate standards for qualification as experts. The Briggs Law in Massachusetts, although not ideal, has been a step forward in the direction of better provision for understanding and disposal of individuals affected by true mental disease or mental defect.

REFERENCES

1. Cook, W. G. H., *Insanity and Mental Deficiency in Relation to Legal Responsibility*. London, Routledge, 1921.
2. Green, M. D., "Public Policies Underlying the Law of Mental Incompetency," *Michigan Law Rev.*, 1940, *38*, 1202–1221.
3. ———, "Judicial Tests of Mental Incompetency," *Missouri Law Rev.*, 1941, *6*, 141–165.
4. ———, "Fraud, Undue Influence and Mental Incompetency: A Study in Related Concepts," *Columbia Law Rev.*, 1943, *43*, 176–205.
5. ———, "Proof of Mental Incompetency and the Unexpressed Major Premise," *Yale Law Jour.*, 1944, *53*, 271–311.
6. Jacoby, G. W., *The Unsound Mind and the Law*. New York, Funk, 1918.
7. Michael, J., and H. Wechsler, *Criminal Law and its Administration*. Chicago, Foundation Press, 1940.
8. Weihofen, H., *Insanity as a Defense in Criminal Law*. New York, Commonwealth Fund, 1933.
9. Zilboorg, G., "Misconceptions of Legal Insanity," *Amer. Jour. Orthopsychiat.*, 1939, *9*, 540–553.

Chapter XXXII

MEDICAL PSYCHOLOGY

PSYCHOLOGY is that division of science which is concerned with behavior and mental life, while psychiatry is a division of medicine dealing with the diagnosis, care, and treatment of those suffering from mental disease. Medical psychology is a portion of the subject matter of general psychology which furnishes the psychological description and dynamics necessary for psychiatry, in the same way that the biological chemistry of nutrition furnishes part of the background for internal medicine.

In a larger sense there is no experiment in the field of psychology which does not have some relevance to the problems of psychopathology. The more anyone knows about human behavior and mental life, the better he is able to understand the behavior of the individual who deviates from that which is considered to be normal. In order to illustrate how research in both psychology and psychiatry has forwarded knowledge in psychopathology, certain selected, but representative, examples will be presented. Some of the greatest contributions and turning points in thought respecting the basic nature of psychopathology have grown out of experiments which were in no way directed toward the immediate problem of mental disorder.

Psychiatry, as such, has progressed largely on the basis of careful clinical observation. This observation has, for the most part, taken one of two forms: either a large group of mentally disordered individuals has been studied and compared and conclusions have been drawn from the grouped material, or intensive studies have been made over comparatively long periods of time of a few individuals who showed symptoms and deviations which had a great deal in common. The psychiatrist is, by definition, a physician trained in the arts and sciences of medicine. His primary objective is to relieve the immediate problems presented by each individual patient. He is motivated most by the idea of rendering service to each individual who comes to him asking for help and health.

Usually the psychologist is not trained or motivated by ideals of individual service. He is following a line of thought which is directed toward scientific goals. If the design of an experiment called for it, he would, on occasion, omit procedures which might be of immediate individual benefit. His scientific objective would be to facilitate a contrast between the results obtained with and without the use of such a procedure. As a scientist he has not had training or experience in the medical arts. Except in special or unusual circumstances, he is not recognized as an individual who has the training or legal responsibility which entitles him to have free access to individuals suffering from mental disorder. Most frequently the experiments which a psychologist conducts with persons suffering from mental disorders are done in collaboration with a physician who is responsible for the ultimate health and welfare of each individual. Ideally, we might expect that anyone who received thorough and adequate training in both psychology and psychiatry would be in a position to make real contributions to our basic knowledge of the mental disorders. A man who did have this combined training and who did make outstanding contributions was Emil Kraepelin.

Emil Kraepelin (1856–1926)

Kraepelin[2, 8, 16] became interested in psychology and psychiatry during his last year at school. He adopted medicine as a career with the definite aim of becoming a psychiatrist. Soon after qualifying as a physician he abandoned clinical work for a time in order to do psychological research with Wundt, the founder of experimental psychology. He spent the year of 1882 in Wundt's laboratory. He was dissuaded by Wundt from continuing a career as an experimental psychologist and returned in 1883 to the Munich clinic. However, he began while with Wundt an elaborate series of studies of the effect of drugs and medications upon the simpler mental processes. After ten years, he brought together his findings in a long monograph. During the next thirty-five years, he published or sponsored more than a hundred studies based upon the experimental method, all designed to illuminate the problems of mental disorder by the use of the methods and findings of experimental psychology.

The general theme which ran through most of these experimental investigations was the integration of psychological functions under the concept of mental employment or psychological work. By this he meant the study of consecutive human performance including the interaction of perceiving, discriminating, remembering, reading, associating, understanding, and acting. He held that these psychological functions were fundamental in everyday human behavior and that their disorders were fundamental to the study of psychopathology.

PLATE 18

EMIL KRAEPELIN (1856–1926)

Making use of the derangements which were produced by drugs, Kraepelin sought to bridge the gap between laboratory experiments and clinical observation. The mental patient often could not, or would not, act as an experimental subject; while the normal person, under the influence of some drug which produced symptoms similar to those of the psychotic, would cooperate. He believed that disorders due to such agents should be set up by measurable dosages and described and measured in psychological terms. In contrast to most investigators he was chiefly interested in how the disordered individual worked rather than in what he did.

As a result of his use of such carefully thought out, systematic plans of study, some have accused Kraepelin of neglecting the total man, the total personality, and of dealing only with simple functions which were abstracted from the entire picture of the disorder. Others have accused him of completely overlooking the individual case, since he was interested in massed data which he accumulated from many individuals. Kraepelin was aware of the shortcomings of his approach to the problems but held that it was necessary to understand the underlying factors before one could pass on to the larger concepts. Kraepelin's work, together with that of his students, is so voluminous that it is impossible to do more than mention briefly certain of the more outstanding of his findings along with their general philosophical impact upon psychological and psychiatric thought, both of his own generation and succeeding generations.

At the time Kraepelin started his work in psychopathology, experimental psychology consisted chiefly of the study of sensory functions and the relationship between physiological activity and psychological occurrences. Psychiatry was largely an observational procedure in which every leader in the field had created a system of classification without too much regard to the systematic efforts of others or to systematic efforts of previous generations. Kraepelin did two things which were of first importance. He made use of the methods of experimental psychology of his day, developed new methods and procedures, and applied those methods to the study of the psychiatric patient. Second, he went on from the experimental studies and clinical observations to build up a system of classification of mental disorders which has been more widely accepted than any other and which today is still considered the best available.

The methods used by experimental psychology in studying sensory abilities and defects produced findings which were of secondary importance to psychopathology. Kraepelin quickly passed by these psychophysical experiments to develop new and more pertinent methods. He devised the *sustained task* which showed wide variation among different mental patients. The sustained task was not regarded as a routine response which was wholly initiated and controlled by the stimulus, but rather as a type of work or action voluntarily laid out and governed by the organism itself. The loss of effective government, whether due to drugs, neurosis, or psychosis, was considered to be open directly for experimental determination and measurement under controlled conditions.

The psychological studies which he sponsored, as well as others which he cited and integrated in his writings, provided a notable increase in factual knowledge concerning fatigue and recovery, practice and learning, motivation to activity, memory, association, and sleep. The effects of many drugs were studied in both normal and psychotic persons. He extended the laboratory methods of psychology to the study of psychotic patients, investigating, for example, the handwriting of the manic-depressive in elation, depression, and remission; perceiving, observing, and remembering in schizophrenics and paretics; the reactions of epileptics; and the character and rate of ideational flow in manic states. Today, most of this material is accepted as part of the routine procedure followed in clinical examination and testing. These tests, however, really grew out of the long, exact, and difficult research carried out by Kraepelin and his students.

In spite of the importance of Kraepelin's experimental work, he is best known for his systematic classification of mental disorders. The first edition of his textbook in psychiatry, published in 1883, was a brief outline of but little more than 100 pages, whereas the ninth edition, which came out in 1927 after his death, consisted of 2425 pages. The basic philosophy on which he based his classification of the mental disorders grew out of the *principle of prediction*. He personally studied many hundreds of cases and reviewed thousands of case histories of mentally deranged individuals. From this study he concluded that, fundamentally, mental disorders could be divided into those caused by external conditions (which are or should be curable) and those caused by inherent constitutional factors (which may be alleviated but are essentially incurable). This viewpoint has in it an element of fatalism; the fatalism of the natural scientist who observes phenomena as they occur and does not quarrel with their occurrence. He cannot reject them but must accept the findings, whether or not they are agreeable to him. Kraepelin assumed that mental diseases exist as separate entities and that fundamentally *the course of any mental disease is predetermined and predictable*. For him, the words curable and incurable were inaccurate since, in the absence of any specific therapy, some patients will naturally recover and others will naturally fail to recover and so deteriorate. Thus, the course of the disease is predetermined in the same way that a chemical reaction is predetermined. The personal side of the patient's illness is incidental or accidental. This hypothesis is scientific, logical, and consistent, and it dominated psychiatric thought for more than a generation.

On the basis of his detailed and voluminous observations which were built into tables and curves, Kraepelin came to the conclusion that there were two major mental diseases which could be differentiated from the large mass of variations found among individual patients in mental institutions. These were dementia praecox and manic-depressive psychosis. He first differentiated the dementia praecox syndrome in the fifth edition of his textbook in 1896, and the manic-depressive psychosis in the sixth edition in 1899.

Neither of these diagnostic groupings met with quick approval or acceptance on the part of his colleagues. Only after years of controversy did acceptance to the degree which exists at present come about. Since the diagnostic groupings in Kraepelin's system were based on symptomatology, their acceptance resulted in a prognostic attitude. Prognosis was included in the diagnosis, and if the prognosis proved ultimately correct, the original diagnosis was thereby confirmed. From this attitude grew a general therapeutic complacency with respect to the manic-depressive psychosis: the patient will get well, so we need to do little but wait. Hopelessness was attached to a diagnosis of dementia praecox: the patient will deteriorate and very little can be done to help him. Kraepelin himself never held to these simple diagnostic and prognostic axioms. He continually changed the system of classification in each new edition of his textbook. He was never satisfied, never hasty, and always a respecter of the weight of the evidence. There was a philosophical eclecticism about his approach which marked him apart from those who were founding the "school" of thought. Kraepelin never started a school of psychiatry. He was a medical scientist in the best sense of the term and singularly free from personal dogma. His approach was a true triumph in that it brought "insanity" into the field of medicine. At the same time it demonstrated that experimental psychology as a natural science had a place in the supporting structure of medicine in the same sense that pathology and physiology have.

Ivan Pavlov (1849–1936)

Another line of thought stems from Pavlov,[10] the great Russian physiologist. In 1914 Shanger-Krestovnikova, a student of Pavlov, was conducting experimental investigations on the conditioned salivary response in dogs. The dog was trained to salivate when a luminous circle was presented. After this conditioned response was established, a differential response was obtained between the circle and an ellipse. The shape of the ellipse was then altered, making it nearer and nearer to that of the circle, while discrimination training continued. When the ellipse became very nearly circular, the discrimination failed to improve and during three weeks of training it became worse. During this time the whole behavior of the dog underwent an abrupt change. The animal, which had been quiet and cooperative, began to squeal, to squirm, and to tear off with its teeth the apparatus used for stimulating the skin. On being taken out of the experimental room, the dog now barked violently in place of going quietly. This change in behavior was held by Pavlov to be the equivalent of an acute neurosis.

Subsequent experimenters have conducted similar experiments with dogs, cats, sheep, pigs, monkeys, and chimpanzees. In all of these animals it has been found possible to bring about a rather abrupt change in behavior when very difficult discrimination was demanded, particularly when the animal being investigated was either kept in close confinement or strapped tightly in a restraining harness. If this type of training was persisted in for several weeks, a disorganization of behavior resulted. The animal became restless, had periods of apparent insomnia, and was not friendly with other animals of its own kind.

Krasnogorski, in 1925, attempted a similar experiment with a six-year-old child, forcing a discrimination between the beating of two metronomes. When the discrimination became difficult, the child was described as taciturn, refused to go to the laboratory, and when forced to do so walked slowly into the apparatus. When the discrimination was made still more difficult or even impossible, the child then became rude, aggressive, disobedient, excited, yawned, closed his eyes, and sometimes fell asleep. Similar experiments were conducted on other children with equivalent results.

In light of experiments such as these, Pavlov[11] went on after he was eighty years old to adapt and apply the ideas which he had gained from his work in physiology to the problems of human psychopathology. Essentially, he made two basic assumptions: (*a*) that animals of different response types exist, and (*b*) that some sort of general neurological processes, which he called "inhibition" and "excitation," mark the activity of the nervous system.

Pavlov's working hypothesis was that types of response shown by dogs to the conditioned reflex technique were equivalent to those shown by human beings. He therefore believed that he had a basis for a fundamental classification of normal as well as psychopathological persons. Among dogs, he held that there were three main types: an excitatory group, an inhibitory group, and a central group. The excitatory and inhibitory tend to be the extremes of a distribution of temperament, with the central at the median. When an animal of the excitatory type is forced in the conditioning process, it becomes ill, retaining only excitatory processes with a disappearance of practically all of the inhibitory ones. Such a condition, he said, was comparable to or identical with neurasthenia in the human. At the opposite extreme where the excitatory processes are weakened and the inhibitory ones prevail, the resulting condition was considered equivalent to hysteria. He also believed that when an animal of the excited type was pushed beyond the normal limits of response, there developed periods of depression or excitement comparable to human manic-depressive psychosis. The inhibited, hysterical type, being highly suggestible, was thought to form the basis for the schizophrenic reaction.

There can be no question concerning the factual observations of Pavlov and his students with respect to the phenomena occurring during the conditioning experiments. Whether or not these observations can be applied in psychopathology is still an open question but one to which a great deal of research effort is being devoted. It is not too clear just what Pavlov meant by excitation or inhibition in physiological and in psychological terms, or whether the meaning in physiology is equivalent to that in psychology. There is a vast amount of experimentation on these topics, but the relationship to psychopathology is still obscure. In any event, Pavlov initiated an entirely new viewpoint which affords both the physiologists and the psychologists an opportunity for application of a definite experimental method to the problems of psychopathology.

The Development and Use of Word Associations

In 1879, Francis Galton[3] reported the first systematic study of the associations which may be derived from the exposure of a single word. His experiments were conducted upon himself. He would allow his mind to play freely for several seconds on one or two ideas and then, while the traces of these ideas were still lingering, he would turn his attention upon them to arrest and scrutinize the exact appearance of the associations which seemed to cluster around the ideas. This study gave him an interesting and unexpected view of a number of the operations of the mind and of the obscure depths at which they took place, of which he had been little conscious before. "The general impression they have left upon me is like that which many of us have experienced when the basement of our house happens to be under thorough sanitary repairs, and we realize for the first time the complex system of drains and gas- and water-pipes, flues, bell-wires, and so forth, upon which our comfort depends, but which are usually hidden out of sight, and of whose existence, so long as they acted well, we had never troubled ourselves."*

On the basis of this exploration of associated ideas, Galton then built up a list of seventy-five words, each of which he wrote on a small piece of paper. He would expose each word momentarily, holding a stop watch in his hand, which he started at the same time the word was exposed. After two or three associations had occurred to him, he stopped the watch and noted down the associations and the elapsed time. He did this on four separate occasions under very different circumstances and at an interval of about a month between each experiment. He found that 4 repetitions of the 75 words gave rise to 505 ideas and 13 instances of blockage in which no idea occurred during 4 seconds. Of the 505 ideas, 216 were the same, which indicates that out of every 100 words, 23 would give rise to the same association in every one of four trials. He concluded that the roadways of the mind are worn into very deep ruts and that the mind is perpetually traveling over familiar ways without the memory retaining any impression of its excursions. "It is apparently always engaged in mumbling over its old stores, and if any one of these is wholly neglected for a while, it is apt to be forgotten, perhaps irrecoverably."†

Galton analyzed so far as possible the time of his life at which each of the associated ideas was first attached to the stimulus word. There were 124 cases in which such identifications could be made satisfactorily. Of these, 39 per cent were first set up during boyhood and youth, 46 per cent during subsequent manhood, and 15 per cent by quite recent events. Those set up during boyhood and youth tended to occur three or four times in the four experiments, while those associated with recent events tended to occur but once.

Galton summarized his experiments as follows:

I have desired to show how whole strata of mental operations that have lapsed out of ordinary consciousness, admit of being dragged into light, recorded and treated statistically, and how the obscurity that attends the

* Galton, F., "Psychometric Experiments," *Brain*, 1880, 2, 151.
† Galton, F., *ibid.*, 155.

initial steps of our thoughts can thus be pierced and dissipated. . . . Perhaps the strongest of the impressions left by these experiments regards the multifariousness of the work done by the mind in a state of half-unconsciousness, and the valid reason they afford for believing in the existence of still deeper strata of mental operations, sunk wholly below the level of consciousness, which may account for such mental phenomena as cannot otherwise be explained. We gain an insight by these experiments into the marvelous number and nimbleness of our mental associations, and we also learn that they are very far indeed from being infinite in their variety. We find that our working stock of ideas is narrowly limited, but that the mind continually recurs to them in conducting its operations, therefore its tracks necessarily become more defined and its flexibility diminished as age advances.*

These studies led Wundt and Kraepelin in 1880 to start word-association experiments. Kraepelin directed the work of several of his colleagues toward the use of this procedure in the exploration of mental disturbances and in the differentiation of clinical types.

The association method was further developed by Jung[4] and his students in order to understand particular pathological processes, especially mental conflicts. Using the method, they were able to discover and isolate emotional complexes which otherwise had not been accessible. The new departure which Jung developed was the application of this method to the elucidation of unconscious mental processes. His assumption was that in the activity of unconscious mental associations there is mirrored the whole psychical essence of the past and of the present, with all its experiences and desires. Over a period of some fifteen years, studies were made of the associations of normal subjects, imbeciles, epileptics, hysterics, and various psychotic patients. Also the accompanying psychogalvanic changes, muscular movements, and respiratory changes were investigated.

In 1910, Kent and Rosanoff[5] compiled a list of one hundred words which were found to be suitable indicators of emotional complexes for use with English-speaking psychiatric patients and which were intended to bring out differences between such patients and normal individuals. They gave this list to one thousand normal people, recording in each instance the first word which was given in reply to the stimulus word. They tabulated these responses and published a series of frequency tables in which they recorded the stimulus word together with the frequency of each word occurring in the responses of the thousand persons.

Following the determination of the standard responses of normal persons, the test was given to 247 psychiatric patients. The comparison

* Galton, F., *ibid.*, 162.

between the normal and the psychotic groups may be presented as follows:

	Common Reactions Per Cent	Doubtful Reactions Per Cent	Individual Reactions Per Cent
1000 normal subjects	91.7	1.5	6.8
247 psychotic subjects	70.7	2.5	26.8

Common reactions consisted of those which were found to occur frequently in the normal group as shown by the larger percentages in the frequency tables. Doubtful reactions referred to hesitations, repetitions of the stimulus word, or of the previous response, whereas individual reactions were those which were not found in the frequency tables. The comparison disclosed more individual reactions in the mental patients than in normal persons. This analysis indicated that the normal range of associations is restricted within a rather limited series of responses. The association method did not provide a sharp distinction between mental health and mental disease; rather, it demonstrated that there was a gradual shading of disturbances in the associative process from the normal to the grossly pathological state.

At the present time it is accepted that complex indicators are valuable as a means of probing into forgotten memories which the patient may have. The method does not provide diagnostic criteria either for classification of the illness or for the therapy which may be used. It is a supplementary tool. In most instances the method of completely free association is now considered preferable to the standard word-association test. In free association the patient is allowed to talk and to recount any idea which may come into his mind. Since he is encouraged, during free association, to lay aside all inhibitions in his reporting, more material of immediate usefulness for the therapist is obtained than may be had from the word-association study.

The Direct Approach in Psychological Investigation

Most of the information about the mental life of abnormal persons comes from personal interviews or from the study of autobiographies. The direct questioning of the mental patient provides a great deal of evidence concerning his mental status. It must always be borne in mind that a mental patient is mentally sick, which means that he either cannot or does not understand his own psychopathological symptoms. If these individuals were able to understand their mental anomalies and could adequately explain them to others, abnormal psychology would be a fairly easy subject. Actually, any material obtained in interviews and from autobiographical accounts must be interpreted by way of comparison with the histories of other people who have shown similar symptoms. This process of evaluation of such material requires extensive experience which can be gained only through personal exploration of the problems and life histories of many mentally deviant persons.

The procedure in obtaining psychiatric data during an interview may be either direct or indirect. When the direct method is used, questions and answers are relied upon to bring out as much relevant information as possible. When the indirect method is used, the patient is encouraged to talk without any particular guidance on the part of the interviewer. It is expected that, if the patient talks long enough, relevant information will be obtained which could not be reached by direct questioning. Since each patient offers a special problem, it is essential to use very flexible methods of interviewing. It may be possible, for example, that the patient is depressed and tends to ascribe his depression to a death in the family. In such a case, the interviewer will attempt to clarify the psychological relations which existed between the patient and the deceased relative. In questioning some other depressed patient, it may be advisable to ignore all the details of family relationships. The skill in obtaining information relevant to the patient's basic problems is a real art.

As a rule, psychiatrists and clinical psychologists have recourse to a more or less standardized procedure in recording the details of a case history. Psychiatrists usually follow a course of investigation that is outlined in some psychiatric handbook or guide. Psychologists prefer to make use of one or more of the standardized questionnaires or of the projective techniques. The general usefulness of questionnaires was briefly mentioned in previous chapters. Here it seems desirable to discuss this method of direct approach more systematically in order to clarify its limitations and its virtues.

The main difficulties of the questionnaire method[7] grow out of the following points. (1) The questionnaire, itself, is rarely an accurate or adequate diagnostic instrument for the individual case. (2) All information obtained by the questionnaire method is affected by the personal psychological processes of the individual answering the questionnaire. (3) No information, even in matters of actually measurable fact, is absolutely certain. It follows, then, that the information obtained by a questionnaire concerning matters which are, for the most part, not open to measurement, is even more uncertain.

These points may be commented on at greater length. The clinician is always interested in the individual case. For this reason he demands that every measurement or measuring instrument which he uses shall be as accurate and informative as possible concerning the particular individual to whom it is applied. Some varieties of psychological procedures, such as the intelligence test, or tests of motor or mechanical ability, have a high predictive value with respect to the performance of any given person. Those questionnaires, however, which deal with personality deviations in the wider sense have not as yet been perfected to a point where the final score affords any degree of certainty with respect to an individual case.

All the answers which an individual gives, either in an interview or to a questionnaire, will be colored by his own experience. They will be tinged with the effect of the answers which he has given to previous questions, and they will be affected by the cooperation or lack of cooperation which he exhibits. One must recognize these facts and deal with them as part of the entire evaluation.

Despite these limitations, the questionnaire method has certain advantages which are of real psychological value to any student of human nature. This is particularly true in dealing with individual problems which involve psychopathology. Briefly, some of these virtues are as follows:

Both the individual answers given and the total questionnaire summation offer a conscious self-portrait, that is, the way in which the person answering the questionnaire pictures himself to himself. The ultimate actuality, the truth or falsity, of this portrait is entirely aside from the major point. The mental operations of the abnormal person may be either excessively logical, as in paranoia, or completely illogical, as in hebephrenia. Logic, rationality, lucidity, and the like, are not in themselves major considerations in descriptive psychopathology. The investigator, at this point, is interested in what the person says or thinks about himself without reference to truth or falsity. The answers which any person gives to a series of questions usually provide a fair amount of revealing self-description.

The questionnaire is a formalized, skeleton interview expressed in a standard fashion. If properly devised, it will give the experienced examiner quite a bit of insight into the mental processes of the individual who has answered the questions. The fact that it is standardized affords opportunity for the comparison of the performance of one individual with that of another, since both individuals met the same set of questions. The differences between their answers will provide illuminating material with respect to each person.

The collected, averaged data obtained by this method from groups of individuals throw light upon the conscious trends of thought and beliefs of the particular groups who have answered the questions. One may find, for example, that paranoid individuals tend to answer questions in a way which is in sharp contrast to the answers given by those of cycloid personality. If this should be true, a start can be made toward a factual understanding of the basic differences between the two attitudes. Elsewhere the notion has been stressed that questionnaires must be "tailor-made" for each particular job. In other words, if it is desired to bring out and establish some common attitudes or beliefs, it can be done by intelligent designing and use of this method.

The direct method of inquiry rather than a standardized questionnaire is the natural way of getting personal information. In dealing with certain groups of mental patients this method fails. It may be that the interviewer does not know what questions to ask, or when and how to ask them. The result will be that the patient, who lacks personal insight, never gives the really relevant information. Other patients have told their story so often and have answered so many questions that they "know all the answers." Still others will present a well-defined problem ("Doctor, I walk in my sleep and I don't know why.") and all direct questioning fails to bring out any pertinent information. For such reasons the indirect approach has received increasing attention in modern psychology and psychiatry.

The Indirect Approach

The account given by any person about himself when the direct method is used can never be a complete story of his personality. Many of the forgotten memories, attitudes, motives, desires, and wishes enter into his report without any conscious awareness of either their entry, or their effect upon his report. Seldom does such a directly obtained account contain material relevant to the fantasy life of the individual. There is much evidence to the effect that unconscious (or not fully conscious) attitudes, motives, or wishes play a significant role in the mental life of both normal and abnormal persons. Recognition of this fact has led to many investigations of the subconscious aspect of mental life. The wishes, daydreams, fantasies, terrors; the triumphs, the hopes, the aspirations; the humiliations and self-reproaches (all that is usually concealed and rationalized), actually influence the behavior and mental life to an extent to which even the most introspective individual is but slightly aware. To get at such material, several new methods have been devised. Some of these follow the conventional rules of science while others pertain less and less to science and more and more to intuitive art.

A method which is widely used today is the Rorschach psychodiagnostic test. Hermann Rorschach,[14] a Swiss psychiatrist, published in 1921 an elaborate study of the responses given by both normal and abnormal persons in the interpretation of specially prepared ink blots. Some of the blots were black and white, some were black, white, and red, and some were multicolored. These ink blots were presented one at a time to the individual being examined. As each was presented, the person was asked: "What might this be?" The explanation, name, or story which the person gave in response to each of the blots was recorded. The given combination of responses was related by Rorschach to all other information available about the subject's personality. Since the ink blots themselves were meaningless, the procedure demanded an organization of imagination. This process frequently offered clues to the personality structure which were not otherwise available. Those who have followed Rorschach in the use of this procedure hold that the method does not reveal an actual personality or behavior picture. It is comparable to an X-ray plate in that it shows the underlying structure. Information concerning this underlying structure makes behavior and personality more understandable.

Klopfer[6] has formalized the Rorschach test and the methods of interpretation in a fashion which is used by many contemporary clinicians. He has emphasized that the responses are indicative of the balance between spontaneity and control, of introversion-extroversion, and of the emotional ties between the inner and the outer life aspects of the individual. Some psychologists have questioned both the basic nature of these personality configurations and the need of formalizing the method to such a degree. They have held that the lack of formal classification and statement has value in itself; that the freedom of expression and freedom of interpretation are of more importance than any formalized or standardized procedure of interpretation or scoring.

It has been shown that the Rorschach method is reliable in that, within limits, a subject will give similar types of interpretations in successive tests. The true validity of the Rorschach test is still a matter of some dispute. Ideally, we should have a series of Rorschach interpretations to be correlated with other measures or indicators of personality which have themselves a high degree of reliability and validity. Although this problem of validation has been approached by various workers, no really satisfactory evidence is at hand at present to justify any definite conclusions.

The Rorschach method has been used in a variety of psychopathological individuals as well as with many normal persons. Beck[1] has shown that the schizophrenic patient tends to report a large number of inaccurately perceived forms and gives unusual rather than popular responses. These results are in line with the bizarre and odd nature of schizophrenic thought and perception as has been demonstrated by many other varieties of psychological study. In depression there is slow reaction time, little originality, little attention to movement or color, and a high percentage of obvious replies. These responses are essentially a reflection of the general retardation which dominates the whole mental life of the depressed patient. In the manic conditions one finds an increased number of responses, more attention to color than to movement, and a higher proportion of responses based on sharply and accurately perceived forms. In neurotics there is a reduction in the number of interpretations indicating movement, a reduction in the form-color responses, an increase in responses determined principally by form, and evidence of *color shock*. Color shock is shown by disturbances of reaction time, exclamations, or peculiar replies given to the ink blots which contain color in addition to black and white. This finding is regarded as an important diagnostic sign of neurosis, particularly useful in distinguishing neurosis from schizophrenia.

Piotrowski[12, 13] believes that the types of response given by patients suffering from organic brain disturbances are different from the responses of those who are suffering from neurosis or psychosis. Among the characteristic differences he has found that the organic cases give a very small number of responses, together with slow reaction time, almost no movement responses, few of the popular types of report, a tendency to name colors, and observable evidence of perplexity or self-distrust during the test.

These findings are but samples of a large and growing volume of research which is being conducted with the Rorschach method. Many able and careful investigators are making use of this method as a way of studying basic personality structure and the deviations of that structure. It is to be expected, therefore, that new evidence is accumulating which will add to the positive value of the procedure and will place it on a more firm scientific basis than it has at present.

Another example of the indirect approach is the method which was introduced in 1935 by Murray[9] and Morgan, and called by them the "Thematic Apperception Test." Their material consists of a series of twenty pictures which the person being studied is asked to use as a starting point for making up a plot or a story. The test is based upon the idea that when a person interprets a pictured ambiguous situation he is apt to expose hidden aspects of his own personality. The stimulus pictures are so composed that there is one or more human figures portrayed on each. The subject can identify himself with any one of these figures in each situation. While he is absorbed in his attempt to explain the picture, he may cease to be conscious of himself and of the scrutiny of others. Therefore, his story will provide the examiner with some knowledge of the wishes, fears, and past experiences which he would otherwise conceal. The subject may be asked not only to make up a story as to how the scene depicted on the picture came about, but also to tell what is going on at the moment, what the characters are feeling, and what the outcome will be.

The results obtained by this procedure have been treated by different investigators[15] in different ways. Some have noted the character of the story which is told. Others have analyzed the language which was used in relating the story. Still others have interpreted the plots produced by the subject in order to understand his conscious and unconscious fantasies. In the application of the test to persons suffering from different mental disorders, the different groups tend to produce stories which are in accordance with their entire personality structures, distorted though they may be.

Summary

Medical psychology partakes of the scientific nature of general psychology; but since it draws most of its human material from clinical observers and observations, it is largely in the stage of scientific development marked by description and tentative classification. Kraepelin developed a scheme of classification of psychiatric disorders which has been generally accepted. He also provided a blueprint of scientific method for the attack on the problems of psychopathology. Much that is undisputed fact in this field today can be directly traced to his work and influence. The ideas which Pavlov gained from the study of animal behavior represent a newer departure in thought but one which is influencing much present-day research.

The diagnostic word-association method is an example of an experimental procedure which produced some information concerning the fundamental nature of mental activity in both normal and abnormal persons. It opened the way for the greater development of free association, questionnaire methods, and indirect or projective techniques. Personal interviews and impersonal questionnaires remain the usual way of obtaining information from mental patients. Both direct questioning and the questionnaire method are far from infallible and often fail to produce relevant material. It is understandable, therefore, that there has been much criticism of the direct method of obtaining psychiatric data. An evaluation of the questionnaire procedure indicates that it has many positive virtues when it is properly used.

The indirect methods of obtaining information from patients are illustrated by the Rorschach test and the Thematic Apperception Test. These newer approaches have caught the attention of many research workers in the field of abnormal psychology. Future scientific clarification and precision of these indirect techniques may be expected.

REFERENCES

1. Beck, S. J., *Rorschach's Test:* I. *Basic Processes.* New York, Grune and Stratton, 1944.
2. Bentley, E. M., and E. V. Cowdry, *The Problem of Mental Disorder.* New York, McGraw-Hill, 1934.
3. Galton, F., "Psychometric Experiments," *Brain,* 1880, *2,* 149–162.
4. Jung, C. G., *Studies in Word-Association.* London, Heinemann, 1918.
5. Kent, G. H., and A. J. Rosanoff, "A Study of Association in Insanity," *Amer. Jour. Insan.,* 1910, *67,* 37–96, 317–390.
6. Klopfer, B., and D. M. Kelley, *The Rorschach Technique.* Yonkers-on-Hudson, World Book, 1942.
7. Landis, C., "Questionnaires and the Study of Personality," *Jour. Nerv. Ment. Dis.,* 1936, *83,* 125–134.
8. Mapother, E., "Emil Kraepelin," *Jour. Ment. Sci.,* 1927, *73,* 509–515.
9. Murray, H. A., *Explorations in Personality.* New York, Oxford, 1938.
10. Pavlov, I. P., *Lectures on Conditioned Reflexes.* New York, International Publishers, 1928.
11. ———, *Conditioned Reflexes and Psychiatry.* New York, International Publishers, 1941.
12. Piotrowski, Z. A., "The Rorschach Inkblot Method in Organic Disturbances of the Central Nervous System," *Jour. Nerv. Ment. Dis.,* 1937, *86,* 525–537.
13. ———, "The Prognostic Possibilities of the Rorschach Method in Insulin Treatment," *Psychiat. Quart.,* 1938, *12,* 679–689.
14. Rorschach, H., *Psychodiagnostics* (English trans.). Berne, Huber, 1942.
15. White, R. W., "The Interpretation of Imaginative Productions. Chapter 6 in J. McV. Hunt, *Personality and the Behavior Disorders.* New York, Ronald, 1944, 214–251.
16. Zilboorg, G., and G. W. Henry, *A History of Medical Psychology.* New York, Norton, 1941.

Chapter XXXIII

PSYCHOTHERAPY

PSYCHOTHERAPY has been described as the acting on the mind of a human being by mental means, with the intention of effecting a cure. The major concern of psychotherapy is that the sufferer shall be relieved of his illness; shall find a form of security in his life; shall gain some self-realization; shall achieve a degree of self-respect and self-confidence greater than that which he has found in his illness. These aims are accomplished in a variety of ways. They may come through identification with some religious faith; through self-discovery or through a discovery of one's own place in the community, culture, or society of which one is a member. In this larger sense psychotherapy is not solely the concern of the psychiatrist or clinical psychologist, but the concern of every human being who attempts to relieve the sufferings of the troubled mind of another person.

Psychologists are and have been interested in psychotherapy for two different reasons, one theoretical and one practical. Theoretically, the subject of psychotherapy is part of general psychology and should be understood by any individual who hopes to have a working knowledge of the science of psychology. From the practical point of view, many psychologists are called upon to do psychotherapeutic work, since it is recognized that they have (or should have) specialized knowledge which provides an understanding of human behavior. The place for therapeutic activities of a psychologist in society, as it is at present organized, is not clear. Psychologists have a fairly well-recognized status as therapists in the use of educational procedures with children. Their status is less well recognized when they are dealing with adult neurotics or psychopathic personalities. They have no recognized status and, as conditions exist at present, no place in dealing with the direct therapy of the major mental disorders, psychoses, and organic conditions.

The history of medical psychology and the methods which have been used for centuries past in dealing with mental defects and mental disorders form a sorry chapter in the record of human progress.[18] Only within the past one hundred years has any notion of tolerance and humanity entered into the care of the mentally sick. The memory of the days of chains, jail sentences, flogging, and, indeed, burning at the stake is still fresh in human experience. There is no point in going into this black chapter of man's inhumanity to man. Our modern orientation is at least humane and does involve improved methods of treatment which produce a fair number of therapeutic successes.

During the centuries of recorded history every conceivable method of treating the mentally sick has been tried. Every new medical, physical, or biological discovery is soon tried out on these unfortunates. Every new psychological approach, every new educational procedure has had its turn. Some have proved to be effective; most have been found wanting. With certain of these approaches, particularly those of a psychological nature, which have been more or less fruitful, we will now concern ourselves. Not too much is known about the way in which these methods operate. Present-day judgment of the effectiveness of almost any form of psychotherapy is in terms of results which have been reported, even though we are not always certain how those results were produced.

Hypnotism and Suggestion

Franz Anton Mesmer[8] (1733–1815) first called to scientific attention a phenomenon which he named *animal magnetism*. In the 1760's he conceived the hypothesis that the two halves of the human body acted like the two poles of a magnet. He thought that if this were true, then anyone might have animal magnetism; and one human being could direct and control the activity of another, in the same way that a magnet will attract or repel iron. Mesmer also assumed that disease was the result of an improper distribution of animal magnetism. He tried passing metallic magnets over the bodies of his patients and found in some an alleviation or even cure of various symptoms about which they had complained. He then tried passing his hands over his patients without using magnets and obtained equally good results. Therefore, he discontinued the use of magnets, believing that the mysterious influence which he had over a patient was a form of animal magnetism. He held that this animal magnetism was a kind of gas or fluid whose distribution and action were under the control of the human will.

Mesmer did not attract too much attention in Vienna, so in 1778 he went to Paris where he opened a clinic for the treatment of all kinds of diseases. This clinic was held in a large room which was draped and darkened with curtains and hangings. In the center of the room was a large oak tub which was several feet high and large enough to permit thirty patients to stand around it. The tub was filled with water in which had been placed iron filings, ground glass, and a number of bottles symmetrically arranged. The tub was covered with a wooden lid through which projected jointed iron rods. The patients would apply the end of one of the rods to whatever part of their body was ailing. While surrounding the tub the patients maintained absolute silence, so that they could listen more attentively to the soft music

PLATE 19

FRANZ ANTON MESMER

(1733–1815)

that was being played. At intervals Mesmer, wearing a brilliant silk robe, would enter the clinic. He would come to each patient in turn, fix his eyes on him, pass his hands over his body, and touch him with a long iron wand. Persons who were suffering from a wide variety of diseases claimed that they were cured by several such treatments.

After a few years a dispute arose between Mesmer and some of his pupils over the right to give lectures dealing with the procedure which he had discovered and was using. Because of the disputes, in 1784 the French Academy of Sciences appointed a committee, of which

Benjamin Franklin was one member, to investigate the existence of animal magnetism which Mesmer claimed to be employing.

As a result of their investigation the commission decided that animal magnetism was not a physical force, and concluded:

The committees, aware that the magnetic fluid could not be noticed by any of our senses, that it had no effect on the members of the committees, nor on the patients who were submitted to it; having assured themselves that the touchings and the pressures [applied by the magnetizers] cause changes rarely favorable to the animal economy and disturbances always harmful to the imagination; having finally demonstrated by decisive experience that imagination without magnetism produces convulsions and that magnetism without imagination produces nothing, [the members of the committees] have unanimously concluded in regard to the question of the existence and usefulness of animal magnetic fluid that such fluid does not exist and therefore cannot be useful, that the violent effects seen in public treatments result from the touching [by the patients], from the imagination which is set into action, and from the machine of incitement, which we must admit against our own desire is the only thing which impressed us. *

This negative report and the civil disturbance in Paris at the onset of the French Revolution caused Mesmer to leave Paris. He went first to Germany, then to Vienna, and finally to Switzerland, and so passed out of the scientific scene. It is evident that Mesmer had made a discovery which he himself misinterpreted, as did the commission which investigated his work.

Mesmer did not actually hypnotize his patients, as we understand the term today. He did produce some very interesting trancelike states. For example, it was reported that "all of the subjects were, to an amazing extent, under the influence of the magnetiser; though they might seem to be asleep, his voice, or a look or sign from him, would arouse them." † One of Mesmer's students was the Marquis de Puységur, who discovered a state which he called "artificial somnambulism" and which was later named *hypnosis* by Braid. De Puységur attempted to apply Mesmer's magnetizing method to a patient who, instead of falling into hysterical convulsions, went into a quiet sleeping trance. From this trance he apparently did not fully awaken for some time, but went about in the fashion of a sleepwalker. When he did awaken he was unable to recall anything that had happened during the trance. Following this discovery in 1784, various physicians and

---

* Zilboorg, G., and G. W. Henry, *A History of Medical Psychology*. New York, Norton, 1941, 345.

† Janet, P., *Psychological Healing*, Vol. I. New York, Macmillan, 1925, 153.

scientists investigated this somnambulistic state. They demonstrated that it was possible to produce, in patients who were in trance, positive hallucinations (seeing things which are not present), negative hallucinations (inability to see things which are really present), anesthesias of any sense, paralyses or loss of voluntary control of any body movement, insensibility to pain, amnesias, and varieties of posthypnotic suggestion. Since the method could be reproduced by practically anyone, it was seized upon by charlatans, quacks, and fakers whose use of the procedure brought it into quick disrepute.

Braid[11] in England in 1841 reestablished scientific interest in mesmerism. He saw a demonstration given by a French magnetizer and, although he originally thought the man was a fake, he convinced himself of the genuine nature of the phenomena in question by producing them himself. He developed a special technique for inducing the trance which is still used. He had the subject look fixedly at some bright object which was held near and slightly above the eyes in such a way that the fixation caused a strain of the eye muscles. This fixation, combined with verbal suggestion, brought on a trance which he named *hypnosis*.

Braid's work attracted the attention of several other physicians and surgeons. It also met bitter, determined opposition from the organized medical profession. In spite of this, mesmeric hospitals were founded in various English cities for the purpose of performing medical and surgical work in conjunction with hypnosis. Amputation of limbs, childbirth, and many other surgical procedures were successfully carried out during hypnotic trance. However, the discovery of anesthetic agents, such as nitrous oxide, chloroform, and ether, was made about this time. Since they did not depend upon a disputed psychological technique, the use of hypnosis as a means of inducing anesthesia for surgical procedures soon virtually disappeared.

Although surgery could dispose of hypnotism, psychological medicine could not do so. The dramatic results obtained in many cases were too impressive to be discounted. When hypnotism was compared to the other procedures, such as purges, bleeding, and drugs, which were used at that time (unsuccessfully) in the mentally ill, it was apparent that the method was useful and productive. Hypnotism unfortunately had (and still has) the reputation of being something mysterious. It seemed to have more than the average possibility of quackery, plus the popular notion that there must be something sinister and evil involved in this psychological phenomenon. The method has encountered continual opposition because the results produced cannot be related to anything which seems definite and objective. Instead they appear to be mysterious and possibly fraudulent.

In the early 1880's two outstanding French physicians began making use of the hypnotic procedure for the care and investigation of mental patients. These two investigators were Charcot and Bernheim. Charcot was head of the neurological service at the Salpêtrière, the leading mental hospital in Paris. He became particularly interested in the study of hysteria and in the use of hypnosis in the investigation and treatment of the hysterical patient. Essentially, he held that hypnosis was possible only in individuals who were actually or potentially hysterical and that hypnosis was closely allied to hysteria.

Bernheim was head of the mental clinic at Nancy. He also made use of hypnotism in the study and treatment of hysterical patients. He believed and taught that both hysteria and hypnotism were merely exaggerated forms of suggestion or autosuggestion. He saw no essential connection between hysteria and hypnosis. He stressed the need for studying the processes of suggestion and the characteristics of suggestibility, since he considered them in no sense limited to hysterical individuals. He was more nearly right in his conclusions than was Charcot. However, Charcot exercised the greater influence because he had among his students both Sigmund Freud and Pierre Janet, each of whom later developed specialized forms of psychotherapy. Their work, in part, grew out of the observations which they had made in Charcot's clinic.

Today hypnotism still carries with it a popular distrust because it is believed to be something mysterious. In spite of all of the experimental work which has been done on the subject during the past century, no one has yet been able to state explicitly just how the hypnotic trance comes about. The phenomenon may be described in terms of conditioned response, exaggerated suggestion, father fixation, or the imposition of the will of one person upon that of another. It is used in a limited way by a few psychiatrists and clinical psychologists. The experience of most practicing psychopathologists who have made use of the method in individuals suffering from mental disorders (particularly hysteria) has been that the immediate condition may be improved but that few lasting benefits accrue. One can suggest to a neurotic patient during hypnosis that the immediate symptoms will no longer bother him. He may even report that he is "cured." However, most of these patients later return to either the same or another therapist complaining of a new set of symptoms. In other words, it is possible to relieve their immediate complaints, but apparently their troubles are too deep-seated for any permanent psychological repair to be effected during hypnosis.

Hypnosis is used in the psychological laboratory today as a procedure for studying personality and, particularly, the so-called unconscious factors which operate in personality. It is possible to reproduce in the hypnotic trance many of the types of behavior and mental aberrations seen in both neurotic and psychotic patients. For example, a hypnotized subject was persuaded to think that he had accidentally burned a hole in a girl's dress with his cigarette. The next day he reported that he was quite upset and had a headache which he said was due to smoking. He believed that he should give up smoking, and was hostile and resentful toward the hypnotist. It was only with difficulty that he could be persuaded to undergo hypnosis a second time, so that the complex about smoking could be explained to him and "cured."[4] Such experiments suggest the possibility of establishing artificial patterns of response which seem quite similar to those shown by a neurotic individual. These patterns influence behavior in the same fashion that a true complex or conflict would.

Since hypnosis is usually viewed as an exaggerated form of suggestion, various kinds of mild hypnotic techniques based mainly upon suggestion have been tried out to replace true hypnosis as a therapeutic procedure. From these modified techniques have developed various forms of psychotherapy which involve suggestion and persuasion.

Psychoanalytic Therapy[7]

Sigmund Freud (1856–1939) became interested in psychotherapy through several months' association in 1885 with Charcot who was at that time employing hypnotic procedures in the treatment of hysterical cases. When Freud resumed his practice of medicine in Vienna he was associated for a short period of time with Breuer who had developed what he called a "cathartic procedure," meaning that during hypnosis the patient was encouraged to talk at length about anything that came into his mind. Freud and Breuer in 1893 published under the title, "The Psychological Mechanisms of Hysterical Phenomena,"[2] the first paper on the subject of psychoanalytic therapy. Originally this therapy consisted of inducing the hysterical patient, while hypnotized, to remember and reproduce forgotten but traumatic experiences which had occurred in his past life. They found that such forgotten material was expressed in the symptoms of hysterical persons. Frequently the physical symptoms were symbolic equivalents of some painful memory that had been repressed. When Freud followed up this type of investigation with other studies which went more deeply into the background of the troubles of such patients, he observed that the symptoms and difficulties usually grew out of some form of sexual maladjustment or repression. Since this element of repressed sexuality was frequently embarrassing and certainly not socially conventional, Breuer dissociated himself from Freud and his studies, while the latter went on in a systematic fashion experimenting with the new procedure.

Freud soon discovered that hypnosis was not a necessary element in the psychotherapeutic procedure; indeed, he became convinced that hypnosis offered a barrier to true understanding and therapeutic results.[7] By a process of trial and error he found that patients would learn a process of free association (a rambling, undirected monologue), during which they could recover memories which had not been part of their ordinary conscious life. The therapy, he believed, was based on the fact that unconscious ideas and mental processes constituted the direct cause of the morbid symptoms. The treatment consisted in the promotion of the self-realization by the patient of the nature of these processes and in helping him to accept or resolve them following their incorporation into his conscious life. The mental resistance which the patient develops in this procedure grows out of the discomfort experienced in admitting into consciousness unpleasant, distasteful, or unconventional thoughts and ideas associated with his own past life. The patient must accept himself through better self-understanding. The fact that he has rejected or more or less inadequately repressed certain memories is considered the main cause of his present unhappiness and mental disability, that is, anxiety, compulsion, hysteria, and the like. When he is encouraged to pursue a course of free association, his forgotten memories are usually found to be either directly or indirectly connected with repressed sexuality.

In essence the psychoanalytical method, as Freud and his followers developed it, aims at enabling a patient to relax and allow his thoughts to drift idly from one idea to the next, without noting or caring where these thoughts are leading him. Although this aim may seem to be simple and easy, it is the most difficult part (and the most essential) in the entire technique of psychoanalysis. It is not an uncommon experience for a person to have to work months before attaining any truly free production of material.

Psychoanalysis has two objectives: One of them is to survey the unconscious material of the patient's mind through the application of the method of free association. The other is to show the influence which this unconscious material has had upon the patient's relationship to other human beings, as well as on his own mental life. On this basis the analyst will first map out the unconscious territory and describe to the patient in an impersonal manner the significant connections which he sees among the various components of the patient's associations. This is the analytical approach to the patient's biographical material. Soon the analyst finds that he has become the storm center of highly significant emotions of the patient. These emotions have to be continuously described, explained, and resolved in order to make it possible for the work on the biographical material to proceed successfully. This emotional storm is called the "transference situation."

From the patient's point of view, the analysis of the transference situation is one of the most valuable of the therapeutic experiences through which he goes. The reason for this is simple. The analyst is, or should be, a person who is little known to the patient. He keeps himself as much in the background as possible, quietly friendly, but always impersonal and reserved. He tries to become a peg on which the patient can hang his fantasies. Therefore, when the patient's emotional relationship to the analyst is being explained and resolved, it is actually not a relationship to a real individual which is involved. The analyst is the object of many unconscious fantasies and feelings which the patient has developed about other persons, particularly his parents. During the psychoanalysis the patient may experience moods of anxiety, anger, hate, affection, or jealousy. By working out the unreasonable storms of feeling which play into his relationship with the analyst, it becomes possible to show him how his unconscious fantasies warp his relationships to other human beings.

The free association and the analysis of the transfer situation reveal the countless interconnections of ideas and feelings which are not accessible by any direct method which attends only to the production of logical and chronological thinking. The insistent reappearance of certain associations connected with observable emotional states gradually makes apparent those unconscious connections which are overloaded with emotion. The unconscious connections may be given special study until their significance is clear. The analyst can watch the course of the undirected associations and their interplay with emotional states, and can guide, in part, the solution of the patient's difficulties. By analogy, at least, it is possible for the analyst to observe in normal people and in those who have minor character disturbances thin rivulets of fantasy and feeling. Their relationship can be traced step by step to the headlong torrents of disorganization shown by the frankly psychotic or psychoneurotic patient.

Out of this procedure, together with the theoretical explanation which Freud and his followers have constructed, grew a radically different psychological viewpoint from that which was held in either objective science or in common sense. Some of this new psychology has been incorporated into ordinary scientific psychology. Some of it is now part of common sense and everyday speech; for example, inferiority complex, repression, or dream symbolism. There is no point in reviewing the controversy which has gone on and still continues concerning the acceptance or rejection of psychoanalytic psychology or psychoanalytic psychiatry. General psychology and clinical psychiatry, the practical approaches to the problems of psychopathology, many of the case histories found in the literature, all these and more, are today replete with psychoanalytic terms and concepts. In fact, most of the explanations advanced in specialized psychopathological studies are phrased in the light of the concepts built up by Freud and his followers. There can be no question but that psychoanalysis has permeated psychiatry, psychopathology, abnormal psychology, and general psychology. Many of the contributions and implications of Freud's clinical observations were so persuasive that they have been accepted without final scientific validation. As years have gone by, some of the material has been directly confirmed by scientific methods.[17] Other theories are still believed correct although the evidence is indirect. Certain claims have been rejected for want of evidence or because further clinical observation has failed to bear out the original hypothesis.

Psychoanalysis has provided a new viewpoint, a new terminology, a new tool, and a new therapy with which to study and treat the mind of the mentally disordered person. Freud and his followers have always maintained that psychoanalysis is itself a science and that its method is a scientific procedure. In comparison to the physical and biological sciences psychoanalysis is, at the best, a poor science and its procedure makes use of the weakest and most unreliable of scientific methods. It must rely upon a technique which does not admit the repetition of observation. It has no self-evident or easily demonstrable validity, and is mixed to an unknown degree with the analyst's own suggestions and with observations which are not directly related to the study of the patient. Such difficulties do not interfere with the therapeutic procedure, but they do weaken the claim that the facts of free association obtained during the analysis are objectively valid. This does not mean that psychoanalysis and the findings obtained by the psychoanalytic method are false. It does indicate, however, that verification must be had either by some more objective experimental approach or by the long-range accumulation of similar reports given by different investigators.

As a method of treatment, the analytic procedure has been relatively successful with hysterical and neurotic patients and with persons suffering from minor character disorders or disabilities.[14] The therapeutic results are not significantly superior to those obtained with other methods in the same groups of individuals, although they are usually thought to be more lasting and even permanent. The application of the procedure to the major mental disorders has been unsuccessful. Freud himself counselled against the use of the analytic method during the acute phase of any psychosis. He indicated that it might be used with the manic-depressive patient when that patient was well, so that he might have a fuller understanding of himself even if future attacks could not be prevented. He advised against the psychoanalysis of schizophrenic patients except as a definite experiment, since the schizophrenic personality structure was considered by him to be so weak that analysis would do more harm than good. It is also true that psychoanalysis has added little or nothing to the therapy of amentia, epilepsy, or any of the organic psychoses.

In summary, Freudian psychoanalysis has contributed to our thinking about the problems of psychopathology and it has provided a therapy of value in hysteria and other forms of neurosis, and in certain minor character anomalies.

Reeducation as a Form of Psychotherapy

In one sense the psychoanalytic therapy is a special form of reeducation.[16] It is a method of directing and leading a person who is unable to control his behavior or emotionality to self-control or to an emotional adjustment which he can tolerate. It is a process of learning that one set of emotional habits has been unsatisfactory and futile and that another set of habits can be acquired which will cause less difficulty in everyday life.

Generally speaking, reeducation of the neurotic person is directed either toward achievement of self-sufficiency or toward the placing of reliance in some group, some person, or some faith which will provide a sense of security when self-sufficiency is impossible. Self-sufficiency in readjustment comes about through an internal reorganization and reevaluation of one's own possibilities, potentialities, and life goals. If a person finally learns to understand himself and his own limitations, he may have strength and integration adequate to meet and to adjust to the problems of everyday life. Another procedure can be adapted to the treatment of the neurotic patient who has not achieved self-sufficiency. Neurotics are incapable of working out their own personal problems and tend to rely on some outer source of strength. This source is expected to supply the necessary balance and reassurance which they themselves are incapable of achieving. For these patients persuasion, moralizing, suggestion, or becoming a member of some group of fellow-sufferers may bring about a fairly satisfactory form of adjustment. The choice between self-sufficiency and reliance on strength-from-without is one which the neurotic himself cannot make (or he would have made it); it must be made for him by some skilled psychotherapist after adequate study of his latent reserves and assets.

It is often difficult for the therapist to decide which attack to make on the problem of a particular neurotic. The choice is easy when the patient is either a relatively strong personality who has gotten into unusual difficulties or when he is a weak, ineffective person. But many are neither clearly strong nor weak. There are persons who seem to possess a natural knack for sizing up the neurotic and giving him advice which will lead to a solution of his problems and to a successful readjustment. This knack is beyond any specialized training in psychology, medicine, religion, or therapy, although any or all of these may contribute to it. There are other persons who, because of close application and long experience, achieve an equal degree of therapeutic efficiency. They have acquired this efficiency at the price of many mistakes which they made in their earlier careers. Except for native endowment or long experience, there is no way of teaching deep sympathy and psychological insight into the problems of other persons. Hamilton stated this point as follows: "I have thus come to know something about the therapeutic methods of practically every American psychopathologist of repute. . . . It is apparent that each of these men has had some patients who worshipped him and patients who damned him, and that none has lacked at least one individually fashioned weapon in his therapeutic armamentarium which all the rest might well covet."*

Reeducation as a therapy is usually not a productive procedure with psychotic patients. If any results are to be obtained with psychotics, then the patient must possess, according to Franz,[5] four particular characteristics. In the first place, he must have some insight; he must realize that he is somehow different from other mem-

---

* Hamilton, G. V., *An Introduction to Objective Psychopathology.* St. Louis, Mosby, 1925, 205.

bers of the community and that this difference must be overcome or compensated for. Next, the patient must have a real desire to get well. If the patient thinks he is a king or if he is preoccupied with listening to imaginary voices, all attempts at reeducation will fail because the patient himself sees no advantage in achieving any other form of adjustment. The third requisite is self-confidence on the part of the patient. He must believe in his capacity for mastering the causes and consequences of his psychosis, and he must have confidence in the ability of his therapist to help him overcome his problems. If the patient is in a deep depression without any evidence of self-confidence, it will be impossible to achieve any degree of reeducation so long as the depression persists. Lastly, the efforts of both the patient and the therapist must be properly directed toward the special difficulties of the given case. The efforts must be directed toward the formation of adequate habits of thought and action in order to enable the patient to adjust in a fashion compatible with his abilities, disabilities, and particular life situation.

Only a few psychotic patients meet these conditions. No psychotic can meet them while he is in the acute phase of his illness. Only after his actual mania, depression, apathy, delusion, or delirium has disappeared can any therapeutic procedure based on reeducation be started. Even then, the number of really psychotic patients who respond favorably to reeducational methods is limited. That intensive persuasion, physiotherapy, and attempts at reeducational procedures are effective with a larger percentage of psychotic patients than is usually believed to be true has been shown by Cheney and Drewry.[3] In other words, although not all psychotics can be helped by such methods, a greater proportion could be helped than are being helped, if only adequate and intensive procedures were applied.

Recent Developments in Psychotherapy

ALCOHOLICS ANONYMOUS

Alcoholics Anonymous[1] is a group of some eight or ten thousand men and women who have themselves recovered from a seemingly hopeless state of mind and body brought about through the intemperate use of alcohol. They found that an ex-alcoholic who had solved his problem and who was properly armed with the facts about himself, could often gain the confidence of another alcoholic. On the basis of this confidence and with the help and understanding which one patient can provide for another, they have achieved some very excellent therapeutic results. Their method essentially consists of bringing the alcoholic patient sharply to the realization that he is a drunkard and that he himself is helpless to control his own obsessional tendency toward alcohol. He must admit to himself his own insufficiency and accept a three point program which they phrase as follows:

1. That we were alcoholic and could not manage our lives.
2. That probably no human power could have relieved our alcoholism.
3. That God could and would if sought.

It is significant that this procedure has been empirically worked out by alcoholics themselves. It is based on an admission of a lack of self-sufficiency and the seeking for, and dependence upon strength from an outside source. The group has demonstrated its effectiveness in a large number of cases. It is a form of nonsectarian religion in which the members have in common a self-acknowledged weakness which they attempt to conquer through mutual assistance and religious sublimation. It would be interesting to know whether or not a similar procedure might be worked out with other mentally disordered individuals, for example, neurotics.

GROUP THERAPY

The need for some psychotherapeutic procedure which can be applied to a fairly large group of mental patients at the same time has often been stressed. Many methods have been tried and promising results have been reported whenever the activities were organized by an enthusiastic psychotherapist, with leadership qualities, who had adequate training and competent assistance. The results show an increase in the number of patients who are able to leave the hospital and an increase in morale of those who must remain in the hospital.

The group-therapy method has recently been extensively used in the treatment of psychoneurotic cases in the Army and Navy. It was particularly appropriate in this situation because it was necessary to treat a large number of acute psychopathological cases with a limited number of therapists. The method was appropriate because of the common elements in the background, symptomatology, and specific problems of adjustment involved.

The program employed in the Army hospitals usually was conducted as follows. A group of ten to thirty patients met with the psychotherapist at regular sessions which lasted about an hour and were held three or more times a week. At the first session the therapist pointed out that these meetings would have value in helping each person get over his nervous condition. The group was told that each individual should bring up any problems that were bothering him and each should feel free to comment on the problems of others in the group. After the patients had been put at their ease and encouraged to talk, the therapist acted as a moderator. He endeavored to guide the group discussion and to build up group identification and solidarity. He had to be familiar with the history and problems of each patient so that he could draw each one into a participating role in the discussion.

The organization of topics to be discussed at each session was defined, so that rambling and incoherent sessions were avoided. Leading questions were used to bring out common symptoms or troubles. Questions such as "What bothers you?" "What makes you angry?" "Why do you think such things scare you?" brought out immediate responses and these were developed by having various members of the group say why they thought such reactions occurred. Among the topics that the therapist introduced were the causes and results of conflict and anxiety, types of motivation, the ways of handling fears, the relation between bodily functions and emotions, and other topics relevant to the psychopathologies involved. During these group discussions, each patient found reassurance from the fact that others had problems similar to his own; he obtained a better understanding of himself; he was given constructive, practical suggestions relevant to his personal problems; and he had an opportunity to "air" his complaints, hostilities, worries, and fears. In brief, the sessions provided a mental catharsis.

One of the main goals of the method of group therapy was to build up the feeling of identification with the group. This feeling not only provided a means of "sharing the guilt" or "sharing the anxiety" but also furnished a stabilizing influence and support. The therapeutic objective was to patch up the personality assets and to return the patient to forms of adjustment which had been effective in previous army or civilian life.

In several hospitals, forms of psychodrama were found valuable as a supplementary method for desensitization and education for the practical, everyday problems that were facing or would face the patient. For example, the situation portrayed might be that of a neuropsychiatric patient returning home and trying to get a job. The embarrassing questions and attitudes that the returning soldier was apt to encounter were represented and ways (both good and bad) of responding in these situations were acted out. The group then criticized the solutions and the behavior. Their criticisms were made into suggestions which were acted out in turn.

These psychotherapeutic sessions were integrated with an extensive program of occupational therapy, vocational guidance and instruction, and physical reconditioning which would develop interests and aptitudes. All of this provided a basis of personal satisfaction and accomplishment.

The group-therapy method used in the armed services was found valuable in relieving hostility, restlessness, and distressing feelings of guilt. It was also useful in reestablishing adequate participation in a social group. It differs from the usual psychotherapy in that a group and not a single individual was treated and in the fact that it tried to "patch up" the psychological weaknesses and repress the disruptive elements in the personality rather than to take apart (analyze) the basic personality problems and rebuild personality structure. That group therapy is immediately effective with many neurotic patients has been demonstrated. How well the "cures" last and how effective the results are as compared to individual therapy remains a question.

PSYCHIATRIC PHARMACOLOGY

Several years ago it was found that following the use of certain of the hypnotic drugs, such as sodium amytal or sodium evipan, a mentally disordered patient may show periods of lucidity or of delirium. During such periods he may describe with intense emotional tone memories which play an important part in his neurosis.[10, 15] The use of sodium evipan [pentothal] in soldiers suffering from traumatic neuroses has produced promising results in some cases.

Such a patient is given an intravenous injection of the drug, after which he goes to sleep for five to fifteen minutes. On arousing, he will sometimes respond readily to questions or enter into a free flow of conversation describing experiences which he previously repressed. Two procedures for dealing with this flow of conversation have been used. The patient may be allowed, as he slowly regains consciousness, to ramble on with remarks which may have the character of a delirium being similar to the grandiose or querulous remarks of an intoxicated person. In this material, compulsive trends of a paranoid character are sometimes laid bare in a fashion which otherwise could not have been achieved. Hence, the therapist can understand more clearly certain of the resentments and complaints which are basic in the motivation of the disordered mental condition.

The second method is to prompt the patient as one might do under hypnosis. He is encouraged to remember and describe certain episodes which are believed to occupy a key position in the production of his neurotic symptoms. The goal is to obtain a restoration of certain periods of amnesia which are active as unconscious motivating forces in neurosis. In order to assure the integration of these revealed facts into the ordinary stream of consciousness, this process of analysis and conversation is continued well into the period of full awakening of ordinary consciousness. Unless this is done, there is a danger that the material discovered will lapse back into unconsciousness. It has occasionally been observed that after the effect of the drug has worn off and another psychotherapeutic session has started, the patient may be completely unaware of what he revealed on the former occasion. If the material disclosed during the narcosis does not become part of the patient's conscious awareness of the facts and attitudes which are acting to produce his disordered state, his emotional release will be only temporary. Much valuable information may be supplied for the psychotherapist, but the immediate effect on the patient will be negligible.

Since much experimental work is being conducted with this particular method, it may be expected that as time goes by there will be an improvement both in the drugs used and in the procedure of questioning and the psychological reeducation.

Summary

The use of psychotherapy implies that we have acted upon the mind of some other individual by psychological means. There is little that is different in the procedures used in psychotherapy from those procedures which are used in getting along with normal people in everyday life.

The story of the discovery and the applications of hypnosis to the treatment of mental disorders typifies the history of many psychotherapeutic procedures. Hypnosis is nonspecific. This means that it does not enter directly into the healing process, but acts as an adjunct or a palliative. Freudian psychotherapy grew out of hypnotic therapy and is nonspecific. It is more effective, generally speaking, than hypnotic therapy. Its effectiveness grows out of a better understanding of the basic psychological problems involved in mental illness, together with a well-rounded reeducational procedure directed to the emotional problems involved.

Hypnosis, psychoanalysis, and the use of hypnotic drugs are but methods of entering past the resistances of a person so that he relates material which he has forgotten. Having retrieved these memories and realized their implication, the patient may be able to make an adequate life adjustment. Reeducation methods, group therapy, the method of Alcoholics Anonymous, and the like, supply the person who is maladjusted because of some essential emotional weakness with a source of support on which he may rely in the absence of self-sufficiency. In brief, the aim of all psychotherapy is to bring the patient to a point of self-sufficiency or to the realization that he must confess his own inadequacy and place reliance on some form of outside strength.

REFERENCES

1. Anon., *Alcoholics Anonymous*. New York, Works Publishing Co., 1939.
2. Breuer, J., and S. Freud, "The Psychic Mechanism of Hysterical Phenomena," in *Collected Works of Sigmund Freud*, Vol. I. London, Hogarth, 1924, 24–41.
3. Cheney, C. O., and P. H. Drewry, Jr., "Results of Non-specific Treatment in Dementia Praecox," *Amer. Jour. Psychiat.*, 1938, *95*, 203–217.
4. Erickson, M. H., "Experimental Demonstration of the Psychopathology of Everyday Life," *Psychoanal. Quart.*, 1939, *8*, 338–353.
5. Franz, S. I., *Nervous and Mental Reeducation*. New York, Macmillan, 1923.
6. Freud, S., *The Problem of Lay Analysis*. New York, Brentano, 1928.
7. ———, *A General Introduction to Psychoanalysis*. New York, Liveright, 1935.
8. Goldsmith, M., *Franz Anton Mesmer*. New York, Doubleday, 1934.
9. Hamilton, G. V., *An Introduction to Objective Psychopathology*. St. Louis, Mosby, 1925.
10. Horsley, J. S., *Narco-analysis*. London, Oxford University Press, 1943.
11. Hull, C. L., *Hypnosis and Suggestibility*. New York, Appleton-Century, 1933.
12. Janet, P., *Psychological Healing*. New York, Macmillan, 1925.
13. Kubie, L. S., "The Psychoanalyst's Point of View." Chapter V in M. Bentley, and E. V. Cowdry, *The Problem of Mental Disorder*. New York, McGraw-Hill, 1934.
14. Landis, C., "A Statistical Evaluation of Psychotherapeutic Methods." Chapter 5 in L. E. Hinsie, *Concepts and Problems of Psychotherapy*. New York, Columbia University Press, 1937.
15. Miller, E., *The Neuroses in War*. New York, Macmillan, 1940, 231–238.
16. Prinzhorn, H., *Psychotherapy*. London, J. Cape, 1932.
17. Sears, R. R., *Survey of Objective Studies of Psychoanalytic Concepts*. New York, Soc. Sci. Res. Council. Bull., #51, 1943.
18. Zilboorg, G. and G. W. Henry, *A History of Medical Psychology*. New York, Norton, 1941.

Chapter XXXIV

MENTAL HYGIENE

THE PRACTICAL applications of abnormal psychology comprise the subject matter of mental hygiene. Mental hygiene is defined as the investigation and systematic practice of measures for the preservation of mental health. Previous chapters have dealt with much of the relevant investigation and, to a certain extent, with methods which have been aimed at the prevention of abnormality. The facts bearing on the preservation of mental health, together with ways which have been found practical and useful in dealing with those who are abnormal, forms the subject matter of this chapter.

Obviously, mental abnormality is no single entity like blindness or diphtheria. All of the different types of psychoses and of neuroses, organic brain damage or infections, endocrine disorders, nutritional defects, and psychopathological states accompanying physical disease are varieties of mental abnormality. The forms of deviant behavior range from unreal fears, anxieties, and guilt feelings to delusions, hallucinations, confusion, and dementia.

The different sorts of abnormalities necessitate different approaches, different forms of guidance, and different interpersonal relationships. Two points should be borne in mind: (a) there is no single rule — each variety of abnormality must be understood and dealt with separately; and (b) each person in each group is an individual and, though general statements for any category may be made, every rule must, on occasion, be modified to meet the particular case.

The Neuroses

Psychologically speaking, the core of any neurosis is a pattern of *persistent, inadequate, nonadjustive emotional reactions*. The neurotic complains of anxiety, guilt feelings, phobias, obsessions, hypochondriasis. He really suffers from his symptoms. Since he usually attempts to inflict his troubles on his friends and relatives, they may "suffer" with him — or they may try to avoid him. Usually the neurotic is quite willing to follow suggestions and to take advice. Almost invariably he follows such guidance only to a point, which demonstrates either that the procedure is valueless in his case, or that it may make him even more uncomfortable than he was before starting the procedure. If he has tried most of the well-meaning advice of friends and relatives for several years, he usually concludes that no simple method is of any value, and has a standard reply, "I tried that and it only made things worse." He will insist that only a new, or a most unusual, or a very expensive method can be of any assistance. He is also convinced that such new, unusual, or expensive methods are practically impossible for him to attain. He cherishes his illness and seems to "enjoy" his sufferings. This is termed *sickness benefit* and is, for the most part, an unconscious mechanism. The normal person will say in exasperation, "He could get well if he wanted to, but he doesn't want to." Actually, he does want to get well, and is seeking health, but usually in an ineffective way.

What can one do to get along with a neurotic? Assuming that efforts have been made to get him interested or diverted by things outside himself; that rest in the country, travel, logical arguments, and attempts at psychotherapy have failed; and that the problem of maladjustment still remains, then three courses of action are open. One can consciously and consistently try to adjust one's own life to endure the neurotic complaints; a further attempt to force a real therapeutic effort may be made: or, one can put as much distance as possible between oneself and the neurotic and maintain that distance.

As a usual thing, trying to get a neurotic individual to adjust adequately to anyone else is like trying to get the mountain to come to Mahomet. Trying to adjust oneself to a neurotic is no easy task, but at least it is a bit more productive than continual, unsuccessful attempts to change him. Neurotic traits can be looked upon in a rational, objective way — as being an unpleasant and unavoidable part of the particular personality. The mere fact that such conduct is viewed in a detached manner enables one to discount it somewhat. Such behavior should not be interpreted as sheer perverseness, nor as an intentional personal attack. One's own psychological flexibility and resistance will determine how well one can adjust to the complaints of a neurotic person.

Psychoanalysis or some similar form of intensive psychotherapy is expensive in both time and money. Part of the effectiveness is said to depend on the fact that the patient must pay, and pay to the point that it adds to his discomfort. The results of intensive psychotherapy are largely determined by the impressiveness and acumen of the therapist, and by the neurotic's age, intelligence, and will to get well. If, then, the neurotic has entered on a course of intensive psychotherapy, his family should be prepared to support the effort, both financially and with psychological understanding and tolerance, for several years. If a serious physical illness required surgery which was expensive and from which recovery would be slow and not too certain, and if this surgery were the only known way, one would not hesitate to follow the medical advice and to pay the price. The same attitude must be adopted if one is going to stand by while a neurotic undergoes intensive psychotherapy. One should be willing to be guided by the therapist so that one will not be a hindrance to the therapy, and may be of assistance. It should be borne in mind that not all neurotics are improved by therapy, and that in spite of the time, money, and care, there may be no improvement — or the condition may become worse.*

The final course open to one who has attempted to deal with a neurotic and failed is to put as much distance as possible between oneself and the neurotic. Suppose, though, that this problem is personal. You are married to the neurotic, or the neurotic is your parent or your child. Actual experience does show that separation is advisable in many instances. It may be that you are an element in the neurosis. Perhaps your absence will do as much to relieve the symptoms as anything else. You must make a rational decision yourself, since the neurotic cannot.

Again, suppose you have a neurosis. What can you do personally about your own mental hygiene? The chances are that your condition has existed in varying degrees of severity most of your life. Since it probably will continue in much the same fashion the rest of your life, an intelligent course of action is to *make the best of it*. Because of the periods of mental turmoil and of acute physical pains, you may miss much of the health and happiness of the average person, but you should be able to find many acceptable substitutes in your achievements. There may be periods in your life when your mental anguish will seem unbearable and uncontrollable. Such periods you must live through. You must discover for yourself the surroundings and the ways in which that can best be done. Other periods will come when you can be productive in the use of your special skills and talents; make the most of them without overdoing things.

¶ * Be cautious in the selection of the therapist. If no adequate source of information is available, apply either to the local county or state medical association, the National Committee for Mental Hygiene, 1790 Broadway, New York, N. Y., or the Psychological Corporation, 522 Fifth Avenue, New York, N. Y.

Neurosis due to trauma or stress is similar to, though not wholly identical with, ordinary overfatigue and exhaustion. Almost any person, otherwise normal, by prolonged, intense physical and mental stress can be reduced to a whining, complaining, emotional, irrational state. It takes much more stress to reduce some people than to reduce others. Everyone has his own level of resistance to stress, and this individual level varies in accordance with physical health, previous strain, and the like.

Let us say that you had never before been a neurotic. Then, together with family difficulties, you had influenza and lost your job. Since then you have had acute anxiety, persistent fatigue, and vague but distressing physical aches and pains. You go to a doctor and tell him that you are afraid you are losing your mind. Your friends and family, realizing something is wrong with you, may have said that you are suffering from "nervous prostration," or have used some similar phrase which you have heard connected with insanity. What can you do about your own condition?

Most persons who have never had a neurotic period previously and who develop one after stress, recover. Rest, a change of scene, temporary release from the responsibility or decisions demanded from one, and chance for physical rehabilitation, reassurance, sympathy, and a degree of self-understanding, all act to speed recovery. The quicker this relief can be obtained, the speedier and surer the recovery. Two conditions are known which may fix or greatly prolong the neurotic episode: continuation in or near the circumstances which precipitated the state, or the conscious (or only partly conscious) belief that a continuation of the state might somehow be of some benefit to you. Let us assume that the neurotic symptoms have appeared after prolonged stress, and that only partial methods have been used to alleviate the stress. Since it is fairly certain that the same old routine is very likely to begin again, these neurotic symptoms are very apt to continue and to become more firmly fixed.

There is a temptation to find that the neurotic symptoms can be a source of sympathy, of financial compensation, of an improved status in the family, or some other benefit which seems to weigh as much or more than the suffering. If you succumb to the temptation, the symptoms may be maintained.

Recovery from this variety of neurosis demands that you have a chance at rehabilitation and self-understanding. Rehabilitation can be sought and found. It need not be expensive and requires but a modicum of imagination. Self-understanding is largely a question of intelligence and one's willingness to face the facts of reality. If you are to realize that your problem is not unique, that help is available, and that there is more to be gained by being healthy than by being an invalid, you are on the way to health.

Psychopathic Personalities

Many family circles include a "black sheep." He (or she) may be the sort of person that goes from job to job, refuses to accept responsibility, signs bad checks, and gets into difficulties which lead to arrest and imprisonment. He may go on drinking sprees which lead to thefts, assaults, and immorality. Such a person should be urged to see a psychotherapist, but all too often, little benefit is obtained, since such deviants rarely respond to therapy. The problem usually resolves itself into how to get along with such a psychopath.

The Old World custom of "remittance men" was one solution. The black sheep of the family was dispatched to some far corner of the world, sent a regular remittance, and told never to come home. Harsh though it seems, it was realistic, and, in the long run, often served the interests of all concerned. Individuals of this type cannot be depended upon; their promises are not kept; they are not deterred by love or affection, nor are moral and ethical considerations of any avail. In dealing with them, one must either resign oneself to heartbreak, bankruptcy, and ultimate defeat, or one must be completely dissociated from such a person. Some families bankrupt themselves through their desire to make good all the black sheep's debts in order to get him out of trouble. It may be commendable that certain families prefer to do this, but at least they should be aware that their efforts afford no permanent solution, and that, in the long run, they are not helping him or themselves. By going to his aid, they solve the immediate problem. Failure to help might provide an incentive toward his improvement because it will force him to face the consequences of his acts.

The Alcoholic*

There is one attitude to assume in dealing with any alcoholic, namely, that the alcoholism is either an illness or a symptom of an illness. This attitude squares with the facts. Most human beings "can take it or leave it alone." There is some basic defect in the person who

* Problems of mental hygiene with alcoholics are dealt with in E. A. Strecker, and F. T. Chambers, *Alcohol: One Man's Meat*, New York, Macmillan, 1938, and *Alcoholics Anonymous*, Works Publishing Company, Church Street Annex P.O. Box 658, New York City.

cannot leave it alone. Alcoholics are a heterogeneous group and must be dealt with in a variety of ways.

Strange as it seems, the first and usually the most difficult problem, is to persuade the alcoholic to recognize and to admit to himself that he is an alcoholic. Until he is convinced of this he can see no reason for concern, no reason for therapy, no reason for reform. All advice is to his ears the croaking of kill-joys and moral reformers. He finds it easy to rationalize and to offer self-justification which helps him resist direct evidence, argument, and well-meant assistance.

A reformed alcoholic seems to be more effective than anyone else in convincing an alcoholic that he is an alcoholic. He speaks the same language and has had the same experiences. In some instances, the experience of being "sobered up" in a general hospital ward for acute alcoholics is an effective warning to a potential drunkard. He can see for himself the end-stages of alcoholic deterioration and the social decline of the chronic alcoholic. Overprotection, covering up, and a hush-hush attitude rarely do any good.

Very few alcoholics have ever been cured by the exhortations and good services of friends or relatives. It is best to make use of those hospitals and clinics which specialize in the treatment of alcoholism, or to get the patient in touch either with the group known as "Alcoholics Anonymous," or with the Salvation Army. Such agencies or groups report excellent results with many persons who come to them.

In brief, alcoholism is a disease which cannot be cured by attempts to hide it. The alcoholic himself must realize his own condition and then put himself (or be put) in contact with a therapeutically minded organization which knows his problems, speaks his language, and can choose a therapy oriented to his problems.

Epileptics*

If a member of your family begins to have seizures, what should you do? Seek competent medical assistance. There has been so much progress in the medical therapy of epilepsy during the past quarter century that a hopeless attitude or one of trying to conceal the illness from the neighbors is unjustified. Where adequate treatment is instituted early in the course of the disease, it is estimated that in 60 to 80 per cent of the cases the seizures may be arrested and the disease kept under control. A careful medical or surgical diagnostic study of

---

* The problems of the epileptic are dealt with in T. J. Putnam, *Convulsive Seizures: How to Deal with Them*. Philadelphia, Lippincott, 1943, and in W. G. Lennox, *Science and Seizures*. New York, Harper, 1941.

each case should be made in order to determine its possible cause and the best regimen of treatment.

Whether an individual case should be institutionalized is a problem that must be considered. In certain, but not all, of the states of the Union, the existence of epilepsy automatically bars the child from the regular public schools. Where school attendance is legal, the type and the frequency of seizures should determine whether the child is allowed to attend school. If the child has very mild *petit mal* attacks, or even *grand mal* attacks that occur only at night, school attendance is usually practical. In every case, some systematic form of education should be instituted. If attendance in special classes or home tutoring is necessary but not possible, then it may be to the best interests of the child to put him in a special school or a state institution where proper education can be provided.

The family must teach the child to adhere to the regimen of treatment that has been found successful. As the epileptic grows older he must understand his condition and learn to accept the limitations which are imposed by his disability. Because he is or has been an epileptic, there will be some activities he must avoid and some professions or vocations he should not consider entering. Proper educational and vocational advice should be sought and followed.

The progress that has been made in the understanding and treatment of epilepsy is outstanding among the types of therapy used in psychopathological disorders. Unfortunately, epilepsy is still popularly considered as a disgrace and calamity. However, modern therapeutic methods give a firm foundation for a feeling of optimism in most cases.

Mental Deficiency

Another problem which some families must face is what to do about a child who shows marked mental retardation. Recognition of mental deficiency is possible at an early age if the child is an idiot or imbecile. The whole course of their physical development — that is, the age at which the child supports his head without help, the age of crawling, and the beginning of speech — is markedly delayed. When the mental defect is not so marked — that is, when the child is either a high-grade imbecile or a moron — the parents may not be aware of the condition until the child begins to have difficulties at school. Most school systems have facilities for giving intelligence and educational tests which will provide a definite estimate of the child's mental ability.

When marked mental defect is present, the question of institutionalization must be considered. The majority of idiots and imbeciles are best cared for in an institution. They constitute a very undesirable influence in a home in which there are other children. Even if there are no other children to be considered, the care of an idiot or imbecile is more than the average mother can successfully undertake. Whether or not morons should be institutionalized depends upon many factors in the specific home situation. These children require a great deal of special protection and control and, if the families are not able to provide it, an institution is preferable. Most of the institutions for the feeble-minded have increased the training facilities available, so that they are really special schools directed toward returning the high-grade mental defective to society. By special emphasis on manual or domestic training, the mentally dull child may learn to be more or less self-sustaining; without this special training he may always be dependent on his family or some relief agency.

The Aged*

Although the physiological and psychological processes of aging are closely associated, the correlation is not perfect. Some old people need, seek, and demand help and attention. Others, old in years, never think of themselves as old, and neither seek nor ask for assistance unless seriously ill. Any elderly person is happier and healthier if he has some activity, some work, some interest which is within his ability. The feeling of uselessness is one of the most distressing features of old age. The aged have lived their lives as productive members of society and they feel lost when it is apparent to them that they are no longer useful. If some occupation or responsibility, either of a paying or non-paying nature, can be obtained for them, they are more apt to be satisfied and hence easier to live with. If neither is possible, then some hobby, church work, Red Cross work, or gardening should be encouraged.

A common and annoying symptom shown by many old people is unnecessary stinginess. They deny themselves, even half-starve themselves, in an effort to save money. This behavior may be only an exaggerated form of lifetime habits of thrift, but often it may be a real change from earlier behavior. In any case, one should try to realize what money means to the aged person. Their earning days are over;

* Lawton, G., *New Goals for Old Age*, New York, Columbia University Press, 1943, and L. J. Martin, and C. DeGruchy, *Salvaging Old Age*, New York, Macmillan, 1930, give valuable information.

they do not know how much longer they will live; and so, to feel secure, they need to conserve what money they have so that it will last until the end. Other peculiarities of the aged may be similarly explained. "Young people are irreverent and dissolute," "The nation is going to pieces," and other similar phrases, are but expressions of envy and impotence — particularly when the aged person has been retired and "put on the shelf." No amount of argument will change these attitudes; but a new interest, a new feeling of being wanted, will often cause such ideas to disappear.

Finally, there is the question of hospitalization or home care after the onset of senile dementia. If the aged person requires close supervision and permanent nursing care which is difficult for the family to provide, institutionalization is advisable even though the psychological effect of being "put away" is unfortunate. Each family has to settle this difficult question in the light of its own circumstances.

The Psychoses*

If there is any reason to suspect that a person has a psychotic condition such as dementia praecox, manic-depressive psychosis, involutional melancholia, or general paresis, there can be no doubt as to the proper line of action. Such a person should be brought to the attention of a competent physician who is qualified to diagnose mental disease. If there is a psychosis, the person should be hospitalized, or provided with special psychiatric nursing care at home. No friend or relative is qualified to treat or care for a psychotic patient. In the acute stages of the illness, regardless of whether or not the psychotic patient is disturbed, continuous supervision is necessary. Suicidal threats and attempts are not uncommon. Such threats and attempts may be only for the purpose of gaining attention, but actual suicide occurs with sufficient frequency to warrant the enforcement of extraordinary precautions at any mental hospital. During every phase of a psychosis, the patient may threaten or attempt homicide or bodily injury to others. This may be only a bluff, but no one who has had experience with such patients ever takes a chance with them. The fact that laws of many years standing state that insane persons are committed to institutions so that they may be protected from themselves and that others may be protected from them, is the fruit of centuries of human experience.

* An excellent and valuable little book dealing in an understanding way with these particular problems is E. M. Stern and S. W. Hamilton, *Mental Illness: A Guide for the Family*. Commonwealth Fund, 41 East 57th Street, New York, N. Y., 1944.

On occasion, parents will plead that their psychotic son has always been a shy, studious, well-behaved boy, and that there is no reason why he should be kept in a hospital. They will say that his illness is due to his shyness and brooding nature, and that it is only temporary. They will make efforts to get him into contact with young people and to lead a normal life. This is usually one of the most unkind things that can be done to a psychotic patient. It may be compared to insistence on vigorous exercise and competitive sports for a patient suffering from active tuberculosis.

The family members may be strongly opposed to "putting their relative away." This prejudice should be avoided. It can be avoided if they can be made to see that the problem is one of mental illness. Neither the family nor the physician should refer to the patient as being "insane" or "crazy." Mental illness is no more nor less a disgrace than any form of physical illness. The chances of recovery vary with the types of the disease, but even the most guarded prognosis is no worse than in many of the serious forms of physical illness.

There are many unfortunate beliefs concerning mental hospitals which years of public education have not been able to change. Mental hospitals are not filled with sane people held there against their wills. Patients are not maltreated and abused. At worst, they may receive too little attention from the doctors and attendants, but even so, the hospital has facilities for treatment and control of patients that make it far superior to treatment and control at home. The physical arrangements of the hospital protect the patient from himself and others from him. Life at the institution is a simple, routine life without the complex problems for adjustment that home life entails. The patient does not have to make decisions for himself and, although to the normal person this represents a prison, to the abnormal it usually represents a haven. One patient wrote, "The steady routine of the hospital soothed my mind. It was a relief not to have to make my own decisions. I knew what time I had to get up, when I was due in the kitchen, when to eat, when to rest or walk. No agony or hesitancy."*

It sometimes happens that friends or relatives blame themselves for the mental illness of another. Only in the rarest instances is such a self-accusation justified. They would not blame themselves if that person had developed cancer or brain tumor. For a mental illness, the same attitude should be taken. Get the patient to competent medical care as soon as possible, and having satisfied yourself that this care is competent and that the hospital is a real hospital and not a custodial

* Krauch, E., *A Mind Restored*, New York, Putnam, 1937, 110.

institution, then you have done all you can and no blame or reproach is warranted. Statements that the patient may make which show resentment must be attributed to his mental condition and not to faults on your part.

How can you personally know whether or not you are "going crazy"? Can, or does, a psychotic person recognize his own illness? If your mind is truly disordered, you will not recognize your own condition, save in a vague way, at the onset of the disease. This is the basis for the old observation which goes, "If a man thinks he's crazy, he's not," or the medical observation, "As long as there is insight, the prognosis is good." If your family insists that you should consult a psychiatrist, comply; and if the psychiatrist advises you to enter a hospital for care and treatment, his advice should be accepted and followed. No one likes to be sick and no one wants to be "crazy," but self-medication and self-treatment have never been too effective for any sort of illness, particularly mental illness.

If you are mentally disturbed, you will find the hospital both a relief and a source of annoyance. At the hospital no one expects you to make decisions, to be very active, or to manage your own affairs. The care you receive may be standardized, but you will be treated as a sick person and be protected from the world and from yourself. You may be annoyed by certain rules, the locked doors, and by other patients, but the annoyance is far less than the relief afforded by the care and protection.

To the best of your ability, follow the advice, counsel, and treatment given by the doctors and nurses, even though they may seem both unreasonable and unpleasant.

Personal mental hygiene enters into these conditions after you have begun to get well, and especially after you have left the hospital. The convalescent period for any mental illness is long. Recovery is slow. The weakness is exasperating. You will be irritated by the advice or activities urged by relatives and friends. Eventually the efficiency which prevailed before the illness will be achieved. Any recovered patient should be able to ignore senseless remarks which imply that he has been "crazy" rather than ill, and that the illness was his fault — which of course it was not.

Suppose you have recovered from schizophrenia, either with or without the use of shock therapy. How can you best guard yourself against future psychotic episodes? As a rule, as a person recovers, he gains weight. The best assurance of a continuing high physical resistance is to keep the weight constant. If you happen to be a married woman, you should not have a child for at least five years, since relapses following childbirth are not uncommon. As normal a life as possible should be led, and not too much concern given to the possibility of another attack. The fact that you recovered once shows you had a fairly high level of resistance.

One who recovers from a manic-depressive psychosis has better than one chance out of two that he will never have another attack. Personal mental hygiene after recovery depends on whether the individual is ordinarily the depressive or hypomanic type of person. When of the depressive type, he should be kept interested so that opportunity for brooding is held at a minimum. (This does not mean overwork.) When of the hypomanic type, the spouse or nearest relative or friend should have an understanding of the manic temperament so that it can be pointed out to the person — and to others when necessary — that there is a tendency to be excitable, to overreact, to say things which will be regretted. The mistakes made by the hypomanic which offend or hurt others should be called to his attention so that he may rectify them. Otherwise, no matter whether depressive or hypomanic, as normal a life as possible should be followed.

Those who have recovered from general paresis have suffered from brain damage. Ordinarily, they cannot be expected to work and think as intelligently and efficiently as they did before the illness. They should adjust themselves to a simpler and less pretentious form of life. They should not be called on for any form of prolonged exertion, either physical or mental. The therapy has cured any latent syphilitic infection, so at least they are free of that.

There is one sure way for the person who has had an alcoholic psychosis to practice mental hygiene. Complete abstinence from alcoholic beverages. If the alcoholism is but a symptom of some other psychosis or neurosis, as is frequently true, then coupled with the abstinence must be the mental hygiene measures appropriate for the neurosis or psychosis.

Mental Hygiene for Everyday Life

Many of the mental mechanisms seen in abnormal persons stand out like caricatures of the same sort of processes seen in the normal person. Rationalization, symbolization, or projection, all common in normal mental life, are grossly exaggerated in mental disease. Other mechanisms found in the abnormal person occur but rarely in the normal person. The apathy of the schizophrenic, the mental disorganization of the senile, or the basic hostility of the manic are not exaggerations of normal mechanisms but are unique products of the disease. In the light of all of the facts of psychopathology, one may conclude that having observed certain mental mechanisms in one's own behavior, or having been told of them by others, still gives little or no understanding of all the phases and types of mental disease.

In brief, the knowledge of psychopathology of everyday life is of more value in dealing with others than in trying to help oneself. It is also of more value in the hands of experts than in the hands of eager amateurs. There is a human tendency to help others who are in distress. Most mental illness seems to the unwary to be nothing more than the expression of queer ideas. "Change your attitudes," "Buck up," "Snap out of it," "Forget it," "Don't take things so seriously," "Face reality squarely," are commonly passed out as therapeutic slogans. Just as it may happen that an occasional headache is due to "eyestrain" and will be alleviated by resting the eyes, so an occasional character deviation may be alleviated by one of these slogans. But it does not happen very often.

In addition to the more obvious neurotic and psychotic types, there are many difficult, queer, odd, or unusual people who enter into our everyday life and with whom we must manage to get along. They are not mentally ill or defective nor in any way in need of psychiatric care and attention. One must somehow attempt to understand them. Many of the following suggestions are truisms which, in spite of their obvious nature, many people never think to try.

One should endeavor to be objective and rational in dealing with any difficult person. You must recognize the possibility that such a person is using different standards from yours. The recognition of the facts of individual differences and of other people's right to their own opinions is something that certain people seem to have naturally and others never gain throughout a lifetime. The difficult person does not react to ordinary values and motives in an expected fashion. One must shift one's viewpoint to look at things the way he does. Frequently, the lack of information about such a person's background and present motivation may make him seem unreasonable. In general, sympathy and empathy depend on mutual similarity. Many of the difficulties arising in interpersonal relations result from the fact that we expect too much of other people, especially stupid people. Placing high standards for others results in exasperation when they fail to meet these standards.

Previously it has been pointed out that it is sometimes necessary to adjust yourself to those who fail to adjust to you. In extreme form, this may amount to trying to fit your life to others' idiosyncrasies to an extent that cannot be seriously defended. The question then is, when does putting up with someone become inadvisable? In specific terms, when is the alcoholic spouse so objectionable that separation is the only solution? When does the senile parent make a normal family life impossible? When must a retarded child be put in an institution? Obviously, there is no set standard with which to answer these questions. The more information anyone has about the lives of his friends and acquaintances, the more he is impressed by how much the human individual can put up with from others and still get along. An increased knowledge of abnormal psychology and insight into the mental mechanisms that are common to both the normal and abnormal person increase anyone's tolerance and understanding. They should provide a sound basis for solving rather than rejecting or avoiding the problem.

The Role of Psychotherapy in Mental Hygiene

The student of abnormal psychology should recognize the assets and the limitations, the virtues and drawbacks of psychotherapy, either as they may apply to others or to himself. He should recognize that "going to see a psychiatrist," or "being psychoanalyzed" is not the accomplishment of a miracle but the application of certain definite psychological principles. The intelligent use of these principles will effect cures in some instances. It will be beneficial for many cases, and of no avail in others. Any person in need of psychotherapy must cooperate to the best of his ability with the therapist. He must, of necessity, put his trust and faith in the ability of the therapist. If he did cooperate, if the therapist has been conscientious and competent, and yet no improvement was obtained, neither the patient nor the therapist should be blamed. Rather, the condition must be considered as one for which the proper therapy is still unknown and the only personal adjustment that the patient can make is to adapt to his difficulty as best he can, following the suggestions provided by the therapist.

Generally speaking, the over-all picture of the improvement of mental health and mental hygiene is a social problem, a public health problem, rather than a series of individual problems. Better hospital, clinic, and institutional care follows an enlightened public opinion and insistent public demand. New discoveries, new or improved methods of treatment, depend on scientific progress, and that progress depends on public support and on the attraction into research of the best possible intellects. As intelligent human beings, we all agree that one unquestioned benefit of civilization and cultural progress is the diminution of disease and the prolongation of healthy life. Much has been done to bring many forms of physical disease under control. Much remains to be done to increase our knowledge of psychopathology and psychotherapy.

REFERENCES

1. Anon., *Alcoholics Anonymous*. New York, Works Publishing Co., 1939.
2. Goddard, H. H., *Psychology of the Normal and Subnormal*. New York, Dodd, 1919.
3. Henderson, D. K., *Psychopathic States*. New York, Norton, 1939.
4. Krauch, E., *A Mind Restored*. New York, Putnam, 1937.
5. Lawton, G., *New Goals for Old Age*. New York, Columbia University Press, 1943.
6. Lennox, W. G., *Science and Seizures*. New York, Harper, 1941.
7. Martin, L. J., and C. De Gruchy, *Salvaging Old Age*. New York, Macmillan, 1930.
8. Putnam, T. J., *Convulsive Seizures: How to Deal With Them*. Philadelphia, Lippincott, 1943.
9. Stern, E. M., and S. W. Hamilton, *Mental Illness: A Guide for the Family*. New York, Commonwealth Fund, 1942.
10. Strecker, E. A., and F. T. Chambers, *Alcohol: One Man's Meat*. New York, Macmillan, 1938.

tioned benefit of civilization and cultural progress is the diminution of disease and the prolongation of healthy life. Much has been done to bring many forms of physical disease under control. Much remains to be done to increase our knowledge of psychopathology and psychotherapy.

REFERENCES

1. Anon., *Alcoholics Anonymous*, New York, Works Publishing Co., 1939.
2. Goddard, H. H., *Psychology of the Normal and Subnormal*, New York, Dodd, 1919.
3. Henderson, D. K., *Psychopathic States*, New York, Norton, 1939.
4. Krauch, E., *A Mind Restored*, New York, Putnam, 1937.
5. Lawton, G., *New Goals for Old Age*, New York, Columbia University Press, 1943.
6. Lennox, W. G., *Science and Seizures*, New York, Harper, 1941.
7. Martin, L. J., and G. De Gruchy, *Salvaging Old Age*, New York, Macmillan, 1930.
8. Putnam, T. J., *Convulsive Seizures: How to Deal With Them*, Philadelphia, Lippincott, 1943.
9. Stern, E. M., and S. W. Hamilton, *Mental Illness: A Guide for the Family*, New York, Commonwealth Fund, 1942.
10. Strecker, E. A., and F. T. Chambers, *Alcohol: One Man's Meat*, New York, Macmillan, 1938.

GLOSSARY

Aboulia; Abulia. Inability to initiate voluntary action or make decisions.

Adjustment. Arranging, composing, and harmonizing the differences, conflicts, and decisions which must be made in everyday life.

Affect. Feeling quality or emotion in general; the dynamic constituent of emotion.

Agnosia. A loss of the ability to recognize objects, persons, or sounds (sensory aphasia).

Agoraphobia. Fear of open or public places.

Agraphia. A disturbance in the ability to write.

Alcoholic Hallucinosis. State of chronic alcoholism marked by active visual and auditory hallucinations.

Alexia. A disturbance in the ability to read or understand written language.

Alzheimer's Disease. A variety of presenile dementia with a marked defect in immediate memory, recall, and speech.

Ambiguous Figure. An outline picture in which certain parts are open to two or more interpretations.

Ambiversion. Personality balanced between the extremes of introversion and extroversion.

Amentia. Feeble-mindedness (*see* Mental deficiency).

Amnesia. Loss of memory.

Amusia. A disturbance in the ability to appreciate or produce music.

Anesthesia. Total or partial loss of sensitivity.

Angina; Angina Pectoris. A disease marked by paroxysmal thoracic pain due to spasm of the systemic arteries or heart.

Anorexia. Diminution or absence of hunger or appetite.

Anterograde Amnesia. Loss of memory due to inattention or inadequate fixation.

Anxiety. Intense apprehension and fearfulness.

Anxiety Neurosis. A type of neurosis in which anxiety is the predominant symptom.

Apathy. Pathological indifference.

Aphasia. A disorder of language in which there is an inability to use articulated speech and/or an inability to comprehend spoken words; the loss of the ability to speak.

Apraxia. The loss of the ability to perform some skilled act in the absence of either motor or sensory paralysis.

Astereognosis. The loss of the ability to recognize objects by cutaneous or kinesthetic sensation, that is, by feeling them.

Asthenic Type. A type of body build which is characterized by being tall, slender, and having little muscular strength.

Athetosis. A constant, recurring series of tentaclelike movements of the hands and feet associated with certain forms of brain damage.

Athletic Type. A type of body build characterized by a strong, solid, muscular appearance.

Aura. Some type of peculiar sensory experience that precedes an overt epileptic attack.

Autism. A form of thinking predominantly subjective in character, where such objective material as does occur is given subjective meaning and emphasis.

Autoeroticism. Masturbation; sexual gratification from one's own body.

Autointoxication. Poisoning by some uneliminated endogenous toxin.

Automatic Writing. Writing without full conscious control.

Autonomic Nervous System. That portion of the nervous system which regulates involuntary or vegetative bodily functions.

Benign Stupor. A stuporous state from which the patient recovers, without evidence of schizophrenia or hysteria.

Bulimia. Abnormally intense hunger sensations.

Castration Complex. Psychoanalytic concept of the conscious and unconscious emotion related to the fear of the loss of the genital organs.

Catalepsy. A state in which sensation and voluntary motion are suspended, the muscles rigid, pulse and respiration slow, and the body cold and pale.

Catatonia. One of the varieties of dementia praecox (schizophrenia); a state of stupor or automatism marked by either negativism or waxy flexibility.

Catharsis. The expression of some unpleasant emotional experience through talking or some other form of behavior, so that the acute unpleasantness is unburdened.

Cathartic Method; Cathexis; Abreaction. The process of working off or discharging pent-up emotion or disagreeable experience by living it through again in speech, action, or feeling.

Causalgia. A sensation of burning pain.

Central Nervous System. Brain and spinal cord.

Cerebral Arteriosclerosis. "Hardening of the arteries" of the brain which leads to sudden onset of confusion, excitement, and other forms of psychotic behavior.

Character Neurosis. A condition in which the personality traits constitute the equivalent of a neurosis.

Choleric. A temperament characterized by grouchy ill-humor and readiness to anger and rage reactions.

Chorea. A state of spasmodic muscular twitchings which are involuntary, irregular, and jerky.

Chromosomes. Microscopic threadlike structures in the nucleus of both the ovum and the spermatozoon which contain the genes.

Chronic Alcoholic Deterioration. Physical and mental disorder subsequent to excessive alcoholism over a long period of time.

Cilia. Hairlike processes on the surface of cells or of unicellular organisms.

Claustrophobia. Morbid fear of closed places.

Co-consciousness. The stream of consciousness which goes with a phase of dissociated personality and which may or may not be connected with the conscious stream of the total integrated personality.

Compulsion. An irresistible impulse to carry out some act.

Compulsion Neurosis. A neurosis in which the patient feels impelled to carry out certain actions over and over, without any logical reason.

Confabulation. The filling in of memory gaps with incorrect, irrelevant, and unconnected details.

Conflict. The mental reaction caused by the action of mutually contradictory or inhibiting instincts or wishes which are part of the Id or unconscious.

Constitution. The relatively constant biological make-up of the individual which governs the adjustment which that individual makes to health or disease. It is the result of the interaction of heredity and environment.

Conversion. Symbolization which takes as its means of expression some physical or physiological representation, for example, psychic blindness.

Convolution. A transversely rounded fold of the cortical surface of the cerebrum or cerebellum, bounded at the sides by fissures.

Cretinism. Mental deficiency associated with thyroid insufficiency.

Culture. The sum total of the attitudes, ideas, and behavior shared and transmitted by the members of a society, together with the material results of such behavior.

Cycloid; Cyclothymic. A personality type characterized by alternation of optimism, cheerfulness and energy with pessimism, sadness, worry, and lack of drive or energy.

Déjà Vu. Illusion of recognition; the illusory feeling of having seen or experienced before.

Delirium Tremens. Condition sometimes following chronic alcoholism in which visual hallucinations, headaches, apprehension, tremors, and occasional convulsions occur.

Delusion. Morbid false belief.

Dementia. The loss or gross disorganization of mental ability.

Dementia Praecox; Schizophrenia. A severe type of mental disease characterized by delusions, hallucinations, withdrawal into fantasy life, and mental deterioration.

Depression. A mood of extreme hopelessness and despondency with feelings of inadequacy and unworthiness.

Dereism. Mental activity that deviates from the laws of logic and experience and fails to take the facts of reality into consideration.

Deterioration. The loss of mental efficiency.

Devolution. A reversal of the process of evolution; a "taking to pieces" in the order from the least organized, the most complex, and most voluntary, toward the most organized, most simple, and most automatic.

Dipsomania. Periodic obsession for and indulgence in alcoholic beverages.

Disease. A condition of body or mind, or some part of body or mind, in which orderly functioning is disturbed or deranged.

Dissociation. Inadequate integration of consciousness so that some ideas or systems of ideas split off from the remainder of consciousness and exist apart from the control of the individual.

Dysplastic. That body type which is neither of the pyknic, asthenic, or athletic type, but a combination of these without adequate blending.

Ego. Self; conscious experience or awareness; "I will."

Elation. Emotional state characterized by intense pleasure and feeling of well-being, along with increased motor activity.

Electroencephalograph; EEG. Record of electrical potentials of the brain usually taken from surface of the scalp.

Emotional Immaturity. Persons who are impulsive, unstable, childish, and show poor emotional control.

Encephalitis. A disease process in which there is inflammation of the brain substance or of its coverings.

Endogenous. Refers to factors originating predominantly within the organism itself and affecting the nervous system directly.

Epilepsy. A condition characterized by convulsions and disturbances in consciousness.

Epileptic Equivalent. Psychic seizure.

Epileptoid. A personality type characterized by being self-centered, pedantic, shallow in emotion, having a tendency to fanaticism, and violent outbursts of anger and hostility.

Etiology. The systematic study of the cause of disease.

Exhibitionism. The public display of the genital region for the purpose of personal sexual satisfaction.

Exogenous. Refers to factors acting either from outside of the body or from another part of the body, outside of the system which is the locus of the morbid condition in question.

Extroversion; Extrovert. A personality type characterized by interests directed mainly toward external environment and social phenomena, rather than toward oneself or one's own experience.

Fetishism. Morbid sexual attraction and stimulation by an inanimate object, usually some article of clothing.

First-Admissions. The number of individuals who are admitted for the first time to some particular institution or group of institutions during some particular period of time.

Fistula. A canal or opening leading from a body cavity to the external surface of the body (it is usually pathological).

Fixation. The arrest or halting of some part of the libido during the ordinary period of growth and development, so that some portion of the behavior or emotional life of the individual remains at a level which was appropriate at an earlier age but is now inappropriate, for example, mother fixation.

Fugue. Episodes of nonremembered activity of considerable duration.

Functional Cause or Basis. The descriptive term used when no organic cause or basis has been found in the etiology of the disease; disorders of function by or through other functions

Furor. An acute excitement with violent outbursts.

Gastric Mucosa. The mucous membrane lining the stomach.

General Paresis. A form of progressive motor paralysis accompanied by a peculiar sort of mental deterioration due to the invasion of the brain by syphilitic disease.

Genes. The factors in the germ cells which are involved in the production of an hereditary character.

Gonad. Sex gland; ovary or testicle.

Grand Mal. A generalized seizure or convulsion in which there is a sudden complete loss of consciousness.

Group Psychotherapy. Application of psychotherapeutic and reeducational methods by a trained therapist to a group, rather than to a single individual.

Hallucination. A false experience of sensation or perception. There is no known adequate stimulus, but the experience seems real.

Health. Soundness of body and mind so that bodily and mental functions are duly discharged.

Hebephrenia. One of the varieties of dementia praecox (schizophrenia).

Heredity. The sum total of physical and mental characteristics which are passed from parent to child by means of the biological carriers, the chromosomes or genes.

Heterosexual. Sexually oriented or attracted to members of the opposite sex.

Homeostasis. The relatively constant internal environment maintained by the coordination of physiological processes.

Homosexual. Sexually attracted to members of one's own sex.

Huntington's Chorea. An hereditary type of disease manifested in adult life which is characterized by jerky, twitching movements and progressive mental deterioration.

Hyperamnesia. Exaggerated memory which may be either general or specific.

Hyperventilation. Forced deep breathing.

Hypnosis. An artificially induced mental state characterized by great suggestibility.

Hypochondriasis. Symptoms and/or illness referred to some part, organ, or organic system of the body when no causal relationship can be established between the complaints and any physical disorder of function or structure.

Hypoplastic Body Form. Underdevelopment of the body.

Hypothyroidism. Insufficient secretion of the thyroid gland.

Hysteria. A neurosis characterized by losses of bodily functions or disturbed and uncontrolled functions, for which no physiological or organic causes can be demonstrated

Id. Unconscious urges, instincts, drives, and motivations; a bundle of incoherent, unorganized cravings predominantly sexual and aggressive in nature which demand motor discharge for satisfaction; "It wants."

Ideation. The process or mental operation of forming ideas.

Identification. The unconscious process of molding or forming one's own Ego after the fashion or pattern of someone taken as an ideal or model.

Idiopathic Epilepsy; Essential Epilepsy. A condition in which convulsions occur with no demonstrable pathology.

Idiot. A low grade of feeble-mindedness with an IQ ranging from 0 to 25.

Idiot Savant. A mental defective with some special ability which is quite outstanding in comparison to his general level of ability.

Illusion. The inexact or inaccurate perception of some actual object or situation.

Imbecile. A medium grade of feeble-mindedness with an IQ ranging from 26 to 50.

Imperception. Failure of stimulation and sensation to arouse their usually associated images, ideas, or responses so that experience has little or no meaning.

Inhibition. The restraint or repression of certain forms of expression.

Insight. A peculiar characteristic of consciousness, which attaches to a belief that is based on adequate evidence, and so is concerned with awareness of psychological changes and with the ability of making a self-judgment as to whether phenomena are natural or morbid.

Intelligence Quotient; IQ. The mental age obtained on an intelligence test, divided by the chronological age, multiplied by 100 to eliminate decimal point.

Introversion; Introvert. A type characterized by the direction of one's energy and interest toward oneself and one's inner world of experience.

Invert. A homosexual.

Involutional Melancholia. An agitated depression occurring commonly between the ages of 45 and 65, without a history of previous mental illness.

Jacksonian Seizure. A convulsion of some part of the body (usually an arm or leg) with no loss of consciousness.

Kahn Test. Laboratory test for syphilitic infection.

Lability of Affect. Rapid shift of emotion.

Law of Regression. Loss of memory proceeds from the unstable to the stable; from the memory of recent events to the memory of remote events; ideas before actions.

Lay-Analyst. Any person, not a physician, who uses psychoanalysis as a psychotherapeutic method.

Lesion. A more or less circumscribed pathological change in the tissues.

Libido. That force by which the sexual instinct is represented in the mind; the energy of those instincts which have to do with all that may be comprised under the word "love."

Little's Disease. Spastic paralysis.

Lunatic. A mentally ill or insane person.

Malingering. The conscious feigning of illness or the intentional exaggeration of some actual physical complaint.

Mania. A state characterized by intense elevation of mood, psychomotor overactivity, flight and overproductivity of ideas.

Manic-Depressive Psychosis. A psychosis characterized by states of mania and/or depression.

Masochism. The procurement of sexual satisfaction by the infliction of pain on oneself.

Masturbation. Self sexual stimulation.

Maturation. Development which accompanies the process of cell differentiation, and which may occur any time during the life of the individual without being directly dependent on growth through use or upon experience.

Megalomania. Delusions of grandeur.

Melancholia. A morbid mental state characterized by depression.

Mendelian Law. A principle of hereditary transmission according to which certain characteristics are transmitted to the offspring in units without change, with a definite ratio for each generation.

Meningitis. A disease marked by inflammation of the membranes which cover the brain and the spinal cord.

Mental Deficiency; Amentia; Oligophrenia. Impairment in the capacity for intellectual development.

Mental Incompetency. Legal term indicating the lack of responsibility for one's acts because of mental disease or defect.

Mental Mechanisms. Unconscious or conscious stylized processes whereby the inner conflict situation is eliminated or reduced in its severity; systematic outlay of mental energy to achieve desires, avoid unpleasantness, or create symptoms in the effort to solve mental conflict.

Mescal; Mescaline. A preparation of cactus, possessing peculiar narcotic properties, especially visual hallucinations.

Mesmerism. Hypnotism.

Microcephaly. A pathological condition in which the head and brain are extremely small (head circumference less than 17 inches); a form of amentia.

Mongolism. Congenital feeble-mindedness in which certain of the facial features resemble those of the Mongolian race, attributed to defective heredity, uterine exhaustion, or nutritional defect in foetal life.

Monoideic. Tendency to revert constantly in thought and action to one idea or subject.

Moral Defective. According to English law, a person with mental defectiveness coupled with strongly vicious or criminal propensities.

Morbid. An abnormal, disordered, or diseased state or condition.

Mores. The customs of a social group.

Moron. The highest grade of feeble-mindedness with an IQ ranging from 50 to 70 or 75.

Multifactorial Genetic Mechanism. Heredity based on the interaction of several or many specific genetic determiners.

Multiple Personality. Dissociated state in which certain memories and sets of ideas break off from normal consciousness and assume independent existence.

Myxedema. A disease characterized by a decreased functioning of the thyroid gland, usually accompanied by mental defect.

Narcissism; Narcism. Exaggerated self-love.

Narco-Analysis; Narco-Synthesis. Treatment in which a drug narcosis is induced during which repressed emotion and memories are brought back and made part of conscious memory.

Negativism; Negativistic. An attitude of resistance to suggestions of other people, sometimes resulting in an opposite reaction to that suggested.

Neologism. A newly coined word which in the case of a psychotic patient has only a private meaning.

Neurasthenia. Type of neurosis characterized by undue fatiguability, feelings of weakness, and numerous bodily complaints of a hypochondriacal nature.

Neurosis. A term used to characterize the milder forms of mental disorders, in which there is usually no actual physical or environmental basis. They are marked by anxieties, obsessions, and phobias which the patient recognizes as abnormal but over which he has no voluntary control.

Neurosyphilis. Syphilis of the central nervous system.

Neurotic Personality. A type characterized by fearfulness, guilt feelings, anxiety, and compulsions, differing from true neurosis in that these symptoms are less pervasive and occur at intervals only.

Nihilistic Delusions. Delusions of nothingness or nonexistence.

Nonspecific Factor. General resistance or lack of resistance which will facilitate the appearance of some genetic character or condition.

Nymphomania. Morbid exaggeration of sexual desire in women.

Obsession. A morbid idea, urge, or emotion that is persistent and irresistible.

Oedipus Complex. Intense emotional attachment to the parent of the opposite sex, with resentment and jealousy of the other parent; this attachment is characteristic of late infancy and early adolescence and normally is outgrown during adolescence.

Oligophrenia. Feeble-mindedness (*see* Mental deficiency).

Organic Cause or Basis. The descriptive term used when there is good evidence indicating that the abnormality is related to a structural change in some one of the bodily systems.

Panophobia. Fear of everything; generalized fearfulness.

Paralysis Agitans; Parkinson's Disease; Shaking Palsy. A disorder marked by tremor of the small muscle groups accompanied by rigidity of the larger body movements, and feelings of restlessness and nervousness.

Paramnesia. Falsification or illusions of memory.

Paranoia. A condition marked by chronic, systematized, gradually developing delusions without hallucinations, and with little tendency to mental deterioration, remission, or recovery.

Paranoid Dementia Praecox. A type of dementia praecox characterized by delusional systems which are less organized than in paranoia and which are usually accompanied by other evidence of mental disorganization.

Parergasia. Synonym for dementia praecox used by A. Meyer.

Paresthesia. False or distorted sensation.

Parorexia. Morbid craving for unusual foods.

Pathological Liar. Person who indulges in falsification which is entirely disproportionate to any discernible end but who is not otherwise mentally or physically ill.

Pathology. The science and study of disease.

Pellagra. A vitamin deficiency disease characterized by dermatitis, diarrhea, and dementia.

Perception. The awareness of external objects on the basis of sensation; the integration of sensory experience with previously acquired knowledge.

Perplexity State. Morbid condition characterized by bewilderment, restlessness, and aimlessness.

Perseveration. The persistent inappropriate repetition or continuation of words, actions, or ideas after they have once occurred.

Petit Mal Epilepsy. A condition in which occur momentary lapses of consciousness, disturbances in expression, and suspension of activity.

Phenylpyruvic Oligophrenia. An hereditary type of mental deficiency characterized by a metabolic disturbance.

Phobia. A morbid fear, one that is an overreaction to a relatively innocuous object.

Phrenology. The pseudo science of reading character from the shape of the head.

Physiognomy. The pseudo science of discerning character from the features of the face.

Pick's Disease. A form of presenile dementia and organic deterioration in which there is a more or less definite and circumscribed area of cortical atrophy of the brain and peculiar disorders of perception and memory.

Polyideic. Tendency to think or act constantly about a limited number of ideas (*see* Monoideic).

Precipitating Cause. The particular incident or incidents which revealed the presence of, or initiated, a disorder or disease.

Predisposing Cause. Some factor or factors, such as heredity, physical illness, or malnutrition which make it possible for a disease to occur.

Predisposition. The basis for and tendency toward exhibiting a particular characteristic, trait, reaction, or disease.

Preformation. The gradual development in the direction of a particular genetically determined characteristic.

Prefrontal Lobotomy. Surgical severing of the nerve tracts connecting the frontal lobes and the thalamus of the brain.

Primary Affect Hunger. Unsatisfied need for love, affection, and feeling of being wanted.

Probate. The official proof of wills.

Prognosis. A forecast of the probable course of events (usually disorder or disease).

Projection. The process of attributing to another person the rejected or unpleasant ideas, emotions, or motives which really belong to oneself.

Provocation. The precipitating cause.

Psychiatrist. A physician (doctor of medicine) who specializes in the diagnosis, care, and treatment of mental disease.

Psychiatry. A division of medicine dealing with the diagnosis, care, and treatment of those suffering from mental disease.

Psychic Seizure; Epileptic Equivalent; Psychomotor Seizure. Attacks that are the equivalent of *grand mal* or *petit mal* seizures, in which automatic motor acts occur and for which the patient has no memory.

Psychoanalysis. A system of psychological theory, and a therapeutic approach devised and named by Freud.

Psychoanalyst. One who uses psychoanalysis as a therapeutic technique in the treatment of psychopathological conditions.

Psychobiology. A term popularized by Adolf Meyer as a system of objective psychology stressing the relationship between the individual and his environment.

Psychology. The division of science which deals with behavior and mental life.

Psychoneurosis. Neurosis.

Psychopathic Personality. A diagnostic category including those whose behavior is socially disturbing and inadequate but who are neither neurotic nor psychotic.

Psychopathology. The science and study of mental disease.

Psychosexuality. The sexual component of personality.

Psychosis. A profound mental illness constituting a disease-entity, usually involving the total personality, during which the patient has little or no insight into his condition.

Psychosomatic Medicine. The medical treatment in which the interaction of mind and body is considered in the diagnosis, care, and treatment of the illness.

Psychotherapy. The acting on the mind of a human being by mental means, with the intention of effecting a cure.

Pyknic. A type of body build characterized by roundness of contour, amplitude of body cavities, and a plentiful endowment of fat.

Rationalization. A process (usually unconscious) which arises from the human need for accounting for or justifying to ourselves certain feelings, ideas, acts, or emotions which are not rational.

Readmissions. The number of persons entering some institution (hospital) two or more times for care or treatment.

Receptors. The endings of afferent neurons which, when adequately stimulated, initiate impulses into the associated afferent nerves.

Recidivist. An habitual criminal; one convicted two or more times.

Regression. Symbolical act of returning to some earlier period in one's life and acting and thinking in a manner appropriate for that earlier period.

Repression. The exclusion of painful and unpleasant material from representation in either behavior or consciousness.

Resident Population. The number of individuals who are residing in some particular place or institution on some particular date.

Retroactive Amnesia. A type of retrograde amnesia in which the memory loss extends backward for a certain limited period preceding the occurrence of the shock or injury which disturbed the memory process.

Retrograde Amnesia. General loss of memory of previously acquired ideas and actions.

Rorschach Test. A technique of personality analysis based on the interpretation given to ink-blots.

Sadism. The procurement of sexual satisfaction through infliction of pain upon others.

Sanguine. A temperament characterized by pleasant feeling-tone, enthusiasm, and changeableness.

Satyriasis. Morbid exaggeration of sexual desire in men.

Scatter. The range of successful performances over different mental-age levels on tests of general intelligence.

Schizoid. A personality type characterized by seclusiveness, lack of adequate emotional attachment to others, diminished initiative, and preoccupation with fantasies.

Schizophrenia. Dementia praecox. Bleuler's term for this disorder, which emphasizes the splitting of the mental life.

Senile Dementia. Morbid intellectual and emotional deterioration in the aged, having a gradual onset and irreversible course.

Sensation. That form of experience aroused from outside the nervous system which cannot be further analyzed by introspection; an element of consciousness.

Sensitive Reference Psychosis. Extreme feelings of inferiority and self-reproach which are projected onto others so that delusions of reference are outstanding, along with general depression, nervousness, and imaginary or real physical ailments.

Shell Shock. Term applied to neurotic and psychotic war casualties in World War I, when they were believed to be due to the effects of physical concussion upon the nervous system.

Sickness Benefit. The exploitation of physical illness and suffering in order to receive attention, affection, or remuneration.

Somatic. Pertaining to the body.

Spastic Paralysis; Infantile Cerebral Palsy; Little's Disease. A gross form of motor disability due to organic brain lesions.

Spasticity. A rigidity of the muscles, associated with inadequate voluntary control.

Specific Factor. A genetic determiner giving rise to some distinct, definite result.

Spes Phthisica. A mental exaltation or euphoria said to occur in tuberculous patients.

Stereotypy. Continued morbid repetition of sounds, words, phrases, or movements.

Stuttering; Stammering. A disorder in the rhythm of verbal expression.

Sublimation. The unconscious exchanging of what would be apparent expressions of sexual desires and wishes for other types of behavior which are socially and ethically approved.

Superego. Conscience; "One must not."

Sydenham's Chorea. St. Vitus's dance.

Symbolization. An unconscious process which is built up on the basis of association and similarity so that one object or idea comes to represent or stand for (symbolize) some other object or idea through some common aspect. The process is usually unconscious.

Symptom. A bodily or mental phenomenon, circumstance, or change of condition arising from and accompanying a disease and constituting an indication or evidence of it.

Syndrome. A combination or concurrence of several symptoms of a disease.

Synesthesia. The arousing of a sensory experience in a modality which is different from that of the primary stimulus.

Testamentary Capacity. Capacity to make a will.

Thanatophobia. Fear of death.

Thymergasia. A synonym for manic-depressive psychosis (A. Meyer).

Tics. Quick, sudden spasms, similar in form to involuntary movements and without known organic basis.

Tort. An offense such as assault and battery, libel, or negligence, in which there is an infringement of personal or civil rights.

Total Admissions. The total number of individuals (first-admissions plus readmissions) admitted to some institution or group of institutions during some particular period of time.

Transference. Establishment of an emotional relationship (love or hate) with some other person because of unconscious identifications.

Transvestite. One who has the morbid obsession to dress in the clothing of the opposite sex.

Trauma. An injury or shock which may be either of physical or psychological origin.

Traumatic Neurosis. A form of neurosis developed following some physical injury, emotional shock, or intense emotional stress.

Twin Index Case. The particular individual who serves as the start of a genetic study based on twins.

Unconscious Fantasy. Fantasy formed or elaborated in the unconscious which appears in a fragmentary fashion in conscious daydreams.

Volition. All that is implied by will, voluntary action, decision, determining tendency, and the like.

Wassermann Test. Laboratory test for syphilitic infection.

Waxy Flexibility. A syndrome occurring in catatonic dementia praecox in which the bodily posture and position may be changed or molded by an outsider and the changes maintained as though the patient were made of wax; the opposite condition of negativism.

Zoophobia. Fear of animals.

INDEX

Cason, H., 342, *351*

Castration anxiety, 184

Causalgia, 307–308

Catalepsy, 319

Catastrophic reactions, 108

Catatonia, 37, 47, 170, 386, 442

Catatonic, dementia praecox, 37–38, 406; hebephrenic group, 268; patients, 385, 395; state, 262, 319; stupor, 394; symptoms, 38

Categorical behavior, 418

Catharsis, 17, 519

Causes of, alcoholic addiction, 182–183; feeblemindedness, 142–143; general paresis, 196; imperception, 309; paralysis agitans, 211; paranoia, 176

Celibacy, 277

Cell, constituents, 144; permeability, 122; structure, 144; walls, 121

Center of consciousness, 101

Central nervous system, 105, 136, 196, 197, 203, 207, 208, 377, 378, 422, 439, 441, 456

Cerebral, arteriosclerosis, 149, 153, 156, 284, 286, 407, 409; atrophy, 128; concussion, 105; cortex, 123, 156, 207, 377, 426, 430; damage, 127, 128; dysfunction, 265; dysrhythmia, 116; hemispheres, 100, 425; lesions, 119, 120, 141; localization, 438, 439; resistance, 128

Cerletti, U., 449, *457*

Chambers, F. T., 535, *545*

Changes in, behavior, 434, 435; general paresis, 199–202; old age, 150; personality, 434; scene, 534; sensory threshold, 310

Chappell, M. N., 236, *240*

Character, 27, 163, 167, 168, 245, 256; changes, 205; deviations, 227; neurosis, 22; traits, 99, 151, 175, 227, 398; vacillation, 396

Characteristics of, alcoholics, 184; cretinism, 140; hands, 212; Huntington's chorea, 217; narcissists, 247; pathological intoxication, 190; psychopaths, 250–251

Charcot, J. M., 81, 82, 93, 94, 100, 319, 518, 519

Chemistry and physiology of dementia praecox, 47–48

Cheney, C. O., 525, *530*

Childbirth, 236–239

Child-guidance clinics, 470, 471

Childhood, 29, 63, 82, 86, 130, 175, 211, 249, 282

Child-of-fourteen-years test, 484

Child psychiatry, 459

Choice between right and wrong, 493

Choleric temperament, 224

Chorea, 217, 218, 317

Chromosomes, 255, 256, 262

Chronic, alcoholic, 181, 182, 186, 187, 192, 194, 265, 397, 406; alcoholic deterioration, 193–194; cardiac, 224, 226; degenerative chorea, 221; delusions, 172; diseases, 239; grouch, 298; irritation, 368; mental fatigue, 74; nature of disease, 226; patients, 175; physical fatigue, 74; pulmonary tuberculosis, 228; shiftlessness, 109

Chronological age, 146, 213

Cimbal, W., 184, *195*

Cimbal's classification, 184

Circular psychosis, 61, 62

Circumstantiality, 416

Civil action, 481, 493

Civilization, 280, 395, 545

Clark, L. P., 142, *148*

Classification, in abnormal psychology, 9–12; of personality, 24; of psychopaths, 290

Claustrophobia, 225, 366

Clinical, observation, 102, 127, 183, 213, 236, 497, 498; psychologists, 20, 506, 513, 518

Clouded consciousness, 156, 157, 237, 309, 403

Clouston, T. S., 232

Cobb, S., *275*

Co-conscious, 96, 348

oral eroticism, 325; psychoanalytic, 326; visualization, 325
Style of life, 86, 88, 299
Subconscious, 16
Subjective, anxiety, 107; emotional experience, 372; experience, 225; type, 25
Sublimation, 18, 35–36
Substitution, 83, 301
Suicide, 172, 208, 210, 217, 220, 245, 281, 282, 286, 289, 394, 539; act, 245; attempt, 193, 358; circumstances, 245; risks, 77; tendencies, 163; threats, 539
Sullivan, E. B., *129*
Sullivan, H. S., 250
Superego, 16, 17, 63, 165, 244
Surgical, extirpation of brain areas, 410; removal of prefrontal lobes, 433; severing of nerve tracts, 431; shock, 170
Sustained task, 498
Sutton, T., 191
Sweating disorders, 84, 106
Swindling, 246
Sydenham's chorea, 217, 317
Symbolic, equivalents, 519; fulfillment, 101; sex wish, 100
Symbolization, 18, 83, 542
Sympathetic nervous system, 378, 379, 383
Symptomatic, alcoholic states, 182; psychoses, 264; psychotic episodes, 236
Symptoms in, anxiety, 75; benign stupor 170; common neuroses, 88; paralysis agitans, 212
Syndrome, 13
Synesthesia, 310
Syntactical defect, 331
Syphilitic, hereditary-congenital, 265; infection, 144; meningoencephalitis, 196

Taboo, 82, 278, 281, 297, 304, 355, 369
Taste buds, 150
Tauber, E. S., *388*
Taylor, J. J., *440*
Taylor, W. S., *89, 103*
Tegelberg, J. J., *387*
Telepathy, 3
Temper tantrums, 175, 476
Temporal lobes, 377, 428, 434, 435, 436, 439
Temporary insanity, 354
Tender-minded type, 25
Terman, L. M., *421*
Terminal dementia, 153, 156, 157, 217, 457
Testamentary capacity, 483–484
Tests of, competency, 483; conceptual thinking, 409; motor ability, 507; physiological function, 377; responsibility, 488
Thanatophobia, 366

Thematic apperception test, 510–511
Thiamin, 452–454, 457
Thomas, W. I., 31, *32*
Thompson, J., 415, *421*
Thompson, L. J., *352*
Thoughts-out-loud, 41–42, 312, 363
Thumb-sucking, 29
Thymergasia, 62
Thyroid, deficiency, 443; disturbance, 183; dysfunction, 64, 380, 444, 456; gland, 64, 139, 379, 443–444; grafting, 443; medication, 140, 457; therapy, 444
Tics, 317, 393
Tietze, C., *88*
Time, ordering of experience, 343; sense, 341
Titley, W. B., 166, *180*
Tjossem, T. D., *336*
Toilet habits, 29
Tort and contract, 481–483, 488
Total admissions, 15
Tough-minded type, 25
Trait, 24, 245, 246, 256, 262
Trance, 93, 94, 102, 375, 516, 517
Transcortical sensory aphasia, 328
Transference, 18, 521
Transvestites, 247
Trauma, 29, 237, 249, 298, 304, 476
Traumatic neuroses, 104–114, 264, 459, 476, 528; civil life, 111–113
Travis, L. E., *320*, 321, 326, *336*
Treatment, causalgia, 308; general paresis, 196, 205; involutional melancholia, 169; mental disorders, 529; peptic ulcers, 233; tuberculosis, 229
Tredgold, A. F., 133, *148, 252*
Trial-and-error learning, 145, 329
Trigger area, 123
Trobriand Islands, 281
Troublemakers, 228, 243, 368
Tryon, R. C., 143, *148*
Tuberculosis, 32, 177, 227–232, 239, 263, 381
Twenty-Pence test, 485
Twin-study method, heredity, 262–263
Types, 24; neurosis, 81; seizures, 118; motivation, 527; reaction, 251; vagrants, 242
Typical description, 7
Typology, 27

Unconscious, 16, 83, 100, 244, 376; connections, 521; factors, 519; fantasies, 19, 511, 521; ideas, 520; imitation, 279; impulse, 487; mechanism, 632; motives, 90, 382; wish, 83, 376, 382
Understanding test, 483
Undue influence, 483